Federal Law

Enforcement

C A R E E R S

Second Edition

Profiles of 250 High-Powered Positions and Tactics for Getting Hired

Thomas H. Ackerman

jIst
Works
America's Career Publisher

Federal Law Enforcement Careers: Profiles of 250 High-Powered Positions and Tactics for Getting Hired, Second Edition

© 2006 by Thomas H. Ackerman

Published by JIST Works, an imprint of JIST Publishing, Inc.
8902 Otis Avenue
Indianapolis, IN 46216-1033
Phone: 1-800-648-JIST   Fax: 1-800-JIST-FAX   E-mail: info@jist.com

Visit our Web site at **www.jist.com** for information on JIST, free job search tips, book chapters, and how to order our many products! For free information on 14,000 job titles, visit **www.careeroink.com**.

Quantity discounts are available for JIST books. Have future editions of JIST books automatically delivered to you on publication through our convenient standing order program. Please call our Sales Department at 1-800-648-5478 for a free catalog and more information.

Trade Product Manager: Lori Cates Hand
Development Editor: Michael Thomas
Interior Designer: Aleata Howard
Page Layout: Trudy Coler, Toi Davis
Cover Designer: Nick Anderson
Proofreaders: Linda Seifert, Jeanne Clark
Indexer: Kelly D. Henthorne

Printed in Canada

11 10 09 08 07 06   9 8 7 6 5 4 3 2 1

Library of Congress Cataloging-in-Publication Data

Ackerman, Thomas H.
  Federal law enforcement careers : profiles of 250 high-powered positions and tactics for getting hired / Thomas H. Ackerman.-- 2nd ed.
        p. cm.
  Rev. ed. of: Guide to careers in federal law enforcement. 1999.
  Includes bibliographical references and index.
ISBN-13: 978-1-59357-256-3 (alk. paper)
ISBN-10: 1-59357-256-5 (alk. paper)
  1. Law enforcement--Vocational guidance--United States. 2. Police--Vocational guidance--United States. 3. Civil service positions--United States. 4. Administrative agencies--United States. I. Ackerman, Thomas H. Guide to careers in federal law enforcement. II. Title.
HV8143.A64 2006
363.2023'73--dc22
                                    2006008427

We have been careful to provide accurate information in this book, but it is possible that errors and omissions have been introduced. Please consider this in making any career plans or other important decisions. Trust your own judgment above all else and in all things.

The views expressed in this book do not necessarily represent the views of any organization, department, or agency of the United States Government.

Previous edition published under the title *Guide to Careers in Federal Law Enforcement.*

ISBN-13: 978-1-59357-256-3
ISBN-10: 1-59357-256-5

ABOUT THIS BOOK

Federal law enforcement officers and support personnel make important decisions every day in carrying out the nation's crime control and national security strategies. Growing concern over crime and increased vigilance in protecting America's borders, coupled with the need to replace federal retirees, will create thousands of federal law enforcement job opportunities in years to come. A more security-conscious society and concern over terrorism also will heighten the need for well-trained personnel to protect federal programs, facilities, assets, and employees. In other words, there has never been a better time to answer the call to public service.

Unfortunately, many people are intimidated, misinformed, or confused about federal job opportunities because they do not have accurate information about the positions, qualification requirements, application and testing procedures, and other important details. Many job seekers also are unaware of special hiring programs for college students, veterans, and Native Americans, and that co-op positions or good grades in college can put you on the fast-track to federal employment. Chapters 1 through 5 provide complete details on federal hiring processes, how to find out about job openings, and strategies for getting hired.

Federal criminal investigators, police officers, intelligence analysts, security specialists, correctional officers, forensic examiners, and others enjoy careers that offer prestige, excellent salaries, and exceptional benefits, as well as opportunities for travel, specialization, and advancement. Careers with more than 140 agencies are profiled in this book, including many with lesser-known agencies most job seekers will never be aware of. Positions with well-respected agencies, such as the EPA Office of Criminal Enforcement, FDA Office of Criminal Investigations, Social Security Administration Office of Inspector General, and National Marine Fisheries Service, are among the best-kept secrets in federal law enforcement. Opportunities with these and other agencies are profiled in chapters 6 through 15.

Federal agencies reward job applicants who emphasize attention to detail and jump through the right hoops at the right time, and you can easily overshadow more highly qualified job applicants simply by having a superior understanding of federal hiring processes. Thorough knowledge of the agencies, the positions, and the federal personnel system are crucial to outshining the competition. This book was written as a virtual roadmap, and it has enabled countless job seekers to gain a competitive edge and land a career in federal law enforcement. I hope you find it helpful in your endeavors to join the ranks of the nation's federal law enforcement personnel—the Feds!

—Thomas H. Ackerman

Dedication: *To Debi, my daughter, whose vision, courage, and commitment make anything possible.*

CONTENTS

Chapter 9: Law Enforcement Technicians and Specialists 259

Chapter 10: General and Compliance Investigators....................289

Chapter 13: Correctional Officers and Specialists 361

Chapter 14: Federal Court Personnel and Prosecutors 373

PART 1

NAVIGATING THE FEDERAL HIRING PROCESS

CHAPTER 1

Federal Hiring Processes

"And so, my fellow Americans, ask not what your country can do for you—ask what you can do for your country."

—*John F. Kennedy*

The federal government is the nation's largest employer, with nearly three million personnel serving throughout the United States and abroad in more than 2,000 different occupations. Federal employees are classified into a wide range of occupational groups and appointment classifications, and are compensated under a variety of pay systems. Hiring procedures also vary from one agency to another, inasmuch as the federal civil service system does not revolve around a standard or unified hiring process or personnel system. Although hiring procedures vary, all are based upon common principles, and all agencies are required to observe certain laws and regulations to ensure that job applicants are evaluated objectively.

This chapter provides an overview of hiring procedures common to most federal law enforcement agencies, including an overview of the federal civil service system, the role of the U.S. Office of Personnel Management (OPM) in personnel administration, types of federal service, occupational classifications, experience requirements, job vacancy announcements, special hiring programs, application formats, written examinations, applicant ratings, personal interviews, polygraph examinations, background investigations, and physical examinations.

The U.S. Office of Personnel Management (OPM)

OPM is the President's advisor for operating and continuously improving the government's system of human resource management. To ensure compliance with personnel laws and regulations, OPM supports agencies in hiring and examining processes in accordance with merit system principles—strict laws designed to ensure that hiring and retention decisions are based on objective job-related criteria and procedures—and that all applicants receive equal opportunity for employment. The agency also provides employment information and job vacancy announcements for many government positions, administers written examinations for certain jobs at the request of agencies, and establishes basic qualification standards for all federal occupations. Although OPM offers support to federal agencies, most agencies conduct their own recruiting and hiring processes.

Among other responsibilities, OPM operates the nation's largest retirement programs, which together cover more than five million active and retired federal employees; administers the Federal Employees Health Benefits program; sets investigation policy for the federal personnel security program, and provides for personnel investigations relating to suitability and security; sets standards for information that goes into employees' Official Personnel Files at agencies; and provides policy direction and guidance on appointments, promotions, reassignments, reinstatements, temporary and term employment, Veterans' Preference, career transition, and other provisions.

Types of Federal Service

The federal civil service system was established in 1883 to replace a patronage system that was wrought with favoritism and abuse. All appointive positions in the executive, judicial, and legislative branches of the federal government are covered under the federal civil service system, except for military positions of the uniformed services. Civil service components consist of the Competitive Service, the Excepted Service, and the Senior Executive Service. The rights, benefits, entitlements, appointment procedures, and job protections of federal personnel are determined based on the variety of service and appointment held. This section provides an overview of the types of federal civilian employment and many of the rules under which federal personnel serve.

Competitive Service Appointments

Federal positions normally filled through open competitive examination under civil service rules and regulations established by OPM are categorized in the Competitive Service. Accordingly, the competitive examination process involves the evaluation of applicants based on their education, experience, and other qualifications, and sometimes includes written tests. Positions in the executive branch of the federal government, which includes most civilian government positions, are in the competitive service unless they are specifically excluded from it. In the competitive service, appointment procedures, merit promotion requirements, and qualification standards are prescribed by law or by OPM, and apply to all agencies.

Excepted Service Appointments

Executive branch positions that are filled outside of competitive service processes are in the Excepted Service. Agencies that hire personnel through excepted service processes are authorized either under federal law, by Presidential Order, or by OPM to establish independent hiring processes to fill certain positions. In the excepted service, only basic requirements are prescribed by law or regulation, and each agency develops specific requirements and procedures for its own jobs. Many agencies hire employees in the competitive service for some jobs and in the excepted service for others. Positions in the legislative and judicial branches are included in the excepted service unless they are specifically included in the competitive service.

Excepted Agencies

While many federal agencies fill position vacancies in both the competitive and excepted service, some are completely excluded from competitive service procedures and have their own hiring systems and evaluation criteria. Agencies that operate independent employment systems are known as Excepted Agencies. Some of the major excepted agencies include the Administrative Office of the U.S. Courts, Agency for International Development, Central Intelligence Agency, Defense Intelligence Agency, Federal Bureau of Investigation, Transportation Security Administration, Federal Reserve Board, Government Accountability Office, National Security Agency, Nuclear Regulatory Commission, Postal Service, Tennessee Valley Authority, Supreme Court of the United States, Peace Corps, and Library of Congress.

Senior Executive Service Appointments

The Civil Service Reform Act (CSRA) established the Senior Executive Service (SES) in 1979 to ensure that executive management of the government is responsive to the needs, policies, and goals of the nation. It was set up as a "third service," completely separate from the existing competitive and excepted services. The SES covers most managerial, supervisory, and policy positions in the executive branch that are classified above GS-15 and do not require Senate confirmation. In other words, SES personnel serve in key positions just below Presidential appointees.

Permanent Appointments

Permanent appointments in the competitive service are classified as either *career-conditional* or *career*. Career-conditional appointments generally are used for initial appointments into the competitive service. Once an employee completes three years of continuous service under a career-conditional appointment, their appointment is converted to career status. Permanent employees may work full-time or part-time schedules; are eligible for retirement benefits, health insurance, and life insurance; and earn annual and sick leave.

Temporary and Term Appointments

Temporary appointments are intended not to exceed one year, although in some situations may be extended for an additional year. The work of temporary appointees must not be permanent in nature. Temporary employees may work full-time or part-time schedules and earn annual leave and sick leave, although they are not entitled to retirement benefits, health insurance, or life insurance.

Term appointments are made for periods of more than one year but cannot exceed four years. These appointments could be appropriate, for example, when there is project work to be completed, when the workload is extraordinary, or when an agency reorganizes. Term employees are permitted to work full-time or part-time schedules. They also earn annual and sick leave, and are eligible for retirement benefits, health insurance, and life insurance.

Competitive Status

Federal employees serving in either career or career-conditional appointments in the competitive service have what is known as *competitive status*. Federal personnel with competitive status who apply for other federal jobs are commonly known as *status applicants* or *status candidates*. Job applicants who are not federal employees, and federal employees who do not qualify for competitive status, are known as *non-status applicants*.

Serving in a position that affords competitive status can pay off in a big way if you plan to move to another federal agency, because oftentimes federal job vacancies are open only to applicants with competitive status. In addition, occasionally only employees of the agency that is filling a vacancy can apply.

Reinstatement Eligibility

Reinstatement Eligibility allows certain former federal employees to apply for federal jobs open only to status candidates, which allows them to reenter the competitive service workforce without competing with the general public in civil service examination processes. Former federal employees with career status and former career-conditional employees who qualify for Veterans' Preference maintain reinstatement eligibility for life. In addition, most nonveterans who were career-conditional employees are eligible for reinstatement for three years after their date of separation. Of course, if you have reinstatement eligibility you can apply for any position that is open to the general public. Reinstatement eligibility does not guarantee a job offer. Excepted service appointees do not have reinstatement eligibility.

Federal Occupational Classifications

OPM has established various occupational groups and series that are used to classify federal jobs. These classifications are made in terms of the variety or subject matter of the work, the level of difficulty or responsibility, and qualification requirements. Position classifications ensure similar personnel administration and pay for positions that involve similar types of work. Occupational groups established for white-collar positions are classified under the General Schedule (GS), and blue-collar jobs fall under the Wage Grade (WG) designation.

Each occupational group level includes up to 100 positions, all of which are classified by a two-letter prefix—GS for General Schedule positions and WG for Wage Grade—and a unique job series number. For example, the Transportation Group of the General Schedule includes positions that range from the GS-2100 through GS-2199 series, such as those concerned with Highway Safety (GS-2125), Transportation Loss and Damage Claims Examining (GS-2135), Air Traffic Control (GS-2152), and Aircraft Operation (GS-2181). General Schedule occupational groups range from the GS-0000 level (Miscellaneous Occupations) to the GS-2200 level (Information Technology). Wage Grade positions range from the WG-2500 group to the WG-9000 group. For example, occupations concerned with the maintenance and repair of aircraft are covered under the Aircraft Overhaul Group (WG-8800 through WG-8899 series), including positions such as Aircraft Propeller Mechanic (WG-8810), Aircraft Parts Mechanic (WG-8840), and Airframe Test Operator (WG-8882).

In terms of the number of personnel serving in occupational groups relating to law enforcement, the largest is the Investigation Group, which includes positions classified in the GS-1800 through GS-1899 series. For example, this group includes positions such as Industry Operations Investigator (GS-1801); Criminal Investigator/Special Agent (GS-1811); Air Safety Investigator (GS-1815); and Border Patrol Agent (GS-1896). The next-largest category falls under the Miscellaneous Occupations group, which includes police and correctional officers, fingerprint specialists, park rangers, and security specialists classified in the GS-0000 through GS-0099 series. A complete schedule of occupational groups for positions in this book can be found online (see the inside back cover of this book).

Both the General Schedule and Wage Grade pay systems consist of 15 grades, each structured in terms of difficulty and responsibility of the work and the qualifications required for its performance, ranging from GS-1 to GS-15 and WG-1 to WG-15, respectively. Additional information concerning federal pay systems is provided in chapter 2, "Salary and Benefits."

Citizenship Requirements

As a general rule, only U.S. citizens and nationals are eligible to hold federal jobs, although limited legal exceptions sometimes apply. The following sections provide a basic overview of citizenship requirements and issues relating to dual citizenship. Questions or issues requiring clarification concerning citizenship status and eligibility requirements for federal jobs should be directed to the agency with which you're seeking employment or to a qualified legal professional.

Qualifying as a U.S. Citizen or National

Generally speaking, U.S. citizens include those who were either

- Born in the United States, the District of Columbia, Puerto Rico, Guam (since 1950), or the U.S. Virgin Islands

- Born outside the United States to parents who are U.S. citizens

- Naturalized as a United States citizen

- Otherwise granted citizenship under the law

Nationals of the United States presently include natives of American Samoa, Swains Island, and the Northern Mariana Islands.

Dual Citizenship

U.S. citizens who possess dual citizenship may or may not qualify for appointment to federal jobs, depending on each applicant's circumstances. Although U.S. laws do not prevent the hiring of dual citizens, the manner in which an applicant has held or exercised his or her dual citizenship status could be relevant when considering him or her for employment. In addition, dual citizenship may be incorporated as one of many factors to be considered in decisions to grant or withhold a security clearance. Federal agencies are required to follow government-wide Executive Orders and adjudicative standards in evaluating dual-citizenship issues, and decisions are made on a case-by-case basis.

Some circumstances relating to dual citizenship that could be of concern and could result in disqualification from the hiring process include the following:

- Possession or use of a foreign passport

- Military service or a willingness to bear arms for a foreign country

- Accepting educational, medical, or other benefits, such as retirement and social welfare, from a foreign country

- Residence in a foreign country to meet citizenship requirements

- Using foreign citizenship to protect financial or business interests in another country

- Seeking or holding political office in a foreign country

- Voting in foreign elections

- Performing or attempting to perform duties to serve the interests of another government in preference to the interests of the United States

Security concerns could be alleviated if the dual citizenship is based solely on parents' citizenship or birth in a foreign country, or if an applicant's previous foreign preference (such as foreign military service) occurred before obtaining U.S. citizenship. An applicant's willingness to renounce his or her foreign citizenship also could be a consideration.

Experience Requirements

Qualification standards for federal law enforcement positions typically specify requirements for experience that is either *general* or *specialized* in nature. Qualifying general and specialized experience varies widely in its degree of specialty from one occupational series to another, and also between salary grades within an occupational series. In addition, position qualification standards often require that a certain amount of the experience be at a level of difficulty and responsibility equivalent to the next lower grade level in the federal service. Job vacancy announcements usually provide detailed descriptions of qualifying general and specialized experience.

General Experience

General experience usually is required at grade levels where the specific knowledge and skills needed to perform the duties of a position are not prerequisites, but where applicants must have demonstrated the *ability* to acquire the particular knowledge and skills. For some occupations, any progressively responsible work experience can be qualifying. Others require experience that provided a familiarity with the subject matter or processes of the occupation, or of the equipment used on the job, although not to the extent required of specialized experience. For example, qualifying general experience for a criminal investigator position with the Internal Revenue Service (IRS) could include responsible accounting or business experience that required knowledge and application of accounting methods, auditing principles, or general business practices.

Specialized Experience

Specialized experience is that which has equipped an applicant with the particular knowledge, skills, and abilities to successfully perform the duties of the position, and which is in or directly related to the line of work of the position. For example, qualifying specialized experience for GS-0083 Police Officer positions at the GS-4 level and above is defined as

> *Experience that provided knowledge of a body of basic laws and regulations, law enforcement operations, practices, and techniques and involved responsibility for maintaining order and protecting life and property. Creditable specialized experience may have been gained in work on a police force; through*

service as a military police officer; in work providing visitor protection and law enforcement in parks, forests, or other natural resource or recreational environments; in performing criminal investigative duties; or in other work that provided the required knowledge and skills.

In contrast to qualifying general experience for the IRS criminal investigator position (as discussed above), for specialized experience an applicant would need to have conducted criminal investigations related to the accounting, auditing, or business practices of suspects, as opposed to experience in business, accounting, or auditing that did not involve criminal investigations.

Substituting Education for Experience

Candidates who possess a bachelor's degree but no specialized experience in the career field of the position sought generally are eligible for appointment at the GS-5 level. However, positions at or above the GS-7 level typically require one year of specialized experience equivalent to the next lower grade level. This means, for example, that in order to qualify for a position at GS-12, an applicant must have had at least one year of specialized experience equivalent to GS-11.

In many cases, applicants can substitute graduate-level education for specialized experience in order to qualify for federal law enforcement careers at the GS-7 level and above. In lieu of specialized experience, one year of graduate study is normally qualifying for appointment to GS-7. Similarly, a master's degree or two years of graduate study can be substituted for specialized experience when applying for positions at the GS-9 level, and either a Ph.D. or three years of graduate education can be substituted for specialized experience when seeking positions at the GS-11 level. In addition, applicants without specialized experience who achieved high academic standing during undergraduate studies qualify for many federal law enforcement jobs at the GS-7 level. This is possible in accordance with Superior Academic Achievement provisions (see "Special Hiring Programs" later in this chapter).

Job Vacancy Announcements

Federal agencies seeking to fill job vacancies coordinate efforts with OPM to create detailed Vacancy Announcements—sometimes referred to as job postings—that provide position details and information concerning qualification requirements, selection criteria, and the application process. While the format varies from one agency to another, most vacancy announcements consist of essentially the same components, as discussed in the following sections. All agencies in the competitive service must post job vacancies with OPM whenever they seek applicants from outside their workforce (except for positions lasting 120 days or less). These vacancies are announced on OPM's USAJobs Web site and elsewhere. See chapter 5, "Sources of Federal Employment Information," for complete details on how to find out about federal job vacancies. An example of a vacancy announcement can be found online (see the inside back cover of this book).

Position Title and Announcement Number

The official title of an advertised position always is shown near the top of the vacancy announcement. Official job titles, which are determined by federal position classification standards, normally are used in vacancy announcements. These sometimes differ from working titles of law enforcement officers and other personnel. For example, criminal investigators in the GS-1811 series are commonly known by their working title of special agent or senior special agent, although most agencies advertise vacancies under the criminal investigator title. However, working titles sometimes are referenced in narrative portions of vacancy announcements.

The top portion of vacancy announcements also includes the announcement number for the advertised position. This number, known also as a posting number, is used by agencies to facilitate the processing of application materials and record-keeping functions. Announcement numbers provide a ready reference for staffing specialists to the exact position title, salary grade, opening and closing dates, location of duty station, and other pertinent data for each announcement. Therefore, it is important to include the announcement number on all application forms and other documents submitted; otherwise agency staffing specialists might have difficulty processing these materials.

Hiring Agency, Duty Location, and Number of Vacancies

The name of the agency filling the position and location (city and state) where the job will be performed are included under these headings. Some vacancy announcements advertise multiple vacancies that will be filled in different locations. These announcements normally include a list of cities to select from. When vacancies exist in more than one duty location, applicants must specify where they are willing to work. In some cases, particularly when special agent vacancies are filled by the FBI and a few other agencies, applicants do not have a choice in duty locations and must be willing to relocate upon accepting the position or completing basic training. Some agencies fill multiple vacancies under the same announcement, while others issue multiple announcements when filling more than one position. Many vacancy announcements provide details about the geographic area surrounding the duty location.

Occupational Series, Salary Grade, and Promotion Potential

The occupational series and salary grade usually are listed adjacent to the position title, in a format such as "Criminal Investigator/GS-1811-07." In this example, the position is classified in the GS-1811 criminal investigator series, and the appointee will be hired at the GS-7 salary grade. When only one salary grade is indicated, applicants must meet the minimum qualifications for the specified grade level and cannot be hired at any other grade. However, vacancy announcements often specify a range of salary grades, such as GS-1811-07/09/11, allowing agencies to fill positions at the highest grade level for which appointees are qualified—in this case, GS-7, GS-9, or GS-11. (See chapter 2 for an explanation of the GS pay scale and a listing of salaries for each grade level.)

Many vacancy announcements also indicate the promotion potential for the position, sometimes referred to as the Full Performance Level, which is the highest grade level to which an employee could expect to advance if their job performance is satisfactory. Advancement to the promotion potential grade is noncompetitive. In other words, there is no need to submit employment applications, take examinations, or compete with other personnel to move from one grade to the next. For example, in the case of a criminal investigator hired at GS-7, and where the promotion potential is GS-12, advancement to GS-9, GS-11, and GS-12 would normally occur at one-year intervals without undergoing testing or competition from other candidates. In many cases, advancement beyond the promotion potential grade is possible if supervisory or management positions are attained.

Opening and Closing Dates

The "open period," in which applications are accepted for federal job vacancies, is marked by the opening and closing dates of vacancy announcements. Opening dates are sometimes referred to as "issue dates" or "announcement dates." This is the first day in which candidates are permitted to submit application materials. Application closing dates are not as straightforward, however, and can be interpreted differently from one agency to another. For example, some agencies require that all job application materials be received by the human resources office on or before the closing date, while others permit applicants to have their materials postmarked no later than the closing date. Announcements must remain open for a minimum of three days, although most law enforcement announcements remain open for at least two weeks.

Area of Consideration and Appointment Tenure

This section specifies who is eligible to apply for a particular vacancy, such as competitive status or non-status candidates, employees of the department or agency issuing the vacancy announcement, or those who qualify under special hiring programs such as Outstanding Scholars, veterans, Native Americans, and others.

Positions that are open to the general public often are indicated by the terms "All Sources" or "Non-Status" in the Area of Consideration block, although current federal employees also can apply for these positions. Vacancies open only to current federal employees and former federal employees with reinstatement eligibility either indicate these details or specify "Status Candidates" in this block. Some vacancies are open only to candidates who reside near the duty location. These announcements typically indicate "Local Commuting Area Only" or similar terminology in the Area of Consideration block. Some agencies use terms such as "Who Can Apply" or "Who May Be Considered" to disclose the area of consideration.

Many vacancy announcements also indicate the appointment tenure, which specifies whether positions are to be filled as full-time permanent, part-time, temporary, or term appointments. The vast majority of federal law enforcement positions are filled as full-time permanent appointments, although agencies such as the National Park Service hire officers for part-time, temporary, or seasonal employment.

Major Duties

The vast majority of vacancy announcements provide an overview of the primary duties and responsibilities of positions being filled. These statements range from a single sentence that provides little or no useful information, to full-page descriptions that include specific details of assignments and tasks performed on the job. Some vacancy announcements also include an overview of the division, branch, or unit where the selectee will serve.

Qualification Requirements

An outline of the basic eligibility standards is incorporated under this heading. These could include a combination of general and specialized experience, education, training, medical requirements, minimum and maximum entry age, and other standards. Applicants must meet the minimum qualification requirements in order to be eligible for further consideration in the application process. Positions advertised under multiple salary grades usually include a breakdown of minimum requirements for each grade. Qualification requirements often are summarized in a format similar to the following example:

> *To qualify for appointment at the GS-5 level, applicants must have completed a four-year course of study above high school leading to a bachelor's degree, or have three years of general experience that was equivalent to at least GS-4 in the Federal service.*

> *For GS-7, applicants must have completed one full year of graduate level education, or have attained superior academic achievement during undergraduate studies, or have one year of specialized experience that was equivalent to at least GS-5 in the Federal service.*

Minimum qualification standards are used by staffing specialists to evaluate candidates' qualifications for positions and to eliminate those who are ineligible for further consideration because they fail to meet basic requirements.

How You Will Be Evaluated

Applicants who meet basic qualification requirements are rated on whether they possess the education, training, experience, or attributes needed for the positions being filled. Ratings are based on particular knowledge, skills, and abilities (KSAs) that are required to perform the duties of the position. The "How You Will Be Evaluated" section includes basic information on evaluation criteria and how application materials will be scored. Agencies rely on information provided in materials such as application forms, resumes, online questionnaires, or narrative statements to evaluate candidates, although the variety of materials used varies from one agency to another. (Application formats and applicant ratings are discussed later in this chapter.) Some agencies use titles such as "Basis of Rating"; "Ranking Factors"; "Knowledge, Skills, and Abilities"; "Selection Criteria"; or "Evaluation Criteria" for this section.

Typically, separate selection criteria are outlined for individual salary grade levels of positions being filled. For example, a recently posted vacancy announcement for a GS-1811 criminal investigator (special agent) position at the GS-7 level specified selection criteria under the heading of "Knowledge, Skills, and Abilities" as follows:

1. Knowledge of investigative techniques, principals, detection methods, and equipment

2. Knowledge of criminal law and rules of criminal procedure

3. Skill in both oral and written communication

4. Ability to analyze and evaluate facts, evidence, and related information and arrive at sound conclusions

5. Ability to deal effectively with individuals and groups at all levels of government and the private sector

While the KSAs listed above are fairly typical of criminal investigator positions at the GS-7 level, vacancy announcements for the same job series and salary grade often vary widely from one agency to another depending upon the nature of positions being filled and agency requirements. In addition, while some vacancy announcements describe selection criteria in detail, others may present KSAs in less explicit terms. For example, the following KSAs were listed in a vacancy announcement for a GS-1811 criminal investigator position at the GS-7 level:

1. Skill in oral communication
2. Skill in written communication
3. Ability to investigate

Supplemental Qualifications Statements

When applying for many federal law enforcement jobs, applicants are required to submit a Supplemental Qualifications Statement along with their application forms, or a resume that describes their education, experience, training, accomplishments, and awards related to the selection criteria. Vacancy announcements usually include instructions pertaining to the format of these statements, which also are known commonly as "KSA Statements." These statements were more common in recent years, although many agencies have replaced them with questionnaires that applicants complete and submit online.

The number of KSAs applicants must address varies from one vacancy announcement to the next. Some applications require candidates to respond to only three or four KSAs, whereas others might ask for six or more responses. (Detailed guidance for completing KSA statements is included in chapter 3, "Standing Out from the Crowd.")

Conditions of Employment

Agencies use this section to advise prospective applicants of special conditions under which hiring decisions and continued employment are based. For example, appointment and retention could be contingent upon passing medical examinations, urinalysis screening for illegal drugs, psychological assessments, written aptitude tests, physical fitness screening, training programs, personal interviews, a polygraph examination, or a pre-employment background investigation. Most agencies require suitability for a security clearance, and many require their personnel to travel extensively or to relocate to other duty stations, if necessary.

How to Apply and Contact Information

This "How to Apply" (or "Application Instructions") section provides detailed information relating to application forms and supporting documentation that must be submitted, the format of supplemental qualifications statements, addresses to which materials should be sent, and other details concerning the application process. Candidates often are directed to send application materials to a human resources office that is located at a site other than the duty station or unit where employment is sought, and many agencies conduct much of the application process online.

Vacancy announcements also include contact information, which usually specifies a street address and sometimes an e-mail address and the name of a person to whom applicants can direct questions or other inquiries. In some cases, a telephone number is provided for access to information regarding the status of the application process, although in some cases callers are connected only to recorded information lines.

Special Hiring Programs and Provisions

The federal government administers a number of special hiring programs that provide preference in hiring for certain groups. Of particular interest to those seeking careers in law enforcement are programs and provisions that apply to college graduates, veterans, and Native Americans, including the following.

The Outstanding Scholar Program

Federal agencies have always looked to educational institutions to recruit candidates who have the skills needed to meet its future staffing needs. The Outstanding Scholar Program is a special hiring authority that is used to attract talented students to certain entry-level positions in the competitive service at the GS-5 and GS-7 grade levels. Applicants who meet Program requirements can be offered a direct appointment by a federal agency without having to go through competitive examining procedures. The direct appointment process cuts through most of the red tape and can save weeks or months of time.

To qualify for consideration, an applicant must be a college graduate and have maintained a grade point average (GPA) of 3.45 or better on a 4.0 scale for all undergraduate coursework, or have graduated in the upper 10 percent of their graduating class in the college, university, or major subdivision (such as the College of Liberal Arts or the School of Criminal Justice). A college degree in any major is qualifying for most of the career fields covered under the Outstanding Scholar Program. A few, however, require some coursework in subjects related to the job. Application can be made a few months before graduation, provided that GPA or class standing requirements are met at such time as a job offer is extended.

Primary law enforcement and investigative career fields covered under the Outstanding Scholar Program include Park Ranger (GS-0025); Security Administration (GS-0080); Intelligence (GS-0132); Wage and Hour Compliance (GS-0249); Internal Revenue Officer (GS-1169); Inspection, Investigation, and Compliance (GS-1801); General Investigations (GS-1810); Criminal Investigations (GS-1811); Game Law Enforcement (GS-1812); Import Specialist (GS-1889); and Customs Inspector (GS-1890).

Additional information concerning the Outstanding Scholar Program—including a chart that includes details concerning law enforcement positions covered under program—is provided in chapter 3, "Standing Out from the Crowd."

Superior Academic Achievement

College students who have achieved high academic standing during undergraduate study may qualify for appointment at the GS-7 level for many federal jobs under Superior Academic Achievement provisions, even if they are lacking job-related experience. Under this provision, unlike the Outstanding Scholar Program, candidates must follow normal competitive hiring procedures and are not eligible for direct appointment.

The Superior Academic Achievement provision applies to those who have completed (or expect to complete within nine months) all the requirements for a bachelor's degree from an accredited college or university. (Students in their senior year of study can apply for positions prior to graduation for consideration based on their grades at the time of application.) Qualification is based upon either class standing, grade-point average, or honor society membership, as follows:

- **Class Standing.** Applicants must be in the upper third of their graduating class in the college, university, or major subdivision (such as the College of Liberal Arts or School of Criminal Justice) based on completed courses.

- **Grade-Point Average.** Applicants must have a grade-point average of 2.95 or higher out of a possible 4.0 for all courses completed at the time of application or during the last two years of the curriculum; or a 3.45 or higher out of a possible 4.0 for all courses completed in the major field of study at the time of application or during the last two years of the curriculum.

- **Honor Society Membership.** Applicants must have membership in one of the national honor societies (other than freshman or sophomore societies) recognized by the Association of College Honor Societies.

Many of the careers that are featured in this book provide for appointment under Superior Academic Achievement provisions. For these positions, eligibility is specified under the Qualifications heading of applicable career profiles.

Veterans' Preference Credit

Since the time of the Civil War, veterans of the armed forces have been given some degree of preference in appointments to federal jobs. By law, veterans who are disabled or who served on active duty during certain time periods are entitled to preference over nonveterans in hiring from competitive lists of eligibles. Preference applies in hiring from civil service examinations and for most excepted service jobs.

Veterans meeting the criteria for preference and who are found eligible (achieve a score of 70 or higher either by a written examination or an evaluation of their experience and education) have either five or ten points added to their numerical ratings depending upon the nature of their preference. Additional details relating to veterans' preference requirements normally are included in vacancy announcements.

Veterans' Readjustment Appointment

The Veterans' Readjustment Appointment (VRA) is a special authority through which agencies can appoint eligible veterans without competitive examination. Candidates need not have been on a list of eligibles, but must meet the basic qualification requirements of the position. Agencies can use the VRA authority to fill positions up through the GS-11 grade level, or at the equivalent grade level under other pay systems. VRA appointments are in the excepted service for a two-year period. Conversion to permanent (career or career-conditional) status is granted after satisfactory completion of the two-year service period and any education or training requirements.

To qualify, candidates must have served on active duty for more than 180 days, all or any part of which occurred after August 4, 1964, and received other than a dishonorable discharge. Some veterans who served fewer than 180 days also are eligible, including those who were discharged or released from active duty as a result of a service-connected disability, as well as Reserve and Guard members who were ordered to active duty under certain circumstances. Vacancy announcements typically include details relating to VRA eligibility.

Thirty Percent or More Disabled Veteran Program

Federal agencies have the authority to provide noncompetitive appointments to veterans who have a service-connected disability of 30 percent or more. Unlike the VRA Program, which limits appointments up to the GS-11 grade, qualifying candidates can be appointed to any salary grade for which they are qualified, without limitation. Candidates must meet all qualifications of the position to which they are appointed, which could include achieving a passing score on a written examination. Appointments are considered temporary for a period of at least 60 days, after which conversion to permanent status can be granted if job performance has been satisfactory.

Native American Preference

In accordance with the Indian Reorganization Act of 1934, preference in filling employment vacancies is given to qualified Native American candidates for all positions in the Bureau of Indian Affairs (BIA), and to other positions in the Department of the Interior directly and primarily related to providing services to Native Americans. Initial appointments under the Act are in the excepted service. Conversion to a career appointment in the competitive service is granted after three years of continuous service and satisfactory performance. Law enforcement careers in the BIA include Correctional Officers, Police Officers, Radio Telecommunication Operators, and Special Agents.

Application Formats

Federal job applicants have several choices when applying for employment consideration, including the Optional Application for Federal Employment (OF-612), a resume, the Standard Form 171 Application for Federal Employment (SF-171), or any other written format of choice. In addition, applications must be submitted online or over the telephone for certain positions, and some agencies require agency-specific application forms. This section provides an overview of application format options. See chapter 3, "Standing Out from the Crowd," for valuable tips on completing application forms and resumes.

OF-612 Optional Application for Federal Employment

The OF-612 application form replaced the SF-171 in 1995 as the standard written format for applying for federal employment. Unlike the cumbersome SF-171, which took hours to complete, the OF-612 is easier to fill out and is printed on two sides of a single sheet of paper. This form requires applicants to describe their employment experience, educational background, and other qualifications, such as job-related training courses, skills, certificates and licenses, honors, awards, and special accomplishments. An OF-612 application form can be found online (see the inside back cover of this book).

The Federal Resume

Along with replacement of the SF-171 application came new rules allowing applicants to submit resumes for job consideration. The federal resume, however, differs significantly from those used in the private sector. For example, while a corporate resume presents a brief synopsis of an applicant's background, a federal resume goes into greater detail and must include specific data that is not normally included in resumes submitted to private industry. Applicants who fail to provide the required information often are eliminated from further consideration. In addition to the information requested in job vacancy announcements, federal resumes must provide essentially the same information as requested in the OF-612 application, including the following:

- **Job Information.** Vacancy announcement number, position title, and salary grade applied for.

- **Personal Information.** Full name, complete mailing address, daytime and evening telephone numbers, Social Security number, country of citizenship, veterans' preference eligibility, reinstatement eligibility, and highest federal civilian grade held (including dates).

- **Education.** Highest grade completed, name and complete address of high school attended, date of diploma or GED, name and complete address of colleges or universities attended, total credits earned (specify whether semester or quarter credits), majors, and type and year of any degrees received. Include a copy of college transcript(s) if requested to do so in vacancy announcements.

- **Paid and Nonpaid Work Experience.** Titles of jobs held (including series and grade, if federal), starting and ending dates (month and year), salary, number of hours per week, employer's name and complete address, supervisor's name and telephone number (indicate whether permission is given to contact the supervisor), and description of duties and accomplishments. Prepare a separate entry for each job.

- **Other Qualifications.** Title and dates of job-related training courses, examples of job-related skills, title and dates of job-related certificates and licenses held, and details of honors, awards, and special accomplishments.

Some agencies that process employment applications online also require candidates to type or paste their resume into a box provided in the application. See chapter 3, "Standing Out from the Crowd," for guidance on the proper format and for tips on creating an outstanding federal resume.

Online Employment Application

Many agencies now accept only online employment applications, inasmuch as these provide a measure of uniformity and facilitate the efficient collection of information needed to evaluate applicants. Candidates without direct access to the Internet can apply for federal jobs online at almost any public or college library, or through federal, state, and local government-sponsored employment offices. Although the format of online applications varies from one agency to the next, most ask for essentially the same information requested in the OF-612 application, and some obtain additional information through extensive online questionnaires.

SF-171 Application for Federal Employment

The Standard Form 171 was created in an effort to standardize job application forms at a time when agencies were using a wide assortment of agency-specific forms. Until January 1995, when it was replaced by the OF-612, applicants had no choice but to submit an SF-171 when applying for most federal jobs. Although the SF-171 is widely regarded as obsolete, some federal agencies allow their employees to use the form when applying for job transfers and promotions.

Telephone Application Processing System

Some federal agencies accept employment applications over the telephone via the OPM Telephone Application Processing System (TAPS), which provides a simple method of applying for federal job vacancies 24 hours a day, seven days a week. Applicant information is entered through a combination of touch-tone telephone keypad and recorded voice responses, including demographic, geographic, and job preference data, along with qualifying education and experience information. This data is downloaded nightly to a local area network and processed. Applicants are evaluated electronically through a rating instrument created for each position, and are referred to agencies for additional processing. TAPS telephone numbers, which vary from one position to another, are provided in job vacancy announcements.

Written Examinations

Several federal law enforcement agencies require candidates to pass a written examination to receive further consideration in the hiring process. Some of the exams are agency-specific, meaning they are designed and used only by a single agency. Such tests include the U.S. Border Patrol Agent Examination, the FBI Phase I test, the U.S. Postal Police Officer Examination, the U.S. Park Police Officer Examination, and the Immigration & Customs Enforcement Special Agent Test Battery. Other exams are generic in nature and are used by multiple agencies. For example, the Treasury Enforcement Agent Examination, the National Police Officer Selection Test, and the Administrative Careers with America Examination are administered to applicants seeking employment with various agencies. Vacancy announcements usually indicate whether written exams are required. See chapter 3, "Standing Out from the Crowd," for additional information concerning these examinations and test-taking guidance.

Initial Applicant Ratings

Federal agencies are required by law to observe merit system principles to ensure that job applicants are rated fairly and objectively. Initial procedures for evaluating and rating applicants depend largely upon whether written examinations are part of the hiring process. Agencies that do not use tests base initial screening decisions on the content of resumes, application forms, information submitted online, and other related materials. On the other hand, agencies that require applicants to take examinations typically rely mostly on the test scores for initial screening and rating purposes. Once initial screening has been completed, the remainder of hiring processes carried out by most agencies tend to follow similar paths regardless of whether written examinations were used.

The Application or Resume

To begin the screening process, federal job applications are reviewed by staffing specialists to determine whether candidates meet minimum qualification requirements. Many agencies use a self-assessment questionnaire for screening purposes as a supplement to application forms or resumes. Oftentimes, these questionnaires are completed online via agency Web sites. Applicants lacking required education, experience, training, or other requirements are eliminated from further consideration, and the remaining applications are evaluated and graded in a numerical scoring process based on qualifications. In some cases, agencies also screen out minimally qualified applicants at this point in the process.

Applications that survive the initial screening process are then reviewed by a rating panel that usually consists of three or more agency staff members who hold positions at or above the grade level of the job being filled. At this point, applicants are evaluated further and are assigned numerical scores for each element of the position selection criteria. As discussed above, candidates who qualify for Veterans' Preference can receive additional points, depending upon their level of preference. After all applications have been reviewed by each panel member, the total scores are calculated and divided by the number of panel members to reach an average score that is known as a rating. Depending on the number of positions being filled, the number of applicants, and agency procedures, a certain number of candidates with the highest scores are then placed on a list of eligibles that is commonly known as the Best Qualified List. These candidates are then referred to the office that will conduct the remainder of the selection process, which oftentimes is the office where the selectee will work. Steps in the remainder of the hiring process depend on the nature of the position being filled and the agency filling the position, although they could include personal interviews, a polygraph examination, a background investigation, a physical fitness test, and final selections.

Written Examination Score

Agencies that require applicants to take a written examination typically screen application materials to ensure that candidates meet minimum requirements (as discussed above) prior to scheduling them for the exam. Those who achieve a passing score on the exam typically are placed on a register of eligibles according to their scores (including Veterans' Preference points). Many agencies maintain eligibility registers for a period of months or even years, from which candidates may be called upon to complete additional phases in the selection process. Those chosen to continue are processed in accordance with individual agency hiring policies. As discussed above, the remaining steps could include interviews, a polygraph examination, a background investigation, a physical fitness test, and other requirements.

Personal Interviews

The vast majority of federal law enforcement agencies interview job applicants as a matter of standard operating procedure. Personal interviews often are conducted in person, although telephone interviews also are common. Two primary types of interviews are used, including *traditional* and *behavioral*. In traditional interviews, applicants are asked "traditional" questions concerning their background, motivations, strengths, weaknesses, accomplishments, and the like. These questions are designed to predict whether applicants are likely to succeed on the job. Behavioral interviews include questions that identify how applicants have acted in situations on and off the job in the past, providing actual evidence relating to job skills, motivations, judgment, integrity, and other characteristics related to job performance. Traditional and behavioral interviews are discussed in greater detail in chapter 3, "Standing Out from the Crowd."

The format of personal interviews varies from one position to another, both in style and level of formality, depending on the position sought and the agency conducting the interview. These range from structured panel interviews to informal one-on-one discussions. Depending on the position being filled, panel interviews could be conducted by field-level personnel who serve in nonsupervisory positions, or by supervisory staff, or by a combination of supervisory and nonsupervisory personnel.

In many cases, interviews are conducted by a single supervisor or manager representing the division or unit where the selectee will serve. The following section offers a brief overview of structured and semi-structured interviews, which are the most common interview formats. See chapter 3 for valuable tips, guidance, and other information concerning personal interviews.

Structured Interviews

Many federal law enforcement agencies use structured interviews in their hiring processes. Such agencies include U.S. Immigration and Customs Enforcement, U.S. Border Patrol, Secret Service, FBI, U.S. Marshals Service, and dozens of smaller agencies. During structured interviews, the interviewers ask every candidate an identical set of questions. This technique allows interviewers to compare and evaluate candidates on a level playing field, and to determine which candidates possess the knowledge, skills, and abilities that are required of the position being filled. Although structured interviews are common during hiring processes for special agent and police officer positions, many agencies use these interviews when filling vacancies at every level, including clerical jobs such as clerk, secretary, typist, administrative assistant, and other positions.

Semi-Structured Interviews

Another common approach to employment interviews is the semi-structured method, which is less formal than the structured interview. Semi-structured interviews typically include a combination of standard questions—similar to the format of a structured interview—although they also include questions that have not been predetermined. Semi-structured interviews are very effective not only for the selection of law enforcement officers, but also of technical and scientific personnel or any position where multiple probes into theoretical questions are posed. An advantage of semi-structured interviews is the flexibility they offer interviewers to examine, explore, and revisit applicants' responses to a variety of open-ended questions tailored to each position.

The Polygraph Examination

A polygraph examination is required by many federal law enforcement agencies, such as the Central Intelligence Agency, Postal Inspection Service, FBI, Air Force Office of Special Investigations, Defense Intelligence Agency, Secret Service, and National Security Agency, among others. Although the nature of polygraph examinations varies from one agency to another, the process typically focuses on verification of information provided by applicants and gathered during the background investigation, national security and counterintelligence issues, illegal drug use and activity, integrity issues, and other areas of concern.

How the Polygraph Works

The polygraph is designed to identify physiological and psychological reactions that are commonly associated with deception. In other words, it records signs of internal stress that people are believed to experience when they respond to questions in a deceptive manner. As a result, data from the examination allows the polygraph examiner to render a diagnostic opinion regarding the honesty or dishonesty of a person.

In technical terms, the polygraph is considered an instrument—not a machine—inasmuch as it is designed to measure changes in cardiovascular activity, respiratory rate, and skin chemistry while the applicant is asked a series of questions. The polygraph normally consists of at least three components, including the following:

- A cardiograph, which monitors pulse and changes in blood pressure

- A pneumograph, which records respiration rate by measuring chest expansions and contractions

- A galvanometer that is normally attached to the hand to measure electrical conductivity through perspiration

The activity monitored by each of the components is recorded in graphic form and interpreted by the examiner. Some polygraph instruments measure gross muscular movements, also.

Phases of the Polygraph

The typical polygraph examination is conducted in three phases, including a pretest, data collection, and data analysis. Most often, the examination begins with a face-to-face pretest interview between the polygraph examiner and the applicant, during which the instrument and the examination are explained. The pretest interview allows the examiner to secure the confidence and cooperation of the applicant, and to evaluate any personal idiosyncrasies that might affect the applicant's examination results. During the data-collection phase, the examiner asks a series of control questions—usually of the "true or false" and "yes or no" variety. Many of the control questions are simple and straightforward. These questions might focus on the applicant's name, place of birth, residence, and other biographical details. The examiner uses the responses to control questions to establish a baseline with which to compare the applicant's reactions to essential questions later.

Control questions are followed by specific questions that explore national security and counterintelligence issues, experience with illegal drugs, and other information provided in application materials. In the final phase, the examiner analyzes the results to determine whether they are indicative of truthfulness or deception. If any responses appear to be deceptive, the examiner might ask the applicant additional questions or ask them to explain these responses. The expertise of the examiner is very important in assessing truthfulness or deception.

Polygraph Results

Most agencies forward results of the polygraph examination to headquarters personnel prior to notifying applicants of whether they passed or failed. This gives the agencies time to review the results and sort out any potential issues. Although applicants who do not fall within acceptable parameters for the polygraph examination usually are disqualified, some agencies will review appeals by applicants who fail the exam, and in limited circumstances offer a second test. Applicants usually are notified in writing as to whether they passed or failed the examination.

The Background Investigation

Every federal law enforcement agency conducts a pre-employment background investigation of selectees prior to bringing them on board. Many agencies conduct their own background investigations, while some agencies have OPM or contractor firms perform the investigations. Background investigators are responsible only for gathering information and reporting their findings in accordance with a standard format, and not for making determinations regarding suitability for employment or granting of a security clearance.

Primary Focus and Time Period Covered

Background investigations are conducted primarily to assess whether applicants are suitable for employment and worthy of a security clearance. Personnel employed by federal law enforcement agencies normally are required to hold a security clearance as a condition of employment. Security clearance determinations are governed by Presidential Executive Orders and Director of Central Intelligence Directives that are extensive and detailed.

Most agencies examine applicants' activities beginning at the age of 18, and earlier years if necessary to fully resolve issues that arise. Background investigations typically include a review of credit history and criminal records; driving record and license inquiries; verification of employment history, licenses, credentials, and certifications; interviews of associates, personal and business references, past and present employers, and neighbors; verification of educational achievements, military records, and medical history; and verification of birth, citizenship, and residency records. Interviews conducted by background investigators almost always are performed in person, although in some circumstances could take place by telephone.

Background investigations can vary somewhat from one agency to another, although there tend to be more similarities than differences in focus and how the investigations are performed. For example, background investigations conducted by the FBI are fairly typical, and place emphasis on the following areas:

- Character, including attributes such as honesty, trustworthiness, judgment, reliability, attitude, discretion, diplomacy, dependability, punctuality, stability, and temperament

- Associates, with emphasis on the types of people, groups, or organizations with which the applicant has been involved or affiliated, and whether any of these associations have been of a disreputable or disloyal nature

- Reputation, relating to the applicant's standing in the community and in their profession or field of work

- Loyalty, in terms of their allegiance toward the United States, employers, and others

- Ability, as far as their level of competency and capacity to perform well in their occupation

- Financial responsibility, meaning the applicant maintains a satisfactory relationship with creditors and has spending habits that are consistent with their means

- Biases or prejudice, which concerns actions and attitude toward people of various racial, ethnic, gender, or religious groups

- Alcohol abuse, which focuses on excessive use of alcoholic beverages and related behavioral issues

- Drug abuse, including the use of any illegal drugs or abuse of prescription medications

Derogatory Information

Discovery of derogatory information is not uncommon, even for the best-qualified applicants. In these instances, background investigators ask follow-up questions and otherwise explore details to elicit all available information. These inquiries often focus on the following:

- The nature, extent, and seriousness of the conduct

- The motivation for and circumstances surrounding the conduct

- The frequency and recentness of the conduct

- The applicant's age and maturity at the time of the conduct

- Whether the conduct was voluntary or whether there was pressure, coercion, or exploitation leading to the conduct

- Whether the applicant has been rehabilitated or has exhibited other pertinent behavioral changes since the conduct

As you can see, investigators endeavor to uncover "the big picture," and derogatory information is not necessarily the kiss of death. In other words, investigators attempt to determine not only the nature and seriousness of the conduct or problem, but whether the applicant has made positive changes in behavior. In the case of derogatory information provided by a person about an applicant, investigators also explore whether there could be animosity or bias toward the applicant on the part of the person providing the information. In the final analysis, the complete background investigation is assessed before a decision on employment is rendered.

Lack of Candor

Without question, lack of candor is one of the most likely pathways to disqualification from the hiring process. Lack of candor occurs when an applicant fails to disclose or conceals derogatory information; misrepresents facts; or provides untruthful information on application forms, during interviews or the polygraph examination, or at any other point along the way. Interestingly enough, a common and fatal mistake applicants often make is failure to be forthright about something that would not have resulted in disqualification if only they had been truthful about it. Therefore, it is important to keep in mind that background investigations are performed by experienced investigators who know exactly how to get to the bottom of things. With this and basic ethics principles in mind, your best bet is to disclose and thoroughly discuss during the application process any information you think could come back to haunt you. In other words, "when in doubt, get it out."

Length of the Background Investigation

Most background investigations are completed in one to four months, although in some cases they can take much longer. The length of the investigation depends on a number of variables, such as the following:

- Accuracy and completeness of application materials

- Issues that arise requiring further investigation

- The extent of foreign travel, or whether the applicant has resided in another country

- The number of residences or employers the applicant has had

- Ability to locate and interview employers, references, or other persons
- Availability of records
- The number of applicants being processed at any given time
- The workload of background investigators

Background Investigation Results

In most cases, applicants are informed of the outcome of their background investigation in writing. Applicants can obtain a copy of the background investigation report in accordance with the Freedom of Information Act (FOIA) and the Privacy Act (PA). Written requests should be mailed to the headquarters of the agency, in care of the office that processes FOIA/PA requests. However, don't be surprised if the agency takes a thick black marker and crosses out the names of individuals and other portions of the report in accordance with FOIA and PA laws. This is known as *redacting* the report, and it is a common practice.

The Medical Examination

Many applicants for employment with federal law enforcement agencies—including some who apply for positions that do not involve law enforcement officer authority—must undergo a medical examination, sometimes referred to as a physical exam. Inasmuch as medical examinations are expensive, they are offered at the end of the hiring process and normally are given only to candidates the agency expects to hire. The following section provides examples of the types of positions for which these exams are required, an overview of exam protocol, and information concerning pre-existing medical conditions.

Positions Requiring a Medical Examination

All candidates for positions that involve exercising law enforcement authority—primarily carrying firearms and making arrests—are required to complete a thorough medical examination prior to appointment. Some examples of these positions include criminal investigator (special agent), customs and border protection officer, deputy U.S. Marshal, nuclear materials courier, park ranger, and police officer. OPM has established general medical requirements for many positions, although agencies are free to create their own standards as long as they are job-related. For example, medical requirements established by OPM for the GS-1811 criminal investigator (special agent) series include the following:

> The duties of positions in this series require moderate to arduous physical exertion involving walking and standing, use of firearms, and exposure to inclement weather. Manual dexterity with comparatively free motion of finger, wrist, elbow, shoulder, hip, and knee joints is required. Arms, hands, legs, and feet must be sufficiently intact and functioning in order that applicants may perform the duties satisfactorily. Sufficiently good vision in each eye, with or without correction, is required to perform the duties satisfactorily. Near vision, corrective lenses permitted, must be sufficient to read printed material the size of typewritten characters. Hearing loss, as measured by an audiometer, must not exceed 35 decibels at 1000, 2000, and 3000 Hz levels. Since the duties of these positions are exacting and responsible, and involve activities

under trying conditions, applicants must possess emotional and mental stability. Any physical condition that would cause the applicant to be a hazard to himself/herself or others is disqualifying.

Most candidates for law enforcement support positions—jobs that do not involve the authority to enforce criminal laws—are not given a pre-employment physical examination. However, the physical demands or hazardous work conditions of some support positions are such that agencies must ensure that certain personnel are physically fit for duty. For example, electronics technician candidates must have a physical exam because they might be required to lift heavy objects or climb ladders, poles, antenna towers, and other objects to mount or service electronic equipment and devices. Other examples of positions that require a medical exam are air safety investigators, diversion investigators, import specialists, mine safety and health inspectors, and pilots. In addition, some positions require a limited medical exam. For example, language specialist candidates are required to undergo a hearing test because they must have adequate hearing in order to translate live and recorded speech.

Medical Examination Protocol

Medical examinations are performed to rule out medical issues or conditions that could potentially affect an applicant's ability to perform the basic functions of the position for which they have applied. The exams usually are coordinated and paid for by the hiring agency, although in some cases they are arranged and paid for by applicants if pre-existing medical conditions are of concern.

Although medical examinations for federal law enforcement job applicants can differ depending on the position being filled, the exams generally include procedures such as the following:

- A review of a medical history questionnaire completed by the applicant

- Measurement of body weight and height

- A complete set of vital signs, including body temperature, heart rate (pulse), blood pressure, respiration rate, and pupil reaction

- Listening to the heart and lungs

- Examination of the ears, nose, throat, mouth, tongue, teeth, and gums

- Examination of the skin, abdomen, lymph nodes, thyroid, prostate, and genitalia

- Evaluation of the spine, musculoskeletal system, neurological functions, joints, flexibility, and posture

- Demonstration of standing, walking, kneeling, bending, pushing, pulling, and muscle coordination

- Lifting and carrying heavy objects (45 pounds or more) or moderately heavy objects (15–44 pounds or more)

- A vision examination that tests near vision, far vision, depth perception, and ability to distinguish basic colors

- An audiometer (hearing) test

- An electrocardiogram (EKG)

- A stress test (treadmill)

- A pulmonary (lung) function test (PFT)
- Laboratory analysis of blood and urine samples

Most commonly, results of the medical examination are turned over to the chief medical officer of the agency, who reviews each candidate's medical history and determines whether they are medically suited for the position. Once on board, most federal law enforcement personnel undergo periodic medical examinations—usually every one to three years, depending on the age of the employee—at agency expense. For example, FBI special agents under age 33 are examined every three years, while those 33 years of age and older are given an exam annually. After age 40, FBI special agents also complete a cardiac stress test every two years.

Preexisting Medical Conditions

Not surprisingly, some federal law enforcement job applicants have preexisting medical conditions that could affect their ability to serve. Oftentimes applicants are aware of these conditions, and occasionally the pre-employment medical examination reveals issues or conditions that were undetected previously. In either case, these issues or conditions could require applicants to undergo additional examination by a medical specialist, oftentimes at the candidate's expense. In these instances, the specialist performs an examination and sends a report of the findings to the agency.

Each candidate's health and fitness, history of surgical procedures, medical records, and other relevant information are reviewed on an individual, case-by-case basis. Although a candidate's doctor also may provide information about a medical condition, the final decision concerning a candidate's ability to serve in federal law enforcement rests solely with the agency. Keep in mind that regardless of whether medical issues or preexisting conditions requiring additional examination are disqualifying in nature, they often result in delay of both application processing and placement in a basic training course.

Pre-employment Physical Fitness Tests

Like many other aspects of federal law enforcement agency hiring processes, whether a pre-employment physical fitness test is required depends on the position applied for and varies from one agency to another. For example, physical fitness tests are administered during the hiring processes for Deputy U.S. Marshals, FBI Special Agents, U.S. Border Patrol Agents, U.S. Customs and Border Protection Officers, and U.S. Park Police Officers, among others. Most fitness tests consist of push-ups, sit-ups, and running, although some include tasks such as a bench-press strength test, lifting heavy objects, a body fat assessment, kneeling, a flexibility evaluation, or a cardiovascular endurance stair-step test. Some agencies, such as the FBI and the U.S. Marshals Service, allow applicants who fail the physical fitness test to be retested later during the same hiring process. On the other hand, agencies such as U.S. Customs and Border Protection do not allow retesting, and applicants who fail the physical fitness test must reapply under future vacancy announcements.

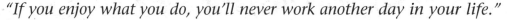

CHAPTER 2

Salary and Benefits

"If you enjoy what you do, you'll never work another day in your life."

—*Confucius*

There are many advantages to a career with the federal government, not the least of which are competitive salaries and a wide range of fringe benefits that surpass those provided by many state and municipal government agencies and firms in the private sector. Indeed, a study conducted by the Congressional Budget Office found that federal benefits are superior to those of many large companies in private industry.

Attractive salaries also make federal employment a good deal. Entry-level salaries for most federal law enforcement clerical support personnel range from $25,000 to $40,000 per year, while annual starting salaries for most law enforcement officers range from $35,000 to $50,000, plus additional locality pay for those who serve in many metropolitan areas. Of course, starting salary is only the beginning, and many employees who remain in the federal workforce earn substantially more than entry-level pay after only a few years on the job. For example, GS-7 level support staff can earn more than $45,000 per year, technical staff at the GS-12 level can earn almost $80,000 per year, and the annual salary for criminal investigator managers at the GS-15 level is $125,000 to $163,000.

The comprehensive benefits package offered to federal personnel helps attract and retain some of the nation's best and brightest talent. Indeed, the federal government offers an excellent combination of benefits to employees, retirees, and their families. In addition to health and life insurance, paid holidays, vacation and sick leave, travel allowances, training, and injury compensation benefits provided to federal employees, many federal law enforcement officers also are covered under special salary and benefit programs. This chapter provides an overview of salary structures and the primary benefits available to federal law enforcement officers and support personnel.

Federal Salary and Wage Systems

Federal law enforcement personnel are compensated under a number of different salary and wage systems, including some established by individual laws and others by administrative determination. The statutory pay systems for white-collar federal personnel are those of the General Schedule, the Foreign Service, and a system that covers certain employees of the Veterans Health Administration of the Department of Veterans Affairs (VA). Salaries under these systems are governed by policies and principles set forth in the United States Code.

The majority of federal law enforcement personnel are covered under the General Schedule pay system. Special Agents and Regional Security Officers of the State Department's Bureau of Diplomatic Security are covered under the Foreign Service pay system. The Veterans Health Administration provides pay plans for VA medical staff. Top-level federal executives and blue-collar personnel are paid in accordance with separate wage and salary systems. An overview of the primary federal salary and wage systems is provided below.

The General Schedule (GS) Pay System

Approximately 75 percent of federal employees are compensated under the General Schedule (GS) pay system, including most white-collar personnel in the executive branch and in certain agencies of the legislative branch. The General Schedule consists of 15 grades, each structured in terms of difficulty and responsibility of the work and the qualifications required for its performance, ranging from GS-1 to GS-15. Progressing from one grade to the next is known as a *grade increase*. Of course, some positions allow for advancement to higher grades than others. A salary range of 10 steps is provided within each grade, with employees normally starting at Step 1 within a particular grade at entry level. Moving to the next step within a grade is known as a *within-grade increase* or *step increase*.

Although most federal jobs are structured so that employees accepting positions at entry level can advance to higher grade levels later on, the manner in which advancement occurs depends on the type of position held. Personnel employed in professional and administrative occupations progress by two-grade increments beginning at grade GS-5 and advancing to grade GS-11, and then in single-grade intervals from grade GS-12 to grade GS-15. For example, the FBI chemist/forensic examiner position is covered by a pay range of GS-7 through GS-13, and also provides for advancement to the next higher grade level in one-year increments. Therefore, chemists hired at the GS-7 level can advance to GS-9 after one year, then to GS-11 one year later, to GS-12 after another year, and finally to GS-13 after another year.

On the other hand, many clerical and technical personnel progress only by single-grade increments, and positions in these categories span lower grade levels overall. For example, the U.S. Secret Service investigative assistant position covers a grade range of GS-5 to GS-7, so an investigative assistant hired at GS-5 would advance to GS-6 after one year and to GS-7 one year later.

Federal personnel whose performance is at an acceptable level can receive periodic within-grade increases in accordance with specified waiting periods. Within-grade increases normally occur after 52 weeks of service in the first three steps in a grade, after 104 weeks in steps 4 through 6, and after 156 weeks in steps 7 and above. Employees also can advance more rapidly within their grades by demonstrating high quality performance and earning "quality step increases." However, an employee can receive only one such increase during any 52-week period. Personnel who reach the highest possible grade in their position continue to receive within-grade increases until they "top-out" at Step 10. Table 2.1 further illustrates the waiting period and manner in which federal personnel move from one step to the next.

Table 2.1: Schedule of Within-Grade Pay Increases	
Advancement From	**Waiting Period**
Step 1 to Step 2	52 weeks of service at Step 1
Step 2 to Step 3	52 weeks of service at Step 2
Step 3 to Step 4	52 weeks of service at Step 3
Step 4 to Step 5	104 weeks of service at Step 4
Step 5 to Step 6	104 weeks of service at Step 5
Step 6 to Step 7	104 weeks of service at Step 6
Step 7 to Step 8	156 weeks of service at Step 7
Step 8 to Step 9	156 weeks of service at Step 8
Step 9 to Step 10	156 weeks of service at Step 9

Federal salary rates normally increase in January each year. Provisions of the Federal Employees Pay Comparability Act of 1990 (FEPCA) require annual increases to be based on changes in the Employment Cost Index, which is maintained by the U.S. Bureau of Labor Statistics as a measure of labor costs in the private sector. However, ongoing disagreements between Congress and the White House concerning FEPCA have led to alternative means of determining pay adjustments. In other words, in recent years the annual federal pay raise has been negotiated by Congress and the President. Most recently, the increase has been tied to the pay raise given to military personnel.

Administratively Determined Pay Systems

Many federal law enforcement personnel are compensated under administratively determined pay systems. Administratively determined pay systems are those for which Congress has authorized heads of agencies to establish compensation for the entire agency or for particular groups of positions without regard to the General Schedule. Some of the agencies establish their own schedules of rates, while others use the General Schedule grade and step structure (although they are not required to do so).

The Federal Wage System (FWS)

Most federal trade, craft, and labor occupations fall under the Federal Wage System (FWS), which covers blue-collar personnel who are paid by the hour. The FWS schedule is designed to compensate these employees so they are paid at the same rate as other federal personnel who perform similar work, and also so their wages are comparable to those of workers in the private sector.

There are 15 grade levels in the FWS schedule. The lowest-paid occupations are represented at Level 1, which includes positions such as janitors and laundry workers, while the highest-paid are at Level 15, such as instrument-makers.

The Senior Executive Service (SES)

The majority of personnel holding supervisory, managerial, and policy positions above the GS-15 level in the executive branch are paid under the Senior Executive Service (SES) pay schedule. SES salary rates are determined by the President, and are adjusted annually at the same time as annual pay raises are authorized for General Schedule personnel. Presently, there are six levels in the SES pay schedule, including salaries that range from $107,550 to $162,100. Positions that require Senate confirmation are not covered under SES.

Locality Payments

Federal employees covered under the General Schedule and many other pay systems receive locality-based comparability payments—known as *locality pay*—in addition to regular salary. Contrary to popular misconceptions, locality pay *does not* serve as a cost-of-living adjustment. Rather, it is designed to cover the difference between prevailing federal and private sector salaries in various geographic locations, although adjustments are made only in areas where the disparity is higher than 5 percent. More than 30 metropolitan areas in the United States are designated as qualifying for locality pay. Personnel employed in all other areas receive locality pay according to the rate established for those in the "Rest of United States" (RUS) category. Locality pay rates are adjusted annually based on data compiled by the U.S. Bureau of Labor Statistics and the nine-member Federal Salary Council, as well as the actions of Congress and the President.

Table 2.2 provides an overview of calendar year 2005 locality pay rates for personnel not employed in RUS locations. In other words, employees in these areas receive the locality pay percentage shown in addition to the RUS rate. Salary schedules shown in tables 2.3, 2.4, and 2.5 also include RUS locality pay.

Table 2.2: Locality Pay Adjustments for 2006. Rates in Metropolitan Areas in Addition to the "Rest of U.S." Rate

Metropolitan Area	Percentage Adjustment
Atlanta–Sandy Springs–Gainesville, GA-AL	2.58%
Boston–Worcester–Manchester, MA-NH-ME-RI	7.47%
Buffalo–Niagara–Cattaraugus, NY	1.00%
Chicago–Naperville–Michigan City, IL-IN-WI	8.63%
Cincinnati–Middletown–Wilmington, OH-KY-IN	4.56%
Cleveland–Akron–Elyria, OH	2.89%
Columbus–Marion–Chillicothe, OH	2.33%
Dallas–Fort Worth, TX	3.87%
Dayton–Springfield–Greenville, OH	1.31%
Denver–Aurora–Boulder, CO	6.97%
Detroit–Warren–Flint, MI	8.48%
Hartford–West Hartford–Willimantic, CT-MA	8.78%
Houston–Baytown–Huntsville, TX	13.85%
Huntsville–Decatur, AL	0.83%
Indianapolis–Anderson–Columbus, IN	0.33%
Los Angeles–Long Beach–Riverside, CA	10.66%
Miami–Fort Lauderdale–Miami Beach, FL	5.32%
Milwaukee–Racine–Waukesha, WI	2.22%

Minneapolis–St. Paul–St. Cloud, MN-WI	4.79%
New York–Newark–Bridgeport, NY-NJ-CT-PA	10.45%
Philadelphia–Camden–Vineland, PA-NJ-DE-MD	5.52%
Phoenix–Mesa–Scottsdale, AZ	0.13%
Pittsburgh–New Castle, PA	1.29%
Portland–Vancouver–Beaverton, OR-WA	4.64%
Raleigh–Durham–Gary, NC	3.05%
Richmond, VA	1.63%
Sacramento–Arden–Arcade–Truckee, CA-NV	5.39%
San Diego–Carlsbad–San Marcos, CA	6.67%
San Jose–San Francisco–Oakland, CA	16.16%
Seattle–Tacoma–Olympia, WA	5.41%
Washington–Baltimore–Northern VA, DC-MD-PA-VA-WV	4.98%

Law Enforcement Salary Rates and Adjustments

Most personnel employed by federal law enforcement agencies are paid according to one of three General Schedule salary tables, including a table that includes a 25 percent salary premium known as Law Enforcement Availability Pay (LEAP), a Law Enforcement Officer Special Rate table, or a standard salary table for support employees. In addition, the majority of personnel whose salary is not based on General Schedule pay tables are compensated under pay systems that mirror salary rates of the General Schedule. The following section provides an overview of the salary rates and adjustments that apply to the vast majority of federal law enforcement agency employees.

Law Enforcement Availability Pay (LEAP)

LEAP, enacted by Congress in 1994, compensates federal criminal investigators for substantial amounts of unscheduled overtime duty they routinely perform, and to ensure the availability of criminal investigators for unscheduled duty based upon the needs of employing agencies. As a result, the vast majority of personnel in the GS-1811 (Criminal Investigating) and GS-1812 (Game Law Enforcement) series receive a salary premium fixed at 25 percent of basic pay. For example, a criminal investigator whose base salary is $52,000 per year receives an additional 25 percent ($13,000) in LEAP, resulting in a total annual salary of $65,000.

To qualify for LEAP, investigators are expected to work, or be available to work, an average of two hours of duty above every regular eight-hour work day. LEAP is a guaranteed employee entitlement that agencies must provide as long as required conditions are met. Some agencies, such as Office of Inspectors General that employ fewer than five criminal investigators, may elect not to cover criminal investigators or are otherwise exempt from LEAP provisions. A salary schedule that incorporates LEAP is shown in table 2.3.

Table 2.3: 2006 General Schedule Annual Salary for Criminal Investigators (Special Agents), Including Law Enforcement Availability Pay (LEAP) and Locality Pay for "Rest of U.S." Geographic Areas

	Step 1	Step 2	Step 3	Step 4	Step 5	Step 6	Step 7	Step 8	Step 9	Step 10
GS-5	43,708	44,889	46,070	47,251	48,433	49,614	50,796	51,978	53,159	54,340
GS-7	49,746	51,209	52,673	54,135	55,598	57,060	58,523	59,986	61,449	62,911
GS-9	55,484	57,274	59,065	60,855	62,645	64,436	66,226	68,018	69,808	71,598
GS-10	61,100	63,070	65,041	67,011	68,981	70,953	72,923	74,894	76,864	78,834
GS-11	64,965	67,131	69,296	71,463	73,629	75,795	77,961	80,128	82,293	84,459
GS-12	77,864	80,459	83,054	85,649	88,244	90,839	93,434	96,029	98,624	101,219
GS-13	92,593	95,679	98,765	101,850	104,936	108,023	111,108	114,194	117,280	120,365
GS-14	109,416	113,063	116,710	120,358	124,004	127,651	131,299	134,945	138,593	142,239
GS-15	128,705	132,995	137,284	141,574	145,864	150,154	154,444	158,734	163,024	167,313

Special Law Enforcement Officer Salary Rates

The Federal Law Enforcement Pay Reform Act of 1990 established special salary rates for law enforcement officers at grades GS-3 through GS-10, including pay enhancements that range from one to seven salary steps above usual General Schedule rates. For example, a police officer who is appointed at grade GS-5 Step 1 under the special rate would receive a starting salary equal to GS-5 Step 8 in the General Schedule. Similarly, Special Rate GS-7 Step 6 is equivalent to GS-7 Step 10 in the General Schedule, and so on. However, salaries for personnel below GS-3 and above GS-10 follow the standard General Schedule rates.

Special salary rates apply to criminal investigators, police officers, correctional officers, field personnel assigned to federal correctional institutions and military detention or rehabilitation facilities, and certain other law enforcement officers and security specialists. A chart that illustrates special salary rates for law enforcement officers is shown in table 2.4.

Table 2.4: 2006 General Schedule Annual Salary for Law Enforcement Officers (Not Including Law Enforcement Availability Pay), Including Special Rates at GS-3 Through GS-10 and Locality Pay for "Rest of U.S." Geographic Areas

	Step 1	Step 2	Step 3	Step 4	Step 5	Step 6	Step 7	Step 8	Step 9	Step 10
GS-3	27,088	27,841	28,594	29,346	30,099	30,852	31,605	32,357	33,110	33,863
GS-4	30,409	31,254	32,099	32,944	33,789	34,634	35,479	36,324	37,169	38,014
GS-5	34,966	35,911	36,856	37,801	38,746	39,691	40,637	41,582	42,527	43,472
GS-6	36,867	37,920	38,974	40,027	41,080	42,133	43,186	44,239	45,293	46,346
GS-7	39,797	40,967	42,138	43,308	44,478	45,648	46,818	47,989	49,159	50,329

GS-8	41,483	42,779	44,075	45,371	46,668	47,964	49,260	50,556	51,853	53,149
GS-9	44,387	45,819	47,252	48,684	50,116	51,549	52,981	54,414	55,846	57,278
GS-10	48,880	50,456	52,033	53,609	55,185	56,762	58,338	59,915	61,491	63,067
GS-11	51,972	53,705	55,437	57,170	58,903	60,636	62,369	64,102	65,834	67,567
GS-12	62,291	64,367	66,443	68,519	70,595	72,671	74,747	76,823	78,899	80,975
GS-13	74,074	76,543	79,012	81,480	83,949	86,418	88,886	91,355	93,824	96,292
GS-14	87,533	90,450	93,368	96,286	99,203	102,121	105,039	107,956	110,874	113,791
GS-15	102,964	106,396	109,827	113,259	116,691	120,123	123,555	126,987	130,419	133,850

Salaries for Support Personnel

The vast majority of law enforcement support personnel are paid under the standard General Schedule pay system at grade levels ranging from GS-5 to GS-15, although some support positions require entry below the GS-5 grade. Examples of support positions include investigative assistants, fingerprint specialists, document analysts, evidence custodians, chemists, compliance investigators, electronics technicians, and intelligence specialists. Employees serving in these occupations are known as "non-sworn personnel," meaning they are not administered an oath of office and do not have the authority to carry firearms or make arrests.

Support personnel are not eligible for LEAP because only federal criminal investigators are authorized to receive this premium pay. Advancement to nonsupervisory, supervisory, and management positions varies from one position to another, depending on salary structures for each position. Although salaries for most support employees are based on the General Schedule, blue-collar support personnel are paid under the FWS. Table 2.5 provides an overview of salaries that apply to support positions.

Table 2.5: 2006 General Schedule Annual Salary for Support Personnel, Including Locality Pay for "Rest of U.S." Geographic Areas

	Step 1	Step 2	Step 3	Step 4	Step 5	Step 6	Step 7	Step 8	Step 9	Step 10
GS-1	18,399	19,014	19,626	20,234	20,847	21,207	21,810	22,420	22,444	23,010
GS-2	20,687	21,179	21,864	22,444	22,694	23,361	24,029	24,696	25,363	26,030
GS-3	22,572	23,324	24,077	24,830	25,583	26,335	27,088	27,841	28,594	29,346
GS-4	25,338	26,183	27,028	27,873	28,718	29,564	30,409	31,254	32,099	32,944
GS-5	28,349	29,295	30,240	31,185	32,130	33,075	34,020	34,966	35,911	36,856
GS-6	31,601	32,654	33,708	34,761	35,814	36,867	37,920	38,974	40,027	41,080
GS-7	35,116	36,287	37,457	38,627	39,797	40,967	42,138	43,308	44,478	45,648
GS-8	38,890	40,187	41,483	42,779	44,075	45,371	46,668	47,964	49,260	50,556
GS-9	42,955	44,387	45,819	47,252	48,684	50,116	51,549	52,981	54,414	55,846
GS-10	47,303	48,880	50,456	52,033	53,609	55,185	56,762	58,338	59,915	61,491

	Step 1	Step 2	Step 3	Step 4	Step 5	Step 6	Step 7	Step 8	Step 9	Step 10
GS-11	51,972	53,705	55,437	57,170	58,903	60,636	62,369	64,102	65,834	67,567
GS-12	62,291	64,367	66,443	68,519	70,595	72,671	74,747	76,823	78,899	80,975
GS-13	74,074	76,543	79,012	81,480	83,949	86,418	88,886	91,355	93,824	96,292
GS-14	87,533	90,450	93,368	96,286	99,203	102,121	105,039	107,956	110,874	113,791
GS-15	102,964	106,396	109,827	113,259	116,691	120,123	123,555	126,987	130,419	133,850

Administratively Uncontrollable Overtime (AUO)

To compensate employees for irregular or occasional overtime inherent in certain occupations, many agencies provide Administratively Uncontrollable Overtime (AUO) pay to qualifying personnel. AUO is a form of premium pay that ranges from 10 to 25 percent of basic pay depending on the average number of hours of overtime performed per week. Qualifying employees must work at least three hours but not more than five hours of overtime per week to receive 10 percent AUO pay; over five but not more than seven hours to receive 15 percent; over seven but not more than nine hours to receive 20 percent; and more than nine hours to receive 25 percent. AUO is paid to Border Patrol Agents and certain other officers, investigators, technicians, and specialists—primarily serving with the Department of Homeland Security—who are involved in field investigative and enforcement activities. Personnel who receive LEAP are not eligible for payment of AUO, and vice versa.

Other Premium Pay

Certain personnel receive overtime pay for work performed beyond a standard workday or service week; compensatory time off in lieu of overtime pay; night shift differential pay; and Sunday premium pay when their regularly scheduled workweek includes Sunday. The nature of premium pay earned depends on the circumstances and the position held.

Holidays, Annual Leave, and Excused Absences

Providing employees with time off from the job is an important aspect of overall efforts to ensure a healthy and productive workforce. When combined, paid holidays and annual leave provide federal personnel with at least 23 workdays off per year, while employees with more than 15 years of federal service end up with more than 36 workdays off. Agencies also can grant excused absences for a variety of purposes.

Paid Holidays

Federal employees receive paid leave for ten holidays annually, including New Year's Day, Martin Luther King's Birthday, Washington's Birthday, Memorial Day, Independence Day, Labor Day, Columbus Day, Veterans Day, Thanksgiving Day, and Christmas Day. If a holiday falls on Saturday, the previous Friday is observed as the legal holiday for employees whose basic workweek is Monday through Friday. Similarly, holidays that fall on Sunday are observed on the following Monday. In the case of employees whose basic workweek is other than Monday through Friday, when a holiday falls on a nonworkday, these personnel receive paid leave on the first workday before the holiday. Employees who must work on a holiday receive Holiday Pay, which is 100 percent of their rate of basic pay (double time).

Annual Leave

Federal employees accumulate paid annual leave for vacations or other purposes based on their years of federal service. Annual leave accrues at the rate of 13 days per year (4 hours per pay period) for employees with fewer than 3 years of service, at 20 days per year (6 hours per pay period) for those with 3 to 15 years of service, and at 26 days per year (8 hours per pay period) for personnel with more than 15 years of service. Employees normally are prohibited from carrying forward more than 240 hours of annual leave from year to year.

Excused Absences

Federal personnel can be granted excused absences or administrative leave for a variety of reasons. For example, employees are eligible for leave to attend court either as a witness or a member of a jury; for bone-marrow, organ, or blood donations; to serve military obligations; or to vote in elections. In 2001, President Bush directed the heads of federal agencies to grant excused absences to federal personnel affected by the attacks on the World Trade Center and the Pentagon. Similarly, in recent years time off has been granted to federal employees immediately upon their return from military active duty to aid in readjustment to civilian life. Time off also can be authorized prior to, during, or after hurricanes, tornadoes, snow storms, or other adverse weather conditions; in response to other disasters or emergency situations; or for other purposes.

Health Care and Wellness Benefits

The federal government provides a comprehensive package of health benefits and other perks to ensure the physical and emotional well-being of its personnel. These include a variety of health insurance plans; long-term care insurance; health and medical services in the workplace; time off for sickness, medical care, maternity and paternity leave, and adoption of a child; and child care services. Many of the health and wellness benefits available to federal employees are discussed in this section.

Federal Employees Health Benefits (FEHB) Program

The Federal Employees Health Benefits (FEHB) Program offers health-care insurance coverage to eligible employees through the largest employer-sponsored health insurance program in the world. The FEHB Program offers the widest selection of health plans in the nation, including managed fee-for-service plans, point of service (POS) plans, and health maintenance organization (HMO) programs. Enrollees are granted coverage without medical examinations or restrictions relating to age or physical condition, and may elect self-only or self-and-family protection. The government contributes between 60 and 75 percent toward the total cost of premiums, depending on the plan. Employees pay their share of premiums through a payroll deduction.

Federal personnel can retain their health-care benefits after retirement as long as they have been continuously enrolled in the FEHB program for the five-year period immediately preceding their retirement. An employee whose date of hire is fewer than five years prior to retirement is also eligible for continuing benefits, provided that they have maintained enrollment continuously until retirement.

Federal Long Term Care Insurance

Federal employees and retirees can purchase comprehensive insurance coverage through the Federal Long Term Care Insurance Program. This optional insurance plan pays for chronic care needed in the event of ongoing illness or disability, whether the care is received in the home or at a nursing home, hospice, adult day-care center, or other assisted-living facility. The plan pays for the services of licensed health-care practitioners, such as assistance with bathing, dressing, or eating, or aid getting in and out of bed, chairs, or a wheelchair. Federal employees and their spouses, children, parents, parents-in-law, and stepparents are eligible to obtain insurance coverage under the program.

Onsite Health Care Units

Many federal agencies provide onsite occupational health services to employees. For example, the FBI offers health and medical services at the J. Edgar Hoover Headquarters Building, the FBI Academy, and the Bureau's 56 field offices. In addition, more than 100 Federal Occupational Health (FOH) centers are located within federal office buildings nationwide, where federal personnel can take advantage of a wide range of health services and resources.

Although the variety of available agency-sponsored or FOH services varies from one location to another, some examples include

- Assessment and treatment of work-related injuries and illnesses
- Health counseling and risk appraisals
- Physical examinations and immunizations
- Health screenings for cholesterol, hypertension, and diabetes
- Classes concerning weight reduction, nutrition, smoking cessation, back care, safety, stress management, ergonomics, workplace violence, and other health and wellness issues
- Referrals to physicians or hospitals

Employee Assistance Programs (EAP)

Every federal agency has an Employee Assistance Program (EAP), a service for federal personnel and their families that is designed to address problems such as alcohol and drug abuse, marital difficulties, legal and financial concerns, and job stress that can adversely affect job performance, reliability, and personal health. The program is staffed by professional counselors who discuss and assess problems and provide short-term counseling. If needed, EAP counselors also provide referrals to other professional services and resources. The EAP also can be helpful in preventing workplace violence incidents, delivering critical incident stress debriefings, and providing assistance to employees during agency restructuring.

The EAP is a confidential program that is protected by strict confidentiality laws and regulations, and by professional ethical standards for counselors. Details of discussions with counselors cannot be released without the written consent of the employee, and EAP records do not become part of any employee security or personnel record. There are no fees for EAP services.

Sick Leave

All full-time federal civilian personnel earn 13 days of paid sick leave per year, in four-hour increments each biweekly pay period. Sick leave can be used for medical, dental, or optical examination or treatment; for incapacitation; to prevent the exposure of communicable diseases; to conduct adoption-related activities; to provide care for ill family members; to make arrangements necessitated by the death of a family member; or to attend the funeral of a family member.

Family and Medical Leave

Under provisions of the Family and Medical Leave Act (FMLA) of 1993, federal employees can take up to 12 weeks of *unpaid* leave per year for the following occurrences:

- The birth of or care of a child

- The placement of a child with the employee for adoption or foster care

- The care of a spouse, son, daughter, or parent of the employee who suffers from a serious health condition

- A serious health condition of the employee that makes him or her unable to perform the essential functions of the position

Family and medical leave is available only to those who have served as federal employees for at least one year. Temporary and intermittent personnel are not eligible for FMLA benefits.

Maternity and Paternity Leave

A number of U.S. Office of Personnel Management (OPM) regulations and agency policies are in place that allow parents to use *paid* sick leave before and after the birth of a child, and to follow alternative work schedules to better manage family obligations. For example, a birth mother can use sick leave for doctor appointments, hospitalization, and her period of incapacitation following childbirth. A birth father can use up to 12 weeks of sick leave each year to accompany the mother to prenatal appointments, to be with her during her period of hospitalization, and to care for her during her recovery period. In addition, both parents can use up to 13 days of sick leave annually to care for a child with minor illnesses or to accompany them to doctor, dental, or optical appointments, and up to 12 weeks of sick leave each year to care for a child with a serious health condition. Agencies also can authorize flexible work schedules so employees can alter their work hours to balance work and family responsibilities.

Child Care Services

Child care services are available to federal employees worldwide, including more than 250 child care centers located in federal office buildings, and more than 800 additional child care centers that are part of the Department of Defense Child Care System. Federal agencies also have policies that provide for time off and flexible work schedules to help employees with their child care responsibilities. These policies are designed to give federal employees the flexibility they need to manage personal and professional responsibilities. In addition, OPM issued regulations in 2003 that permit agencies to spend appropriated funds to assist lower-income employees with the costs of child care, and to make direct payments to child care centers to cover these costs.

Death and Disability Benefits

Life insurance, workers' compensation benefits, and disability retirement benefits are designed to protect federal employees and their families in the event of serious injuries, illnesses, or fatalities. In addition, Congress enacted the Public Safety Officers' Benefits (PSOB) Act and the Federal Law Enforcement Dependents Assistance (FLEDA) Act to provide benefits to the families of officers whose deaths or disabilities are the result of injuries sustained in the line of duty. These laws were enacted in recognition of the low level of benefits provided by many state and local governments to public safety officers and their families, and also the negative impact this could have on attracting qualified individuals into public service and providing adequate protection for communities. Congress also enacted provisions to allow federal officers to attend funerals for fellow law enforcement personnel during duty hours and at government expense.

Life Insurance

Most federal civilian personnel are eligible to participate in the Federal Employees' Group Life Insurance (FEGLI) Program, a plan that offers both life insurance and accidental death and dismemberment coverage. Premiums are based on the employee's age and are paid through regular payroll deductions. Participants can purchase additional life insurance to cover eligible family members, although accidental death and dismemberment coverage is not included.

The amount of basic life insurance coverage is equal to an employee's annual basic pay plus $2,000, although employees can purchase additional insurance equal to as much as five times their annual basic pay. The government pays approximately one-third of the premium for basic life insurance, and the remaining two-thirds is withheld from the employee's pay by payroll deduction. FEGLI policies build no cash or loan value, and participants are not permitted to borrow against life insurance benefits.

Although life insurance is available from FEGLI and private companies, federal personnel also can obtain insurance through nonprofit organizations such as the Special Agents Mutual Benefit Association (SAMBA) and the Worldwide Assurance for Employees of Public Agencies (WAEPA).

The Public Safety Officers' Benefits (PSOB) Program

The PSOB Program provides eligible federal law enforcement officers with death and disability benefits. PSOB was enacted to assist in the recruitment and retention of law enforcement officers and firefighters. The Act was designed not only to offer peace of mind to those seeking careers in law enforcement and firefighting, but also to send a message about the value society places on the contributions of public safety officers who serve their communities and the nation in dangerous occupations.

The PSOB Program provides a one-time payment to the eligible survivors of public safety officers whose deaths are the result of injury sustained in the line of duty. The Program provides the same benefit to those who have been permanently and totally disabled by a catastrophic personal injury sustained in the line of duty if the injury permanently prevents them from performing any gainful work. Since 1988, the benefit has been adjusted annually to reflect the percentage of change in the Consumer Price Index. As of October 1, 2005, the benefit amount was $283,385.

Law enforcement officers eligible for PSOB Program benefits include, but are not limited to, police, corrections, probation, parole, judicial, and other law enforcement officers of federal, state, county, and local public agencies, as well as the District of Columbia, the Commonwealth of Puerto Rico, and any U.S. territory or possession.

The Federal Law Enforcement Dependents Assistance (FLEDA) Program

Congress enacted the Federal Law Enforcement Dependents Assistance (FLEDA) Act of 1996 to provide financial assistance for higher education to the spouses and children of federal law enforcement officers killed or disabled in the line of duty. FLEDA benefits are intended for the sole purpose of paying for educational expenses, including tuition, room and board, books, supplies, and fees for dependents who attend a qualifying program of education at an eligible institution. Assistance under the Program is available for a period of 45 months of full-time education or training or for a proportional period for a part-time program. As of October 1, 2005, the amount payable for each full-time student was $827 per month of class attendance—up to $9,924 per year.

Federal Workers' Compensation Benefits

The Federal Employees' Compensation Act (FECA) provides benefits to federal personnel who become disabled as a result of any personal injury or occupational disease that is *job-related*. FECA is administered by the Office of Workers' Compensation Programs (OWCP) of the U.S. Department of Labor. All permanent and temporary federal employees are covered under the Act, regardless of their length of employment or the type of position held.

FECA benefits cover the costs of medical and surgical treatment, rehabilitation, and other necessary expenses. For permanent disabilities, employees who have no dependants generally receive two-thirds of their pre-disability gross wages, while employees who have one or more dependants are paid three-fourths of their pre-disability gross wages. Permanent disability payments are tax-free. FECA also provides compensation to injured employees' dependents if the injury or disease causes death. Disabilities that are not job-related are covered under federal disability retirement benefit programs.

Federal Disability Retirement Benefits

Federal employees who become permanently disabled as a result of *any* injury or medical condition—whether or not the injury or condition is job-related—can receive disability retirement benefits instead of FECA payments. However, unlike workers' compensation provisions, employees cannot receive disability retirement benefits unless they meet certain length-of-employment requirements. Personnel covered under the Civil Service Retirement System (CSRS) must have at least five years of creditable federal service to be eligible for a disability retirement, while employees covered under the Federal Employees Retirement System (FERS) must have at least 18 months of federal service to be eligible. (Additional information concerning CSRS and FERS is provided under "General Retirement Benefits," below.)

A federal employee whose disability is a result of an injury or disease sustained on the job could qualify for disability retirement benefits *and* FECA payments, although in most cases they must decide whether to draw benefits from one or the other. Compensation under FECA tends to be superior to disability retirement, however, inasmuch as the payments often are higher and are tax-free. Federal disability retirement benefits are administered by OPM.

Funeral Leave for Law Enforcement Officers

Federal law enforcement officers may be excused from duty, without loss of pay or leave, to attend the funeral of a fellow law enforcement officer who was killed in the line of duty. Attendance at such a service is considered to be an official duty, and employing agencies are authorized under the United States Code to pay the costs of travel and subsistence for those who attend (Title 5, U.S. Code, Section 6328).

General Retirement Benefits

The government offers federal employees a comprehensive retirement benefits package that often exceeds coverage provided by firms in the private sector. Most federal civilian employees are eligible to receive an unreduced retirement annuity at age 60 with 20 years of service, and at age 62 with five years of service. Upon completing five years of civilian service, prior military service can be counted toward the service requirements under certain circumstances.

With 30 years of service, those who are covered under the Federal Employees' Retirement System (FERS)—which includes most employees hired after December 31, 1983—can retire at age 55 to 57, depending on their year of birth. FERS is a three-tiered plan consisting of a basic annuity benefit, the Thrift Savings Plan, and Social Security. Employees who are covered under the Civil Service Retirement System (CSRS), the predecessor to FERS, can retire at age 55 with 30 years of service. There is no mandatory retirement age for support employees.

The Basic Retirement Annuity Benefit

Federal employees receive a basic annuity benefit upon retirement based on the length of their federal service and their earnings history. If an employee reaches the minimum retirement age and has at least 20 years of creditable service, he or she can retire and begin receiving the basic annuity benefit immediately. However, this benefit is reduced if the employee retires under the age of 62, unless he or she retires under one of the following conditions:

- With 20 years of service at age 60
- With 30 years of service at the minimum retirement age
- Following an involuntary separation through no fault of the employee after completing 25 years of service (or 20 years if at least age 50)

An employee also is entitled to a basic annuity benefit at any age if approved for disability retirement, although some restrictions apply. Cost-of-living adjustments are paid to regular retirees over age 62, as well as disabled retirees and survivors at any age.

The Federal Thrift Savings Plan (TSP)

The Federal Retirement Thrift Investment Board administers the Federal Thrift Savings Plan (TSP), a retirement savings and investment plan for federal personnel that provides the same type of savings and tax benefits that many private corporations offer their employees under 401(k) plans. The TSP offers tax-deferred investment earnings, a choice of investment funds, a loan program, portable benefits upon leaving government service, and a choice of withdrawal options. All contributions to an employee's TSP account earn interest and can be divided among six funds, including the following:

- Government Securities Investments (G) Fund
- Fixed Income Index Investment (F) Fund
- Common Stock Index Investment (C) Fund
- Small Capitalization Stock Index Investment (S) Fund
- International Stock Index Investment (I) Fund
- Lifecycle (L) Funds

Employees covered under FERS are permitted to contribute up to 15 percent of their basic pay each pay period to a TSP account, although contributions are restricted by annual limits prescribed by the Internal Revenue Code. Contributions by FERS employees are either partially or fully matched by the government, depending upon the percentage of income contributed. The government matches each employee contribution dollar for dollar on the first 3 percent contributed, and 50 cents on the dollar for the next 2 percent. CSRS personnel can contribute up to 10 percent of their basic pay, although they do not receive any agency matching contributions and contributions also are restricted by annual IRS limits.

Employee contributions, agency matching funds, and earnings on all TSP accounts are deferred from income taxes until funds are withdrawn. An employee who leaves the government prior to retirement can either obtain a refund of their contributions or leave the contributions in his or her account and allow the account to earn interest. Employee contributions, agency matching funds, and earnings on all TSP accounts are deferred from income taxes until funds are withdrawn. Employees also have the opportunity to borrow against their TSP contributions in certain circumstances.

Social Security Benefits

Social Security is a component of the retirement system for FERS personnel, and also for some CSRS employees who are eligible as a result of their employment in the military or other Social Security-covered jobs. All new federal personnel are automatically covered under the Social Security system. An employee can apply for regular Social Security benefits as early as age 62, while disability Social Security benefits are conditionally available at any age. Cost-of-living adjustments increase the amount of Social Security benefits in January each year.

Special Retirement Benefits

Congress enacted special retirement coverage that applies to federal criminal investigators and many other federal law enforcement and correctional officers "...whose primary duties involve the investigation, apprehension, or detention of individuals suspected or convicted of offenses against the criminal laws of the United States." As a result of these laws, federal criminal investigators and certain other federal officers must retire by age 57. These personnel also can voluntarily retire earlier than support personnel—in some cases prior to age 50. Similar mandatory and voluntary early-retirement provisions also apply to federal firefighters and air traffic controllers.

The majority of sworn federal law enforcement officers are covered under special provisions that provide for voluntary and mandatory retirement at an earlier age than other government employees. These provisions apply only to personnel who serve in certain "covered" positions, including most criminal investigators, police officers, correctional officers, field personnel assigned to federal correctional institutions and military detention or rehabilitation facilities, and certain other law enforcement officers and security specialists.

Qualifying law enforcement personnel who are covered under FERS can receive an unreduced retirement annuity at age 50 with 20 years of federal law enforcement service, or any age with 25 years of such service. Those covered under CSRS also can retire at age 50 with 20 years of service, although they are not permitted to retire at an earlier age. Retirement is mandatory for law enforcement officers covered under both systems at the end of the month in which they turn 57. In most cases, personnel serving in covered positions must be appointed prior to their 37th birthday. However, applicants over the age of 37 who have previous service creditable under special law enforcement retirement provisions sufficient to allow them to retire at age 57 with 20 years of creditable service also can be eligible. The maximum entry age for covered positions is an exception to provisions against age discrimination within the Age Discrimination in Employment Act of 1967.

Cost-of-living adjustments are paid at all ages under special retirement provisions. In addition, considering that retirees normally are not eligible to receive Social Security payments until age 62, special retirement rules also allow law enforcement officers under age 62 to receive a supplement that equals the estimated Social Security benefit.

Travel and Commuting Allowances

Federal law enforcement officers and many support employees must travel on official business from time to time. All federal agencies provide full reimbursement for airfare, lodging, rental cars, parking, taxis, and other expenses for travel throughout the United States and worldwide. Federal employees also can receive subsidies to help pay the costs of traveling to and from work.

Travel Allowances and Reimbursements

Federal employees who travel on official business normally receive reimbursement for transportation and lodging expenses plus a daily allowance for meals and incidental expenses (M&IE). This allowance applies to travel undertaken during the course of investigative assignments, attendance in training programs, and other activities in furtherance of federal agencies' missions. Most hotel chains and many independent establishments offer discounted lodging rates for government travelers. M&IE allowances are paid at a government-wide flat daily rate that varies from one locality to another depending on prevailing costs in the area visited.

Public Transportation Subsidies

Most federal agencies offer public transportation subsidies to their personnel to encourage the use of mass transit and to defray the costs of commuting. Employees are eligible to receive the subsidy if they travel to and from work via subway, bus, train, commuter vehicles occupied by six or more adults (such as van pools), or other qualifying transportation modes.

Legal Protection

There are many risks associated with careers in law enforcement. In addition to the most obvious risks—the possibility of suffering personal injuries or even death—law enforcement officers also run the risk of being sued or charged criminally for their actions. Of course, lawsuits against law enforcement officers are no different than those targeting any other individuals or groups, inasmuch as some suits are justified and others are frivolous. Although federal law enforcement officers who act within the scope of their responsibilities normally are represented in civil actions by the U.S. Department of Justice (DOJ), many officers find peace of mind in having a private attorney in their corner. Private counsel can either augment DOJ representation in civil actions or serve as sole representation if DOJ does not provide a defense.

Protection from civil and criminal liability begins first with carrying out law enforcement duties in a responsible manner. However, law enforcement officers also should be protected through expert legal representation in all serious matters and carry professional liability insurance as an additional measure of security. Federal agents most often turn to the Federal Law Enforcement Officers Association (FLEOA) for legal protection. In addition, some professional liability insurance policies available to federal personnel cover the cost of legal representation, and federal officers holding membership in organizations such as the Fraternal Order of Police (FOP) can purchase legal defense coverage through them.

The Federal Law Enforcement Officers Association (FLEOA)

FLEOA is a nonpartisan association that represents more than 20,000 federal law enforcement officers from about 60 federal agencies. This organization not only provides its members with immediate expert legal advice and representation following critical incidents or other legal matters, it also works on legislative action and issues affecting federal law enforcement officers. FLEOA's primary credo is that "legal assistance and representation are only a phone call away," and the organization stands behind this promise with help around the clock, 365 days a year. This includes assistance not only with matters that could result in civil or criminal liability, but also to protect members' employee rights and to ensure fair and appropriate treatment on the job. Legal services are provided at no cost to FLEOA members whose membership is in good standing at the time of an occurrence for which services are requested. Membership is open to nonsupervisory and supervisory personnel.

Professional Liability Insurance

Federal agencies reimburse law enforcement officers, supervisors, and managers for one-half the cost of professional liability insurance premiums. A number of companies offer professional liability insurance policies to federal employees, including firms such as Mass Benefits Consultants and Wright & Company, among others.

Generally speaking, these policies are designed to pay for covered damages awarded in civil courts against policyholders personally, as well as the costs associated with legal defense of policyholders in civil and administrative matters. However, these policies typically are limited to coverage arising only out of acts carried out *within the scope* of employment. In addition, some policies exclude coverage for bodily injuries arising out of car accidents, or for damage to property that is owned either by the government or the policyholder, or for accidents caused by nuclear materials, or for many other reasons. Therefore, it is critical to compare policies carefully, and to review all exclusions from coverage and other policy details before signing on the dotted line.

CHAPTER 3

Standing Out from the Crowd

"The difference between a successful person and others is not a lack of strength, not a lack of knowledge, but rather a lack of will."

—Vince Lombardi

Your likelihood of succeeding in any career search often depends less on your qualifications than your ability to stand out from the crowd. To gain an advantage in the highly competitive federal law enforcement application process, you must fully understand federal civil service procedures and be able to communicate, both orally and in writing, that you are the best choice.

This concept might not be as simple as it appears. Standing out from the crowd does not necessarily mean that you must always be better qualified than other candidates. Indeed, if you know how to sell yourself properly you can outshine competitors who have stronger credentials. Standing out from the crowd begins with responsibility, good judgment, and integrity. It also requires investing wisely in getting organized, targeting your career search, maintaining detailed records, evaluating your career skills and carefully matching them to targeted positions, and networking. Of course, you'll also need to craft an application or resume using the right terminology and perform well during interviews. It is a well-known fact that federal agencies do not always hire the best-qualified applicants—they often choose those who have a better understanding of the hiring process than other applicants and who invest the time and effort to conduct a more effective job search.

This chapter probably contains the most important information in the book, because it provides details of specific strategies you can use to launch a successful campaign and land a rewarding career in federal law enforcement. The strategies are not difficult, although they can be time-consuming. Rest assured that most applicants will not fully understand the ins and outs of the hiring process, or they will not invest the time it takes to come out on top—to win. This is where their loss can be your gain.

Responsibility

Any search for a career in law enforcement starts with responsibility, long before the first application is submitted. In fact, carrying out your personal and business affairs in a responsible manner is at least as important as any qualifications or accomplishments you could possibly achieve. How could this be true? Because even the best-qualified applicant will be disqualified from the hiring process if he or she has been convicted of a felony or major misdemeanor offense, defaulted on a student loan, failed a drug test or polygraph examination, or was caught cheating on their income taxes.

The plain truth is that society holds law enforcement officers to the highest standards—because law enforcement is a high calling—and character, honesty, integrity, and loyalty are more important to most federal agencies than any amount of experience, education, or skill that applicants might have. A history of poor job performance or bad credit also can derail your career search, and falsifying information during the hiring process or failing to be forthright about previous problems or issues also are likely to result in disqualification. Such behavior is inconsistent with everything federal law enforcement agencies stand for.

It is critical that you "keep it clean" before applying for federal law enforcement jobs, otherwise your background investigation could end in disappointment. This is not to suggest that you must have lived a squeaky-clean life. Agency personnel who carry out the hiring processes realize that everyone has made mistakes. Nonetheless, your chances of succeeding in the hiring process increase dramatically if you have little or no significant "baggage" in your background. If there are background issues you must overcome, your best bet is to be forthright about them, to openly discuss lessons learned, and to put your best foot forward.

Getting Organized

One of the most important aspects of a federal law enforcement job search is to get organized—and *stay* organized. Getting organized consists not only of gathering and arranging job search materials, but also targeting your career search, learning about the federal civil service process, and maintaining meticulous records of personal contacts and important information along the way. It is also important to locate records relating to your education, employment, training, and accomplishments. Time invested in these tasks early on will enable you to conduct a more efficient and productive campaign.

Target Your Career Search

The first step in the search process is to define your career goals and target the type of job you would like to obtain. This will enable you to focus your search on a particular field or position and to cover territory more efficiently, rather than spreading your efforts too thin. This advice might seem like a page right out of "Job Search 101," but you would be surprised at the number of job seekers who have not decided what they would like to do for a living. If you can't decide whether you would like to become a federal agent, firefighter, campground manager, fitness trainer, or stock broker, you probably are a good candidate for an occupational assessment to identify and make the most of your interests, priorities, motivations, transferable skills, cognitive strengths, and other abilities. There are ten career categories in this book, and each provides a wide range of positions from which to choose. It will be to your advantage to set your sights on positions within one or two of these categories and then target your search efforts accordingly.

Learn About the Federal Hiring Process

Considering that federal hiring processes differ substantially from those of the private sector, it is important to understand exactly how the processes function prior to navigating your way through them. Reading this book is a good first step because it provides an overview of civil service procedures and offers many tips and techniques for conducting your search. It is also important to read vacancy announcements carefully and to follow instructions to the letter. Considering that hiring processes sometimes change, you should also obtain pamphlets from individual agencies, speak to recruiters about the nature of their hiring processes, consult with career counselors or advisors at your school, or visit agency Web sites for information. In addition, some trade periodicals, such as *Federal Jobs Digest* and *Federal Career Opportunities*, publish articles that include advice for federal job seekers (see chapter 5, "Sources of Employment Information").

Assemble Job Search Materials

After defining your goals, the next step is to gather materials such as high school and college transcripts, diplomas, certificates, awards, occupational licenses, job descriptions, employment performance evaluations, work products, military discharge documents, professional and character reference lists, birth certificate, Social Security card, and other information. These documents and similar materials will serve as the basis for your resumes, employment applications, and job interviews. It is very likely that you'll need to present copies (and possibly originals) of these documents as you progress through the hiring process. You also will need addresses and phone numbers of schools, employers, references, friends, and places you have lived. If the positions you apply for require a security clearance, you also will need contact information for your former spouses, immediate relatives, doctors, and possibly your creditors to complete the SF-86 Questionnaire for National Security Positions (see the inside back cover of this book for instructions on finding this form online).

If you put these tasks on the back burner instead of assembling the materials early, the quality of your employment applications and resumes will suffer. Besides, it is much less stressful to locate these materials in advance than to search for them on the day that an application is due or an hour before attending an interview.

Maintain a Record of Agency Contacts

Among the most important aspects of an efficient and successful career search is to maintain good records of all contacts with prospective employers and others who can assist you with your career search. You should record the details of each contact, including the date, agency name, telephone number, names of those contacted and their titles, results of the contact, and any other comments or special notes. (See the inside back cover for instructions on accessing a handy "Agency Contact Record" that you can use for this purpose.) An aggressive career search campaign should include numerous contacts that must remain organized and readily available for future reference and follow-up. Count on your competitors to record this information on sticky notes, the backs of envelopes, and paper bags—and then to lose them.

Again, you must be committed to maintaining a dedicated and systematic job search if you plan to set yourself apart from other applicants. With this in mind, if you have no use for this form because your contacts have been few and far between, you probably are not working hard enough toward your goal and should consider reassessing your priorities.

Networking

While networking is an important strategy in any career search, it can be an especially effective tool when attempting to get into the vast federal workforce. As discussed in chapter 4, "The Five Quickest Ways to Get Hired," research studies show time and again that personal networking is the most effective tool you can use to land a job. With this in mind, you must take full advantage of your communication skills to get the most out of this crucial technique.

Establish a Base of Contacts

Networking involves forming alliances—making periodic contact with friends, associates, professionals in your chosen field, and any others who could become aware of hiring opportunities or provide sources of information. To establish your base of contacts, begin by speaking to friends, family members, neighbors, classmates, and people you know through social or religious groups, regardless of the field in which they are employed. Don't be concerned if their line of work has nothing to do with law enforcement or the federal government. Keep in mind that you are looking for information from them—not a job—and that the people closest to you might lead you to others who can help with your career search. Reach out to as many people as possible, even if you have not spoken to them for a while. They will be glad you approached them; most will be flattered when you ask for guidance.

Expand Your Base of Contacts

The next step is to expand your base of contacts, which is fundamental to successful networking. This is the appropriate time to contact the professors, instructors, advisors, internship coordinators, and career placement office staff at your school, as well as personnel specialists at agencies you are interested in working for. This group of people has one thing in common—they make a living preparing others to make a living. Rest assured that you will not be the first person to approach them—they know the drill and they probably know others who can help. Indeed, the greatest benefit to working with this group is that each of them probably has an expansive contact base of their own.

You should also contact law enforcement personnel whom you have come to know during the course of internships, co-op positions, career fairs, or through other channels. Former supervisors and members of alumni groups also can be good sources of information and contacts. Similar to the manner in which you interacted with people when establishing your contact base, you should tell them about your goals and ask for referrals to others who might be able to help.

Participate in Professional and Academic Organizations

Becoming active in professional and academic organizations also is an excellent way to establish communication with criminal justice professionals. Many of these groups hold conferences and seminars that are likely to put you face to face with law enforcement officers and others who can provide you with up-to-date information on recruiting efforts and—perhaps most importantly—referrals to others who are "in the loop."

For example, the Academy of Criminal Justice Sciences (ACJS) holds an annual conference in cooperation with the Alpha Phi Sigma Criminal Justice Honor Society, a national organization for college students pursuing degrees in criminal justice. Each year, the ACJS/Alpha Phi Sigma conference brings together more than 2,000 participants, including criminal justice professors, researchers, policymakers, law enforcement and correctional officers, court personnel, and students. In addition to presentations concerning the latest research and developments in all criminal justice disciplines, typically the conference also features workshops of value to participants seeking employment, including some that are dedicated only to students. As with other criminal justice conferences and seminars, many students and practitioners have landed new careers because they met the right people or otherwise made the right connections at this conference. However, keep in mind that *joining* professional and academic organizations will get you only a certificate on the wall. You must *actively participate*.

Network Online

The advent of the Internet has literally opened up the entire world to networking possibilities. However, if you use it only to gather facts and figures from Web sites, you will miss the boat. There are a variety of Internet bulletin boards, newsgroups, and chat rooms that enable law enforcement job seekers to exchange information and ideas with one another for mutual benefit. In addition, these Web sites often include private messaging (PM) capabilities, and many offer other systems that facilitate e-mail communication so users can engage in discussion one on one.

The best example of an Internet bulletin board that also combines private messaging for law enforcement job seekers is the 911HotJobs.com Employment Portal, which was created by a police officer to assist others in landing a career in law enforcement. This Web site has thousands of well-informed members—including law enforcement professionals and job seekers alike—who provide up-to-the-minute information concerning recruiting and hiring efforts by law enforcement agencies. Of particular value, most members readily share complete details of their job-hunting successes and failures, which can reduce the learning curve for others substantially. In addition, members commonly "PM" the moderators and one another to discuss their situations and seek advice. See chapter 5, "Sources of Federal Employment Information," for additional information regarding the 911HotJobs.com Employment Portal.

The Application vs. Resume Debate

Standing out from the crowd depends largely on your ability to assemble a comprehensive written application package that not only emphasizes your skills and attributes, but also demonstrates that you will be a good fit for the position and the agency. An effective application or resume starts with a thorough evaluation of your strengths, accomplishments, and career skills. Whether you are filling out an application, applying online, or crafting a resume, to be competitive you *must* carefully match your skills to the targeted position and create a powerful written account of what you have to offer. Using dynamic and industry-specific terminology also will make an impact. Of course, you must decide which format to use—application vs. resume—unless the agency decides for you.

As discussed in chapter 1, there are several ways to apply for most federal jobs, including the OF-612 Application for Employment, a resume, online applications, touch-tone telephone application systems, and sometimes the SF-171 application form. However, telephone application processing and the SF-171 are rarely used and could become obsolete in the near future. Therefore, aside from situations in which agencies accept *only* applications submitted online, you must weigh the pros and cons in the application vs. resume debate. Interestingly enough, oftentimes online application processes *also* require applicants to cut and paste a resume into the application, so it is important not only to know how to compose a quality resume, but also to understand the resume formatting limitations of online application systems.

Although there are subtle advantages to one application format or the other depending upon your background, the format you choose is far less important than the content of your application package.

The OF-612 Application for Employment

Unless vacancy announcements specify that you must apply electronically or over the telephone, federal job applicants must first decide whether to submit an application form or a resume. In these cases, the OF-612 can be a good choice because it covers all the bases in a straightforward and organized manner, and it is easy to navigate. The OF-612 also is appropriate if your resume-writing skills are unremarkable and either you do not know anyone who could compose a quality resume for you or you cannot afford to hire a professional resume writer.

However, it is important to note that many sections of the OF-612 do not provide adequate space for the information requested. For example, the "Work Experience" and "Additional Work Experience" sections of the current edition of the form afford enough space for only two jobs, and you are given only one inch of space to insert complete details of your duties and accomplishments. So, unless your jobs involved only licking envelopes, you'll need much more space to adequately describe your responsibilities and receive full credit for your accomplishments. Similarly, the "Other Qualifications" section has only a one-inch block for details relating to *all* of your job-related skills, leadership activities, certificates and licenses earned, honors and awards received, special accomplishments, publications, professional memberships, computer skills, public speaking experience, foreign languages spoken, and other information.

Therefore, if you prefer to use the OF-612 instead of a resume, it is best to indicate "see attachment" in any block that provides inadequate space for your responses, and type the details on a plain sheet of letter-size (8 ½" × 11") paper, as shown in figure 3.1.

Edward R. Applicant, Jr.
123-45-6789

ATTACHMENT TO OF-612 APPLICATION FOR EMPLOYMENT

Continuation of Section B—Work Experience

SAFETY OPTIONS, INC.
BRIGHTON, MICHIGAN

Work Description: _____

_____

_____

_____

_____

Figure 3.1: Suggested format for extra attachments to the application.

Resumes

Resumes are most appropriate for those who are adept at documenting their background without the structure inherent in formal application forms. This format offers flexibility and the opportunity to emphasize skills and accomplishments in a unique manner. It is important to realize, however, that a *federal resume* differs significantly from those used in the private sector. As discussed in chapter 1, federal resumes must include specific personal data, job information, and other details that normally are not included in resumes submitted to private industry. In addition, although one-page resumes are the rule of thumb in the private sector, in most situations a one-page federal resume would not sufficiently cover the elements and detail required of federal job applicants.

Overall, if you are familiar with resume writing, or if you can either hire a pro or get help from a friend who is experienced at the craft, a resume probably is a better choice for you than the OF-612. Of course, nearly all bookstores, public libraries, college libraries, and career resource centers have resume books on hand. Two good resources for writing resumes for federal jobs are *Federal Resume Guidebook* by Kathryn Kraemer Troutman and *Expert Resumes for Military-to-Civilian Transitions* by Wendy S. Enelow and Louise M. Kursmark, both published by JIST Publishing.

Strategies for Applications and Resumes

Whether your application or resume stand alone or both are required, they must be exceptional. If the hiring process does not involve an online application, your resume will be the first document reviewed and it will serve as the basis for your rating. If you submit a resume along with an online application, both will be used to evaluate and rate your qualifications. Either way, you must understand that your rating will be based *only* on the information you submit, and also that rating panel members are prohibited from making any assumptions about your background or experience based only on your job titles.

As discussed in chapter 1, a federal resume must include many details that normally are not included in resumes submitted to companies or government agencies at the state and local levels. As with many other aspects of federal hiring processes, you must learn the rules and understand the ins and outs of the system first. The tips and techniques offered in the following sections can spell the difference between making the Best Qualified List and failing to make it over the first hurdle.

Carefully Evaluate Your Career Skills

The first—and most important—step in composing an effective resume or application is to evaluate your background and experience to determine what career skills you have to offer. To begin step one, carefully analyze the tasks you performed and your accomplishments at each job you held and create an exhaustive list of the skills you developed. Do not limit your list to full-time employment experience; include any part-time or volunteer work, internship experience, and co-op positions. Also list all professional memberships, achievements, awards, certificates, licenses, leadership activities, proficiency in foreign languages, special skills, public speaking experience, and other activities that could set you apart from others.

Be sure to think carefully about all of your work experience and the skills you performed, regardless of the career field. Many jobs that are unrelated to criminal justice require skills that are applicable to careers in law enforcement, investigations, corrections, security, and compliance work. You will be more competitive if you can demonstrate that you have experience that is related to the responsibilities of the position you are applying for, even if your experience has nothing to do with law enforcement or careers in the criminal justice system. Also list your extracurricular activities and hobbies if *any* of the skills you developed during these endeavors could be applied to your chosen field.

To complete step one, examine each item on your list and think about the skills or talents that are involved. Take your time. All jobs, internships, extracurricular activities, hobbies, and other pursuits require particular knowledge, skills, and abilities— many of which are transferable to careers in law enforcement. Write them all down. Also list any schools, training seminars, and workshops you attended (including dates and locations), and any degrees, honors, fellowships, or certificates you earned. Many of the skills you developed in educational and training settings also can be useful in federal law enforcement careers.

The quality of the finished product depends largely upon the depth and thoroughness of your effort in both aspects of step one. Indeed, this step is similar to the mathematics class you attended in high school—if you do not follow along and do the work properly in the beginning, you'll be lost the rest of the way.

Match Your Skills to the Position

Once you have prepared a list of your career skills, you must match them to those needed for the positions you are seeking. As discussed in chapter 1, most vacancy announcements include a list of the knowledge, skills, and abilities (KSAs) involved. In addition, the "Major Duties" section of virtually every vacancy announcement also offers many clues concerning the varieties of education, training, and experience that are of value. If you carefully read these sections you should know *exactly* what the agencies are looking for and the criteria with which applicants will be evaluated. If your efforts in this step fall short, you are likely to join the ranks of most other applicants in the pool—failing to make the Best Qualified List—which is *not* the place to be.

Therefore, it is critical that you tailor your resume to the specific requirements of each targeted position, highlighting all of your education, training, experience, talents, and accomplishments that demonstrate your ability to perform the job skills. Do not make the mistake of providing generic job descriptions that present little or no information about your individual accomplishments. Instead, clearly describe your specific responsibilities and achievements, including activities, projects, and initiatives you participated in and how your contributions made a difference in the outcome. When possible, use simple phrases instead of long-winded sentences to describe your background and experience.

Do not overlook any experience and accomplishments that are related in any way to the career you are pursuing. These could include tasks such as interacting with the public, gathering and organizing information, resolving complaints, troubleshooting, solving problems, writing reports, making oral presentations, using computers, establishing and attaining goals, following organizational policies and procedures, and coordinating projects with other people or organizations. Also highlight any experience that demonstrates communication skills, initiative, leadership, dependability, persistence, innovation, and the ability to perform in stressful situations.

Use Appropriate Keywords

Using appropriate keywords is an effective method of matching your skills to the position. Many federal employment applications—especially those submitted online—are scanned for keywords for scoring purposes. Agencies follow this procedure to increase the speed of application processing, regardless of whether the scanning is carried out with computer hardware and software or by personnel assigned to read applications. Therefore, the presence or absence of certain words in these materials can determine whether you make it over the first hurdle in the hiring process.

Fortunately, it is not difficult to figure out which keywords will be used, because most of them are included in vacancy announcements. To identify probable keywords, simply study the "Major Duties," "Qualification Requirements," and "How You Will be Evaluated" sections. These sections will have phrases including the keywords that are likely to be used when applications are scored. For example, the following details were included in a recent vacancy announcement for a criminal investigator position with an Office of Inspector General agency. The probable keywords are underlined.

> DUTIES:
>
> Responsible for <u>coordinating</u> and <u>conducting criminal investigations</u>. Works on cases involving a variety of specific investigative functions. <u>Investigates allegations</u> of crimes and <u>official misconduct</u> in a variety of settings. Investigates crimes involving <u>high technology</u>. <u>Gathers information</u> and determines <u>facts</u> in various types of investigations. Conducts <u>crime scene searches</u> for <u>evidence</u>; makes a record of evidence discovered at <u>crime scenes</u> through <u>photographs</u>, <u>sketches</u>, and <u>evidence logs</u>, and <u>collects and preserves physical evidence</u>,

as appropriate. Also must <u>conduct searches</u>, participate in <u>surveillance</u>, or operate in an <u>undercover</u> role.

Performs appropriate <u>investigative planning</u> and <u>analysis</u> and <u>makes recommendations</u> on necessary actions to be taken, depending on the circumstances. <u>Researches</u> and <u>analyzes facts</u> and other information, determines appropriate investigative steps, <u>documents findings</u>, formalizes reports, and follows other appropriate protocol. <u>Prepares reports</u> and <u>presents findings</u> of investigative activities to other criminal investigators, managers, <u>prosecutors</u>, <u>high-level officials</u>, and <u>grand juries</u>.

KNOWLEDGE, SKILLS, AND ABILITIES:

Ability to <u>communicate</u> effectively.

Ability to <u>conduct investigations</u>, <u>analyze evidence</u>, and <u>prepare reports</u>.

Ability to <u>research</u>, <u>interpret</u>, and <u>apply rules, regulations, and policies</u>.

Knowledge of U.S. <u>laws</u>, <u>regulations</u>, and <u>policies</u> applicable to the organization's <u>law enforcement</u>, <u>inspection</u>, or <u>compliance</u> mission.

Experience in conducting <u>physical and electronic surveillance</u> utilizing a variety of <u>audio, video,</u> and <u>photographic</u> equipment.

Review vacancy announcements carefully, either underline or highlight probable keywords, and use the keywords in your application materials when describing your education, training, experience, skills, and other qualifications.

Use Targeted Action Verbs

Similarly to keywords, using targeted *action verbs* can improve your chances of being selected for the Best Qualified List. Phrases that begin with well-chosen action verbs provide power and direction to resumes, application forms, and cover letters. Choose words that emphasize experience, skills, and activities *that are related to the targeted position*. Targeted action verbs are highly effective in conveying leadership, responsibility, and accomplishment. In some cases, depending on the phraseology of vacancy announcements, there will be an overlap between keywords and action verbs. An extensive list of job-specific action verbs that are useful for federal resumes and application forms can be found online (see the inside back cover of this book).

Don't Undersell Yourself

Among the biggest mistakes that federal job applicants make is to undersell themselves. As a result, they lose consideration for employment—not because they aren't qualified, but because they fail to spell out their qualifications in writing. This often is because either they misunderstand the federal job application rating process, under which applicants are scored based on the information provided in their applications or resumes, or because they fail to adequately evaluate and describe their knowledge, skills, and abilities.

Keep in mind that rating panel members are forbidden to make assumptions or use personal knowledge in the rating process, no matter what positions you held. The panel is allowed to use only the written information you submit. So, unless your background is clearly spelled out on your application or resume, you will not receive credit for it. Consider details submitted by an applicant for a federal police officer position about their experience as a plainclothes security officer at a retail store:

Processed persons detained for shoplifting by selecting and preparing appropriate forms depending on the circumstances. Wrote incident reports that were examined and approved by my supervisor. Filled out other forms and wrote incident reports for a variety of other types of incidents. These also were reviewed and approved by my supervisor. The various reports and forms, along with many other tasks I performed, served as the basis for my performance evaluations. Over the two-year period I served with the company, my performance was evaluated every six months. All of my performance evaluation ratings were above average.

This is a typical example of information submitted by someone unfamiliar with federal hiring processes. In particular, the applicant has not matched their skills to the position, and seems unaware that rating panel members cannot assume that he or she, as a plainclothes security officer, performed tasks that provided skills transferable to the position of federal police officer. More than likely, the applicant mistakenly assumes that everyone knows what plainclothes security officers do on the job and that his or her experience will be noted accordingly. However, this applicant will be given credit *only* for experience in the areas discussed in the application— filling out forms and writing reports—not other experience that has prepared them to perform the duties of a federal police officer. If this applicant has responsibilities like those in similar positions, he or she will not receive credit for experience in areas such as the following:

- Using observation skills in performing a variety of covert surveillance techniques

- Maintaining surveillance logs and activity logs

- Communicating with other personnel via portable radio and dispatching equipment, while using appropriate terminology, codes, and protocol

- Coordinating with other personnel for safely approaching and confronting persons suspected of committing larceny offenses, fraud, assaults, malicious destruction of property, staging false accidents, and other crimes

- Applying knowledge of legal subjects, such as criminal law, juvenile law, laws of arrest, admissions and confessions, custody and detention, civil rights, and civil liability

- Performing arrests, searches incident to arrests, and resulting seizures of contraband

- Using defensive tactics and subject control techniques to protect himself or herself, or others

- Interviewing witnesses

- Interrogating arrested persons

- Working with the local police department to transfer custody of arrested persons

- Coordinating prosecution efforts with the local police department and the prosecutor's office

- Testifying in court under oath during hearings, trials, and sentencing functions

- Responding to calls for service or assistance, and to suspicious circumstances

- Resolving disputes involving customers, store personnel, and others

- Assisting with the safe and orderly evacuation of store occupants during weather emergencies, power outages, bomb threats, and other circumstances

- Applying first-aid and CPR to injured persons in medical incidents and emergencies

As you can see, the applicant has failed to discuss in his or her application or resume the knowledge, skills, and abilities he or she acquired on the job—every one of which is *exactly* the type of experience federal agencies look for when filling police officer positions. Although examples like this are both unfortunate and typical, they can work in your favor if your competition does not know the difference.

Include Community Service and Volunteer Work

Community service and volunteer work are among the most commonly overlooked resume entries, even though they often involve valuable hands-on experience and transferable skills. This sort of experience should be listed and described as employment in the same manner as paid positions. Do not list these positions as extracurricular activities; this approach will not provide an adequate accounting of your accomplishments or responsibilities. Instead, under separate headings for each position, provide details of your activities and place emphasis on the specific tasks you performed and your achievements.

List and Describe Internships Properly

Similarly to volunteer and community service work, internships frequently are given inadequate attention or no mention at all on resumes. This can be a big mistake, because internships often represent the only job-related experience for many recent college graduates and those making a career change. Unless you have extensive experience related to the position you're applying for, you should list any job-related internships as separate positions on your application or resume.

Many job applicants also make the mistake of simply listing company or agency divisions, groups, activities, or job functions they were exposed to during internships. This is a fine start, but it is critical that you describe exactly *what you did*, not just the kinds of things you were *exposed to*. Under separate headings for each internship, provide complete details of your activities with emphasis on specific tasks performed and accomplishments. A description of activities might include operating technical equipment and communications devices, assisting with investigations, conducting surveillance, performing patrol duties, reviewing financial records and other documents, participating in personal interviews, assisting with trial preparation, answering inquiries from the public, searching databases, and solving problems. These and other tasks performed during internships should not be overlooked, because they often provide valuable hands-on experience that is directly related to the career you are seeking.

Customize Every Resume or Application

It is critical that you tailor *every* resume or application to the specific requirements of each position. Again, you must study the KSAs, major duties, and qualifications for each position because they will vary from one position to the next. In fact, the criteria used to evaluate applicants can vary significantly even if the positions being filled are the same as one another. This is because agencies often target different skill sets, depending on their mission and the ways in which they operate.

In addition, most agencies make adjustments in the skill sets they look for, depending on their needs at any given time. A perfect example is the FBI special agent hiring process, which sometimes allows *only* applicants with certain skills and experience to apply based on projected needs. Indeed, the FBI and other agencies evaluate and reevaluate their needs in response to changes in mission or priorities, special projects or initiatives planned or underway, projected retirements, and other factors. Therefore, considering that each application must be a custom fit for the position being filled, it is not wise to use exactly the same resume or application material twice.

Get a Second Opinion

After you have completed your application or resume, have it proofread and critiqued by someone such as a college faculty member, career placement office advisor, professional in the field of the career you are seeking, family member, or friend, if you think they can be objective. Have them check for appearance, format, grammar, punctuation, style, misspelled words, and typographical errors. Many colleges and universities offer proofreading and critiquing free of charge to enrolled students and alumni, and many companies and individuals offer this service for a small fee. Remember that your application or resume will be the first document reviewed—and that first impressions are crucial.

Fill Out Application Forms Completely

It is very important to fill out application forms completely and follow all instructions carefully. Do not omit any requested information, and make sure that all the information you provide is correct. Candidates often are eliminated from consideration for jobs because they failed to follow application directions or omitted pertinent information. It would be a shame if you carefully followed the strategies discussed above and did not make it over the first hurdle because of a minor technicality.

Also, if you must submit both an online application and resume, be sure to provide consistent information in both documents, and also in other materials that could be required, such as the SF-86 Questionnaire for National Security Positions. Otherwise, you could end up spending a great deal of time explaining the inconsistencies.

Understand the Limitations of Cut-and-Paste Resumes

Unlike hard-copy resumes, there are limitations to the length and formatting of resumes submitted with online applications. For example, most federal application processes that require candidates to paste a resume into a text box presently allow a maximum of around 12,000 to 16,000 characters, which is equivalent to about 5 to

8 pages of continuous text or 8 to 12 pages for typical resume formats. This should be adequate space to describe your background, provided that your resume is well organized and written in plain English.

As far as formatting is concerned, simple is best. Keep in mind that you will be pasting information into an online text box, and that special formatting is likely to be lost. Therefore, you should not use bold, italics, underlining, bullets, indenting, or centering of lines or text. Plain fonts, such as Arial or Times New Roman, tend to work best.

Strategies for Composing KSA Statements

One of the most significant differences between federal and private-sector hiring processes is the use of KSA statements—formally known as Supplemental Qualifications Statements—to evaluate applicants' knowledge, skills, and abilities. A KSA statement is a one- to two-page response in which the applicant details his or her experience with respect to each criterion in the job posting. As discussed in chapter 1, many agencies that use online application processes no longer request KSA statements, and instead ask targeted questions that result in a similar assessment of applicants' knowledge, skills, and abilities. For example, FBI special agent applicants must submit the same information formerly addressed in KSA statements by answering online application questions and submitting a resume.

KSA Statement Criteria

Obviously, the nature of KSA statements varies from one position to another. However, the criteria that must be addressed in these statements also can vary from one agency to the next for the *same* position, depending on the agencies' needs and hiring goals. KSA statements typically require applicants to write about their experience, education, training, and other qualifications relating to about three to six main criteria of the position. For example, an applicant for the position of investigative assistant could be faced with KSA requirements such as the following:

- Knowledge of basic criminal investigation techniques
- Ability to gather and sort through facts and other data
- Ability to organize and plan assignments
- Skill in the use of computer software and the Internet, including databases, search engines, and Web sites relating to public records
- Ability to communicate orally and in writing in order to obtain and share information, serve as a liaison to other law enforcement agencies, and write reports

Preparing KSA Statements

There are many similarities between the art of preparing KSA statements, composing a federal resume, and responding to essay questions in an online application form. The importance of matching your knowledge, skills, and abilities to those addressed in vacancy announcements cannot be overstated. The bottom line is that although the job interview often serves as the deciding factor in hiring decisions, you are not likely to make it to the interview stage if you do not fit the mold. Regardless of the positions you apply for, you can actually outshine more qualified competition if you take the time to properly match your experience and other qualifications to those of the KSAs for the position. Therefore, when preparing KSA statements it is critical to follow exactly the same strategies for composing applications and resumes discussed earlier in this chapter.

Length and Format of KSA Statements

If matching your skills to the position is the greatest challenge in preparing KSA statements, then composing responses to each of the criteria in a clear and concise manner runs a close second. On one hand, considering that your initial rating depends *only* on the information you provide in writing, and because you don't want to undersell yourself, it would seem that "more is better." This logic is true to some extent, because you are not likely to receive a high rating if you do not have much to say. On the other hand, as with many things in life, too much of a good thing can be bad. Put another way, when asked by students about the appropriate length for midterm papers, a popular criminal justice professor at Michigan State University often replied: "About like a dress—long enough to cover everything and short enough to be interesting."

With this in mind, as a general rule your response to each KSA component should be about one to two pages in length, single spaced, with one-inch margins. Writing style varies from one person to another, but if you submit less than three-quarters of a page or so per element, you probably did not adequately consider the applicability of your experience. If this is the case, the information presented earlier in this chapter on evaluating your career skills, matching them to the position, and not underselling yourself should help you to overcome this situation. However, if you use more than two pages to discuss each element, chances are good that you need to be more concise. Even the most experienced applicant should have little or no trouble limiting each KSA element response to less than two pages. Frankly, the problem with long-winded responses is that nobody wants to read them, and rating panel members cringe when the KSA statement equivalent of *War and Peace* lands on their desks. Therein lies the dilemma. Nonetheless, composing KSA responses that are one to two pages per element should not be too difficult.

Aside from one-inch margins and single-line spacing, the format of KSA statements should be simple. Begin by reiterating the criterion text verbatim, either in bold type, capital letters, or underlined, so it will stand out from your response. Next, skip a line and type your response in paragraph form using standard English.

Cover Letters

You should send cover letters with resumes or applications as a way to introduce yourself and explain how your talents will benefit the organization. A cover letter should convey serious interest and enthusiasm, and must be short—no more than one page—and to the point. It also should capture the reader's attention, follow a business letter format, identify the position sought, and highlight your credentials and any unique qualifications. Cover letters must be individually tailored for each position. If you qualify under special hiring programs, such as those for veterans or the Outstanding Scholar Program, you should highlight this in your cover letters.

Written Examinations

Application processes for most jobs with federal law enforcement agencies do not involve written examinations. In recent years, many agencies have replaced these tests with online application questions that are used to identify each applicant's knowledge, skills, abilities, and experience. However, several agencies require candidates for criminal investigator and police officer positions to take a written test, and candidates for some support positions must take either written or practical skills examinations geared specifically to the positions sought. Vacancy announcements include basic information concerning written examinations and any other tests that might be required.

The following sections provide an overview of the examinations given by many federal law enforcement agencies, as well as tips for answering multiple-choice questions. In addition, strategies for answering mathematical reasoning and logical reasoning questions—the two most common types of questions presented in federal law enforcement employment exams—offer many insights that should improve your score.

Note that the information and strategies presented in the following sections are not designed to teach you everything there is to know about federal law enforcement employment exams. Unfortunately, there simply is not enough space in one book to adequately cover every aspect of every test. Fortunately, however, there are many study guides that can pick up where this book leaves off.

Study Guides

Even though you might be unfamiliar with federal law enforcement employment exams, the good news is that other standardized exams you probably have taken are quite similar, and there are countless study guides that should prove helpful. In particular, several books relating to examinations such as the American College Test (ACT), the Scholastic Aptitude Test (SAT), the Graduate Management Admission Test (GMAT), the Graduate Record Examination (GRE), and the Law School Admissions Test (LSAT) are very useful. These guides focus on competencies that are similar to those evaluated in federal law enforcement employment exams, such as verbal reasoning, mathematical reasoning, reading comprehension, and English grammar. Most study guides also include sample questions, full-length practice tests, answers, analyses, and other useful features.

Overview of Examinations

Written examinations are required for criminal investigator positions with a few agencies, including the FBI, Internal Revenue Service, Treasury Inspector General for Tax Administration, and Secret Service, among others. Agencies such as the U.S. Border Patrol, U.S. Park Police, and U.S. Postal Service administer written tests to applicants for border patrol agent and police officer positions. Some agencies require electronics engineer candidates to pass the Fundamentals of Engineering Examination (formerly known as the Engineering-in-Training Exam), or a written test required for professional registration administered by the boards of engineering examiners in the various states. FBI language specialist and contract linguist candidates must pass a hearing test, as well as a battery of language tests that focus on listening comprehension, reading comprehension, and translation.

Federal law enforcement employment exams are constructed mostly of multiple-choice and true-or-false questions that focus primarily on logical reasoning (known also as verbal reasoning or critical reasoning), mathematical reasoning, problem-solving, judgment, knowledge of English grammar and punctuation, reading comprehension, observation skills, and analytical abilities. An overview of the most common written examinations is included in the following sections.

Treasury Enforcement Agent Examination

The Treasury Enforcement Agent (TEA) examination is divided into three parts that measure verbal reasoning, arithmetic reasoning, and analytical abilities. Passing scores range from 70 to 100 points before the addition of Veterans' Preference points (see chapter 1). Historically, the TEA Examination has been used by law enforcement agencies within the U.S. Department of the Treasury as part of their special agent hiring processes. Indeed, the Criminal Investigation Division of the Internal Revenue Service (IRS-CID) and the Treasury Inspector General for Tax Administration (TIGTA) still use the TEA exam today. The exam also is used by the Bureau of Alcohol, Tobacco, Firearms and Explosives (ATF), which was a component of the Treasury Department until the agency was transferred to the U.S. Department of Justice in 2003. Similarly, the U.S. Secret Service still uses the exam, even though in 2003 the agency was transferred from the Treasury Department to the Department of Homeland Security (DHS).

FBI Special Agent Examination

Applicants for FBI special agent positions are given three written exams during Phase I of the hiring process. These consist of a Biographical Data Inventory, a three-part Cognitive Ability Test, and a Situational Judgment Test. The Biographical Data Inventory measures the ability to organize, plan, and prioritize; the ability to maintain a positive image; the ability to evaluate information and make judgment decisions; initiative and motivation; and the ability to adapt to changing situations. The Cognitive Ability Test measures mathematical reasoning and problem-solving skills, including the ability to interpret data from tables and graphs, mathematical knowledge, attention to detail, and the ability to evaluate information and make decisions. In the Situational Judgment Test, candidates are faced with hypothetical problem situations and are asked to choose their most likely and least likely courses of action among a number of alternatives. This test measures the ability to organize, plan, and prioritize; the ability to relate effectively with others; the ability to maintain a positive image; the ability to evaluate information and make judgment decisions; the ability to adapt to changing situations; and integrity.

The FBI exam is scored on a "pass or fail" basis. Additional information concerning the exam and how to land a career with the Bureau is available in *FBI Careers*, the companion book to *Federal Law Enforcement Careers* (also published by JIST Works).

U.S. Immigration and Customs Enforcement Special Agent Test Battery

Applicants for special agent vacancies with U.S. Immigration and Customs Enforcement (ICE), a component of DHS, must take the three-part ICE Special Agent Test Battery written exam early in the hiring process. This 4.5-hour test assesses logical reasoning, mathematical reasoning, and writing skills. Logical reasoning and mathematical reasoning questions are similar to those presented in graduate-level college admission tests. The writing skills assessment does not require candidates to submit a writing sample. Instead, this portion of the test includes written passages from which candidates must identify errors in English grammar, usage, sentence structure, punctuation, and other basics. The DHS Special Agent Exam is scored on a "pass or fail" basis. DHS offers the test quarterly in cooperation with the Office of Personnel Management (OPM).

U.S. Border Patrol Test

Border Patrol Agent candidates must pass a three-part examination that assesses logical reasoning skills, Spanish language proficiency or the ability to learn Spanish, and experience that is related to or useful for the work of Border Patrol agents. Logical reasoning questions are designed to evaluate how well candidates read, understand, and apply critical thinking skills to factual situations. These questions assess whether candidates can draw logical conclusions based on facts that are presented in various paragraphs. Spanish language proficiency questions focus on vocabulary and grammar. Candidates who are not fluent in Spanish are given an artificial language test that is based on grammatical structures of the Spanish Language. The artificial language test does not measure Spanish language proficiency; rather, it is used to predict the ability to learn a foreign language.

U.S. Park Police Officer Examination

Candidates for the position of U.S. Park Police Officer who meet minimum experience, education, and age requirements must pass a three-part written examination administered by OPM. This exam takes approximately 2.5 hours to complete, and consists of multiple-choice questions that measure aptitude in name and number comparison, reading comprehension, and mathematical reasoning. Name and number comparison questions require candidates to identify names and numbers that are similar or alike. The reading comprehension section includes questions relating to the content of narrative passages. Questions in the mathematical reasoning section test the ability to sort through information, apply analytical skills, and solve problems with mathematics. A minimum score of 70 percent is required to advance to the next phase of the hiring process.

U.S. Customs and Border Protection Officer Test

There are five components of the U.S. Customs and Border Protection (CBP) Officer Test. The first three sections evaluate logical reasoning, arithmetic reasoning, and writing skills. The logical reasoning and arithmetic reasoning questions are similar to those presented in other federal law enforcement employment tests, such as the ICE Special Agent Test Battery and the TEA Examination. In each of these sections, you are given one hour and 15 minutes to answer 27 questions. The writing skills assessment focuses on the proper use of grammar, syntax, punctuation, spelling, organization of sentences in a paragraph, and organization of paragraphs in a passage. You are given 50 minutes to answer 30 questions in this section. The CBP Officer Test contains two additional components, known as the *Applicant Assessment* and the *Applicant Experience Record,* that are used to provide overall assessments of candidates' knowledge, skills, abilities, experience, and competitiveness.

U.S. Postal Police Officer Examination

The Postal Police Officer Examination is a multiple-choice test that focuses on reading comprehension, name and number comparison proficiency, and arithmetic reasoning. Reading comprehension questions require candidates to draw inferences and distinguish between essential and peripheral information presented in narrative passages. These questions are similar to those presented in undergraduate-level college admission tests. Name and number comparison questions require candidates to examine a series of similar names and numbers to determine which are different or alike. The arithmetic reasoning section requires analysis of information that is presented in the form of either story problems or straight calculations. A minimum score of 70 percent (exclusive of Veterans' Preference) is required to be placed on a register of eligibles.

National Police Officer Selection Test

The National Police Officer Selection Test was designed by Stanard & Associates, a company based in Chicago, following extensive research and development concerning the skills necessary for police officers to perform successfully. It is used as an entry-level examination by federal agencies such as the U.S. Capitol Police, Bureau of Engraving and Printing, Bureau of Indian Affairs, and U.S. Secret Service Uniformed Division, and also by many state, county, and municipal police departments nationwide. This four-part written test, which is based on a 12th-grade level of difficulty, includes questions that are directly related to the tasks performed by police officers. The test is designed to measure cognitive skills that are critical to the successful learning and performance of the job, including arithmetic reasoning; reading comprehension; grammar, punctuation, and spelling proficiency; and report writing abilities.

Administrative Careers with America Examination

The Administrative Careers with America (ACWA) test is administered for entry-level GS-5 and GS-7 professional and administrative jobs that fall into six occupational groups. These groups include fields such as law enforcement, health, writing and public information, business, finance, management, personnel administration, and information technology. A separate test was developed for each group.

Federal law enforcement agencies can use the ACWA test when filling positions such as criminal investigator (special agent), industry operations investigator, intelligence specialist, park ranger, police officer, security specialist, and telecommunications specialist, among others. The test consists of two parts, including an evaluation of job-related abilities and an Individual Achievement Record (IAR). The job-related abilities section is tailored for each occupational group, and evaluates verbal reasoning (reading) and quantitative reasoning (mathematics) skills. The IAR is a multiple-choice questionnaire that focuses on applicants' experience, skills, educational achievements, employment history, and other activities. This section is designed to supplement the job-related abilities test by providing an assessment of additional job-relevant characteristics.

General Test-Taking Concepts

Regardless of the format of written examinations or the types of questions presented, by applying a number of general test-taking concepts you are likely to increase your score right out of the gate. The following strategies have been used by many former applicants who passed written examinations and went on to land careers with various federal law enforcement agencies.

Conquering Test Anxiety

If you are like most people, you have firsthand experience with test anxiety, whether in school, applying for a job, obtaining a driver's license, or in another setting. Test anxiety is simply a reaction to stress that accompanies test taking. Some applicants experience symptoms such as nervousness, muscle tension, headaches, stomach discomfort, rapid heartbeat, or sweating. The most detrimental of symptoms is mental blocking, which can affect memory, reasoning skills, perception, and the ability to focus.

Interestingly enough, test anxiety is not necessarily bad news. According to many highly regarded research studies, a moderate amount of pretest stress actually boosts performance, although either too little or excessive amounts can diminish performance. In other words, applicants who are able to recognize, manage, and channel test anxiety can use it to their advantage.

Most often, the root of test anxiety is fear of failure. Recognizing that fear is the culprit, and confronting it, are the primary challenges in conquering test anxiety. Although it is easier said than done, many test takers overcome pretest fear by putting the outcome of the hiring process into perspective. It is important to keep in mind that, in the worst-case scenario, failing a pre-employment test will not be the most difficult experience of your life. Indeed, nobody will take away your family or your education, you will not lose your job, and your pets will still worship you. In addition, more than likely you will have an opportunity to take the test again down the road. So, although you should do everything within reason to ensure your success in the hiring process, it is important to maintain appropriate perspective on things. Maintaining a positive outlook and employing the techniques discussed in the following sections should help you to overcome test anxiety.

Always Prepare

Oftentimes the most stressful part of an event—whether you're going out on a blind date or moving your family across the country—boils down to fear of the unknown. After the event is over, you often find that the stress was for naught. Therefore, it only stands to reason that conquering test anxiety will be easier if you have a firm understanding of what lies ahead. Adequate preparation also leads to an increase in confidence, and it is far easier to have confidence going into a situation if you understand the challenges you are facing and expect to succeed. Although the steps you should take will vary from one test to another, most often it is wise to brush up on your math skills, understand strategies for mastering multiple-choice questions, gain insight from others who have taken the same or similar tests, and review the other test-taking tips offered in this chapter. Also, study with someone else periodically. Discussing the material with others is not only an effective tool for reinforcing the information, it also reduces test anxiety and usually results in higher scores for everyone involved.

Never Cram for the Exam

Without question, preparing for tests is far less efficient if you don't budget enough time and attention to it. Therefore, it is best to space studying over a period of weeks or even months instead of cramming for the test the night before. Cramming is most often the result of procrastination. Unfortunately, cramming can increase anxiety significantly, which always interferes with clear thinking. Procrastination itself also increases stress—and excessive stress reduces test scores. On the other hand, studies have repeatedly shown that students absorb more information when studying takes place over a period of time. A simple and effective technique is to schedule study periods into your daily routine leading up to an exam and, most importantly, to exercise discipline in adhering to your study schedule as closely as possible.

Reduce Pre-Test Stress

Many people experience a gradual buildup of stress in the days—or even weeks—leading up to an important exam. Even if you do not fit into this category, it is still a good idea to reduce stress in your life to the greatest extent possible prior to the test. This could include tactics such as getting organized well in advance, working fewer hours, following a nutritious diet, exercising, and getting plenty of rest. It is especially important to get enough sleep the night before and to eat breakfast on the day of the test. Many people also have found over-the-counter stress-formula vitamin supplements to be helpful. Visualization techniques—visualizing success and maintaining a positive attitude—also can get you off on the right foot. Ideally, you should follow these strategies not only prior to the test, but also afterward as a part of your everyday routine.

Relax During the Exam

Reducing test anxiety and other forms of stress often can be accomplished through various relaxation techniques. Although a number of approaches can be used, a common method of relaxing tense muscles is known as the *Progressive Muscular Relaxation* (PMR) technique, which has proven effective in studies by university researchers. The PMR technique involves tightening a group of muscles, holding them in a state of tension for a few seconds, and then relaxing them completely. You can achieve this best by working head to toe and waiting about 30 seconds between muscle groups. The PMR method also can be used in conjunction with slow, deep breathing, which also aids in relaxation. Many doctors and other health professionals also can offer suggestions for applying relaxation techniques.

Strategies for Multiple-Choice Questions

Virtually all law enforcement examinations include multiple-choice questions that are designed to test your ability to recognize and sort out information, apply facts and concepts, and identify knowledge. Indeed, multiple-choice questions are the backbone of most standardized tests. The following strategies should be helpful in tackling multiple-choice questions on any law enforcement test.

Follow Directions

One of the most important test-taking skills is the ability to follow directions—which also happens to be one of the most important traits of law enforcement personnel. Unfortunately, some candidates are so anxious to get the test over with that they skip the directions. This often is a costly mistake. Always be sure to read and listen to all directions carefully before starting the test. A very important and often overlooked piece of information given in the instructions concerns whether your score is based only on the total number of correct answers, or whether deductions are made for incorrect answers. If you don't know whether you will be penalized for guessing, you could get yourself into trouble very quickly. In other words, getting off to a good start begins before you answer the first question.

Read the Questions and Choices Carefully

Failure to read questions carefully is a common cause for selecting incorrect answers on multiple-choice tests. As much as multiple-choice questions examine your knowledge and problem-solving skills, they are also designed to test your ability to review information carefully and thoroughly. Read difficult or confusing questions more than once, if necessary, and resist the temptation to jump to conclusions about what you think the questions ask. Instead, rely only on the information presented and decide which answers are best. Also, read all the answers before making a selection—even if the first or second choice appears correct—because the best answer might be listed last. Keep in mind that more than one correct answer could be presented and that you must choose the *best* answer from among the choices.

Make Educated Guesses

Most multiple-choice questions are scored on the total number of correct answers. If this is the case for the test you are taking, you should answer every question—even if you have to guess—because there is no penalty for guessing. If you do not know the answer, keep in mind that eliminating only one or two of the choices will increase the probability of selecting the correct answer. Simply cross off the incorrect answers on the test booklet and go from there.

Skip Difficult Questions

Work through questions quickly but also carefully. If you come to a question that you can't answer or are unsure about, it is best to skip the question for the time being and to return to it after answering the other questions. Tackling difficult questions is often easier when you are more relaxed after answering easier questions. In addition, your answers to easier questions could jog your memory or provide clues to those that are more difficult.

Fill in Answers Carefully

Many tests are paper-and-pencil variety in which an answer booklet is accompanied by a machine-readable answer sheet. Therefore, it is critical that you make sure that the number you are answering corresponds to the number of the question. If you skip a question, be sure to leave the space for that question blank. Although this is a matter of common sense, many test takers have been thrown off by one question in a sequence and marked one incorrect answer after another. Also be sure to fill in the answer ovals completely so that the grading machine can easily record your responses, and avoid making extra marks on the answer sheet because these could cause scoring errors.

Strategies for Mathematical Reasoning Questions

Questions that focus on mathematical reasoning—known also as arithmetic reasoning—are among the most common type of examination questions used in hiring processes by law enforcement agencies. The significance of mathematical reasoning in its applicability to law enforcement goes far beyond the ability to perform arithmetic calculations. This type of question is used to evaluate skills relating to assessing situations, gathering and organizing evidence, recognizing patterns, identifying relevant information, solving problems, reaching logical conclusions, developing solutions, and recognizing ways in which solutions can be applied. In other words, mathematical reasoning involves reaching logical conclusions from a set of facts, which is essential for solving problems in law enforcement and investigations careers.

Mathematical reasoning questions are used in tests such as the U.S. Park Police Officer Examination, U.S. Postal Police Officer Examination, National Police Officer Selection Test, FBI Special Agent Examination, TEA Examination, and the ICE Special Agent Test Battery.

Format of Mathematical Reasoning Questions

Questions that focus on mathematical reasoning are presented in paragraph form, commonly known as word problems or story problems. These questions typically involve the application of basic arithmetic concepts, although some tests also include basic algebra and geometry problems. For example, mathematical reasoning problems could require you to perform addition, subtraction, multiplication, and division; to perform calculations with fractions, percentages, decimals, ratios, and proportions; to calculate the area of an object; solve distance, time, and rate problems; and to solve problems with formulas or equations. Mathematical reasoning questions normally do not require mathematical abilities that extend beyond the high-school level. The exams do not include problems requiring knowledge of calculus, trigonometry, or other advanced mathematical principles and techniques.

Mathematical Reasoning Question Examples

Although there are many varieties of mathematical reasoning questions presented in federal law enforcement employment examinations, the following examples provide an overview of many question types used. As discussed previously, study guides for standardized tests offer additional sample questions and practice tests that also should be helpful.

1. Hunter Carnley weighed 8 pounds, 10 ounces at birth. Jack Blackwell weighed 7 pounds, 3 ounces at birth. What is the ratio of Hunter Carnley's birth weight to Jack Blackwell's birth weight?

   A. 4/5

   B. 5/4

   C. 6/5

   D. 6/7

   E. 7/8

2. An amateur wrestler was champion of his weight class in a tournament that qualified him to enter an international wrestling competition. The maximum weight for his weight class is 119 pounds. However, for the international tournament he must convert his weight into kilograms. If the formula for conversion is .45 kilograms for each pound, what is the wrestler's weight in kilograms (rounded to the nearest whole number)?

   A. 54

   B. 74

   C. 173

   D. 262

   E. 264

3. A rectangular pool 24 feet long, 8 feet wide, and 4 feet deep is filled with water. Water is leaking from the pool at a rate of 0.4 cubic feet per minute. At this rate, how many hours will it take for the water level to drop 1 foot?

A. 4

B. 8

C. 12

D. 16

E. 32

4. A savings account earns 1 percent interest per month on the sum of the initial amount deposited plus any accumulated interest. If a savings account is opened with an initial deposit of $1,000 and no other deposits or withdrawals are made, what will be the amount in this account at the end of 6 months?

A. $1,054.60

B. $1,060.00

C. $1,060.60

D. $1,061.52

E. $1,072.14

5. Barry served in a management position with General Motors (GM) Corporation in Lansing, Michigan. He and his wife, Christy, lived in Portland, Michigan. In 2004, Barry received notice from GM that he would be transferred to a facility in Mansfield, Ohio. To prepare their home for sale, Christy, a highly skilled interior designer, spent $4,887.50 for paint, wallpaper, carpeting, and window treatments. According to their real estate agent, Christy's improvements increased the value by $15,000. GM purchased the home for $250,000. What percentage of the sales price can be attributed to Christy's improvements?

A. 3%

B. 6%

C. 9%

D. 12%

E. 17%

Answers to Mathematical Reasoning Question Examples

1. **(C).** Hunter weighed 8 pounds, 10 ounces, which is 138 ounces ($8 \times 16 = 128 + 10 = 138$). Jack weighed 7 pounds, 3 ounces, which is 115 ounces ($7 \times 16 = 112 + 3 = 115$). The difference is 23 ounces. 138 pounds ÷ 23 = 6, and 115 pounds ÷ 23 = 5. Therefore, the ratio is 6 to 5. Also, considering that Hunter weighed more than Jack, and that answers B and C are the only choices in which the first number is higher than the second, it is obvious that answers A, D, and E should be eliminated from the start.

2. **(A).** $119 \times .45 = 53.55$. The nearest whole number is 54.

3. **(B).** Calculate the total cubic feet in the pool ($24 \times 8 \times 4 = 768$). The pool is 4 feet deep, so a one-foot drop is 1/4 of the pool's volume ($768 \div 4 = 192$). Divide 192 by 0.4 to calculate the number of minutes it will take for the water level to drop 1 foot ($192 \div 0.4 = 480$). Divide 480 by 60 to calculate the number of hours ($480 \div 60 = 8$).

4. **(D).** 1,000 × 1.01 = 1,010 (one month) × 1.01 = 1,020.10 (two months) × 1.01 = 1,030.301 (three months) × 1.01 = 1,040.604 (four months) × 1.01 = 1,051.01 (five months) × 1.01 = 1,061.52 (six months).

5. **(B).** $15,000 divided into $250,000 = .06 (6%). The amount Christy spent on improvements is irrelevant, as are all other details in this question. (See "Sort out the clutter" in the following section.)

Tips for Mathematical Reasoning Questions

Considering that the vast majority of mathematical reasoning questions are presented in a multiple-choice format, strategies for multiple-choice questions also are applicable. In addition, the following tips apply specifically to mathematical reasoning questions.

- **Brush up on your math skills.** If you follow only one tip to prepare yourself for mathematical reasoning questions, this should be the one. Although the math skills required for most tests are not especially difficult for most candidates, the level of difficulty is likely to be compounded if it has been a while since you practiced math calculations similar to those you will be asked to perform on the test. High-school math textbooks can be helpful study aids, and preparation manuals for the SAT, GRE, and GMAT tests also should be useful.

- **Sort out the clutter.** Mathematical reasoning questions often contain irrelevant information that is designed to obscure the facts and cause distraction. (A good example is shown in question 5, above.) Sorting out essential and nonessential information will make it easier to identify the correct answers. Don't assume that everything included in the passage is to be considered in determining an answer. Instead, ignore irrelevant details.

- **Read all the choices before answering.** Many questions are easier to answer by examining the choices and skipping the calculations. This technique often enables you to immediately eliminate choices that are incorrect. Also remember that many questions can be answered through approximations rather than time-consuming calculations. For example, if you estimate that the answer is about 50 percent, and the choices are 16 percent, 25 percent, 53 percent, 86 percent, and 92 percent, you should select 53 percent and move on to the next question instead of performing the calculations.

- **Don't get stuck on a question.** Most mathematical reasoning questions can be answered without lengthy or complicated calculations. If you cannot answer a question by performing a few rough calculations or estimates, you probably will be better off guessing than spending an excessive amount of time on the question.

- **Use the process of elimination.** In many cases you can systematically discard incorrect choices and narrow down your options to one or two by following the process of elimination. This technique is useful when certain choices are obviously incorrect. For example, if you determine that the correct answer will be a positive number and three of the five choices are negative numbers, you can narrow the number of choices to two. In fact, even eliminating only one choice increases your odds of selecting the correct answer.

- **Check your work.** Be sure to check your calculations if you can do so quickly. However, for complicated problems requiring more than a quick once-over to check your work, move on to the next question and examine your calculations only if you have time left over after completing all other problems. Oftentimes, you can detect errors simply by asking yourself whether your answers make sense.

Strategies for Logical Reasoning Questions

Many law enforcement examinations use questions that focus on logical reasoning—known also as verbal reasoning or critical reasoning—to determine how well job applicants read, understand, and apply critical thinking skills to factual situations. The skills evaluated through logical reasoning questions are similar in many ways to those concerned with mathematical reasoning. Logical reasoning is among the most critical skills that law enforcement officers must have and apply because it is useful in virtually every aspect of their work, especially in decision-making and problem-solving tasks. Examinations such as the ICE Special Agent Test Battery, the U.S. Border Patrol Test, and the TEA Examination use logical reasoning questions.

Format of Logical Reasoning Questions

These questions begin with a reading passage that normally ranges in length from one sentence to a paragraph of four or five sentences. Each passage is followed by either a positive or negative "lead-in phrase" that prompts you to select from among five answers labeled (a) through (e).

Positive lead-in phrases are presented in this manner:

From the information given above, it CAN be validly concluded that...

Negative lead-in phrases are presented in this manner:

From the information given above, it CANNOT be validly concluded that...

Logical reasoning questions require you to draw conclusions based on facts presented in the passages. You are expected to accept every fact in the passages as true. As shown above, the style of the lead-in question determines the nature of the conclusion from which to choose. In other words, positive lead-in questions are followed by one valid conclusion and four invalid conclusions, and negative lead-in questions are accompanied by one invalid conclusion and four valid conclusions. Regardless of the lead-in question style, there can be only one correct response to each question.

Logical Reasoning Question Examples

The following examples illustrate the nature of logical reasoning questions. The first example is a positive lead-in question, and the second example a negative.

1. In 2005, there were 450,000 immigrants from Finland living in Sweden. Although most of these immigrants were not employed in professional occupations, many of them were. For instance, many were engineers or nurses. Very few of these immigrants were librarians, another professional occupation.

   From the information given above, it CAN be validly concluded that during 2005 in Sweden:

A. Most immigrants from Finland were either engineers or nurses.

B. It is not the case that some of the Finnish immigrants were nurses.

C. None of the Finnish immigrants were engineers.

D. Most of the population not employed in professional occupations were Finnish immigrants.

E. Some engineers were Finnish immigrants.

2. A rapidly changing technical environment in government is promoting greater reliance on electronic mail (e-mail) systems. As this usage grows, there are increasing chances of conflict between the users' expectations of privacy and public access rights. In some investigations, access to all e-mail, including those messages stored in archival files and messages outside the scope of the investigation, has been sought and granted. In spite of this, some people send messages through e-mail that would never be said face-to-face or written formally.

From the information given above, it CANNOT be validly concluded that:

A. Some e-mail messages that have been requested as part of investigations have contained messages that would never be said face-to-face.

B. Some messages that people would never say face-to-face are sent in e-mail messages.

C. Some e-mail messages have been requested as part of investigations.

D. E-mail messages have not been exempted from investigations.

E. Some e-mail messages contain information that would be omitted from formal writing.

Answers to Logical Reasoning Question Examples

1. **(E).** Answer E is correct because it restates the third sentence in terms of the overlap between Finnish immigrants and engineers. Answer A says that most Finnish immigrants are engineers or nurses, which are professional occupations. However, the second sentence says that most Finnish immigrants are not employed in professional occupations, so answer A is false. Answer B is false because it denies any overlap between Finnish immigrants and nurses, even though this overlap is clear from the third sentence of the paragraph. Answer C is false because it denies the overlap between Finnish immigrants and engineers. Because the paragraph does not give complete information about the nonprofessionals (immigrant and nonimmigrant) in Sweden, answer D is invalid.

2. **(A).** This is an example of a question with a negative lead-in statement. It asks for the conclusion that is NOT supported by the paragraph, meaning that four of the statements are valid conclusions and one is not. Response B is a valid conclusion because it restates a fact given in the last sentence of the paragraph. Response E is valid because it restates the other fact in the last sentence. The third sentence is the source of both response C and response D. Both of these choices restate information in that sentence, based on the fact that access to e-mail messages was sought and granted.

This leaves only the first option, response A. This is the only choice that does NOT represent a valid conclusion, because even though we know from the paragraph that there is a group of e-mail messages that are requested in investigations and also that there is a group of messages that contain information that people would not say face-to-face, there is nothing that says that these groups overlap.

Tips for Logical Reasoning Questions

In addition to applying the strategies for multiple-choice questions suggested above, here are some tips that should be helpful when responding to logical reasoning questions.

- **Never assume anything.** It is very important to understand that the questions are not intended to evaluate your knowledge of the subject matter presented in the reading passages, but rather your ability to read and reason on the basis of a set of facts. In addition, you are expected to accept all information as true. Therefore, you must rely *only* on the information included in the passages, and not on any subject-matter knowledge you might have.

- **Sort out the clutter.** Similarly to mathematical reasoning questions, many logical reasoning questions offer irrelevant details that can be distracting and confusing. Therefore, you must sort out relevant and irrelevant details and concentrate only on the information necessary to solve the problem.

- **Take a systematic approach.** Considering that logical reasoning questions often are confusing and always require attention to details, it is wise to employ a systematic approach that involves reading the passages at least twice. During the first reading you should identify the general theme of the passage and the essential information. After reading the answers, do not rely only upon your memory of the passage to select an answer. Instead, read the entire passage again to verify your answer.

- **Pay attention to key words.** You must give particular attention to words such as "none," "some," "few," "many," "most," "all," "every," "could," "should," "must," and "only" when reading not only the passages, but also the answers. These words often are crucial in identifying the facts—including how two or more groups are related—and establishing the foundation for your reasoning. For example, in the statement, "All prisoners detained in large prisons are federal prisoners," the first group, consisting of prisoners detained in large prisons, is totally included in the second group, consisting of federal prisoners.

- **Answer the question that is asked.** One of the most common mistakes you can make on the test is failing to read the questions carefully. Many logical reasoning questions include choices that appear correct if you misinterpret their meaning. Although time limits can be demanding, you must be sure that you understand what is being asked before determining the answer.

Interviewing Strategies

The application process for the majority of federal law enforcement careers—whether for law enforcement officer or support positions—includes one or more personal interviews. Agencies conduct interviews to further assess competitive applicants toward the end of the application process, and to allow candidates an opportunity to learn more about the targeted position and the agency. Of course, the greatest emphasis in job interviews is on determining whether candidates have appropriate knowledge, skills, and abilities for the positions being filled. However, considering that most careers in federal law enforcement require confidence and interpersonal skills, interviewers also will evaluate these attributes.

There are several varieties of employment interviews used by federal law enforcement agencies, with each designed for different purposes. Generally speaking, interviews are either traditional or behavioral in nature. Within these types, the interviews can be carried out by a single person, known commonly as a one-on-one interview; by a small group, such as three or four interviewers, in what is known as a panel interview; or by a large group, often consisting of those the selectee will be assigned to work with, also known as a team interview.

Regardless of the format used, personal interviews provide knowledgeable and well-prepared applicants with a golden opportunity to showcase their qualifications. Strategies discussed in the following sections should help you to perform well and make a positive impression.

Overview of Traditional Interviews

Most job applicants are quite familiar with traditional interviews, a method that is used by many federal law enforcement agencies. This approach has been around since the dawn of time, and involves a series of planned or unplanned questions designed to determine how applicants measure up to the job criteria and whether they will be an appropriate fit for the organization. For example, the traditional interview usually includes questions such as the following:

- Why do you want to work for this agency?
- How has your experience and education prepared you for this job?
- What motivates you?
- What are your strengths?
- What are your greatest accomplishments?
- What are your weaknesses?
- Would you prefer to work alone or as a member of a team?
- Why should we hire you?

Traditional interviews also vary widely in terms of their level of formality, including structured, unstructured, and semi-structured. Structured interviews consist of a standard set of questions that are asked of every applicant, usually in the same order. The goal of this technique is to be as objective as possible by placing all applicants on an identical, level playing field. Unstructured interviews are more conversational than question-and-answer in format, with no prepared questions. In this type of interview, questions arise spontaneously depending on the flow of the conversation. Semi-structured interviews, as the title suggests, are a cross between structured and unstructured approaches. In this method, interviewers ask a number of prepared questions, although also move with the flow of the conversation and ask many unplanned questions depending on candidates' responses. As discussed in chapter 1, most federal law enforcement agencies conduct semi-structured or structured interviews.

Strategies for Traditional Interviews

For many job applicants, traditional interviews are easier to prepare for because many of the questions are predictable. However, it is important to consider that having a feel for the types of questions you are likely to be asked will take you only so far, and that you must employ many other tactics if you want to stand out from the crowd. The following tips and techniques should help you to put your best foot forward.

Learn About the Organization

Job applicants who take time to learn about the agency and the position are more likely to adequately articulate what they have to offer, while also sending the message that they are serious about a career with the organization. Many applicants conduct no more than minimal research about the careers they are seeking, and it shows. It is best to present yourself in the most positive light by showing that you have done your homework. Remember that your goal is to demonstrate that you are the best fit for the job, so it only stands to reason that you will make a more positive impact if you are knowledgeable about the agency, division, or unit filling the position and how it can use your skills. This can be particularly helpful when applying for positions with small, lesser-known agencies, as it shows that you truly want to work for them as opposed to getting a foot in the door and moving on to a larger agency down the road.

Present a Professional Image

The saying "You never get a second chance to make a good first impression" is true. Research shows that job interviewers evaluate applicants not only on their responses to questions, but also on their appearance and demeanor. It is very important to wear professional business attire to the interview, such as a suit and tie for males and a suit, dress, or pantsuit for females. You must be aware that every aspect of your performance will be judged, including the manner in which you present yourself. Be sure to greet the interviewers with confidence and a firm handshake, and to maintain good posture throughout the interview. You should also maintain eye contact with every member of the interview panel in an alternating manner while you answer questions.

Review Your Resume or Application

Always take the time to carefully review your resume and application prior to the interview because many questions are likely to be based on information you provided in these documents. In fact, interviewers often start off by confirming information you provided—in many cases a few months prior to the interview. Brush up on the details so as not to provide contradictory information, otherwise you are likely to be embarrassed. In addition, be prepared to discuss any significant changes that occurred after you submitted your resume and application. These could include developments such as a promotion or other change of positions, a change of employers, degrees or professional certifications earned, or any awards or professional recognition received.

Prepare Answers to Broad Questions About Yourself

Most traditional interviews include several broad questions pertaining to education, work experience, job-related skills, and career goals. To avoid surprises, review these areas prior to interviews and anticipate probable questions, then write down your answers. Many interviews include questions relating to your motivation for changing jobs, the skills and abilities you have to offer, your accomplishments, how you can improve the organization, how well you perform under stress, and your ability to work with others in a team environment. Although there is no need to rehearse your responses, anticipating the questions and writing out your answers will help you to organize your thoughts and recall details that might not occur to you on the spur of the moment.

Focus on the Positive

One of the most effective strategies you can apply is to focus on the positive during the interview. In other words, answer questions in a direct and positive manner and speak positively of present and former employers whenever possible. You can express a positive attitude and interest in the position using information you gathered to prepare for the interview. Explain how your experience, education, and training will make you productive in a short period of time with minimal supervision. Also be sure to sell yourself with specific examples of your skills and accomplishments.

Keep in mind that interviews also could—and often do—focus on failures or mistakes. Your best bet is to readily admit that you have not had 100 percent success in everything you have done. Just be sure to turn negatives into positives by explaining what you learned from your mistakes and how these lessons will serve you and the agency well in the future.

Listen Carefully

Not listening well probably is the fastest way to get yourself into trouble during a job interview. After all, if you cannot follow instructions or if you give answers to questions other than those actually asked, your interviewers will have a good indication of what they could expect from you on the job.

Candidates who perform well during job interviews owe much of their success to good listening skills. Those who make an effort to listen attentively for information about the position and the agency also tend to ask better questions, which sets them apart from others. Unfortunately, many candidates are so anxious to respond to questions during the interview that they overlook the importance of good listening skills. You must listen carefully to each question to understand the meaning and context presented, and then take a brief moment to collect your thoughts before responding. Interviewers expect you to give adequate thought to the questions, and they are interested not only in your answers, but also the manner in which you construct your answers. Pausing to collect your thoughts and prepare a response—even if only briefly—usually results in better-organized answers.

Tell It Like It Is

Would you issue a traffic ticket to your mother? If the answer is no, and if you were asked this question during the interview, then you must tell it like it is. One of the most common mistakes applicants make during job interviews is to anticipate what the interviewers would like to hear rather than answering questions with sincerity and candor. As a result, attempting to outguess the interview panel often leads to failure. Keep in mind that there are no "right" and "wrong" answers to most questions, and that every candidate is evaluated on whether they possess the critical skills, abilities, maturity, judgment, and personality traits the agencies are looking for.

The interviewers also would like to know whether you are honest, down-to-earth, sincere, and—perhaps most important of all—the kind of person they would like to work with. In other words, if you have what it takes, you will be much better off providing a true snapshot of yourself than putting on an act.

Ask Questions

An exchange of information is appropriate for virtually all job interviews, and applicants should be prepared to ask meaningful questions about the agency and the position. Indeed, employers expect applicants to ask questions about the agency, working conditions, training programs, advancement opportunities, job performance measures, and other issues. Having the confidence to ask appropriate questions during an interview not only will make a positive impression, but also will enable you to become more informed about the agency and the position. After all, a one-way job interview that consists only of questions asked by the employer and none by the applicant is more of an interrogation than an interview.

Provide Requested Information

It is common for interviewers to ask applicants to send them copies or originals of certificates, diplomas, transcripts, licenses, references, or other materials. Unfortunately, it also is common for applicants to fail to provide them as requested. Perhaps needless to say, failing to follow through almost certainly will bring an end to your candidacy for the position. Demonstrate responsibility and reliability by providing the requested information as soon as possible after an interview.

Send a Follow-up Letter

Career counselors, advisors, and other experts have long held that you should send a follow-up letter to the organization immediately after a job interview. The experts are right on the money. You should always write a brief letter of appreciation following an interview and send it to your primary contact. In the letter, be sure to thank the participants for their time and reiterate your interest in the position. Keep it simple, and mail it within twenty-four hours of the interview.

Frankly, it is unlikely that the text of your follow-up letter will mean much. More importantly, however, your letter will demonstrate your professionalism, etiquette, and willingness to take the time to follow through.

Evaluate Your Performance

In an effort to make each interview a learning experience, evaluate your performance by asking yourself whether you prepared adequately, presented your qualifications effectively, listened well, asked appropriate questions, and learned all that you needed to know about the position. After answering these questions as objectively as possible, make a list of specific ways you can improve and review the list before your next interview.

Although it might seem trivial, this exercise—essentially a self-debriefing—really can pay big dividends toward improving your performance in future interviews.

Overview of Behavioral Interviews

Many federal law enforcement agencies have abandoned traditional interviews in favor of behavioral interviewing. In a nutshell, behavioral interviews are designed to identify examples of your behavior in previous circumstances, which provides more accurate information concerning the presence or absence of skills than traditional interview questions. As a result, behavioral interviews tend to present a more reliable indication of how you will behave in similar circumstances in the future.

Traditional vs. Behavioral Questions

Traditional interview questions often require "yes" or "no" answers, or ask you to describe what you would do in a particular situation. These questions only require you to *speculate how you would behave,* which offers much less insight than information about *how you actually behaved* in a given set of circumstances. For example, a traditional interview could include a question such as this:

> *How would you motivate your co-workers while working together on a project?*

This question asks you to imagine yourself in the situation and to predict your response. In traditional interviews, questions of this variety tend to be answered with only a brief supposition of the best way to handle the matter—often based on the applicant's perception of what the interviewer would like to hear—after which the interviewer moves on to the next question. On the other hand, a similar behavioral interview question could be presented like this:

> *Tell me about a situation you have experienced during which you successfully motivated your co-workers while working together on a project.*

As you can see, behavioral questions are designed to identify actual evidence of your ability to perform and succeed on the job—or your lack of these abilities—as opposed to mere guesswork. In addition, considering that behavioral questions require you to describe actual experiences instead of making a quick guess, you will do most of the talking and the interviewer will do most of the listening, rather than the other way around. Behavioral interviewing is effective in determining whether job applicants have attained particular knowledge, skills, and abilities, and also is more reliable than traditional interviewing as a basis for predicting future behavior and job success.

Sample Behavioral Interview Questions

Behavioral interviews focus on your actions in a wide range of situations. The following questions are fairly typical of the variety of life experiences you are likely to be asked about.

1. Give an example of a situation during which you used your communication skills to present complex information so that it was easy to understand.

2. Give an example of a time you approached someone to discuss a difficult or unpleasant situation, and how you handled the matter.

3. Tell about a time when being organized and prepared contributed to your success.

4. Give an example of a situation that required you to gather a great deal of information to solve a problem or present a proposal.

5. Tell about an occasion when you analyzed a situation and identified the appropriate steps to take to achieve positive results.

6. Discuss how you completed a project on schedule because you prioritized tasks effectively.

7. Describe a successful project that required you to focus on many tasks at the same time.

8. Tell about a time when you established rapport or a positive relationship with a difficult person.

9. Tell about a time during which a group of people you worked with had a serious conflict or could not agree on a course of action, and how you approached the matter.

10. Describe a situation that required you to compromise in order to resolve a problem or disagreement.

11. Tell about a time when your efforts improved teamwork.

12. Give an example of a time during which you maintained a positive attitude when others did not.

13. Describe an occasion during which your organization was looked upon favorably as a result of your actions.

14. Describe a situation when you prevented a small problem from becoming a large problem.

15. Describe a significant mistake you have made, how you could have avoided it, and what you learned from the experience.

16. Give an example of circumstances that required you to weigh various options to make an important decision.

17. Give an example of a significant personal goal you set and how you accomplished it.

18. Give an example of an important idea or project that was implemented primarily as a result of your efforts.

19. Describe a situation that caused you to modify your planned actions in order to respond to the needs of another person.

20. Tell about a situation when you made a quick decision under difficult or dangerous circumstances.

21. Give an example of a situation that caused you a great deal of stress, and how you reacted to the situation and the stress.

22. Tell about a situation during which you reacted successfully to circumstances that were changing rapidly and beyond your control.

23. Tell about an occasion when you conformed to a policy or followed a supervisor's orders even though you disagreed with the policy or order.

24. Give an example of a challenging situation during which you exercised integrity.

25. Discuss what you have done to maintain physical fitness and good health.

Strategies for Behavioral Interviews

The strategies suggested earlier in this chapter for traditional interviews also will be helpful during behavioral interviews. However, there are a number of additional steps you should take to prepare for behavioral interviews.

Although there is no way to know exactly what you will be asked during the interview, you can prepare some of your responses in advance nonetheless. These revolve around knowing in advance what you would like to discuss, presenting your answers in an appropriate format, getting the most mileage out of your experiences, putting your best foot forward, listening, and not attempting to be anyone but yourself. In addition, it is very important to be honest rather than telling the interviewers what you believe they would like to hear.

Catalog Your Experiences

An effective method of preparing for behavioral interview questions is to recall incidents that required you to evaluate a situation and choose a course of action while you were under stress, in difficult or emotional circumstances, responding to emergencies, or faced with moral or ethical dilemmas. It is also important to present your responses in an organized manner, including an introduction to the situation, a detailed description of your actions, and an explanation of the outcome.

Although many behavioral questions are tailor-made for responses based on your experience in the workplace, many questions also lend themselves to experience that is not career-related. For example, many of your responses could revolve around your experience as a student, parent, member or coach of an athletic team, instructor, member or leader of a Girl Scout or Boy Scout troop, Parent-Teacher Association board member, volunteer police officer or firefighter, homeowners association board member, or other position. In other words, just about any experience that involves employment, community service, education, troubleshooting, problem-solving, teamwork, coaching, teaching, leadership, responding to emergencies, or thinking on your feet is likely to fit in nicely.

Give careful thought to how your experiences match these and similar environments and it should pay off during the interview. Among other benefits, discussing your experiences outside of the workplace should give the impression that you are well-rounded.

Use the STAR Technique

The STAR technique is a systematic method of answering behavioral interview questions. The acronym STAR stands for

- **S**ituation
- **T**ask
- **A**ction
- **R**esult

To apply the STAR technique, first describe the situation you encountered and then identify the task that is appropriate for the situation. For example, you could discuss a conflict between two of your co-workers (the situation) and how you helped them to resolve it (the task). Be sure to provide sufficient detail so that the interviewers understand the circumstances completely.

Next, explain the specific action you took toward resolving the situation. The focus of the action should be on what you actually did or suggested. In the scenario involving your co-workers, you could describe a compromise that you suggested.

Finally, describe the result of the situation. In this case, you could discuss the terms of the compromise and how each worker accepted the outcome, as well as what you accomplished or learned from the incident.

The STAR technique enables you to frame your responses to behavioral questions in a straightforward, organized, and informative manner. As a rule of thumb, your description of the situation or task should encompass about 20 to 25 percent of your response overall; your explanation of the action taken should cover about 50 to 60 percent of your response; and describing the results should comprise the remaining 20 to 25 percent. The following example illustrates the STAR technique in action:

> *Interviewer's Question: Describe a situation in which you exercised good judgment and integrity.*
>
> *Situation: Last month, I participated in the execution of a search warrant at a convenience store in Chicago that was involved in food stamp trafficking. I was assigned to search a small office at the rear of the store. While I was alone in the office, I opened a desk drawer and discovered a cigar box that contained more than $100,000 in cash.*
>
> *Task: My objective was to seize the evidence in the most appropriate manner. I am aware that being alone in the room could have resulted in baseless accusations by the suspect that I took some of the cash. Of course, this sort of accusation—even if unfounded—could have caused a great deal of unnecessary discussion between the defense attorney, the prosecutor, and my agency, and almost certainly would have cast a dark cloud over the investigation. I also had an obligation to follow my agency's policy concerning the handling of cash evidence.*
>
> *Action: As soon as I noticed that the cigar box contained cash, I placed it back in the drawer, stood in the doorway leading into the office, and notified the team leader of my discovery. I remained in the doorway until he arrived, explained the circumstances, and then pointed out the box. After I photographed it, we counted the cash together and seized it in accordance with our agency's policy manual.*
>
> *Result: Considering that I didn't handle, count, or seize the cash until a witness was present, it is unlikely that anyone will question whether I pocketed any of the money. Not only did I use good judgment and maintain my integrity in the situation, the integrity of the evidence—including the chain of custody—also was maintained at all times. In other words, I acted within the law and agency policies, and the prosecutor intends to use the cash as evidence.*

As demonstrated in this example, the STAR technique enables you to respond to the question clearly, concisely, and in an organized manner. In addition to addressing judgment and integrity, the response also focuses on other traits that federal law enforcement agencies look for during the interview, such as oral communication skills and the ability to evaluate and adapt to changing situations.

Prior to the interview you must think carefully about several scenarios in which you have been involved, including the action you took and the outcome, and write down the details. Writing about the incidents will help you to collect and organize the details. This exercise might seem like a lot of work, but the rewards are well worth it. Preparing your responses and using the STAR technique should pay big dividends during the interview because you will already have a number of situations in mind when you are asked to discuss your experiences, and you will present them in an appropriate manner.

Admit Your Failures

In addition to questions that focus on your successes in evaluating, responding to, and adapting to various circumstances, you are likely to be asked about experiences that resulted in negative outcomes. In other words, be prepared to discuss situations in which your actions brought results that were somehow unsatisfactory, and any shortcomings that might have caused negative results. The interviewers realize that no applicant has led a life of perfection, and they will be interested in how you address negative outcomes.

If you are asked these types of questions, it is best to readily admit to your failures and to explain what you learned from them. This will give you a golden opportunity to turn negatives into positives, and also to exhibit maturity and humbleness. Rest assured that the interviewers neither want nor expect to hear that you have never made poor choices or otherwise taken the wrong path. If nothing else, failing to admit your mistakes will convince the interviewers that you are not the kind of person they will want to work with.

Additional Strategies for Internship Applicants

Not surprisingly, many federal law enforcement personnel got a foot in the door through an internship prior to landing a full-time career—including the author of this book. Regardless of the agency you would like to work for or the type of career you are interested in, internship experience can make you more competitive in the selection process for the career you are seeking.

This section is entitled "*Additional* Strategies for Internship Applicants" because virtually all the information and guidance presented earlier in this chapter also can be helpful for those seeking internships. With this in mind, consider the following strategies to increase your chances of landing an internship with a federal law enforcement agency.

Make Your Own Opportunities

If you plan on serving an internship, it is critical to get the ball rolling on your own—and early. Countless college students who are close to graduation approach professors or internship coordinators and expect to obtain an internship on the way out the door. In most cases, because they failed to get started two or three years earlier, these students almost always graduate with no internship or practical experience under their belts, and often with little direction in their career search. Of course, such lateness is a big disadvantage.

Planning for an internship should begin early in your academic career, preferably as a freshman and no later than your sophomore year. This is the time to get acquainted with internship coordinators, professors, or other staff who are responsible for arranging internship opportunities. Although it is true that preference usually is given to students in their junior or senior years, or to graduate students, internships sometimes begin earlier. Also, keep in mind that internship application processes often are similar in many ways to those for full-time jobs, which means they can be time consuming. For example, the application process for FBI internships begins 10 to 12 months prior to the starting date, which would require you to apply during your sophomore year for an internship during your junior year. Also realize that internship coordinators, professors, and advisors typically are swamped with many projects and responsibilities, and that internships—just like full-time careers—often go to students who are persistent and make themselves known.

Get the Facts

Many college students who are interested in landing a career with a federal law enforcement agency are unaware of the broad range of internship opportunities available to graduate and undergraduate students. If you take the time to find out about the opportunities that exist—rather than waiting for others to come to you with the information—you will be ahead of the game. Internship coordinators and many professors have ongoing contact with agencies that offer internships. You can also learn about internship opportunities by visiting career fairs attended by federal law enforcement agencies, or through your networking contacts, or by contacting the agencies directly. When you know what is available and how to take the steps to land an internship, you are halfway there.

Describing Your Experience

Whether you are submitting application forms or a resume, you must carefully evaluate your experience and education before completing these materials. Be sure to include all full-time and any part-time employment, volunteer work, community service you have performed, and your involvement in professional organizations. Also provide details of any achievements, awards, leadership activities, licenses or certificates, or special skills you possess. In other words, you should follow the same protocol for applying for a full-time job, with no less of an effort.

As discussed earlier in this chapter, if you completed an internship previously, be sure to list and describe it as a separate position on your application or resume (as if it were employment), because this will allow adequate space to describe your experiences in detail. In doing so, it is crucial that you describe exactly what you did rather than what you observed. Under separate headings for each internship, provide complete details of your activities and place emphasis on the specific tasks you performed and any accomplishments. These descriptions provide evidence of valuable hands-on experience that could place you ahead of other applicants.

Submitting Application Materials

Most internship application processes involve submitting an application and other documents, such as a resume, an essay, transcripts, letters of recommendation, written agreements, and a photograph. Background investigations also are common. *Always* provide truthful and accurate information in your application materials, and be sure to meet all deadlines; otherwise, you run the risk of delaying the application process or losing consideration for the position.

After you have spent hours putting together your application package, it would be unfortunate if it were misdirected or lost. One of the most important aspects of the application process is to be sure that you send the package to the right address. Mail that is misdirected—either at the agency or on the way there—could be delayed for days or weeks before it ends up in the right hands. Also, submit all your application materials via first-class mail or through a major package courier service, such as UPS or FedEx. Mailed packages should be sent either certified with "return receipt" service, or by Priority Mail with "delivery confirmation" service. UPS and FedEx provide both tracking and delivery confirmation automatically. Spending a few extra pennies will give you assurance that your materials were received by the agency, as well as peace of mind.

Tips for Internship Interviews

Virtually every internship application process includes a personal interview. Although most interviews are conducted face to face, sometimes they are carried out over the telephone. The nature of interview questions depends mostly on the type of internship for which you are applying. In addition to questions that are targeted specifically to the internship, you should be prepared to answer a number of general questions, such as the following:

- What can you tell me about yourself?
- What can you tell me about the agency?
- What would you like to accomplish during the internship?
- Do you have any particular qualities that will be helpful during your internship?
- What are your major strengths and weaknesses?
- What accomplishment are you most proud of?
- What kinds of tasks, assignments, or projects motivate you the most?
- Why have you chosen to pursue a career in this field?
- What are your career goals?
- How would your most recent supervisor describe you?
- What can you tell me about yourself that is not on your resume or application?
- Do you have any questions about the internship?

In addition to the "traditional" questions in the preceding list, it also is possible that you will be asked behavioral questions during the internship interview. Therefore, you should review the behavioral interview information presented previously in this chapter so that you will have a general idea of what to expect. Regardless of the interview format, if you keep in mind the knowledge, skills, and abilities the interviewers are looking for, you should be able to predict many—if not most—of the questions.

Preparation, eye contact, listening skills, and a positive attitude are vital to your success during internship interviews. Of course, guidance on these and other techniques presented earlier in this chapter also is applicable to internship interviews.

Asking Questions During the Interview

More than likely, you will be given an opportunity toward the end of the interview to ask questions. Asking questions serves not only as a means of gathering information, but also demonstrates your interest in the internship. Be careful, however, not to ask questions that have already been answered during the interview or questions with obvious answers. Interviewers can assess your maturity, communication skills, and professionalism based on your questions, so it is important to be prepared and to ask questions that you truly would like answered. Also, have several questions in mind, because the interviewer might answer some of them during the interview. Here are a few examples of questions you could ask:

- Could you describe a typical day for interns?
- What sort of assignments or projects do interns work on?
- Do interns have an opportunity to participate in training or seminars?
- What have interns found to be most satisfying or rewarding in their internships?
- How do you measure the performance of interns?

Of course, the questions you ask will depend on your interests and whether the interviewers spend time providing details about the internship. Nonetheless, feel free to ask questions that are geared toward learning more about the internship and the agency if the opportunity presents itself.

Perseverance

Perseverance is one of the most important traits of law enforcement officers and other personnel who serve with law enforcement agencies. It also can mean the difference between standing out from the crowd and being among the masses during the hiring process.

Stay the Course

Searching for a position in federal law enforcement is not only hard work, but often a lengthy and discouraging process. Although competition for these prestigious careers is intense, the rewards are plentiful for those who take an organized approach and stick with it. Take advantage of your personal network, keep good records, contact as many agencies as possible, and try every method you can to get your foot in the door. You must exercise steady persistence in spite of difficulties, obstacles, or setbacks along the way. In order to stand out from the crowd you must remain focused on your goal. If you are qualified and determined, your perseverance will pay off.

Those Who Can, Do

Time and again, victory is achieved by those who have a greater hunger to win than their opponents. Countless federal law enforcement officers and support personnel owe their success in landing a career with "the feds" to ambition, determination, purpose, and conviction as much as their qualifications. In other words, the "can do" state of mind can be as important as any of your credentials, whether during your job search or throughout your career.

The quotation at the beginning of this chapter attributed to Vince Lombardi, the legendary coach of the Green Bay Packers football team, says it all: "The difference between a successful person and others is not a lack of strength, not a lack of knowledge, but rather a lack of will." If you do exactly what it takes to stand out from the crowd, success is likely to follow.

CHAPTER 4

The Five Quickest Ways to Get Hired

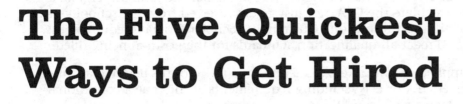

"Even if you are on the right track, you'll get run over if you just sit there."

—*Will Rogers*

The road to a career in federal law enforcement can be a fast track for candidates who either qualify for certain hiring programs or position themselves in the right place at the right time. The fast track often is traveled by college graduates with good grades or those who wisely invested their time in a paid or unpaid internship related to their field of interest, as well as current and former federal employees who have served in any occupation. Among the primary benefits of these pathways over traditional approaches is that they usually allow qualifying candidates to compete in applicant pools that are considerably smaller. So, carefully examine each of the following fast-track strategies, then consider whether you presently qualify under any of them or are willing to trade your time for the opportunity to slip in through the back door later.

Fast Track Number 1: The Outstanding Scholar Program

The Outstanding Scholar Program is perhaps the best kept secret in the federal law enforcement job search arena. This program allows agencies to hire college graduates at the GS-5 or GS-7 levels directly, without having to conduct competitive examining processes (written examinations). Many agencies prefer to hire personnel though the Outstanding Scholar Program because it allows them to recruit bright candidates, while also eliminating some of the time-consuming tasks associated with hiring processes. First and foremost, the program significantly reduces the number of applications to be processed, while at the same time ensuring that only applicants with good grades can apply. As a result, job seekers who qualify under the program are more likely to land a career in federal law enforcement simply because they are eligible for a common pathway of entry that is not available to many others. Fortunately for those who meet the program's minimum qualifications, in many cases position vacancies are open *only* to Outstanding Scholar candidates.

Outstanding Scholar Program Eligibility

Outstanding Scholar Program applicants must have graduated with a grade point average (GPA) of 3.45 or better on a 4.0 scale for all undergraduate coursework; or have graduated in the upper 10 percent of their graduating class in the college, university, or major subdivision (such as the College of Liberal Arts). All undergraduate grades are used to calculate the GPA, not just grades received from the school granting the degree. In addition to meeting Outstanding Scholar Program requirements, applicants must also meet all qualification standards for the position being filled.

Candidates can apply any time after graduation, or a few months before graduation as long as they meet GPA or class standing requirements at the time a conditional job offer is made. However, a conditional job offer means just that—an appointment is conditional upon successful completion of a bachelor's degree with qualifying grades or class standing. For example, if a conditional appointment is made six weeks prior to graduation, and if the candidate selected does not meet GPA or class standing eligibility upon graduating, the conditional offer must be rescinded. Grades earned for courses completed in graduate school cannot be used in calculating the GPA or determining class standing, although graduate education can be considered for competitiveness purposes along with other knowledge, skills, and abilities for candidates who qualify under the program otherwise.

Qualifying Law Enforcement Positions

The Outstanding Scholar Program is applicable only for certain positions. In addition to careers in business, finance, management, human resources administration, and other administrative fields, a number of law enforcement and investigative career vacancies are filled under the program. Table 4.1 provides a list of occupations relating to federal law enforcement that are eligible.

Table 4.1: General Schedule Law Enforcement Positions Eligible Under the Outstanding Scholar Program

Occupational Group	Occupational Series	Examples of Positions
Park Ranger	GS-0025	Park Ranger, River Ranger
Security Administration	GS-0080	Industrial Security Specialist, Information Security Specialist, Personnel Security Specialist, Physical Security Specialist, Security Specialist
Social Science	GS-0101	Correctional Treatment Specialist, Drug Treatment Specialist
Intelligence	GS-0132	Intelligence Analyst, Intelligence Operations Specialist, Intelligence Research Analyst, Intelligence Research Specialist, Intelligence Specialist

Psychology	GS-0180	Clinical Psychologist
Wage and Hour Compliance	GS-0249	Wage and Hour Compliance Specialist
Miscellaneous	GS-0301	Crime Prevention Specialist, Firearms Enforcement Technician, Seizure and Forfeiture Specialist, Victim-Witness Program Specialist
Telecommunications	GS-0391	Telecommunications Specialist
Paralegal Specialist	GS-0950	Paralegal Specialist
Internal Revenue Officer	GS-1169	Revenue Officer
Inspection, Investigation,	GS-1801	Aviation Accident Investigator, Commercial Fishing Vessel Examiner, Compliance Investigator, Compliance Officer, Customs Import Specialist, Deportation Officer, Diversion Investigator, Explosives Enforcement Specialist, Federal Air Marshal, Field Investigator, Futures Trading Investigator, Immigration Enforcement Agent, Industry Operations Investigator, Labor Investigator, Law Enforcement Ranger, Marine Accident Investigator, Market Surveillance Specialist, Museum Security Specialist, Pension Investigator, Pipeline Accident Investigator, Product Safety Investigator, Seized Property Specialist, Technical Enforcement Officer, Wildlife Inspector
General Investigator	GS-1810	Background Investigator, Civil Investigator, Investigator
Criminal Investigator	GS-1811	Criminal Investigator, Deputy U.S. Marshal, Detective, Investigator, Special Agent
Game Law Enforcement	GS-1812	Special Agent, Special Agent Pilot
Import Specialist	GS-1889	Import Specialist

How to Apply as an Outstanding Scholar

Application instructions and other details normally are specified in vacancy announcements under the *Area of Consideration* heading. The instructions often ask applicants to mail or fax a copy of college transcripts to a particular person. Typically, the authenticity of college transcripts is verified during the background investigation. Whether applicants are responding to a formal job vacancy announcement or sending unsolicited resumes or other materials to agencies, those who qualify under the Outstanding Scholar Program should *always* attach a cover letter that explains that they qualify under the program, and should also attach a photocopy of their college transcript. In many cases, agencies that do not have current job vacancies will take notice of candidates who qualify under the program and will retain these materials for further consideration once an opening occurs.

Fast Track Number 2: Acquire Federal Competitive Status

As discussed in chapter 1, federal employees who are serving in either career or career-conditional appointments in the competitive service have *competitive status,* and all other job seekers are classified as *non-status candidates.* Many job vacancies in federal law enforcement are open only to applicants with competitive status (known as *status applicants),* or in some cases only to employees of the agency that is filling the position. In other words, federal personnel are eligible to compete for many jobs in what amounts to an internal job market, and non-status candidates are effectively shut out of the process. In addition, many *former* federal employees also have reinstatement eligibility, which allows them to reenter the competitive service workforce without competing with the general public in civil service examination processes.

In consideration of the clear advantage held by federal employees in obtaining certain jobs, it only makes sense that in order to compete on a level playing field one must first acquire a position *somewhere* in the federal system. This strategy is used by many candidates who are serious about landing a federal law enforcement career and are willing to invest a year or two in a job that might not have been their first choice. Once on the inside, these employees have access to internal job postings and also learn about job vacancies with other agencies that often go unnoticed outside of the government, and they can apply for jobs that are not open to competition from the general public. In addition, if the federal job initially obtained requires a background investigation or a security clearance, federal law enforcement agencies often will take notice of this and realize that bringing such a candidate on board is likely to streamline the hiring process.

Obtain a Position Related to Law Enforcement

Although accepting a job in a field unrelated to law enforcement will extend competitive status, it is best for applicants to seek employment that is in some way related to their career of choice. For example, if your goal is to become a special agent with the U.S. Secret Service and you have an opportunity to accept a position as a security specialist, then you should strongly consider taking the job. Once inside the organization you can watch for postings for special agent vacancies that might be open only to federal employees or, better yet, only to Secret Service personnel. Similarly, accepting a position as a federal police officer, probation officer, compliance investigator, seized property specialist, dispatcher, or any other position related to law enforcement not only will provide competitive status, but also could allow you to gain experience related to the position you hope to apply for down the road. Accepting such a position also affords an opportunity to interact with law enforcement personnel from other agencies—and to find out about openings with these agencies as well.

Obtain Federal Employment in Any Field

Even accepting federal employment in a position that is not related to law enforcement will provide competitive status, experience, and also the opportunity to apply for other positions that are open only to federal personnel or those of the employing agency. This strategy is especially appropriate for those who are either unemployed or underemployed. Unless you already have a good job and law enforcement experience, waiting empty-handed for your ultimate career appointment to come along makes little sense. Instead of passing up the opportunity to accept a federal job that is not your first choice, you should strongly consider getting your foot in the door first—and gaining experience and competitive status in doing so.

Fast Track Number 3: The Student Career Experience Program

Many federal law enforcement agencies offer opportunities for students through the Student Career Experience Program (SCEP), an arrangement that provides meaningful work experience and leads directly to employment after graduation. This type of appointment—sometimes referred to as a "co-op position" in recognition of the former Cooperative Education Program that was similar to SCEP—provides many benefits to students and federal agencies alike. Students who participate in the program benefit from the integration of classroom instruction with practical professional experience in their major field of study, and later on from a full-time career in government service. On the other hand, federal agencies benefit by having the opportunity to evaluate students' skills and performance in actual work situations, and also the opportunity to bring educated personnel into the federal workforce. Whether in the public or private sectors, most employers prefer to hire educated applicants who also have professional experience related to the jobs they are filling. Most federal agencies are involved in the program, and many use it as a primary recruiting strategy.

How the SCEP Program Works

Federal agencies seeking candidates to fill most law enforcement and professional support positions tend to fill SCEP positions with undergraduate students in their junior or senior year of study, and to graduate students pursuing a master's or Ph.D. degree. Depending on the program format and recruiting needs of employing agencies, students normally alternate between periods of paid work experience and classroom study for at least two academic terms, and sometimes for up to two years. SCEP participants usually earn a salary that is either slightly below or equal to that of the entry level for the occupation in which they serve. All students earn annual leave and sick leave, and many are eligible for health insurance and life insurance benefits as well. College credit is awarded in most cases.

Typically, federal agencies allocate funds prior to bringing SCEP participants on board with the expectation of filling anticipated job vacancies down the line. Initially, students are appointed to paid positions in the excepted service. Although students who perform in a satisfactory manner usually are offered employment upon graduation, they are under no obligation to accept employment and the agencies are not required to offer employment. Students who accept a full-time position are appointed without any competition and their employment is converted to permanent status in the competitive service. On the other hand, students who are not offered or do not accept a full-time position still gain valuable experience that will be helpful when seeking employment elsewhere.

Participants normally perform many of the primary duties of an occupation under the supervision of experienced personnel. For example, many federal investigative agencies allow SCEP students to participate in virtually every aspect of criminal investigations, including tasks such as performing record checks, participating in interviews, reviewing financial records and creating spreadsheets, conducting surveillance, operating technical investigative equipment, participating in intelligence-gathering activities, assisting with the execution of search warrants, recovering and processing evidence, and meeting with Assistant United States Attorneys. In many instances, SCEP students also participate in training exercises along with full-time personnel. Agencies are required to establish performance plans and conduct performance evaluations for every student to document what they are expected to do and to advise them on how well they are performing.

SCEP Eligibility

The program is open to students attending a high school, accredited technical or vocational school, two- or four-year college or university, or a graduate or professional school. Of course, students enrolled in high school or vocational programs would qualify mostly for clerical and blue-collar jobs after graduation, while students graduating with bachelor's and graduate degrees are more likely to be placed in positions that lead to professional, administrative, or technical careers. All students must be enrolled in school at least half-time. Except in rare circumstances, noncitizens cannot participate in the program, and only U.S. citizens and natives of American Samoa or Swains Island can be converted to permanent employment.

The SCEP Application Process

Considering that initial appointments are in the excepted service, agencies are free to establish their own qualification standards. However, agencies normally adopt the same qualification standards as those for the full-time position the student will fill after graduation. Placement into the program usually is very competitive. In addition to screening processes that are conducted by participating colleges and universities, federal law enforcement agencies usually require candidates to undergo a formal application process that includes personal interviews, a background investigation, drug testing, and sometimes a medical examination. In most cases, candidates must also submit application forms and academic transcripts. There are no written exams for entry into the program or conversion to full-time employment.

Agencies are not required to a post vacancy announcement or any other public notice when filling SCEP positions. Instead, they work directly with schools to implement the program. Information concerning SCEP opportunities with federal law enforcement agencies is available from college cooperative education offices, job placement offices, or criminal justice faculty. Most college criminal justice departments also have advisors on staff who can answer questions and assist students in obtaining SCEP positions.

Fast Track Number 4: College Internships

In a similar manner to SCEP positions, internships also provide an opportunity for students to enhance their education and make practical application of classroom theory—often leading to full-time careers. Internships usually involve one or two academic semesters of unpaid field study in which students observe and participate in various tasks associated with a career in their academic major. This experience allows students to explore their career interests under actual working conditions, and to make informed choices before moving into the workforce. Internship opportunities tend to be more plentiful and easier to obtain than SCEP positions.

Although internships usually are not designed to lead directly to employment, many lead to employment *indirectly*. In other words, internship experience allows students to showcase their skills and potential, and also to get their foot in the door when seeking employment after college. As a result, interns gain the inside track with the agency they served, and often have an advantage over applicants who are unknown. In fact, many interns are hired by the same agency into full-time careers after graduation through the Federal Career Intern Program (as discussed under "Fast Track Number 5," on the next page). Other interns who perform well often acquire referrals to other agencies seeking qualified candidates.

Variety of Internship Opportunities

Criminal justice internships cover disciplines such as uniformed law enforcement, criminal investigation, intelligence, behavioral sciences, juvenile justice, probation and parole, forensic sciences, court administration, corrections, security, radio communications, research, and many other fields. While responsibilities vary depending upon the agency and type of work involved, interns perform tasks such as searching databases; examining financial records; observing undercover activities; organizing intelligence information; observing interviews with victims or witnesses; participating in search warrant execution; assisting with investigations and surveillance operations; analyzing evidence; observing legal proceedings; performing patrol duty (sometimes in uniform); assisting with prisoner handling, transportation, and processing; performing laboratory tests; operating security equipment; assisting with security surveys; creating audiovisual materials; operating communications equipment; conducting research projects; participating in training programs; and completing various clerical assignments.

A wide variety of federal agencies have provided internships to college students in the past, including USDA Forest Service; USDA Office of Inspector General; Central Intelligence Agency; EPA Criminal Investigation Division; Federal Protective Service; HUD Office of Inspector General; U.S. Park Police; Drug Enforcement Administration; Federal Bureau of Investigation; U.S. Marshals Service; U.S. Postal Inspection Service; Bureau of Alcohol, Tobacco, Firearms and Explosives; Internal Revenue Service; U.S. Secret Service; Federal Law Enforcement Training Center; State Department Bureau of Diplomatic Security; and State Department Office of Inspector General, among others.

Personal Networking

Criminal justice internships enable students to establish valuable contacts with professionals in the field that can lead to a successful job search. By interacting with those on the inside, interns can find out about advertised and unadvertised job vacancies, obtain advice, and seek referrals to other individuals or agencies. In many cases, these contacts can significantly reduce the amount of time it takes to obtain employment, and often spell the difference between landing a great career or none at all. In fact, information published recently in the Federal Register based on national statistics disclosed that personal networking—good old fashioned word-of-mouth—is the most effective way to find a job. Indeed, a substantial percentage of those serving with federal law enforcement agencies today attribute personal networking as the key to their successful job search, and many of them used internships as the foundation of their networking campaign.

Internship Application and Placement Processes

Selection processes for internships can be very competitive, and placement opportunities vary from year to year and from one school to another. Preference usually is given to junior and senior class members and graduate students, although many internship opportunities are available to freshmen and sophomores as well. Agencies often require intern candidates to submit application forms, transcripts, an essay, and other materials anywhere from four months to one year in advance. Background checks usually are required. Students should inquire about internship opportunities early in their academic careers in order to properly plan for this experience, and should apply for these positions as early as possible in the application process. Most college criminal justice programs have internship coordinators or advisors on staff who can provide guidance and specific details about placement opportunities.

Fast Track Number 5: The Federal Career Intern Program

The Federal Career Intern Program (FCIP) was established by President Clinton "...to attract exceptional men and women to the federal workforce who have diverse professional experiences, academic training, and competencies, and to prepare them for careers in analyzing and implementing public programs." The program is another example of federal efforts to recruit high-caliber talent into government jobs, to develop their professional abilities, and to retain them in a variety of federal careers where they can meet the future challenges of public service.

How the FCIP Program Works

First, it should be noted that FCIP internships are very different than the "Fast Track Number 4" college internships discussed previously. The primary differences are that FCIP internships typically are served *after* graduation from college (although it is possible to qualify for some positions without a bachelor's degree by virtue of experience) and are *full-time paid employment*. In addition, those hired under FCIP perform the same work for the same pay and benefits as others hired through "traditional" hiring processes.

FCIP was designed to give agencies some flexibility in hiring processes by allowing them to make initial appointments into excepted service positions. Indeed, although agencies must follow certain regulations set forth in the Code of Federal Regulations (CFR), the CFR allows agencies to hire candidates "...in accordance with any regulations or practices that the head of the agency concerned finds necessary." In other words, the agencies are not required to follow many of the rules that apply to competitive service appointments. For example, public notice and vacancy announcements are not required when filling these positions. Although the flexibilities are applied in many ways and for a variety of purposes, one important result is that agencies can use FCIP as a means to hire their former college interns after graduation. This feature alone can put you on the fast track, because if an agency wants to hire you after your internship, it is highly unlikely that you will have to compete in a large pool of applicants for the job.

FCIP candidates are appointed at either the GS-5, GS-7, or GS-9 level (or equivalent), depending on applicants' qualifications. Except in rare circumstances, initial appointments are made for a two-year period. During this period, interns carry out various responsibilities of the position in accordance with the performance elements of their assigned grade level. In addition, interns participate in formal training programs to develop competencies that are appropriate to the agency's mission and needs. For example, training could include attending programs at the Federal Law Enforcement Training Center, such as the Criminal Investigator Training Program (CITP), or on-the-job experience, mentoring with senior personnel, rotational assignments, attending conferences and seminars, or completing other training programs.

Agencies are required to establish performance plans and to conduct performance evaluations for interns to document agency expectations and inform interns of their progress. After two years, interns who have performed in a satisfactory manner must be converted to permanent status in the competitive service without the need to take examinations or undergo any other competitive processes. However, agencies are not required to retain any intern whose performance has not been fully successful.

FCIP Eligibility

Generally speaking, eligibility standards for FCIP internships are the same as those established for positions filled through traditional hiring processes. For example, a candidate who is hired under the program into a GS-1811 criminal investigator (special agent) position must meet minimum qualifications normally set forth for the position. In other words, unless the hiring agency has special requirements, the following qualifications would apply:

- Must be a U.S. citizen or a native of American Samoa or Swains Island.

- Must be at least 21 years of age and under the age of 37. (Candidates over age 37 who have previous service creditable under special law enforcement retirement provisions may also be eligible.)

- Must have sufficiently good vision in each eye, with or without correction. Corrected or uncorrected near vision must be sufficient to read printed material the size of typewritten characters. Hearing loss must not exceed 35 decibels at 1,000, 2,000, and 3,000 Hertz.

- Requirements for appointment to GS-5 level include completion of a four-year course of study leading to a bachelor's degree, OR three years of general experience, one year of which was equivalent to GS-4; for GS-7, one full year of graduate education, or superior academic achievement during undergraduate studies, or one year of specialized experience equivalent to GS-5; for GS-9, a master's degree or two years of graduate education, OR one year of specialized experience equivalent to GS-7. In some cases, qualifying education may be substituted for experience, and vice versa.

- Tentative appointees must qualify for a security clearance and pass a background investigation, drug screening test, and medical exam.

The FCIP Application Process

Each agency is responsible for establishing rules and procedures regarding the application process, including the announcement of vacancies and acceptance of applications. In most cases, agencies follow similar protocol used to fill other positions, although they often elect not to post formal vacancy announcements through OPM. In other words, candidates typically must submit an application form or resume and possibly other materials, and application processes will vary depending on the positions being filled and the agency filling them. Those interested in the program should contact agencies directly to determine whether FCIP positions are to be filled. Prospective applicants also should consult with their college advisors or internship coordinators, because agencies can—and often do—use FCIP to hire their former college interns.

CHAPTER 5

Sources of Federal Employment Information

"Knowledge is of two kinds. We know a subject ourselves, or we know where we can find information upon it."

—*Samuel Johnson*

Federal law enforcement agencies are constantly searching for talented individuals to fill vacancies in critical occupations. The key to finding out about career opportunities in the federal workforce is knowing where to look. Recruiting information can be obtained from career periodicals that are geared exclusively to federal job seekers, telephone-based systems that provide up-to-date details on job vacancies, high-tech Web sites that make use of sophisticated search capabilities, and resources such as newspaper classified advertisements and agency personnel offices. This chapter offers an overview of many sources of information that will make your federal law enforcement career search more productive.

The U.S. Office of Personnel Management

The U.S. Office of Personnel Management (OPM) maintains an extensive collection of information pertaining to federal employment and civil service procedures. The public can access this information free of charge either at OPM service centers, on the Internet, via computer modem access to an electronic bulletin board, or through automated telephone response and fax systems. The OPM Web site is located at www.opm.gov.

USAJOBS by Phone

USAJOBS by Phone is the federal government's official telephone-based source for job openings and employment information. This system provides instant access to current information on federal job opportunities worldwide, including positions with all federal law enforcement agencies. Users are guided through a series of prompts that allow searches for position vacancies by occupational category, job series, agency, or position title. New jobs are added daily. USAJOBS by Phone also offers information concerning qualification requirements, applications, student employment and other special hiring programs, employment policies and procedures, benefits, and other subjects. If you would like copies of vacancy announcements or other information sent to you, OPM will mail or fax it within 24 hours. USAJOBS by Phone can be reached at (703) 724-1850, 24 hours a day, seven days a week.

Federal Job Information Touch-Screen Computers

Another way to obtain federal employment information is to access OPM computer kiosks in public buildings. These computers employ touch-screen technology to disseminate job vacancy information. They are located at OPM Federal Employment Information Centers in major cities nationwide, at many state employment service centers and social service agencies, and within job placement offices at some colleges and universities.

Resources on the World Wide Web

The World Wide Web offers a vast supply of information that can be very helpful in your federal job search. You can obtain extensive background information on federal law enforcement agencies and careers by conducting keyword searches using popular Internet search engines such as Google, Yahoo!, Excite, and Lycos, among others. Although locating these resources is easy, obtaining current and reliable information presents an entirely different challenge. Most college and university criminal justice programs host Web sites that provide general information on criminal justice careers and links to federal law enforcement agencies, and many commercial Web sites and message boards contain a mixed bag of information that varies from current and accurate to outdated and inaccurate. If you do not have a computer or Internet access, you can use a computer to access the Web at virtually all public and college libraries. The following Web sites are among the best and have proven helpful to many federal law enforcement career-seekers.

USAJOBS Web Site

One of the best resources for federal career information is the USAJOBS Web site, which is maintained by OPM. This site provides users with access to information on current job openings listed in the Federal Jobs Database, full-text vacancy announcements, salary schedules, answers to frequently asked questions about federal employment and special hiring programs, and other information. Users can search for job vacancies by title, occupational category or series, department or agency, or geographic area. This site also allows users to print hard copies of vacancy announcements and other documents. Serious job hunters should make the USAJOBS Web site a regular stop on the road to landing a federal law enforcement career. You can access USAJOBS at www.usajobs.opm.gov.

The 911HotJobs.com Employment Portal

The 911HotJobs.com Web site was created in 1997 by Robert Amaral, a police officer who realized it was difficult to find police department employment information on the Internet and wanted to make it easier for job-seekers. Over the years, Amaral's Web site has expanded to include job postings for positions with law enforcement agencies, fire departments, and emergency medical service providers at the municipal, county, state, and federal levels. A wide range of federal agencies have posted job vacancy announcements on the 911HotJobs.com Web site. The site also offers for sale more than 100 employment books; dozens of videotapes, CDs, and DVDs; software; and an assortment of online practice tests.

The 911JobForums.com Message Board

In February 2000, the 911HotJobs.com Web site added an interactive message board for job-seekers interested in exchanging information on employment opportunities. Today, 911JobForums.com has more than 20 employment forums and other interactive specialty areas concerned with federal law enforcement, state police and highway patrol, sheriff departments, corrections, probation and parole, the military, fire and emergency medical services, dispatch, physical fitness, firearms and equipment, news, and other topics. Message board members can post questions and answers relating to employment issues and other subjects, read responses posted by other members, poll members about their job search experiences and concerns, and contact one another through a private message system. About one-half of employment-related message board activity revolves around federal law enforcement. More than 30 volunteer moderators—all seasoned veterans in their particular areas of expertise—monitor message board activity, answer questions, and offer their assistance. Membership is free.

FedWorld Information Network

FedWorld was established by the National Technical Information Service, an agency of the U.S. Department of Commerce, to serve as an online inventory of information disseminated by the federal government. The FedWorld Information Network supports a federal job announcement database that uses files created by OPM in Macon, Georgia. This search engine allows users to locate job vacancy information by keyword, occupational series, salary grade, or geographic area. The FedWorld Web site also has links to government reports, tax forms, U.S. Supreme Court decisions, and other resources. FedWorld can be accessed on the Web at www.fedworld.gov.

Federal Agency Web Sites

Many federal law enforcement agencies maintain Web sites that provide a general overview and history of the organization, information relating to specific careers, an overview of recruiting processes, and a listing of current job opportunities. Some also provide recruiting bulletins, profiles of famous cases, summaries of enforcement activities, training information, internal search engines, links to other sources of information, and access to policy manuals, reports, strategic plans, and other documents. Agency Web site addresses are listed at the end of each career profile included in this book.

IG Net

IG Net is a Web site that is dedicated to the work of more than 50 Inspector General agencies that conduct investigations, inspections, and audits. This site provides an extensive listing of job vacancies in the Inspector General community, full text vacancy announcements, salary schedules, information on training seminars and workshops, a profile of the Inspector General Criminal Investigator Academy, a search engine, and links to home pages of various agencies and other online resources. Considering that many of the best careers in federal law enforcement are with Inspector General agencies, this Web site should be viewed regularly during your career search. Access the IG Net site at www.ignet.gov.

Career Periodicals and Newspapers

A few publications provide up-to-date information on federal job vacancies worldwide. These are available by subscription through the mail or online, and some are sold in bookstores or maintained in public and college libraries. The following section offers an overview of the most popular publications.

Federal Career Opportunities

Federal Career Opportunities is a biweekly newspaper that includes details on thousands of federal job vacancies, ranging from entry-level through the Senior Executive Service, that are located nationwide and overseas. Listings are organized first by department or agency, and then by the job series classification. Every issue also includes several articles pertaining to federal hiring practices, employment trends, recruiting drives, and other related subjects. An online version also is accessible by subscription. *Federal Career Opportunities* is published every two weeks and is available from Federal Research Service, P.O. Box 1708, Annandale, VA 22003. Federal Research Service can be reached by phone at (800) 822-5027. An online version also is accessible by subscription at www.fedjobs.com.

Federal Jobs Digest

Federal Jobs Digest is published every two weeks with details of thousands of federal job vacancies located nationwide and overseas. Each 32-page newspaper also includes around a dozen articles and features relating to agency hiring plans, advice on preparing federal resumes and application forms, and news items related to federal employment. The *Federal Jobs Digest* Web site also provides job vacancy information online, recruiting information, and access to various job search services. *Federal Jobs Digest* is available from Breakthrough Publications, 326 Main St., Emmaus, PA 18049. *Federal Jobs Digest* can be reached by telephone at (800) 824-5000. The *Federal Jobs Digest* Web site is located at www.federaljobsdigest.com.

The Federal Times

The Federal Times is a weekly newspaper devoted to the issues and events that impact the federal workplace. Each 24-page issue includes dozens of articles relating to federal salary and benefits, actions in Congress and OPM, legal updates, and other news and information of interest to federal employees and job applicants. Informative articles pertaining to federal law enforcement matters appear regularly in this publication. *The Federal Times* normally includes a listing of approximately 100 current job vacancies in all career areas that are open to current or former federal employees. Subscription information is available from *Federal Times*, 6883 Commercial Dr., Springfield, VA 22159. The phone number for *Federal Times* is (800) 368-5718, and its Web site address is www.federaltimes.com.

Newspaper Classified Advertisements

Many federal agencies advertise job vacancies in the classified section of local and national newspapers such as the *New York Times, Washington Post, Wall Street Journal, Los Angeles Times, USA Today, Chicago Tribune,* and *Detroit News.* These advertisements often provide few details beyond the job title, basic qualifications, application deadline, and contact information. Some agencies also provide a brief outline of position duties, salary and benefits, number of vacancies, Web site information, and other details. Although details in newspaper classified ads often are limited, they should not be overlooked as a resource for federal job vacancy information.

Other Sources of Information

Details on federal job vacancies also are available from a number of other sources, such as federal personnel offices, state job service centers, and college career placement offices, among others. A handful of these sources of federal employment information are discussed below.

Federal Agency Personnel Offices

Information pertaining to current job vacancies, minimum qualification requirements, recruiting plans, training, and other employment-related matters is available from virtually all federal agency personnel offices. Although many of these offices are located within headquarters operations in and around Washington, D.C., federal employment information also can be obtained from many regional and local offices nationwide. Some federal agency personnel offices also operate 24-hour employment hotlines that provide current job vacancy details and other recruiting information over the telephone. You can obtain information concerning the availability of walk-in service, telephone hotlines, and other sources of information by calling individual agencies or visiting their Web sites. Telephone numbers for federal agencies normally are listed in the Government Listings section of telephone directories.

State Employment Service Centers

State Employment Service Centers or Employment Security Offices also provide information relating to current federal job vacancies. Some offices have OPM Touch-Screen Computers on site, while others provide personal computers with Internet service that allow access to the OPM Web site. Information concerning the location of these service centers and the services offered typically is available on the Internet by accessing state government Web sites. Service center phone numbers usually are listed in the Government Listings section of telephone directories.

College Career Placement Offices

All colleges and universities provide career placement services to their students and alumni. Career placement offices usually provide information relating to job vacancies in business, nonprofit organizations, and government agencies. Many also provide career counseling services, conduct mock interviews, maintain career resource libraries, sponsor job search workshops and career fairs, and arrange on-campus interviews. Visit career placement offices early in your academic pursuits to take full advantage of these services. Academic advisors, internship coordinators, and many professors also can be helpful in your career search.

Professional Organizations

Professional and trade organizations are excellent resources for finding out about job vacancies and establishing contacts with professionals in the field. Most of these groups hold regular meetings, conduct training seminars and conferences, and publish informative journals or newsletters that include job vacancy information. Some also offer career placement services and maintain job hotlines. Many well-known criminal justice organizations offer special membership categories and reduced rates for students, such as the Academy of Criminal Justice Sciences, American Correctional Association, American Society of Criminology, American Society for Industrial Security, and International Association of Law Enforcement Intelligence Analysts, among others. Many personnel presently employed by federal law enforcement agencies landed their careers partially as a result of networking efforts with members of these organizations. Active membership in professional organizations also demonstrates interest and involvement in the field.

Career Fairs

Career fairs remain an integral part of the recruiting effort for many agencies that are seeking the best and brightest candidates. Attending career fairs provides a unique opportunity for job-seekers to learn about federal law enforcement agencies and employment opportunities, to meet professionals in the field, and to develop a networking contact base. While all career fairs have professionals on hand to answer questions and pass out literature, some also conduct on-the-spot employment interviews or mock interviews. Be sure to obtain business cards from those who represent agencies you are interested in so you will have a contact for future reference, and inquire about other individuals you could contact for further information.

PART 2

CAREER PROFILES

CHAPTER 6

Criminal Investigators

"You can get a lot more done with a kind word and a gun than with a kind word alone."

—Al Capone

Federal criminal investigators in the United States are among the most respected and highly trained law enforcement officers in the world. These personnel—known commonly as federal agents—perform duties such as gathering and examining evidence of federal crimes, serving subpoenas, interviewing witnesses, conducting surveillance, participating in undercover operations, monitoring wiretaps, infiltrating criminal organizations, executing search and arrest warrants, interrogating suspects, testifying before grand juries, working with assistant U.S. attorneys to prosecute criminals, and so on. They also participate in task force operations with law enforcement agencies at the federal, state, local, and tribal levels, and provide security for high-ranking government officials and visiting foreign dignitaries. This chapter includes profiles of criminal investigation careers with 75 agencies.

Most federal agents are granted authority to carry firearms and make arrests through statutes that are tailored to specific agencies or activities, such as the FBI, U.S. Marshals Service, Department of Agriculture Office of Inspector General, Drug Enforcement Administration, and U.S. Postal Inspection Service, although some agents are deputized by the U.S. Department of Justice in lieu of statutory authority. The majority of federal agents are classified in the GS-1811 series and serve under the working title of *special agent*, while others have titles such as criminal investigator, special investigator, detective, deputy U.S. marshal, and postal inspector. Most agents also are covered under special retirement provisions for federal law enforcement officers and receive 25 percent Law Enforcement Availability Pay in addition to base salary.

Every candidate who navigates the federal hiring process and graduates from basic training becomes one of America's finest—a federal agent—a reward that provides innumerable opportunities to protect and serve the nation with honor.

Criminal Investigator (GS-1811)

Office of Inspector General, Defense Information Systems Agency, U.S. Department of Defense

The Defense Information Systems Agency (DISA), a combat support agency of the U.S. Department of Defense (DoD), is responsible for planning, developing, and supporting command, control, communications, and information systems that serve the needs of the president, vice president, secretary of defense, joint chiefs of staff, and all DoD components. DISA field operations include the White House Communications Agency, Defense Information Technology Contracting Organization, DISA Space Command, and others.

Criminal investigators serving with the DISA Office of Inspector General (OIG) conduct sensitive and complex criminal and general investigations of federal laws concerning fraud, waste, abuse, or mismanagement in DISA programs and operations. Investigations often focus on allegations of fraud pertaining to DISA contracts and procurement, public corruption, illegal use of government purchase cards, conflict of interest, money laundering, mail fraud, wire fraud, false statements, giving or receiving illegal gratuities, violations of the Uniform Code of Military Justice (UCMJ), and other crimes. DISA criminal investigators conduct investigations jointly with agencies such as the Defense Criminal Investigative Service (DCIS) and other Defense Department investigative agencies; Social Security OIG; and various federal, state, and local law enforcement agencies. This is a civilian position and does not require active duty military service.

Qualifications and Salary Levels

GS-5: Completion of a four-year course of study leading to a bachelor's degree; or three years of general experience, one year of which was equivalent to at least GS-4. **GS-7:** One full year of graduate education, or superior academic achievement during undergraduate studies, or one year of specialized experience equivalent to at least GS-5. **GS-9:** A master's degree, or two years of graduate education, or one year of specialized experience equivalent to at least GS-7. **GS-11:** A Ph.D. or equivalent doctoral degree, or three years of graduate education, or one year of specialized experience equivalent to at least GS-9. **GS-12:** One year of specialized experience equivalent to at least GS-11. **GS-13:** One year of specialized experience equivalent to at least GS-12.

Qualifying education can be substituted for experience, and vice versa. Eyesight requirements include good distant vision in each eye, near vision that is sufficient to read print the size of typewritten characters, normal depth perception and peripheral vision, and the ability to distinguish basic colors. Eyeglasses and contact lenses are permitted. Hearing loss must not exceed 35 decibels at the 1000, 2000, and 3000 Hertz levels. Tentative appointees must qualify for a security clearance and pass a background investigation and drug test.

Training

DISA-OIG criminal investigators attend the 11-week Criminal Investigator Training Program at the Federal Law Enforcement Training Center (FLETC) in Glynco, Georgia (see chapter 16). In-service training includes instruction relating to the UCMJ, contract and procurement fraud investigations, financial crimes, money laundering, and other subjects. DISA-OIG special agents also can attend the three-week Inspector General Investigator Training Program at FLETC (see chapter 16).

Contact: Office of Inspector General; Defense Information Systems Agency; U.S. Department of Defense; 701 S. Courthouse Rd.; Arlington, VA 22204; phone: (703) 607-6300; Internet: www.disa.mil/main/ig.html/

Criminal Investigator (GS-1811)
United States Navy, U.S. Department of Defense

United States Navy (USN) installations are staffed by criminal investigators who are responsible for investigations at USN air fields, communication facilities, supply centers, and other facilities worldwide. These personnel—known also as field office or base investigators—carry out a full range of investigative and other law enforcement operations in accordance with the particular activities of individual installations or regions.

Navy criminal investigators typically investigate general crimes that occur within their base of operations, and they also conduct investigations off-site pertaining to violations of the Uniform Code of Military Justice (UCMJ). The variety and complexity of investigations vary from one location to another, although they often focus on crimes such as aggravated assault, theft, vandalism, robbery, weapons offenses, sabotage, narcotics violations, burglary, sexual assault, fraud, arson, financial crimes, and other offenses. Navy criminal investigators coordinate investigative and intelligence-gathering efforts with the Naval Criminal Investigative Service (NCIS), Army Criminal Investigation Command, Defense Criminal Investigative Service, Air Force Office of Special Investigations, and other agencies. Many Navy criminal investigators are assigned to NCIS evidence teams. Navy criminal investigators are authorized to conduct surveillance and undercover operations, carry firearms, make arrests, execute search warrants, and serve subpoenas. This is a civilian position and does not require active duty military service.

Qualifications and Salary Levels

GS-5: Completion of a four-year course of study leading to a bachelor's degree; or three years of general experience, one year of which was equivalent to at least GS-4. **GS-7:** One full year of graduate education, or superior academic achievement during undergraduate studies, or one year of specialized experience equivalent to at least GS-5. **GS-9:** A master's degree, or two years of graduate education, or one year of specialized experience equivalent to at least GS-7. **GS-11:** A Ph.D. or equivalent doctoral degree, or three years of graduate education, or one year of specialized experience equivalent to at least GS-9. **GS-12:** One year of specialized experience equivalent to at least GS-11. **GS-13:** One year of specialized experience equivalent to at least GS-12.

Applicants must be at least 21 years of age and under age 37. However, candidates over age 37 who have previous service creditable under special law enforcement retirement provisions also may be eligible. Eyesight requirements include good distant vision in each eye, near vision that is sufficient to read print the size of typewritten characters, normal depth perception and peripheral vision, and the ability to distinguish basic colors. Eyeglasses and contact lenses are permitted. Hearing loss must not exceed 35 decibels at the 1000, 2000, and 3000 Hertz levels. Applicants must pass a medical examination, drug screening test, and background investigation, and qualify for a security clearance.

Training

Navy criminal investigators attend either a state-certified police academy training program in the state where they will be employed, or the 11-week Criminal Investigator

Training Program at the Federal Law Enforcement Training Center in Glynco, Georgia (see chapter 16). Initial training typically is followed by agency-specific instruction and on-the-job training at the duty station, which focuses on subjects such as the UCMJ, Navy regulations, state law violations, search and seizure, counterterrorism, financial investigations, sex crimes, and use of force.

Contact: Civilian Human Resources; United States Navy; U.S. Department of Defense; 1200 Navy Pentagon; Washington, DC 20350; phone: (800) 378-4559; Internet: www.navy.mil/

Criminal Investigator (GS-1811)
Office of Protection Services, Smithsonian Institution

Criminal investigators serving within the Security Services Division of the Smithsonian Institution (SI) Office of Protection Services (OPS) conduct investigations and perform security functions to protect SI assets and personnel. SI-OPS criminal investigators carry out these tasks within the museums, galleries, and other facilities that encompass the largest museum complex in the world.

SI-OPS criminal investigators investigate crimes and other matters occurring within or affecting SI museums, galleries, research facilities, the Kennedy Center for the Performing Arts, the National Zoo, or other facilities located in Washington, DC; Massachusetts; New York; Florida; Arizona; Hawaii; and the Republic of Panama. Investigations typically are concerned with theft of SI artifacts and property, vandalism, purse snatching, burglaries, accidents where tort claims are likely, and other serious crimes. SI-OPS criminal investigators gather intelligence concerning criminal activity and threats, share intelligence information with other law enforcement agencies, protect dignitaries and other VIPs, and conduct crime prevention surveys. They also provide armed security during the movement of SI collections and other valuable artifacts to or from SI facilities nationwide. SI-OPS criminal investigators are authorized to conduct surveillance and undercover operations, carry firearms, make arrests, execute search warrants, and serve subpoenas. They work closely with the U.S. Park Police, Metropolitan Police Department of the District of Columbia, FBI, museum law enforcement and security personnel nationwide, and other law enforcement agencies to coordinate investigations and locate, identify, and recover missing artwork.

Qualifications and Salary Levels

GS-5: Completion of a four-year course of study leading to a bachelor's degree; or three years of general experience, one year of which was equivalent to at least GS-4. **GS-7:** One full year of graduate education, or superior academic achievement during undergraduate studies, or one year of specialized experience equivalent to at least GS-5. **GS-9:** A master's degree, or two years of graduate education, or one year of specialized experience equivalent to at least GS-7. **GS-11:** A Ph.D. or equivalent doctoral degree, or three years of graduate education, or one year of specialized experience equivalent to at least GS-9. **GS-12:** One year of specialized experience equivalent to at least GS-11. **GS-13:** One year of specialized experience equivalent to at least GS-12.

Applicants can use equivalent combinations of specialized experience and education to meet total experience requirements. Eyesight requirements include good distant vision in each eye, near vision that is sufficient to read print the size of typewritten characters, normal depth perception and peripheral vision, and the ability to distinguish basic colors. Eyeglasses and contact lenses are permitted. Hearing loss must not exceed 35 decibels at the 1000, 2000, and 3000 Hertz levels. Tentative appointees must qualify for a security clearance and pass a background investigation, drug screening test, and medical examination.

Training

SI-OPS criminal investigators attend the 11-week Criminal Investigator Training Program at the Federal Law Enforcement Training Center in Glynco, Georgia (see chapter 16). They also attend in-service courses that focus on SI physical security, protective operations, criminal law, criminal procedure, and other subjects.

Contact: Office of Protection Services; Smithsonian Institution; 750 9th St. NW; Washington, DC 20560; phone: (202) 357-3062; Internet: www.si.edu/

Deputy United States Marshal (GS-0082/GS-1811)
United States Marshals Service, U.S. Department of Justice

The U.S. Marshals Service—the nation's oldest federal law enforcement agency—was established by the first Congress in the Judiciary Act of 1789. That year, President George Washington appointed the first 13 U.S. marshals. Deputy U.S. Marshals (DUSMs) are involved in virtually every aspect of the federal criminal justice system, including fugitive investigations, court security, custody of federal prisoners, witness security, asset forfeiture operations, service of federal court orders, and law enforcement operations support. They are based in every federal judicial district nationwide, and in Guam, the Northern Mariana Islands, Puerto Rico, the Virgin Islands, and the District of Columbia. DUSMs apprehend the majority of the nation's federal fugitives through independent investigations and extensive fugitive task force initiatives. These domestic and international operations result in the capture of tens of thousands of fugitives each year who have escaped from custody; have violated conditions of probation, parole, or bond; have failed to appear in court; or are wanted by law enforcement agencies for other reasons. DUSMs provide support and protection for the federal courts, including security for 800 judicial facilities; almost 2,000 judges and magistrates; and countless jurors, attorneys, and other court personnel and visitors.

Their role in prisoner custody involves housing and transporting federal prisoners from the time they are brought into federal custody through acquittal or sentencing processes, and includes transporting convicted offenders to prison. In accordance with the Witness Security Program, DUSMs protect witnesses (and their immediate dependents) who risk their lives to testify in court against organized crime members, drug traffickers, terrorists, and other major criminals. DUSMs also serve federal subpoenas, court orders, and arrest warrants; and seize, manage, and sell property forfeited by drug traffickers and other criminals. Many DUSMs participate in the Marshals Service Special Operations Group, a tactically trained mobile reaction team that responds to emergencies of national significance requiring federal intervention, such as terrorist incidents, natural disasters, riots, and other crisis situations. DUSMs are authorized to carry firearms and to make arrests for federal and state crimes. They coordinate operations frequently with agencies such as the Drug Enforcement Administration; Bureau of Alcohol, Tobacco, Firearms and Explosives; Department of Agriculture Office of Inspector General; and other agencies.

DUSMs typically are hired as GS-0082 personnel at the GS-5 or GS-7 level, and they can advance to the journeyman grade of GS-11. The primary responsibilities at these levels include court security; transporting, processing, and monitoring prisoners; and serving subpoenas and court orders. After gaining experience in the GS-0082 series, they can apply for promotion to the GS-1811 DUSM position. DUSM "1811s" focus primarily on fugitive investigations, threat investigations, protecting witnesses, and assisting other law enforcement agencies. However, the tasks carried out by all DUSMs can vary widely from one judicial district to another, and in many districts there is no significant difference between the responsibilities of GS-0082 and GS-1811 DUSMs.

Only those serving in the GS-1811 series are covered under special retirement provisions for law enforcement officers and receive 25 percent Law Enforcement Availability Pay.

Qualifications and Salary Levels

GS-5: Completion of a four-year course of study leading to a bachelor's degree; or three years of general experience, one year of which was equivalent to at least GS-4. **GS-7:** One full year of graduate education, or superior academic achievement during undergraduate studies, or one year of specialized experience equivalent to at least GS-5. **GS-9:** A master's degree, or two years of graduate education, or one year of specialized experience equivalent to at least GS-7. **GS-11:** A Ph.D. or equivalent doctoral degree, or three years of graduate education, or one year of specialized experience equivalent to at least GS-9. **GS-12:** One year of specialized experience equivalent to at least GS-11. **GS-13:** One year of specialized experience equivalent to at least GS-12.

Experience and education can be combined to meet total experience requirements for positions at grades GS-5 and GS-7. Applicants must be at least 21 years of age and under age 37. However, candidates over age 37 who have previous service creditable under special law enforcement retirement provisions also may be eligible. Eyesight requirements include uncorrected distant vision not worse than 20/200 (Snellen) in each eye, and corrected distant vision not worse than 20/20 binocular; normal depth perception and peripheral vision; and the ability to distinguish basic colors. The eligibility of candidates who have undergone eye surgery is determined on a case-by-case basis depending on the outcome of the surgery. Hearing loss must not exceed 30 decibels in either ear at 500, 1000, or 2000 Hertz, and 40 decibels in either ear at 3000 Hertz. The hiring process includes a written examination, medical examination, physical fitness assessment, drug screening test, background investigation, and security clearance determination. The physical fitness assessment consists of sit-ups, pushups, running, and a flexibility measurement.

Training

Initial training for all DUSMs includes the seven-week DUSM Integrated Training Program at the Federal Law Enforcement Training Center (FLETC) in Glynco, Georgia. This program is followed by the three-week DUSM Basic Training Program at FLETC. These programs focus on prisoner search, restraint, and transportation; court security; witness protection, high-threat-level trials; law; building entry techniques; asset forfeiture; and other subjects. Appointees to the DUSM GS-1811 position must also attend the 11-week Criminal Investigator Training Program at FLETC (see chapter 16). All DUSMs receive ongoing in-service training relating to their specific responsibilities and the operations of the agency.

Contact: United States Marshals Service; U.S. Department of Justice; 600 Army-Navy Dr.; Arlington, VA 22202; phone: (202) 307-9437; Internet: www.usmarshals.gov/; e-mail: us.marshals@usdoj.gov

Detective (GS-1811)
Naval Air Systems Command, United States Navy, U.S. Department of Defense

The U.S. Naval Air Systems Command (NAVAIR) provides engineering, research, development testing, and logistics support to the Navy and Marine Corps for aircraft, airborne weapon systems, avionics, electronic warfare systems, photographic and support equipment, ranges, and targets worldwide. NAVAIR is based at eight principal sites in the U.S. and has overseas operations in Japan and Italy.

Detectives conduct criminal and administrative investigations pertaining to Naval personnel and firms conducting business with NAVAIR components. Investigations often pertain to violations of Navy and Department of Defense (DoD) standards of conduct and the Uniform Code of Military Justice; fraudulent claims for line-of-duty injury compensation; sonic boom investigations involving damage allegedly caused by aircraft; and crimes such as larceny, drug possession, weapons offenses, sexual assault, and domestic assault involving Naval personnel. Detectives also review audit and inspection reports produced by the Defense Contract Audit Agency, DoD Office of Inspector General, and Government Accountability Office to identify issues relating to the integrity of NAVAIR programs and operations. Detectives are authorized to conduct surveillance and undercover operations, carry firearms, make arrests, execute search warrants, and serve subpoenas. Many investigations are conducted with special agents of the Naval Criminal Investigative Service and the Defense Criminal Investigative Service, and other federal, state, and local law enforcement agencies. This is a civilian position and does not require active duty military service.

Qualifications and Salary Levels

GS-5: Completion of a four-year course of study leading to a bachelor's degree; or three years of general experience, one year of which was equivalent to at least GS-4. **GS-7:** One full year of graduate education, or superior academic achievement during undergraduate studies, or one year of specialized experience equivalent to at least GS-5. **GS-9:** A master's degree, or two years of graduate education, or one year of specialized experience equivalent to at least GS-7. **GS-11:** A Ph.D. or equivalent doctoral degree, or three years of graduate education, or one year of specialized experience equivalent to at least GS-9. **GS-12:** One year of specialized experience equivalent to at least GS-11. **GS-13:** One year of specialized experience equivalent to at least GS-12.

Equivalent combinations of education and experience can be used to meet minimum experience requirements. Eyesight requirements include good distant vision in each eye, near vision that is sufficient to read print the size of typewritten characters, normal depth perception and peripheral vision, and the ability to distinguish basic colors. Eyeglasses and contact lenses are permitted. Hearing loss must not exceed 35 decibels at the 1000, 2000, and 3000 Hertz levels. Tentative appointees must qualify for a security clearance and pass a background investigation, drug screening test, and medical examination.

Training

NAVAIR detectives attend either a state-certified police academy training program in the state where they will be employed, or the 11-week Criminal Investigator Training Program at the Federal Law Enforcement Training Center in Glynco, Georgia (see chapter 16). In-service training includes courses in subjects such as report writing, child sexual abuse, legal issues and updates, supervision and leadership, firearms proficiency, and defensive tactics.

Contact: Naval Air Systems Command; United States Navy; U.S. Department of Defense; 21936 Bundy Rd.; Patuxent River, MD 20670; phone: (301) 757-4669; Internet: www.navair.navy.mil/

Detective

AMTRAK Police Department, National Railroad Passenger Corporation

The AMTRAK Police Department is a vital component of the National Railroad Passenger Corporation (NRPC), a government corporation established to develop the potential for modern rail service and meet the nation's intercity passenger transportation needs. AMTRAK serves more than 500 station locations in 46 states, and operates trains over a system of nearly 22,000 route miles. With police personnel assigned to 29 field locations in 16 states and the District of Columbia, the AMTRAK Police Department serves as the law enforcement and security arm of the NRPC, performing crime prevention functions and providing protection of railroad passengers, property, and personnel. The Department also is responsible for planning, assessing, and evaluating AMTRAK passenger, critical infrastructure, and station security, and for developing and implementing AMTRAK emergency response plans.

AMTRAK detectives investigate a wide range of crimes occurring on trains, in train stations or other facilities, or on other property owned or controlled by AMTRAK. These include offenses such as assault, larceny, burglary, robbery, weapons offenses, drug trafficking, arson, vandalism, obstructions placed on tracks, and bomb threats. AMTRAK detectives conduct surveillance and undercover operations, and occasionally perform uniformed patrol duty. They also coordinate operations with other departments and agencies, such as the Transportation Security Administration and other components of the U.S. Department of Homeland Security, and the Federal Railroad Administration and other Department of Transportation agencies. AMTRAK detectives are authorized to carry firearms, make arrests, execute search warrants, and serve subpoenas.

Qualifications and Salary Levels

Employment as an AMTRAK detective is open to noncitizens who are authorized to work in the United States. AMTRAK detectives are appointed through excepted service hiring processes. The qualifications and salaries of the position are similar to those of GS-1811 criminal investigators with other federal agencies. Applications typically are accepted only from AMTRAK police officers. Applicants must be at least 21 years of age at the time of appointment, and have an associate's degree or at least 60 semester credits from an accredited college or university. A bachelor's degree is preferred. The application process includes a written examination, background investigation, psychological evaluation, medical examination, and drug screening test.

Training

AMTRAK detectives attend either the 11-week Criminal Investigator Training Program at the Federal Law Enforcement Training Center in Glynco, Georgia (see chapter 16), or a state-certified criminal investigator training program at a police academy in the state where they will be employed. In-service training covers subjects such as surveillance techniques, undercover operations, drug interdiction, terrorism, emergency preparedness, crisis management, intelligence gathering, firearms proficiency, and arrest techniques.

Contact: AMTRAK Police Department; 900 Second St.—Room 101; Washington, DC 20002; phone: (800) 331-0008; Internet: www.amtrak.com/

Enlisted Special Agent
Criminal Investigation Command, United States Army, U.S. Department of Defense

The U.S. Army Criminal Investigation Command (Army-CID) provides a full range of investigative services to all Army elements worldwide. In addition to conducting field tasks traditionally associated with criminal investigations, Army-CID operates a forensic laboratory, a protective services unit, and a crime records center; employs computer crime specialists; collects and analyzes criminal intelligence; and performs polygraph examinations. Army-CID also has a corps of civilian special agents (see "Special Agent, Criminal Investigation Command," later in this chapter).

Enlisted special agents serving with Army-CID conduct sensitive and special interest investigations of serious crimes that occur on military installations or that involve Army personnel elsewhere. Investigations focus on crimes such as assault, robbery, homicide, drug trafficking, procurement fraud, war crimes, and terrorism. They also provide personal security for the secretary of defense and other Defense Department (DoD) officials. Enlisted special agents are battle-ready, and they provide front-line support to Army divisions during operational deployments. They are authorized to conduct surveillance and undercover operations, carry firearms, make arrests, execute search warrants, and serve subpoenas. Although Army-CID maintains a staff of civilian criminal investigators, enlisted special agent positions are staffed by soldiers serving on active duty. Enlisted special agents often conduct investigations jointly with other military, federal, state, and local law enforcement agencies.

Qualifications and Salary Levels

Candidates for enlisted special agent positions must be 21 years of age and currently serving in the Army, with at least two years of military service. Additional requirements include six months of experience with a military police unit, or completion of a six-month internship with a CID unit, or one year of experience with a civilian police force; no record of psychological or pathological personality disorders; no record of unsatisfactory credit; suitable character as established by a background investigation; no civil court or court-martial convictions; physical fitness; normal color vision; 60 semester hours of college credit; and willingness to complete a five-year tour of duty after completing apprentice special agent training. Promotion to warrant officer special agent requires 24 months as an enlisted special agent demonstrating exceptional performance, a bachelor's degree (although this requirement can be waived to 60 semester hours if otherwise fully qualified), and demonstrated potential to serve in a supervisory capacity. All enlisted special agents must maintain a top-secret security clearance.

Training

Enlisted special agents attend a 15-week Apprentice Special Agent Course at the U.S. Military Police School in Fort McClellan, Alabama, which covers subjects such as criminal law and procedure, crime scene processing, drug trafficking, report writing, and war fighting. They also attend in-service training programs that cover subjects such as hostage negotiation, terrorism on military installations, child abuse investigation, criminal and civil law, firearms proficiency, and defensive tactics. Enlisted special agents can complete advanced in-service courses at facilities such as the DoD

Polygraph Institute, FBI National Academy, Metropolitan Police Academy at Scotland Yard, Federal Law Enforcement Training Center, Defense Acquisition University, Canadian Police College, and Army Logistics Management College.

Contact: Criminal Investigation Command; United States Army; U.S. Department of Defense; 6010 6th St.; Ft. Belvoir, VA 22060; phone: (703) 806-0416; Internet: www.cid.army.mil/; e-mail: mailcicg@cidc.belvoir.army.mil

Postal Inspector
United States Postal Inspection Service, U.S. Postal Service

The U.S. Postal Inspection Service (USPIS) is one of the nation's oldest and most prestigious federal law enforcement agencies. As the primary law enforcement arm of the U.S. Postal Service, USPIS exercises investigative jurisdiction over more than 200 postal-related statutes pertaining to assaults against the Postal Service or its employees and misuse of the postal system. Postal inspectors work with USPIS forensic scientists, other USPIS personnel, federal and state prosecutors, and other law enforcement agencies to ensure the prosecution of criminals who attack the nation's postal system.

Criminal investigations conducted by postal inspectors focus on crimes such as mail fraud, mail theft, assaults upon Postal Service personnel, burglary of Postal Service facilities, bombs and explosives sent through the mails, trafficking in narcotics and other controlled substances through the mails, theft of postal money orders and postage stamps, embezzlement, and money laundering. Postal inspectors are authorized to conduct surveillance and undercover operations, carry firearms, make arrests, execute search warrants, and serve subpoenas. They work closely with agencies such as the U.S. Postal Service Office of Inspector General (OIG), Department of Agriculture OIG, FBI, Department of Justice OIG, U.S. Immigration and Customs Enforcement, Department of Transportation OIG, and other agencies.

Postal inspectors are covered under special retirement provisions for law enforcement officers, and they qualify for 25 percent Law Enforcement Availability Pay.

Qualifications and Salary Levels

Postal inspectors are appointed through excepted service hiring processes. Salaries for this position are similar to those of GS-1811 special agents at the GS-9 through GS-13 levels with other federal agencies. Applicants must be at least 21 years of age and under age 37. However, candidates over age 37 who have previous service creditable under special law enforcement retirement provisions also may be eligible. Eyesight requirements include uncorrected distant vision not worse than 20/100 (Snellen) in each eye, uncorrected binocular distant vision not worse than 20/40, and corrected distant vision not worse than 20/20 binocular; normal depth perception and peripheral vision; and the ability to distinguish basic colors. Hearing loss must not exceed 30 decibels in either ear at 500, 1000, or 2000 Hertz. Weight must be proportionate to height.

Applicants must qualify under at least one of the following entry programs, including Foreign Language Skills, which requires fluency in a foreign language for which USPIS has a current need; Postal Service Experience, which is limited to those who have been a Postal Service employee, contractor, or intern within the previous two years; Specialized Nonpostal Experience, which includes candidates with experience in the practice of law, accounting, auditing, computer sciences, law enforcement, or bioterrorism investigations; and Academic Achievement, which is open to candidates with a bachelor's degree and two years of full-time work experience, or a master's degree or Ph.D. and one year of full-time work experience, or a bachelor's degree and a cumulative grade point average of 3.0 or higher on a 4.0 scale. The application process includes a written examination, polygraph examination, drug screening test, medical examination, and background investigation.

Training

Postal Inspectors attend the 12-week Postal Inspector Basic Training Program at the USPIS Training Academy in Potomac, Maryland (see chapter 16). Ongoing in-service training for postal inspectors includes instruction in subjects such as mail processing and flow; information technology; hazardous materials; biohazard detection systems; technical surveillance operations; threat management; officer survival; and defensive tactics.

Contact: United States Postal Inspection Service; U.S. Postal Service; 475 L'Enfant Plaza SW; Washington, DC 20260; phone: (703) 292-3803; Internet: www.usps.com/postalinspectors/

Special Agent (GS-1811)
Office of Inspector General, U.S. Agency for International Development

The U.S. Agency for International Development (USAID) is an independent agency that administers U.S. foreign economic and humanitarian assistance programs in the developing world, Central and Eastern Europe, and the New Independent States of the former Soviet Union. USAID supports programs in the areas of population growth, health care, broad-based economic growth, environment, and democracy. Special agents of the USAID Office of Inspector General (OIG) investigate fraud, corruption, and other crimes relating to the agency's resources and programs, and also those of the Millennium Challenge Corporation, the African Development Foundation, and the Inter-American Foundation.

USAID-OIG special agents are responsible primarily for investigating fraud in the agency's procurement, contract, and grant programs. These investigations are concerned with violations of the Procurement Integrity Act, a federal law aimed at enforcing ethical conduct in the government contracting process; the Foreign Corrupt Practices Act, which prohibits U.S. firms from making corrupt payments to foreign officials; embezzlement of project funds; theft of commodities and government property; serious misconduct by USAID personnel; and other offenses. USAID-OIG special agents are based in Washington, DC, and overseas field offices in Hungary, Egypt, Senegal, the Philippines, South Africa, and El Salvador. They are authorized to conduct surveillance and undercover operations, carry firearms, make arrests, execute search warrants, and serve subpoenas. USAID-OIG special agents often are assisted by foreign law enforcement agencies, and they conduct investigations jointly with agencies such as the IRS Criminal Investigation Division, U.S. Immigration and Customs Enforcement, State Department Bureau of Diplomatic Security, FBI, and other agencies.

USAID-OIG special agents are covered under special retirement provisions for law enforcement officers, and they qualify for 25 percent Law Enforcement Availability Pay.

Qualifications and Salary Levels

GS-5: Completion of a four-year course of study leading to a bachelor's degree; or three years of general experience, one year of which was equivalent to at least GS-4. **GS-7:** One full year of graduate education, or superior academic achievement during undergraduate studies, or one year of specialized experience equivalent to at least GS-5. **GS-9:** A master's degree, or two years of graduate education, or one year of specialized experience equivalent to at least GS-7. **GS-11:** A Ph.D. or equivalent doctoral degree, or three years of graduate education, or one year of specialized experience equivalent to at least GS-9. **GS-12:** One year of specialized experience equivalent to at least GS-11. **GS-13:** One year of specialized experience equivalent to at least GS-12.

Equivalent combinations of education and experience can be used to meet minimum experience requirements. Applicants must be at least 21 years of age and under age 37. However, candidates over age 37 who have previous service creditable under special law enforcement retirement provisions also may be eligible. Eyesight requirements include good distant vision in each eye, near vision that is sufficient to read print the size of typewritten characters, normal depth perception and peripheral vision, and the ability to distinguish basic colors. Eyeglasses and contact lenses are permitted. Hearing loss must not exceed 35 decibels at the 1000, 2000, and 3000 Hertz levels. Tentative appointees must qualify for a top-secret security clearance and pass a background investigation, drug screening test, and medical examination.

Training

USAID-OIG special agents attend the 11-week Criminal Investigator Training Program at the Federal Law Enforcement Training Center (FLETC) in Glynco, Georgia (see chapter 16). Ongoing in-service training includes instruction pertaining to USAID program investigations, international issues and events, white-collar crime, search and seizure, law, computer forensics, financial investigations, personnel misconduct, and other subjects. USAID-OIG special agents also can attend the three-week Inspector General Investigator Training Program at FLETC (see chapter 16).

Contact: Office of Inspector General; U.S. Agency for International Development; 1300 Pennsylvania Ave. NW; Washington, DC 20523; phone: (202) 712–1023; Internet: www.usaid.gov/; e-mail: inquiries@usaid.gov

Special Agent (GS-1811)
Forest Service, U.S. Department of Agriculture

Special agents of the U.S. Department of Agriculture (USDA) Forest Service (FS) investigate criminal activity on 191 million acres of national forests, grasslands, and land utilization projects located in 44 states, the Virgin Islands, and Puerto Rico. National Forest lands are divided administratively into nine regions, with each region led by a special agent–in-charge (SAC). Each SAC is responsible for FS law enforcement operations regionwide, including supervision of all special agents and uniformed law enforcement officers.

Investigations carried out by FS special agents focus on timber theft, arson, accidents, unauthorized mining claims, violations of the Archeological Resources Protection Act, embezzlement, theft of government property or funds, infractions of USDA and agency regulations by FS personnel, and origins of wildland fires. In cooperation with other agencies in carrying out the National Drug Control Strategy, FS special agents also investigate the manufacture, distribution, and use of narcotics and other controlled substances on National Forest System lands, including marijuana cultivation, weapons and booby trap violations, and production of illegal drugs in clandestine laboratories. FS investigations and intelligence-gathering efforts also concentrate on international drug trafficking organizations that have been linked to operations on FS lands. USDA Forest Service special agents are authorized to conduct surveillance and undercover operations, carry firearms, make arrests, execute search warrants, and serve subpoenas. Investigations often are conducted jointly with agencies such as the Department of Agriculture Office of Inspector General, Drug Enforcement Administration, National Guard, and many other federal, state, and local law enforcement and regulatory agencies.

FS special agents are covered under special retirement provisions for law enforcement officers, and they qualify for 25 percent Law Enforcement Availability Pay.

Qualifications and Salary Levels

GS-5: Completion of a four-year course of study leading to a bachelor's degree; or three years of general experience, one year of which was equivalent to at least GS-4. **GS-7:** One full year of graduate education, or superior academic achievement during undergraduate studies, or one year of specialized experience equivalent to at least GS-5. **GS-9:** A master's degree, or two years of graduate education, or one year of specialized experience equivalent to at least GS-7. **GS-11:** A Ph.D. or equivalent doctoral degree, or three years of graduate education, or one year of specialized experience equivalent to at least GS-9. **GS-12:** One year of specialized experience equivalent to at least GS-11. **GS-13:** One year of specialized experience equivalent to at least GS-12.

Qualifying education can be substituted for experience, and vice versa. Applicants must be at least 21 years of age and under age 37. However, candidates over age 37 who have previous service creditable under special law enforcement retirement provisions also may be eligible. Vision standards include distant visual acuity not worse than 20/40 (Snellen) in one eye and 20/20 in the other eye, with or without correction; near vision sufficient to read print the size of typewritten characters, with or without correction; the ability to distinguish basic shades of colors; and normal depth perception and peripheral vision. Hearing loss must not exceed 35 decibels at the 1000, 2000, and 3000 Hertz levels. Tentative appointees must qualify for a security clearance and pass a drug screening test and medical examination.

Training

FS special agents attend the 11-week Criminal Investigator Training Program at the Federal Law Enforcement Training Center (FLETC) in Glynco, Georgia (see chapter 16), followed by a two-week course at FLETC that covers various aspects of FS law enforcement operations. FS special agents receive at least 40 hours of in-service training annually in subjects such as non-lethal control techniques, impact weapons, aerosol subject restraint, controlled substance enforcement, survival and rescue tactics, photography, and firearms. Many FS special agents attend the FBI National Academy training program (see chapter 16).

Contact: For further information, contact the FS ranger district where employment is sought, or the Forest Service; U.S. Department of Agriculture; 1400 Independence Ave. SW; Washington, DC 20250; phone: (202) 205-8333; Internet: www.fs.fed.us/; e-mail: fsjobs@fs.fed.us.

Special Agent (GS-1811)
Office of Inspector General, U.S. Department of Agriculture

The U.S. Department of Agriculture (USDA) Office of Inspector General (OIG) investigates fraud and other violations of federal law relating to approximately 300 programs. USDA-OIG agents are prepared to respond to national emergencies, terrorism incidents, and other attacks affecting USDA personnel, programs, operations, regulated industries, and the nation's agriculture infrastructure. They also protect the secretary of agriculture throughout the world. USDA-OIG is one of the most versatile and respected agencies in federal law enforcement.

Investigations carried out by USDA-OIG special agents focus primarily on programs concerned with food assistance, food safety and inspection, farm subsidies and loans, rural housing assistance, agriculture price support, federal crop insurance, smuggling of animal and plant products, research grants, child care feeding assistance, and USDA Forest Service contracting operations, among others. Particular emphasis is given to the investigation of Food Stamp Program violations, including retailers and others that exchange food stamp benefits for cash, contraband, and other goods. USDA-OIG special agents investigate threats and assaults upon USDA personnel and allegations of serious official misconduct by USDA employees. Personnel misconduct investigations focus on offenses such as embezzlement, conflict of interest, misuse of official position, bribery, collusion with program participants, time and attendance fraud, and misuse or theft of government property. Other USDA-OIG investigations have resulted in prosecutions for offenses such as homicide, tampering with food products, trafficking in endangered species, mail fraud, and violations of Racketeer Influenced and Corrupt Organization statutes.

USDA-OIG special agents conduct investigations with agencies such as the FBI, USDA Forest Service, U.S. Fish and Wildlife Service, Drug Enforcement Administration, Postal Inspection Service, U.S. Immigration and Customs Enforcement, IRS Criminal Investigation Division, U.S. Secret Service, U.S. Marshals Service, and many other law enforcement and regulatory agencies. Investigations often involve undercover operations and electronic surveillance, and collection of intelligence information from informants and law enforcement agencies. Special agents are authorized to carry firearms, make arrests, execute search warrants, and serve subpoenas.

USDA-OIG special agents are covered under special retirement provisions for law enforcement officers, and they qualify for 25 percent Law Enforcement Availability Pay.

Qualifications and Salary Levels

GS-5: Completion of a four-year course of study leading to a bachelor's degree; or three years of general experience, one year of which was equivalent to at least GS-4. **GS-7:** One full year of graduate education, or superior academic achievement during undergraduate studies, or one year of specialized experience equivalent to at least GS-5. **GS-9:** A master's degree, or two years of graduate education, or one year of specialized experience equivalent to at least GS-7. **GS-11:** A Ph.D. or equivalent doctoral degree, or three years of graduate education, or one year of specialized experience equivalent to at least GS-9. **GS-12:** One year of specialized experience equivalent to at least GS-11. **GS-13:** One year of specialized experience equivalent to at least GS-12.

Qualifying education can be substituted for experience, and vice versa. Applicants must be at least 21 years of age and under age 37. However, candidates over age 37 who have previous service creditable under special law enforcement retirement provisions also may be eligible. Eyesight requirements include good distant vision in each eye, near vision that is sufficient to read print the size of typewritten characters, normal depth perception and peripheral vision, and the ability to distinguish basic colors. Eyeglasses and contact lenses are permitted. Hearing loss must not exceed 35 decibels at the 1000, 2000, and 3000 Hertz levels. The application process includes a drug screening test, medical examination, background investigation, and top-secret security clearance determination.

Training

Initial training for USDA-OIG special agents includes the 11-week Criminal Investigator Training Program at the Federal Law Enforcement Training Center (FLETC) in Glynco, Georgia (see chapter 16). Many special agents also attend the three-week Inspector General Investigator Training Program at FLETC. Other in-service training focuses on subjects such as USDA program investigations, undercover operations, criminal and civil law, white-collar crime, employee integrity investigations, firearms proficiency, arrest techniques, defensive tactics, and other topics.

Contact: Office of Inspector General; U.S. Department of Agriculture; 1400 Independence Ave. SW—Room 117W; Washington, DC 20250; phone: (202) 720-3079; Internet: www.usda.gov/oig/; e-mail: oigjobs@oig.usda.gov

Special Agent (GS-1811)
Office of Export Enforcement, Bureau of Industry and Security, U.S. Department of Commerce

The Commerce Department's Office of Export Enforcement (OEE), a component of the Bureau of Industry and Security, investigates violations of export control laws relating to strategically sensitive non-agricultural commodities and technology. OEE concentrates its efforts on violations posing significant threats to U.S. national security, foreign policy objectives, and economic interests. OEE also investigates restrictive trade practices, reviews visa applications of foreign nationals to prevent illegal technology transfers, and conducts cooperative enforcement activities on an international basis.

OEE special agents investigate violations of the International Emergency Economic Powers Act, Export Administration Act, Arms Export Control Act, Fastener Quality Act, Trading with the Enemy Act, and other export control and public safety statutes prohibiting the shipment of certain goods and materials out of the U.S. For example, OEE special agents have investigated schemes to export military vehicles to Vietnam, bomb-making materials to Iraq, thermal imaging cameras to Lebanese terrorists, industrial equipment to Iran and Libya, handcuffs to the Republic of Croatia, and gas masks to Japan. They devote particular attention to investigations involving exports of weapons and military goods, technological goods that can be used in the development of weapons of mass destruction, and exports to embargoed nations or state sponsors of terrorism such as North Korea, Cuba, Iran, Libya, Sudan, and Syria. OEE special agents are authorized to carry firearms, make arrests, execute search warrants, and serve subpoenas. They conduct investigations jointly with the FBI; Defense Criminal Investigative Service; U.S. Immigration and Customs Enforcement; and other federal, state, and local law enforcement and regulatory agencies.

Special agents serving with OEE are covered under special retirement provisions for law enforcement officers, and they qualify for 25 percent Law Enforcement Availability Pay.

Qualifications and Salary Levels

GS-5: Completion of a four-year course of study leading to a bachelor's degree; or three years of general experience, one year of which was equivalent to at least GS-4. **GS-7:** One full year of graduate education, or superior academic achievement during undergraduate studies, or one year of specialized experience equivalent to at least GS-5. **GS-9:** A master's degree, or two years of graduate education, or one year of specialized experience equivalent to at least GS-7. **GS-11:** A Ph.D. or equivalent doctoral degree, or three years of graduate education, or one year of specialized experience equivalent to at least GS-9. **GS-12:** One year of specialized experience equivalent to at least GS-11. **GS-13:** One year of specialized experience equivalent to at least GS-12.

Applicants can use equivalent combinations of specialized experience and education to meet total experience requirements. Applicants must be at least 21 years of age and under age 37. However, candidates over age 37 who have previous service creditable under special law enforcement retirement provisions also may be eligible. Eyesight requirements include good distant vision in each eye, near vision that is sufficient to read print the size of typewritten characters, normal depth perception and peripheral vision, and the ability to distinguish basic colors. Eyeglasses and contact lenses are permitted. Hearing loss must not exceed 35 decibels at the 1000, 2000, and 3000 Hertz levels. Tentative appointees must qualify for a security clearance and pass a background investigation, personal interview, drug screening test, and medical examination.

Training

OEE special agents attend the 11-week Criminal Investigator Training Program at the Federal Law Enforcement Training Center in Glynco, Georgia (see chapter 16). They also attend in-service training programs that cover subjects such as terrorism; missile technology; chemical, biological, and radiological weapons; identification and handling of chemical materials; and firearms proficiency.

Contact: Office of Export Enforcement; Bureau of Industry and Security; U.S. Department of Commerce; 14th St. and Constitution Ave. NW; Washington, DC 20230; phone: (202) 482-1208; Internet: www.bis.doc.gov/enforcement/eeprogrm.htm/

Special Agent (GS-1811)
National Marine Fisheries Service, National Oceanic and Atmospheric Administration, U.S. Department of Commerce

As a component of the National Oceanic and Atmospheric Administration (NOAA), the National Marine Fisheries Service (NMFS) administers programs that support domestic and international conservation and management of living marine resources. NMFS special agents enforce more than 30 statutes and several international treaties concerned with the protection of ocean ecosystems over areas that encompass more than three million square miles of water.

Special agents of the NMFS Office for Law Enforcement investigate violations of federal laws pertaining to the conservation and protection of ocean fisheries, marine mammals, and endangered species of fish and wildlife. These investigations—which most often focus on commercial fishermen, fishing companies, recreational boaters, and sport fishermen—pertain to laws such as the Endangered Species Act; Marine Mammal Protection Act; Lacey Act; Marine Protection, Research, and Sanctuaries Act; and Convention on International Trade in Endangered Species of Wild Fauna and Flora.

For example, criminal investigations carried out by NMFS special agents are concerned with fishing in conservation areas, Exclusive Economic Zones, and other prohibited areas; using illegal fishing methods and equipment; landing fish out of season or in excess of legal limits; capturing, injuring, or killing protected species; possessing undersized fish; and the illegal importation of fish and other products.

To monitor compliance with international treaties and agreements, NMFS special agents conduct surveillance of foreign fishing operations within a protected 200-mile conservation and fishery management territory along the U.S. coastline. Investigations often include undercover operations involving extensive covert investigative procedures. NMFS special agents are authorized to board surface vessels and aircraft within the protected zone, carry firearms, make arrests, execute search warrants, and serve subpoenas. Many operations are conducted jointly with the U.S. Fish and Wildlife Service; Coast Guard Investigative Service; U.S. Customs and Border Protection; U.S. Immigration and Customs Enforcement; FBI; and other federal, state, and local law enforcement and regulatory agencies.

NMFS special agents are covered under special retirement provisions for law enforcement officers, and they qualify for 25 percent Law Enforcement Availability Pay.

Qualifications and Salary Levels

GS-5: Completion of a four-year course of study leading to a bachelor's degree; or three years of general experience, one year of which was equivalent to at least GS-4. **GS-7:** One full year of graduate education, or superior academic achievement during undergraduate studies, or one year of specialized experience equivalent to at least GS-5. **GS-9:** A master's degree, or two years of graduate education, or one year of specialized experience equivalent to at least GS-7. **GS-11:** A Ph.D. or equivalent doctoral degree, or three years of graduate education, or one year of specialized experience equivalent to at least GS-9. **GS-12:** One year of specialized experience equivalent to at least GS-11. **GS-13:** One year of specialized experience equivalent to at least GS-12.

Equivalent combinations of education and experience can be used to meet minimum experience requirements. Applicants must be at least 21 years of age and under age 37. However, candidates over age 37 who have previous service creditable under special law enforcement retirement provisions also may be eligible. Eyesight requirements include distant vision not worse than 20/200 (Snellen) in each eye without correction, and 20/20 in each eye with correction. Normal depth perception, peripheral vision, and the ability to distinguish shades of color are required. Hearing loss must not exceed 30 decibels at 500, 1000, and 2000 Hertz; and 40 decibels at 3000 Hertz. Tentative appointees must qualify for a security clearance and pass a background investigation, drug screening test, and medical examination.

Training

Initial training for NMFS special agents includes the 11-week Criminal Investigator Training Program at the Federal Law Enforcement Training Center (FLETC) in Glynco, Georgia (see chapter 16). After completing this course, special agents attend the four-week Marine Law Enforcement Training Program at FLETC, which includes instruction in seamanship, nautical terminology, vessel identification, vessel pursuit and boarding procedures, radar, emergency procedures, waterborne arrest techniques, and other subjects. This program is followed by a four-week course presented by NMFS staff that focuses on laws enforced by the agency, as well as NOAA and NMFS regulations, policies, and procedures. In-service training covers subjects such as nautical procedures, vessel intercepts, global positioning systems, computer forensics, and photography.

Contact: Office for Law Enforcement; National Marine Fisheries Service; National Oceanic and Atmospheric Administration; U.S. Department of Commerce; 8484 Georgia Ave.—Suite 415; Silver Spring, MD 20910; phone: (301) 427-2300; Internet: www.nmfs.noaa.gov/ole/

Special Agent (GS-1811)
Office of Inspector General, U.S. Department of Commerce

The U.S. Department of Commerce (DOC) encourages, serves, and promotes the nation's international trade, economic growth, environment, ocean resources, and technological advancement through a variety of programs. DOC Office of Inspector General (OIG) special agents conduct investigations to identify fraud and other forms of criminal or improper activity in DOC programs and operations. The agency is among several DOC components—including the Bureau of Industry and Security, Bureau of the Census, National Institutes of Standards and Technology, and National Marine Fisheries Service—that rely on law enforcement and security personnel to accomplish DOC's mission.

DOC-OIG special agents conduct investigations that focus primarily on fraud in DOC programs, internal misconduct, and computer offenses. Fraud investigations are concerned mostly with corruption committed by contractors, grantees, and others conducting business with DOC. These investigations identify fraudulent billing, falsification of contractor payrolls, altered invoices, misappropriation of funds, loan fraud, and other schemes. Internal misconduct cases are concerned with time and attendance fraud, theft or misuse of government property, embezzlement, conflict of interest, kickbacks, bribery, collusion, and other violations of DOC standards of conduct. Many DOC-OIG computer-related investigations also focus on wrongdoing by DOC personnel, including employees who access or download sexually explicit material on the Department's computers. DOC-OIG special agents are authorized to conduct undercover operations, carry firearms, make arrests, execute search warrants, and serve subpoenas. They conduct investigations with agencies such as the FBI, Department of Labor OIG, Department of Transportation OIG, IRS Criminal Investigation Division, and other agencies.

DOC-OIG special agents are covered under special retirement provisions for law enforcement officers, and they qualify for 25 percent Law Enforcement Availability Pay.

Qualifications and Salary Levels

GS-5: Completion of a four-year course of study leading to a bachelor's degree; or three years of general experience, one year of which was equivalent to at least GS-4. **GS-7:** One full year of graduate education, or superior academic achievement during undergraduate studies, or one year of specialized experience equivalent to at least GS-5. **GS-9:** A master's degree, or two years of graduate education, or one year of specialized experience equivalent to at least GS-7. **GS-11:** A Ph.D. or equivalent doctoral degree, or three years of graduate education, or one year of specialized experience equivalent to at least GS-9. **GS-12:** One year of specialized experience equivalent to at least GS-11. **GS-13:** One year of specialized experience equivalent to at least GS-12.

Experience and education can be combined to meet total experience requirements. Applicants must be at least 21 years of age and under age 37. However, candidates over age 37 who have previous service creditable under special law enforcement retirement provisions also may be eligible. Eyesight requirements include good distant vision in each eye, near vision that is sufficient to read print the size of typewritten characters, normal depth perception and peripheral vision, and the ability to distinguish basic colors. Eyeglasses and contact lenses are permitted. Hearing loss must not exceed 35 decibels at the 1000, 2000, and 3000 Hertz levels. Successful completion of a background investigation, drug test, medical examination, and security clearance process also are required.

Training

DOC-OIG special agents attend the 11-week Criminal Investigator Training Program at the Federal Law Enforcement Training Center (FLETC) in Glynco, Georgia (see chapter 16). They also attend in-service training programs relating to DOC program investigations, personnel misconduct investigations, financial investigations, computer hardware and software, defensive tactics, arrest techniques, and other subjects. Many DOC-OIG special agents also attend the three-week Inspector General Investigator Training Program at FLETC (see chapter 16).

Contact: Office of Inspector General; U.S. Department of Commerce; 1401 Constitution Ave. NW; Washington, DC 20230; phone: (202) 482-4661; Internet: www.oig.doc.gov/; e-mail: jobs@oig.doc.gov

Special Agent
Office of Inspector General, Corporation for National and Community Service

The Corporation for National and Community Service (CNCS) awards grants for national service programs to address the nation's education, human, public safety, and environmental needs. CNCS carries out its mission through three major program areas, including AmeriCorps, Learn and Serve America, and National Senior Service Corps. CNCS Office of Inspector General (OIG) special agents investigate fraud, waste, and abuse by CNCS employees, grantees, contractors, and other recipients of funds under or relating to the agency's programs and operations.

CNCS-OIG special agents conduct criminal, civil, and administrative investigations that are concerned with unlawful activities and other improprieties by CNCS employees, contractors, grantees, and volunteers. These investigations focus on offenses such as embezzlement, theft, misuse of government property, forgery, conversion, bribery, extortion, blackmail, false claims, misappropriation of funds, credit card fraud, unauthorized destruction of government records, abuse of authority, and other criminal and noncriminal activity affecting the agency. CNCS-OIG special agents conduct investigations jointly with agencies such as the FBI; Defense Criminal Investigative Service; Health and Human Services OIG; U.S. Office of Special Counsel; and other federal, state, and local law enforcement agencies.

Qualifications and Salary Levels

CNCS-OIG special agents are appointed through excepted service hiring processes. The qualifications and salaries of the position are similar to those of GS-1811 special agents at the GS-7 through GS-13 levels with other federal agencies. The agency seeks candidates with knowledge, skills, and abilities in areas such as fraud investigation, investigative planning, interviewing, oral briefings, and report writing. Tentative appointees must qualify for a security clearance and undergo a background investigation.

Training

Newly appointed CNCS-OIG special agents attend the 11-week Criminal Investigator Training Program at the Federal Law Enforcement Training Center (FLETC) in Glynco, Georgia (see chapter 16). In-service training includes the three-week Inspector General Investigator Training Program at FLETC (see chapter 16), as well as courses that cover subjects such as grant administration, white-collar crime, personnel misconduct investigations, and other topics.

Contact: Office of Inspector General; Corporation for National and Community Service; 1201 New York Ave. NW—Suite 830; Washington, DC 20525; phone: (202) 606-9390; Internet: www.cns.gov/; e-mail: info@cncsig.gov

Special Agent (GS-1811)
Office of Special Investigations, United States Air Force, U.S. Department of Defense

The U.S. Air Force Office of Special Investigations (AFOSI) conducts major criminal investigations and counterintelligence, counterterrorism, and counterespionage activities for the protection of Air Force and Defense Department resources, technology, and personnel worldwide. AFOSI accomplishes its mission with the expertise of forensic specialists, behavioral scientists, information technology specialists, polygraph examiners, antiterrorism teams, and other technical specialists.

Investigations carried out by AFOSI special agents pertain to crimes such as robbery, sexual assault, drug use and trafficking, arson, homicide, espionage, terrorism, computer infiltration, and violations of the Uniform Code of Military Justice. A significant amount of AFOSI investigative resources are dedicated to economic crime investigations, including violations involving Air Force contracting matters, theft or misuse of government funds, pay and allowance matters, procurement and property disposal activities, and major administrative irregularities. AFOSI special agents also provide personal security for high-ranking Air Force officials and their guests. They are authorized to conduct surveillance and undercover operations, carry firearms, make arrests, execute search warrants, and serve subpoenas. Agencies that participate in AFOSI investigations include the FBI; Defense Criminal Investigative Service; NASA Office of Inspector General; Bureau of Alcohol, Tobacco, Firearms and Explosives; and other U.S. and foreign law enforcement agencies. AFOSI special agents serve in 154 locations worldwide, including all major Air Force installations and many special operating locations.

Special agents serving with AFOSI are covered under special retirement provisions for law enforcement officers, and they qualify for 25 percent Law Enforcement Availability Pay. Although this position is staffed by civilian personnel, AFOSI also maintains a cadre of military active duty special agents.

Qualifications and Salary Levels

GS-7: One full year of graduate education, or superior academic achievement during undergraduate studies, or one year of specialized experience equivalent to at least GS-5. **GS-9:** A master's degree, or two years of graduate education, or one year of specialized experience equivalent to at least GS-7. **GS-11:** A Ph.D. or equivalent doctoral degree, or three years of graduate education, or one year of specialized experience equivalent to at least GS-9. **GS-12:** One year of specialized experience equivalent to at least GS-11. **GS-13:** One year of specialized experience equivalent to at least GS-12.

Equivalent combinations of education and experience can be used to meet minimum experience requirements. Applicants must be at least 21 years of age and under age 37. However, candidates over age 37 who have previous service creditable under special law enforcement retirement provisions also may be eligible. Eyesight requirements include good distant vision in each eye, near vision that is sufficient to read print the size of typewritten characters, normal depth perception and peripheral vision, and the ability to distinguish basic colors. Eyeglasses and contact lenses are permitted. Hearing loss must not exceed 35 decibels at the 1000, 2000, and 3000 Hertz levels. Tentative appointees must qualify for a top-secret security clearance and pass a background investigation, drug screening test, and medical examination.

Training

Basic training for AFOSI special agents consists of the 11-week Criminal Investigator Training Program at the Federal Law Enforcement Training Center (FLETC) in Glynco, Georgia (see chapter 16). This program is followed by six weeks of agency-specific training at FLETC presented by AFOSI staff, which includes instruction in military law, crimes against property and persons, computer crime, forensics, fraud investigations, environmental crime, force protection, interrogation, and ethics. Ongoing in-service training includes courses in economic and environmental crime investigations, technical services, protective operations, surveillance and countersurveillance, firearms, defensive tactics, and other subjects. Many AFOSI special agents attend a 12-week technical training program to acquire skills in electronics, photography, and technical surveillance countermeasures.

Contact: Office of Special Investigations; United States Air Force; U.S. Department of Defense; 1535 Command Dr.—Suite C-309; Andrews AFB, MD 20762; phone: (240) 857-0989; Internet: http://public.afosi.amc.af.mil/; e-mail: civilian.recruiting@ogn.af.mil

Special Agent (GS-1811)
Criminal Investigation Command, United States Army, U.S. Department of Defense

Civilian special agents of the U.S. Army Criminal Investigation Command (Army-CID) investigate offenses primarily concerning Army contracting, procurement, and acquisition programs. These special agents are assigned to Army-CID's Major Procurement Fraud Unit (MPFU), which is the agency's only all-civilian investigative element.

MPFU investigations often pertain to wrongdoing by civilian contractors who research, develop, test, manufacture, and install weapons systems or equipment for the Army. These investigations focus on crimes relating to product substitution, overcharging for goods and services, misappropriation of funds, falsification of contractors' certified payrolls, charging personal expenses to Department of Defense (DoD) contracts, bribery, embezzlement, antitrust violations, racketeering, collusion, larceny, and organized crime. Civilian special agents are strategically located near contracting and defense production centers. Army-CID special agents are authorized to conduct surveillance and undercover operations, carry firearms, make arrests, execute search warrants, and serve subpoenas. They often conduct investigations jointly with other DoD components, the FBI, and other law enforcement agencies. Although this position is staffed by civilian personnel, Army-CID also maintains a staff of special agents who are enlisted soldiers or warrant officer soldiers (see "Enlisted Special Agent" earlier in this chapter).

Army-CID special agents are covered under special retirement provisions for law enforcement officers, and they qualify for 25 percent Law Enforcement Availability Pay.

Qualifications and Salary Levels

GS-9: A master's degree, or two years of graduate education, or one year of specialized experience equivalent to at least GS-7. **GS-11:** A Ph.D. or equivalent doctoral degree, or three years of graduate education, or one year of specialized experience equivalent to at least GS-9. **GS-12:** One year of specialized experience equivalent to at least GS-11. **GS-13:** One year of specialized experience equivalent to at least GS-12.

Applicants must be at least 21 years of age and under age 37. However, candidates over age 37 who have previous service creditable under special law enforcement retirement provisions also may be eligible. Qualifying education can be substituted for experience, and vice versa. Eyesight requirements include good distant vision in each eye, near vision that is sufficient to read print the size of typewritten characters, normal depth perception and peripheral vision, and the ability to distinguish basic colors. Eyeglasses and contact lenses are permitted. Hearing loss must not exceed 35 decibels at the 1000, 2000, and 3000 Hertz levels. The application process includes a drug screening test, background investigation, and top-secret security clearance determination.

Training

Army-CID special agents attend a 15-week Apprentice Special Agent Course at the U.S. Military Police School in Fort McClellan, Alabama, which covers subjects such as criminal law and procedure, crime scene processing, physical and testimonial evidence, property and person crimes, drug trafficking, report writing, and protective services. They also attend in-service training programs that cover subjects such as criminal and civil law, financial investigations, procurement fraud, the Bank Secrecy Act, the Financial Crimes Enforcement Network, terrorism, and arrest techniques. In-service training can be completed at institutions such as the FBI National Academy, Canadian Police College, Metropolitan Police Academy at Scotland Yard, Federal Law Enforcement Training Center, and Army Logistics Management College.

Contact: Criminal Investigation Command; United States Army; U.S. Department of Defense; 6010 6th St.; Ft. Belvoir, VA 22060; phone: (703) 806-0416; Internet: www.cid.army.mil/; e-mail: mailcicg@cidc.belvoir.army.mil

Special Agent (GS-1811)
Defense Criminal Investigations Activity, Defense Logistics Agency, U.S. Department of Defense

The Defense Logistics Agency (DLA) supports the logistics requirements of the military services and their acquisition of weapons and other materiel, and also provides technical and logistics services to several civilian federal agencies. DLA supply centers consolidate the requirements of all military service branches and procure goods such as clothing, fuel, food, construction materials, and medical supplies. Special agents assigned to DLA's Defense Criminal Investigations Activity (DCIA) investigate violations of federal laws, DLA and Department of Defense (DoD) directives, and various export laws. DCIA maintains offices worldwide.

DCIA special agents conduct criminal and administrative investigations of offenses and irregularities that involve DLA programs, personnel, and resources when the primary DoD investigative agency declines investigative responsibility or accedes to a joint investigation. These investigations pertain primarily to offenses such as contract fraud, bribery, antitrust violations, labor law violations, workers' compensation fraud, and violations of the Federal Acquisition Regulation, Export Administration Regulation, International Traffic in Arms Regulation, or Arms Export Control Act. They also perform crime prevention surveys and lead or participate in protective missions. DCIA special agents work closely with agencies such as the FBI, Defense Criminal Investigative Service, Army Criminal Investigation Command, Naval Criminal Investigative Service, Department of Labor Office of Inspector General, IRS Criminal Investigation Division, and Postal Inspection Service. DCIA special agents are authorized to carry firearms.

Qualifications and Salary Levels

GS-5: Completion of a four-year course of study leading to a bachelor's degree; or three years of general experience, one year of which was equivalent to at least GS-4. **GS-7:** One full year of graduate education, or superior academic achievement during undergraduate studies, or one year of specialized experience equivalent to at least GS-5. **GS-9:** A master's degree, or two years of graduate education, or one year of specialized experience equivalent to at least GS-7. **GS-11:** A Ph.D. or equivalent doctoral degree, or three years of graduate education, or one year of specialized experience equivalent to at least GS-9. **GS-12:** One year of specialized experience equivalent to at least GS-11. **GS-13:** One year of specialized experience equivalent to at least GS-12.

Applicants can use equivalent combinations of specialized experience and education to meet total experience requirements. Eyesight requirements include good distant vision in each eye, near vision that is sufficient to read print the size of typewritten characters, normal depth perception and peripheral vision, and the ability to distinguish basic colors. Eyeglasses and contact lenses are permitted. Hearing loss must not exceed 35 decibels at the 1000, 2000, and 3000 Hertz levels. The application process includes a drug test, medical examination, background investigation, and security clearance determination.

Training

DCIA special agents attend the 11-week Criminal Investigator Training Program at the Federal Law Enforcement Training Center in Glynco, Georgia (see chapter 16). In-service training includes instruction relating to the Uniform Code of Military Justice, export laws and regulations, computer fraud, personnel investigations, interviewing and interrogation, and other subjects.

Contact: Defense Criminal Investigations Activity; Defense Logistics Agency; U.S. Department of Defense; 8725 John L. Kingman Rd.—Suite 2358; Fort Belvoir, VA 22060; phone: (703) 767-5440; Internet: www.dla.mil/dcia/

Special Agent (GS-1811)
Naval Criminal Investigative Service, United States Navy, U.S. Department of Defense

The Naval Criminal Investigative Service (NCIS) is the primary law enforcement and counterintelligence arm of the U.S. Navy. This agency provides criminal investigative, counterintelligence, law enforcement, physical security, and personnel security support to the Navy and Marine Corps worldwide, both ashore and afloat. NCIS special agents are stationed at more than 150 locations around the world, as well as on aircraft carriers and other major combatants.

Investigations conducted by NCIS special agents encompass a wide range of offenses committed by or against the personnel or property of the Navy or Marine Corps, including federal crimes and violations of the Uniform Code of Military Justice. NCIS investigations are divided among several disciplines, including property and person crimes, white-collar crimes, drug interdiction, counterterrorism and counterintelligence, and computer crimes. Property and person crimes are concerned with offenses such as larceny, robbery, arson, domestic assault, child abuse, kidnapping, sexual assault, and homicide. White-collar crime investigations focus on procurement fraud, bribery, kickbacks, product substitution, and other financial crimes. Drug interdiction investigations target the sale and use of illegal narcotics and other drugs on or near Navy and Marine Corps installations and at ports of call. Counterintelligence and counterterrorism investigations focus primarily on vulnerability assessments, force protection, terrorist threats, espionage, sabotage, and security violations. Investigations of computer crimes pertain to computer intrusions, malicious virus incidents, manipulation of software, and other offenses committed primarily by hackers, organized criminal groups, foreign intelligence services, terrorists, and Navy personnel.

NCIS special agents also perform technical investigative services such as polygraph examinations, electronic surveillance, and forensic laboratory procedures; and provide personal security for the secretary of the Navy, senior military commanders, foreign dignitaries, and other officials. NCIS special agents are authorized to carry firearms and make arrests. Many joint operations are conducted with other Defense Department agencies; the FBI; NASA Office of Inspector General; and other federal, state, and local law enforcement agencies.

Special agents serving with NCIS are covered under special retirement provisions for law enforcement officers, and they qualify for 25 percent Law Enforcement Availability Pay. This is a civilian position and does not require active duty military service.

Qualifications and Salary Levels

GS-7: One full year of graduate education, or superior academic achievement during undergraduate studies, or one year of specialized experience equivalent to at least GS-5. **GS-9:** A master's degree, or two years of graduate education, or one year of specialized experience equivalent to at least GS-7. **GS-11:** A Ph.D. or equivalent doctoral degree, or three years of graduate education, or one year of specialized experience equivalent to at least GS-9. **GS-12:** One year of specialized experience equivalent to at least GS-11. **GS-13:** One year of specialized experience equivalent to at least GS-12.

Qualifying education can be substituted for experience, and vice versa. Applicants must be at least 21 years of age and under age 37. However, candidates over age 37 who have previous service creditable under special law enforcement retirement provisions also may be eligible. Eyesight requirements include binocular distant vision correctable to 20/20 (Snellen), near vision that is sufficient to read print the size of typewritten characters, normal depth perception and peripheral vision, and the ability to distinguish basic colors. Eyeglasses and contact lenses are permitted. Hearing loss must not exceed 35 decibels at the 1000, 2000, and 3000 Hertz levels. The application process includes a written examination, background investigation, medical examination, drug screening test, and a polygraph examination. Appointees must be willing to serve at any of the 150 offices worldwide, including locations throughout the U.S., overseas, or on aircraft carriers or other major combatants.

Training

NCIS special agents attend the 11-week Criminal Investigator Training Program at the Federal Law Enforcement Training Center (FLETC) in Glynco, Georgia (see chapter 16), followed by an eight-week NCIS course at FLETC, which includes instruction in the NCIS report-writing system, databases, and courses related to specific job tasks. They also attend in-service training programs that cover subjects such as homicide investigation, crime scene processing, domestic security, critical incident stress debriefing, technical surveillance countermeasures, drug interdiction, counterintelligence, and arrest techniques.

Contact: Naval Criminal Investigative Service; United States Navy; U.S. Department of Defense; 716 E. Sicard St. SE; Washington Navy Yard; Washington, DC 20388; phone: (202) 433-9162; Internet: www.ncis.navy.mil/

Special Agent (GS-1811)
Defense Criminal Investigative Service, Office of Inspector General, U.S. Department of Defense

The Defense Criminal Investigative Service (DCIS) is the criminal investigation component of the Department of Defense (DoD) Office of Inspector General (OIG). DCIS conducts investigations of major criminal violations focusing mainly on terrorism, contract and procurement fraud, cybercrimes, computer intrusions, illegal technology transfers, bribery, corruption, and major theft.

Criminal investigations carried out by DCIS special agents typically concentrate on violations of federal laws committed by DoD personnel and contractors. Contract and procurement investigations focus on fraud in major construction projects, cost mischarging, defective pricing, defective or unapproved parts, product substitution, collusion, bribery, and kickbacks. DCIS special agents investigate economic espionage, antitrust violations, gambling, healthcare fraud, sexual assault, labor law violations, government purchase card fraud, unlawful disclosure of classified information, and other misconduct by DoD personnel. They also participate in Joint Terrorism Task Force and Anti-Terrorism Task Force operations nationwide, and investigate the illegal transfer of high technology, weapons systems, explosive devices, munitions, and information to terrorist organizations and nations that pose a threat to national security. DCIS special agents are authorized to conduct surveillance and undercover operations, carry firearms, make arrests, execute search warrants, and serve subpoenas. Investigative and intelligence-gathering operations are coordinated with other DoD investigative agencies, the U.S. intelligence community, and agencies such as the Department of Agriculture Office of Inspector General (OIG), U.S. Immigration and Customs Enforcement, National Aeronautics and Space Administration OIG, and Department of Transportation OIG, among others.

DCIS special agents are covered under special retirement provisions for law enforcement officers, and they qualify for 25 percent Law Enforcement Availability Pay. This is a civilian position and does not require active duty military service.

Qualifications and Salary Levels

GS-5: Completion of a four-year course of study leading to a bachelor's degree; or three years of general experience, one year of which was equivalent to at least GS-4.
GS-7: One full year of graduate education, or superior academic achievement during undergraduate studies, or one year of specialized experience equivalent to at least

GS-5. **GS-9:** A master's degree, or two years of graduate education, or one year of specialized experience equivalent to at least GS-7. **GS-11:** A Ph.D. or equivalent doctoral degree, or three years of graduate education, or one year of specialized experience equivalent to at least GS-9. **GS-12:** One year of specialized experience equivalent to at least GS-11. **GS-13:** One year of specialized experience equivalent to at least GS-12.

Qualifying education can be substituted for experience, and vice versa. Applicants must be at least 21 years of age and under age 37. However, candidates over age 37 who have previous service creditable under special law enforcement retirement provisions also may be eligible. Eyesight requirements include good distant vision in each eye, near vision that is sufficient to read print the size of typewritten characters, normal depth perception and peripheral vision, and the ability to distinguish basic colors. Eyeglasses and contact lenses are permitted. Hearing loss must not exceed 35 decibels at the 1000, 2000, and 3000 Hertz levels. Candidates must successfully undergo a background investigation, qualify for a top-secret security clearance, and pass a drug test and medical examination prior to appointment.

Training

Initial training for DCIS special agents includes the 11-week Criminal Investigator Training Program (CITP) at the Federal Law Enforcement Training Center (FLETC) in Glynco, Georgia (see chapter 16). This program is followed by the DCIS Special Agent Basic Training Program at FLETC, which introduces special agents to the DoD organization and techniques for the investigation of terrorism, product substitution, computer crimes, illegal transfer of DoD technology, theft, fraud, bribery, and corruption. DCIS special agents also attend the three-week Inspector General Investigator Training Program at FLETC about six months after completing the CITP course. Additional in-service training includes courses in DoD program investigations, financial investigations, procurement fraud, personnel misconduct, interviewing techniques, legal issues and updates, firearms proficiency, arrest techniques, and defensive tactics.

Contact: Defense Criminal Investigative Service; Office of Inspector General; U.S. Department of Defense; 400 Army-Navy Dr.—Room 901E; Arlington, VA 22202; phone: (703) 604-8600; Internet: www.dodig.mil/

Special Agent (GS-1811)
Pentagon Police Department, Pentagon Force Protection Agency, U.S. Department of Defense

The Pentagon Force Protection Agency (PFPA) was established in 2002 in the wake of the terrorist attacks on the World Trade Center and the Pentagon of September 11, 2001. PFPA provides force protection, security, and law enforcement for the personnel, facilities, infrastructure, and other resources at the Pentagon and for Department of Defense (DoD) activities and facilities within the National Capitol Region (NCR) that are not under the jurisdiction of a military department. These include resources within the Pentagon; Hoffman Building; Army Materiel Command; dozens of other buildings in the NCR area; and the DoD Alternate Joint Communications Center in Pennsylvania, which is a secure facility designed for continuation of operations in the event of a terrorist attack or national emergency.

Special agents serving with the Pentagon Police Department (PPD), a component of PFPA, investigate personnel misconduct and criminal acts occurring within the Pentagon reservation and other DoD facilities in the NCR. In addition to violations of the U.S. Code and the Code of Federal Regulations, criminal investigations handled by

PPD special agents occasionally pertain to violations under the criminal codes of Virginia, Maryland, and the District of Columbia. To defend DoD personnel and assets from terrorist attacks, PPD special agents develop antiterrorism (AT) programs; collect, analyze, and disseminate AT threat information; conduct AT vulnerability assessments; serve as AT subject matter experts; and present AT training to PFPA and DoD personnel. PFPA special agents also participate in background investigations of applicants for PFPA police officer positions. They are authorized to carry firearms, make arrests, execute search warrants, and serve subpoenas.

PPD special agents are covered under special retirement provisions for law enforcement officers, and they qualify for 25 percent Law Enforcement Availability Pay.

Qualifications and Salary Levels

GS-7: One full year of graduate education, or superior academic achievement during undergraduate studies, or one year of specialized experience equivalent to at least GS-5. **GS-9:** A master's degree, or two years of graduate education, or one year of specialized experience equivalent to at least GS-7. **GS-11:** A Ph.D. or equivalent doctoral degree, or three years of graduate education, or one year of specialized experience equivalent to at least GS-9. **GS-12:** One year of specialized experience equivalent to at least GS-11. **GS-13:** One year of specialized experience equivalent to at least GS-12.

Equivalent combinations of education and experience can be used to meet minimum experience requirements. Applicants must be at least 21 years of age and under age 37. However, candidates over age 37 who have previous service creditable under special law enforcement retirement provisions also may be eligible. Eyesight requirements include good distant vision in each eye, near vision that is sufficient to read print the size of typewritten characters, normal depth perception and peripheral vision, and the ability to distinguish basic colors. Eyeglasses and contact lenses are permitted. Hearing loss must not exceed 35 decibels at the 1000, 2000, and 3000 Hertz levels. The application process includes a drug screening test, background investigation, medical examination, and top-secret security clearance determination.

Training

Newly appointed PPD special agents attend the 11-week Criminal Investigator Training Program at the Federal Law Enforcement Training Center in Glynco, Georgia (see chapter 16). Ongoing in-service training includes courses relating to crime scene processing and photography, surveillance techniques, federal and state criminal law and procedure, search and seizure, laws of arrest, interviewing and interrogation, and other subjects.

Contact: Pentagon Police Department; Pentagon Force Protection Agency; U.S. Department of Defense; Washington, DC 20301; phone: (703) 693-3685; Internet: www.pfpa.mil/; e-mail: PFPArecruiting@pfpa.mil

Special Agent (GS-1811)
Office of Inspector General, U.S. Department of Education

The U.S. Department of Education (ED) ensures equal access to education and promotes educational excellence. ED also establishes policies for federal financial aid programs for education, and distributes and monitors funding for these programs. Special agents of the ED Office of Inspector General (OIG) investigate fraud, waste, and abuse in programs and operations administered or financed by the Department.

Investigations carried out by ED-OIG special agents focus primarily on allegations of fraud in ED assistance programs—typically involving ED contractors, educational or financial institutions, or grantees—and on official misconduct committed by ED employees. For example, ED-OIG special agents investigate schemes involving school personnel who obtain Federal Pell Grants or other financial aid for ineligible students, or for students who dropped out of school, or for persons who are not students. Other investigations targeting school personnel focus on those who embezzle student financial aid funds, receive funds for courses that were not held, or falsely certify that student-athletes participated in the Federal Work-Study Program. Investigations of students often pertain to those who fraudulently obtain financial aid by using multiple Social Security numbers or the identities of other persons, or by submitting fraudulent transcripts or other false information. ED-OIG special agents also perform internal investigations relating to allegations of misconduct by ED personnel, including offenses such as embezzlement, bribery, kickbacks, and conflict of interest. ED-OIG special agents participate in Justice Department intergovernmental fraud task forces, and conduct investigations jointly with agencies such as the FBI, Postal Inspection Service, IRS Criminal Investigation Division, Social Security Administration OIG, U.S. Immigration and Customs Enforcement, and other agencies. They are authorized to conduct surveillance and undercover operations, carry firearms, make arrests, execute search warrants, and serve subpoenas.

ED-OIG special agents are covered under special retirement provisions for law enforcement officers, and they qualify for 25 percent Law Enforcement Availability Pay.

Qualifications and Salary Levels

GS-5: Completion of a four-year course of study leading to a bachelor's degree; or three years of general experience, one year of which was equivalent to at least GS-4. **GS-7:** One full year of graduate education, or superior academic achievement during undergraduate studies, or one year of specialized experience equivalent to at least GS-5. **GS-9:** A master's degree, or two years of graduate education, or one year of specialized experience equivalent to at least GS-7. **GS-11:** A Ph.D. or equivalent doctoral degree, or three years of graduate education, or one year of specialized experience equivalent to at least GS-9. **GS-12:** One year of specialized experience equivalent to at least GS-11. **GS-13:** One year of specialized experience equivalent to at least GS-12.

Qualifying education can be substituted for experience, and vice versa. Applicants must be at least 21 years of age and under age 37. However, candidates over age 37 who have previous service creditable under special law enforcement retirement provisions also may be eligible. Eyesight requirements include good distant vision in each eye, near vision that is sufficient to read print the size of typewritten characters, normal depth perception and peripheral vision, and the ability to distinguish basic colors. Eyeglasses and contact lenses are permitted. Hearing loss must not exceed 35 decibels at the 1000, 2000, and 3000 Hertz levels. Tentative appointees must qualify for a security clearance and pass a background investigation, drug screening test, and medical examination.

Training

ED-OIG special agents attend the 11-week Criminal Investigator Training Program at the Federal Law Enforcement Training Center (FLETC) in Glynco, Georgia (see chapter 16). They also attend in-service training programs that cover subjects such as employee integrity investigations, ED program investigations, procurement fraud, financial investigations, arrest techniques, defensive tactics, and firearms proficiency. Many

ED-OIG special agents also attend the three-week Inspector General Investigator Training Program at FLETC (see chapter 16).

Contact: Office of Inspector General; U.S. Department of Education; 400 Maryland Ave. SW; Washington, DC 20202; phone: (202) 245-6900; Internet: www.ed.gov/about/offices/list/oig/

Special Agent (GS-1811)
Office of Inspector General, U.S. Department of Energy

The Department of Energy (DOE) manages programs pertaining to energy conservation and research, radioactive waste management, fossil energy, national security, and pipeline construction projects. DOE Office of Inspector General (OIG) special agents investigate allegations of fraud, waste, and abuse in DOE programs and operations, with particular emphasis on contract and grant fraud; environmental, health, and safety violations; computer crimes; and issues that reflect on DOE integrity and credibility.

Many investigations conducted by DOE-OIG special agents are concerned with fraud in DOE programs committed by the Department's contractors or grantees. These investigations often identify offenses such as falsification of contractors' certified payrolls, overcharging for goods and services, charging nonqualifying expenses to DOE contracts, product substitution, and participation in DOE contracts by debarred firms. Special agents assigned to the DOE-OIG Technology Crimes Section investigate complex computer crimes and provide computer forensic support during other investigations. Computer crime investigations pertain to intrusions into computer networks and systems, malicious cyber attacks, misuse of DOE computer systems for illegal gain, and other offenses. DOE-OIG special agents also investigate official misconduct committed by DOE personnel, including violations such as embezzlement, theft of office equipment and supplies, and fraudulent travel reimbursement claims. DOE special agents are authorized to conduct surveillance and undercover operations, carry firearms, make arrests, execute search warrants, and serve subpoenas. They often work with agencies such as the FBI; IRS Criminal Investigation Division; Environmental Protection Agency; and other federal, state, and local law enforcement and regulatory agencies.

DOE-OIG special agents are covered under special retirement provisions for law enforcement officers, and they qualify for 25 percent Law Enforcement Availability Pay.

Qualifications and Salary Levels

GS-5: Completion of a four-year course of study leading to a bachelor's degree; or three years of general experience, one year of which was equivalent to at least GS-4. **GS-7:** One full year of graduate education, or superior academic achievement during undergraduate studies, or one year of specialized experience equivalent to at least GS-5. **GS-9:** A master's degree, or two years of graduate education, or one year of specialized experience equivalent to at least GS-7. **GS-11:** A Ph.D. or equivalent doctoral degree, or three years of graduate education, or one year of specialized experience equivalent to at least GS-9. **GS-12:** One year of specialized experience equivalent to at least GS-11. **GS-13:** One year of specialized experience equivalent to at least GS-12.

Applicants can use equivalent combinations of specialized experience and education to meet total experience requirements. Applicants must be at least 21 years of age and under age 37. However, candidates over age 37 who have previous service creditable under special law enforcement retirement provisions also may be eligible. Eyesight requirements include good distant vision in each eye, near vision that is sufficient to read print the size of typewritten characters, normal depth perception and peripheral vision, and the ability to distinguish basic colors. Eyeglasses and contact lenses are permitted. Hearing loss must not exceed 35 decibels at the 1000, 2000, and 3000 Hertz levels. Successful completion of a background investigation, drug test, medical examination, and security clearance process also are required.

Training

DOE-OIG special agents attend the 11-week Criminal Investigator Training Program at the Federal Law Enforcement Training Center (FLETC) in Glynco, Georgia (see chapter 16). They also attend in-service training programs concerning DOE program investigations, procurement fraud, personnel misconduct, financial investigations, search and seizure, computer forensics, and first aid. DOE-OIG special agents also can attend the three-week Inspector General Investigator Training Program at FLETC (see chapter 16).

Contact: Office of Inspector General; U.S. Department of Energy; 1000 Independence Ave. SW; Washington, DC 20585; phone: (202) 586-9939; Internet: www.ig.doe.gov/

Special Agent (GS-1811)
Criminal Investigation Division; Office of Criminal Enforcement, Forensics and Training; U.S. Environmental Protection Agency

Criminal violations of federal environmental laws are investigated by special agents of the U.S. Environmental Protection Agency's Criminal Investigation Division (EPA-CID). These agents investigate crimes that pose a significant threat to human health and the environment—the nation's air, water, and land resources—with emphasis on egregious and willful violations. EPA-CID special agents serve within EPA's Office of Criminal Enforcement, Forensics and Training (OCEFT). Special agents and other personnel assigned to OCEFT present training programs to EPA employees and those of other federal, state, local, and foreign law enforcement, intelligence, and regulatory agencies.

Environmental investigations carried out by EPA-CID special agents are concerned primarily with hazardous waste disposal practices and industrial discharges in violation of the Clean Air Act, Clean Water Act, Toxic Substances Control Act, National Emissions Standards for Hazardous Air Pollutants, and other environmental statutes. In support of these efforts, EPA-CID special agents participate in more than 90 environmental crime task forces nationwide with federal, state, and local law enforcement agencies. They also support the U.S. Secret Service, FBI, and other law enforcement agencies with counterterrorism planning and prevention during special events such as the Super Bowl and the Olympic Games. The FBI relies on EPA-CID special agents for environmental crime expertise when responding to crime scenes and during investigations related to chemical, biological, and radiological weapons. They are authorized to conduct surveillance and undercover operations, carry firearms, make arrests, execute search warrants, and serve subpoenas.

EPA-CID special agents are covered under special retirement provisions for law enforcement officers, and they qualify for 25 percent Law Enforcement Availability Pay.

Qualifications and Salary Levels

GS-5: Completion of a four-year course of study leading to a bachelor's degree; or three years of general experience, one year of which was equivalent to at least GS-4. **GS-7:** One full year of graduate education, or superior academic achievement during undergraduate studies, or one year of specialized experience equivalent to at least GS-5. **GS-9:** A master's degree, or two years of graduate education, or one year of specialized experience equivalent to at least GS-7. **GS-11:** A Ph.D. or equivalent doctoral degree, or three years of graduate education, or one year of specialized experience equivalent to at least GS-9. **GS-12:** One year of specialized experience equivalent to at least GS-11. **GS-13:** One year of specialized experience equivalent to at least GS-12.

Experience and education can be combined to meet total experience requirements. Applicants must be at least 21 years of age and under age 37. However, candidates over age 37 who have previous service creditable under special law enforcement retirement provisions also may be eligible. Eyesight requirements include good distant vision in each eye, near vision that is sufficient to read print the size of typewritten characters, normal depth perception and peripheral vision, and the ability to distinguish basic colors. Eyeglasses and contact lenses are permitted. Hearing loss must not exceed 35 decibels at the 1000, 2000, and 3000 Hertz levels. The application process includes a medical examination, drug screening test, background investigation, and security clearance determination.

Training

EPA-CID special agents attend the 11-week Criminal Investigator Training Program at the Federal Law Enforcement Training Center (FLETC) in Glynco, Georgia (see chapter 16), followed by an eight-week EPA Basic Environmental Investigation Course at FLETC. EPA-CID special agents also attend advanced courses at FLETC, including the five day EPA Special Agent In-Service Training program, and a variety of courses at EPA's National Enforcement Training Institute (see chapter 16). These courses cover investigative techniques, evidence collection, hot-zone forensics, personal protection equipment, and other subjects. Additional in-service training focuses on firearms proficiency, arrest techniques, and defensive tactics.

Contact: Criminal Investigation Division; Office of Criminal Enforcement, Forensics and Training; U.S. Environmental Protection Agency; 1200 Pennsylvania Ave. NW; Washington, DC 20460; phone: (202) 564-2490; Internet: www.epa.gov/compliance/criminal/

Special Agent (GS-1811)
Office of Inspector General, U.S. Environmental Protection Agency

The U.S. Environmental Protection Agency (EPA) protects human health and safeguards the nation's air, water, and land resources by controlling and abating pollution caused by solid waste, pesticides, radiation, toxic substances, and other sources. Special agents of the EPA Office of Inspector General (EPA-OIG) investigate fraud and other crimes in the programs and operations administered or financed by EPA.

Criminal investigations conducted by EPA-OIG special agents often focus on fraudulent reports submitted by laboratories, contract and financial fraud, computer crimes, and EPA employee integrity matters. Laboratory fraud investigations frequently pertain to organizations that monitor compliance with federal environmental laws and provide the results of laboratory testing to the EPA. These investigations often identify falsified test reports, false calibrations, improper testing, and false billing. Contract and financial fraud investigations are concerned with kickback schemes, overcharging, charging nonqualifying expenses, misappropriation of funds, embezzlement, bid-rigging, and other schemes carried out by contractors, grantees, and other organizations that receive EPA funds. Computer crime investigations identify offenses relating to software piracy, EPA computer system intrusions, EPA employees who access and download pornographic material, and other crimes. Employee integrity investigations also focus on misuse of EPA computers, as well as bribery, kickbacks, fraudulent claims for travel reimbursements, embezzlement, and theft or misuse of government purchase cards. EPA-OIG special agents are authorized to conduct surveillance and under-cover operations, carry firearms, make arrests, execute search warrants, and serve subpoenas. They often coordinate investigations with agencies such as the FBI, Defense Criminal Investigative Service, U.S. Army Criminal Investigation Command, Department of Agriculture OIG, and EPA Criminal Investigation Division.

EPA-OIG special agents are covered under special retirement provisions for law enforcement officers, and they qualify for 25 percent Law Enforcement Availability Pay.

Qualifications and Salary Levels

GS-5: Completion of a four-year course of study leading to a bachelor's degree; or three years of general experience, one year of which was equivalent to at least GS-4. **GS-7:** One full year of graduate education, or superior academic achievement during undergraduate studies, or one year of specialized experience equivalent to at least GS-5. **GS-9:** A master's degree, or two years of graduate education, or one year of specialized experience equivalent to at least GS-7. **GS-11:** A Ph.D. or equivalent doctoral degree, or three years of graduate education, or one year of specialized experience equivalent to at least GS-9. **GS-12:** One year of specialized experience equivalent to at least GS-11. **GS-13:** One year of specialized experience equivalent to at least GS-12.

Qualifying education can be substituted for experience, and vice versa. Applicants must be at least 21 years of age and under age 37. However, candidates over age 37 who have previous service creditable under special law enforcement retirement provisions also may be eligible. Eyesight requirements include good distant vision in each eye, near vision that is sufficient to read print the size of typewritten characters, normal depth perception and peripheral vision, and the ability to distinguish basic colors. Eyeglasses and contact lenses are permitted. Hearing loss must not exceed 35 decibels at the 1000, 2000, and 3000 Hertz levels. Tentative appointees must qualify for a security clearance and pass a background investigation, drug screening test, and medical examination.

Training

EPA-OIG special agents attend the 11-week Criminal Investigator Training Program at the Federal Law Enforcement Training Center (FLETC) in Glynco, Georgia (see chapter 16). In-service training could include courses at EPA's National Enforcement Training Institute (see chapter 16) and other locations that focus on environmental crimes and investigations, EPA program regulations, white-collar crime, and other subjects. EPA-OIG special agents also can attend the three-week Inspector General Investigator Training Program at FLETC (see chapter 16).

Contact: Office of Inspector General; U.S. Environmental Protection Agency; 1200 Pennsylvania Ave. NW; Washington, DC 20460; phone: (202) 566-0847; Internet: www.epa.gov/oigearth/

Special Agent (GS-1811)

Office of Inspector General, Equal Employment Opportunity Commission

The Equal Employment Opportunity Commission (EEOC) enforces laws that prohibit discrimination in hiring, promoting, firing, setting wages, testing, training, apprenticeship, and all other terms and conditions of employment. The EEOC conducts investigations of alleged discrimination, makes determinations based on gathered evidence, attempts conciliation when discrimination has taken place, files lawsuits, and conducts voluntary assistance programs for employers, unions, and community organizations. EEOC Office of Inspector General (OIG) special agents perform complex investigations related to the integrity of EEOC programs and operations, including misconduct by the Commission's personnel.

A significant proportion of EEOC-OIG investigations are concerned with provisions of Title VII of the Civil Rights Act of 1964, which prohibits employment discrimination based on race, color, religion, gender, national origin, disability, or age. Other investigations identify violations of the Equal Pay Act, Age Discrimination in Employment Act, Title I and Title V of the Americans with Disabilities Act, Sections 501 and 505 of the Rehabilitation Act, and other laws. EEOC-OIG special agents also investigate official misconduct by EEOC employees, including allegations of bribery, conflict of interest, theft or misuse of government property, misuse of official position for private gain, falsification of travel vouchers and time and attendance reports, and other violations. EEOC-OIG special agents conduct investigations jointly with agencies such as the FBI; Office of Personnel Management OIG; Government Accountability Office; and other federal, state, and local law enforcement and regulatory agencies.

Qualifications and Salary Levels

GS-5: Completion of a four-year course of study leading to a bachelor's degree; or three years of general experience, one year of which was equivalent to at least GS-4. **GS-7:** One full year of graduate education, or superior academic achievement during undergraduate studies, or one year of specialized experience equivalent to at least GS-5. **GS-9:** A master's degree, or two years of graduate education, or one year of specialized experience equivalent to at least GS-7. **GS-11:** A Ph.D. or equivalent doctoral degree, or three years of graduate education, or one year of specialized experience equivalent to at least GS-9. **GS-12:** One year of specialized experience equivalent to at least GS-11. **GS-13:** One year of specialized experience equivalent to at least GS-12.

Equivalent combinations of education and experience can be used to meet minimum experience requirements. Eyesight requirements include good distant vision in each eye, near vision that is sufficient to read print the size of typewritten characters, normal depth perception and peripheral vision, and the ability to distinguish basic colors. Eyeglasses and contact lenses are permitted. Hearing loss must not exceed 35 decibels at the 1000, 2000, and 3000 Hertz levels. Candidates must successfully undergo a background investigation and qualify for a security clearance.

Training

Initial training for EEOC-OIG special agents includes the 11-week Criminal Investigator Training Program at the Federal Law Enforcement Training Center (FLETC) in Glynco, Georgia (see chapter 16). In-service training includes the three-week Inspector General Investigator Training Program at FLETC, and courses that focus on communication skills, accounting methods, computer forensics, information security, and other subjects.

Contact: Office of Inspector General; Equal Employment Opportunity Commission; 1801 L St. NW; Washington, DC 20507; phone: (202) 663-4379; Internet: www.eeoc.gov/

Special Agent
Office of Inspector General, Farm Credit Administration

The Farm Credit Administration (FCA) is responsible for ensuring the safe and sound operation of the banks, associations, affiliated service organizations, and other entities that collectively comprise what is known as the Farm Credit System, and for protecting the interests of the public and those who borrow from FCA institutions or invest in FCA securities. The FCA Office of Inspector General (OIG) is an independent agency that is responsible for investigating fraud and abuse by FCA employees, contractors, and other recipients of funds under or relating to FCA programs and operations.

FCA-OIG special agents conduct investigations concerning a variety of matters, although most investigations are concerned with allegations of wrongdoing by FCA personnel. Employee integrity investigations focus on offenses such as larceny; conversion; misappropriation of funds; misuse of government purchase cards, travel cards, funds, or property; violation of Merit System Principles; and mismanagement. FCA-OIG special agents are authorized to conduct surveillance and undercover operations, carry firearms, make arrests, execute search warrants, and serve subpoenas. They coordinate operations occasionally with agencies such as the FBI; Federal Reserve Board OIG; U.S. Secret Service; Postal Inspection Service; and other federal, state, and local law enforcement agencies.

FCA-OIG special agents are covered under special retirement provisions for law enforcement officers, and they qualify for 25 percent Law Enforcement Availability Pay.

Qualifications and Salary Levels

FCA-OIG special agents are appointed through excepted service hiring processes. The qualifications and salaries of the position are similar to those of GS-1811 special agents with other federal agencies. Applicants must be at least 21 years of age and under age 37. However, candidates over age 37 who have previous service creditable under special law enforcement retirement provisions also may be eligible. Eyesight requirements include good distant vision in each eye, near vision that is sufficient to read print the size of typewritten characters, normal depth perception and peripheral vision, and the ability to distinguish basic colors. Eyeglasses and contact lenses are permitted. Hearing loss must not exceed 35 decibels at the 1000, 2000, and 3000 Hertz levels. Candidates must successfully undergo a background investigation and qualify for a security clearance.

Training

FCA-OIG special agents attend the 11-week Criminal Investigator Training Program at the Federal Law Enforcement Training Center (FLETC) in Glynco, Georgia (see chapter 16). They also attend in-service training programs that cover subjects such as investigative techniques, legal updates, white-collar crime, employee integrity investigations, and defensive tactics. FCA-OIG special agents also can attend the three-week Inspector General Investigator Training Program at FLETC (see chapter 16).

Contact: Office of Inspector General; Farm Credit Administration; 1501 Farm Credit Dr.; McLean, VA 22102; phone: (703) 883-4030; Internet: www.fca.gov/oiginvestigations.htm/; e-mail: ig_information@fca.gov

Special Agent
Office of Inspector General, Federal Deposit Insurance Corporation

The Federal Deposit Insurance Corporation (FDIC) promotes and preserves public confidence in U.S. financial institutions by insuring bank and thrift deposits; examining state-chartered banks that are not members of the Federal Reserve System for safety, soundness, and compliance with consumer protection laws; and liquidating assets of failed institutions to reimburse the insurance funds for the cost of failures. Special agents serving with the FDIC Office of Inspector General (OIG) investigate activities that harm or threaten to harm the integrity of FDIC and its operations, with particular emphasis on white-collar crime.

The majority of FDIC-OIG investigations pertain to financial institution fraud. These investigations focus on FDIC-supervised institutions, and frequently involve fraud by officers, directors, or their employees; obstruction of FDIC examinations; fraud leading to the failure of institutions; fraud affecting multiple institutions; and fraud involving monetary losses that could significantly affect institutions. FDIC-OIG special agents also investigate FDIC-supervised institutions that conceal their assets from the FDIC to avoid paying court-ordered criminal restitution. Other investigations pertain to criminal or serious noncriminal misconduct by FDIC employees. Agents assigned to FDIC-OIG's Electronic Crimes Unit conduct computer-related investigations affecting FDIC—including cases involving computer abuse by FDIC personnel—and provide computer forensic support to investigations nationwide. FDIC-OIG special agents are authorized to conduct surveillance and undercover operations, carry firearms, make arrests, execute search warrants, and serve subpoenas. They conduct most investigations jointly with the FBI, although they also work closely with agencies such as the IRS Criminal Investigation Division, Treasury Department OIG, Federal Reserve Board OIG, Postal Inspection Service, and other law enforcement and regulatory agencies.

FDIC-OIG special agents are covered under special retirement provisions for law enforcement officers, and they qualify for 25 percent Law Enforcement Availability Pay.

Qualifications and Salary Levels

FDIC-OIG special agents are appointed through excepted service hiring processes. The qualifications and salaries of the position are similar to those of GS-1811 special agents at the GS-5 through GS-13 levels with other federal agencies. Applicants must be at least 21 years of age and under age 37. However, candidates over age 37 who have previous service creditable under special law enforcement retirement provisions also may be eligible. Eyesight requirements include good distant vision in each eye, near vision that is sufficient to read print the size of typewritten characters, normal depth perception and peripheral vision, and the ability to distinguish basic colors. Eyeglasses and contact lenses are permitted. Hearing loss must not exceed 35 decibels at the 1000, 2000, and 3000 Hertz levels. The application process includes a drug screening test, medical examination, background investigation, and security clearance determination.

Training

Initial training for FDIC-OIG special agents consists of the 11-week Criminal Investigator Training Program at the Federal Law Enforcement Training Center (FLETC) in Glynco, Georgia (see chapter 16). In-service training includes instruction in subjects such as computer fraud, computer intrusions, federal bank regulations, firearms proficiency, and various courses presented by the National Association of Certified Fraud Examiners. FDIC-OIG special agents also can attend the three-week Inspector General Investigator Training Program at FLETC (see chapter 16).

Contact: Office of Inspector General; Federal Deposit Insurance Corporation; 801 17th St. NW; Washington, DC 20434; phone: (202) 416-4255; Internet: www.fdicig.gov/

Special Agent
Office of Inspector General, Federal Reserve Board

The Board of Governors of the Federal Reserve System—known commonly as the Federal Reserve Board (FRB)—determines general monetary, credit, and operating policies for the System as a whole, and formulates the regulations necessary to carry out provisions of the Federal Reserve Act. FRB's principal duties consist of monitoring credit conditions; supervising Federal Reserve banks, member banks, and bank holding companies; and regulating the implementation of certain consumer credit protection laws. Special agents of the FRB Office of Inspector General (OIG) investigate allegations of administrative, civil, and criminal misconduct related to the programs and operations administered or financed by FRB, as well as violations of FRB personnel standards of conduct.

FRB-OIG special agents investigate a wide range of criminal and administrative allegations, such as the use of fraudulent Social Security numbers to establish bank accounts at institutions regulated by FRB, bank fraud, loan fraud, obstruction of bank examiners, threats against FRB staff and property, contract fraud, theft of uncirculated Federal Reserve Notes, misuse of FRB computers or other property, and other offenses. FRB-OIG special agents are authorized to conduct surveillance and undercover operations, carry firearms, make arrests, execute search warrants, and serve subpoenas. They conduct investigations jointly with agencies such as the FBI, U.S. Secret Service, Drug Enforcement Administration, Treasury Inspector General for Tax Administration, State Department OIG, Department of Homeland Security OIG, and IRS Criminal Investigation Division.

FRB-OIG special agents are covered under special retirement provisions for law enforcement officers.

Qualifications and Salary Levels

FRB-OIG special agents are appointed through excepted service hiring processes. The qualifications and salaries of the position are similar to those of GS-1811 special agents at the GS-5 through GS-13 levels with other federal agencies that do not receive Law Enforcement Availability Pay. Applicants must be at least 21 years of age and under age 37. However, candidates over age 37 who have previous service creditable under special law enforcement retirement provisions also may be eligible. Eyesight requirements include good distant vision in each eye, near vision that is sufficient to read print the size of typewritten characters, normal depth perception and peripheral vision, and the ability to distinguish basic colors. Eyeglasses and contact lenses are permitted. Hearing loss must not exceed 35 decibels at the 1000, 2000, and 3000 Hertz levels. The application process includes a drug screening test, background investigation, medical examination, and top-secret security clearance determination.

Training

FRB-OIG special agents attend the 11-week Criminal Investigator Training Program at the Federal Law Enforcement Training Center (FLETC) in Glynco, Georgia (see chapter 16). In-service training includes courses such as the three-week Inspector General Investigator Training Program at FLETC (see chapter 16); instruction relating to FRB program investigations, procurement fraud, money laundering, computer forensics, legal issues and updates, or personnel misconduct; or courses presented by the Association of Certified Fraud Examiners, the Institute for Internal Auditors, or the Inspector General Criminal Investigator Academy (see chapter 16).

Contact: Office of Inspector General; Federal Reserve Board; 20th St. and Constitution Ave. NW; Washington, DC 20551; phone: (202) 452-3000; Internet: www.federalreserve.gov/oig/

Special Agent (GS-1811)
Office of Inspector General, U.S. General Services Administration

The U.S. General Services Administration (GSA) manages government property, records, and buildings; procures and distributes supplies government-wide; operates transportation and travel management programs for federal agencies; stockpiles strategic materials; and manages government data processing resources. The investigations division of GSA's Office of Inspector General (OIG) manages a nationwide program to prevent and detect illegal and improper activities involving GSA programs, operations, and personnel.

GSA-OIG special agents conduct criminal and noncriminal investigations pertaining primarily to GSA contracts, contractors, and their employees, although they also investigate other matters. Investigations frequently uncover falsification of contractors' certified payrolls; fraudulent deviation from contract specifications; manipulation of books and records by individuals, partnerships, corporations, and other entities; contract overcharges; and failure to conduct required inspections. Oftentimes, contract fraud investigations identify crimes committed by GSA personnel, including embezzlement, bribery, conflict of interest, and kickbacks relating to contracts for building construction and maintenance; heating, cooling, plumbing, and electrical systems; surplus property programs; training programs; office supplies, equipment, and furniture; telecommunications services; computer software; and other goods and services. GSA-OIG special agents often investigate theft and misuse of GSA fleet and purchase cards that are used to buy gasoline, automobile parts and supplies, and other goods. They are authorized to conduct surveillance and undercover operations, carry firearms, make arrests, execute search warrants, and serve subpoenas. Investigations often are coordinated with agencies such as the Defense Criminal Investigative Service, Army Criminal Investigation Command, FBI, Department of Agriculture OIG, Department of Transportation OIG, and IRS Criminal Investigation Division.

GSA-OIG special agents are covered under special retirement provisions for law enforcement officers, and they qualify for 25 percent Law Enforcement Availability Pay.

Qualifications and Salary Levels

GS-5: Completion of a four-year course of study leading to a bachelor's degree; or three years of general experience, one year of which was equivalent to at least GS-4. **GS-7:** One full year of graduate education, or superior academic achievement during undergraduate studies, or one year of specialized experience equivalent to at least GS-5. **GS-9:** A master's degree, or two years of graduate education, or one year of specialized experience equivalent to at least GS-7. **GS-11:** A Ph.D. or equivalent doctoral degree, or three years of graduate education, or one year of specialized experience equivalent to at least GS-9. **GS-12:** One year of specialized experience equivalent to at least GS-11. **GS-13:** One year of specialized experience equivalent to at least GS-12.

Experience and education can be combined to meet total experience requirements. Applicants must be at least 21 years of age and under age 37. However, candidates over age 37 who have previous service creditable under special law enforcement retirement provisions also may be eligible. Eyesight requirements include good distant vision in each eye, near vision that is sufficient to read print the size of typewritten characters, normal depth perception and peripheral vision, and the ability to distinguish basic colors. Eyeglasses and contact lenses are permitted. Hearing loss must not exceed 35 decibels at the 1000, 2000, and 3000 Hertz levels. Candidates must successfully undergo a background investigation, qualify for a security clearance, and pass a drug test and medical examination prior to appointment.

Training

GSA-OIG special agents attend the 11-week Criminal Investigator Training Program at the Federal Law Enforcement Training Center (FLETC) in Glynco, Georgia (see chapter 16). They also attend in-service training programs that cover subjects such as contract and procurement fraud, GSA program investigations, computer crime, criminal and civil law, and personnel misconduct. Many GSA-OIG special agents also attend the three-week Inspector General Investigator Training Program at FLETC (see chapter 16).

Contact: Office of Inspector General; General Services Administration; 1800 F St. NW; Washington, DC 20405; phone: (202) 501-1397; Internet: www.gsa.gov/

Special Agent (GS-1811)
Office of Forensic Audits and Special Investigations, U.S. Government Accountability Office

The U.S. Government Accountability Office (GAO)—formerly known as the General Accounting Office—was established to independently audit government agencies, and serves as the investigative arm of the U.S. Congress. The GAO Office of Forensic Audits and Special Investigations (FSI) conducts congressional oversight investigations of alleged violations of federal criminal law, misconduct, and serious wrongdoing, including all matters concerning the receipt, disbursement, and use of public funds.

GAO-FSI special agents conduct investigations of government programs and activities, prepare written reports and detailed analyses, and assist GAO auditors and evaluators when they encounter criminal wrongdoing. Fraud investigations carried out by GAO-FSI special agents focus on programs that receive federal funds, such as those concerned with healthcare, information technology, natural resources, environmental protection, education, defense, and national security. GAO-FSI special agents also investigate conflicts of interest and mismanagement relating to government contracting and procurement activities; fraud pertaining to government grants, loans, and entitlements; violations of federal standards of ethical conduct and ethics regulations by federal employees; and the integrity of federal law enforcement and investigative programs. GAO-FSI special agents conduct investigations jointly with the FBI; Pension Benefit Guaranty Corporation Office of Inspector General (OIG); Office of Personnel Management OIG; U.S. Secret Service; Drug Enforcement Administration; and other federal, state, and local law enforcement agencies.

GAO-FSI special agents are covered under special retirement provisions for law enforcement officers, and they qualify for 25 percent Law Enforcement Availability Pay.

Qualifications and Salary Levels

GS-11: A Ph.D. or equivalent doctoral degree, or three years of graduate education, or one year of specialized experience equivalent to at least GS-9. **GS-12:** One year of specialized experience equivalent to at least GS-11. **GS-13:** One year of specialized experience equivalent to at least GS-12. **GS-14:** One year of specialized experience equivalent to at least GS-13.

Equivalent combinations of education and experience can be used to meet minimum experience requirements. Applicants must be at least 21 years of age and under age 37. However, candidates over age 37 who have previous service creditable under special law enforcement retirement provisions also may be eligible. Eyesight requirements include good distant vision in each eye, near vision that is sufficient to read print the size of typewritten characters, normal depth perception and peripheral vision, and the ability to distinguish basic colors. Eyeglasses and contact lenses are permitted. Hearing loss must not exceed 35 decibels at the 1000, 2000, and 3000 Hertz levels. The application process includes a drug screening test, medical examination, background investigation, and security clearance determination.

Training

GAO-FSI special agents attend the 11-week Criminal Investigator Training Program at the Federal Law Enforcement Training Center in Glynco, Georgia (see chapter 16). Ongoing in-service training covers subjects such as auditing techniques, Defense Department programs, healthcare fraud, financial investigations, and procurement fraud. GAO-FSI special agents also attend courses presented by the Association of Certified Fraud Examiners.

Contact: Office of Forensic Audits and Special Investigations; U.S. Government Accountability Office; 441 G St. NW; Washington, DC 20548; phone: (202) 512-3000; Internet: www.gao.gov/; e-mail: recruit@gao.gov

Special Agent
Office of Inspector General, U.S. Government Printing Office

With operations centered around the largest general printing plant in the world, the U.S. Government Printing Office (GPO) produces and procures printed and electronic publications for Congress and the departments and establishments of the federal government. The GPO Office of Inspector General (OIG) conducts investigations relating to employee misconduct and monetary or material losses occurring in GPO programs and operations. The subjects of these investigations typically are contractors, program participants, GPO management, and other agency employees.

Investigations conducted by GPO-OIG special agents are concerned mostly with workers' compensation fraud, procurement fraud, and employee misconduct. Workers' compensation fraud investigations focus on GPO employees who submit false claims and make false statements to receive workers' compensation benefits. Procurement fraud cases typically involve GPO contractors who illegally substitute products, submit inflated claims, make false statements, engage in bid collusion or illegal subcontracting, and commit violations of the Small Disadvantaged Business Program. Employee misconduct investigations often are concerned with offenses such as misuse of government computers, theft of GPO funds and property, kickbacks, misappropriation of funds, travel voucher fraud, time and attendance fraud, and gambling. GPO-OIG special agents also investigate intrusions into GPO computers and other attacks on the agency's assets and personnel. They participate with other federal OIG agencies, Defense Department investigative agencies, other federal law enforcement agencies, and federal prosecutors in a federal procurement fraud working group formed by the U.S. Attorney's Office. They are authorized to conduct surveillance and undercover operations, carry firearms, make arrests, execute search warrants, and serve subpoenas.

GAO-OIG special agents are covered under special retirement provisions for federal law enforcement officers.

Qualifications and Salary Levels

Appointments to the GPO-OIG special agent position are carried out through excepted service hiring processes. The qualifications and salaries of the position are similar to those of GS-1811 special agents at the GS-5 through GS-13 levels with other federal agencies. Applicants must be at least 21 years of age and under age 37. However, candidates over age 37 who have previous service creditable under special law enforcement retirement provisions also may be eligible. Eyesight requirements include good distant vision in each eye, near vision that is sufficient to read print the size of typewritten characters, normal depth perception and peripheral vision, and the ability to distinguish basic colors. Eyeglasses and contact lenses are permitted. Hearing loss must not exceed 35 decibels at the 1000, 2000, and 3000 Hertz levels. Tentative appointees must qualify for a security clearance and pass a background investigation, drug screening test, and medical examination.

Training

GPO-OIG special agents attend the 11-week Criminal Investigator Training Program at the Federal Law Enforcement Training Center (FLETC) in Glynco, Georgia (see chapter 16). They attend in-service training programs that cover subjects such as GPO program and financial investigations, corruption, computer fraud, contract and procurement fraud, and workers' compensation program laws. GPO-OIG special agents also attend the three-week Inspector General Investigator Training Program at FLETC (see chapter 16).

Contact: Office of Inspector General; U.S. Government Printing Office; 732 N. Capitol St. NW; Washington, DC 20401; phone: (202) 512-0039; Internet: www.gpo.gov/oig/

Special Agent (GS-1811)

Food and Drug Administration, U.S. Department of Health and Human Services

The Food and Drug Administration (FDA) protects the nation's public health by assuring the safety and security of human and veterinary drugs, biological products, medical devices, the food supply, cosmetics, and products that emit radiation. The FDA Office of Criminal Investigations is responsible for all criminal investigations conducted by the FDA, including those involving the agency's programs and operations, food and drug tampering incidents, and products regulated by the FDA.

Criminal investigations carried out by FDA special agents focus on violations of the Food, Drug, and Cosmetic Act; Federal Anti-Tampering Act; Prescription Drug Marketing Act; Safe Medical Devices Act; Controlled Substances Act; and many other laws. Investigations of these and other violations are concerned with misbranded, adulterated, diluted, or counterfeit drugs; the unlawful sale, theft, or diversion of hospital drugs, drug samples, anabolic steroids, narcotics, or other controlled substances; kickback schemes involving federal healthcare programs; mail-order pharmacies and other operations that sell drugs without prescriptions; and other offenses. The responsibilities of FDA special agents also include the investigation of misconduct and crimes committed by FDA personnel concerning the agency's programs and operations, including offenses such as bribery, conflict of interest, embezzlement, and misappropriation of federal funds.

FDA special agents participate in many national and international law enforcement and intelligence task forces, and they work closely with agencies such as the FBI, Drug Enforcement Administration, Department of Agriculture Office of Inspector General (OIG), Postal Inspection Service, Health and Human Services OIG, Defense Criminal Investigative Service, and other agencies. They are authorized to conduct surveillance and undercover operations, carry firearms, make arrests, execute search warrants, and serve subpoenas.

FDA special agents are covered under special retirement provisions for law enforcement officers, and they qualify for 25 percent Law Enforcement Availability Pay.

Qualifications and Salary Levels

GS-5: Completion of a four-year course of study leading to a bachelor's degree; or three years of general experience, one year of which was equivalent to at least GS-4. **GS-7:** One full year of graduate education, or superior academic achievement during undergraduate studies, or one year of specialized experience equivalent to at least GS-5. **GS-9:** A master's degree, or two years of graduate education, or one year of specialized experience equivalent to at least GS-7. **GS-11:** A Ph.D. or equivalent doctoral degree, or three years of graduate education, or one year of specialized experience equivalent to at least GS-9. **GS-12:** One year of specialized experience equivalent to at least GS-11. **GS-13:** One year of specialized experience equivalent to at least GS-12.

Qualifying education can be substituted for experience, and vice versa. Applicants must be at least 21 years of age and under age 37. However, candidates over age 37 who have previous service creditable under special law enforcement retirement provisions also may be eligible. Eyesight requirements include good distant vision in each eye, near vision that is sufficient to read print the size of typewritten characters, normal depth perception and peripheral vision, and the ability to distinguish basic colors. Eyeglasses and contact lenses are permitted. Hearing loss must not exceed 35 decibels at the 1000, 2000, and 3000 Hertz levels. The application process includes a drug screening test, medical examination, background investigation, and security clearance determination.

Training

FDA special agents attend the 11-week Criminal Investigator Training Program at the Federal Law Enforcement Training Center in Glynco, Georgia (see chapter 16). In-service training is geared toward FDA regulations; updates to the Food, Drug, and Cosmetic Act and other laws; FDA program investigations; financial investigations; undercover operations; search and seizure; first aid and CPR; arrest techniques; defensive tactics; and firearms proficiency.

Contact: Office of Criminal Investigations; Food and Drug Administration; U.S. Department of Health and Human Services; 7500 Standish Place—Suite 250N; Rockville, MD 20855; phone: (301) 294-4030; Internet: www.fda.gov/

Special Agent (GS-1811)
Office of Inspector General, U.S. Department of Health and Human Services

The U.S. Department of Health and Human Services (HHS) is the federal government's principal agency for protecting the health of Americans and providing essential human services. HHS operates more than 300 programs that cover a wide range of activities, and it is the largest grant-making agency in the federal government. Special agents of the HHS Office of Inspector General (OIG) conduct criminal and civil investigations to identify fraud and other forms of criminal or improper activity in HHS programs and operations.

Many of the investigations performed by HHS-OIG special agents are concerned with crimes committed by hospitals, nursing homes, clinics, doctors, dentists, medical equipment suppliers, and other healthcare providers associated with Medicare and Medicaid programs. These include false claims, embezzlement, contract and procurement fraud, kickbacks, and many other illegal practices. Medicare and Medicaid investigations often focus on crimes such as patient dumping or abuse; billing for services that were unallowable, medically unnecessary, or not rendered; upcoding claims to indicate higher levels of service than provided; and illegal prescription drug pricing.

Employee integrity investigations are concerned with official misconduct by HHS personnel, including offenses such as bribery, collusion, conflict of interest, misuse of government purchase cards, and time and attendance fraud. HHS-OIG special agents also investigate fraud relating to grants for scientific research, contract fraud, failure to pay court-ordered child support, and many other offenses. They are authorized to conduct surveillance and undercover operations, carry firearms, make arrests, execute search warrants, and serve subpoenas. Investigations often are conducted with agencies such as the FBI; Food and Drug Administration; Office of Personnel Management OIG; Department of Agriculture OIG; Department of Veterans Affairs OIG; and other federal, state, and local law enforcement and regulatory agencies.

HHS-OIG special agents are covered under special retirement provisions for law enforcement officers, and they qualify for 25 percent Law Enforcement Availability Pay.

Qualifications and Salary Levels

GS-5: Completion of a four-year course of study leading to a bachelor's degree; or three years of general experience, one year of which was equivalent to at least GS-4. **GS-7:** One full year of graduate education, or superior academic achievement during undergraduate studies, or one year of specialized experience equivalent to at least GS-5. **GS-9:** A master's degree, or two years of graduate education, or one year of specialized experience equivalent to at least GS-7. **GS-11:** A Ph.D. or equivalent doctoral degree, or three years of graduate education, or one year of specialized experience equivalent to at least GS-9. **GS-12:** One year of specialized experience equivalent to at least GS-11. **GS-13:** One year of specialized experience equivalent to at least GS-12.

Qualifying education can be substituted for experience, and vice versa. Applicants must be at least 21 years of age and under age 37. However, candidates over age 37 who have previous service creditable under special law enforcement retirement provisions also may be eligible. Eyesight requirements include good distant vision in each eye, near vision that is sufficient to read print the size of typewritten characters, normal depth perception and peripheral vision, and the ability to distinguish basic colors. Eyeglasses and contact lenses are permitted. Hearing loss must not exceed 35 decibels at the 1000, 2000, and 3000 Hertz levels. Candidates must successfully undergo a background investigation, qualify for a security clearance, and pass a drug test and medical examination prior to appointment.

Training

HHS-OIG special agents attend the 11-week Criminal Investigator Training Program at the Federal Law Enforcement Training Center (FLETC) in Glynco, Georgia (see chapter 16). They also attend the three-week Inspector General Investigator Training Program at FLETC, and take courses in subjects such as report writing, HHS program investigations, Medicare and Medicaid fraud, and interviewing techniques.

Contact: Office of Inspector General; U.S. Department of Health and Human Services; 330 Independence Ave. SW; Washington, DC 20201; phone: (202) 619-3210; Internet: www.hhs.gov/oig/

Special Agent (GS-1811)
United States Coast Guard Investigative Service, U.S. Department of Homeland Security

The U.S. Coast Guard—a military organization within the U.S. Department of Homeland Security—protects the public, the environment, and U.S. economic interests in the nation's ports and inland waterways, along the coasts, on international waters, or in any maritime region as required to support U.S. national security. The Coast Guard is staffed by active duty, reserve, civilian, and auxiliary personnel who serve the agency in times of peace and war. The Coast Guard Investigative Service (CGIS) is the criminal investigation arm of the Coast Guard.

CGIS special agents conduct criminal and personnel security investigations, perform counterintelligence operations, and provide personal protection to high-ranking Coast Guard officials. They are based in seven regional offices and 23 smaller offices—known as resident agencies—nationwide. Criminal investigations carried out by CGIS special agents focus on felony violations of the Uniform Code of Military Justice, drug trafficking activities, illegal immigrant smuggling operations, violent crimes, terrorism, piracy, fishing violations, marine environmental crimes and other maritime criminal offenses, fraud and other crimes in Coast Guard programs, and official misconduct by Coast Guard employees. CGIS special agents participate with the FBI, Drug Enforcement Administration, IRS Criminal Investigation Division, U.S. Immigration and Customs Enforcement, and other law enforcement agencies in Organized Crime Drug Enforcement Task Force operations nationwide. They also participate in personal protective operations with the U.S. Secret Service and State Department, and in other operations with agencies such as the National Marine Fisheries Service, Naval Criminal Investigative Service, Air Force Office of Special Investigations, Department of Transportation Office of Inspector General (OIG), and other law enforcement and regulatory agencies. They are authorized to conduct surveillance and undercover operations, carry firearms, make arrests, execute search warrants, and serve subpoenas.

CGIS special agents are covered under special retirement provisions for law enforcement officers, and they qualify for 25 percent Law Enforcement Availability Pay. Although the Coast Guard also maintains a staff of active duty military special agents, this is a civilian position and does not require active duty service.

Qualifications and Salary Levels

GS-5: Completion of a four-year course of study leading to a bachelor's degree; or three years of general experience, one year of which was equivalent to at least GS-4. **GS-7:** One full year of graduate education, or superior academic achievement during undergraduate studies, or one year of specialized experience equivalent to at least GS 5. **GS-9:** A master's degree, or two years of graduate education, or one year of specialized experience equivalent to at least GS-7. **GS-11:** A Ph.D. or equivalent doctoral degree, or three years of graduate education, or one year of specialized experience equivalent to at least GS-9. **GS-12:** One year of specialized experience equivalent to at least GS-11. **GS-13:** One year of specialized experience equivalent to at least GS-12.

Experience and education can be combined to meet total experience requirements. Applicants must be at least 21 years of age and under age 37. However, candidates over age 37 who have previous service creditable under special law enforcement retirement provisions also may be eligible. Eyesight requirements include good distant vision in each eye, near vision that is sufficient to read print the size of typewritten characters, normal depth perception and peripheral vision, and the ability to distinguish basic colors. Eyeglasses and contact lenses are permitted. Hearing loss must not exceed 35 decibels at the 1000, 2000, and 3000 Hertz levels. Tentative appointees must qualify for a top-secret security clearance and pass a background investigation, drug screening test, and medical examination.

Training

CGIS special agents attend the 11-week Criminal Investigator Training Program at the Federal Law Enforcement Training Center in Glynco, Georgia (see chapter 16). In-service training includes on-the-job and formal instruction in areas such as drug trafficking, homicide, sexual assault, financial crimes, counterterrorism, informant development, and other topics.

Contact: Coast Guard Investigative Service; United States Coast Guard; U.S. Department of Homeland Security; 2100 Second St. SW; Washington, DC 20593; phone: (202) 267-1890; Internet: www.uscg.mil/

Special Agent (GS-1811)
United States Immigration and Customs Enforcement, U.S. Department of Homeland Security

U.S. Immigration and Customs Enforcement (ICE)—the largest investigative arm of the Department of Homeland Security—prevents and investigates terrorism, smuggling, and other crimes, and identifies vulnerabilities in the nation's critical infrastructure industries and border security. ICE components include the Office of Detention and Removal, the Federal Protective Service, the Office of Intelligence, and the Office of Investigations. ICE special agents are based throughout the U.S. and in more than 20 countries.

Investigations carried out by ICE special agents are concerned primarily with smuggling, national security, and financial crimes. Smuggling investigations identify, disrupt, and dismantle criminal organizations that smuggle narcotics, contraband, and humans into the U.S. and threaten the nation's critical infrastructure. National security investigations focus on terrorism and preventing the illegal importation, exportation, and transfer of weapons of mass destruction, arms and munitions, and high technology. Financial investigations pertain to vulnerabilities in the nation's financial infrastructure, including offenses such as money laundering, bulk cash smuggling, intellectual property rights violations, insurance schemes, counterfeit goods trafficking, and other financial crimes. Investigations carried out by ICE special agents target child pornography and exploitation; cargo theft; organized crime; sophisticated alien smuggling operations; international criminal activities conducted on the Internet; trafficking in stolen art, antiquities, and ancient artifacts; government document fraud; and many other crimes and schemes. ICE special agents are authorized to conduct surveillance and undercover operations, carry firearms, make arrests, execute search warrants, and serve subpoenas. They often coordinate operations with agencies such as U.S. Customs and Border Protection, Drug Enforcement Administration, Postal Inspection Service, FBI, Department of Agriculture Office of Inspector General (OIG), Social Security Administration OIG, and other agencies.

ICE special agents are covered under special retirement provisions for law enforcement officers, and they qualify for 25 percent Law Enforcement Availability Pay.

Qualifications and Salary Levels

GS-5: Completion of a four-year course of study leading to a bachelor's degree; or three years of general experience, one year of which was equivalent to at least GS-4. **GS-7:** One full year of graduate education, or superior academic achievement during undergraduate studies, or one year of specialized experience equivalent to at least GS-5. **GS-9:** A master's degree, or two years of graduate education, or one year of specialized experience equivalent to at least GS-7. **GS-11:** A Ph.D. or equivalent doctoral degree, or three years of graduate education, or one year of specialized experience equivalent to at least GS-9. **GS-12:** One year of specialized experience equivalent to at least GS-11. **GS-13:** One year of specialized experience equivalent to at least GS-12.

Qualifying education can be substituted for experience, and vice versa. Applicants must be at least 21 years of age and under age 37. However, candidates over age 37 who have previous service creditable under special law enforcement retirement provisions also may be eligible. Eyesight requirements include uncorrected distant vision not worse than 20/200 (Snellen) binocular, corrected distant vision not worse than 20/30 in one eye and 20/20 in the other eye, and near vision that is sufficient to read Jaeger Type 2 at 14 inches. Eyeglasses and contact lenses are permitted. Hearing loss must not exceed 30 decibels at the 500, 1000, and 2000 Hertz levels. The application process includes the ICE Special Agent Test Battery written examination (see chapter 3) and a drug screening test, medical examination, background investigation, and top-secret security clearance determination.

Training

Initial training for ICE special agents consists of the 11-week Criminal Investigator Training Program (CITP) at the Federal Law Enforcement Training Center (FLETC) in Glynco, Georgia (see chapter 16), followed by the 11-week ICE Special Agent Training (ICE-SAT) program at FLETC's ICE Academy. The ICE-SAT course includes instruction relating to customs law, immigration law, DHS and ICE policies and procedures, law enforcement computer database systems, and various agency-specific topics. In-service training consists of advanced instruction in many subjects covered during CITP and ICE-SAT courses, as well as training to prepare ICE special agents for special assignments.

Contact: Office of Investigations; United States Immigration and Customs Enforcement; U.S. Department of Homeland Security; 425 I St. NW; Washington, DC 20536; phone: (202) 514-0078; Internet: www.ice.gov/

Special Agent (GS-1811)
Federal Protective Service, United States Immigration and Customs Enforcement, U.S. Department of Homeland Security

The Federal Protective Service (FPS)—one of the nation's oldest federal law enforcement agencies—was transferred to the Department of Homeland Security in 2003. As a component of U.S. Immigration and Customs Enforcement, FPS is responsible for law enforcement and security within more than 8,800 federally owned and leased buildings and facilities nationwide. FPS special agents protect these assets through complex and sensitive investigations and close cooperation with other federal, state, and local law enforcement agencies.

FPS special agents conduct investigations and gather intelligence relating primarily to crimes committed in and around government buildings and facilities, security threats, and terrorism. They also take proactive measures to protect federal personnel, visitors, and assets. FPS special agents accomplish these objectives by sharing intelligence information with other law enforcement agencies, participating in local and national antiterrorism task forces, conducting comprehensive vulnerability and security assessments, implementing appropriate security threat countermeasures, performing surveillance, analyzing crime statistics, and recommending enhanced levels of protection to FPS management and other agencies. They also investigate incidents involving theft, vandalism, arson, bomb threats, assaults, weapons offenses, and other crimes. FPS special agents coordinate investigations and intelligence operations with agencies such as the FBI, Drug Enforcement Administration, U.S. Marshals Service, U.S. Customs and Border Protection, Defense Criminal Investigative Service, State Department Bureau of Diplomatic Security, and many other agencies. They are authorized to conduct surveillance and undercover operations, carry firearms, make arrests, execute search warrants, and serve subpoenas.

FPS special agents are covered under special retirement provisions for law enforcement officers, and they qualify for 25 percent Law Enforcement Availability Pay.

Qualifications and Salary Levels

GS-5: Completion of a four-year course of study leading to a bachelor's degree; or three years of general experience, one year of which was equivalent to at least GS-4. **GS-7:** One full year of graduate education, or superior academic achievement during undergraduate studies, or one year of specialized experience equivalent to at least GS-5. **GS-9:** A master's degree, or two years of graduate education, or one year of specialized experience equivalent to at least GS-7. **GS-11:** A Ph.D. or equivalent doctoral degree, or three years of graduate education, or one year of specialized experience equivalent to at least GS-9. **GS-12:** One year of specialized experience equivalent to at least GS-11. **GS-13:** One year of specialized experience equivalent to at least GS-12.

Qualifying education can be substituted for experience, and vice versa. Applicants must be at least 21 years of age and under age 37. However, candidates over age 37 who have previous service creditable under special law enforcement retirement provisions also may be eligible. Eyesight requirements include uncorrected distant vision not worse than 20/200 (Snellen) binocular, corrected distant vision not worse than 20/30 in one eye and 20/20 in the other eye, and near vision that is sufficient to read Jaeger Type 2 at 14 inches. Eyeglasses and contact lenses are permitted. Hearing loss must not exceed 30 decibels at the 500, 1000, and 2000 Hertz levels. The application process includes a drug screening test, medical examination, background investigation, and top-secret security clearance determination.

Training

FPS special agents attend the 11-week Criminal Investigator Training Program at the Federal Law Enforcement Training Center in Glynco, Georgia (see chapter 16). In-service training consists of instruction in subjects relating to vulnerability assessments, counterterrorism, intelligence gathering, law enforcement computer databases, white-collar crime, and forensic photography, among others.

Contact: Federal Protective Service; United States Immigration and Customs Enforcement; U.S. Department of Homeland Security; 801 I St. NW—Suite 900; Washington, DC 20536; phone: (202) 514-2648; Internet: www.ice.gov/fps/

Special Agent (GS-1811)
Office of Inspector General, U.S. Department of Homeland Security

The U.S. Department of Homeland Security (DHS) was created in the aftermath of the terrorist attacks of September 11, 2001. The mission of DHS is to protect the nation from terrorism and other threats to national security by securing U.S. borders, synthesizing intelligence activities, coordinating communication between law enforcement and other government agencies, training and equipping first responders, and managing federal emergency response activities. The DHS Office of Inspector General (OIG) conducts audits, investigations, and inspections relating to DHS programs and operations.

Special agents serving with DHS-OIG investigate employee misconduct, fraud, and other crimes committed against DHS components such as the Federal Emergency Management Agency (FEMA), U.S. Customs and Border Protection, Transportation Security Administration, U.S. Immigration and Customs Enforcement, U.S. Secret Service, Domestic Nuclear Detection Office, and U.S. Citizenship and Immigration

Services. Many DHS-OIG investigations are concerned with fraud relating to DHS contracts and grants, disaster assistance programs for individuals and government agencies, mortgage and rental assistance programs, the National Flood Insurance Program, the National Hurricane Program, and other DHS operations. DHS-OIG special agents devote particular attention to the investigation of criminal wrongdoing and violations of DHS standards of ethical conduct committed by the Department's personnel. For example, DHS-OIG special agents investigate bribery, assaults, excessive force and other civil rights violations, alien smuggling and harboring illegal aliens, sale of counterfeit immigration documents, and other crimes. DHS-OIG special agents conduct investigations with agencies such as the Postal Inspection Service OIG, Department of Justice OIG, and other agencies. They are authorized to conduct surveillance and undercover operations, carry firearms, make arrests, execute search warrants, and serve subpoenas.

DHS-OIG special agents are covered under special retirement provisions for law enforcement officers, and they qualify for 25 percent Law Enforcement Availability Pay.

Qualifications and Salary Levels

GS-5: Completion of a four-year course of study leading to a bachelor's degree; or three years of general experience, one year of which was equivalent to at least GS-4. **GS-7:** One full year of graduate education, or superior academic achievement during undergraduate studies, or one year of specialized experience equivalent to at least GS-5. **GS-9:** A master's degree, or two years of graduate education, or one year of specialized experience equivalent to at least GS-7. **GS-11:** A Ph.D. or equivalent doctoral degree, or three years of graduate education, or one year of specialized experience equivalent to at least GS-9. **GS-12:** One year of specialized experience equivalent to at least GS-11. **GS-13:** One year of specialized experience equivalent to at least GS-12.

Qualifying education can be substituted for experience, and vice versa. Applicants must be at least 21 years of age and under age 37. However, candidates over age 37 who have previous service creditable under special law enforcement retirement provisions also may be eligible. Eyesight requirements include good distant vision in each eye, near vision that is sufficient to read print the size of typewritten characters, normal depth perception and peripheral vision, and the ability to distinguish basic colors. Eyeglasses and contact lenses are permitted. Hearing loss must not exceed 35 decibels at the 1000, 2000, and 3000 Hertz levels. The application process includes a drug screening test, medical examination, background investigation, and top-secret security clearance determination.

Training

DHS-OIG special agents attend the 11-week Criminal Investigator Training Program at the Federal Law Enforcement Training Center (FLETC) in Glynco, Georgia (see chapter 16). Many special agents also attend the three-week Inspector General Investigator Training Program at FLETC, as well as training programs relating to personnel misconduct investigations, DHS program fraud, white-collar crime, procurement fraud, report writing, and other subjects.

Contact: Office of Inspector General; U.S. Department of Homeland Security; 245 Murray Dr.—Bldg. 410; Washington, DC 20528; phone: (202) 254-4100; Internet: www.dhs.gov/

Special Agent (GS-1811)
United States Secret Service, U.S. Department of Homeland Security

The U.S. Secret Service (USSS) is mandated under federal law and executive order to carry out missions involving protection and investigation, and is designated under a presidential decision directive as the lead agency for coordinating federal antiterrorism and counterterrorism assets for national events.

USSS special agents provide protection around the clock for the president, vice president, president-elect, and vice president–elect, and their immediate families; former presidents and their spouses and minor children; visiting heads of foreign governments and their spouses traveling with them; other distinguished foreign visitors to the U.S.; official representatives of the U.S. performing special missions abroad; and major presidential and vice presidential candidates and their spouses during an election year. In carrying out protective assignments, USSS special agents gather intelligence information; serve on "advance teams" that survey each site to be visited; determine personnel and equipment needs, the location of hospitals, and evacuation routes for emergencies; alert public safety agencies in the area; establish a command post; and coordinate operations with federal, state, local, and military law enforcement agencies. Investigations focus on counterfeiting of U.S. currency, securities, and government identification documents; forgery of Social Security checks, savings bonds, and other government disbursements; fraud pertaining to credit cards, banks, electronic funds transfers, telecommunications, and telemarketing; money laundering; and computer crime. USSS special agents are authorized to conduct surveillance and undercover operations, carry firearms, make arrests, execute search warrants, and serve subpoenas. They often work with agencies such as the IRS Criminal Investigation Division, FBI, U.S. Immigration and Customs Enforcement, Drug Enforcement Administration, Social Security Administration Office of Inspector General (OIG), and Department of Agriculture OIG, among others.

USSS special agents are covered under special retirement provisions for law enforcement officers, and they qualify for 25 percent Law Enforcement Availability Pay.

Qualifications and Salary Levels

GS-5: Completion of a four-year course of study leading to a bachelor's degree; or three years of general experience, one year of which was equivalent to at least GS-4. **GS-7:** One full year of graduate education, or superior academic achievement during undergraduate studies, or one year of specialized experience equivalent to at least GS-5. **GS-9:** A master's degree, or two years of graduate education, or one year of specialized experience equivalent to at least GS-7. **GS-11:** A Ph.D. or equivalent doctoral degree, or three years of graduate education, or one year of specialized experience equivalent to at least GS-9. **GS-12:** One year of specialized experience equivalent to at least GS-11. **GS-13:** One year of specialized experience equivalent to at least GS-12.

Equivalent combinations of education and experience can be used to meet minimum experience requirements. Applicants must be at least 21 years of age and under age 37. However, candidates over age 37 who have previous service creditable under special law enforcement retirement provisions also may be eligible. Eyesight requirements include uncorrected binocular distant vision of at least 20/60 (Snellen), correctable to 20/20 in each eye; normal depth perception and peripheral vision; the ability to distinguish shades of color; and near vision sufficient to read Jaeger type 2 at 14 inches. Candidates who have undergone LASIK eye surgery must be free from residual effects three months after surgery, while those who have had other forms of refractive eye surgery must be free from residual effects one year after surgery. Hearing loss must not exceed 30 decibels at the 500, 1000, and 2000 Hertz levels. The application process includes the Treasury Enforcement Agent Examination (see chapter 3) and a drug screening test, medical examination, background investigation, polygraph examination, and top-secret security clearance determination.

Training

USSS special agents attend the 11-week Criminal Investigator Training Program at the Federal Law Enforcement Training Center in Glynco, Georgia (see chapter 16), followed by an 11-week agency-specific course at USSS training facilities in Laurel, Maryland, that is concerned primarily with protective operations; fraud involving credit cards, checks, and computers; financial investigations; and other agency-specific training. In-service training consists of courses in defensive driving, criminal investigation, intelligence gathering, surveillance, and other topics.

Contact: United States Secret Service; U.S. Department of Homeland Security; 950 H St. NW; Washington, DC 20223; phone: (202) 406-5800; Internet: www.secretservice.gov/; e-mail: jobs@secretservice.gov

Special Agent (GS-1811)
Office of Inspector General, U.S. Department of Housing and Urban Development

The U.S. Department of Housing and Urban Development (HUD) is the principal federal agency responsible for programs concerned with the nation's housing needs, fair housing opportunities, and improvement and development of America's communities. HUD provides assistance for housing, insures mortgages for dwellings, extends loans for home improvement, provides federal housing subsidies for low- and moderate-income families, and provides community development grants to states and communities.

Special agents of the HUD Office of Inspector General (OIG) conduct criminal, civil, and administrative investigations of irregularities concerning programs funded by HUD and other Department operations. These investigations are concerned primarily with fraud committed by contractors, grantees, and individuals who participate in HUD programs, as well as official misconduct by HUD employees. HUD-OIG special agents investigate mortgage loan fraud, property-flipping schemes, equity skimming, rental assistance fraud, identity theft, bank fraud, gang activity in public housing projects, violent crimes, and other matters. HUD-OIG special agents are authorized to conduct surveillance and undercover operations, carry firearms, make arrests, execute search warrants, and serve subpoenas. They investigate many crimes through multi-agency task force operations with agencies such as the Drug Enforcement Administration, IRS Criminal Investigation Division, Postal Inspection Service, FBI, and other agencies.

HUD-OIG special agents are covered under special retirement provisions for law enforcement officers, and they qualify for 25 percent Law Enforcement Availability Pay.

Qualifications and Salary Levels

GS-5: Completion of a four-year course of study leading to a bachelor's degree; or three years of general experience, one year of which was equivalent to at least GS-4. **GS-7:** One full year of graduate education, or superior academic achievement during undergraduate studies, or one year of specialized experience equivalent to at least GS-5. **GS-9:** A master's degree, or two years of graduate education, or one year of specialized experience equivalent to at least GS-7. **GS-11:** A Ph.D. or equivalent doctoral degree, or three years of graduate education, or one year of specialized experience equivalent to at least GS-9. **GS-12:** One year of specialized experience equivalent to at least GS-11. **GS-13:** One year of specialized experience equivalent to at least GS-12.

Applicants can use equivalent combinations of specialized experience and education to meet total experience requirements. Applicants must be at least 21 years of age and under age 37. However, candidates over age 37 who have previous service creditable under special law enforcement retirement provisions also may be eligible. Eyesight requirements include good distant vision in each eye, near vision that is sufficient to read print the size of typewritten characters, normal depth perception and peripheral vision, and the ability to distinguish basic colors. Eyeglasses and contact lenses are permitted. Hearing loss must not exceed 35 decibels at the 1000, 2000, and 3000 Hertz levels. Tentative appointees must qualify for a security clearance and pass a background investigation, personal interview, drug screening test, and medical examination.

Training

Initial training for HUD-OIG special agents includes the 11-week Criminal Investigator Training Program at the Federal Law Enforcement Training Center (FLETC) in Glynco, Georgia (see chapter 16). In-service courses pertain to subjects such as HUD program investigations, criminal law and procedure, search and seizure, asset forfeiture, and financial investigations. Many HUD-OIG special agents attend the three-week Inspector General Investigator Training Program at FLETC (see chapter 16).

Contact: Office of Inspector General; U.S. Department of Housing and Urban Development; 451 7th St. SW; Washington, DC 20410; phone: (202) 708-0390; Internet: www.hud.gov/offices/oig/

Special Agent (GS-1811)
Bureau of Indian Affairs, U.S. Department of the Interior

The Department of the Interior's Bureau of Indian Affairs (BIA) is the principal bureau within the federal government responsible for the administration of federal programs for recognized Indian tribes, and for promoting Indian self-determination. In addition, the Bureau has a trust responsibility emanating from treaties and other agreements with Native American groups.

BIA special agents investigate violations of federal, state, tribal, and natural resources conservation laws on Native American lands, reservations, allotments, and communities throughout Indian Country. BIA special agents perform criminal investigations and other tasks that are similar to those carried out by most of the nation's police detectives, including a combination of crimes against persons, property crimes, white-collar crimes, and other matters. Investigations focus on offenses such as assault, burglary, auto theft, child sexual abuse, homicide, drug trafficking, arson, kidnapping, fraud, and criminal activity related to gaming operations and other legitimate businesses operating within Indian Country. BIA special agents often perform surveillance and undercover investigations, including operations with agencies such as the Bureau of Land Management; U.S. Fish and Wildlife Service; Department of Interior Office of Inspector General; National Park Service; Drug Enforcement Administration; FBI; and other agencies at the federal, state, local, and tribal levels. They are authorized to carry firearms, make arrests, execute search warrants, and serve subpoenas.

BIA special agents are covered under special retirement provisions for law enforcement officers, and they qualify for 25 percent Law Enforcement Availability Pay.

Qualifications and Salary Levels

GS-5: Completion of a four-year course of study leading to a bachelor's degree; or three years of general experience, one year of which was equivalent to at least GS-4. **GS-7:** One full year of graduate education, or superior academic achievement during undergraduate studies, or one year of specialized experience equivalent to at least GS-5. **GS-9:** A master's degree, or two years of graduate education, or one year of specialized experience equivalent to at least GS-7. **GS-11:** A Ph.D. or equivalent doctoral degree, or three years of graduate education, or one year of specialized experience equivalent to at least GS-9. **GS-12:** One year of specialized experience equivalent to at least GS-11. **GS-13:** One year of specialized experience equivalent to at least GS-12.

Under the Indian Reorganization Act of 1934, qualified Native American applicants are given hiring preference for BIA positions, although applications from non–Native American candidates are encouraged. Qualifying education can be substituted for experience, and vice versa. Applicants must be at least 21 years of age and under age 37. However, candidates over age 37 who have previous service creditable under special law enforcement retirement provisions also may be eligible. Eyesight requirements include good distant vision in each eye, near vision that is sufficient to read print the size of typewritten characters, normal depth perception and peripheral vision, and the ability to distinguish basic colors. Eyeglasses and contact lenses are permitted. Hearing loss must not exceed 35 decibels at the 1000, 2000, and 3000 Hertz levels. Candidates must successfully undergo a background investigation, qualify for a security clearance, and pass a drug test and medical examination prior to appointment.

Training

Newly appointed BIA special agents attend the 11-week Criminal Investigator Training Program at the Federal Law Enforcement Training Center in Glynco, Georgia (see chapter 16). They also attend in-service training programs that cover subjects such as tribal and criminal law, civil law, fish and game laws, environmental crimes, drug trafficking investigations, and technical investigative equipment.

Contact: Bureau of Indian Affairs; U.S. Department of the Interior; 1849 C St. NW; Washington, DC 20240; phone: (202) 208-3710; Internet: www.doi.gov/bureau-indian-affairs.html/

Special Agent (GS-1811)
Bureau of Land Management, U.S. Department of the Interior

The Bureau of Land Management (BLM) administers public lands in accordance with the Federal Land Policy and Management Act of 1976, and other laws. BLM manages 264 million surface acres of land—about one-eighth of America's land surface—located primarily in 12 western states, including Alaska. The agency also manages 300 million acres of below-ground mineral resources.

BLM special agents investigate criminal activity relating to the Endangered Species Act, Archaeological Resources Protection Act, migratory bird hunting violations, and other crimes on public lands and resources managed by the Bureau. These investigations are concerned with offenses such as timber theft, theft of archaeological artifacts, unlawful sale or treatment of wild horses or burros, violation of conservation laws, hazardous waste dumping, theft of oil and gas, motor vehicle theft, assault, and homicide. BLM special agents also investigate clandestine drug laboratory operations, marijuana cultivation, and other drug trafficking activities. Many investigations focus on vandalism to ancient dwellings; cultural, prehistoric, and historic sites; ancient dwellings; historic trails; wilderness areas; and burial sites. BLM special agents are authorized to conduct surveillance and undercover operations, carry firearms, make arrests, execute search warrants, and serve subpoenas. They conduct investigations and share intelligence information with agencies such as the U.S. Fish and Wildlife Service; Department of Interior Office of Inspector General; Environmental Protection Agency; National Park Service; Bureau of Indian Affairs; and other law enforcement agencies at the federal, state, and local levels.

BLM special agents are covered under special retirement provisions for law enforcement officers, and they qualify for 25 percent Law Enforcement Availability Pay.

Qualifications and Salary Levels

GS-5: Completion of a four-year course of study leading to a bachelor's degree; or three years of general experience, one year of which was equivalent to at least GS-4. **GS-7:** One full year of graduate education, or superior academic achievement during undergraduate studies, or one year of specialized experience equivalent to at least GS-5. **GS-9:** A master's degree, or two years of graduate education, or one year of specialized experience equivalent to at least GS-7. **GS-11:** A Ph.D. or equivalent doctoral degree, or three years of graduate education, or one year of specialized experience equivalent to at least GS-9. **GS-12:** One year of specialized experience equivalent to at least GS-11. **GS-13:** One year of specialized experience equivalent to at least GS-12.

Equivalent combinations of education and experience can be used to meet minimum experience requirements. Applicants must be at least 21 years of age and under age 37. However, candidates over age 37 who have previous service creditable under special law enforcement retirement provisions also may be eligible. Eyesight requirements include good distant vision in each eye, near vision that is sufficient to read print the size of typewritten characters, normal depth perception and peripheral vision, and the ability to distinguish basic colors. Eyeglasses and contact lenses are permitted. Hearing loss must not exceed 35 decibels at the 1000, 2000, and 3000 Hertz levels. Candidates must successfully undergo a background investigation, qualify for a security clearance and pass a drug test and medical examination prior to appointment.

Training

BLM special agents attend the 11-week Criminal Investigator Training Program at the Federal Law Enforcement Training Center in Glynco, Georgia (see chapter 16). They complete a minimum of 40 hours of in-service training annually, including courses in subjects such as evidence photography, archaeological crime scene processing, domestic terrorism, critical incidents, environmental crimes investigation, and investigative techniques. Special agents also can attend a variety of courses at the BLM National Training center in Phoenix, Arizona.

Contact: Office of Law Enforcement and Security; Bureau of Land Management; U.S. Department of the Interior; 1849 C St. NW; Washington, DC 20240; phone: (202) 208-3269; Internet: www.blm.gov/; e-mail: woinfo@blm.gov

Special Agent (GS-1811)
National Park Service, U.S. Department of the Interior

The National Park Service is dedicated to conserving the nation's cultural and natural resources at nearly 400 locations that encompass the National Park System. Many national parks offer public tours, educational programs, films, exhibits, publications, and other interpretive media, as well as lodging, food, and transportation services.

NPS special agents investigate a wide range of criminal offenses and other matters pertaining to NPS programs and operations. Investigations focus on incidents that occur on the grounds of national parks and monuments, scenic parkways, preserves, historic sites, and other areas. For example, NPS special agents investigate violations of the Archaeological Resources Protection Act, Endangered Species Act, and Migratory Bird Treaty Act; NPS recreation and use violations; hazardous waste disposal and other environmental crimes; marijuana cultivation and other drug offenses; vandalism; arson; and other property and personal crimes. NPS special agents also participate in local and regional drug task force operations, and conduct investigations jointly with agencies such as the U.S. Fish and Wildlife Service, U.S. Park Police, Bureau of Land Management, Department of Interior Office of Inspector General, Environmental Protection Agency, Bureau of Indian Affairs, and Drug Enforcement Administration. They are authorized to conduct surveillance and undercover operations, carry firearms, make arrests, execute search warrants, and serve subpoenas.

NPS special agents are covered under special retirement provisions for law enforcement officers, and they qualify for 25 percent Law Enforcement Availability Pay.

Qualifications and Salary Levels

GS-5: Completion of a four-year course of study leading to a bachelor's degree; or three years of general experience, one year of which was equivalent to at least GS-4. **GS-7:** One full year of graduate education, or superior academic achievement during undergraduate studies, or one year of specialized experience equivalent to at least GS-5. **GS-9:** A master's degree, or two years of graduate education, or one year of specialized experience equivalent to at least GS-7. **GS-11:** A Ph.D. or equivalent doctoral degree, or three years of graduate education, or one year of specialized experience equivalent to at least GS-9. **GS-12:** One year of specialized experience equivalent to at least GS-11. **GS-13:** One year of specialized experience equivalent to at least GS-12.

Applicants can use equivalent combinations of specialized experience and education to meet total experience requirements. Eyesight requirements include uncorrected distant vision not worse than 20/100 (Snellen) in each eye, and corrected binocular distant vision not worse than 20/20; normal depth perception and peripheral vision; and the ability to distinguish basic colors. Candidates who have undergone LASIK eye surgery must be free from residual effects three months after surgery, while those who have had other forms of refractive eye surgery must be free from residual effects one year after surgery. Hearing loss must not exceed 30 decibels in either ear at 500, 1000, or 2000 Hertz, and 40 decibels in either ear at 3000 Hertz. (Hearing aids cannot be used during the test.) The application process includes a drug screening test, background investigation, security clearance determination, and medical examination.

Training

Initial training for NPS special agents consists of the 11-week Criminal Investigator Training Program at the Federal Law Enforcement Training Center in Glynco, Georgia (see chapter 16). Ongoing in-service training includes a minimum of 40 hours of coursework annually that covers subjects such as environmental crimes, covert wildlife investigations, Archaeological Resources Protection Act violations, drug trafficking, and background investigations.

Contact: Division of Personnel Management; National Park Service; Department of the Interior; 1849 C St. NW; Washington, DC 20240; phone: (202) 208-6843; Internet: www.nps.gov/

Special Agent (GS-1811)
Office of Inspector General, U.S. Department of the Interior

The Department of the Interior (DOI) manages the nation's public lands and minerals, national parks, national wildlife refuges, and western water resources, and upholds federal trust responsibilities to Native American tribes. Special agents of the DOI Office of Inspector General (OIG) investigate criminal, civil, and administrative matters that could compromise the Department's mission or threaten the integrity of DOI programs.

Special agents serving with DOI-OIG investigate allegations of waste, fraud, abuse, and mismanagement in the programs and operations of agencies such as the National Park Service, U.S. Fish and Wildlife Service, Bureau of Indian Affairs, and Bureau of Reclamation. The majority of DOI-OIG investigations are concerned with contractors, grantees, firms, or individuals doing business with DOI, or the Department's employees who have access to or responsibility for monies or financial systems. These investigations often focus on offenses such as false claims, obtaining loans by fraudulent means, grant fraud, using government computers to view pornography, and workers' compensation fraud. DOI-OIG special agents are authorized to conduct surveillance and undercover operations, carry firearms, make arrests, execute search warrants, and serve subpoenas. They conduct investigations jointly with agencies such as the FBI; Defense Criminal Investigative Service; Environmental Protection Agency; IRS Criminal Investigation Division; and other federal, state, and local law enforcement and regulatory agencies.

DOI-OIG special agents are covered under special retirement provisions for law enforcement officers, and they qualify for 25 percent Law Enforcement Availability Pay.

Qualifications and Salary Levels

GS-5: Completion of a four-year course of study leading to a bachelor's degree; or three years of general experience, one year of which was equivalent to at least GS-4. **GS-7:** One full year of graduate education, or superior academic achievement during undergraduate studies, or one year of specialized experience equivalent to at least GS-5. **GS-9:** A master's degree, or two years of graduate education, or one year of specialized experience equivalent to at least GS-7. **GS-11:** A Ph.D. or equivalent doctoral degree, or three years of graduate education, or one year of specialized experience equivalent to at least GS-9. **GS-12:** One year of specialized experience equivalent to at least GS-11. **GS-13:** One year of specialized experience equivalent to at least GS-12.

Equivalent combinations of education and experience can be used to meet minimum experience requirements. Applicants must be at least 21 years of age and under age 37. However, candidates over age 37 who have previous service creditable under special law enforcement retirement provisions also may be eligible. Eyesight requirements include good distant vision in each eye, near vision that is sufficient to read print the size of typewritten characters, normal depth perception and peripheral vision, and the ability to distinguish basic colors. Eyeglasses and contact lenses are permitted. Hearing loss must not exceed 35 decibels at the 1000, 2000, and 3000 Hertz levels. Tentative appointees must qualify for a security clearance and undergo a background investigation, drug screening test, and medical examination.

Training

DOI-OIG special agents attend the 11-week Criminal Investigator Training Program at the Federal Law Enforcement Training Center (FLETC) in Glynco, Georgia (see chapter 16). They attend various in-service training programs that focus on DOI program investigations, surveillance and undercover operations, conservation law, archaeological resources investigations, firearms proficiency, defensive tactics, and other subjects. DOI-OIG special agents also can attend the three-week Inspector General Investigator Training Program at FLETC (see chapter 16).

Contact: Office of Inspector General; U.S. Department of the Interior; 1849 C St. NW; Washington, DC 20240; phone: (202) 208-5313; Internet: www.oig.doi.gov/

Special Agent (GS-1811)
United States Fish and Wildlife Service, U.S. Department of the Interior

The U.S. Fish and Wildlife Service (FWS) is responsible for the conservation, protection, and enhancement of fish, wildlife, migratory birds, endangered species, and certain marine mammals, and their habitat. FWS manages more than 95 million acres of land and water resources consisting of wildlife refuges, wetlands, fish hatcheries, inland sport fisheries, and other special management areas.

FWS special agents investigate a wide range of violations of federal fish and wildlife laws, such as those concerning the illegal taking, importing, and commercialization of wildlife. These laws are covered under the Endangered Species Act, Convention on International Trade in Endangered Species, Lacey Act, Airborne Hunting Act, and other laws. The violations investigated by FWS special agents often are committed by organized groups that carry out clandestine operations and complex conspiracies. Investigations pertain to international and domestic smuggling rings involved in illegal trafficking of protected species, violations of federal migratory game bird hunting laws, illegal importing and commercialization of wildlife, habitat destruction, hazardous materials dumping and other environmental crimes, and other offenses. FWS special agents are authorized to conduct surveillance and undercover operations, carry firearms, make arrests, execute search warrants, and serve subpoenas. They coordinate investigations and share intelligence information with agencies such as the National Marine Fisheries Service; Department of Interior Office of Inspector General (OIG); Department of Agriculture OIG; and other federal, state, local, tribal, and foreign agencies.

FWS special agents are covered under special retirement provisions for law enforcement officers, and they qualify for 25 percent Law Enforcement Availability Pay.

Qualifications and Salary Levels

GS-7: One full year of graduate education, or superior academic achievement during undergraduate studies, or one year of specialized experience equivalent to at least

GS-5. **GS-9:** A master's degree, or two years of graduate education, or one year of specialized experience equivalent to at least GS-7. **GS-11:** A Ph.D. or equivalent doctoral degree, or three years of graduate education, or one year of specialized experience equivalent to at least GS-9. **GS-12:** One year of specialized experience equivalent to at least GS-11. **GS-13:** One year of specialized experience equivalent to at least GS-12.

Qualifying education can be substituted for experience, and vice versa. Eyesight requirements include uncorrected distant vision not worse than 20/100 (Snellen) in each eye, and corrected binocular distant vision not worse than 20/20; normal depth perception and peripheral vision; and the ability to distinguish basic colors. Candidates who have undergone LASIK eye surgery must be free from residual effects three months after surgery, while those who have had other forms of refractive eye surgery must be free from residual effects one year after surgery. Hearing loss must not exceed 30 decibels in either ear at 500, 1000, or 2000 Hertz, and 40 decibels in either ear at 3000 Hertz. (Hearing aids cannot be used during the test.) The application process includes a drug screening test, medical examination, background investigation, and security clearance determination.

Training

FWS special agents attend the 11-week Criminal Investigator Training Program at the Federal Law Enforcement Training Center (FLETC) in Glynco, Georgia (see chapter 16), followed by the eight-week FWS Special Agent Basic School at FLETC, which covers the laws and treaties enforced by FWS law enforcement personnel, FWS policies and regulations, wildlife identification, law enforcement authority, and other agency-specific topics. In-service training includes at least 40 hours of coursework annually, including instruction in covert wildlife investigations, undercover operations, first aid and CPR, firearms proficiency, arrest techniques, and defensive tactics.

Contact: Office of Law Enforcement; United States Fish and Wildlife Service; U.S. Department of the Interior; 4401 N. Fairfax Dr.; Arlington, VA 22203; phone: (703) 358-1949; Internet: www.fws.gov/le/

Special Agent (GS-1811)
Bureau of Alcohol, Tobacco, Firearms and Explosives; U.S. Department of Justice

The Bureau of Alcohol, Tobacco, Firearms and Explosives (ATF) is dedicated to preventing terrorism and reducing violent crime by enforcing federal criminal laws; regulating the firearms and explosives industries; and providing investigative, forensic, and training assistance to federal, state, local, military, and foreign law enforcement agencies. ATF's investigative and enforcement operations are geared primarily toward reducing crime involving firearms and explosives, acts of arson, and illegal trafficking of alcohol and tobacco products.

ATF special agents investigate violations of the Gun Control Act of 1968, National Firearms Act, Arms Export Control Act, and many other laws. ATF special agents devote special attention to the investigation of illegal trafficking of firearms, armed narcotics traffickers, repeat offenders who possess firearms, arson-for-profit schemes affecting interstate commerce, ethnic street gangs, animal rights groups and environmental extremists involved in arson and domestic terrorism activities, and other matters. Many ATF special agents are assigned to the agency's national and international response teams, which assist other law enforcement agencies with crime scene processing and the investigation of significant arson and explosives incidents. ATF special agents are authorized to conduct surveillance and undercover operations, carry firearms, make arrests, execute search warrants, and serve subpoenas. Investigations frequently are conducted jointly with agencies such as the Drug Enforcement Administration; U.S. Marshals Service; FBI; Department of Agriculture Office of Inspector General (OIG); IRS Criminal Investigation Division; and other federal, state, local, and military law enforcement and regulatory agencies.

ATF special agents are covered under special retirement provisions for law enforcement officers, and they qualify for 25 percent Law Enforcement Availability Pay.

Qualifications and Salary Levels

GS-5: Completion of a four-year course of study leading to a bachelor's degree; or three years of general experience, one year of which was equivalent to at least GS-4. **GS-7:** One full year of graduate education, or superior academic achievement during undergraduate studies, or one year of specialized experience equivalent to at least GS-5. **GS-9:** A master's degree, or two years of graduate education, or one year of specialized experience equivalent to at least GS-7. **GS-11:** A Ph.D. or equivalent doctoral degree, or three years of graduate education, or one year of specialized experience equivalent to at least GS-9. **GS-12:** One year of specialized experience equivalent to at least GS-11. **GS-13:** One year of specialized experience equivalent to at least GS-12.

Qualifying education can be substituted for experience, and vice versa. Applicants must be at least 21 years of age and under age 37. However, candidates over age 37 who have previous service creditable under special law enforcement retirement provisions also may be eligible. Eyesight requirements include uncorrected distant vision not worse than 20/100 (Snellen) in each eye, and corrected distant vision not worse than 20/30 in one eye and 20/20 in the other eye; normal depth perception and peripheral vision; the ability to distinguish shades of color; and near vision sufficient to read Jaeger type 2 at 14 inches. Candidates who have undergone LASIK eye surgery must be free from residual effects three months after surgery, while those who have had other forms of refractive eye surgery must be free from residual effects one year after surgery. Hearing loss must not exceed 30 decibels at 500, 1000, and 2000 Hertz. Candidates must pass the Treasury Enforcement Agent Examination (see chapter 3), undergo a background investigation and medical examination, qualify for a top-secret security clearance, and pass a polygraph examination and drug test prior to appointment.

Training

Basic training for newly hired ATF special agents is a six-month process, including the 11-week Criminal Investigator Training Program at the Federal Law Enforcement Training Center (FLETC) in Glynco, Georgia (see chapter 16), followed by the 14-week ATF Special Agent Basic Training (SABT) program at FLETC. The SABT course focuses on firearms laws, explosives, surveillance, undercover operations, technical investigative equipment, and other subjects pertaining to ATF enforcement operations. ATF special agents also attend a variety of in-service courses that focus on similar subjects and topics related to special assignments.

Contact: Bureau of Alcohol, Tobacco, Firearms and Explosives; U.S. Department of Justice; 650 Massachusetts Ave. NW—Room 4100; Washington, DC 20226; phone: (202) 927-5690; Internet: www.atf.gov/; e-mail: persdiv@atf.gov

Special Agent (GS-1811)
Drug Enforcement Administration, U.S. Department of Justice

The Drug Enforcement Administration (DEA) is the lead federal agency responsible for enforcing the nation's narcotics and controlled substances laws and regulations. To accomplish its mission, DEA special agents are strategically placed along known routes of illicit drug trafficking, including more than 200 U.S. cities and 79 foreign posts of duty in 58 countries. The DEA manages a national drug intelligence system in cooperation with federal, state, local, and foreign officials to collect, analyze, and disseminate strategic and operational drug intelligence information.

DEA special agents enforce major violations of the Controlled Substances Act through complex investigations of individuals and organizations involved in the growing, manufacture, or distribution of controlled substances. DEA special agents pursue sophisticated organized criminal enterprises, criminal gangs, and others through carefully planned investigations that involve intelligence operations, extensive surveillance and undercover operations, infiltration of illicit drug channels, working closely with informants, financial analysis, and seizure of drug trafficking proceeds. Veteran DEA special agents can be assigned to posts overseas. DEA special agents often participate in task force and joint operations with agencies such as the IRS Criminal Investigation Division; U.S. Immigration and Customs Enforcement; U.S. Coast Guard; Bureau of Alcohol, Tobacco, Firearms and Explosives; and other federal, state, local, military, and foreign law enforcement agencies. They are authorized to conduct surveillance and undercover operations, carry firearms, make arrests, execute search warrants, and serve subpoenas.

DEA special agents are covered under special retirement provisions for law enforcement officers, and they qualify for 25 percent Law Enforcement Availability Pay.

Qualifications and Salary Levels

GS-7: One full year of graduate education, or superior academic achievement during undergraduate studies, or one year of specialized experience equivalent to at least GS-5. **GS-9:** A master's degree, or two years of graduate education, or one year of specialized experience equivalent to at least GS-7. **GS-11:** A Ph.D. or equivalent doctoral degree, or three years of graduate education, or one year of specialized experience equivalent to at least GS-9. **GS-12:** One year of specialized experience equivalent to at least GS-11. **GS-13:** One year of specialized experience equivalent to at least GS-12.

Equivalent combinations of education and experience can be used to meet minimum experience requirements. Applicants must be at least 21 years of age and under age 37. However, candidates over age 37 who have previous service creditable under special law enforcement retirement provisions also may be eligible. Eyesight requirements include uncorrected binocular distant vision not worse than 20/200 (Snellen), and corrected distant vision not worse than 20/20 in one eye and 20/40 in the other eye; normal depth perception and peripheral vision; and the ability to distinguish basic colors. Hearing loss must not exceed 35 decibels at the 1000, 2000, and 3000 Hertz levels. The application process includes a drug screening test, medical examination, physical task test, background investigation, polygraph examination, psychological assessment, and top-secret security clearance determination.

Training

Initial training for DEA special agents includes the 16-week DEA Basic Agent Training program in Quantico, Virginia (see chapter 16). In-service training includes the one-week Advanced Agent Training School at the DEA Academy, which includes instruction in electronic surveillance techniques, confidential informants, tactical training, legal updates, and other topics. Other in-service training is concerned with subjects such as interviewing techniques, ethics and integrity, financial investigations, clandestine laboratory operations, asset forfeiture, firearms proficiency, and undercover operations.

Contact: Recruiting information can be obtained from any DEA field office, or by contacting the Office of Personnel; Drug Enforcement Administration; U.S. Department of Justice; 2401 Jefferson Davis Hwy.; Alexandria, VA 22301; phone: (202) 307-1000; Internet: www.dea.gov/.

Special Agent (GS-1811)
Federal Bureau of Investigation, U.S. Department of Justice

The Federal Bureau of Investigation (FBI) investigates violations of federal criminal law; protects the nation from foreign intelligence and terrorist activities; and provides leadership and law enforcement assistance to federal, state, local, and international agencies. The FBI is responsible for investigating all federal crimes that have not been specifically assigned by Congress to other federal agencies. In other words, the Bureau is the lead federal agency for investigations of crimes such as kidnapping and bank robbery, although the U.S. Secret Service investigates currency counterfeiting, the Department of Agriculture Office of Inspector General handles food stamp trafficking investigations, the Postal Inspection Service investigates mail fraud, and so on. FBI operations are based in 56 field offices nationwide, about 400 satellite offices known as Resident Agencies, specialized field installations, and foreign liaison posts known as Legal Attaches.

FBI special agents investigate more than 260 federal statutes, with emphasis on terrorism, foreign counterintelligence, cybercrimes, public corruption, civil rights violations, organized crime enterprises, white-collar offenses, and violent crime. Within these priority areas, FBI investigations focus on racketeering enterprises, domestic security, financial institution fraud and embezzlement, healthcare fraud and other forms of fraud against the government, air piracy, environmental crimes, copyright matters, bankruptcy fraud, homicide, and many other offenses. FBI special agents are organized into investigative squads that specialize in certain types of crimes. They also can be assigned to special response units, such as the Bureau's scuba team, evidence response team, hazardous materials unit, hostage rescue team, special weapons and tactics teams, and crisis negotiation unit, among others. FBI special agents conduct many investigations through task force or joint operations with other law enforcement agencies, and through cooperation with law enforcement agencies in foreign countries. They are authorized to conduct surveillance and undercover operations, carry firearms, make arrests, execute search warrants, and serve subpoenas.

FBI special agents are covered under special retirement provisions for law enforcement officers, and they qualify for 25 percent Law Enforcement Availability Pay.

Qualifications and Salary Levels

FBI special agents normally enter service at the GS-10 level, regardless of prior education or experience. Applicants must have a bachelor's degree and qualify under at least one of five entry programs, including Law, which requires a Juris Doctorate degree from an accredited resident law school; Accounting, which requires a bachelor's degree in accounting or a related discipline; Language, which requires a bachelor's degree in any discipline and fluency in a foreign language for which the FBI has a current need; Computer Science/Information Technology, which requires a bachelor's degree related to computer science or information technology, or a bachelor's degree in electrical engineering, or certification as either a Cisco Certified Network Professional (CCNP) or Cisco Certified Internetworking Expert (CCIE); and Diversified, which requires a bachelor's degree in any discipline and three years of full-time work experience, or an advanced degree and two years of full-time work experience. The FBI gives priority to applicants who possess certain critical skills, depending on the needs of the Bureau at any time. Applicants must be at least 23 years of age and under age 37. However, candidates over age 37 who have previous service creditable under special law enforcement retirement provisions also may be eligible.

Eyesight requirements include uncorrected binocular distant vision not worse than 20/200 (Snellen), and corrected distant vision not worse than 20/20 in one eye and 20/40 in the other eye. However, the FBI may grant a waiver to applicants with uncorrected vision worse than 20/200 if (a) soft contact lenses are worn and have been worn for a period of more than one year, (b) the minimum corrected vision requirement (shown above) has been met, and (c) there are no indications of corneal change that might require discontinuation of contact lenses in the future. Applicants seeking a waiver are evaluated on a case-by-case basis, and no formal Snellen scale limit has been established. Normal depth perception and peripheral vision and the ability to distinguish basic colors also are required. Applicants who have undergone surgical vision correction are evaluated on a case-by-case basis. Hearing loss must not exceed 25 decibels at 1000, 2000, and 3000 Hertz; a single reading of 35 decibels at 1000, 2000, and 3000 Hertz; a single reading of 35 decibels at 500 Hertz; and a single reading of 45 decibels at 4000 Hertz. Candidates must qualify for a top-secret security clearance and pass a background investigation, polygraph examination, drug screening test, medical examination, and battery of tests (see chapter 3).

Training

FBI special agents attend the 18-week New Agents' Training Program at the FBI Academy in Quantico, Virginia (see chapter 16). They also attend various in-service training programs at the FBI Academy and other locations throughout their careers depending on the needs of individual agents, their responsibilities and special assignments, and the needs of the Bureau at any time. These include courses that focus on counterterrorism, counterintelligence, cybercrime, leadership, ethics, information technology, critical incident stress, hate crimes, bloodborne pathogens, and other subjects.

Contact: Recruiting information can be obtained from any FBI field office, or by contacting the Federal Bureau of Investigation; U.S. Department of Justice; 935 Pennsylvania Ave. NW; Washington, DC 20535; phone: (202) 324-2727; Internet: www.fbi.gov/.

Special Agent (GS-1811)
Office of Inspector General, U.S. Department of Justice

The U.S. Department of Justice (DOJ) is the world's largest law office and the central agency for enforcement of federal laws. DOJ agencies play a key role in protecting the nation against criminals and subversion, ensuring healthy business competition, safeguarding consumers, and enforcing drug and immigration laws. The DOJ Office of Inspector General (OIG) conducts independent audits, investigations, inspections, and special reviews of DOJ personnel and programs to detect and deter waste, fraud, abuse, and misconduct, and to promote integrity, economy, efficiency, and effectiveness in Department operations.

Special agents serving with DOJ-OIG investigate violations of laws and ethical standards that govern DOJ employees, grantees, and contractors relating to operations of the FBI; Drug Enforcement Administration; U.S. Marshals Service; Bureau of Alcohol Tobacco, Firearms and Explosives; U.S. Attorney's Office; Federal Bureau of Prisons; and other DOJ components. Employee integrity investigations focus on embezzlement, theft, unlawful disclosure of information, excessive force during arrests and other civil rights violations, workers' compensation fraud, bribery of U.S. Customs and Border Protection officers, abuse of prisoners, smuggling contraband into prisons, misuse of government vehicles or other property, and many other offenses. External investigations most often are concerned with fraud committed by DOJ contractors and grantees. DOJ-OIG special agents are authorized to conduct surveillance and undercover operations, carry firearms, make arrests, execute search warrants, and serve subpoenas. They conduct many investigations jointly with the FBI and other federal, state, and local law enforcement agencies.

DOJ-OIG special agents are covered under special retirement provisions for law enforcement officers, and they qualify for 25 percent Law Enforcement Availability Pay.

Qualifications and Salary Levels

GS-5: Completion of a four-year course of study leading to a bachelor's degree; or three years of general experience, one year of which was equivalent to at least GS-4. **GS-7:** One full year of graduate education, or superior academic achievement during undergraduate studies, or one year of specialized experience equivalent to at least GS-5. **GS-9:** A master's degree, or two years of graduate education, or one year of specialized experience equivalent to at least GS-7. **GS-11:** A Ph.D. or equivalent doctoral degree, or three years of graduate education, or one year of specialized experience equivalent to at least GS-9. **GS-12:** One year of specialized experience equivalent to at least GS-11. **GS-13:** One year of specialized experience equivalent to at least GS-12.

Experience and education can be combined to meet total experience requirements. Applicants must be at least 21 years of age and under age 37. However, candidates over age 37 who have previous service creditable under special law enforcement retirement provisions also may be eligible. Eyesight requirements include good distant vision in each eye, near vision that is sufficient to read print the size of typewritten characters, normal depth perception and peripheral vision, and the ability to distinguish basic colors. Eyeglasses and contact lenses are permitted. Hearing loss must not exceed 35 decibels at the 1000, 2000, and 3000 Hertz levels. Candidates must successfully undergo a background investigation, qualify for a top-secret security clearance, and pass a drug test and medical examination prior to appointment.

Training

Initial training for DOJ-OIG special agents includes the 11-week Criminal Investigator Training Program at the Federal Law Enforcement Training Center (FLETC) in Glynco, Georgia (see chapter 16). They also attend a variety of in-service courses that are concerned with white-collar crime, computer forensics, criminal and civil law, investigative techniques, technical investigative equipment, and other subjects. Many DOJ-OIG special agents also attend the three-week Inspector General Investigator Training Program at FLETC (see chapter 16).

Contact: Office of the Inspector General; U.S. Department of Justice; 1425 New York Ave.—Suite 7100; Washington, DC 20530; phone: (202) 616-4760; Internet: www.usdoj.gov/oig/

Special Agent (GS-1811)
Office of Inspector General, U.S. Department of Labor

The U.S. Department of Labor (DOL) administers a variety of federal labor laws guaranteeing workers' rights to safe and healthful working conditions, freedom from employment discrimination, unemployment insurance, a minimum hourly wage and overtime pay, and workers' compensation. Special agents of the DOL Office of Inspector General (OIG) conduct investigations to identify fraud and other forms of criminal or improper activity in DOL programs and operations.

DOL-OIG investigations pertain to wrongdoing in more than 100 DOL programs concerned with pension and welfare benefit plans; the unemployment insurance system; employment and training services; occupational safety and health; veterans' employment and training services; mine safety; and provisions of the Federal Employees Compensation Act, Davis-Bacon Act, Black Lung Benefits Act, and other laws. DOL-OIG special agents frequently investigate allegations of contract fraud, theft, bribery, kickbacks, false claims, healthcare provider fraud, and violations of law and DOL standards of conduct by Department employees. Special agents assigned to DOL-OIG's Labor Racketeering Section investigate organized crime activities, labor racketeering, extortion by labor union officials, and embezzlement from employee benefit plans. DOL-OIG special agents are authorized to conduct surveillance and undercover operations, carry firearms, make arrests, execute search warrants, and serve subpoenas. They work closely with agencies such as the FBI; Housing and Urban Development OIG; Social Security Administration OIG; Pension Benefit Guaranty Corporation OIG; and other federal, state, and local law enforcement and regulatory agencies.

DOL-OIG special agents are covered under special retirement provisions for law enforcement officers, and they qualify for 25 percent Law Enforcement Availability Pay.

Qualifications and Salary Levels

GS-5: Completion of a four-year course of study leading to a bachelor's degree; or three years of general experience, one year of which was equivalent to at least GS-4. **GS-7:** One full year of graduate education, or superior academic achievement during undergraduate studies, or one year of specialized experience equivalent to at least GS-5. **GS-9:** A master's degree, or two years of graduate education, or one year of specialized experience equivalent to at least GS-7. **GS-11:** A Ph.D. or equivalent doctoral degree, or three years of graduate education, or one year of specialized experience equivalent to at least GS-9. **GS-12:** One year of specialized experience equivalent to at least GS-11. **GS-13:** One year of specialized experience equivalent to at least GS-12.

Equivalent combinations of education and experience can be used to meet minimum experience requirements. Applicants must be at least 21 years of age and under age 37. However, candidates over age 37 who have previous service creditable under special law enforcement retirement provisions also may be eligible. Eyesight requirements include good distant vision in each eye, near vision that is sufficient to read print the size of typewritten characters, normal depth perception and peripheral vision, and the ability to distinguish basic colors. Eyeglasses and contact lenses are permitted. Hearing loss must not exceed 35 decibels at the 1000, 2000, and 3000 Hertz levels. Tentative appointees must qualify for a security clearance and pass a background investigation, drug screening test, and medical examination.

Training

DOL-OIG special agents attend the 11-week Criminal Investigator Training Program at the Federal Law Enforcement Training Center (FLETC) in Glynco, Georgia (see chapter 16). Topics of in-service training include white-collar crime, labor laws, contract fraud, internal investigations, healthcare provider fraud, legal issues and updates, financial investigations, first aid and CPR, firearms proficiency, arrest techniques, use of force, and other subjects. Many DOL-OIG special agents attend the Inspector General Investigator Training Program at FLETC (see chapter 16).

Contact: Office of Inspector General; U.S. Department of Labor; 200 Constitution Ave. NW; Washington, DC 20210; phone: (202) 693-5100; Internet: www.oig.dol.gov/

Special Agent (GS-1811)
Office of Inspector General, National Aeronautics and Space Administration

The National Aeronautics and Space Administration (NASA) develops, constructs, tests, and operates aeronautical and space vehicles, and conducts research relating to the exploration of space and flight within and outside the earth's atmosphere. NASA's Office of Inspector General (OIG) investigates allegations of crime, cybercrime, fraud, waste, abuse, and misconduct affecting NASA programs, projects, operations, and resources.

Special agents serving with NASA-OIG conduct investigations relating to NASA programs, operations, contractors, grantees, and employees. A significant amount of OIG activity and resources are directed toward the investigation of procurement irregularities and contract fraud. These investigations pertain to offenses such as false claims, bid rigging, falsification of contractors' certified payrolls, fraudulent deviation from NASA contract specifications, product substitution, false certifications of inspections and testing, billing for unallowable costs, and other schemes. Investigations of NASA personnel are concerned with offenses such as embezzlement, theft or misuse of government property or purchase cards, downloading pornography on NASA computers, kickbacks, conflict of interest, and travel voucher fraud. NASA-OIG special agents also investigate unlawful intrusion into NASA computer and electronic communication systems. They are authorized to conduct surveillance and undercover operations, carry firearms, make arrests, execute search warrants, and serve subpoenas. Investigations often are conducted with agencies such as the FBI; Defense Criminal Investigative Service; Naval Criminal Investigative Service; Air Force OSI; Army Criminal Investigations Command; Social Security Administration OIG; and other federal, state, and local law enforcement agencies.

NASA-OIG special agents are covered under special retirement provisions for law enforcement officers, and they qualify for 25 percent Law Enforcement Availability Pay.

Qualifications and Salary Levels

GS-7: One full year of graduate education, or superior academic achievement during undergraduate studies, or one year of specialized experience equivalent to at least

GS-5. **GS-9:** A master's degree, or two years of graduate education, or one year of specialized experience equivalent to at least GS-7. **GS-11:** A Ph.D. or equivalent doctoral degree, or three years of graduate education, or one year of specialized experience equivalent to at least GS-9. **GS-12:** One year of specialized experience equivalent to at least GS-11. **GS-13:** One year of specialized experience equivalent to at least GS-12.

Qualifying education can be substituted for experience, and vice versa. Applicants must be at least 21 years of age and under age 37. However, candidates over age 37 who have previous service creditable under special law enforcement retirement provisions also may be eligible. Eyesight requirements include good distant vision in each eye, near vision that is sufficient to read print the size of typewritten characters, normal depth perception and peripheral vision, and the ability to distinguish basic colors. Eyeglasses and contact lenses are permitted. Hearing loss must not exceed 35 decibels at the 1000, 2000, and 3000 Hertz levels. Candidates must successfully undergo a background investigation, qualify for a security clearance, and pass a drug test and medical examination prior to appointment.

Training

NASA-OIG special agents attend the 11-week Criminal Investigator Training Program at the Federal Law Enforcement Training Center (FLETC) in Glynco, Georgia (see chapter 16). They also attend in-service training programs that cover subjects such as contract and procurement fraud, search and seizure in the workplace, handling and processing of seized computer evidence, export control laws and regulations, internal investigations, use of force, and other subjects. NASA-OIG special agents also attend the three-week Inspector General Investigator Training Program at FLETC (see chapter 16).

Contact: Office of Inspector General; National Aeronautics and Space Administration; 300 E St. SW; Washington, DC 20546; phone: (202) 358-1500; Internet: www.oig.nasa.gov/

Special Agent (GS-1811)
Office of Inspector General, National Archives and Records Administration

The National Archives and Records Administration (NARA) is responsible for managing federal government records, maintaining historically valuable documents, managing the Presidential Library System, and operating educational programs and exhibits for the benefit of the public, researchers, scholars, educators, and their students. The NARA Office of Inspector General (OIG) performs investigations of criminal, civil, and administrative misconduct related to NARA programs and operations.

NARA-OIG special agents investigate fraud, theft, violations of employee standards of conduct, and other forms of criminal or improper activity relating to NARA programs and personnel, contracts, contractors and their employees, and grantees. Many investigations involve allegations of fraud or other misconduct by NARA personnel, including theft, misuse of government purchase cards, downloading pornography on NARA computers, time and attendance fraud, unauthorized release of government records, and other allegations or offenses. Investigations of contract and grant fraud focus on false claims, false certifications, false statements on applications and other documents, fraudulent deviation from or failure to comply with contract specifications, and other crimes. NARA-OIG special agents also investigate intrusion into NARA computer systems; bomb threats; threats sent by mail or e-mail; arson; and theft of records, historical documents, artwork, classified documents, and other NARA property and assets. NARA special agents are authorized to conduct surveillance and undercover operations, carry firearms, make arrests, execute search warrants, and serve subpoenas. Some investigations are conducted jointly with the FBI, Federal Protective Service, General Services Administration, and other law enforcement agencies.

NARA-OIG special agents are covered under special retirement provisions for law enforcement officers, and they qualify for 25 percent Law Enforcement Availability Pay.

Qualifications and Salary Levels

GS-7: One full year of graduate education, or superior academic achievement during undergraduate studies, or one year of specialized experience equivalent to at least GS-5. **GS-9:** A master's degree, or two years of graduate education, or one year of specialized experience equivalent to at least GS-7. **GS-11:** A Ph.D. or equivalent doctoral degree, or three years of graduate education, or one year of specialized experience equivalent to at least GS-9. **GS-12:** One year of specialized experience equivalent to at least GS-11. **GS-13:** One year of specialized experience equivalent to at least GS-12.

Applicants can use equivalent combinations of specialized experience and education to meet total experience requirements. Applicants must be at least 21 years of age and under age 37. However, candidates over age 37 who have previous service creditable under special law enforcement retirement provisions also may be eligible. Eyesight requirements include good distant vision in each eye, near vision that is sufficient to read print the size of typewritten characters, normal depth perception and peripheral vision, and the ability to distinguish basic colors. Eyeglasses and contact lenses are permitted. Hearing loss must not exceed 35 decibels at the 1000, 2000, and 3000 Hertz levels. The application process includes a drug screening test, medical examination, background investigation, and security clearance determination.

Training

NARA-OIG special agents attend the 11-week Criminal Investigator Training Program at the Federal Law Enforcement Training Center (FLETC) in Glynco, Georgia (see chapter 16). They also attend in-service training programs that cover subjects concerned with contract and procurement fraud, internal investigations, criminal and civil law, financial investigations, computer forensics, arrest techniques, defensive tactics, use of force, and firearms proficiency. NARA-OIG special agents also can attend the three-week Inspector General Investigator Training Program at FLETC (see chapter 16).

Contact: Office of Inspector General; National Archives and Records Administration; 8601 Adelphi Rd.—Room 1300; College Park, MD 20740; phone: (301) 837-3000; Internet: www.nara.gov/oig/investigations.html/

Special Agent
AMTRAK Office of Inspector General, National Railroad Passenger Corporation

The National Railroad Passenger Corporation (AMTRAK) Office of Inspector General (OIG) is responsible for detecting and investigating fraud, waste, and abuse concerning AMTRAK programs and operations. AMTRAK-OIG special agents are based in Washington, DC; Baltimore; Wilmington; Philadelphia; New York; Boston; Chicago; and Los Angeles.

The majority of investigations carried out by AMTRAK-OIG special agents are concerned with criminal activity and other misconduct by AMTRAK employees. These investigations focus largely on theft of cash funds and embezzlement, although they also target offenses such as time and attendance fraud, kickbacks, abuse of position, and accessing pornographic Web sites using AMTRAK computers. Among the most common investigations are those concerned with theft of cash fares by conductors and assistant conductors, embezzlement by ticket agents, and theft of cash funds by food service personnel. AMTRAK-OIG special agents also investigate fraud and other crimes committed by AMTRAK contractors, vendors, and customers, including cases involving tickets purchased with stolen credit cards, forgery or counterfeiting of tickets and monthly rail passes, and fraud committed by AMTRAK contractors. Some investigations are conducted jointly with agencies such as the Railroad Retirement Board OIG; Department of Transportation OIG; Postal Inspection Service; and other federal, state, and local law enforcement and regulatory agencies. AMTRAK-OIG special agents are authorized to carry firearms, make arrests, execute search warrants, and serve subpoenas.

Qualifications and Salary Levels

AMTRAK-OIG special agents are appointed through excepted service hiring processes. The qualifications and salaries of the position are similar to those of GS-1811 special agents at the GS-5 through GS-13 levels with other federal agencies that do not receive Law Enforcement Availability Pay. Eyesight requirements include good distant vision in each eye, near vision that is sufficient to read print the size of typewritten characters, normal depth perception and peripheral vision, and the ability to distinguish basic colors. Eyeglasses and contact lenses are permitted. Hearing loss must not exceed 35 decibels at the 1000, 2000, and 3000 Hertz levels. Tentative appointees must qualify for a security clearance and pass a background investigation, drug screening test, and medical examination.

Training

AMTRAK-OIG special agents attend the 11-week Criminal Investigator Training Program at the Federal Law Enforcement Training Center (FLETC) in Glynco, Georgia (see chapter 16). Ongoing in-service training includes courses such as the two-week Criminal Investigations in an Automated Environment Training Program at FLETC, and training in employee integrity investigations, financial investigations, contract and procurement fraud, terrorism indicators, criminal and civil law, and other subjects. AMTRAK-OIG special agents also attend the three-week Inspector General Investigator Training Program at FLETC (see chapter 16).

Contact: AMTRAK Office of Inspector General; National Railroad Passenger Corporation; 10 G St. NE; Washington, DC 20002; phone: (202) 906-4863; Internet: www.amtrakoig.com/

Special Agent (GS-1811)
Office of Inspector General, National Science Foundation

The National Science Foundation (NSF) is an independent agency that was created to increase the nation's base of scientific and engineering knowledge and its ability to conduct scientific research, and to develop science and engineering education programs. With an annual budget of more than $5 billion, NSF funding accounts for about 20 percent of all federally supported research conducted by America's colleges and universities. The NSF Office of Inspector General (OIG) investigates wrongdoing by organizations and individuals that receive funding from, conduct business with, or are employed by NSF. To accomplish its mission, NSF-OIG also employs scientists to respond to allegations, assist with investigations, and monitor administration of NSF programs.

NSF-OIG special agents conduct investigations relating to NSF proposals, awards, programs, operations, grantees, and employees. These investigations often focus on violations of federal law committed by scientists, researchers, and academic administrators. For example, many investigations focus on overbilling for research expenses or billing for unallowable costs; misappropriation of funds; using grant funds for personal expenses; and embezzlement of grant funds by university administrators, researchers, bookkeepers, or other personnel. Personnel misconduct investigations are concerned with misuse of NSF purchase cards, vehicles, or other government property; time and attendance fraud; bribery; kickbacks; conflict of interest; and other offenses. Investigations often are conducted with agencies such as the FBI, Defense Criminal Investigative Service, National Aeronautics and Space Administration OIG, Department of Education OIG, and other agencies.

NSF-OIG special agents are covered under special retirement provisions for law enforcement officers, and they qualify for 25 percent Law Enforcement Availability Pay.

Qualifications and Salary Levels

GS-5: Completion of a four-year course of study leading to a bachelor's degree; or three years of general experience, one year of which was equivalent to at least GS-4. **GS-7:** One full year of graduate education, or superior academic achievement during undergraduate studies, or one year of specialized experience equivalent to at least GS-5. **GS-9:** A master's degree, or two years of graduate education, or one year of specialized experience equivalent to at least GS-7. **GS-11:** A Ph.D. or equivalent doctoral degree, or three years of graduate education, or one year of specialized experience equivalent to at least GS-9. **GS-12:** One year of specialized experience equivalent to at least GS-11. **GS-13:** One year of specialized experience equivalent to at least GS-12.

Experience and education can be combined to meet total experience requirements. Applicants must be at least 21 years of age and under age 37. However, candidates over age 37 who have previous service creditable under special law enforcement retirement provisions also may be eligible. Eyesight requirements include good distant vision in each eye, near vision that is sufficient to read print the size of typewritten characters, normal depth perception and peripheral vision, and the ability to distinguish basic colors. Eyeglasses and contact lenses are permitted. Hearing loss must not exceed 35 decibels at the 1000, 2000, and 3000 Hertz levels. The application process includes a medical examination and background investigation.

Training

NSF-OIG special agents attend the 11-week Criminal Investigator Training Program at the Federal Law Enforcement Training Center (FLETC) in Glynco, Georgia (see chapter 16). In-service training includes instruction in NSF program fraud, money laundering, financial investigations, interviewing and interrogation, Affirmative Civil Enforcement, employee integrity investigations, and other topics. NSF-OIG special agents also attend the three-week Inspector General Investigator Training Program at FLETC (see chapter 16).

Contact: Office of Inspector General; National Science Foundation; 4201 Wilson Blvd.—Room 1135; Arlington, VA 22230; phone: (703) 292-7100; Internet: www.nsf.gov/oig/; e-mail: info@nsf.gov

Special Agent
Office of Inspector General, U.S. Nuclear Regulatory Commission

The U.S. Nuclear Regulatory Commission (NRC) Office of Inspector General (OIG) is responsible for investigations relating to NRC operations. This agency conducts investigations concerning the integrity of NRC-administered or -financed programs and other activities. NRC-OIG also conducts investigative inspections—known as event inquiries—which examine NRC regulations and identify institutional weaknesses that led to or allowed a problem to occur. Event inquiries do not focus on individual misconduct.

The majority of investigations carried out by NRC-OIG special agents focus on violations of law and misconduct by NRC employees and contractors. Inasmuch as NRC's mission is to protect the health and safety of the public, NRC-OIG special agents place particular emphasis on NRC staff misconduct that could adversely affect the agency's handling of matters related to health and safety. These investigations frequently involve allegations of misconduct by managers, inspectors, and other high-ranking NRC officials whose positions directly affect public health and safety; failure by NRC management to ensure that health and safety matters are appropriately addressed; conflict of interest by NRC employees; favorable or unfavorable treatment of NRC contractors, licensees, or vendors, or those proposing to do business with NRC; acceptance of gratuities; fraud in NRC procurement processes; and other crimes or wrongdoing by NRC employees, contractors, licensees, or vendors. NRC-OIG investigations also are concerned with false claims and overbilling by contractors, licensees, or vendors; fraudulent workers' compensation claims by NRC personnel; unauthorized use of NRC computers; sexual harassment; and other offenses. NRC-OIG special agents are authorized to conduct surveillance and undercover operations, carry firearms, make arrests, execute search warrants, and serve subpoenas. They conduct investigations with agencies such as the FBI, Department of Energy OIG, Department of Labor OIG, and other agencies.

Special agents serving with NRC-OIG are covered under special retirement provisions for law enforcement officers, and they qualify for 25 percent Law Enforcement Availability Pay.

Qualifications and Salary Levels

NRC-OIG special agents are appointed through excepted service hiring processes. The qualifications and salaries of the position are similar to those of GS-1811 special agents at the GS-5 through GS-13 levels with other federal agencies. Applicants must be at least 21 years of age and under age 37. However, candidates over age 37 who have previous service creditable under special law enforcement retirement provisions also may be eligible. Eyesight requirements include good distant vision in each eye, near vision that is sufficient to read print the size of typewritten characters, normal depth perception and peripheral vision, and the ability to distinguish basic colors. Eyeglasses and contact lenses are permitted. Hearing loss must not exceed 35 decibels at the 1000, 2000, and 3000 Hertz levels. Successful completion of a background investigation, drug test, and security clearance process also are required.

Training

NRC-OIG special agents attend the 11-week Criminal Investigator Training Program at the Federal Law Enforcement Training Center (FLETC) in Glynco, Georgia (see chapter 16). They also attend in-service training programs that cover subjects such as radiation safety, nuclear reactor security systems, quality assurance, employee integrity investigations, NRC program investigations, and procurement fraud. Many NRC-OIG special agents also attend the three-week Inspector General Investigator Training Program at FLETC (see chapter 16).

Contact: Office of Inspector General; U.S. Nuclear Regulatory Commission; 11545 Rockville Pike; Rockville, MD 20852; phone: (301) 415-5930; Internet: www.nrc.gov/insp-gen.html/

Special Agent
Office of Investigations, U.S. Nuclear Regulatory Commission

The Office of Investigations (OI) within the U.S. Nuclear Regulatory Commission (NRC) investigates violations, accidents, and incidents occurring at facilities licensed by the NRC. The agency conducts these investigations—which also focus on applicants for NRC licenses and the contractors and vendors of licensees or applicants—to ensure compliance with NRC regulations and federal laws relating to the use of nuclear materials. NRC-OI investigations normally are not concerned with NRC employees or those who have contracts directly with NRC.

Investigations carried out by NRC-OI special agents pertain primarily to organizations that possess radioactive materials, conduct operations involving emission of radiation, or dispose of radioactive waste. These investigations are concerned with public utilities that operate nuclear power plants; fuel-cycle facilities; medical facilities; colleges and universities; organizations that use industrial radiography in construction, oil and gas, utility, and aerospace applications; laboratories; and other organizations. For example, NRC-OI investigations focus on failure to ensure that radiation safety activities are performed in accordance with NRC regulations; failure to provide radiation safety training to licensee personnel; failure to perform required inspections or maintain required records; and other prohibited activities. NRC-OI special agents also investigate allegations of employment discrimination within NRC. All violations are subject to civil enforcement and can also result in criminal prosecution. Although the origins of investigations vary, many are initiated as a result of NRC inspections of licensed facilities. Some investigations are conducted in cooperation with other law enforcement agencies, such as the Defense Criminal Investigative Service, Naval Criminal Investigative Service, and Department of Energy Office of Inspector General. Many NRC-OI special agents participate in antiterrorism advisory councils related to national security concerns and counterterrorism.

NRC-OI special agents are covered under special retirement provisions for federal law enforcement officers, and they are eligible to receive 25 percent Law Enforcement Availability Pay.

Qualifications and Salary Levels

NRC-OI special agents are appointed through excepted service hiring processes. The qualifications and salaries of the position are similar to those of GS-1811 special agents at the GS-5 through GS-13 levels with other federal agencies. Applicants must be at least 21 years of age and under age 37. However, candidates over age 37 who have previous service creditable under special law enforcement retirement provisions also may be eligible. Eyesight requirements include good distant vision in each eye, near vision that is sufficient to read print the size of typewritten characters, normal depth perception and peripheral vision, and the ability to distinguish basic colors. Eyeglasses and contact lenses are permitted. Hearing loss must not exceed 35 decibels at the 1000, 2000, and 3000 Hertz levels. The application process includes a background investigation, drug test, and security clearance determination.

Training

Initial training for NRC-OI special agents includes the 11-week Criminal Investigator Training Program at the Federal Law Enforcement Training Center in Glynco, Georgia (see chapter 16). They also attend in-service training programs that cover subjects such as nuclear reactor construction and operations, radiography systems, quality assurance, radiation safety, nuclear reactor security systems, white-collar crime, interviewing techniques, and other topics.

Contact: Office of Investigations; U.S. Nuclear Regulatory Commission; Washington, DC 20555; phone: (301) 415-2373; Internet: www.nrc.gov/

Special Agent (GS-1811)
Office of Inspector General, U.S. Office of Personnel Management

As the federal government's human resources agency, the U.S. Office of Personnel Management (OPM) is responsible for providing up-to-date federal employment information; for ensuring that the nation's civil service system remains free of political influence and that federal employees are selected and treated fairly and on the basis of merit; and for managing federal retirement systems and the Federal Employees Health Benefits (FEHB) Program.

Special agents of the OPM Office of Inspector General (OIG) investigate fraud, corruption, and other criminal or improper activities relating to the FEHB, Civil Service Retirement System, Federal Employees Retirement System, and other OPM programs and operations. The OPM-OIG investigations division has two components, including the Healthcare and Life Insurance Branch, and the Retirement and Special Investigations Branch. Healthcare fraud cases often pertain to healthcare providers who carry out schemes involving fraudulent billings, including overcharging; billing for services that were unallowable, medically unnecessary, or not performed; coding claims to indicate higher levels of service than actually provided; billing for services provided by unlicensed personnel; and other offenses. Retirement fraud investigations typically target family members who receive retirement benefits after an annuitant's death. OPM-OIG special agents also investigate employee misconduct, including crimes such as embezzlement, larceny, misappropriation of funds, conflict of interest, and bribery. OPM-OIG special agents are authorized to conduct surveillance and undercover operations, carry firearms, make arrests, execute search warrants, and serve subpoenas. Investigations are conducted on a regular basis with agencies such as the FBI, Health and Human Services OIG, and other law enforcement and regulatory agencies.

OPM-OIG special agents are covered under special retirement provisions for law enforcement officers, and they qualify for 25 percent Law Enforcement Availability Pay.

Qualifications and Salary Levels

GS-5: Completion of a four-year course of study leading to a bachelor's degree; or three years of general experience, one year of which was equivalent to at least GS-4. **GS-7:** One full year of graduate education, or superior academic achievement during undergraduate studies, or one year of specialized experience equivalent to at least GS-5. **GS-9:** A master's degree, or two years of graduate education, or one year of specialized experience equivalent to at least GS-7. **GS-11:** A Ph.D. or equivalent doctoral degree, or three years of graduate education, or one year of specialized experience equivalent to at least GS-9. **GS-12:** One year of specialized experience equivalent to at least GS-11. **GS-13:** One year of specialized experience equivalent to at least GS-12.

Qualifying education can be substituted for experience, and vice versa. Applicants must be at least 21 years of age and under age 37. However, candidates over age 37 who have previous service creditable under special law enforcement retirement provisions also may be eligible. Eyesight requirements include good distant vision in each eye, near vision that is sufficient to read print the size of typewritten characters, normal depth perception and peripheral vision, and the ability to distinguish basic colors. Eyeglasses and contact lenses are permitted. Hearing loss must not exceed 35 decibels at the 1000, 2000, and 3000 Hertz levels. Tentative appointees must qualify for a security clearance and pass a background investigation, drug screening test, and medical examination.

Training

OPM-OIG special agents attend the 11-week Criminal Investigator Training Program at the Federal Law Enforcement Training Center (FLETC) in Glynco, Georgia (see chapter 16). They also attend in-service training programs that cover subjects such as healthcare and disability insurance fraud, legal issues and updates, white-collar crime, financial investigations, and firearms proficiency. OPM-OIG special agents also can attend the three-week Inspector General Investigator Training Program at FLETC (see chapter 16).

Contact: Office of Inspector General; U.S. Office of Personnel Management; 1900 E St. NW—Room 6400; Washington, DC 20415; phone: (202) 606-1200; Internet: www.opm.gov/

Special Agent
Office of Inspector General, Peace Corps

The Peace Corps promotes world peace and friendship by providing qualified and trained volunteers to serve abroad in six program areas including education, agriculture, health, small business development, urban development, and the environment. Thousands of Peace Corps volunteers serve throughout the world in program areas geared toward health and education, HIV/AIDS, agriculture, environment, information technology, and business development. The Peace Corps Office of Inspector General (OIG) serves as the law enforcement arm of the agency and works closely with the Department of State, the Department of Justice, and other federal agencies.

Special agents of the Peace Corps Office of Inspector General (OIG) conduct criminal, civil, and administrative investigations concerning alleged or suspected violations of federal laws concerned with domestic and international Peace Corps programs and operations. Peace Corps OIG special agents investigate criminal and noncriminal misconduct committed by the agency's employees, trainees, and volunteers based in the

U.S. and more than 70 countries. These investigations are concerned with offenses such as theft, forgery, fraud, acceptance of gratuities, and significant violations of Peace Corps regulations. Peace Corps OIG special agents also investigate violent crimes and other serious crimes against the agency's personnel, including sexual assault, aggravated assault, robbery, kidnapping, disappearance, and homicide. The majority of investigations pertain to offenses committed overseas, which requires Peace Corps OIG special agents to travel extensively. Peace Corps special agents are authorized to conduct surveillance and undercover operations, carry firearms, make arrests, execute search warrants, and serve subpoenas. They often coordinate investigations with the FBI, Department of Labor OIG, Office of Personnel Management OIG, State Department Bureau of Diplomatic Security, and other U.S. government and foreign law enforcement agencies.

Peace Corps OIG special agents are covered under special retirement provisions for law enforcement officers, and they qualify for 25 percent Law Enforcement Availability Pay.

Qualifications and Salary Levels

Peace Corps OIG special agents are appointed through excepted service hiring processes. The qualifications and salaries of the position are similar to those of GS-1811 special agents at the GS-5 through GS-13 levels with other federal agencies. Eyesight requirements include good distant vision in each eye, near vision that is sufficient to read print the size of typewritten characters, normal depth perception and peripheral vision, and the ability to distinguish basic colors. Eyeglasses and contact lenses are permitted. Hearing loss must not exceed 35 decibels at the 1000, 2000, and 3000 Hertz levels. The application process includes a background investigation and top-secret security clearance determination.

Training

Peace Corps OIG special agents attend the 11-week Criminal Investigator Training Program at the Federal Law Enforcement Training Center (FLETC) in Glynco, Georgia (see chapter 16). In-service training focuses on subjects such as Peace Corps programs, sex crimes, homicide investigation, financial investigations, international issues, and investigative techniques. Many Peace Corps OIG special agents attend the three-week Inspector General Investigator Training Program at FLETC (see chapter 16), depending on their previous training and experience.

Contact: Office of Inspector General; Peace Corps; 1111 20th St. NW; Washington, DC 20526; phone: (202) 692-2915; Internet: www.peacecorps.gov/; e-mail: oig@peacecorps.gov

Special Agent (GS-1811)
Office of Inspector General, Pension Benefit Guaranty Corporation

The Pension Benefit Guaranty Corporation (PBGC), a wholly owned government corporation, insures most private-sector pension plans that provide a benefit based on factors such as age, years of service, and salary. PBGC administers insurance programs that protect the retirement incomes of more than 40 million American workers in more than 30,000 pension plans. The PBGC Office of Inspector General (OIG) investigates violations of laws and regulations, mismanagement, gross waste of funds, abuses of authority, and other matters relating to PBGC operations.

PBGC-OIG special agents investigate violations of federal law relating to the Employee Retirement Income Security Act (ERISA); official misconduct by PBGC personnel; misuse of grant funds; or fraud committed by PBGC contractors, subcontractors, or vendors. ERISA investigations focus on fraud in pension insurance programs administered by PBGC, including the Single Employer Program and the Multiemployer Program. These investigations often involve allegations of fiduciary breaches, such as instances in which pension plan administrators unlawfully remove plan funds resulting in shortages, or pension plan participants who submit false information or commit other forms of fraud to unlawfully obtain retirement or disability benefits. Many investigations focus on family members or others who receive retirement benefits after an annuitant's death. Employee integrity investigations are concerned with offenses such as bribery, collusion, embezzlement, kickbacks, time and attendance fraud, misuse of government computers, and inflated claims for travel reimbursement. PBGC-OIG special agents also investigate matters involving theft of pension checks or government property, threats against PBGC, and other crimes. Many investigations are conducted jointly with the Department of Labor OIG, Office of Personnel Management OIG, Government Accountability Office, and other law enforcement and regulatory agencies.

PBGC-OIG special agents are covered under special retirement provisions for law enforcement officers.

Qualifications and Salary Levels

GS-5: Completion of a four-year course of study leading to a bachelor's degree; or three years of general experience, one year of which was equivalent to at least GS-4. **GS-7:** One full year of graduate education, or superior academic achievement during undergraduate studies, or one year of specialized experience equivalent to at least GS-5. **GS-9:** A master's degree, or two years of graduate education, or one year of specialized experience equivalent to at least GS-7. **GS-11:** A Ph.D. or equivalent doctoral degree, or three years of graduate education, or one year of specialized experience equivalent to at least GS-9. **GS-12:** One year of specialized experience equivalent to at least GS-11. **GS-13:** One year of specialized experience equivalent to at least GS-12.

Applicants can use equivalent combinations of specialized experience and education to meet total experience requirements. Applicants must be at least 21 years of age and under age 37. However, candidates over age 37 who have previous service creditable under special law enforcement retirement provisions also may be eligible. Eyesight requirements include good distant vision in each eye, near vision that is sufficient to read print the size of typewritten characters, normal depth perception and peripheral vision, and the ability to distinguish basic colors. Eyeglasses and contact lenses are permitted. Hearing loss must not exceed 35 decibels at the 1000, 2000, and 3000 Hertz levels. Tentative appointees must qualify for a security clearance and pass a background investigation and medical examination.

Training

PBGC-OIG special agents attend the 11-week Criminal Investigator Training Program at the Federal Law Enforcement Training Center (FLETC) in Glynco, Georgia (see chapter 16). Ongoing in-service training includes the three-week Inspector General Investigator Training Program (see chapter 16), and courses concerning ERISA provisions, white-collar fraud, interviewing techniques, criminal and civil law, computer hardware and software, and the investigation of fraud and personnel misconduct.

Contact: Office of Inspector General; Pension Benefit Guaranty Corporation; 1200 K St. NW—Suite 470; Washington, DC 20005; phone: (202) 326-4030; Internet: www.pbgc.gov/

Special Agent
Office of Inspector General, U.S. Postal Service

The U.S. Postal Service (USPS) Office of Inspector General (OIG) prevents, detects, and investigates fraud, waste, and program abuse, and promotes efficiency in the operations of the Postal Service. USPS-OIG also has oversight responsibility for all activities of the U.S. Postal Inspection Service, including internal affairs investigations.

USPS-OIG special agents conduct criminal investigations pertaining to USPS operations and programs, with particular emphasis on fraud committed by contractors and vendors, workers' compensation fraud, healthcare provider fraud, and employee integrity matters. Contract and vendor fraud cases often are concerned with vehicle repair shops and fuel suppliers that submit fraudulent fleet credit card charges for repairs and fuel not provided; other firms that overcharge or bill USPS for goods or services not provided; falsification of certified payroll records; product substitution; and other schemes. Workers' compensation investigations typically target USPS personnel who feign disability and submit fraudulent claims for benefits. Healthcare provider fraud investigations often involve false claims for the treatment of USPS employees that was medically unnecessary, unallowable, or not provided; and upcoding claims to indicate higher levels of service than provided. Employee integrity cases often pertain to USPS personnel who accept bribes or gratuities from contractors or subcontractors, steal money from postage stamp vending machines, embezzle funds or USPS money orders, or violate other standards of conduct. USPS-OIG special agents also investigate serious incidents and tort claims which could have significant liability implications on USPS. They are authorized to conduct surveillance and undercover operations, carry firearms, make arrests, execute search warrants, and serve subpoenas. Many investigations are conducted with agencies such as the FBI, Postal Inspection Service, Department of Labor OIG, U.S. General Services Administration OIG, and other agencies.

USPS-OIG special agents are covered under special retirement provisions for law enforcement officers, and they qualify for 25 percent Law Enforcement Availability Pay.

Qualifications and Salary Levels

USPS-OIG special agents are appointed through excepted service hiring processes. The qualifications and salaries of the position are similar to those of GS-1811 special agents at the GS-5 through GS-13 levels with other federal agencies. Eyesight requirements include good distant vision in each eye, near vision that is sufficient to read print the size of typewritten characters, normal depth perception and peripheral vision, and the ability to distinguish basic colors. Eyeglasses and contact lenses are permitted. Hearing loss must not exceed 35 decibels at the 1000, 2000, and 3000 Hertz levels. The application process includes a background investigation, medical examination, drug test, and security clearance determination.

Training

USPS-OIG special agents attend the 11-week Criminal Investigator Training Program at the Federal Law Enforcement Training Center (FLETC) in Glynco, Georgia (see chapter 16). They also attend in-service training programs that cover subjects such as internal fraud, financial investigations, workers' compensation fraud, investigative techniques, and personnel misconduct. USPS-OIG special agents also can attend the three-week Inspector General Investigator Training Program at FLETC (see chapter 16).

Contact: Office of Inspector General; United States Postal Service; 1735 N. Lynn St.— 10th Floor; Arlington, VA 22209; phone: (703) 248-2100; Internet: www.uspsoig.gov/

Special Agent (GS-1811)
Office of Inspector General, Railroad Retirement Board

The Railroad Retirement Board (RRB) is an independent agency that administers comprehensive retirement, survivor, unemployment, and sickness benefit programs for the nation's railroad workers and their families. The RRB Office of Inspector General (OIG) conducts audits, management reviews, and investigations of RRB programs and operations.

RRB-OIG special agents investigate violations of a wide range of federal laws and irregularities pertaining to the administration of RRB programs, including provisions of the Railroad Retirement Act and Railroad Unemployment Insurance Act. Many RRB-OIG investigations pertain to the theft of retirement benefits by someone other than the authorized RRB annuitant—frequently a relative of a deceased annuitant. Disability investigations often involve sophisticated schemes carried out by annuitants who conceal income that, if reported, would exceed allowable earnings limitations. Investigations of unemployment insurance (UI) and sickness insurance (SI) fraud often focus on individuals who are receiving UI or SI benefits while employed. RRB-OIG special agents also investigate employee misconduct involving unethical behavior, conflict of interest, abuses of authority, failure to report outside employment, and other offenses. RRB-OIG special agents are authorized to conduct surveillance and undercover operations, carry firearms, make arrests, execute search warrants, and serve subpoenas. They work closely with agencies such as the FBI, Health and Human Services OIG, Postal Inspection Service, Social Security Administration OIG, Department of Labor OIG, Office of Personnel Management OIG, and other agencies.

RRB-OIG special agents are covered under special retirement provisions for law enforcement officers, and they qualify for 25 percent Law Enforcement Availability Pay.

Qualifications and Salary Levels

GS-5: Completion of a four-year course of study leading to a bachelor's degree; or three years of general experience, one year of which was equivalent to at least GS-4. **GS-7:** One full year of graduate education, or superior academic achievement during undergraduate studies, or one year of specialized experience equivalent to at least GS-5. **GS-9:** A master's degree, or two years of graduate education, or one year of specialized experience equivalent to at least GS-7. **GS-11:** A Ph.D. or equivalent doctoral degree, or three years of graduate education, or one year of specialized experience equivalent to at least GS-9. **GS-12:** One year of specialized experience equivalent to at least GS-11. **GS-13:** One year of specialized experience equivalent to at least GS-12.

Experience and education can be combined to meet total experience requirements. Applicants must be at least 21 years of age and under age 37. However, candidates over age 37 who have previous service creditable under special law enforcement retirement provisions also may be eligible. Eyesight requirements include good distant vision in each eye, near vision that is sufficient to read print the size of typewritten characters, normal depth perception and peripheral vision, and the ability to distinguish basic colors. Eyeglasses and contact lenses are permitted. Hearing loss must not exceed 35 decibels at the 1000, 2000, and 3000 Hertz levels. The application process includes a drug screening test, medical examination, background investigation, and top-secret security clearance determination.

Training

RRB-OIG special agents attend the 11-week Criminal Investigator Training Program at the Federal Law Enforcement Training Center (FLETC) in Glynco, Georgia (see chapter 16). In-service training includes courses that focus on fraudulent claims, technical investigative equipment, interviewing techniques, computer forensics, and other topics. RRB-OIG agents also attend the three-week Inspector General Investigator Training Program at FLETC (see chapter 16).

Contact: Office of Inspector General; Railroad Retirement Board; 844 N. Rush St.—4th Floor; Chicago, IL 60611; phone: (312) 751-4350; Internet: www.rrb.gov/mep/oig.asp/

Special Agent (GS-1811)
Office of Inspector General, U.S. Small Business Administration

The U.S. Small Business Administration (SBA) assists and protects the interests of small business, and ensures that small businesses receive a fair portion of federal government purchases, contracts, and subcontracts. SBA also makes loans to small businesses, state and local development organizations, and the victims of floods or other catastrophes. The Investigations Division of SBA's Office of Inspector General (OIG) manages a program to detect and deter fraud, corruption, and other illegal and improper activities involving SBA programs, operations, and personnel.

SBA-OIG special agents carry out a full range of investigative and law enforcement functions. The majority of investigations focus on applicants or participants in the SBA Section 7(a) Loan Guaranty Program or the Disaster Loan Program. Fraud investigations often focus on those who submit false tax returns or other false information to obtain loans or benefits; use funds for purposes other than those for which loans were granted; misrepresent U.S. citizenship to gain loan approval; obtain loans for damage that was not incurred; or commit other offenses. In addition, many investigations pertain to large companies that misrepresent the size of their operations to qualify for small business loans. SBA-OIG investigations often involve complex conspiracies and result in criminal charges for offenses such as conversion, bank fraud, money laundering, false claims, false statements, conspiracy, and conflict of interest. SBA-OIG special agents also investigate SBA employee integrity matters, including offenses such as bribery, conflict of interest, embezzlement, and abuses of authority. They are authorized to conduct surveillance and undercover operations, carry firearms, make arrests, execute search warrants, and serve subpoenas. In addition to participating in federal task force operations, SBA-OIG special agents conduct investigations with agencies such as the FBI, Department of Homeland Security OIG, Social Security Administration OIG, Postal Inspection Service, IRS Criminal Investigation Division, and other law enforcement agencies.

SBA-OIG special agents are covered under special retirement provisions for law enforcement officers, and they qualify for 25 percent Law Enforcement Availability Pay.

Qualifications and Salary Levels

GS-5: Completion of a four-year course of study leading to a bachelor's degree; or three years of general experience, one year of which was equivalent to at least GS-4. **GS-7:** One full year of graduate education, or superior academic achievement during undergraduate studies, or one year of specialized experience equivalent to at least GS-5. **GS-9:** A master's degree, or two years of graduate education, or one year of specialized experience equivalent to at least GS-7. **GS-11:** A Ph.D. or equivalent doctoral degree, or three years of graduate education, or one year of specialized experience equivalent to at least GS-9. **GS-12:** One year of specialized experience equivalent to at least GS-11. **GS-13:** One year of specialized experience equivalent to at least GS-12.

Qualifying education can be substituted for experience, and vice versa. Applicants must be at least 21 years of age and under age 37. However, candidates over age 37 who have previous service creditable under special law enforcement retirement provisions also may be eligible. Eyesight requirements include good distant vision in each eye, near vision that is sufficient to read print the size of typewritten characters, normal depth perception and peripheral vision, and the ability to distinguish basic colors. Eyeglasses and contact lenses are permitted. Hearing loss must not exceed 35 decibels at the 1000, 2000, and 3000 Hertz levels. The application process includes a drug screening test, medical examination, background investigation, and security clearance determination.

Training

SBA-OIG special agents attend the 11-week Criminal Investigator Training Program at the Federal Law Enforcement Training Center (FLETC) in Glynco, Georgia (see chapter 16). They also attend in-service training programs that focus on subjects such as criminal and civil law, SBA loan programs, investigative techniques, and non-lethal subject control techniques. SBA-OIG special agents also attend the three-week Inspector General Investigator Training Program at FLETC (see chapter 16).

Contact: Office of Inspector General; U.S. Small Business Administration; 409 3rd St. SW; Washington, DC 20416; phone: (202) 205-6220; Internet: www.sba.gov/ig/; e-mail: oig@sba.gov

Special Agent (GS-1811)
Office of Inspector General, Smithsonian Institution

In carrying out its mission to protect the integrity of the Smithsonian Institution (SI), special agents of the SI Office of Inspector General (OIG) investigate violations of federal laws and regulations, gross waste of funds, abuses of authority and other misconduct, and mismanagement concerning SI programs and operations. The SI-OIG Investigations Division also identifies fraud indicators, and recommends measures to management to improve SI's ability to protect itself against fraud and other wrongdoing.

Investigations conducted by SI-OIG special agents often pertain to wrongdoing by SI employees, such as theft, embezzlement, misuse of government vehicles or property, use of public office for private gain, trafficking in museum objects, destruction or removal of official records, using controlled substances or alcohol on SI property, and other offenses. SI-OIG special agents also investigate fraud relating to SI contracts, grants, and other business matters, including offenses such as theft of SI property or funds, false claims, false statements, bribery, kickbacks, misappropriation of funds, deviation from or failure to comply with contract specifications, and other crimes. SI-OIG special agents are authorized to conduct surveillance and undercover operations, carry firearms, make arrests, execute search warrants, and serve subpoenas. They conduct investigations jointly with agencies such as the FBI; U.S. General Services Administration OIG; IRS Criminal Investigation Division; U.S. Fish and Wildlife Service; and other federal, state, or local law enforcement agencies.

Qualifications and Salary Levels

GS-7: One full year of graduate education, or superior academic achievement during undergraduate studies, or one year of specialized experience equivalent to at least GS-5. **GS-9:** A master's degree, or two years of graduate education, or one year of specialized experience equivalent to at least GS-7. **GS-11:** A Ph.D. or equivalent doctoral degree, or three years of graduate education, or one year of specialized experience equivalent to at least GS-9. **GS-12:** One year of specialized experience equivalent to at least GS-11. **GS-13:** One year of specialized experience equivalent to at least GS-12.

Applicants can use equivalent combinations of specialized experience and education to meet total experience requirements. Eyesight requirements include good distant vision in each eye, near vision that is sufficient to read print the size of typewritten characters, normal depth perception and peripheral vision, and the ability to distinguish basic colors. Eyeglasses and contact lenses are permitted. Hearing loss must not exceed 35 decibels at the 1000, 2000, and 3000 Hertz levels. Tentative appointees must qualify for a security clearance and pass a background investigation, drug screening test, and medical examination.

Training

Newly appointed SI-OIG special agents attend the 11-week Criminal Investigator Training Program at the Federal Law Enforcement Training Center (FLETC) in Glynco, Georgia (see chapter 16). They also attend the three-week Inspector General Investigator Training Program at FLETC (see chapter 16), and in-service courses that focus on SI programs and operations, computer forensics, data mining, fraud involving SI contracts and grants, internal investigations, and other subjects.

Contact: Office of Inspector General; Smithsonian Institution; 750 9th St. NW—Suite 4200; Washington, DC 20560; phone: (202) 275-2244; Internet: www.si.edu/oig/

Special Agent (GS-1811)
Office of Inspector General, Social Security Administration

The Social Security Administration (SSA) manages the nation's retirement, survivor, and disability insurance programs; administers the Supplemental Security Income program for the aged, blind, and disabled; assigns Social Security numbers to U.S. citizens; and maintains earnings records for workers. The SSA Office of Inspector General (OIG) conducts investigations related to fraud, waste, abuse, and mismanagement in SSA programs and operations.

SSA-OIG special agents investigate criminal wrongdoing by SSA program applicants and beneficiaries; physicians, interpreters, representative payees, contractors, grantees, and others who receive funds from SSA; and SSA employees. Many SSA-OIG investigations pertain to counterfeiting of Social Security cards, obtaining Social Security numbers based on false information, misusing Social Security numbers to obtain government benefits, theft and forgery of benefit checks, feigned disabilities, scams involving deceased payees, and other schemes. Investigations of SSA employees are concerned with offenses such as embezzlement, misappropriation of funds during the processing of overpayments, fraudulent issuance or sale of Social Security cards, unauthorized access to confidential information, and other violations. SSA-OIG special agents are authorized to conduct surveillance and undercover operations, carry firearms, make arrests, execute search warrants, and serve subpoenas. They work closely with agencies such as the FBI, Health and Human Services OIG, Department of Labor OIG, Railroad Retirement Board OIG, Department of Agriculture OIG, and other agencies.

SSA-OIG special agents are covered under special retirement provisions for law enforcement officers, and they qualify for 25 percent Law Enforcement Availability Pay.

Qualifications and Salary Levels

GS-5: Completion of a four-year course of study leading to a bachelor's degree; or three years of general experience, one year of which was equivalent to at least GS-4. **GS-7:** One full year of graduate education, or superior academic achievement during undergraduate studies, or one year of specialized experience equivalent to at least GS-5. **GS-9:** A master's degree, or two years of graduate education, or one year of specialized experience equivalent to at least GS-7. **GS-11:** A Ph.D. or equivalent doctoral degree, or three years of graduate education, or one year of specialized experience equivalent to at least GS-9. **GS-12:** One year of specialized experience equivalent to at least GS-11. **GS-13:** One year of specialized experience equivalent to at least GS-12.

Qualifying education can be substituted for experience, and vice versa. Applicants must be at least 21 years of age and under age 37. However, candidates over age 37 who have previous service creditable under special law enforcement retirement provisions also may be eligible. Eyesight requirements include good distant vision in each eye, near vision that is sufficient to read print the size of typewritten characters, normal depth perception and peripheral vision, and the ability to distinguish basic colors. Eyeglasses and contact lenses are permitted. Hearing loss must not exceed 35 decibels at the 1000, 2000, and 3000 Hertz levels. Candidates must successfully undergo a background investigation, qualify for a security clearance, and pass a drug test and medical examination prior to appointment.

Training

SSA-OIG special agents attend the 11-week Criminal Investigator Training Program at the Federal Law Enforcement Training Center (FLETC) in Glynco, Georgia (see chapter 16). In-service training includes instruction in subjects such as healthcare fraud, SSA program updates, criminal and civil law, white-collar crime, and employee integrity investigations. Many SSA-OIG special agents also attend the three-week Inspector General Investigator Training Program at FLETC (see chapter 16).

Contact: Office of Inspector General; Social Security Administration; 6401 Security Blvd.—Suite 300; Baltimore, MD 21235; phone: (410) 966-8385; Internet: www.ssa.gov/oig/

Special Agent (GS-1811)
Bureau of Diplomatic Security, U.S. Department of State

As the State Department's primary law enforcement and security arm, the Bureau of Diplomatic Security (DS) is responsible for providing a secure environment for the conduct of U.S. foreign policy, performing criminal and counterterrorism investigations, and protecting the secretary of state and certain foreign dignitaries during their visits to the United States. DS—the only law enforcement agency with representation in nearly every country throughout the world—also trains foreign civilian law enforcement officers to reduce the threat of terrorism.

DS special agents conduct criminal investigations related primarily to statutes protecting the integrity of U.S. passport and entry visa documents, and they perform background investigations and personnel security investigations of individuals seeking appointment to or continued employment with the State Department. Passport and visa investigations often are related to fugitives and criminals involved in international terrorism operations, alien smuggling rings, organized crime activities, and drug traffickers operating in the U.S. and abroad who change identities and conceal their movements. DS special agents typically coordinate counterterrorism and counterintelligence investigations with U.S. agencies that participate in joint terrorism task force operations, and with foreign law enforcement agencies. They are authorized to conduct surveillance and undercover operations, carry firearms, make arrests, execute search warrants, and serve subpoenas. Investigations, counterintelligence activities, and protective operations often are conducted jointly with agencies such as the FBI, U.S. Immigration and Customs Enforcement, Drug Enforcement Administration, Social Security Administration Office of Inspector General, and other agencies. Following initial training, DS special agents normally are assigned to a domestic field office or resident agency, although they must be willing to accept assignments throughout the world.

DS special agents are covered under special retirement provisions for federal law enforcement officers, and they are eligible to receive 25 percent Law Enforcement Availability Pay.

Qualifications and Salary Levels

GS-5: Completion of a four-year course of study leading to a bachelor's degree; or three years of general experience, one year of which was equivalent to at least GS-4. **GS-7:** One full year of graduate education, or superior academic achievement during undergraduate studies, or one year of specialized experience equivalent to at least GS-5. **GS-9:** A master's degree, or two years of graduate education, or one year of specialized experience equivalent to at least GS-7. **GS-11:** A Ph.D. or equivalent doctoral degree, or three years of graduate education, or one year of specialized experience equivalent to at least GS-9. **GS-12:** One year of specialized experience equivalent to at least GS-11. **GS-13:** One year of specialized experience equivalent to at least GS-12.

Equivalent combinations of education and experience can be used to meet minimum experience requirements. Applicants must be at least 21 years of age and under age 37. However, candidates over age 37 who have previous service creditable under special law enforcement retirement provisions also may be eligible. Eyesight requirements include uncorrected distant vision not worse than 20/100 (Snellen) in each eye, corrected to 20/20 in one eye and 20/30 in the other eye, near vision that is sufficient to read print the size of typewritten characters, normal depth perception and peripheral vision, and the ability to distinguish basic colors. Hearing loss must not exceed 30 decibels at the 500, 1000, and 2000 Hertz levels. Tentative appointees must qualify for a top-secret security clearance and pass a background investigation, drug screening test, written examination, physical fitness test, and medical examination.

Training

DS special agents complete a six-month basic training program that begins with an orientation in Washington, DC, followed by the 11-week Criminal Investigator Training Program at the Federal Law Enforcement Training Center in Glynco, Georgia (see chapter 16). DS special agents then attend a three-month specialized training program at State Department facilities and other sites in the Washington, DC, area, consisting of courses in passport and visa fraud, investigative techniques, officer safety, emergency medical techniques, and other subjects. Ongoing on-the-job and in-service training focuses on investigative techniques, counterterrorism, protective operations, threat assessments, questioned documents, and other topics.

Contact: Bureau of Diplomatic Security; U.S. Department of State; 2201 C St. NW; Washington, DC 20520; phone: (202) 647-7277; Internet: www.state.gov/m/ds/; e-mail: DSrecruitment@state.gov

Special Agent (GS-1811)
Office of Inspector General, U.S. Department of State

The State Department advises the president on foreign policy, promotes the security of the United States, gathers intelligence relating to America's overseas interests, negotiates treaties and agreements with foreign nations, and represents the United States in the United Nations and other international organizations. The State Department Office of Inspector General (OIG) is an independent agency that audits, inspects, and investigates the programs and activities of all elements of the Department and the Broadcasting Board of Governors for International Broadcasting.

Special agents of the State Department Office of Inspector General (OIG) investigate criminal activity relating primarily to employee misconduct by State Department employees and fraud in the Department's contract and procurement operations. Employee integrity investigations pertain to offenses such as embezzlement, theft or misuse of government property or vehicles, false travel voucher claims, and unemployment fraud. Contract and procurement fraud cases are concerned with product substitution, billing for unallowable expenses or for goods or services not received, falsification of contractors' certified payrolls, false claims, bribery, kickbacks, and other fraudulent schemes. State Department OIG special agents are authorized to conduct surveillance and undercover operations, carry firearms, make arrests, execute search warrants, and serve subpoenas. They often work with agencies such as the State Department Bureau of Diplomatic Security, U.S. Agency for International Development OIG, Department of Labor OIG, IRS Criminal Instigation Division, U.S. Immigration and Customs Enforcement, FBI, Drug Enforcement Administration, and foreign law enforcement agencies.

State Department OIG special agents are covered under special retirement provisions for federal law enforcement officers, and they are eligible to receive 25 percent Law Enforcement Availability Pay.

Qualifications and Salary Levels

GS-5: Completion of a four-year course of study leading to a bachelor's degree; or three years of general experience, one year of which was equivalent to at least GS-4.

GS-7: One full year of graduate education, or superior academic achievement during undergraduate studies, or one year of specialized experience equivalent to at least GS-5. **GS-9:** A master's degree, or two years of graduate education, or one year of specialized experience equivalent to at least GS-7. **GS-11:** A Ph.D. or equivalent doctoral degree, or three years of graduate education, or one year of specialized experience equivalent to at least GS-9. **GS-12:** One year of specialized experience equivalent to at least GS-11. **GS-13:** One year of specialized experience equivalent to at least GS-12.

Applicants can use equivalent combinations of specialized experience and education to meet total experience requirements. Applicants must be at least 21 years of age and under age 37. However, candidates over age 37 who have previous service creditable under special law enforcement retirement provisions also may be eligible. Eyesight requirements include good distant vision in each eye, near vision that is sufficient to read print the size of typewritten characters, normal depth perception and peripheral vision, and the ability to distinguish basic colors. Eyeglasses and contact lenses are permitted. Hearing loss must not exceed 35 decibels at the 1000, 2000, and 3000 Hertz levels. The application process includes a drug screening test, medical examination, background investigation, and top-secret security clearance determination.

Training

State Department OIG special agents attend the 11-week Criminal Investigator Training Program at the Federal Law Enforcement Training Center (FLETC) in Glynco, Georgia (see chapter 16). They also attend in-service training programs that cover subjects such as financial fraud investigations, technical investigative equipment, computer software and databases, seizing of computers, and interviewing techniques. Many State Department OIG special agents also attend the three-week Inspector General Investigator Training Program at FLETC (see chapter 16).

Contact: Office of Inspector General; U.S. Department of State; 2201 C St. NW—Suite 8100; Washington, DC 20522; phone: (202) 663-0340; Internet: www.oig.state.gov/

Special Agent
Office of Inspector General, Tennessee Valley Authority

Special agents of the Tennessee Valley Authority (TVA) Office of Inspector General (OIG) conduct criminal and administrative investigations pertaining to waste of funds, fraud, and abuses of authority in the programs and operations of TVA, a wholly owned government corporation that is the nation's largest single producer of electric power.

TVA-OIG special agents investigate financial and internal matters relating to personnel misconduct, workers' compensation fraud, harassment and intimidation, contract fraud, environmental crimes, and other offenses pertaining to TVA's servicing of large industries, federal installations, and 160 power distributors located in the Tennessee Valley region. These investigations focus on loan fraud, contract fraud, billing for goods or services not provided, conspiracy, misuse of TVA purchase cards, and other offenses. TVA-OIG special agents also investigate fraud in TVA's self-insured healthcare plan. Healthcare fraud investigations typically are concerned with healthcare professionals, pharmacies, and suppliers that upcode claims to indicate higher levels of service than provided; bill for goods or services that were unallowable, medically unnecessary, not rendered, or provided by unlicensed personnel; inflated billing; and other schemes. TVA-OIG special agents work closely with agencies such as the FBI, Department of Energy OIG, Department of Labor OIG, U.S. General Services Administration OIG, and Environmental Protection Agency Criminal Investigation

Division. They also participate in the Environmental Crimes Joint Task Force and a healthcare task force sponsored by the United States Attorney for the Eastern District of Tennessee, and the FBI Joint Terrorism Task Force. They are authorized to conduct surveillance and undercover operations, carry firearms, make arrests, execute search warrants, and serve subpoenas.

Qualifications and Salary Levels

TVA-OIG special agents are appointed through excepted service hiring processes. The qualifications and salaries of the position are similar to those of GS-1811 special agents at the GS-5 through GS-13 levels with other federal agencies. Eyesight requirements include good distant vision in each eye, near vision that is sufficient to read print the size of typewritten characters, normal depth perception and peripheral vision, and the ability to distinguish basic colors. Eyeglasses and contact lenses are permitted. Hearing loss must not exceed 35 decibels at the 1000, 2000, and 3000 Hertz levels. Tentative appointees must qualify for a security clearance and pass a background investigation, drug screening test, and medical examination.

Training

TVA-OIG special agents attend the 11-week Criminal Investigator Training Program at the Federal Law Enforcement Training Center (FLETC) in Glynco, Georgia (see chapter 16). In-service training covers TVA operations and subjects such as workers' compensation fraud, financial investigations, environmental offenses, white-collar crime, and investigative techniques. They also attend courses presented by the Association of Certified Fraud Examiners. TVA-OIG special agents attend the three-week Inspector General Investigator Training Program at FLETC (see chapter 16).

Contact: Office of Inspector General; Tennessee Valley Authority; 400 W. Summit Hill Dr.; Knoxville, TN 37902; phone: (865) 632-7720; Internet: www.oig.tva.gov/

Special Agent (GS-1811)
National Highway Traffic Safety Administration, U.S. Department of Transportation

The National Highway Traffic Safety Administration (NHTSA) carries out programs relating to the safety of motor vehicles, drivers, occupants, and pedestrians in accordance with the National Traffic and Motor Vehicle Act and the Highway Safety Act. Through its Office of Odometer Fraud Investigation, NHTSA also administers provisions of federal vehicle odometer laws to protect purchasers of vehicles having altered odometers.

NHTSA special agents pursue odometer fraud investigations nationwide and assist prosecutors with related criminal prosecution and civil litigation. These investigations are concerned with the interstate movement of large numbers of vehicles and vehicle title documents through automobile dealerships and subsidiaries that engage in systematic and programmed odometer fraud. Investigations typically result in criminal charges for interstate transportation of stolen property and fraudulent securities, mail fraud, and wire fraud, and in many cases involve bribery of state government officials, false statements, and tax evasion. Many odometer fraud investigations focus on foreign organized criminal enterprises operating throughout the U.S. and internationally. NHTSA special agents are authorized to conduct surveillance and undercover operations, carry firearms, make arrests, execute search warrants, and serve subpoenas. They frequently participate in task force and sting operations with other federal, state, and local law enforcement and regulatory agencies, and provide assistance to other agencies with investigations and prosecutions at the state and local levels. They often coordinate federal investigative activities with agencies such as the FBI, U.S. Immigration and Customs Enforcement, Postal Inspection Service, State Department Bureau of Diplomatic Security, and U.S. Marshals Service.

NHTSA special agents are covered under special retirement provisions for law enforcement officers, and they qualify for 25 percent Law Enforcement Availability Pay.

Qualifications and Salary Levels

GS-14: One year of specialized experience equivalent to at least GS-13. **GS-15:** One year of specialized experience equivalent to at least GS-14.

NHTSA special agent positions are filled only at the GS-14 and GS-15 levels. Applicants must be at least 21 years of age and under age 37. However, candidates over age 37 who have previous service creditable under special law enforcement retirement provisions also may be eligible. Eyesight requirements include good distant vision in each eye, near vision that is sufficient to read print the size of typewritten characters, normal depth perception and peripheral vision, and the ability to distinguish basic colors. Eyeglasses and contact lenses are permitted. Hearing loss must not exceed 35 decibels at the 1000, 2000, and 3000 Hertz levels. The application process includes a background investigation, medical examination, drug test, and security clearance determination.

Training

NHTSA appoints only trained and experienced criminal investigators to the special agent position. They complete on-the-job training and a variety of courses throughout their careers concerning subjects such as motor vehicle titling, questioned documents, tracing of funds through financial institutions, white-collar fraud, sources of information, criminal and civil law, search and seizure, and courtroom testimony. NHTSA special agents also attend courses presented at conferences sponsored by the National Odometer and Title Fraud Enforcement Association.

Contact: Office of Odometer Fraud Investigation; National Highway Traffic Safety Administration; U.S. Department of Transportation; 400 7th St. SW—Room 6130; Washington, DC 20590; phone: (202) 366-4761; Internet: www.nhtsa.dot.gov/

Special Agent (GS-1811)
Office of Inspector General, U.S. Department of Transportation

The U.S. Department of Transportation (DOT) establishes the nation's transportation policy and operates programs relating to highway planning, development, and construction; motor carrier safety; urban mass transit; railroads; aviation; and the safety of oil and gas pipelines, waterways, and ports. Special agents of the DOT Office of Inspector General (OIG) investigate contract and grant fraud, employee integrity matters, and other allegations of fraud, waste, abuse, and mismanagement in a broad range of the Department's programs and operations.

Many investigations conducted by DOT-OIG special agents are concerned with Federal Aviation Administration contract and procurement functions, including contracts to build airport control towers, runways, terminals, and maintenance facilities, or fraud relating to the manufacturing and distribution of aircraft parts. Investigations of Federal Highway Administration programs focus on areas such as highway and bridge construction, motor carrier safety programs, and transportation of hazardous materials. Federal Railroad Administration program investigations pertain primarily to AMTRAK construction, procurement, and railcar safety programs. DOT-OIG investigations of U.S. Coast Guard programs often focus on fraud relating to construction and replacement of Coast Guard stations, aircraft hangars, and docking facilities. Other investigations are concerned with fraud and other crimes affecting the Federal Transit Administration, National Highway Traffic Safety Administration, Maritime Administration, and other DOT components. DOT-OIG special agents also conduct employee integrity investigations involving offenses such as bribery, conflict of interest, and abuses of authority. They are authorized to conduct surveillance and undercover operations, carry firearms, make arrests, execute search warrants, and serve subpoenas. Many investigations are conducted with agencies such as the FBI, Postal Inspection Service, Environmental Protection Agency, and Defense Criminal Investigative Service, among others.

DOT-OIG special agents are covered under special retirement provisions for law enforcement officers, and they qualify for 25 percent Law Enforcement Availability Pay.

Qualifications and Salary Levels

GS-5: Completion of a four-year course of study leading to a bachelor's degree; or three years of general experience, one year of which was equivalent to at least GS-4. **GS-7:** One full year of graduate education, or superior academic achievement during undergraduate studies, or one year of specialized experience equivalent to at least GS-5. **GS-9:** A master's degree, or two years of graduate education, or one year of specialized experience equivalent to at least GS-7. **GS-11:** A Ph.D. or equivalent doctoral degree, or three years of graduate education, or one year of specialized experience equivalent to at least GS-9. **GS-12:** One year of specialized experience equivalent to at least GS-11. **GS-13:** One year of specialized experience equivalent to at least GS-12.

Experience and education can be combined to meet total experience requirements. Applicants must be at least 21 years of age and under age 37. However, candidates over age 37 who have previous service creditable under special law enforcement retirement provisions also may be eligible. Eyesight requirements include good distant vision in each eye, near vision that is sufficient to read print the size of typewritten characters, normal depth perception and peripheral vision, and the ability to distinguish basic colors. Eyeglasses and contact lenses are permitted. Hearing loss must not exceed 35 decibels at the 1000, 2000, and 3000 Hertz levels. The application process includes a drug screening test, medical examination, background investigation, and security clearance determination.

Training

Initial training for DOT-OIG special agents includes the 11-week Criminal Investigator Training Program at the Federal Law Enforcement Training Center (FLETC) in Glynco, Georgia (see chapter 16). They also attend a variety of in-service courses concerning subjects such as DOT program investigations, hazardous materials, white-collar crime, contract and procurement fraud, and internal investigations. DOT-OIG special agents also attend the three-week Inspector General Investigator Training Program at FLETC (see chapter 16).

Contact: Office of Inspector General; U.S. Department of Transportation; 400 7th St. SW—Room 9210; Washington, DC 20590; phone: (202) 366-1959; Internet: www.oig.dot.gov/

Special Agent (GS-1811)
Internal Revenue Service, U.S. Department of the Treasury

The Criminal Investigation Division (CID) of the Internal Revenue Service (IRS) is the law enforcement arm of the IRS. Special agents serving with IRS-CID investigate violations of federal tax, money laundering, and Bank Secrecy Act laws through programs that target tax crimes related to legal sources of income, financial crimes related to narcotics trafficking and other illegal sources of income, and terrorism financing.

IRS-CID special agents have exceptional expertise in following money trails to establish unreported income and the flow of assets. They investigate offenses such as money laundering, illegal political campaign contributions, illegal tax shelters, financial institution fraud, savings and loan scandals, bankruptcy fraud, currency reporting violations, and telemarketing fraud. Many investigations focus on tax protesters, organized crime activities, and public corruption. IRS-CID special agents are an integral component of the nationwide Organized Crime and Drug Enforcement Task Forces (OCDETF) and FBI Joint Terrorism Task Forces (JTTF), as well as task forces that focus on High Intensity Money Laundering and Financial Crime Areas (HIFCA) and High Intensity Drug Trafficking Areas (HIDTA). To combat international money-laundering related to drug trafficking, terrorism, and other crimes, IRS-CID special agents are based in countries such as Canada, Mexico, Germany, Hong Kong, Columbia, and France. IRS-CID special agents are authorized to conduct surveillance and undercover operations, carry firearms, make arrests, execute search warrants, and serve subpoenas. They work closely with agencies such as the U.S. Secret Service; U.S. Immigration and Customs Enforcement; Bureau of Alcohol, Tobacco, Firearms and Explosives; FBI; Drug Enforcement Administration; Department of Agriculture Office of Inspector General (OIG); and most other federal law enforcement agencies.

IRS-CID special agents are covered under special retirement provisions for law enforcement officers, and they qualify for 25 percent Law Enforcement Availability Pay.

Qualifications and Salary Levels

GS-5: Completion of a four-year course of study leading to a bachelor's degree, with at least 15 semester hours in accounting and nine semester hours in related business subjects (such as tax law, finance, economics, business law, or banking); or three years of accounting or business experience that required the application of accounting or auditing principles and general business practices; or certification as a Certified Public Accountant. **GS-7:** All requirements under GS-5 and either one full year of graduate education, or superior academic achievement during undergraduate studies, or one year of specialized experience equivalent to at least GS-5. **GS-9:** All requirements under GS-5 and either a master's degree, or two years of graduate education, or a law degree, or one year of specialized experience equivalent to at least GS-7. **GS-11:** All requirements under GS-5 and either a Ph.D. or equivalent doctoral degree, or three years of graduate education, or one year of specialized experience equivalent to at least GS-9. **GS-12:** All requirements under GS-5 and one year of specialized experience equivalent to at least GS-11. **GS-13:** All requirements under GS-5 and one year of specialized experience equivalent to at least GS-12.

Qualifying education can be substituted for experience, and vice versa. Applicants must be at least 21 years of age and under age 37. However, candidates over age 37 who have previous service creditable under special law enforcement retirement provisions also may be eligible. Eyesight requirements include uncorrected distant vision not worse than 20/200 (Snellen) in each eye, correctable to 20/30 in one eye and 20/20 in the other eye; normal depth perception and peripheral vision; ability to distinguish shades of color; and near vision sufficient to read Jaeger type 2 at 14 inches. Hearing loss must not exceed 30 decibels at the 500, 1000, and 2000 Hertz levels. The application process includes the Treasury Enforcement Agent Examination (see chapter 3) and a drug screening test, medical examination, background investigation, security clearance determination, and tax audit.

Training

IRS-CID special agents attend the 11-week Criminal Investigator Training Program at the Federal Law Enforcement Training Center (FLETC) in Glynco, Georgia (see chapter 16), followed by a 16-week agency-specific course at FLETC that covers subjects such as tax law, tax fraud, money laundering, computer fraud, surveillance techniques, and courtroom testimony. IRS-CID special agents also attend a wide range of in-service courses, including instruction concerning the Internal Revenue Code; OCDETF, JTTF, HIFCA, and HIDTA task force operations; asset forfeiture laws and procedures; firearms proficiency; defensive tactics; and other training programs related to the responsibilities of individual agents.

Contact: Criminal Investigation Division; Internal Revenue Service; U.S. Department of the Treasury; 1111 Constitution Ave. NW; Washington, DC 20224; phone: (202) 622-7796; Internet: www.treas.gov/irs/ci/

Special Agent (GS-1811)
Office of Inspector General, U.S. Department of the Treasury

The U.S. Department of the Treasury Office of Inspector General (OIG) is responsible for investigations concerning official misconduct by Treasury personnel, and financial crimes, corruption, and other criminal activity relating to Treasury programs and operations. Treasury OIG special agents also promote crime prevention and integrity awareness among the Department's employees.

Many investigations carried out by Treasury OIG special agents pertain to contract and procurement fraud schemes involving Treasury vendors and contractors. These investigations typically focus on offenses such as theft, embezzlement, bribery, product substitution, false claims, and other crimes. Personnel misconduct investigations encompass a range of allegations such as theft of U.S. currency or postage stamps from the Bureau of Engraving and Printing, bribery, embezzlement, time and attendance fraud, and conflict of interest. Treasury OIG special agents also investigate offenses such as credit card fraud, theft and forgery of Treasury checks, predatory lending practices, money laundering, and other crimes. They are authorized to conduct surveillance and undercover operations, carry firearms, make arrests, execute search warrants, and serve subpoenas. Many investigations are conducted jointly with various Treasury Department offices and bureaus, and agencies such as the FBI, Department of Housing and Urban Development OIG, Postal Inspection Service, and other agencies.

Treasury OIG special agents are covered under special retirement provisions for law enforcement officers, and they qualify for 25 percent Law Enforcement Availability Pay.

Qualifications and Salary Levels

GS-5: Completion of a four-year course of study leading to a bachelor's degree; or three years of general experience, one year of which was equivalent to at least GS-4. **GS-7:** One full year of graduate education, or superior academic achievement during undergraduate studies, or one year of specialized experience equivalent to at least GS-5. **GS-9:** A master's degree, or two years of graduate education, or one year of specialized experience equivalent to at least GS-7. **GS-11:** A Ph.D. or equivalent doctoral degree, or three years of graduate education, or one year of specialized experience equivalent to at least GS-9. **GS-12:** One year of specialized experience equivalent to at least GS-11. **GS-13:** One year of specialized experience equivalent to at least GS-12.

Experience and education can be combined to meet total experience requirements. Applicants must be at least 21 years of age and under age 37. However, candidates over age 37 who have previous service creditable under special law enforcement retirement provisions also may be eligible. Eyesight requirements include good distant vision in each eye, near vision that is sufficient to read print the size of typewritten characters, normal depth perception and peripheral vision, and the ability to distinguish basic colors. Eyeglasses and contact lenses are permitted. Hearing loss must not exceed 35 decibels at the 1000, 2000, and 3000 Hertz levels. Candidates must successfully undergo a background investigation, qualify for a security clearance, and pass a drug test and medical examination prior to appointment.

Training

Treasury OIG special agents attend the 11-week Criminal Investigator Training Program at the Federal Law Enforcement Training Center (FLETC) in Glynco, Georgia (see chapter 16). They also attend in-service training programs that cover subjects such as employee integrity investigations, criminal and civil law, procurement fraud, financial investigations, and other topics. Treasury OIG special agents also attend the three-week Inspector General Investigator Training Program at FLETC (see chapter 16).

Contact: Office of Inspector General; U.S. Department of the Treasury; 740 15th St. NW—Suite 500; Washington, DC 20220; phone: (202) 927-5260; Internet: www.treas.gov/inspector-general/

Special Agent (GS-1811)
Treasury Inspector General for Tax Administration, U.S. Department of the Treasury

The Treasury Inspector General for Tax Administration (TIGTA) provides independent oversight of Internal Revenue Service (IRS) activities. TIGTA was established in 1999 to replace the IRS Internal Security Division as part of the IRS Restructuring and Reform Act of 1998.

TIGTA special agents conduct criminal and noncriminal investigations involving serious official misconduct by IRS employees, threats and assaults upon the IRS and its personnel, and external attempts to corruptly interfere with federal tax administration. Employee integrity investigations are concerned with offenses such as bribery; extortion attempts by IRS employees against taxpayers; unlawful inspection, disclosure, or destruction of tax return or taxpayer information; illegal drug activities; and abuses of authority. They also investigate impersonation of IRS personnel; threats and assaults against IRS employees and facilities; fraud in IRS contracting and procurement programs; unlawful intrusions into IRS computer systems; accidents involving IRS property or personnel; and other matters. TIGTA special agents are authorized to conduct surveillance and undercover operations, carry firearms, make arrests, execute search warrants, and serve subpoenas. They conduct many investigations with other federal, state, and local law enforcement agencies.

TIGTA special agents are covered under special retirement provisions for law enforcement officers, and they qualify for 25 percent Law Enforcement Availability Pay.

Qualifications and Salary Levels

GS-5: Completion of a four-year course of study leading to a bachelor's degree; or three years of general experience, one year of which was equivalent to at least GS-4. **GS-7:** One full year of graduate education, or superior academic achievement during undergraduate studies, or one year of specialized experience equivalent to at least GS-5. **GS-9:** A master's degree, or two years of graduate education, or one year of specialized experience equivalent to at least GS-7. **GS-11:** A Ph.D. or equivalent doctoral degree, or three years of graduate education, or one year of specialized experience equivalent to at least GS-9. **GS-12:** One year of specialized experience equivalent to at least GS-11. **GS-13:** One year of specialized experience equivalent to at least GS-12.

Qualifying education can be substituted for experience, and vice versa. Applicants must be at least 21 years of age and under age 37. However, candidates over age 37 who have previous service creditable under special law enforcement retirement provisions also may be eligible. Eyesight requirements include uncorrected distant vision not worse than 20/200 (Snellen) in each eye, correctable to 20/20 binocular; normal depth perception and peripheral vision; ability to distinguish shades of color; and near vision sufficient to read Jaeger type 2 at 14 inches. Hearing loss must not exceed 30 decibels at the 500, 1000, and 2000 Hertz levels. The application process includes a drug screening test, medical examination, background investigation, and security clearance determination.

Training

TIGTA special agents attend the 11-week Criminal Investigator Training Program at the Federal Law Enforcement Training Center (FLETC) in Glynco, Georgia (see chapter 16). This program is followed by the four-week TIGTA Special Agent Basic Training program at FLETC, which covers subjects such as employee integrity investigations, report writing, photography, interviewing techniques, and legal matters. TIGTA special agents also attend the three-week Inspector General Investigator Training Program at FLETC (see chapter 16), and in-service training relating to subjects such as surveillance, undercover operations, technical investigative equipment, and computer crime.

Contact: Treasury Inspector General for Tax Administration; U.S. Department of the Treasury; 1125 15th St. NW—Room 700; Washington, DC 20005; phone: (202) 927-7160; Internet: www.treas.gov/tigta/

Special Agent (GS-1811)
Office of Inspector General, U.S. Department of Veterans Affairs

The U.S. Department of Veterans Affairs (VA) operates programs to benefit veterans and their families. VA programs consist of compensation payments for disabilities or death related to military service, pensions, education and rehabilitation, home loan guaranty, burial, and a medical care program incorporating nursing homes, clinics, and medical centers.

Special agents of the VA Office of Inspector General (OIG) conduct investigations to identify fraud and other criminal or improper activity in VA programs and operations. Program fraud investigations focus on persons who use the identities of veterans to obtain benefits for medical care, pensions, mortgages, or other assistance; relatives of veterans or their beneficiaries who receive benefits of deceased payees; spouses of deceased payees who continue to receive benefits after remarriage; fraud in the VA Home Loan Guarantee Program; theft and forgery of VA benefit checks; healthcare fraud; fraudulent claims for educational assistance or disability benefits; and other fraudulent schemes. Employee integrity investigations focus on patient abuse; theft, diversion, or use of controlled substances by VA physicians, nurses, pharmacists, or other employees; theft of computers, equipment, supplies, human remains, or other items from VA facilities; workers' compensation fraud; time and attendance fraud; bribery; embezzlement; and other crimes or official misconduct. VA-OIG special agents also investigate contract fraud, which often pertains to product substitutions, false billings, false claims, and other offenses. VA-OIG special agents are authorized to conduct surveillance and undercover operations, carry firearms, make arrests, execute search warrants, and serve subpoenas. They work closely with the VA Police Department and agencies such as the Social Security Administration OIG, Department of Labor OIG, Department of Health and Human Services OIG, and other agencies.

VA-OIG special agents are covered under special retirement provisions for law enforcement officers, and they qualify for 25 percent Law Enforcement Availability Pay.

Qualifications and Salary Levels

GS-5: Completion of a four-year course of study leading to a bachelor's degree; or three years of general experience, one year of which was equivalent to at least GS-4. **GS-7:** One full year of graduate education, or superior academic achievement during undergraduate studies, or one year of specialized experience equivalent to at least GS-5. **GS-9:** A master's degree, or two years of graduate education, or one year of specialized experience equivalent to at least GS-7. **GS-11:** A Ph.D. or equivalent doctoral degree, or three years of graduate education, or one year of specialized experience equivalent to at least GS-9. **GS-12:** One year of specialized experience equivalent to at least GS-11. **GS-13:** One year of specialized experience equivalent to at least GS-12.

Applicants can use equivalent combinations of specialized experience and education to meet total experience requirements. Applicants must be at least 21 years of age and under age 37. However, candidates over age 37 who have previous service creditable under special law enforcement retirement provisions also may be eligible. Eyesight requirements include good distant vision in each eye, near vision that is sufficient to read print the size of typewritten characters, normal depth perception and peripheral vision, and the ability to distinguish basic colors. Eyeglasses and contact lenses are permitted. Hearing loss must not exceed 35 decibels at the 1000, 2000, and 3000 Hertz levels. Tentative appointees must qualify for a security clearance and pass a background investigation, drug screening test, and medical examination.

Training

VA-OIG special agents attend the 11-week Criminal Investigator Training Program at the Federal Law Enforcement Training Center (FLETC) in Glynco, Georgia (see chapter 16). In-service training includes courses concerning VA program fraud investigations, workers' compensation fraud, investigative techniques, drug enforcement, and other subjects. Many VA-OIG special agents also attend the three-week Inspector General Investigator Training Program at FLETC (see chapter 16).

Contact: Office of Inspector General; U.S. Department of Veterans Affairs; 810 Vermont Ave. NW; Washington, DC 20420; phone: (202) 565-8620; Internet: www.va.gov/oig/

Special Agent Pilot (GS-1811)
United States Fish and Wildlife Service, U.S. Department of the Interior

Aviation operations are crucial to the U.S. Fish and Wildlife Service's (FWS's) mission to conserve and protect the nation's fish, wildlife, migratory birds, endangered species, marine mammals, and other natural resources. FWS special agent pilots carry out challenging aviation missions over more than 95 million acres of wetlands, fish hatcheries, inland sport fisheries, wildlife refuges, and other areas.

FWS special agent pilots operate light aircraft in support of the agency's law enforcement and other operations nationwide. Their primary responsibility is aerial surveillance to detect violations relating to the illegal taking, importing, and commercializing of wildlife, while working closely with other FWS special agents in criminal investigations. Their aviation missions are a critical component of investigations that target wildlife smuggling, trafficking in protected species, violations of federal migratory game bird hunting laws, hazardous materials dumping and other environmental crimes, and many other offenses. When not engaged in flight operations, FWS special agent pilots conduct criminal investigations (see "Special Agent, United States Fish and Wildlife Service," earlier in this chapter). FWS special agent pilots are authorized to conduct surveillance and undercover operations, carry firearms, make arrests, execute search warrants, and serve subpoenas. They coordinate aviation operations, investigations, and intelligence activities with agencies such as the Bureau of Land Management; U.S. Immigration and Customs Enforcement; Forest Service; National Marine Fisheries Service; and other federal, state, local, tribal, and foreign agencies.

FWS special agent pilots are covered under special retirement provisions for law enforcement officers, and they qualify for 25 percent Law Enforcement Availability Pay.

Qualifications and Salary Levels

GS-5: Completion of a four-year course of study leading to a bachelor's degree; or three years of general experience, one year of which was equivalent to at least GS-4. **GS-7:** One full year of graduate education, or superior academic achievement during undergraduate studies, or one year of specialized experience equivalent to at least GS-5. **GS-9:** A master's degree, or two years of graduate education, or one year of specialized experience equivalent to at least GS-7. **GS-11:** A Ph.D. or equivalent doctoral degree, or three years of graduate education, or one year of specialized experience equivalent to at least GS-9. **GS-12:** One year of specialized experience equivalent to at least GS-11. **GS-13:** One year of specialized experience equivalent to at least GS-12.

Applicants must have a current Federal Aviation Administration (FAA) Commercial Pilot Certificate with ratings appropriate for the duties performed, an instrument rating, and a current Class I Medical Certificate, and must meet all Department of the Interior Aviation Management Directorate (AM) requirements for pilots. Flight time requirements include 1,500 hours of total flight time, including 1,200 hours as pilot-in-command; 75 hours of night flying experience, including at least 25 hours as pilot-in-command; 75 hours of actual or simulated instrument time, including at least 50 hours in actual flight; 100 hours as pilot-in-command during the previous 12 months; and 200 hours as pilot-in-command in low-level operations (within 500 feet of the surface of typical terrain), or 10 hours of low-level flight instruction within the previous five years followed by a low-level flight check by an AM pilot inspector. Applicants must submit a Form OAS-61, Record of Aeronautical Experience.

Eyesight requirements include uncorrected distant vision not worse than 20/100 (Snellen) in each eye, and corrected binocular distant vision not worse than 20/20; normal depth perception and peripheral vision; and the ability to distinguish basic colors. Candidates who have undergone LASIK eye surgery must be free from residual effects three months after surgery, while those who have had other forms of refractive eye surgery must be free from residual effects one year after surgery. Hearing loss must not exceed 30 decibels in either ear at 500, 1000, or 2000 Hertz, and 40 decibels in either ear at 3000 Hertz. (Hearing aids cannot be used during the test.) The application process includes a drug screening test, medical examination, background investigation, and security clearance determination.

Training

FWS special agent pilots attend the 11-week Criminal Investigator Training Program at the Federal Law Enforcement Training Center (FLETC) in Glynco, Georgia (see chapter 16), followed by the eight-week FWS Special Agent Basic School at FLETC, which covers FWS policies and regulations, law enforcement authority, laws and treaties enforced by FWS law enforcement personnel, wildlife identification, and other agency-specific topics. Ongoing in-service training includes at least 40 hours of coursework annually, including instruction relating to aviation safety, aircraft capabilities and limitations, mission planning, interagency operations, crash survival, and other topics.

Contact: Office of Law Enforcement; United States Fish and Wildlife Service; U.S. Department of the Interior; 4401 N. Fairfax Dr.; Arlington, VA 22203; phone: (703) 358-1949; Internet: www.fws.gov/le/

Special Investigator
Office of Inspector General, Central Intelligence Agency

To safeguard national security, the Central Intelligence Agency (CIA) collects, evaluates, and disseminates intelligence information relating to political, military, economic, scientific, and other developments throughout the world. CIA personnel conduct covert actions at the direction of the president to preempt national security threats or achieve U.S. policy objectives.

Special investigators of the CIA Office of Inspector General (OIG) investigate allegations of waste, fraud, abuse, mismanagement, and violations of federal law pertaining to CIA programs and operations. Investigations carried out by CIA-OIG special investigators often are related to official misconduct by Agency personnel, including offenses such as conflict of interest, time and attendance fraud, theft or misuse of government property, bribery, kickbacks, embezzlement, and other crimes or violations of CIA standards of conduct. CIA-OIG special investigators also investigate employee grievances that have reached the appeal level, and appellate decisions of various Agency boards. In addition to employee integrity investigations, CIA special investigators conduct investigations relating to fraud in the agency's contracting and procurement activities.

Although CIA special investigators are authorized to conduct surveillance and serve subpoenas, they are prohibited by law to have arrest authority. Many investigations are conducted jointly with agencies such as the FBI; State Department Bureau of Diplomatic Security; Drug Enforcement Administration; Defense Criminal Investigative Service; and other federal, state, and local law enforcement agencies.

Qualifications and Salary Levels

CIA-OIG special investigators are appointed through excepted service hiring processes. Salaries for this position are similar to those of GS-1811 special agents at the GS-12 through GS-14 levels with other federal agencies. Applicants must have a bachelor's degree; at least five years of investigative experience, preferably with a federal law enforcement agency; strong research and analytical capabilities; the ability to assemble and assimilate large quantities of information, discern key issues, and draw conclusions; exceptional written and verbal communication skills; and the ability to produce coherent, articulate, and well-organized reports that are sometimes complex and lengthy. Applicants must also qualify for a top-secret security clearance and pass a writing test, background investigation, polygraph examination, medical examination, and psychological examination.

Training

Initial training for CIA-OIG special investigators includes a four-week program conducted by CIA staff which focuses on CIA policies and procedures, federal court processes, criminal law and procedure, OIG subpoena authority, evidence processing and control, fraud, bribery and gratuities, financial investigations, interviewing techniques, civil proceedings, trial preparation, Financial Crimes Enforcement Network operations, and other topics. In-service training is concerned with subjects such as computer crimes, white-collar offenses, personnel misconduct investigations, contractor fraud, legal issues and updates, and various courses offered by the Federal Law Enforcement Training Center (FLETC) or FBI Academy. CIA-OIG special investigators also can attend the three-week Inspector General Investigator Training Program at FLETC (see chapter 16).

Contact: Office of Inspector General; Central Intelligence Agency; Washington, DC 20505; phone: (703) 874-2555; Internet: www.cia.gov/; e-mail: oiginv@ucia.gov

CHAPTER 7

Intelligence Analysts

"Three may keep a secret—if two of them are dead."

—Benjamin Franklin

Intelligence analysts in federal law enforcement play a vital role in the effort to protect our nation's citizens from foreign and domestic threats. These skilled specialists are responsible for data collection, analysis, interpretation, and dissemination of information relating to criminal activity and other matters that directly or indirectly affect national security. Depending upon the mission of employing agencies, intelligence analysts conduct intelligence work pertaining to drug trafficking, terrorism, low-intensity conflict, alien smuggling, passport fraud, organized crime, money laundering, arson rings, cargo theft, espionage, transportation security, and a broad range of other matters. Intelligence analysts also compose data collection manuals, process requests for intelligence information, determine the distribution of raw intelligence data and finished intelligence reports, and perform liaison functions within the U.S. intelligence community. Although all intelligence organizations carry out similar processes, each agency is geared toward producing intelligence within its own sphere of operations.

Intelligence analysts are required to have a basic knowledge and understanding of one or more of the natural or social sciences, engineering, military science, history, political science, or law enforcement. They must also have a fundamental knowledge of research techniques, the ability to express ideas orally and in writing, and a demonstrated potential for learning the methods and techniques characteristic of intelligence work.

Intelligence Analyst (GS-0132)
Federal Bureau of Investigation, U.S. Department of Justice

Intelligence analysts with the Federal Bureau of Investigation (FBI) examine and interpret national security information in support of the criminal intelligence, foreign counterintelligence, counterterrorism, and organized crime missions of the Bureau. FBI intelligence analysts collect and analyze information from sources such as criminal investigations, seized documents, financial records, surveillance reports, witness interviews, informants, and court-ordered wiretaps. They also use intelligence data to prepare strategic and operational analyses, case studies, and threat assessments that are distributed within the FBI; to federal, state, and local law enforcement agencies; and throughout the U.S. intelligence community.

With three areas of specialization in which to serve, these professional support personnel are assigned as either an all-source analyst, operations specialist, or reports officer. FBI all-source analysts are responsible for projects and activities that are geared to a specifically defined geographical or functional area in support of the criminal intelligence, foreign counterintelligence, counterterrorism, and organized crime missions of the FBI. In addition to receiving and processing intelligence on investigative targets within the United States, all-source analysts also obtain intelligence data concerning situations in foreign countries, such as implications of a recent presidential election, revolution, uprising, or coup. Operations specialists lend direct support to investigations by providing case management assistance and critical front-line intelligence. They participate along with FBI special agents in intelligence and investigative operations, including multi-agency task force operations, by collecting, analyzing, evaluating, and disseminating intelligence information. Reports officers are responsible for reviewing investigative and intelligence reports, briefing notes, bulletins, memoranda, correspondence, and other documents; summarizing the information; and formatting it for dissemination to intelligence and law enforcement agencies.

Qualifications and Salary Levels

FBI intelligence analysts are appointed through excepted service hiring processes, although they are paid in accordance with general schedule (GS) pay system rates. All applicants must possess at least one of the following qualifications:

1. A bachelor's degree in any discipline from an accredited college or university; or,

2. Present or former federal employment in a GS-0132 occupational (intelligence analysis) series position for a minimum of one year, or service in a temporary duty assignment to a GS-0132 position for a minimum of one year; or,

3. At least one year of experience as an intelligence analyst; or,

4. Experience in the United States Armed Services under an intelligence Military Occupational Specialty (MOS) code.

In addition, the following salary grade requirements apply: **GS-7:** One full year of graduate-level education, or superior academic achievement during undergraduate studies; and either one year of specialized experience, or two years of experience in a position that involves the exercise of analytical ability, judgment, discretion, and personal responsibility equivalent to at least GS-5. **GS-9:** A master's degree, or a law degree (JD or LL.B.), or two years of graduate-level education; and either one year of specialized experience, or two years of experience in a position that involves the exercise of analytical ability, judgment, discretion, and personal responsibility equivalent to at least GS-7. **GS-11:** A Ph.D. or equivalent doctoral degree, or three years of graduate-level education; and either one year of specialized experience, or two years of experience in a position that involves the exercise of analytical ability, judgment, discretion, and personal responsibility equivalent to at least GS-9. **GS-12**: One year of specialized experience equivalent to at least GS-11. **GS-13:** One year of specialized experience equivalent to at least GS-12. **GS-14:** One year of specialized experience equivalent to at least GS-13. **GS-15:** One year of specialized experience equivalent to at least GS-14. Tentative appointees must qualify for a top-secret security clearance and pass a background investigation, drug screening test, and polygraph exam.

Training

Training for FBI intelligence analysts begins with a seven-week Analytical Cadre Education Strategy (ACES) course at the FBI Academy's College of Analytical Studies in Quantico, Virginia. This course focuses primarily on the intelligence cycle—the components of intelligence requirements, collection, analysis, reporting, and dissemination—and how intelligence advances national security goals. The ACES course also includes instruction on strategic and tactical analysis, asset vetting, report writing, the intelligence community, and various analytical methodologies. In-service training varies widely depending on analysts' particular area of specialty and unit of assignment, although it could include instruction concerning terrorist groups, sleeper cells, weapons of mass destruction, animal rights and environmental extremists, economic espionage, theft of U.S. technology and sensitive economic information by foreign intelligence services, attacks on the nation's critical infrastructure, gang activity, organized criminal enterprises, healthcare fraud, cybercrime, insurance fraud, the behavioral sciences, terrorist threats, and other topics. Intelligence analysts also can attend advanced versions of the ACES course, other programs at the FBI Academy, and courses offered by other organizations.

Contact: Recruiting information can be obtained from any FBI field office, or by contacting the Office of Intelligence; Federal Bureau of Investigation; 935 Pennsylvania Ave. NW; Washington, DC 20535; phone: (202) 324-3000; Internet: www.fbi.gov/.

Intelligence Operations Specialist
Transportation Security Administration, U.S. Department of Homeland Security

Transportation Security Administration (TSA) intelligence operations specialists are assigned to the agency's Transportation and Security Intelligence Service, where they plan, organize, and conduct intelligence assessments in support of TSA field elements throughout the world.

In furtherance of TSA's mission to protect America's transportation systems, intelligence operations specialists oversee indication and warnings operations; review and analyze domestic and international intelligence that relates to U.S. transportation and public transit systems, including airports and aviation systems, railroads, seaports, bus systems, pipelines, and highways; interact and exchange intelligence information with agencies and organizations such as the Central Intelligence Agency, FBI, National Security Agency, Defense Intelligence Agency, Terrorist Threat Integration Center, and Terrorist Screening Center; and provide oral briefings and written presentations to senior officials within TSA, the Department of Homeland Security, and the U.S. Intelligence and Law enforcement communities. TSA intelligence operations specialists also identify significant intelligence trends and gaps; maintain databases of intelligence information; and research, evaluate, and integrate intelligence data for articles, papers, and studies, including those presented in TSA's "Transportation Security Information Report."

TSA intelligence operations specialists participate in a variety of conferences, meetings, and working groups, such as the Interagency Intelligence Committee on Terrorism, the National Joint Terrorism Task Force (JTTF), and FBI field office JTTFs. Their responsibilities also include providing classified and unclassified intelligence information on a daily basis to federal security directors at U.S. airports concerning aviation threat data received from the intelligence community and law enforcement agencies. Some of this information is used to brief airport security personnel.

Qualifications and Salary Levels

TSA intelligence operations specialists are appointed through excepted service hiring processes. The qualifications and salaries for this position are similar to those of intelligence analysts at the GS-7, GS-9, GS-11, GS-12, and GS-13 levels with other federal agencies. TSA is especially interested in candidates with knowledge and experience in the areas of risk analysis; vulnerability assessment; contingency planning; domestic and international intelligence relating to transportation systems; terrorist groups, tactics, methodologies, and ideologies; Middle Eastern terrorism activities; written and oral communications; and team building. Candidates must successfully complete a background investigation, qualify for a top-secret security clearance, and pass a drug test prior to appointment.

Training

Initial training for TSA intelligence operations specialists includes the two-week Intelligence Analyst Training Program at the Federal Law Enforcement Training Center in Glynco, Georgia (see chapter 16). Ongoing professional development includes training in areas such as aviation, maritime, and transit system threat indicators; chemical, biological, and nuclear threat awareness; international terrorism; operational planning; analytical methods; legal issues; computer database information retrieval; and electronic sources of information.

Contact: Transportation Security Administration; U.S. Department of Homeland Security; 601 S. 12th St.; Arlington, VA 22202; phone: (800) 887-1895; Internet: www.tsa.gov/

Intelligence Operations Specialist (GS-0132)
Bureau of Intelligence and Research, U.S. Department of State

The Bureau of Intelligence and Research (BIR) is the focal point in the Department of State for coordination of sensitive civilian and military intelligence operations, analysis, and research for the Department and other federal agencies. BIR intelligence operations specialists serve as liaison concerning operational intelligence programs related to counterterrorism with the U.S. intelligence community, the National Security Council, and various State Department bureaus. Their intelligence activities also support foreign policy, U.S. diplomacy, and national security purposes.

Some of their responsibilities include researching, analyzing, and evaluating intelligence reports; interpreting intelligence findings and making recommendations for actions to be taken; serving as a liaison representative with intelligence community organizations to ensure that State Department views on counterterrorism are well understood; gathering information on terrorist incidents and other criminal activities to determine potential threats to State Department employees and facilities; drafting memoranda for Department principals attending National Security Council meetings on intelligence operational programs related to counterterrorism; representing the Bureau at interagency meetings on operational counterterrorism practices; and other activities to protect United States national interests from foreign security threats. Although a substantial effort is directed toward intelligence gathering, analysis, and dissemination for law enforcement purposes, intelligence operations involving national security matters are more prevalent.

Qualifications and Salary Levels

GS-7: One full year of graduate education, or superior academic achievement during undergraduate studies, or one year of specialized experience equivalent to GS-5. **GS-9:** A master's degree, or two years of graduate education, or one year of specialized experience equivalent to GS-7. **GS-11:** A Ph.D. or equivalent doctoral degree, or three years of graduate education, or one year of specialized experience equivalent to GS-9. **GS-12:** One year of specialized experience equivalent to GS-11. **GS-13:** One year of specialized experience equivalent to GS-12. Experience and education can be combined to meet total experience requirements. Those tentatively selected must qualify for a security clearance and pass a background investigation.

Training

Intelligence operations specialists attend a one-week training program conducted by State Department staff that includes instruction in subjects such as crime reporting, drafting intelligence assessments, computer techniques, legal aspects of intelligence, sources of information, databases, information management, intelligence dissemination, and report writing. In-service training includes courses in foreign policy, advanced computer techniques, State Department regulations, and other subjects related to specific duties of the position.

Contact: Bureau of Intelligence and Research; U.S. Department of State; 2201 C St. NW; Washington, DC 20520; phone: (202) 261-8888 or (202) 647-7284; Internet: www.state.gov/employment/

Intelligence Operations Specialist (GS-0132)
Office of Inspector General, U.S. Department of State

The Security and Intelligence Oversight division of the State Department Office of Inspector General (OIG) is responsible for evaluating the effectiveness of intelligence activities of the State Department and of mission chiefs worldwide, and for ensuring that intelligence operations and related activities are conducted in a manner consistent with law and executive directives.

State Department OIG intelligence operations specialists gather data and conduct interviews with Department, intelligence community, and other officials to develop working hypotheses and recommend issues to be examined during the course of intelligence inspections; plan and conduct intelligence oversight reviews; evaluate the ability of overseas posts to respond to threats from terrorism, organized crime, intelligence penetration, physical intrusion, and other criminal activity; determine whether adequate internal controls are in place to prevent or reduce the incidence of waste, fraud, and mismanagement; evaluate functional and individual performance in intelligence activities under review, highlighting potential problems and presenting viable solutions; draft detailed written reports; and meet with State Department managers to present findings and resolve conflicts.

Qualifications and Salary Levels

GS-7: One full year of graduate education, or superior academic achievement during undergraduate studies, or one year of specialized experience equivalent to GS-5. **GS-9:** A master's degree, or two years of graduate education, or one year of specialized experience equivalent to GS-7. **GS-11:** A Ph.D. or equivalent doctoral degree, or three years of graduate education, or one year of specialized experience equivalent to GS-9. **GS-12:** One year of specialized experience equivalent to GS-11. **GS-13:** One year of specialized experience equivalent to GS-12. Equivalent combinations of education and experience can be used to meet minimum experience requirements. Candidates must successfully complete a background investigation and qualify for a security clearance prior to appointment.

Training

Initial training for State Department intelligence operations specialists includes a one-week course presented by the Defense Intelligence Agency that provides an overview of intelligence operations. They also attend a variety of training courses throughout their careers involving State Department operations and programs, intelligence gathering and dissemination, operations of federal intelligence organizations, memoranda of understanding, ambassador authority, and other subjects that focus on specific responsibilities of the position.

Contact: Office of Inspector General; U.S. Department of State; 2201 C St. NW; Washington, DC 20520; phone: (202) 663-0340 or (202) 647-7284; Internet: www.oig.state.gov/

Intelligence Research Analyst (GS-0132)
United States Coast Guard, U.S. Department of Homeland Security

As the primary maritime law enforcement agency in the United States, the U.S. Coast Guard (USCG) employs intelligence research analysts to conduct extensive studies in support of a wide range of law enforcement and other USCG operations. Operating within Coast Guard Headquarters, Maritime Intelligence Fusion Centers, and Field Intelligence Support Teams, intelligence research analysts collect, analyze, and disseminate intelligence pertaining to individuals and organizations involved in drug trafficking activities, illegal alien smuggling operations, terrorism, piracy, marine environmental crimes, and other maritime criminal activity.

Their responsibilities also include producing all-source assessments on threats to maritime interests and Coast Guard forces operating throughout the world, and representing the Coast Guard in interagency operations with the United States intelligence community on issues of terrorism, counterintelligence, crime, and low-intensity conflict. Coast Guard intelligence research analysts gather intelligence from classified and unclassified library sources, documents, photographs, databases, and other sources. They present the results of their research orally or in writing to senior USCG officers and civilian personnel, and to representatives of other organizations in high-level interagency meetings. USCG intelligence research analysts also maintain liaison and share intelligence with agencies such as the Central Intelligence Agency, Defense Intelligence Agency, FBI, Marine Corps Intelligence, and National Security Agency, among others.

Qualifications and Salary Levels

GS-7: One full year of graduate education, or superior academic achievement during undergraduate studies, or one year of specialized experience equivalent to GS-5. **GS-9:** A master's degree, or two years of graduate education, or one year of specialized experience equivalent to GS-7. **GS-11:** A Ph.D. or equivalent doctoral degree, or three years of graduate education, or one year of specialized experience equivalent to GS-9.

GS-12: One year of specialized experience equivalent to GS-11. **GS-13:** One year of specialized experience equivalent to GS-12. Qualifying education can be substituted for experience, and vice versa. The application process includes a background investigation and top-secret security clearance determination.

Training

Initial training for intelligence research analysts includes a one-week course conducted by USCG staff in effective report writing and format. They also complete orientation training that covers the Coast Guard's history, mission, culture, internal processes, customs, organizational structure, personnel system, and other topics. In-service training consists of courses pertaining to internal intelligence gathering and dissemination policies and procedures, intelligence information management, handling classified information, computer software and hardware systems, link analysis, event charting, and other subjects depending upon the needs of the Coast Guard and individual personnel.

Contact: Civilian Personnel Management Division; United States Coast Guard; 2100 Second St. SW; Washington, DC 20593; phone: (202) 267-1310; Internet: www.uscg.mil/

Intelligence Research Specialist (GS-0132)
Office of Border Patrol, United States Customs and Border Protection, U.S. Department of Homeland Security

Border Patrol intelligence research specialists serving with United States Customs and Border Protection (CBP) are responsible for producing and analyzing intelligence concerning illegal immigration, terrorists, weapons of mass destruction, illegal drugs, and other threats to national security and CBP personnel.

Armed with information from a wide variety of sources, Border Patrol intelligence research specialists consolidate and evaluate incoming reports, intelligence data, and information involving Border Patrol operations; select and isolate pertinent information; organize and summarize investigative material to identify needs, trends, patterns, and profiles; ensure that necessary follow-up actions are initiated; and select or recommend intelligence dissemination methods that are appropriate for the intelligence developed. Border Patrol intelligence research specialists prepare written intelligence reports and contribute to statistical compilations. They present written reports and oral briefings to the Chief Border Patrol Agent on a regular basis, from which the results are used by high-level Border Patrol staff to devise and implement appropriate responses to threats to national security and CBP personnel. They also maintain working relationships with counterparts and colleagues throughout the intelligence community, exchange information, and provide free flow of intelligence on matters of mutual interest. For example, Border Patrol intelligence research specialists coordinate operations with agencies such as the FBI, U.S. Coast Guard, National Park Service, U.S. Immigration and Customs Enforcement, and Drug Enforcement Administration.

Qualifications and Salary Levels

GS-7: One full year of graduate education, or superior academic achievement during undergraduate studies, or one year of specialized experience equivalent to GS-5. **GS-9:** A master's degree, or two years of graduate education, or one year of specialized experience equivalent to GS-7. **GS-11:** A Ph.D. or equivalent doctoral degree, or three years of graduate education, or one year of specialized experience equivalent to GS-9. **GS-12:** One year of specialized experience equivalent to GS-11. **GS-13:** One year of specialized experience equivalent to GS-12. Experience and education can be combined to meet total experience requirements. Tentative appointees must pass a background investigation and drug screening test, and qualify for a security clearance.

Training

Border Patrol Intelligence Research Specialists attend the two-week Intelligence Analyst Training Program at the Federal Law Enforcement Training Center in Glynco, Georgia (see chapter 16). Ongoing in-service and on-the-job training focuses on subjects such as intelligence gathering, terrorism indicators, false documents, threat assessment, Border Patrol operations and regulations, legal issues, and other matters related to specific duties of the position and nature of assignment.

Contact: Office of Border Patrol; United States Customs and Border Protection; U.S. Department of Homeland Security; 1300 Pennsylvania Ave. NW; Washington, DC 20229; phone: (202) 344-1250; Internet: www.cbp.gov/

Intelligence Research Specialist (GS-0132)
Drug Enforcement Administration, U.S. Department of Justice

In coordination with other federal, state, local, and foreign law enforcement organizations, Drug Enforcement Administration (DEA) intelligence research specialists collect, analyze, and disseminate drug-related intelligence pertaining to individuals and organizations involved in the growing, manufacture, or distribution of controlled substances.

Working closely with DEA special agents during the course of criminal investigations, DEA intelligence research specialists gather and analyze information from a variety of sources, including criminal investigations, seized documents, financial records, surveillance reports, cooperating sources, and court-ordered wiretaps. They manage complex research projects in areas such as drug cultivation and production, methods of transportation, trafficking routes, major conspiracies, and the structure and analysis of trafficker organizations. Case development is enhanced through the use of sophisticated databases and unique methods of data manipulation. Intelligence research specialists present intelligence data orally or in writing to case agents, supervisory personnel, prosecuting attorneys, grand juries, and high-level decision-makers. DEA intelligence research specialists are stationed in most major U.S. cities, and in foreign countries that cultivate drug crops, produce drugs, or are transit points.

Qualifications and Salary Levels

GS-7: One full year of graduate education, or superior academic achievement during undergraduate studies, or one year of specialized experience equivalent to GS-5. **GS-9:** A master's degree, or two years of graduate education, or one year of specialized experience equivalent to GS-7. **GS-11:** A Ph.D. or equivalent doctoral degree, or three years of graduate education, or one year of specialized experience equivalent to GS-9. **GS-12:** One year of specialized experience equivalent to GS-11. **GS-13:** One year of specialized experience equivalent to GS-12. Applicants can use equivalent combinations of specialized experience and education to meet total experience requirements. Tentative appointees must qualify for a top-secret security clearance and pass a background investigation, drug screening test, and polygraph examination. Intelligence research specialists must sign a DEA Mobility Agreement and must be willing to accept reassignment to any location depending on the needs of the DEA and the Intelligence Program.

Training

Newly hired personnel attend the nine-week Basic Intelligence Research Specialist course at the DEA Academy in Quantico, Virginia. This program covers the mission and functions of the DEA, sources of information, legal aspects of intelligence, computer databases and software, information management, report writing, intelligence dissemination, and other aspects of drug trafficking and violent crime intelligence operations. DEA intelligence research specialists also attend various advanced courses throughout their careers that include instruction in legal issues, analytical tools and methodologies, DEA computer systems, law enforcement databases, critical thinking, operational and tactical procedures, personal integrity and responsibility, internal regulations, and other subjects related to specific duties.

Contact: Direct inquiries to the DEA field office where employment is sought, or to the Office of Personnel; Drug Enforcement Administration; U.S. Department of Justice; 2401 Jefferson Davis Hwy.; Alexandria, VA 22301; phone: (202) 307-1000; Internet: www.dea.gov/

Intelligence Research Specialist (GS-0132)
United States Immigration and Customs Enforcement, U.S. Department of Homeland Security

The U.S. Immigration and Customs Enforcement (ICE) Office of Intelligence (OI) is tasked with the collection, integration, analysis, and dissemination of information on critical homeland security vulnerabilities that could be exploited by terrorist and criminal organizations.

Operating within OI headquarters and ICE field intelligence units, intelligence research specialists concentrate their efforts on the movement of people, money, and goods into, within, and out of the United States to provide accurate intelligence data to ICE leadership, field agents, and other law enforcement agencies. By applying their expertise in data and threat analysis, foreign languages, financial investigations, counterterrorism, and other areas, ICE intelligence research analysts obtain and process information from a wide range of sources to assess patterns, trends, and developments in areas such as illegal immigration, human smuggling and trafficking, criminal aliens, counterfeiting of immigration documents, air and marine smuggling, cargo theft, drug smuggling, financial crimes and money laundering, illicit transportation of currency in support of criminal enterprise, commercial fraud, Internet crimes, child pornography, arms trafficking and high-technology transfers, terrorism, and security at federal facilities.

Their responsibilities include evaluating raw intelligence data; performing file research to identify patterns, trends, and associations; drawing conclusions based on incoming data; recognizing leads, detecting discrepancies, and identifying relevant evidence; operating computer systems and using databases to facilitate the collection and development of information; and preparing written reports and oral presentations. Intelligence research specialists assigned to the Intelligence Support Division provide senior ICE management with daily reports on significant activities, and staff the 24-hour ICE Operations Center to handle incoming incident reports and facilitate the exchange of intelligence between ICE and other agencies.

Qualifications and Salary Levels

GS-7: One full year of graduate education, or superior academic achievement during undergraduate studies, or one year of specialized experience equivalent to GS-5. **GS-9:** A master's degree, or two years of graduate education, or one year of specialized experience equivalent to GS-7. **GS-11:** A Ph.D. or equivalent doctoral degree, or three years of graduate education, or one year of specialized experience equivalent to GS-9. **GS-12:** One year of specialized experience equivalent to GS-11. **GS-13:** One year of specialized experience equivalent to GS-12. Qualifying education can be substituted for experience, and vice versa. Candidates must successfully complete a background investigation, qualify for a top-secret security clearance, and pass a drug test prior to appointment.

Training

ICE intelligence research specialists attend a five-week basic intelligence course at the Federal Law Enforcement Training Center in Glynco, Georgia. This program covers subjects such as criminal law, legal aspects of intelligence operations, intelligence collection and cycles, link analysis and charting, event analysis, intelligence computer programs, crime scene investigation, interviewing and interrogation, oral briefing techniques, computer security, and terrorism. In-service training includes instruction concerning import and export fraud, smuggling operations, legal issues and updates, advanced intelligence analysis, case methodologies, and other pertinent and timely subjects.

Contact: Office of Intelligence; United States Immigration and Customs Enforcement; U.S. Department of Homeland Security; 425 I St. NW; Washington, DC 20536; phone: (202) 514-2648; Internet: www.ice.gov/

Intelligence Research Specialist (GS-0132)
Bureau of Alcohol, Tobacco, Firearms and Explosives, U.S. Department of Justice

The Bureau of Alcohol, Tobacco, Firearms and Explosives (ATF) employs intelligence research specialists to conduct complex analytical studies in support of investigative operations and ATF's national intelligence strategy. ATF intelligence research specialists collect, analyze, and evaluate information relating to national and international organizations and individuals involved in the trafficking of firearms, explosives, and narcotics; arson rings; traditional and nontraditional organized crime enterprises; terrorist organizations; and others involved in complex criminal conspiracies.

Using information from various sources, ATF intelligence research specialists are responsible for producing detailed strategic analyses that describe and predict violent criminal activity patterns. This involves tasks such as planning and developing intelligence programs and collection methods; applying various information processing and link analysis techniques; providing technical advice and consultation to ATF special agents and federal prosecutors; participating in working groups, task force operations, and conferences; and following appropriate dissemination protocol. Intelligence research studies typically include estimates of the scope of each type of criminal activity under various demographic, geopolitical, and other scenarios, and assessments of their long-term impact on the ATF enforcement mission. ATF intelligence research specialists use sophisticated computer systems and programs to facilitate the collection and development of information. They communicate their research findings to law enforcement personnel, prosecuting attorneys, and grand juries in the form of written reports, charts, graphs, spreadsheets, and organized oral presentations.

Qualifications and Salary Levels

ATF intelligence research specialists are appointed through excepted service hiring processes. The qualifications and salaries for this position are similar to those of intelligence analysts at the GS-7, GS-9, GS-11, GS-12, and GS-13 levels with other federal agencies. ATF seeks candidates with the ability to apply facts derived from a variety of sources to solve problems, as well as experience in research techniques, intelligence operations, computer databases, and report writing. Candidates must successfully complete a background investigation, qualify for a top-secret security clearance, and pass a drug test prior to appointment.

Training

ATF intelligence research specialists attend the two-week Intelligence Analyst Training Program at the Federal Law Enforcement Training Center in Glynco, Georgia (see chapter 16). In-service training includes various courses, conferences, and workshops pertaining to link analysis, analytical charting methods, concealed income analysis, case management, court testimony, pen register operations and analysis, firearms trafficking investigations, organized crime, legal issues and updates, and other subjects.

Contact: Personnel Division; Bureau of Alcohol, Tobacco, Firearms and Explosives; U.S. Department of Justice; 650 Massachusetts Ave. NW—Room 4100; Washington, DC 20226; phone: (202) 927-8610; Internet: www.atf.gov/; e-mail: persdiv@atf.gov

Intelligence Research Specialist (GS-0132)
Financial Crimes Enforcement Network, U.S. Department of the Treasury

The Financial Crimes Enforcement Network (FinCEN) was created by the Treasury Department to provide a government-wide, multi-source intelligence and analytical network to support law enforcement and regulatory agencies in the detection, investigation, and prosecution of financial crimes, with particular emphasis on money-laundering activities relating to drug trafficking operations and terrorism.

FinCEN intelligence research specialists collect, analyze, and disseminate intelligence information gathered from databases and other sources, such as the Treasury Department Financial Database, which includes reports filed under requirements of the Federal Bank Secrecy Act; databases administered by federal law enforcement and regulatory agencies; and commercial, publicly available databases containing business and marketing records, and demographic information. FinCEN intelligence research specialists disseminate intelligence information to U.S. and international law enforcement agencies to assist in building investigations, preparing prosecutions, and developing and implementing strategies to combat money laundering and other financial crimes. They also work on an interagency basis to support and execute U.S. strategies for combating money laundering, terrorist financing, and other financial crimes; promote international anti-money laundering and counter-terrorist financing standards; and provide training and assistance to countries seeking to legislate against financial crimes by implementing an effective legal and institutional framework, including the establishment of financial intelligence units. In addition to maintaining a permanent core of intelligence research specialists, dozens of personnel are assigned to FinCEN on long-term details from various federal law enforcement and regulatory agencies.

Qualifications and Salary Levels

GS-7: One full year of graduate education, or superior academic achievement during undergraduate studies, or one year of specialized experience equivalent to GS-5. **GS-9:** A master's degree, or two years of graduate education, or one year of specialized experience equivalent to GS-7. **GS-11:** A Ph.D. or equivalent doctoral degree, or three years of graduate education, or one year of specialized experience equivalent to GS-9. **GS-12:** One year of specialized experience equivalent to GS-11. **GS-13:** One year of specialized experience equivalent to GS-12. Equivalent combinations of education and experience can be used to meet minimum experience requirements. The application process includes a drug screening test, background investigation, and top-secret security clearance determination.

Training

FinCEN Intelligence Research Specialists attend the two-week Intelligence Analyst Training Program at the Federal Law Enforcement Training Center in Glynco, Georgia (see chapter 16). In-service training is concerned with topics such as financial fraud, banking regulations, money laundering, legal issues, international terrorist activity and terrorism financing, intelligence databases, and other subjects related to specific duties of the position.

Contact: Financial Crimes Enforcement Network; U.S. Department of the Treasury; 2070 Chain Bridge Rd.; Vienna, VA 22182; phone: (703) 905-3591; Internet: www.fincen.gov/

Intelligence Specialist (GS-0132)
Naval Criminal Investigative Service, U.S. Department of Defense

Intelligence specialists of the Naval Criminal Investigative Service (NCIS) perform intelligence analysis and production tasks related to criminal investigations, counterintelligence, and terrorism activities in support of Navy and Marine Corps operations in the United States and overseas.

Operating within a worldwide field structure that provides counterintelligence support both offshore and afloat, NCIS intelligence specialists develop, collate, and analyze data collected from criminal investigations and other sources; review case files of counterintelligence investigations and operations to evaluate, extract, and disseminate information and provide analytical support; develop investigative targets; operate automated databases; and perform link analysis to determine relationships concerning information gathered by NCIS special agents and other investigators.

Their responsibilities also include producing analytical reviews, flow charts, spreadsheets, and timelines of complex cases; assisting in the prosecution of criminal cases; monitoring trends in criminal activity; participating in interagency conferences; and maintaining liaison with other agencies in the U.S. intelligence community to discuss mutual intelligence problems and operations. NCIS intelligence specialists also are assigned to the Navy's Multiple Threat Alert Center, which provides indications and warning of threats to Navy and Marine Corps personnel and assets around the world. This facility operates 24 hours a day to identify terrorist activity, foreign intelligence threats, and criminal threats that could affect naval operations or U.S. national security. NCIS intelligence specialists provide their research results to other federal, state, and local law enforcement agencies on a reciprocal basis.

This is a civilian position and does not require active duty military service.

Qualifications and Salary Levels

GS-7: One full year of graduate education, or superior academic achievement during undergraduate studies, or one year of specialized experience equivalent to GS-5. **GS-9:** A master's degree, or two years of graduate education, or one year of specialized experience equivalent to GS-7. **GS-11:** A Ph.D. or equivalent doctoral degree, or three years of graduate education, or one year of specialized experience equivalent to GS-9. **GS-12:** One year of specialized experience equivalent to GS-11. **GS-13:** One year of specialized experience equivalent to GS-12. Experience and education can be combined to meet total experience requirements. Tentative appointees must pass a background investigation and drug screening test, and qualify for a top-secret security clearance. A polygraph exam also could be required.

Training

NCIS Intelligence Specialists complete 10 weeks of initial training that is conducted by the Defense Intelligence Agency in Washington, D.C. This comprehensive program consists of a two-week National Intelligence Course, a three-week Intelligence Analysis Course, a three-week Counterterrorism Analysis Course, and a two-week Counterintelligence Course. These courses focus on intelligence analysis fundamentals, tools and techniques used in data collection, terrorist threats and issues, counterterrorism analysis, civilian and military intelligence activities, functions and interdependent relationships among counterintelligence organizations, and other subjects. In-service training consists of similar courses, as well as various updates, conferences, and symposia.

Contact: Counterintelligence Directorate; Naval Criminal Investigative Service; 716 Sicard St. SE; Washington Navy Yard; Washington, DC 20388; phone: (202) 433-8800; Internet: www.ncis.navy.mil/; e-mail: jobs@ncis.navy.mil

CHAPTER 8

Uniformed Law Enforcement Officers

"Only in a police state is the job of a policeman easy."

—Orson Welles

Uniformed federal law enforcement officers ensure compliance with and enforce laws, regulations, and agency rules while also providing a visible deterrent to crime on and around federal property and other locations. These officers are responsible for preserving the peace and protecting civil rights; conducting patrols; preventing, detecting, and investigating crimes; arresting violators; assisting in the prosecution of criminals; and providing assistance to citizens in emergency situations. Many uniformed federal officers also control traffic, investigate accidents, respond to crime scenes, engage in search and rescue missions, screen visitors in federal buildings, monitor electronic security devices, counsel persons in need of assistance, and manage activities related to wildlife and natural resources.

Uniformed federal officers perform work in a wide variety of settings that range from federally owned and leased office buildings to military installations, Native American lands, hospitals, training academies, national parks, forests, international borders, campgrounds, recreational areas, historic residences and landmarks, train tracks and stations, roads and highways, power plants, hydroelectric dams, and printing facilities, among others.

Air Interdiction Agent (GS-1881)
United States Customs and Border Protection, U.S. Department of Homeland Security

In October 2005, more than two years after the U.S. Department of Homeland Security was established, the Border Patrol Air Operations unit and the former U.S. Customs Aviation Program combined personnel, aircraft, and other resources to create CBP Air, the largest law enforcement air force in the world. As a result, Border Patrol agent pilots and U.S. Customs special agent pilots were consolidated into the air interdiction agent position. In furtherance of the U.S. Customs and Border Protection (CBP) mission, air interdiction agents provide crucial aerial support to Department of Homeland Security operations by working with air, marine, and ground units to interdict people, vehicles, aircraft, and watercraft illegally crossing U.S. borders. These enforcement operations focus on illegal immigration, alien smuggling, drug trafficking enterprises, terrorist activities, and other crimes. CBP air interdiction agents operate a fleet that includes more than 250 fixed-wing aircraft and helicopters.

Air interdiction agents carry out aerial patrols—largely over areas adjacent to the international boundaries of the United States—that involve surveillance, tracking, pursuits, and search and rescue operations. They also provide support to airspace security operations for designated areas and national security events, such as the Olympic Games, Super Bowl, and presidential inaugurations. Air interdiction agents accomplish these tasks by using sophisticated electronic devices, including night scopes, remote sensor systems, video cameras, fiberoptic scopes, radar instruments, and mobile radio communications equipment. As fully commissioned law enforcement officers, these personnel also perform a wide range of traditional ground-based border enforcement tasks, such as gathering intelligence; conducting interviews and interrogations; searching persons, vehicles, vessels, and cargo for weapons and contraband; making arrests; writing reports; preparing cases for prosecution; and testifying in court. They also provide air and ground support to other federal, state, local, and foreign law enforcement agencies. Air interdiction agents are authorized to carry firearms and make arrests.

Air Interdiction Agents are covered under special retirement provisions for federal law enforcement officers, and they are eligible to receive Law Enforcement Availability Pay.

Qualifications and Salary Levels

Grade levels for this position—which range from GS-9 to GS-13—are based on the nature of experience and number of flight hours logged. For all grade levels, candidates must have a Commercial Pilot Certificate or the appropriate military rating for the type of aircraft to be operated; an instrument rating; a minimum of 1,500 hours of total flight time, including 250 hours as pilot-in-command, 75 hours of instrument flying, 75 hours of night flying, and 100 hours of flying time in the last 12 months; and an FAA Class II Medical Certificate. Applicants must be at least 21 years of age and under age 37. However, candidates over age 37 who have previous service creditable under special law enforcement retirement provisions also may be eligible. Tentative appointees must qualify for a security clearance and pass a background investigation, drug screening test, and medical examination.

Training

CBP air interdiction agents attend the 11-week Criminal Investigator Training Program at the Federal Law Enforcement Training Center (FLETC) in Glynco, Georgia (see chapter 16). This course is followed by specialized training conducted by CBP instructors at FLETC, which includes instruction in areas such as immigration law, search and seizure, patrol and surveillance techniques, drug trafficking, alien smuggling, interdiction techniques, defensive tactics, CBP operations, and other subjects. Ongoing inservice training is geared toward various aspects of CBP Air operations, terrorism, and specific responsibilities of the position.

Contact: United States Customs and Border Protection; U.S. Department of Homeland Security; 1300 Pennsylvania Ave. NW; Washington, DC 20229; phone: (202) 344-1250; Internet: www.cbp.gov/

Border Patrol Agent (GS-1896)
Office of Border Patrol, United States Customs and Border Protection,U.S. Department of Homeland Security

Prior to the terrorist attacks of September 11, 2001, the primary mission of the Border Patrol was to detect and prevent the smuggling and unlawful entry of undocumented aliens into the United States. Today, the Border Patrol is concerned principally with homeland security—specifically with preventing terrorists and terrorist weapons from entering the United States—although the interdiction of illegal aliens remains a high priority for the agency. As a uniformed and mobile law enforcement arm of U.S. Customs and Border Protection (CBP), Border Patrol agents patrol about 6,000 miles of international land border with Canada and Mexico and nearly 2,000 miles of coastal border.

Border Patrol agents conduct patrols in vehicles, aircraft, and boats, as well as on foot and horseback. In search of undocumented aliens—including terrorists who enter the United States unlawfully—Border Patrol agents conduct surveillance, farm and ranch inspections, traffic observation, and city patrols; respond to electronic sensor alarms; use infrared scopes and low-light camera systems at night; and follow tracks and other physical evidence. In an effort to intercept drug smugglers, Border Patrol agents carry out extensive drug interdiction efforts along the nation's borders, including operations that are coordinated with agencies such as the U.S. Coast Guard, National Park Service, U.S. Immigration and Customs Enforcement, FBI, and Drug Enforcement Administration. Border Patrol agents rely heavily on tactical, operational, and strategic intelligence to assess risks to national security and target enforcement efforts. The initial tour-of-duty for Border Patrol agents normally is along the U.S. border with Mexico. They are authorized to conduct undercover operations, carry firearms, and make arrests.

Border Patrol agents are covered under special retirement provisions for law enforcement officers, and they are eligible to receive Administratively Uncontrollable Overtime Pay.

Qualifications and Salary Levels

GS-5: Completion of a four-year course of study leading to a bachelor's degree; or three years of general experience, one year of which was equivalent to GS-4. **GS-7:** One full year of graduate education, or superior academic achievement during undergraduate studies, or one year of specialized experience equivalent to GS-5. **GS-9:** A master's degree, or two years of graduate education, or one year of specialized experience equivalent to GS-7. **GS-11:** A Ph.D. or equivalent doctoral degree, or three years of graduate education, or one year of specialized experience equivalent to GS-9. **GS-12:** One year of specialized experience equivalent to GS-11.

Qualifying education can be substituted for experience, and vice versa. Applicants must be at least 21 years of age and under age 37. However, candidates over age 37 who have previous service creditable under special law enforcement retirement provisions also may be eligible. Eyesight requirements include uncorrected distant visual acuity not worse than 20/100 (Snellen) in each eye. Binocular distant vision must be correctable to 20/20 with glasses or contact lenses. Corrected or uncorrected near vision must be sufficient to read Jaeger Type 2 at 14 inches. Normal peripheral vision, depth perception, and the ability to distinguish basic shades of color are required. A history of refractive surgery to correct vision defects is permissible if an examination by a board-certified ophthalmologist or optometrist determines there are no postoperative complications. Hearing loss must not exceed 30 decibels in either ear at 500, 1000, and 2000 Hertz; or 40 decibels in either ear at 3000 Hertz. (Hearing aids cannot be used during the test.) Candidates must achieve a passing score on the Border Patrol Agent Examination to advance in the hiring process (see chapter 3). The application process also includes a physical fitness test, drug screening, medical examination, and background investigation.

Training

USBP agents attend the 19-week Border Patrol Integrated Training Program within the Border Patrol Academy at the Federal Law Enforcement Training Center in Artesia, New Mexico (see chapter 16). Ongoing in-service training focuses on subjects such as alien smuggling operations, narcotics trafficking, immigration law updates, terrorism operations, criminal law, laws of arrest, search and seizure, use of force, patrol and surveillance techniques, first aid, firearms proficiency, and defensive tactics.

Contact: Office of Border Patrol; United States Customs and Border Protection; U.S. Department of Homeland Security; 1300 Pennsylvania Ave. NW; Washington, DC 20229; phone: (202) 344-1250; Internet: www.cbp.gov/

Capitol Police Officer
Patrol Division, U.S. Capitol Police

Officers of the U.S. Capitol Police (USCP) are responsible for protecting people and government property; preventing, detecting, and investigating criminal acts; and enforcing traffic regulations within a 190-acre area that encompasses the U.S. Capitol Building, a large complex of congressional buildings, and many area parks and roadways. As the agency with the sole statutory responsibility for providing protective and law enforcement services for the U.S. Congress, USCP officers monitor closed circuit television surveillance monitors, alarms, and intrusion detection devices; screen visitors and packages entering buildings; perform patrols on foot and in vehicles; respond to crimes in progress, disturbances, protests, demonstrations, bomb threats, and emergency situations; conduct traffic control and enforcement; assist the U.S. Secret Service with operations for the protection of the president, vice president, immediate family members of the president and vice president, and visiting dignitaries on Capitol grounds; and provide personal protection for members of Congress and their families in the Capitol complex and throughout the United States. In order to provide for the protection of national security information, the USCP conducts special operations to ensure that Congress operates free from the threat of surreptitious and clandestine listening devices and monitoring systems. After more than one year on the job, USCP officers can be assigned to responsibilities involving dignitary protection, criminal or special investigations, intelligence, threat response, drug enforcement, canine handling, communications, the Emergency Response Team, hazardous devices and electronic countermeasures, or bicycle patrol. USCP officers are authorized to carry firearms and make arrests.

Retirement benefits for Capitol police officers are equivalent to that of personnel in the competitive service who are covered under special retirement provisions for federal law enforcement officers.

Qualifications and Salary Levels

USCP officers are appointed through excepted service hiring processes. The U.S. Capitol Police Pay Plan is identical to the Supreme Court Police Pay Plan (see later in this chapter). Salaries under these pay systems are similar to GS-9 through GS-12, which are significantly higher than salaries for most GS-0083 federal police officers who perform similar work and are compensated under the General Schedule pay system. Applicants must be at least 21 years of age and under age 37. However, candidates over age 37 who have previous service creditable under special law enforcement retirement provisions also may be eligible. A high school diploma or GED certificate is required. Uncorrected visual acuity must be no worse than 20/100 (Snellen), correctable to 20/20 in each eye. Weight must be proportionate to height. Applicants must pass the National Police Officer Selection Test (see chapter 3). The application process also includes an oral interview, polygraph examination, background investigation, medical examination, and psychological evaluation.

Training

USCP officers attend the 10-week Mixed Basic Police Training Program at the Federal Law Enforcement Training Center in Glynco, Georgia (see chapter 16). Basic training is followed by a 10-week course at the Capitol Police Training Academy in Washington, DC, which focuses primarily on the District of Columbia Code, police procedures, and traffic law enforcement. This course is followed by a field training program in which new officers perform their duties accompanied by experienced field training officers. In-service training could include courses in public relations, legal issues and updates, protective operations, firearms proficiency, first aid, physical fitness and defensive tactics, and many other subjects.

Contact: Recruiting Section; United States Capitol Police; 119 D St. NE; Washington, DC 20510; phone: (866) 561-8727 or (202) 224-9819; Internet: www.uscapitolpolice.gov/; e-mail: recruiting@cap-police.senate.gov

Customs and Border Protection Canine Officer (GS-1895)
United States Customs and Border Protection, U.S. Department of Homeland Security

Among the most innovative and unique operations within U.S. Customs and Border Protection (CBP) is the Canine Enforcement Program, which is staffed by uniformed CBP canine officers and specially trained detector dogs that are used to combat terrorist threats, interdict illegal drugs and contraband, and detect concealed persons at our nation's borders, land ports, seaports, airports, and international mail facilities.

Functioning within the largest canine program in U.S. federal law enforcement, CBP canine teams—each of which consists of one canine officer and one detector dog—are trained to detect explosives; chemicals used in weapons of mass destruction; narcotics and other illegal drugs; currency, including money being smuggled out of the United States to circumvent monetary reporting requirements; fruits, vegetables, meats, soil, or other prohibited items that could carry animal or plant diseases, insects, or pests that could harm U.S. agriculture resources; and concealed persons attempting to enter the United States illegally. CBP canine officers also participate with Border Patrol Search, Trauma, and Rescue (BORSTAR) teams in responding to emergency incidents involving distressed Border Patrol agents and migrants along the border. CBP canine teams save countless staff-hours by promptly and efficiently detecting smuggled items in motor vehicles, watercraft, aircraft, mail, baggage, and cargo, and they account for a significant proportion of narcotic seizures made by CBP. Canine enforcement operations often are coordinated with U.S. Immigration and Customs Enforcement special agents and other federal, state, and local law enforcement officers. CBP officers are authorized to carry firearms and make arrests.

Qualifications and Salary Levels

GS-5: Completion of a four-year course of study leading to a bachelor's degree; or three years of general experience, one year of which was equivalent to GS-4. **GS-7:** One full year of graduate education, or superior academic achievement during undergraduate studies, or one year of specialized experience equivalent to GS-5. **GS-9:** A master's degree, or two years of graduate education, or one year of specialized experience equivalent to GS-7. **GS-11:** A Ph.D. or equivalent doctoral degree, or three years of graduate education, or one year of specialized experience equivalent to GS-9. **GS-12:** One year of specialized experience equivalent to GS-11.

Equivalent combinations of education and experience can be used to meet minimum experience requirements. Eyesight requirements include binocular distant vision not worse than 20/100 (Snellen) uncorrected and 20/30 corrected; corrected binocular near vision not worse than 20/40; and the ability to distinguish primary colors as defined by color perception Ishihara Pseudoisochromatic plate tests. Candidates who have undergone LASIK eye surgery must be free from residual effects three months after surgery, while those who have had other forms of refractive eye surgery must be free from residual effects one year after surgery. Uncorrected bilateral hearing loss must not exceed 25 decibels for the average of 500, 1000, 2000, and 3000 Hertz, and must not exceed 45 decibels hearing loss at 4000 and 6000 Hertz in either ear. The difference in hearing levels between the better ear thresholds and worse ear thresholds cannot exceed 15 decibels for the average of 500, 1000, 2000, and 3000 Hertz, and must not exceed 30 decibels hearing loss at 4000 and 6000 Hertz. (Hearing aids cannot be used during the test.) Candidates must achieve a passing score on the U.S. Customs and Border Protection Officer Test early in the hiring process (see chapter 3). Appointment is contingent upon passing a background investigation, medical examination, fitness test, and drug screening. The fitness test, which is held immediately after the medical examination, includes a Kneel and Stand Test, a Lift and Lower Test, and a Step Test. The Kneel and Stand Test consists of three positions—kneeling on both knees, kneeling on one knee, and standing—and making changes between these positions in timed exercises. The Lift and Lower Test requires lifting a 50-pound crate from the floor and placing it on a table eight times in 60 seconds. The Step Test requires candidates to step up to and down from a 12-inch-high step continuously for five minutes.

Training

CBP canine officers attend the 14-week U.S. Customs and Border Protection Integrated Training Program within the CBP Academy at the Federal Law Enforcement Training Center (FLETC) in Glynco, Georgia (see chapter 16). They also receive training relating to canine enforcement techniques at facilities such as the CBP Canine Enforcement Training Center in Front Royal, Virginia (see chapter 16); the Border Patrol National Canine Facility in El Paso, Texas; the USDA National Detector Dog Training Center in Orlando, Florida; or the FLETC campus in Glynco, Georgia. For example, the Canine Enforcement Training Center offers a 13-week Basic Narcotics Detection Course that includes instruction in canine behavior and handling; detection of heroin, cocaine, marijuana, hashish, and methamphetamine; search techniques concerning vehicles, aircraft, freight containers, luggage, mail, and other locations; border inspection and control procedures; passenger and cargo facilitation; legal matters; communications systems; firearms; and non-lethal defense techniques. A seven-week Passenger Processing Course at FLETC includes instruction concerning procedures for screening passengers, pedestrians, and their hand-carried items with detector dogs. The USDA National Detector Dog Training Center offers training in the detection of agriculture products, soil, and threats to agriculture industry. CBP canine officers can attend training at the Border Patrol National Canine Facility that is geared toward the detection of concealed aliens and illegal drugs. Canine training also is presented by many law enforcement agencies, state and local police training academies, and private firms.

Contact: United States Customs and Border Protection; U.S. Department of Homeland Security; 1300 Pennsylvania Ave. NW; Washington, DC 20229; phone: (202) 344-1250; Internet: www.cbp.gov/

Customs and Border Protection Officer (GS-1895)
United States Customs and Border Protection, U.S. Department of Homeland Security

U.S. Customs and Border Protection officers—commonly known as CBP officers—are responsible primarily for the duties that were performed by customs inspectors and immigration inspectors prior to the merger in 2003 of the U.S. Immigration and Naturalization Service and the U.S. Customs Service into the Department of Homeland Security. CBP officers detect and prevent terrorists and contraband from entering the United States; enforce and administer laws relating to the right of persons to enter, reside in, or depart from the United States, Puerto Rico, Guam, or the U.S. Virgin Islands; and enforce laws concerning the importation or exportation of merchandise. They carry out these responsibilities at land border ports shared with Mexico and Canada; at international airports throughout the continental United States, Alaska, Hawaii, Puerto Rico, Guam, and the Virgin Islands; at seaports along the Atlantic and Pacific Oceans, the Gulf of Mexico, and the Great Lakes; and at passenger pre-clearance sites and designated foreign Container Security Initiative (CSI) cargo locations outside of the United States.

Some of the tasks performed by CBP officers include obtaining information about the description, characteristics, value, and country of origin of imported merchandise or agricultural products; admitting, holding, or releasing merchandise at ports of entry; monitoring, examining, and processing cargo containers at ports of entry to facilitate importing of merchandise; classifying and assessing duty and taxes on dutiable merchandise; conducting interviews and examining documents to determine citizenship and immigration status; determining the admissibility of aliens into the United States; searching people, baggage, cargo, ships, aircraft, and vehicles entering or leaving the United States; seizing narcotics, currency, equipment, vehicles, vessels, and contraband; and detaining or arresting persons who violate federal laws concerning immigration, customs, agriculture products, and other goods. Many activities are coordinated with U.S. Immigration and Customs Enforcement special agents, CBP canine officers, and other federal, state, and local law enforcement officers. CBP officers are authorized to carry firearms and make arrests.

Qualifications and Salary Levels

GS-5: Completion of a four-year course of study leading to a bachelor's degree; or three years of general experience, one year of which was equivalent to GS-4. **GS-7:** One full year of graduate education, or superior academic achievement during undergraduate studies, or one year of specialized experience equivalent to GS-5. **GS-9:** A master's degree, or two years of graduate education, or one year of specialized experience equivalent to GS-7. **GS-11:** A Ph.D. or equivalent doctoral degree, or three years of graduate education, or one year of specialized experience equivalent to GS-9. **GS-12:** One year of specialized experience equivalent to GS-11.

Equivalent combinations of education and experience can be used to meet minimum experience requirements. Eyesight requirements include binocular distant vision not worse than 20/100 (Snellen) uncorrected and 20/30 corrected; corrected binocular near vision not worse than 20/40; and the ability to distinguish primary colors as defined by color perception Ishihara Pseudoisochromatic plate tests. Candidates who have undergone LASIK eye surgery must be free from residual effects three months after surgery, while those who have had other forms of refractive eye surgery must be free from residual effects one year after surgery. Uncorrected bilateral hearing loss must not exceed 25 decibels for the average of 500, 1000, 2000, and 3000 Hertz, and must not exceed 45 decibels hearing loss at 4000 and 6000 Hertz in either ear. The difference in hearing levels between the better ear thresholds and worse ear thresholds cannot exceed 15 decibels for the average of 500, 1000, 2000, and 3000 Hertz, and must not exceed 30 decibels hearing loss at 4000 and 6000 Hertz. (Hearing aids cannot be used during the test.) Candidates must achieve a passing score on the U.S. Customs and Border Protection Officer Test early in the hiring process (see chapter 3). Appointment is contingent upon passing a background investigation, medical examination, fitness test, and drug screening. The fitness test, which is held immediately after the medical examination, includes a Kneel and Stand Test, a Lift and Lower Test, and a Step Test. The Kneel and Stand Test consists of three positions—kneeling on both knees, kneeling on one knee, and standing—and making changes between these positions in timed exercises. The Lift and Lower Test requires lifting a 50-pound crate from the floor and placing it on a table eight times in 60 seconds. The Step Test requires candidates to step up to and down from a 12-inch-high step continuously for five minutes.

Training

Initial training for CBP officers includes the 14-week U.S. Customs and Border Protection Integrated Training Program within the CBP Academy at the Federal Law Enforcement Training Center in Glynco, Georgia (see chapter 16). Ongoing in-service training could include courses relating to border search operations; passenger processing; inspection profiling; interviewing techniques; hazardous material cargo; detection of radioactive materials; legal updates; bombs and explosives; detection of contraband, narcotics, and dangerous drugs; the behavioral sciences; arrest authority and techniques; domestic and international terrorism; defensive tactics; bloodborne pathogens; firearms; and other topics.

Contact: United States Customs and Border Protection; U.S. Department of Homeland Security; 1300 Pennsylvania Ave. NW; Washington, DC 20229; phone: (202) 344-1250; Internet: www.cbp.gov/

Enforcement Officer (GS-1812)

National Marine Fisheries Service, National Oceanic and Atmospheric Administration, U.S. Department of Commerce

The Office for Law Enforcement of the National Marine Fisheries Service (NMFS) ensures that commercial fishermen, fishing companies, recreational boaters, sport fishermen, and other ocean users comply with fishing statutes and other laws that protect ocean ecosystems. NMFS enforcement officers enforce dozens of federal laws and various international treaties related to the protection and conservation of marine resources over areas that encompass more than 3 million square miles of water. These officers conduct marine patrols and other activities along 23 coastal states and territories and the high seas to enforce laws such as the Magnuson-Stevens Fishery Conservation and Management Act; the Endangered Species Act; the Marine Mammal Protection Act; the Lacey Act; the Marine Protection, Research, and Sanctuaries Act; the Atlantic Salmon Convention Act; and the Convention on International Trade in Endangered Species of Wild Fauna and Flora.

The responsibilities of enforcement officers include conducting patrols up to 200 miles offshore in vessels and aircraft; boarding commercial and recreational fishing vessels at sea and in ports; inspecting fish and other marine resource products within vessels and other areas; conducting searches and seizures of vessels and products; interviewing witnesses; collecting and preserving evidence; writing reports; and referring criminal violations to the U.S. Attorney's Office, and civil cases to the National Oceanic and Atmospheric Administration (NOAA) Office of General Counsel. NMFS enforcement officers also inspect fish processing plants, review sales of wildlife products on the Internet, and inspect shipments of marine resource products entering the United States at ports of entry, including border crossings, airports, and harbors. Enforcement operations often are coordinated with federal law enforcement agencies such as the U.S. Coast Guard, U.S. Customs and Border Protection, U.S. Immigration and Customs Enforcement, Food and Drug Administration, Drug Enforcement Administration, and FBI; other federal, state, local, tribal, and international law enforcement agencies; the Civil Air Patrol; and various private environmental organizations. NMFS enforcement officers are authorized to carry firearms and make arrests.

Qualifications and Salary Levels

GS-5: Completion of a four-year course of study leading to a bachelor's degree; or three years of general experience, one year of which was equivalent to GS-4. **GS-7:** One full year of graduate education, or superior academic achievement during undergraduate studies, or one year of specialized experience equivalent to GS-5. **GS-9:** A master's degree or two years of graduate education, or one year of specialized experience equivalent to GS-7. **GS-11:** A Ph.D. or equivalent doctoral degree, three years of graduate education, or one year of specialized experience equivalent to GS-9.

Equivalent combinations of education and experience can be used to meet minimum experience requirements. Eyesight standards include distant vision not worse than 20/200 (Snellen) in each eye without correction, and 20/20 in each eye with correction; near vision sufficient to read printed material the size of typewritten characters, with or without correction; normal depth perception and peripheral vision; and the ability to distinguish basic shades of color. Hearing loss must not exceed 30 decibels at 500, 1000, and 2000 Hertz; and 40 decibels at 3000 Hertz. Tentative appointees must qualify for a security clearance, and pass a drug screening test and medical examination.

Training

Training for NMFS enforcement officers begins with the 16-week Natural Resources Police Training Program at the Federal Law Enforcement Training Center (FLETC) in Glynco, Georgia (see chapter 16). After completing this course, enforcement officers attend the four-week Marine Law Enforcement Training Program at FLETC, which includes instruction in seamanship, nautical terminology, navigation, nautical chart interpretation, vessel handling, vessel identification, marine communications, vessel pursuits and boarding procedures, meteorology and heavy weather, radar, emergency procedures, waterborne arrest techniques, and other subjects. This program is followed by a four-week course presented by NMFS staff that focuses on laws enforced by the agency, as well as NOAA and NMFS regulations, policies, and procedures. In-service training covers subjects such as nautical procedures, vessel intercepts, legal updates, global positioning systems, Spanish language, computer forensics, photography, officer survival afloat, arrest techniques, defensive tactics, and firearms proficiency.

Contact: Office for Law Enforcement; National Marine Fisheries Service; National Oceanic and Atmospheric Administration; U.S. Department of Commerce; 8484 Georgia Ave.—Ste. 415; Silver Spring, MD 20910; phone: (301) 427-2300; Internet: www.nmfs.noaa.gov/ole/

Immigration Enforcement Agent (GS-1801)
United States Immigration and, Customs Enforcement, U.S. Department of Homeland Security

In 2003, when the Immigration and Naturalization Service (INS) was transferred from the U.S. Department of Justice to the U.S. Department of Homeland Security, the responsibilities of INS immigration agents and INS detention enforcement officers were consolidated and reclassified into the immigration enforcement agent position. Immigration enforcement agents are responsible for various tasks associated with the processing, deporting, and removal of illegal aliens from the United States.

Serving within the Immigration and Customs Enforcement (ICE) Detention and Removal Program, immigration enforcement agents gather intelligence and evidence relating to immigration violations; participate in task force operations and fugitive investigations; conduct interviews and interrogations; apprehend aliens who are employed in the United States without authorization, and those who have absconded from immigration proceedings; handle detainee intake and transfer processing; counsel detainees regarding personal and family matters; present cases to the U.S. Attorney's Office; initiate criminal proceedings against immigration violators; ensure the security of detainees; transport detainees to and from jails, prisons, medical appointments, and court hearings; and escort them to their country of citizenship. Investigative and enforcement operations often are conducted jointly with ICE special agents, Border Patrol agents, and other federal, state, and local law enforcement officers. The responsibilities of immigration enforcement agents can vary considerably from one office to another, depending on local dynamics, priorities, and initiatives underway at any given time. Although these personnel are issued uniforms, they carry out many tasks and special assignments in plain clothes. They are authorized to carry firearms and make arrests.

Immigration enforcement agents earn Administratively Uncontrollable Overtime pay, and they are covered under special retirement provisions for law enforcement officers.

Qualifications and Salary Levels

GS-5: Completion of a four-year course of study leading to a bachelor's degree; or three years of general experience, one year of which was equivalent to GS-4. **GS-7:** One full year of graduate education, or superior academic achievement during undergraduate studies, or one year of specialized experience equivalent to GS-5. **GS-9:** A master's degree, or two years of graduate education, or one year of specialized experience equivalent to GS-7. **GS-11:** A Ph.D. or equivalent doctoral degree, or three years of graduate education, or one year of specialized experience equivalent to GS-9.

Applicants must be at least 21 years of age and under age 37. However, candidates over age 37 who have previous service creditable under special law enforcement retirement provisions also may be eligible. Experience and education can be combined to meet total experience requirements. Uncorrected distant vision must be 20/200 (Snellen) or better in each eye, and uncorrected distant vision must be no worse than 20/30 in one eye and 20/40 in the other eye. Near vision must be sufficient to read Jaeger Type 2 at 14 inches. Candidates also must have normal depth perception and peripheral vision, and the ability to distinguish basic colors. Candidates who have undergone LASIK eye surgery must be free from residual effects three months after surgery, while those who have had other forms of refractive eye surgery must be free from residual effects one year after surgery. Hearing loss must not exceed 30 decibels at 500, 1000, and 2000 Hertz. The ability to hear the conversational voice at 15 feet without a hearing aid also is required. Tentative appointees must pass a medical examination, drug screening test, background investigation, and qualify for a security clearance.

Training

Immigration enforcement agents attend the 12-week ICE Detention and Removal Operations Training Program at the Federal Law Enforcement Training Center in Glynco, Georgia (see chapter 16). In-service training could include courses concerning legal issues and updates, interviewing and investigative techniques, firearms proficiency, arrest techniques, defensive tactics, and other subjects.

Contact: United States Immigration and Customs Enforcement; U.S. Department of Homeland Security; 801 I St. NW—Ste. 900; Washington, DC 20536; phone: (202) 305-2734; Internet: www.ice.gov/

Law Enforcement Officer (GS-1801)
Forest Service, U.S. Department of Agriculture

Law enforcement officers of the U.S. Department of Agriculture (USDA) Forest Service conduct patrols to prevent, detect, and enforce violations of federal laws and regulations concerning the protection and safe uses of National Forest System lands and resources. Forest Service law enforcement officers have jurisdiction on more than 191 million acres of national forests, grasslands, and land utilization projects managed by the Forest Service in 44 states, the Virgin Islands, and Puerto Rico.

The primary responsibilities of Forest Service law enforcement officers include general patrol; responding to calls for service, suspicious circumstances, crimes in progress, alarms, motor vehicle accidents, plane crashes, and medical emergencies; handling domestic and civil disputes; traffic enforcement; engaging in search and rescue operations; enforcing violations relating to natural resources laws, timber theft, arson, unauthorized mining claims, dumping of hazardous materials, marijuana cultivation, production of illegal drugs in clandestine laboratories, and provisions of the Archeological Resources Protection Act; executing search and arrest warrants; and conducting informational and educational programs. They also perform crime scene investigations, prepare incident reports, and testify in criminal and civil court proceedings, hearings, and trials. Forest Service law enforcement officers are authorized to carry firearms and make arrests. Law enforcement operations often are coordinated with Forest Service special agents and other federal, state, and local law enforcement agencies.

This position is covered under special retirement provisions for law enforcement officers.

Qualifications and Salary Levels

GS-5: Completion of a four-year course of study leading to a bachelor's degree; or three years of general experience, one year of which was equivalent to GS-4. **GS-7:** One full year of graduate education, or superior academic achievement during undergraduate studies, or one year of specialized experience equivalent to GS-5. **GS-9:** A master's degree, or two years of graduate education, or one year of specialized experience equivalent to GS-7. **GS-11:** A Ph.D. or equivalent doctoral degree, or three years of graduate education, or one year of specialized experience equivalent to GS-9.

Applicants must be at least 21 years of age and under age 37. However, candidates over age 37 who have previous service creditable under special law enforcement retirement provisions also may be eligible. Applicants can use equivalent combinations of specialized experience and education to meet total experience requirements. Vision standards include distant visual acuity not worse than 20/20 (Snellen) in one eye and 20/40 in the other eye, with or without correction; corrected or uncorrected near vision sufficient to read printed material the size of typewritten characters; normal depth perception and peripheral vision; and the ability to distinguish basic colors. Hearing loss must not exceed 35 decibels at 1000, 2000, and 3000 Hertz in each ear. (Hearing aids cannot be used during the test.) The application process includes a background investigation and drug test.

Training

Training for Forest Service law enforcement officers begins with the 16-week Natural Resources Police Training Program (NRPTP) at the Federal Law Enforcement Training Center (FLETC) in Glynco, Georgia (see chapter 16). After graduating from the NRPTP course, Forest Service law enforcement officers attend a two-week Forest Service Basic Law Enforcement Officer Training Program at FLETC that covers various aspects of Forest Service law enforcement operations not addressed in the NRPTP course. They also attend at least 40 hours of in-service training annually, including courses in subjects such as officer safety, non-lethal control techniques, impact weapons, aerosol subject restraint, off-road and emergency vehicle operation, mountain bicycle patrol, firearms proficiency, first aid, controlled substance investigations, criminal and civil law, photography, protection of archaeological resources, search and rescue management, and Spanish language. Law enforcement officers at the GS-11 level are encouraged to attend the FBI National Academy training program in Quantico, Virginia.

Contact: For further information, contact the Forest Service ranger district where employment is sought, or Forest Service; U.S. Department of Agriculture; 1400 Independence Ave. SW; Washington, DC 20250; phone: (202) 205-8333; Internet: www.fs.fed.us/; e-mail: fsjobs@fs.fed.us.

Law Enforcement Officer
Federal Reserve Bank Police, U.S. Federal Reserve System

The Federal Reserve System—which is the central bank of the United States—is responsible for formulating and administering the nation's credit and monetary policy, while also performing functions such as the transfer of funds, handling of government deposits and debt issues, supervising and regulating banks, and acting as a lender of last resort. Federal Reserve Bank (FRB) law enforcement officers protect FRB assets, property, employees, tenants, and visitors at Federal Reserve district banks in Atlanta, Boston, Chicago, Cleveland, Dallas, Kansas City, Minneapolis, New York, Philadelphia, Richmond, San Francisco, and St. Louis, and at branch banks located in 25 cities throughout the United States.

The primary responsibilities of FRB law enforcement officers vary from one district to another, although they generally include screening visitors and controlling access to secure areas of the bank; inspecting briefcases, packages, and other containers brought into FRB facilities; operating x-ray equipment and metal detectors; conducting static post duty and foot patrols; maintaining a control room post; monitoring alarm systems, intrusion control devices, intercoms, radios, closed-circuit surveillance monitors, and other specialized equipment and systems; maintaining post logs; inspecting vehicles entering security-sensitive areas for unauthorized personnel or contents; overseeing the transfer of assets to and from armored cars; and gathering intelligence information. They also respond to intrusion and fire alarms, emergencies, disturbances, and other incidents; participate in building evacuation drills; coordinate bomb searches; investigate thefts and other incidents; write detailed reports; escort personnel in possession of cash and securities to the post office and financial institutions; and perform CPR and first aid. FRB law enforcement officers are authorized to carry firearms and make arrests.

Qualifications and Salary Levels

FRB law enforcement officers are appointed through excepted service hiring processes. The qualifications and salaries of the position are similar to those of GS-0083 police officers at the GS-4 through GS-8 levels with other federal agencies. Applicants must be at least 21 years of age. Requirements for appointment to FRB law enforcement officer include a high school diploma or GED certificate; experience with computers; excellent written and oral communication skills; a stable employment history reflecting excellent performance and attendance; and familiarity with firearms. Candidates with experience in law enforcement, internal security or other security-related field, or the military are preferred. Tentative appointees must pass a background investigation, medical examination, and psychological evaluation.

Training

Initial training for FRB law enforcement officers varies from one district to another, although it consists of about a six-week course presented by FRB staff. Examples of subjects introduced during this program include an overview of the Federal Reserve System mission; FRB policies, procedures, and rules; bank layout and design; security post and screening procedures; electronic security and surveillance systems; laws and regulations; terrorism; conflict resolution; stress management; ethics; report writing; first aid and CPR; firearms proficiency; use of force; and other matters related to the dynamics of particular facilities served. Ongoing in-service training focuses on topics such as information security, legal issues and updates, security equipment and procedures, tactical operations, response to bomb threats, bloodborne pathogens, CPR and first-aid techniques and equipment, and firearms proficiency. FRB law enforcement officers also can complete refresher training in legal subjects through an online independent study course.

Contact: Inquiries should be directed to the personnel office of the Federal Reserve district or branch bank where employment is sought, or to Personnel Division; Federal Reserve System; 20th St. and Constitution Ave. NW; Washington, DC 20551; phone: (202) 452-3000; Internet: www.federalreserve.gov/.

Law Enforcement Ranger (GS-1801)
Bureau of Land Management, U.S. Department of the Interior

Law enforcement rangers of the Bureau of Land Management (BLM) enforce federal laws and regulations relating to public lands and resources managed by the Bureau. They perform these activities on 270 million acres of public lands and an additional 300 million acres where mineral rights are owned by the federal government.

In carrying out the BLM Office of Law Enforcement and Security mission—including the objectives of the Federal Land Policy and Management Act of 1976—BLM law enforcement rangers perform general patrol in marked vehicles, aircraft, and boats, and also on foot, horseback, motorcycles, and all-terrain vehicles; respond to calls for service, accidents, and emergencies; issue traffic and parking citations; conduct surveillance; investigate and enforce violations relating to natural resources offenses, trespassing, timber theft, arson, vandalism; protect cultural and historical sites; and engage in search and rescue operations. They also locate and eradicate drug manufacturing laboratories and marijuana cultivation sites, and enforce other drug-control laws as they relate to lands and resources managed by BLM. Law enforcement rangers often carry out field work over remote or rugged terrain; in conservation, wilderness, canyon, isolated, and desert areas; on wild and scenic rivers; and at high altitudes where climatic conditions are variable and extreme. Operations often are coordinated with BLM special agents and other federal, state, and local law enforcement agencies. BLM law enforcement rangers are authorized to carry firearms and make arrests.

This position is covered under special retirement provisions for law enforcement officers.

Qualifications and Salary Levels

GS-5: Completion of a four-year course of study leading to a bachelor's degree; or three years of general experience, one year of which was equivalent to GS-4. **GS-7:** One full year of graduate education, or superior academic achievement during undergraduate studies, or one year of specialized experience equivalent to GS-5. **GS-9:** A master's degree, or two years of graduate education, or one year of specialized experience equivalent to GS-7. **GS-11:** A Ph.D. or equivalent doctoral degree, or three years of graduate education, or one year of specialized experience equivalent to GS-9. **GS-12:** One year of specialized experience equivalent to GS-11.

Candidates must be at least 21 years of age and under age 37. However, those over age 37 who have previous service creditable under special law enforcement retirement provisions also may be eligible. Eyesight requirements include distant vision not worse than 20/40 (Snellen) in one eye and 20/100 in the other eye, with or without correction; near vision sufficient to read printed material the size of typewritten characters, with or without correction; and the ability to distinguish basic shades of colors.

Hearing loss must not exceed 30 decibels in either ear at 500, 1000, or 2000 Hertz. The application process includes a background investigation, drug test, medical examination, and top-secret security clearance determination.

Training

BLM law enforcement rangers attend the 16-week Natural Resources Police Training Program at the Federal Law Enforcement Training Center (FLETC) in Glynco, Georgia (see chapter 16). They also receive at least 40 hours of in-service training annually, which could include courses at FLETC, other law enforcement academies, the BLM National Training Center in Arizona, colleges and universities, or other locations. Examples of in-service training subjects include evidence photography, archaeological crime scene processing, domestic terrorism, legal updates, search and rescue techniques, serious accident investigation, judgment pistol shooting, defensive tactics, firearms proficiency, armorer certification, and various topics concerning the protection of natural resources.

Contact: Office of Law Enforcement and Security; Bureau of Land Management; U.S. Department of the Interior; 1849 C St. NW; Washington, DC 20240; phone: (202) 208-3269; Internet: www.blm.gov/; e-mail: woinfo@blm.gov

Mint Police Officer
United States Mint, U.S. Department of the Treasury

The United States Mint (USM) produces and circulates coinage to enable the nation to conduct its trade and commerce. As the law enforcement and security force for USM operations, mint police officers are responsible for protecting USM plant facilities, other properties, personnel, visitors, and assets—including more than $100 billion in gold, silver, and coinage. The USM distributes U.S. coins to Federal Reserve banks and branches nationwide.

In carrying out the mission of the USM Police Division, mint police officers perform static post, vehicle, and foot patrol duties; screen visitors entering USM facilities; observe closed-circuit surveillance monitors; maintain a control room post; respond to emergency situations, bomb threats, fires, crimes in progress, and calls for service; interview witnesses and suspects; prepare written reports; perform searches and seizures; escort visitors and contractors through restricted areas; and oversee the transfer of coinage to armored cars for shipment to Federal Reserve banks. In addition, many mint police officers are assigned collateral duties that involve responsibilities such as bicycle patrol, serving on the USM Police Special Response Team, performing as a firearms instructor, or overseeing the development of new hires while serving as a field training officer. To protect the Mint from terrorism and other threats, mint police officers coordinate security reviews with the Secret Service; the FBI; and the Bureau of Alcohol, Tobacco, Firearms and Explosives. USM police officers are authorized to carry firearms and make arrests. They are stationed at facilities in Denver, Colorado; Philadelphia, Pennsylvania; San Francisco, California; Fort Knox, Kentucky; West Point, New York; and Washington, DC.

Qualifications and Salary Levels

USM police officers are appointed through excepted service hiring processes. These officers are covered under a pay system administered by the Secretary of the Treasury. Salaries under this pay system are similar to GS-7 through GS-12, which are higher than salaries for most GS-0083 federal police officers who perform similar work and are compensated under the General Schedule pay system. Eyesight requirements include uncorrected distant vision not worse than 20/70 (Snellen) in each eye, with correction to at least 20/20; corrected or uncorrected near vision sufficient to read Jaeger Type 2 at 14 inches; the ability to distinguish basic colors; and normal depth perception and peripheral vision. Hearing loss must not exceed 30 decibels in one ear at 500, 1000, or 2000 Hertz. (A hearing aid is permitted in the other ear.) Candidates must successfully undergo a background investigation and medical examination, qualify for a security clearance, and pass a drug test prior to appointment.

Training

Mint police officers attend the 10-week Mixed Basic Police Training Program at the Federal Law Enforcement Training Center in Glynco, Georgia (see chapter 16). After completing this course, mint police officers report to their respective posts of duty for an additional five weeks of specialized training that is geared toward various aspects of local and national USM police operations. Thereafter, in-service training includes instruction in areas such as agency policies and procedures, the USM computer network, law enforcement jurisdiction, officer safety, terrorism, federal and local court operations, professionalism, public relations, radio communications, firearm proficiency, and physical fitness. Weapons training includes practice and qualification with pistols, shotguns, Uzi submachine guns, and non-lethal weapons.

Contact: Recruiting Division; U.S. Mint Police; U.S. Department of the Treasury; 801 Ninth St. NW—8th Floor; Washington, DC 20220; phone: (202) 354-7300; Internet: www.usmint.gov/

Park Police Officer
United States Park Police, National Park Service, U.S. Department of the Interior

As a law enforcement unit of the National Park Service, the U.S. Park Police (USPP) exercises jurisdiction over National Park Service areas and certain other federal and state lands. USPP officers provide a wide range of uniformed patrol and law enforcement services in the vicinity of national parks, monuments, memorials, historic residences, highways, and other federal property in Washington, DC, and Maryland; within the Gateway National Recreation Area in New York City; and also on the grounds of the Golden Gate National Recreation Area in San Francisco.

In addition to performing patrols in cars, USPP officers conduct patrols on foot, horses, motorcycles, scooters, bicycles, and all-terrain vehicles, as well as in boats and helicopters. They respond to emergencies and other matters; enforce traffic laws; investigate traffic accidents and crimes; collect and preserve evidence; perform crowd control and provide security at special events, parades, festivals, celebrations, and demonstrations; conduct search and rescue operations and medevac missions; gather intelligence, conduct threat assessments, and share intelligence information with other law enforcement agencies; and provide full-time protective services for the U.S. Secretary of the Interior. In addition, USPP officers frequently participate in protective operations for the president and vice president of the United States and visiting dignitaries. Experienced USPP officers can be assigned to the Special Forces Branch, which consists of a Special Weapons and Tactics (SWAT) team and motorcycle, aviation, and canine units; or the Criminal Investigations Branch, which comprises sections including Major Crimes, Identification, Special Investigations, Narcotics and Vice, and Asset Forfeiture. USPP officers are authorized to carry firearms and make arrests.

This position is covered under special retirement provisions for federal law enforcement officers.

Qualifications and Salary Levels

USPP officers are appointed through excepted service hiring processes. The U.S. Park Police Pay System—which is identical to the Secret Service Uniformed Division Pay System—is established in the District of Columbia Code. Salaries under these pay systems are similar to GS-7 through GS-12, which are higher than salaries for most GS-0083 federal police officers who perform similar work and are compensated under the General Schedule pay system. Applicants must be at least 21 years of age and under age 37. However, those over age 37 who have previous service creditable under special law enforcement retirement provisions also may be eligible. Minimum qualifications include two years of progressively responsible experience that demonstrated the ability to learn and apply detailed and complex regulations and procedures that involve making sound judgments; or two years of active-duty military experience; or two years of education above high school; or a combination of at least two years of experience and education. Completion of a federal, state, county, or municipal police academy can be substituted for three months of experience. Eyesight requirements include uncorrected distant vision not worse than 20/100 (Snellen) in each eye, and corrected binocular distant vision not worse than 20/20; normal depth perception and peripheral vision; and the ability to distinguish basic colors. The use of soft contact lenses can be considered a reasonable accommodation for candidates who have worn soft contact lenses for at least one year. Candidates who have undergone LASIK eye surgery must be free from residual effects three months after surgery. Hearing loss must not exceed 30 decibels in either ear at 500, 1000, or 2000 Hertz, and 40 decibels in either ear at 3000 Hertz. (Hearing aids cannot be used during the test.) Candidates must achieve a passing score on the U.S. Park Police Officer Examination to advance in the hiring process (see chapter 3). Tentative appointees must qualify for a security clearance and pass a background investigation, drug screening test, and medical examination.

Training

USPP officers attend the 18-week U.S. Park Police Basic Training Program at the Federal Law Enforcement Training Center (FLETC) in Glynco, Georgia, which is conducted by FLETC and USPP staff. This course includes instruction in subjects such as patrol procedures, crowd control, criminal law, report writing, hostage situations, communications, stress, narcotics, officer safety and survival, firearms, driver training, physical fitness, and defensive tactics. In-service training includes at least 40 hours of instruction annually in subjects such as automobile theft, domestic violence, police baton techniques, traffic radar operation, alcohol traffic enforcement, legal issues and updates, crime scene investigation, defensive tactics, first aid and CPR, and firearms proficiency.

Contact: U.S. Park Police; National Park Service; U.S. Department of the Interior; 1100 Ohio Dr. SW; Washington, DC 20240; phone: (202) 619-7056; Internet: www.nps.gov/uspp/

Park Ranger (GS-0025)
National Park Service, U.S. Department of the Interior

National Park Service (NPS) park rangers are responsible for law enforcement and natural resources management duties at more than 300 locations that encompass the National Park System and other federally managed sites. NPS park rangers are stationed at national parks and monuments, scenic parkways, preserves, trails, campgrounds, battlefields, seashores, lakeshores, recreational areas, and historic sites nationwide.

Examples of responsibilities carried out by NPS park rangers include conducting patrols in vehicles or on foot, bicycles, or horseback; protecting historical, archeological, and natural resources; responding to traffic accidents, medical emergencies, alarms, and fires; performing traffic enforcement and control tasks; investigating offenses such as larceny, assault, vandalism, trespassing, drug possession and trafficking, and weapons offenses; overseeing security checkpoints; and performing search and rescue operations and crowd control. They also perform natural resource management tasks, such as presenting educational programs to park visitors concerning points of interest, historical and natural resources, and park activities; and tasks related to habitat and wildlife monitoring, rescue, and rehabilitation. The nature of duties depends largely on the size and particular needs of areas served. The NPS employs full-time, part-time, and seasonal park rangers, including those with or without law enforcement authority. Those with law enforcement authority are authorized to carry firearms and make arrests.

Full-time park rangers assigned to law enforcement duties are covered under special retirement provisions for law enforcement officers.

Qualifications and Salary Levels

GS-5: Completion of a four-year course of study leading to a bachelor's degree that included at least 24 semester hours of coursework related to law enforcement, criminal investigation, criminology, police science, law, or similar subjects; or three years of general experience, one year of which was equivalent to GS-4. **GS-7:** One full year of graduate education related to the subject-areas listed under GS-5, or superior academic achievement during undergraduate studies, or one year of specialized experience equivalent to GS-5. **GS-9:** A master's degree, or two years of graduate education related to the subject-areas listed above, or one year of specialized experience equivalent to GS-7. **GS-11:** A Ph.D. or equivalent doctoral degree, or three years of graduate education related to the subject-areas listed under GS-5, or one year of specialized experience equivalent to GS-9. **GS-12:** One year of specialized experience equivalent to GS-11.

Equivalent combinations of education and experience can be used to meet minimum experience requirements for positions at grades GS-5 through GS-11. Applicants must be at least 21 years of age and under age 37. However, candidates over age 37 who have previous service creditable under special law enforcement retirement provisions also may be eligible. Eyesight requirements include uncorrected distant vision not worse than 20/100 (Snellen) in each eye, and corrected binocular distant vision not worse than 20/20; normal depth perception and peripheral vision; and the ability to distinguish basic colors. The use of soft contact lenses can be considered a reasonable accommodation for candidates who have worn soft contact lenses for at least one year. Candidates who have undergone LASIK eye surgery must be free from residual effects three months after surgery, while those who have had other forms of refractive eye surgery must be free from residual effects one year after surgery. Hearing loss must not exceed 30 decibels in either ear at 500, 1000, or 2000 Hertz, and 40 decibels in either ear at 3000 Hertz. (Hearing aids cannot be used during the test.) The application process includes a drug screening test, background investigation, and medical examination.

Training

NPS park rangers attend the 16-week Natural Resources Police Training Program at the Federal Law Enforcement Training Center in Glynco, Georgia (see chapter 16). Park rangers also receive a minimum of 40 hours of in-service training annually, including courses in subjects such as traffic accident investigation, criminal law, search and seizure, laws of arrest, patrol techniques, computerized criminal information systems, crime victim and witness assistance, detention facility operations, oleoresin capsicum agents, firearms proficiency, flying while armed, defensive tactics, and first aid.

Contact: Division of Personnel Management; National Park Service; U.S. Department of the Interior; 1849 C St. NW; Washington, DC 20240; phone: (202) 208-6843; Internet: www.nps.gov/

Police Officer
National Institute of Standards and Technology, U.S. Department of Commerce

The National Institute of Standards and Technology (NIST) assists industry in developing technology to improve product quality, modernize manufacturing processes, ensure product reliability, and facilitate rapid commercialization of products based on new scientific discoveries. NIST is a nonregulatory federal agency within the Commerce Department's Technology Administration.

NIST police officers are responsible for the protection of NIST personnel, visitors, facilities, and property on the agency's 600-acre campus in Gaithersburg, Maryland, and the 200-acre campus in Boulder, Colorado. Law enforcement and public welfare functions that NIST police officers perform include general patrol; responding to crimes in progress, suspicious circumstances, calls for service, medical emergencies, accidents, fires, and other incidents; detecting and investigating federal and state crimes; traffic control and enforcement; parking control; accident investigation; apprehending violators; and assisting area police departments with hazardous materials incidents and other emergencies. Security duties carried out by NIST police officers include preventing theft, trespass violations, sabotage, espionage, fire, destruction of property, and accidents. Police officers also inspect and search vehicles arriving on NIST campuses when events or meetings are held that are open to the public. NIST police officers are authorized to carry firearms and make arrests.

Qualifications and Salary Levels

NIST police officers are appointed through excepted service hiring processes. Appointments are made at Pay Bands II, III, and IV, which are similar to the GS-3 through GS-8 salary levels. For Pay Band II, candidates must have either six months of general experience that demonstrated the ability to acquire the particular knowledge and skills needed to perform police duties, or one year above high school that included at least six semester hours of study related to law enforcement. Requirements for

Pay Band III include either one year of experience in law enforcement equivalent to the GS-4 level, or four years of education above high school. For Pay Band IV, applicants must have one year of experience in law enforcement equivalent to the GS-6 level. Tentative appointees must qualify for a security clearance and pass a drug screening test, medical examination, and background investigation, and also a driving test administered by the NIST Safety Office.

Training

NIST police officers attend the 10-week Mixed Basic Police Training Program at the Federal Law Enforcement Training Center in Glynco, Georgia (see chapter 16). In-service training includes courses in areas such as security procedures, criminal law, laws of arrest, search and seizure, patrol techniques, traffic accident investigation, defensive tactics, firearms proficiency, first aid, and other subjects relating to law enforcement, security, and emergency preparedness. Some in-service training is held in cooperation with area police departments. For example, NIST police officers often attend training exercises with police, fire, and emergency management personnel from various agencies in Montgomery County, Maryland.

Contact: Office of Human Resources Management; National Institute of Standards and Technology; U.S. Department of Commerce; 100 Bureau Dr.—Mail Stop 1720; Gaithersburg, MD 20899; phone: (301) 975-3058; Internet: www.nist.gov/; e-mail:inquiries@nist.gov

Police Officer (GS-0083)
United States Army, U.S. Department of Defense

Civilian U.S. Army police officers perform a wide range of law enforcement and security functions to maintain order and safety at Army facilities such as forts, posts, weapons testing facilities, training facilities, hospitals, and other locations. They are sworn law enforcement officers who are authorized to carry firearms and make arrests for federal and state offenses.

Army police officers conduct vehicle and foot patrols; respond to crimes in progress, emergency situations, and accidents; detect and investigate federal and state crimes; collect and preserve evidence for use in investigations and prosecutions; conduct interviews and interrogations; apprehend violators; testify in court; intervene in and mediate domestic disputes and disturbances; perform first aid and CPR; perform traffic control and enforcement; conduct traffic accident investigations; monitor closed-circuit television, alarm panels, and other security systems; perform physical security inspections and crime prevention tasks; and ensure that all persons and vehicles entering Army installations are identified and cleared for access. Some of the offenses Army police officers respond to and investigate include assaults, larceny, malicious destruction of property, trespassing, weapons violations, armed robbery, homicide, drug trafficking, sabotage, espionage, and violations of the Uniform Code of Military Justice. Army police officers also are responsible for controlling access to restricted areas containing highly sensitive or classified information, which if sabotaged or subjected to espionage could have an adverse impact on national security. The range of responsibilities of these personnel can vary considerably depending on the type of installation and the needs of areas served. Army police officers are authorized to carry firearms and make arrests. While the Army also maintains a corps of active-duty military police officers, this position does not require active-duty service.

Qualifications and Salary Levels

GS-4: Six months of general experience and six months of specialized experience; or two years of education above high school with at least 12 semester hours of coursework related to law enforcement, criminal investigation, criminology, police science, law, or similar subjects. **GS-5:** Completion of a four-year course of study leading to a bachelor's degree; or three years of specialized experience, one year of which was equivalent to GS-4. **GS-6:** One year of specialized experience equivalent to GS-5. **GS-7:** One year of specialized experience equivalent to GS-6. **GS-8:** One year of specialized experience equivalent to GS-7.

Experience and education can be combined to meet specialized experience requirements for positions at grades GS-4 and GS-5. Prior completion of a police academy training program can be substituted for three months of specialized experience or six months of general experience. No substitution of education or training may be made for the required specialized experience for appointment to positions at GS-6 and above. Applicants must have good near and distant vision, the ability to distinguish basic colors, and the ability to hear the conversational voice. Appointees must pass a drug screening test, medical examination, and background investigation, and qualify for a security clearance.

Training

Depending primarily upon the threat level and nature of responsibilities at the assigned post of duty, Army police officers attend either a state-certified police academy training program in the state where they will be employed; or the 10-week Mixed Basic Police Training Program at the Federal Law Enforcement Training Center in Glynco, Georgia (see chapter 16); or an in-house training program conducted by Army or Defense Department staff. Examples of in-service training include courses relating to search and seizure, traffic accident investigation, patrol techniques, legal updates, firearms proficiency, defensive tactics, first aid, responding to riots and other disturbances, sabotage, and counterterrorism.

Contact: Apply directly to the Army installation where employment is sought, or contact Army Personnel and Employment Service; 6800 Army Pentagon; Washington, DC 20310; phone: (703) 697-5081; Internet: www.army.mil/.

Police Officer (GS-0083)
Defense Logistics Agency, U.S. Department of Defense

The Defense Logistics Agency (DLA) provides supplies to all branches of the military and many other federal agencies, and supports their acquisition of weapons and materiel such as food, clothing, electronic supplies, fuel, industrial supplies, construction materials, and medical supplies. DLA police officers perform law enforcement and security functions nationwide at Agency installations such as supply and distribution centers.

Their responsibilities consist of a wide range of tasks, such as performing vehicle and foot patrol; responding to incidents ranging from simple rule violations to felony offenses and accidents; taking charge of crime scenes; responding to calls for service, disturbances, emergency situations, and other incidents; performing traffic control and enforcement, and traffic accident investigations; conducting preliminary investigations of federal and state crimes; and apprehending violators. DLA police officers also are responsible for controlling access to DLA-managed installations, buildings, facilities, and parking lots; verifying security clearance status of persons requiring entry into restricted areas; accounting for and evacuating building occupants during threat conditions; and many other security and crime prevention tasks. The variety of responsibilities depends largely on the characteristics of the installation served. DLA police officers are authorized to carry firearms and make arrests. This is a civilian position and does not require active-duty military service.

Qualifications and Salary Levels

GS-5: Completion of a four-year course of study leading to a bachelor's degree related to law enforcement, criminal investigation, criminology, police science, law, or similar subjects; or three years of specialized experience, one year of which was equivalent to GS-4. **GS-6:** One year of specialized experience equivalent to GS-5. **GS-7:** One year of specialized experience equivalent to GS-6. **GS-8:** One year of specialized experience equivalent to GS-7.

Equivalent combinations of education and experience can be used to meet minimum experience requirements for positions at grades GS-4 and GS-5. Prior completion of a police academy training program can be substituted for three months of specialized experience or six months of general experience. No substitution of education or training may be made for the required specialized experience for appointment to positions at GS-6 and above. Applicants must have good near and distant vision, the ability to distinguish basic colors, and the ability to hear the conversational voice. Appointees must pass a drug screening test, medical examination, and background investigation, and qualify for a security clearance.

Training

Newly appointed DLA police officers attend the 10-week Mixed Basic Police Training Program at the Federal Law Enforcement Training Center (FLETC) in Glynco, Georgia (see chapter 16). In-service training can include courses that focus on installation security procedures, driver training, traffic accident investigation, patrol techniques, vehicle stops, legal updates, firearms proficiency, defensive tactics, first aid, terrorist attacks, emergency management exercises, and other subjects. Many DLA police officers attend advanced security training programs at FLETC.

Contact: For further information, contact the DLA installation where employment is sought, or Defense Logistics Agency; 8725 John J. Kingman Rd.—Ste. 2533; Fort Belvoir, VA 22060; phone: (703) 767-6200; Internet: www.dla.mil/.

Police Officer
National Security Agency, U.S. Department of Defense

As one of the most unique organizations in the world, the National Security Agency (NSA) employs the nation's premier codebreakers and codemakers, intelligence analysts, computer scientists, mathematicians, language analysts, and other highly skilled personnel to protect U.S. Government information systems and produce foreign signals intelligence information. In support of NSA's mission to understand the secret communications of foreign adversaries while protecting U.S. communications, NSA police officers provide crucial security and law enforcement services within the Agency's office complexes in and around Fort Meade, Maryland.

NSA police officers are responsible for patrolling NSA property and a broad range of other tasks geared toward the protection of NSA assets, personnel, and facilities. The responsibilities of these personnel involve counterterrorism and force protection; controlling access of persons and vehicles to NSA buildings and property; responding to security issues, medical emergencies, fires, bomb threats, and other matters; managing critical incidents; enforcing laws and regulations relating to the protection of NSA assets; and conducting security inspections of vehicles, facilities, and property. Experienced officers can be assigned to specialized units such as the Emergency Response Team, Chemical and Biological Rapid Response Team, Canine Unit, Communication Center, Bicycle Patrol Unit, or Training Unit. NSA police officers are authorized to carry firearms and make arrests.

Qualifications and Salary Levels

NSA police officers are appointed through excepted service hiring processes and are compensated under an NSA pay plan that mirrors the General Schedule pay system. The qualifications and salaries of the position are similar to those of GS-0083 police officers at the GS-5 through GS-9 levels with other federal agencies. Applicants must be at least 21 years of age and have a high school diploma or GED, as well as either two years of education above the high school level, or honorable active-duty military experience, or two years of progressively responsible experience that demonstrated the ability to learn and apply detailed and complex regulations and procedures. Uncorrected binocular distant vision must be no worse than 20/125 (Snellen), and corrected vision must be no worse than 20/20. The application process includes a background investigation, top-secret security clearance determination, medical examination, psychological screening, drug test, and polygraph examination.

Training

Initial training for NSA police officers consists of the 10-week Mixed Basic Police Training Program at the Federal Law Enforcement Training Center (FLETC) in Glynco, Georgia (see chapter 16). They also attend various in-service courses throughout their careers to learn new skills and to develop existing competencies, although the nature of training depends on the needs of individual personnel, agency requirements, and availability of courses.

Contact: Office of Recruitment and Staffing; National Security Agency; U.S. Department of Defense; Ft. Meade, MD 20755; phone: (866) 672-4473; Internet: www.nsa.gov/careers/; e-mail: customercare@nsa.gov

Police Officer (GS-0083)
United States Naval Academy, U.S. Department of Defense

The U.S. Naval Academy (USNA) operates a four-year undergraduate education and training program that prepares young men and women to serve as professional officers in the Navy and Marine Corps. USNA police officers are responsible for a broad range of law enforcement and security functions on the grounds of the USNA in Annapolis, Maryland, a 338-acre campus located 33 miles east of Washington, DC.

USNA police officers perform vehicle and foot patrols; enforce federal, state, and military criminal laws, including provisions of the Uniform Code of Military Justice; respond to calls for service, alarms, and emergency situations; perform first aid and CPR; secure and take charge of crime scenes; collect and preserve evidence for investigative and prosecution purposes; interview and take statements from victims and witnesses; interrogate suspects; enforce traffic laws and parking regulations; investigate traffic accidents; prepare written incident and accident reports; assist prosecutors with criminal actions; and testify in court proceedings. USNA police officers conduct preliminary criminal investigations and enforce laws relating to crimes such as larceny, burglary, assault, vandalism, weapons offenses, and trespass violations. USNA police officers participate in a well-coordinated community policing program that includes patrols on foot and bicycles, seatbelt and child safety seat education, bicycle safety instruction, alcohol impaired driving prevention education, crime prevention presentations and security surveys, and a gun safety program. USNA police officers are authorized to carry firearms and make arrests. This is a civilian position and does not require active-duty military service.

Qualifications and Salary Levels

GS-4: Six months of general experience and six months of specialized experience; or two years of education above high school with at least 12 semester hours of coursework related to law enforcement, criminal investigation, criminology, police science, law, or similar subjects. **GS-5:** Completion of a four-year course of study leading to a bachelor's degree in the subject-areas listed under GS-4; or three years of specialized experience, one year of which was equivalent to GS-4. **GS-6:** One year of specialized experience equivalent to GS-5. **GS-7:** One year of specialized experience equivalent to GS-6. **GS-8:** One year of specialized experience equivalent to GS-7.

Experience and education can be combined to meet specialized experience requirements for positions at grades GS-4 and GS-5. Prior completion of a police academy training program can be substituted for three months of specialized experience or six months of general experience. No substitution of education or training may be made for the required specialized experience for appointment to positions at GS-6 and above. Applicants must have good near and distant vision, the ability to distinguish basic colors, and the ability to hear the conversational voice. Appointees must pass a drug screening test, medical examination, and background investigation, and qualify for a security clearance.

Training

Initial training for USNA police officers includes a two-week in-house training program that focuses on patrol procedures, motor vehicle stops, criminal law, juvenile law, laws of arrest, domestic violence, arrest and detention procedures, crowd control, bomb threats, traffic enforcement, traffic accident investigation, sex crimes, firearms, expandable batons, defensive tactics, and other subjects. Many USNA police officers also attend the 10-week Mixed Basic Police Training Program at the Federal Law Enforcement Training Center in Glynco, Georgia (see chapter 16). In-service training consists of at least 40 hours of coursework annually, which includes subjects concerning terrorism, use of force, report writing, hazardous materials, traffic radar, alcohol traffic enforcement, emergency vehicle operation, public relations, and legal updates, among other topics.

Contact: USNA Police Headquarters; 257 Longshaw Rd.; Annapolis, MD 21402; Phone: (410) 293-5767; Internet: www.usna.edu/; e-mail: secweb@usna.edu

Police Officer (GS-0083)
United States Navy, U.S. Department of Defense

United States Navy (USN) police officers are responsible for law enforcement and security functions on the grounds of USN installations such as shipyards, air fields, supply centers, hospitals, and communication facilities. Largely because of the terrorist attacks of September 11, 2001, much of the work of Navy police officers involves antiterrorism and other efforts to protect the Navy from threats to national security.

Navy police officers control the movement of persons and vehicles into and off of USN property and facilities; perform vehicle and foot patrols; respond to calls for service, alarms, and emergency situations; enforce federal, state, and military criminal laws; perform undercover and surveillance operations; administer first aid and CPR; take command of crime scenes; collect and preserve evidence; interview victims, witnesses, and suspects; prepare written statements; enforce traffic laws and parking regulations; investigate traffic accidents; prepare written incident and accident reports; assist prosecutors with criminal actions; and testify in court proceedings. They also conduct preliminary investigations of offenses such as theft, assault, robbery, sabotage, weapons offenses, malicious destruction of property, and narcotics violations. Navy police officers are authorized to carry firearms and make arrests. This is a civilian position and does not require active-duty military service.

Qualifications and Salary Levels

GS-4: Six months of general experience and six months of specialized experience; or two years of education above high school with at least 12 semester hours of coursework related to law enforcement, criminal investigation, criminology, police science, law, or similar subjects. **GS-5:** Completion of a four-year course of study leading to a bachelor's degree in the subject-areas listed under GS-4; or three years of specialized experience, one year of which was equivalent to GS-4. **GS-6:** One year of specialized experience equivalent to GS-5. **GS-7:** One year of specialized experience equivalent to GS-6. **GS-8:** One year of specialized experience equivalent to GS-7.

Equivalent combinations of education and experience can be used to meet minimum experience requirements for positions at grades GS-4 and GS-5. Prior completion of a police academy training program can be substituted for three months of specialized experience or six months of general experience. No substitution of education or training may be made for the required specialized experience for appointment to positions at GS-6 and above. Applicants must have good near and distant vision, the ability to distinguish basic colors, and the ability to hear the conversational voice. Appointees must pass a drug screening test, medical examination, and background investigation, and qualify for a security clearance.

Training

Initial training for Navy police officers includes either a state-certified police academy training program in the state where they will be employed; or the 10-week Mixed Basic Police Training Program at the Federal Law Enforcement Training Center in Glynco, Georgia (see chapter 16); or an in-house police training course conducted by Navy staff. In-service training focuses on subjects such as crime scene processing, criminal investigation, police science and technology, analysis of criminal behavior, tactical operations, police and community relations, criminal law, laws of arrest, search and seizure, traffic accident investigation, firearms proficiency, defensive tactics, first aid, and other subjects.

Contact: Direct inquiries to the Human Resources Office where employment is sought, or contact Civilian Human Resources; United States Navy; U.S. Department of Defense; 1200 Navy Pentagon; Washington, DC 20350; phone: (800) 378-4559; Internet: www.navy.mil/.

Police Officer (GS-0083)

Pentagon Police Department, Pentagon Force Protection Agency, U.S. Department of Defense

The Pentagon's police force—formerly known as the Defense Protective Service—was absorbed by the newly created Pentagon Force Protection Agency (PFPA) in May 2002. PFPA police officers protect the people, facilities, infrastructure, and other Defense Department interests in the National Capitol Region that are not under the jurisdiction of a military department, including the Pentagon, Hoffman Building, Army Materiel Command, and dozens of other buildings. They are also assigned to the Defense Department's Alternate Joint Communications Center—known as the Raven Rock Mountain complex—in Adams County, Pennsylvania, a secure facility designed for continuation of operations in the event of a terrorist attack or national emergency.

PFPA police officers control access to the Pentagon and other government buildings and facilities—including sensitive areas within these locations—to prevent unauthorized entry; perform patrols and surveillance; search and secure buildings; conduct bomb searches; respond to calls for service, alarms, and emergency situations; regulate pedestrian and vehicular traffic, issue citations, and investigate traffic accidents; prepare written incident and accident reports; interview complainants and interrogate suspects; enforce federal and state laws, rules, and Defense Department regulations; make arrests; and perform crisis management tasks, including the safe movement, control, and evacuation of personnel during drills and actual emergencies. PFPA police officers also are responsible for protecting the Secretary of Defense, other Defense Department officials, and dignitaries doing business with the Defense Department. Experienced officers can be assigned to the PFPA Canine Division, which is the explosives detection unit for the Department of Defense in and around the Washington, DC, area; the Emergency Response Team, a tactical response group that is trained to handle crowd-control situations, dignitary protection, special building entries, hostage situations, and other matters; or the Protective Services Unit, which provides personal protection for Defense Department leaders. Other special assignments are available with the Motorcycle Squad, Bicycle Squad, Traffic Enforcement Unit, and in other areas. PFPA police officers are authorized to carry firearms. This is a civilian position and does not require active-duty military service.

Qualifications and Salary Levels

PFPA police officers are appointed through excepted service hiring processes. These officers are covered under a pay system administered by the Secretary of Defense. Salaries under this pay system are similar to GS-9 through GS-12, which are higher than salaries for most GS-0083 federal police officers who perform similar work and are compensated under the General Schedule pay system. Eyesight requirements include uncorrected distant vision not worse than 20/100 (Snellen) in each eye, and corrected binocular distant vision not worse than 20/20; normal depth perception and peripheral vision; and the ability to distinguish basic colors. Hearing loss must not exceed 30 decibels in either ear at 500, 1000, or 2000 Hertz, and 40 decibels in either ear at 3000 Hertz. Weight must be proportionate to height. The application process includes a medical examination, physical fitness evaluation, drug test, background investigation, and security clearance determination.

Training

Newly appointed PFPA police officers undergo two weeks of initial processing and orientation at the Pentagon, and then attend the 10-week Mixed Basic Police Training Program at the Federal Law Enforcement Training Center in Glynco, Georgia (see chapter 16). This program is followed by one week of additional agency-specific training at the Pentagon. Various in-service courses focus on subjects such as chemical, biological, and radiological weapons; terrorism threats; vulnerability assessments; criminal law; laws of arrest; traffic accident investigation; security procedures; firearms proficiency; defensive tactics; and first aid. Officers assigned to special units attend ongoing in-service training that is presented by organizations such as Heckler and Koch, the International Association of Chiefs of Police, the Special Weapons and Tactics (SWAT) teams of the U.S. Park Police and the District of Columbia Metropolitan Police Department, various Defense Department agencies, and other providers.

Contact: Pentagon Police Department; Pentagon Force Protection Agency; U.S. Department of Defense; Washington, DC 20301; phone: (703) 693-3685; Internet: www.pfpa.mil/; e-mail: PFPArecruiting@pfpa.mil

Police Officer
Metropolitan Police Department, District of Columbia

Officers of the Metropolitan Police Department of the District of Columbia (MPDC) exercise jurisdiction over most areas within the District, with the exception of property under the control of federal agencies that maintain police departments such as the Supreme Court, U.S. Capitol, Library of Congress, National Zoological Park, and Government Printing Office. Although MPDC police officers are not federal employees, they serve as the primary law enforcement agency within the District—which is a federal enclave—and operations are coordinated extensively with federal law enforcement agencies in the DC area.

MPDC police officers perform all functions traditionally associated with urban police department operations, including conducting vehicle and foot patrols; responding to calls for service, crimes in progress, and emergency situations; making arrests; performing traffic control and enforcement; sponsoring community policing functions; performing crowd control at demonstrations and public events; protecting VIPs as assigned; and engaging in crime prevention activities. MPDC officers also can be assigned to specialized units that are concerned with harbor patrol, traffic control and enforcement, police training, special events, escort and security for the president and vice president of the United States, tactical incidents, bicycle patrol, motorcycle patrol, canine handler duties, and criminal investigations. MPDC police officers coordinate operations on an ongoing basis with the U.S. Secret Service, U.S. Park Police, Capitol Police, FBI, National Zoological Park Police, various Defense Department agencies, AMTRAK Police, and many other federal, state, and local agencies. MPDC police officers are authorized to carry firearms and make arrests.

Qualifications and Salary Levels

Salaries for MPDC police officers are similar to that of GS-0083 police officer positions of federal law enforcement agencies. Applicants must have reached the age of 20 years and six months at the time of application, and age 21 at the time of appointment; have completed at least two years of college (60 semester hours) in any field of study; and pass a written examination. Uncorrected visual acuity must be no worse than 20/100 (Snellen), correctable to 20/30 in both eyes. Height and weight must be proportionate. The application process includes a medical examination, psychological evaluation, background investigation, and drug-screening test.

Training

Initial training consists of a 24-week Basic Police Officer Training Course at the MPDC Academy, which includes courses in subjects such as criminal law, the District of Columbia Code, laws of arrest, search and seizure, traffic regulations, human relations, community policing, ethics, first aid, self-defense, firearms proficiency, communications, and emergency vehicle operation. In-service training includes courses in subjects such as criminal law, laws of arrest, traffic accident investigation, firearms proficiency, defensive tactics, and first aid.

Contact: Office of Recruiting; Metropolitan Police Department of the District of Columbia; 300 Indiana Ave. NW—Room 2169; Washington, DC 20001; phone: (202) 727-2767 or (800) 994-6732; Internet: www.mpdc.dc.gov/; e-mail: recruits.mpd-recruit@mpdc.org

Police Officer
Uniformed Police Branch, U.S. Government Printing Office

With operations that are centered around the largest general printing plant in the world, the U.S. Government Printing Office (GPO) produces and procures printed and electronic publications for Congress and the departments and establishments of the federal government. As the law enforcement branch of the GPO, uniformed police officers perform loss prevention functions and provide protection for GPO employees, visitors, buildings, and grounds.

Some examples of the responsibilities carried out by GPO police officers include conducting vehicle and foot patrols; responding to intrusion, fire, and other emergency alarms; investigating terrorist threats, disturbances, accidents, robberies, thefts, assaults, vandalism, and other crimes; coordinating bomb searches; standing guard at money-handling facilities; protecting classified materials; inspecting briefcases, packages, and other containers brought into GPO facilities by employees, visitors, and contractors to prevent the introduction of illegal materials; issuing identification badges to visitors; operating x-ray and metal detection equipment used to screen incoming and outgoing personnel and property; testing fire alarms; performing first aid and CPR; and investigating misconduct or violations of laws by GPO employees that do not involve fraud, waste, abuse, or mismanagement. GPO police officers are authorized to carry firearms and make arrests.

Qualifications and Salary Levels

GPO police officers are appointed through excepted service hiring processes. The qualifications and salaries of the position are similar to those of GS-0083 police officers at the GS-4 through GS-8 levels with other federal agencies. Applicants must have good near and distant vision, the ability to distinguish basic colors, and the ability to hear the conversational voice. The application process includes a medical examination, drug test, and background investigation.

Training

GPO police officers attend the 10-week Mixed Basic Police Training Program at the Federal Law Enforcement Training Center in Glynco, Georgia (see chapter 16). They also can attend in-service training programs that focus on subjects such as antiterrorism, crisis management, patrol procedures, legal issues and updates, hazardous materials, emergency response procedures, and officer safety.

Contact: Uniformed Police Branch; Government Printing Office; 732 N. Capitol St. NW; Washington, DC 20401; phone: (202) 512-1800; Internet: www.gpo.gov/; e-mail: recruitment@gpo.gov

Police Officer (GS-0083)
National Institutes of Health, U.S. Department of Health and Human Services

The Division of Police within the National Institutes of Health (NIH) operates a full-service police department that exercises law enforcement jurisdiction over the NIH campus in Bethesda, Maryland. The NIH enclave consists of 75 buildings on more than 300 acres, and includes a research hospital, outpatient clinic, pediatric treatment center, numerous research and education facilities, and the National Library of Medicine.

Uniformed NIH police officers perform a wide range of law enforcement and security functions, including patrolling on foot and bicycles, and in marked and unmarked police cars; responding to traffic accidents, calls for service, crimes in progress, and emergency situations; conducting preliminary investigations of criminal matters; coordinating security for special events and VIP visits; traffic enforcement and control; performing first aid and CPR; and providing police escorts. Experienced NIH police officers can be assigned to the Police Investigations Section, which is staffed by plain-clothes detectives who process crime scenes and conduct criminal investigations, surveillance, interviews, and interrogations. In addition, NIH police has canine teams that assist with patrol functions and bomb detection operations, and a Traffic Unit that handles traffic flow and enforcement. NIH police officers are authorized to carry firearms and make arrests.

Qualifications and Salary Levels

GS-4: Six months of general experience and six months of specialized experience; or two years of education above high school with at least 12 semester hours of coursework related to law enforcement, criminal investigation, criminology, police science, law, or similar subjects. **GS-5:** Completion of a four-year course of study leading to a bachelor's degree in the subject-areas listed under GS-4; or three years of specialized experience, one year of which was equivalent to GS-4. **GS-6:** One year of specialized experience equivalent to GS-5. **GS-7:** One year of specialized experience equivalent to GS-6. **GS-8:** One year of specialized experience equivalent to GS-7.

Experience and education can be combined to meet specialized experience requirements for positions at grades GS-4 and GS-5. Prior completion of a police academy training program can be substituted for three months of specialized experience or six months of general experience. No substitution of education or training may be made for the required specialized experience for appointment to positions at GS-6 and above. Applicants must have good near and distant vision, the ability to distinguish basic colors, and the ability to hear the conversational voice. Appointees must pass a drug screening test, medical examination, and background investigation.

Training

NIH police officers attend the 10-week Mixed Basic Police Training Program at the Federal Law Enforcement Training Center in Glynco, Georgia (see chapter 16). Professional development includes at least 40 hours of in-service training annually, including instruction on topics such as traffic enforcement and accident investigation, VIP protection, criminal law, laws of arrest, search and seizure, firearms proficiency, defensive tactics, and first aid.

Contact: Division of Police; National Institutes of Health; U.S. Department of Health and Human Services; 31 Center Dr.—Building B3B17; Bethesda, MD 20892; phone: (301) 496-2387; Internet: www.ser.ors.od.nih.gov/div_police.htm/

Police Officer (GS-0083)
Federal Protective Service, U.S. Immigration and Customs Enforcement,U.S. Department of Homeland Security

The Federal Protective Service (FPS) traces its roots to the late 1700s, and is one of the oldest federal law enforcement agencies. Until March 2003, when FPS was transferred to U.S. Immigration and Customs Enforcement (ICE), the Agency had been the law enforcement and security arm of the Public Buildings Service, U.S. General Services Administration (GSA), for more than 30 years. FPS provides law enforcement and security services within more than 8,800 federally owned and leased buildings and facilities nationwide.

FPS police officers patrol areas in and around federal buildings and facilities in cars, on motorcycles and bicycles, and on foot; monitor intrusion and fire alarm systems, x-ray equipment, metal detectors, and closed-circuit television systems; conduct traffic enforcement and control; respond to traffic accidents, calls for service, crimes in progress, emergency situations, protests, and demonstrations; perform first aid and CPR; conduct undercover and surveillance operations; secure crime scenes; collect and preserve evidence; interview victims and witnesses; interrogate suspects; and process prisoners. FPS police officers respond to criminal offenses such as trespassing, theft, robbery, burglary, arson, assault, sexual assault, weapons offenses, vandalism, threats, gambling, drug activity, and homicide. They also provide protection support for presidential inaugurations and events such as the Olympic Games and the Kentucky Derby. FPS special response teams are trained to manage hostage situations, civil unrest, demonstrations, bomb threats, counterterrorism operations, hazardous materials and weapons of mass destruction incidents, and situations that call for canine support. FPS police officers participate in antiterrorism task forces and other operations jointly with ICE special agents and agencies such as the Drug Enforcement Administration, U.S. Marshals Service, and other federal, state, and local law enforcement agencies. FPS police officers are authorized to carry firearms and make arrests.

Qualifications and Salary Levels

GS-5: Completion of a four-year course of study leading to a bachelor's degree related to law enforcement, criminal investigation, criminology, police science, law, or similar subjects; or three years of specialized experience, one year of which was equivalent to

GS-4. **GS-6:** One year of specialized experience equivalent to GS-5. **GS-7:** One year of specialized experience equivalent to GS-6. **GS-8:** One year of specialized experience equivalent to GS-7. **GS-9:** One year of specialized experience equivalent to GS-8. **GS-10:** One year of specialized experience equivalent to GS-9.

Equivalent combinations of education and experience can be used to meet minimum experience requirements for positions at grade GS-5. Prior completion of a police academy training program can be substituted for three months of specialized experience or six months of general experience. No substitution of education or training may be made for the required specialized experience for appointment to positions at GS-6 and above. Applicants must have good near and distant vision, the ability to distinguish basic colors, and the ability to hear the conversational voice. Appointees must pass a drug screening test, medical examination, and background investigation, and qualify for a security clearance.

Training

Newly appointed FPS police officers attend the 10-week Mixed Basic Police Training Program at the Federal Law Enforcement Training Center (FLETC) in Glynco, Georgia (see chapter 16). In-service training could include the two-week Advanced Physical Security Training Program at FLETC, as well as courses pertaining to crime prevention, electronic security systems, oral briefing techniques, written communication skills, contract administration, security procedures and equipment, legal issues and updates, weapons of mass destruction, international and domestic terrorism, firearms proficiency, judgment pistol shooting, defensive tactics, first aid, and other topics.

Contact: Federal Protective Service; United States Immigration and Customs Enforcement; U.S. Department of Homeland Security; 801 I St. NW—Ste. 900; Washington, DC 20536; phone: (202) 514-2648; Internet: www.ice.gov/fps/

Police Officer (GS-0083)
Bureau of Indian Affairs, U.S. Department of the Interior

Law enforcement on Native American reservations is significantly different from the environments in which most federal police officers carry out their duties, and it presents unique challenges. Bureau of Indian Affairs (BIA) police officers enforce federal, state, tribal, and conservation laws on Native American lands, reservations, allotments, and communities throughout Indian Country. They must always be aware of tribal norms, traditions, cultural issues, politics, and economies in carrying out their duties.

BIA police officers respond to calls for service, disturbances, traffic accidents, fires, and emergency situations; conduct patrols in vehicles and on foot; operate traffic radar and perform traffic enforcement functions; conduct night surveillance using technical equipment in high-crime areas; coordinate traffic and crowd control activities at religious and ceremonial gatherings; and conduct preliminary investigations of offenses such as hunting and fishing violations, larceny, burglary, vandalism, assault, auto theft, child sexual abuse, murder, sexual assault, robbery, liquor violations, and drug trafficking. BIA police officers do not patrol Native American lands that are served by tribes that maintain police departments, although they often provide assistance to tribal police agencies in emergency situations and a variety of other circumstances. BIA police officers frequently carry out their duties in remote areas, at high altitudes, and over mountains and rugged terrain where climatic conditions are variable and extreme. They are authorized to carry firearms and make arrests.

BIA police officers are covered under special retirement provisions for law enforcement officers.

Qualifications and Salary Levels

GS-3: Six months of general experience; or one year of education above high school with at least six semester hours of coursework related to law enforcement, criminal investigation, criminology, police science, law, or similar subjects. **GS-4:** Six months of general experience and six months of specialized experience, or two years of education above high school with at least 12 semester hours of coursework in the subject-areas listed under GS-3. **GS-5:** Completion of a four-year course of study leading to a bachelor's degree in the subject-areas listed under GS-3; or three years of specialized experience, one year of which was equivalent to GS-4. **GS-6:** One year of specialized experience equivalent to GS-5. **GS-7:** One year of specialized experience equivalent to GS-6. **GS-8:** One year of specialized experience equivalent to GS-7.

Under the Indian Reorganization Act of 1934, qualified Native American applicants are given hiring preference for BIA positions, although applications from non-Native American candidates are encouraged. Applicants must be at least 21 years of age and under age 37. However, candidates over age 37 who have previous service creditable under special law enforcement retirement provisions also may be eligible. Experience and education can be combined to meet specialized experience requirements for positions at grades GS-4 and GS-5. Prior completion of a police academy training program can be substituted for three months of specialized experience or six months of general experience. No substitution of education or training may be made for the required specialized experience for appointment to positions at GS-6 and above. Applicants must have good near and distant vision, the ability to distinguish basic colors, and the ability to hear the conversational voice. Candidates must achieve a passing score on the National Police Officer Selection Test to advance in the hiring process (see chapter 3). Appointees must pass a drug screening test, medical examination, and background investigation.

Training

BIA police officers attend the 16-week Basic Police Officer Training Program—Indian Police Academy at the Federal Law Enforcement Training Center in Artesia, New Mexico, which includes instruction in subjects such as Indian Country law, conflict management, narcotics violations, officer safety and survival, criminalistics, search and seizure, collection and preservation of evidence, civil rights, detention and arrest, ethics, stress, firearms, defensive tactics, and defensive driving. In-service training focuses on subjects such as crime scene investigation, domestic assault, traffic enforcement, accident investigation, police administration, criminal law, laws of arrest, firearms proficiency, defensive tactics, first aid, and other courses relating to law enforcement in Native American communities.

Contact: Direct inquiries to the personnel office where employment is sought, or contact Office of Personnel; Bureau of Indian Affairs; U.S. Department of the Interior; 1849 C St. NW; Washington, DC 20240; phone: (202) 208-3710; Internet: www.doi.gov/bureau-indian-affairs.html/.

Police Officer (GS-0083)
Bureau of Reclamation, U.S. Department of the Interior

The mission of the Bureau of Reclamation (BR) is to manage, develop, and protect water and related resources in an environmentally and economically sound manner. BR police officers are responsible for law enforcement and security functions for the protection of BR facilities, employees, and visitors nationwide.

With law enforcement jurisdiction over water conveyances and distribution facilities, storage reservoirs, and hydroelectric power plants (including the Hoover Dam), BR police officers enforce federal and state laws; control access to restricted areas; perform vehicle and foot patrols; monitor alarm systems and intrusion control devices; respond to calls for service, alarms, disturbances, traffic accidents, fires, material spills, and emergency situations; operate fire apparatus; direct traffic and investigate motor vehicle accidents; secure crime scenes; preserve and collect evidence; conduct investigations, surveillance, interviews and interrogations; perform first aid and CPR; and exercise antiterrorism measures. BR police officers also are stationed at inspection checkpoints along U.S. Highway 93 on both sides of the Hoover Dam in Arizona, where they inspect vehicle passenger areas, trunks, cargo areas, engine compartments, and undercarriages, including closed or locked containers within these areas. BR police officers are authorized to carry firearms and make arrests.

Qualifications and Salary Levels

GS-4: Six months of general experience and six months of specialized experience; or two years of education above high school with at least 12 semester hours of coursework related to law enforcement, criminal investigation, criminology, police science, law, or similar subjects. **GS-5:** Completion of a four-year course of study leading to a bachelor's degree in the subject-areas listed under GS-4; or three years of specialized experience, one year of which was equivalent to GS-4. **GS-6:** One year of specialized experience equivalent to GS-5. **GS-7:** One year of specialized experience equivalent to GS-6. **GS-8:** One year of specialized experience equivalent to GS-7.

Equivalent combinations of education and experience can be used to meet minimum experience requirements for positions at grades GS-4 and GS-5. Prior completion of a police academy training program can be substituted for three months of specialized experience or six months of general experience. No substitution of education or training may be made for the required specialized experience for appointment to positions at GS-6 and above. Applicants must have good near and distant vision, the ability to distinguish basic colors, and the ability to hear the conversational voice. Appointees must pass a drug screening test, medical examination, and background investigation, and qualify for a security clearance.

Training

BR police officers attend the 16-week Natural Resources Police Training Program at the Federal Law Enforcement Training Center in Glynco, Georgia (see chapter 16). In-service training may include courses in traffic enforcement and accident investigation, search and seizure, criminal law, laws of arrest, firearms proficiency, defensive tactics, first aid, and other topics concerning specific responsibilities.

Contact: Security, Safety, and Law Enforcement Office; Bureau of Reclamation; U.S. Department of the Interior; Denver Federal Center—PO Box 25007; Denver, CO 80225; phone: (303) 445-3736; Internet: www.usbr.gov/

Police Officer (GS-0083)
Federal Bureau of Investigation, U.S. Department of Justice

The Federal Bureau of Investigation (FBI) maintains a force of uniformed police officers whose primary mission is to maintain law and order, and to protect life, property, and the civil rights of FBI personnel and visitors at FBI buildings and facilities. FBI police officers are stationed at the Bureau's Headquarters Building in Washington, DC; the Washington, DC, Field Office; the FBI Training Academy in Quantico, Virginia; two buildings occupied by the New York City Field Office; and at the Bureau's Criminal Justice Information Services Division complex in Clarksburg, West Virginia.

FBI police officers are assigned to fixed posts, patrols, and control-desk duties on rotating shifts around the clock, through which they protect government property and national security information from acts of sabotage, espionage, terrorism, trespass, theft, fire, and accidental or malicious damage or destruction. They conduct patrols on foot and in vehicles to check for unsecured windows and doors, detect and prevent illegal entry, identify suspicious persons and vehicles, and respond to other conditions. They also answer calls for service, respond to crimes in progress and emergency situations, conduct physical security escorts, and administer first aid and CPR to sick or injured persons. When crimes are detected, FBI police officers secure the crime scenes, collect and preserve evidence, interview victims and witnesses, and process prisoners. Fixed-post duty involves access-control tasks, such as checking the identification of FBI employees and screening visitors seeking access to secure areas. Officers are also assigned to a control center where they monitor electronic intrusion-detection devices and communications systems. FBI police officers are authorized to carry firearms and make arrests.

Qualifications and Salary Levels

GS-5: Completion of a four-year course of study leading to a bachelor's degree related to law enforcement, criminal investigation, criminology, police science, law, or similar subjects; or three years of specialized experience, one year of which was equivalent to GS-4. **GS-6:** One year of specialized experience equivalent to GS-5. **GS-7:** One year of specialized experience equivalent to GS-6. **GS-8:** One year of specialized experience equivalent to GS-7. **GS-9:** One year of specialized experience equivalent to GS-8.

Applicants must be at least 21 years of age and have a high school diploma or its equivalent. Eyesight requirements include uncorrected distant vision not worse than 20/200 (Snellen), corrected vision not worse than 20/20 in one eye and 20/40 in the other eye, and the ability to distinguish basic shades of colors. Candidates who have undergone LASIK eye surgery must be free from residual effects one year after surgery. All applicants who have undergone any form of surgical vision correction are evaluated on a case-by-case basis by the FBI's Health Care Programs Unit. Hearing loss must not exceed 25 decibels at 1000, 2000, and 3000 Hertz; a single reading of 35 decibels at 1000, 2000, and 3000 Hertz; a single reading of 35 decibels at 500 Hertz; and a single reading of 45 decibels at 4000 Hertz. Tentative appointees must pass a polygraph examination, drug screening test, medical examination, and background investigation, and qualify for a security clearance.

Training

FBI police officers attend the 10-week Mixed Basic Police Training Program at the Federal Law Enforcement Training Center in Glynco, Georgia (see chapter 16). In-service training covers topics concerning patrol techniques, responding to emergencies, driving skills, law, weapons proficiency and qualification, defensive tactics, physical security functions, and other subjects relating to specific duties.

Contact: FBI Police; Federal Bureau of Investigation; 935 Pennsylvania Ave. NW; Washington, DC 20535; phone: (202) 324-3000; Internet: www.fbi.gov/

Police Officer
Library of Congress Police, The Library of Congress

The Library of Congress (LC) is the national library of the United States, offering diverse materials for research, including the world's most extensive collections in areas such as American history, music, and law. LC police officers perform a variety of law enforcement and security functions around the clock within Library buildings and grounds.

Some of the responsibilities carried out by LC police officers include protecting the lives, property, and civil rights of LC staff and patrons; maintaining law and order; protecting LC property and collections; monitoring intrusion detection, closed-circuit television, and other security and access control systems; conducting patrols to detect and report unlawful or unsafe actions and conditions; maintaining fixed exterior posts; subduing unruly persons; performing first aid and CPR in cases of accident or acute illness; participating in fire drills and inspections; drafting official reports pertaining to accidents, incidents, conditions, or unusual circumstances; and managing the LC Police Communications Center. They also provide law enforcement and security support to library functions and special events, including the National Book Festival, Congressional events, visits from heads of state, and presidential inaugural events, among others. LC police officers are authorized to carry firearms and make arrests.

Qualifications and Salary Levels

LC police officers are appointed through excepted service hiring processes. The qualifications and salaries of the position are similar to those of GS-0083 police officers with other federal agencies. Applicants must be at least 21 years of age and have a high school diploma or GED certificate. Requirements include at least 18 months of full-time law enforcement or security experience. Qualifying work experience includes service with a federal, state, or local police agency; private security organization; or service in the armed forces as a military police officer. One year of college or 30 semester credits in criminal justice or law enforcement courses can be substituted for nine months of experience. Applicants must have good near and distant vision, the ability to distinguish basic colors, and ability to hear the conversational voice. Tentative appointees must pass a written examination, medical examination, and background investigation.

Training

LC police officers attend the 10-week Mixed Basic Police Training Program at the Federal Law Enforcement Training Center in Glynco, Georgia (see chapter 16).

In-service training focuses on criminal law, search and seizure, laws of arrest, interviewing techniques, firearms proficiency, defensive tactics, first aid, and other subjects.

Contact: Library of Congress Police; The Library of Congress; 101 Independence Ave. SE; Washington, DC 20540; phone: (202) 707-9089; Internet: www.loc.gov/

Police Officer
AMTRAK Police Department, National Railroad Passenger Corporation

With police personnel assigned to 29 field locations in 16 states and the District of Columbia, the AMTRAK Police Department serves as the law enforcement and security arm of the federal government's National Railroad Passenger Corporation. AMTRAK police officers perform crime prevention functions and provide protection of passengers, property, and personnel, while maintaining jurisdiction over more than 500 train stations in 46 states, and over a rail system of nearly 22,000 route miles.

The primary responsibilities of AMTRAK police officers include riding trains; performing foot, bicycle, and vehicle patrols of train stations, railroad right-of-way, and maintenance facilities to detect criminal activity; preventing and detecting vandalism to tracks, trains, signals, and other property; responding to incidents involving larceny, robbery, purse snatching, assault, weapons offenses, panhandling, drug trafficking, murder, arson, bomb threats, obstructions placed on tracks, and other crimes committed on trains, in train stations, or on AMTRAK property; conducting surveillance; exchanging intelligence information with other law enforcement agencies; preserving the peace; performing preliminary criminal investigations; apprehending offenders; responding to emergency situations and accidents; and performing first aid and CPR. Experienced AMTRAK police officers also can be assigned to the Bicycle Patrol Unit, the Canine Unit, and the Detective Division (see chapter 6). AMTRAK police officers conduct many operations jointly with other federal, state, local, and transit law enforcement agencies. They are authorized to carry firearms and make arrests.

Qualifications and Salary Levels

Employment as an AMTRAK police officer is open to noncitizens who are authorized to work in the United States. AMTRAK police officers are appointed through excepted service hiring processes. The qualifications and salaries of the position are similar to those of GS-0083 police officers at the GS-4 through GS-8 levels with other federal agencies. Applicants must be at least 21 years of age at the time of appointment. A high school diploma or GED is required, although an associate's degree or at least 60 semester credits from an accredited college or university are preferred. Applicants must pass a written examination, background investigation, psychological evaluation, medical examination, and drug screening test.

Training

Newly appointed AMTRAK police officers attend either the 10-week Mixed Basic Police Training Program at the Federal Law Enforcement Training Center in Glynco, Georgia (see chapter 16), or a state-certified police academy training program in the same state as the post of duty. In-service training includes periodic courses relating to topics such as railroad operations and signal reading, drug interdiction, disaster response, crisis management, safety procedures, bloodborne pathogens, legal issues and updates, firearms proficiency, defensive tactics, arrest techniques, and first aid.

Contact: AMTRAK Police Department; 900 Second St.—Room 101; Washington, DC 20002; phone: (800) 331-0008; Internet: www.amtrak.com/

Police Officer (GS-0083)
National Zoological Park Police, Smithsonian Institution

National Zoological Park Police (NZPP) officers protect one of the oldest branches of the Smithsonian Institution—the National Zoo—which encompasses 163 acres along Rock Creek in Northwest Washington, DC, and contains more than 2,700 animals and 435 different species. The National Zoological Park is open to the public 364 days per year, and receives about two million visitors annually.

NZPP officers are responsible for a wide range of law enforcement and security functions on Zoo property, including protecting animals and exhibits; maintaining order and enforcing Zoo rules; inspecting Zoo buildings, locker rooms, restrooms, and other facilities; locating lost children, other missing persons, and lost property; providing assistance to Zoo visitors; directing pedestrian and motor vehicle traffic; investigating traffic accidents; performing crowd control; conducting vehicular and foot patrols; responding to calls for service, crimes in progress, and emergency situations; administering first aid and CPR; writing detailed incident and accident reports; and preparing criminal cases for prosecution. They also participate in crime prevention and law enforcement operations with the Metropolitan Police Department of the District of Columbia (MPDC), including patrols, crime scene searches and evidence processing, investigations, prisoner transportation, traffic enforcement, and other matters. NZPP officers are authorized to carry firearms and make arrests.

Qualifications and Salary Levels

NZPP police officers are appointed through excepted service hiring processes. The qualifications and salaries for these officers are determined by the Secretary of the Smithsonian Institution, and are similar to those of GS-0083 police officers with other federal agencies. Prior completion of a police academy training program can be substituted for three months of specialized experience or six months of general experience. Applicants must have good near and distant vision, the ability to distinguish basic colors, and the ability to hear the conversational voice. Appointees must pass a medical examination and background investigation.

Training

NZPP officers attend the 10-week Mixed Basic Police Training Program at the Federal Law Enforcement Training Center in Glynco, Georgia (see chapter 16). In-service training focuses on topics such as National Zoological Park policies and procedures, traffic accident investigation, criminal law, the District of Columbia Code, search and seizure, laws of arrest, firearms proficiency, defensive tactics, and first aid.

Contact: Office of Human Resources; Smithsonian Institution; 3001 Connecticut Ave. NW; Washington, DC 20008; Phone: (202) 275-1102; internet: www.nationalzoo.si.edu/

Police Officer

Supreme Court Police, Supreme Court of the United States

The Supreme Court of the United States is the highest tribunal in the nation for all cases and controversies arising under the Constitution or the laws of the United States. As the final arbiter of the law, the Supreme Court ensures the promise of equal justice under law and also functions as guardian and interpreter of the Constitution. Officers of the Supreme Court Police are responsible for the protection of personnel, visitors, and property at the Supreme Court, which is located across the street from the U.S. Capitol Building in Washington, DC.

Supreme Court police officers perform many law enforcement and security functions, including conducting foot and vehicle patrols of the Supreme Court Building, grounds, and adjacent streets; providing personal protection throughout the United States of the chief justice and associate justices of the Supreme Court, official Supreme Court guests, and officers or employees of the Supreme Court while these personnel are engaged in their duties; ensuring overall building security and surveillance; providing courtroom security; responding to crimes in progress, disturbances, bomb threats, and emergency situations; policing protests and demonstrations on Supreme Court Building grounds; performing first aid and CPR; and providing assistance to Supreme Court visitors. Supreme Court police officers are authorized to carry firearms and make arrests.

Retirement benefits for Supreme Court police officers are equivalent to those of personnel in the competitive service who are covered under special retirement provisions for federal law enforcement officers.

Qualifications and Salary Levels

Supreme Court police officers are appointed through excepted service hiring processes. The Supreme Court Police Pay Plan is identical to the U.S. Capitol Police Pay Plan. Salaries under these pay systems are similar to GS-9 through GS-12, which are significantly higher than salaries for most GS-0083 federal police officers who perform similar work and are compensated under the General Schedule pay system. Applicants must be at least 21 years of age and under age 37. However, candidates over age 37 who have previous service creditable under special law enforcement retirement provisions also may be eligible. Applicants must have a high school diploma. Two years of college education and prior law enforcement or security experience is preferred. Applicants must pass a medical examination and background investigation.

Training

Supreme Court police officers attend the 10-week Mixed Basic Police Training Program at the Federal Law Enforcement Training Center in Glynco, Georgia (see chapter 16). Basic training is followed by a six-month orientation and field training program at the Supreme Court that includes courses related to specific duties of the position, as well as foot and vehicular patrol duty with an experienced field training officer, and assignment to various posts of duty. In-service training could include courses in security procedures, personal protective operations, legal issues and updates, firearms proficiency, defensive tactics, first aid, and other subjects.

Contact: Personnel Office; Supreme Court of the United States; 1 First St. NE; Washington, DC 20543; phone: (202) 479-3404; Internet: www.supremecourtus.gov/

Police Officer

TVA Police, Tennessee Valley Authority

The Tennessee Valley Authority (TVA), a wholly owned government corporation, is the nation's largest single producer of electric power. It provides electric service to large industries, federal installations, and 158 power distributors within an 80,000-square mile area in Tennessee and parts of Mississippi, Alabama, Georgia, North Carolina, Virginia, and Kentucky. As fully commissioned uniformed personnel, TVA police officers are responsible for maintaining order and protecting TVA personnel, property, assets, and the public, including more than 100 million annual users of TVA recreational facilities.

TVA police officers carry out patrols and other duties in and around three nuclear power plants, 29 hydroelectric dams, 11 coal plants, 100 public recreation areas, dozens of reservoirs and the 290,000 acres of land surrounding them, 13 customer service centers, and other offices and facilities throughout the Tennessee Valley region. TVA police officers perform a wide range of law enforcement and security functions, including ensuring access control to prevent unauthorized entry to TVA property or restricted areas; conducting foot and vehicle patrols to prevent sabotage, theft of nuclear materials, civil disorders, vandalism, assaults, and other crimes; responding to crimes in progress, alarms, disturbances, bomb threats, accidents, and emergency situations; conducting traffic control and enforcement; performing first aid and CPR; and investigating crimes and accidents. Experienced officers can be assigned to marine patrol, bicycle patrol, and investigative duties, as well as community policing responsibilities. TVA police officers are authorized to carry firearms and make arrests.

Qualifications and Salary Levels

TVA police officers are appointed through excepted service hiring processes. The qualifications and salaries of the position are similar to those of GS-0083 police with other federal agencies. Applicants must be at least 21 years of age; have an associate's degree (or at least 65 semester hours of college credit) and two years of related law enforcement experience, or a bachelor's degree; and have basic computer skills. Eyesight and hearing requirements include the ability to see with sufficient clarity to monitor electronic equipment panels, light bars, screens, monitors, and other equipment and devices; and the ability to discriminate between differing sounds, such as various alarms and speech. Applicants must pass a written examination, background investigation, psychological evaluation, medical examination, drug and alcohol screening, physical fitness test, and swimming test.

Training

Newly appointed TVA police officers attend the 16-week Natural Resources Police Training Program (NRPTP) at the Federal Law Enforcement Training Center in Glynco, Georgia (see chapter 16). This training is followed by a 10-week field training program at the assigned TVA post of duty. In-service training could focus on topics such as nuclear security, access control procedures, intrusion detection devices, terrorism, marine patrol techniques, traffic control and enforcement, accident investigation, legal issues and updates, interviewing techniques, gang awareness, firearms proficiency, first aid, and defensive tactics.

Contact: TVA Police; 400 W. Summit Hill Dr.; Knoxville, TN 37902; phone: (800) 824-3861; Internet: www.tva.gov/abouttva/tvap/

Police Officer
Bureau of Engraving and Printing, U.S. Department of the Treasury

The Bureau of Engraving and Printing (BEP) designs, prints, and finishes all of the nation's paper currency, as well as U.S. postage stamps, Treasury securities, naturalization certificates, U.S. Coast Guard water use licenses, presidential appointment certificates, White House invitations, military identification cards, and other security documents. To protect these operations, BEP police officers are responsible for law enforcement and security functions at the Agency's headquarters facility in Washington, DC, and a currency manufacturing plant in Fort Worth, Texas.

BEP police officers are assigned to the Police Operations Division within the Office of Security. Some examples of the responsibilities carried out by BEP police officers include protecting Bureau assets, plant facilities, property, personnel, and visitors; maintaining order; conducting static post and foot patrol duty; responding to suspicious circumstances, calls for service, crimes in progress, and emergency situations; enforcing federal and municipal laws, Treasury Department regulations, and Bureau security rules; conducting preliminary investigations of incidents involving theft, vandalism, fire, and other security and safety hazards; writing detailed reports concerning crimes, emergency situations, security and safety violations, and other incidents; screening visitors entering Bureau facilities; and monitoring alarm systems, intrusion control devices, and closed-circuit surveillance monitors. BEP police officers also provide support to other components of the Office of Security, including the Product Integrity Division, the Technical Security Division, and the Personnel Security Division. BEP police officers are authorized to carry firearms and make arrests.

Qualifications and Salary Levels

BEP police officers are appointed through excepted service hiring processes. These officers are covered under a pay system administered by the Secretary of the Treasury. Salaries under this pay system are similar to GS-7 through GS-12, which are higher than salaries for most GS-0083 federal police officers who perform similar work and are compensated under the General Schedule pay system. Applicants must be at least 21 years of age. Prior completion of a police academy training program can be substituted for three months of specialized experience or six months of general experience. Eyesight requirements include uncorrected visual acuity no worse than 20/50 (Snellen), correctable to 20/20 in both eyes, and the ability to distinguish basic colors. Hearing loss must not exceed 45 decibels at the average of 4000 Hertz and 6000 Hertz. (Hearing aids cannot be used during the test.) Applicants must achieve a passing score on the National Police Officer Selection Test (see chapter 3). The application process also includes a drug screening test, medical examination, background investigation, and security clearance determination.

Training

Initial training for police officer recruits consists of a two-week orientation program conducted by BEP staff, followed by the 10-week Mixed Basic Police Training Program at the Federal Law Enforcement Training Center (FLETC) in Glynco, Georgia (see chapter 16). After graduation from FLETC, BEP police officers complete eight weeks of field training at their assigned posts of duty. They also receive at least two weeks of in-service training annually, including in-house instruction and other courses relating to subjects concerning criminal law, laws of arrest, search and seizure, BEP policies, physical security procedures, terrorism threat assessment, responding to emergencies, firearms proficiency, first aid, defensive tactics, and other topics.

Contact: Police Officer Recruiting Unit; Bureau of Engraving and Printing; U.S. Department of the Treasury; 14th and C St. SW; Washington, DC 20228; phone: (202) 927-2170; Internet: www.moneyfactory.gov/; e-mail: BEPjobs@BEP.treas.gov

Police Officer (GS-0083)
Office of Security and Law Enforcement, U.S. Department of Veterans Affairs

The Department of Veterans Affairs (VA) operates hundreds of healthcare facilities in the United States, Puerto Rico, and the Philippines to benefit veterans and members of their families. VA police officers are responsible for the physical protection of patients, visitors, and employees at VA facilities that include medical centers, domiciliaries, out-patient clinics, nursing home care units, cemeteries, and Vietnam veteran outreach centers.

The primary law enforcement duties of VA police officers include conducting patrols in vehicles and on foot; enforcing federal, state, and municipal criminal laws and VA regulations; responding to disturbances, assaults by patients and visitors, accidents, alarms, bomb threats, demonstrations, fires, crimes in progress, and emergency situations; making arrests; providing traffic and crowd control; investigating accidents; writing reports; conducting interviews and interrogations; collecting and preserving evidence; and investigating criminal incidents and other matters. Some of the laws VA police officers enforce include trespassing, larceny, assault, disorderly conduct, firearms violations, vandalism, driving while intoxicated, and parking violations. Security duties include monitoring surveillance camera systems, escorting employees and visitors between buildings and parking areas, controlling access to secure areas, con-ducting physical security surveys, participating in crime prevention programs, handling emergency preparedness responsibilities, and other tasks.

VA police officers often coordinate operations with agencies such as the National Park Service, FBI, U.S. Park Police, Secret Service, Drug Enforcement Administration, and U.S. Marshals Service. The varieties of law enforcement and security activities vary widely from one location to another, and depend largely on the size and particular needs of facilities served. VA police officers are authorized to carry firearms and make arrests.

Qualifications and Salary Levels

GS-5: Completion of a four-year course of study leading to a bachelor's degree related to law enforcement, criminal investigation, criminology, police science, law, or similar subjects; or three years of specialized experience, one year of which was equivalent to GS-4. **GS-6:** One year of specialized experience equivalent to GS-5. **GS-7:** One year of specialized experience equivalent to GS-6. **GS-8:** One year of specialized experience equivalent to GS-7.

Experience and education can be combined to meet specialized experience require-ments for positions at grade GS-5. Prior completion of a police academy training pro-gram can be substituted for three months of specialized experience or six months of general experience. No substitution of education or training may be made for the required specialized experience for appointment to positions at GS-6 and above.

Applicants must have good near and distant vision, the ability to distinguish basic colors, and the ability to hear the conversational voice. Tentative appointees must pass a drug screening test, medical examination, psychological evaluation, and background investigation.

Training

Initial training for VA police officers includes two weeks of introductory training at the assigned post of duty, followed by a five-week Basic Police Officer Training Course at the VA Law Enforcement Training Center on the campus of the Central Arkansas Veterans Healthcare System in North Little Rock, Arkansas. Conducting basic training in an actual healthcare setting enables police officer recruits to interact with VA patients, staff, and visitors in an environment that cannot be duplicated at police academies or other training facilities. Basic training emphasizes human behavior; encounters with persons who are intoxicated, assaultive, destructive, mentally ill, irrational, or disturbed; conflict resolution; use of force; criminal law; laws of arrest; patrol techniques; firearms handling and qualification; and other topics pertaining to security and policing in a healthcare environment and other settings. VA police officers complete at least 40 hours of in-service training annually that focuses on first aid and CPR, hazardous materials, conflict resolution, firearms, chemical weapons, side-handle batons, patrol techniques, bicycle patrols, and other subjects.

Contact: Inquiries should be directed to the facility where employment is sought, or to Office of Security and Law Enforcement; U.S. Department of Veterans Affairs; 810 Vermont Ave. NW; Washington, DC 20420; phone: (202) 273-4800; Internet: www.va.gov/osle/.

Postal Police Officer
United States Postal Inspection Service, U.S. Postal Service

As the uniformed law enforcement branch of the U.S. Postal Service, postal police officers perform a wide range of functions pertaining to the security of postal personnel, customers, buildings, vehicles, property, and mail. They enforce postal laws and regulations while also providing a mobile response to emergency situations involving postal operations.

Examples of responsibilities carried out by postal police officers include controlling access to postal facilities and secure areas within these areas; preventing prohibited items from being brought onto postal premises, and confiscating these items; monitoring electronic security devices that provide surveillance and alarm protection; performing static post, vehicular, and foot patrols on postal property; conducting surveillance of persons in and around postal property to prevent assaults on postal employees and other crimes; responding to emergency situations and crimes in progress, accidents, injuries, illnesses, fires, disturbances, burglaries, robberies, bomb threats, and other circumstances threatening life or property; maintaining order to prevent assaults, injuries, and damage to property; collecting and preserving evidence; performing first aid in emergency situations; ensuring the security of mail-handling areas; and escorting shipments of high-value mail that are in transit between postal units and airports. Postal police officers are authorized to carry firearms and make arrests.

Qualifications and Salary Levels

Postal police officers are appointed through excepted service hiring processes. The qualifications and salaries of the position are similar to those of GS-0083 police officers with other federal agencies. Applicants must be at least 21 years of age. Eyesight requirements include uncorrected distant vision no worse than 20/100 (Snellen) in each eye, correctable to 20/20 in one eye and 20/40 in the other, and good color perception. Applicants must be able to hear the conversational voice without the use of a hearing aid. Weight must be proportionate to height. Applicants must qualify for a security clearance and pass the U.S. Postal Police Officer Examination (see chapter 3), a drug screening test, and a background investigation.

Training

Newly appointed postal police officers attend a six-week basic training program presented by the Postal Inspection Service Career Development Division at the William F. Bolger Training Center in Potomac, Maryland (see chapter 16). In-service training includes advanced versions of subjects presented during basic training, as well as other courses related to specific responsibilities of the position.

Contact: Postal Police; U.S. Postal Inspection Service; 475 L'Enfant Plaza SW; Washington, DC 20260; phone: (703) 292-3803; Internet: www.usps.com/postalinspectors/

Refuge Law Enforcement Officer (GS-0025)
United States Fish and Wildlife Service, U.S. Department of the Interior

The National Wildlife Refuge System protects America's refuge resources and ensures the safety of visitors and government personnel. Refuge law enforcement officers of the U.S. Fish and Wildlife Service (FWS) are responsible for preventing and detecting violations of federal, state, and local fish and wildlife laws on more than 500 national wildlife refuges encompassing more than 30 million acres.

FWS refuge law enforcement officers respond to and investigate violations involving illegal hunting and fishing; illegal importing and commercialization of wildlife; poaching by individuals and interstate market hunting rings; over-bagging of waterfowl; theft and disturbance of archeological resources; timber theft; illegal harvesting of plants and animals; hazardous materials dumping; arson; firearms violations; vandalism; burglary; marijuana cultivation; possession, use, distribution, trafficking, cultivation, and manufacture of controlled substances on FWS lands; traffic violations; and other offenses. Some of the tasks refuge law enforcement officers perform include patrolling refuge areas in vehicles and on foot; conducting surveillance; participating in raids; interviewing witnesses and interrogating suspects; documenting legal water uses; ensuring compliance with refuge water management plans; monitoring upstream water use to protect refuge water rights from illegal diversions; presenting cases for prosecution to the U.S. Attorney's Office; handling homeland security matters; and conducting fire, health, and safety inspections. They also operate small watercraft and special-purpose vehicles, participate in aerial surveillance operations that involve flying as a passenger in FWS aircraft to identify suspects and illegal activity, and engage in search and rescue missions. Operations carried out by refuge law enforcement officers often are coordinated with FWS special agents and other federal, state, and local law enforcement agencies. Refuge law enforcement officers are authorized to carry firearms and make arrests.

This position is covered under special retirement provisions for federal law enforcement officers.

Qualifications and Salary Levels

GS-5: Completion of a four-year course of study leading to a bachelor's degree that included at least 24 semester hours of coursework related to law enforcement, criminal investigation, criminology, police science, law, or similar subjects; or three years of general experience, one year of which was equivalent to GS-4. **GS-7:** One full year of graduate education related to the subject-areas listed under GS-5, or superior academic achievement during undergraduate studies, or one year of specialized experience equivalent to GS-5. **GS-9:** A master's degree or two years of graduate education related to the subject-areas listed under GS-5, or one year of specialized experience equivalent to GS-7. **GS-11:** A Ph.D. or equivalent doctoral degree, or three years of graduate education related to the subject-areas listed under GS-5, or one year of specialized experience equivalent to GS-9. **GS-12:** One year of specialized experience equivalent to GS-11.

Applicants must be at least 21 years of age and under age 37. However, candidates over age 37 who have previous service creditable under special law enforcement retirement provisions also may be eligible. Experience and education can be combined to meet total experience requirements for positions at grades GS-5 through GS-11. Eyesight requirements include uncorrected distant vision not worse than 20/100 (Snellen) in each eye, and corrected binocular distant vision not worse than 20/20; normal depth perception and peripheral vision; and the ability to distinguish basic colors. The use of soft contact lenses can be considered a reasonable accommodation for candidates who have worn soft contact lenses for at least one year. Candidates who have undergone LASIK eye surgery must be free from residual effects three months after surgery. Hearing loss must not exceed 30 decibels in either ear at 500, 1000, or 2000 Hertz, and 40 decibels in either ear at 3000 Hertz. (Hearing aids cannot be used during the test.) The application process includes a psychological evaluation, drug screening test, medical examination, and background investigation.

Training

Refuge officers attend the 16-week Natural Resources Police Training Program at the Federal Law Enforcement Training Center (FLETC) in Glynco, Georgia (see chapter 16). Officers then complete a two-week Refuge Officer Basic School either at FLETC, or the FWS National Conservation Training Center in Shepherdstown, West Virginia, or a similar facility. This course covers topics such as law, relevant treaties, waterfowl identification, tracking and sign recognition, subject control techniques, FWS policies, and enforcement problems unique to national wildlife refuges. In-service training includes at least 40 hours annually in subjects such as wildlife investigation, archaeological resources protection, marine law enforcement, Spanish language, legal issues and updates, firearms proficiency, first aid, defensive tactics, and other topics.

Contact: Office of Law Enforcement; U.S. Fish and Wildlife Service; 4401 N. Fairfax Dr.; Arlington, VA 22203; phone: (703) 358-1949; Internet: www.fws.gov/le/

River Ranger (GS-0025)
National Park Service, U.S. Department of the Interior

River rangers play an important—and interesting—role in National Park Service (NPS) operations relating to interpretive and recreational programs. These personnel patrol water resources managed by NPS, which involves enforcing federal and state laws concerning the protection of natural and cultural resources, including endangered species. River rangers are responsible for many tasks that enable NPS to operate meaningful programs for the benefit and protection of its visitors and personnel.

River rangers conduct back-country patrols on Class II, III, and IV white-water rivers—primarily in white-water rafts—which involves preparing equipment and conveyances; rowing and paddling rafts; identifying problems, complaints, disturbances, and violations of laws and park regulations; explaining laws and regulations to park visitors, and taking other actions necessary to preserve the peace; performing search and rescue operations; providing emergency medical assistance to injured persons; participating in river campground, back-country, and boating permit programs; and maintaining equipment used in park law enforcement operations. They also investigate and enforce violations of laws such as larceny, assault, malicious destruction of property, weapons offenses, drug use and possession, arson, and other crimes. When they are not engaged in river patrol functions, river rangers conduct traditional vehicle and foot patrol duties. In addition, river rangers perform many tasks unrelated to law enforcement or security, such as presenting information and educational programs to park visitors concerning points of interest, including cultural, historical, and natural resources, and park activities; and carrying out conservation programs relating to habitat and wildlife monitoring, rescue, and rehabilitation. River rangers are authorized to carry firearms and make arrests.

Qualifications and Salary Levels

GS-5: Completion of a four-year course of study leading to a bachelor's degree that included at least 24 semester hours of coursework related to law enforcement, criminal investigation, criminology, police science, law, or similar subjects; or three years of general experience, one year of which was equivalent to GS-4. **GS-7:** One full year of graduate education related to the subject-areas listed under GS-5, or superior academic achievement during undergraduate studies, or one year of specialized experience equivalent to GS-5. **GS-9:** A master's degree or two years of graduate education related to the subject-areas listed under GS-5, or one year of specialized experience equivalent to GS-7. **GS-11:** A Ph.D. or equivalent doctoral degree, or three years of graduate education related to the subject-areas listed under GS-5, or one year of specialized experience equivalent to GS-9. **GS-12:** One year of specialized experience equivalent to GS-11. Applicants must be at least 21 years of age. Experience and education can be combined to meet total experience requirements for positions at grades GS-5 through GS-11. Appointment is contingent upon passing a background investigation, medical examination, and drug test.

Training

NPS river rangers attend an orientation program that covers the mission, policies, procedures, and rules of the post of duty and the National Park Service. This is followed by on-the-job training that is monitored by experienced NPS park rangers and river rangers. They also can attend formal training courses that are presented at Grand Canyon National Park or other NPS training centers; at the Federal Law Enforcement Training Center in Glynco, Georgia; or other locations.

Contact: Division of Personnel Management; National Park Service; U.S. Department of the Interior; 1849 C St. NW; Washington, DC 20240; phone: (202) 208-6843; Internet: www.nps.gov/

Security Protective Officer
CIA Security Protective Service, Central Intelligence Agency

Overview

The Central Intelligence Agency (CIA) collects, evaluates, and disseminates vital intelligence information on political, military, economic, scientific, and other developments abroad needed to safeguard national security, and provides the information to the president and national policymakers. Within this mission, security protective officers play a crucial role in the CIA's effort to provide a comprehensive, worldwide security program that protects Agency personnel, programs, information, facilities, and activities. Security protective officers are responsible for protecting CIA assets and personnel by enforcing federal laws and Agency regulations within and around CIA installations.

Many of the law enforcement and security functions carried out by these personnel—such as providing patrols, maintaining checkpoints and static posts, and responding to calls for service and emergencies—are similar to those performed by police and security officers employed by the Pentagon Force Protection Agency, Defense Logistics Agency, Army, Navy, Secret Service Uniformed Division, and other agencies. For example, security protective officers ensure that access to CIA property is controlled and restricted to Agency employees and other persons with proper authorization; inspect vehicles, packages, briefcases, and other containers to ensure that prohibited items are not brought onto or removed from CIA property; enforce the unauthorized possession of weapons, cameras, other visual or audio recording devices, and electronic transmitting equipment on CIA property; enforce traffic and parking laws and regulations; and operate a security communications center. Security protective officers also can be assigned to special units, including the Explosive Ordnance Disposal Unit, which screens mail, packages, and vehicles; the Canine Unit, which is responsible for searching for explosives; and the Security Protective Service (SPS) Honor Guard, which includes a select group of officers who present the American flag at CIA ceremonies and funerals. Security protective officers are authorized to carry firearms and make arrests.

Qualifications and Salary Levels

Applicants must be physically fit, at least 21 years of age, and have a high school diploma or the equivalent. Requirements also include military experience (preferably as a military police officer or Marine Corps security guard), or police experience, or other significant security experience. An associate's or bachelor's degree in criminal justice or a related field is preferred. This position requires a 36-month commitment to the SPS before seeking other opportunities within the CIA. Excellent oral and written communication skills, a high level of integrity and trustworthiness, and strong interpersonal skills also are required. The application process includes a medical examination, personality evaluation, psychological screening, polygraph interview, background investigation, and top-secret security clearance determination.

Training

Newly appointed security protective officers attend the 10-week Mixed Basic Police Training Program at the Federal Law Enforcement Training Center (FLETC) in Glynco, Georgia (see chapter 16). This program is followed by specialized in-house training presented at SPS training facilities. Security protective officers also attend an annual in-service training program that focuses on security and law enforcement tactics, legal issues and updates, firearms proficiency, and other subjects. They also can attend advanced courses at FLETC, other law enforcement training academies, colleges and universities, and other locations.

Contact: Recruitment Center; Central Intelligence Agency; Washington, DC 20505; phone: (703) 482-1100; Internet: www.cia.gov/

Uniformed Division Officer
United States Secret Service, U.S. Department of Homeland Security

Uniformed Division (UD) officers of the United States Secret Service (USSS) are an integral component of USSS protective operations. Formerly known as the Executive Protective Service and the White House Police, the UD is responsible for a broad range of security operations at the White House Complex, the vice president's residence, buildings in which presidential offices are located, the U.S. Treasury Building and its annex facility, foreign diplomatic missions and embassies located in the Washington, DC, metropolitan area and throughout the United States, and the USSS James J. Rowley Training Center in Laurel, Maryland. UD officers accomplish their mission through operations coordinated by the Division's three branches, including the White House Branch, Naval Observatory Branch, and Foreign Mission Branch.

UD officers carry out their protective responsibilities through special support programs and a network of foot patrols, vehicular patrols, and fixed posts, and are closely involved in almost every phase of the USSS protective mission. Officers screen visitors and operate magnetometers at the White House and at other sites to prevent persons from taking weapons into secure areas; and monitor closed-circuit television surveillance monitors and intrusion detection devices. UD officers assigned to the Canine Unit respond to bomb threats, suspicious packages, and other situations where explosive detection is necessary. Opportunities also are available with other specialized units including the Emergency Response Team, Bicycle Patrol Unit, Honor Guard Unit, Motorcycle Support Unit, Countersniper Team, Special Operations Section, Human Resources and Training Unit, Magnetometer Operations Section, and Crime Scene Search Unit. UD officers are authorized to carry firearms and make arrests.

This position is covered under special retirement provisions for law enforcement officers.

Qualifications and Salary Levels

UD police officers are appointed through excepted service hiring processes. The Secret Service Uniformed Division Pay System—which is identical to the U.S. Park Police Pay System—is established in the District of Columbia Code. Salaries under these pay systems are similar to GS-7 through GS-12, which are higher than salaries for most GS-0083 federal police officers who perform similar work and are compensated under the General Schedule pay system. Applicants must be at least 21 years of age and under age 37. However, candidates over age 37 who have previous service creditable under special law enforcement retirement provisions also may be eligible. Applicants must have a high school diploma or GED certificate and be in excellent health and physical condition. Weight must be proportionate to height. Uncorrected binocular visual acuity must be no worse than 20/60 (Snellen), correctable to 20/20 in each eye. Candidates who have undergone LASIK eye surgery must be free from residual effects three months after surgery, while those who have had other forms of refractive eye surgery must be free from residual effects one year after surgery. Law enforcement or military experience is preferable but not required. Applicants must pass the National Police Officer Selection Test (see chapter 3). The application process also includes a polygraph examination, background investigation, medical examination, drug screening test, and a top-secret security clearance determination.

Training

Initial training for UD officers includes the 10-week Mixed Basic Police Training Program at the Federal Law Enforcement Training Center in Glynco, Georgia (see chapter 16). This program is followed by 11 weeks of agency-specific specialized instruction at Secret Service's James J. Rowley Training Center. Topics covered during this program and advanced in-service training are concerned with subjects such as protective operations, physical security and law enforcement procedures, diplomatic immunity, international treaties and protocol, international and domestic terrorism, the District of Columbia Code, laws of arrest, search and seizure, psychology, police-community relations, firearms proficiency, emergency medicine, physical fitness, subject control tactics, and other subjects.

Contact: Inquiries can be directed to any USSS field office, or to Uniformed Division Recruiting; United States Secret Service; U.S. Department of Homeland Security; 950 H St. NW; Washington, DC 20223; phone: (202) 406-7540; Internet: www.secretservice.gov/; e-mail: udjobs@usss.treas.gov.

CHAPTER 9

Law Enforcement Technicians and Specialists

"Give us the tools and we will finish the job."

—*Winston Churchill*

The missions of federal law enforcement agencies are highly specialized, and they vary considerably from one agency to another. Although the visions and goals of each agency are different, they share a common need for specially trained personnel whose expertise provides the technical capabilities agencies must have to carry out their law enforcement and regulatory functions. This chapter covers a wide variety of specialized careers that involve technical support for criminal investigation and law enforcement operations. Most of these positions are with the nation's largest law enforcement agencies, such as the Drug Enforcement Administration; FBI; Naval Criminal Investigative Service; Bureau of Diplomatic Security; U.S. Secret Service; and Bureau of Alcohol, Tobacco, Firearms and Explosives.

Depending on the nature of their expertise, skilled federal law enforcement technicians and specialists examine fingerprint evidence; operate aircraft during patrol operations, search and rescue missions, and medical evacuations; analyze evidence gathered at the scenes of terrorist bombings; determine the cause and origin of explosions and fires; examine firearms and ammunition; identify handwriting and counterfeit documents; analyze samples of blood, saliva, stains, gunshot residue, paint, fibers, controlled substances, and other evidence; take surveillance photographs during foreign counterintelligence operations; obtain records and other evidence; and perform many other tasks to assist special agents with criminal investigations.

Airplane Pilot (GS-2181)
National Park Service, U.S. Department of the Interior

National Park Service (NPS) airplane pilots are responsible for flight activities over the natural, historical, and recreational areas that encompass the National Park System. NPS airplane pilots carry out various assignments in support of law enforcement patrol operations, including surveillance and drug interdiction functions; search and rescue operations; medical evacuations; resource protection; wildfire detection; missions to transport law enforcement personnel, other employees, and supplies to remote areas; game census activities; and mapping operations in areas under the juris-diction of NPS.

NPS airplane pilots fly local, statewide, and cross-country missions in aircraft equipped with floats, skis, or wheels, under hazardous conditions and over unfavorable moun-tainous terrain, through narrow or twisting canyons, under challenging wind condi-tions, in extreme desert heat, and occasionally during unpredicted storms. In addition, pilots often conduct air patrols, searches, and resource protection flights at low alti-tudes—occasionally below 500 feet—and conduct landings in isolated areas on dirt roads or snow that are considered marginal airstrips. NPS airplane pilots also are responsible for maintaining airworthiness of aircraft, complying with Federal Aviation Administration (FAA) safety procedures and regulations, maintaining logs and flight reports, performing pre-flight and post-flight checks, and assisting with aircraft maintenance.

Qualifications and Salary Level

Grade levels for this position—GS-11, GS-12, and GS-13—are based on the nature of experience and number of flight hours logged. For all grade levels, candidates must have a current FAA Commercial Pilot Certificate with ratings appropriate for the duties performed, an instrument rating, and a current FM Class I Medical Certificate, and must meet all Department of the Interior Aviation Management Directorate (AM) requirements for pilots. Requirements for appointment to the GS-11 level and above include 1,500 hours of total flight time, including 1,200 hours as pilot-in-command; 75 hours of night flying experience, including at least 25 hours as pilot-in-command; 75 hours of actual or simulated instrument time, including at least 50 hours in actual flight; 100 hours as pilot-in-command during the previous twelve months; and 200 hours as pilot-in-command in low-level operations (within 500 feet of the surface of typical terrain), or 10 hours of low-level flight instruction within the previous five years followed by a low-level flight check by an AM pilot inspector. Applicants must submit a Form OAS-61, Record of Aeronautical Experience. A drug screening test also is required.

Training

NPS airplane pilots complete a wide range of training courses, seminars, and work-shops throughout their careers. These programs cover subjects concerned with airplane and helicopter safety, aircraft capabilities and limitations, accident prevention, crash survival methods, water ditching, personal survival vests and flotation devices, emer-gency locator transmitters, hazardous materials, fuel-handling procedures, sling load cargo transportation, departmental and agency aviation policies and procedures, and aviation resources. NPS pilots are also required to complete a one-week refresher course every three years that focuses on safety topics, policy information, aviation pro-gram updates, and other subjects.

Contact: Division of Personnel Management; National Park Service; Department of the Interior; 1849 C St. NW; Washington, DC 20240; phone: (202) 208-6843; Internet: www.nps.gov/

Airplane Pilot (GS-2181)
United States Marshals Service, U.S. Department of Justice

United States Marshals Service (USMS) airplane pilots are responsible for flying aircraft in support of the USMS Justice Prisoner and Alien Transportation System (JPATS), one of the largest transporters of prisoners in the world. JPATS pilots respond to more than 1,000 requests every day to move prisoners between judicial districts, correctional institutions, and foreign countries. As the only government-operated, scheduled passenger airline in the United States, JPATS serves 40 domestic and international cities, as well as other cities on an as-needed basis. USMS coordinates air operations from hubs in Oklahoma, Louisiana, Arizona, and the Virgin Islands.

In a cooperative effort between the USMS, Federal Bureau of Prisons (BOP), and U.S. Immigration and Customs Enforcement (ICE), USMS airplane pilots transport prisoners and protected witnesses for the USMS, BOP, ICE, other federal agencies, the U.S. military, and state and local governments with a fleet of turbine-powered, turboprop, and multi-engine fixed-wing aircraft. These pilots transport prisoners to hearings, court appearances, and detention facilities nationwide; fly overseas to remove deported aliens from the United States; and operate aircraft in response to national emergencies and various Department of Justice missions. The responsibilities of USMS airplane pilots include providing support for USMS Special Operations Group missions; transporting cargoes of ammunition, pyrotechnics, and chemical munitions; maintaining aircraft; writing reports; and performing other duties to accomplish the mission of the USMS Air Operations Branch. These personnel fly aircraft in and out of all types of airfields, over favorable and unfavorable terrain, during day and nighttime hours.

Qualifications and Salary Level

Grade levels for this position—GS-11, GS-12, and GS-13—are based on the nature of experience and number of flight hours logged. For all grade levels, candidates must have an Airline Transport Pilot (ATP) certificate or the appropriate military rating; a turbojet rating; a minimum of 1,500 hours of total flight time, including 500 hours of flying time in a multi-engine airplane, 250 hours as pilot-in-command, 75 hours of instrument flying, 75 hours of night flying, and 100 hours of flying time in the last 12 months; and a Federal Aviation Administration Class II Medical Certificate. Applicants must pass a background investigation, drug screening test, and medical examination.

Training

Initial training for airplane pilots includes an orientation to USMS operations, and approximately three weeks of ground school simulation exercises in the types of aircraft to be operated. In-service training consists of annual ground school simulation refresher exercises, as well as courses that cover subjects such as cockpit resources management, prisoner handling and transportation, safety and survival, firearms familiarization, and other topics.

Contact: Human Resources Division; United States Marshals Service; U.S. Department of Justice; 600 Army-Navy Dr.; Arlington, VA 22202; phone: (202) 307-9437; Internet: www.usmarshals.gov/; e-mail: us.marshals@usdoj.gov

Biologist (Forensic Examiner) (GS-0401)
Federal Bureau of Investigation, U.S. Department of Justice

FBI biologists support the Bureau's criminal investigation and foreign counterintelligence missions, and provide expert technical assistance to other federal, state, and local law enforcement agencies. These skilled technicians are assigned to the FBI Laboratory, which is one of the largest and most comprehensive forensic science facilities in the world, and the only full-service federal forensic laboratory. Biologists perform more than one million examinations at the FBI Laboratory every year.

The primary responsibilities of the Bureau's biologists include examination and analysis of body tissues, body fluids, and stains recovered as evidence in violent crimes. In carrying out these processes, biologists apply a full range of scientific theories and principles, serological techniques, and biochemical analysis. For example, FBI biologists perform mitochondrial DNA analysis or other analytical techniques on forensic specimens such as human hair, bone, teeth, blood, semen, urine, and other tissues, body fluids, or substances. In addition, they compare results of analyses to known blood or saliva samples obtained from crime victims or suspects. Biologists also locate, identify, reconstruct, and preserve evidence obtained at crime scenes; conduct evidence inventories; calibrate and operate analytical instruments to analyze and identify samples; prepare and present oral briefings and detailed written reports to FBI special agents, other law enforcement officers, prosecutors, and grand juries; provide expert testimony in evidentiary hearings and criminal trials in support of their findings; and conduct research at the FBI Forensic Science Research and Training Center—a component of the FBI Academy—to improve and develop the methodology of forensic analyses.

Qualifications and Salary Level

GS-7: One full year of graduate education; or superior academic achievement during undergraduate studies in a curriculum related to biochemistry, biological sciences, biotechnology, or a related discipline with at least 24 semester hours in biochemistry or the biological sciences; or a bachelor's degree in one of the above-listed disciplines and one year of specialized experience in one of the same. **GS-9:** A master's degree, or two years of graduate education, or a bachelor's degree in one of the previously discussed disciplines and one year of specialized experience equivalent to at least GS-7. **GS-11:** A Ph.D. or equivalent doctoral degree, or three years of graduate education, or a bachelor's degree in one of the previously discussed disciplines and one year of specialized experience equivalent to at least GS-9. **GS-12:** A bachelor's degree in one of the previously discussed disciplines and one year of specialized experience equivalent to at least GS-11. **GS-13:** A bachelor's degree in one of the previously discussed disciplines and one year of specialized experience equivalent to at least GS-12. Tentative appointees must pass a background investigation, drug screening test, and polygraph examination, and qualify for a top-secret security clearance.

Training

Professional development for FBI biologists consists of on-the-job and in-service training relating to various scientific theories and principles, serological techniques, biochemical analysis, mitochondrial DNA analysis, preservation of evidence, courtroom testimony, and other subjects. Biologists also attend training programs concerning the latest technology, instruments, and equipment used in the FBI Laboratory. Courses, seminars, and workshops are presented by FBI staff at the Forensic Science Research and Training Center, although classes and seminars also are available at colleges and universities, at state and local police academies, and through other organizations.

Contact: Laboratory Division; Federal Bureau of Investigation; U.S. Department of Justice; 935 Pennsylvania Ave. NW; Washington, DC 20535; phone: (202) 324-2727; Internet: www.fbi.gov/

Chemist/Forensic Examiner (GS-1320)
Federal Bureau of Investigation, U.S. Department of Justice

FBI chemists carry out forensic science activities in support of FBI operations, as well as criminal investigations conducted by other law enforcement agencies worldwide. The analyses conducted by these personnel often result in prosecutions for crimes such as homicide, bank robbery, drug trafficking, terrorism, product tampering, and financial fraud. The work of chemists, biologists, and other FBI Laboratory staff can be dangerous because they are exposed periodically to hazardous materials, bloodborne pathogens, and toxic substances.

FBI chemists analyze the composition, molecular structure, and properties of substances; the transformations they undergo; and the amounts of matter and energy included in these transformations. Chemists assigned to the laboratory's general chemistry subunit identify dyes, chemicals, and marking materials used in bank security devices; controlled substances associated with drug investigations; ink from pens, typewriters, stamp pads, and other sources; and other solids and liquids. In the toxicology subunit, they analyze specimens of food products to detect drugs, drug metabolites, pharmaceuticals, poisons, biological tissues and fluids, and substances associated with product tampering investigations. Analyses in the paints and polymers subunit include paint chips, plastics, petroleum products, tapes, adhesives, caulks, and sealants. This subunit maintains the National Automotive Paint File, which stores samples of car paints and is used to locate vehicles involved in hit-and-run accidents. Chemists assigned to the instrumentation operation and support subunit calibrate and maintain analytical instruments used to analyze and identify samples, maintain databases, and evaluate new technologies.

Chemists assigned to all subunits present oral briefings and written reports to FBI special agents and other law enforcement officers, prosecutors, and grand juries; and provide expert testimony in evidentiary hearings and criminal trials. They also conduct scientific research at the Forensic Science Research and Training Center; present their findings to the forensic science community; and conduct training for prosecuting attorneys, judges, police officers, and forensics examiners of other law enforcement agencies.

Qualifications and Salary Level

To qualify for the chemist position, applicants must have one of the following:

A.   A bachelor's degree in the physical sciences or life sciences, or engineering that included 30 semester hours in chemistry, supplemented by coursework in mathematics through differential and integral calculus, and at least six semester hours of physics.

B.   A combination of education, experience, and coursework equivalent to a college major as outlined in item A, including at least 30 semester hours in chemistry, supplemented by coursework in mathematics through differential and integral calculus, and at least six semester hours of physics.

To qualify under item B, the quality of the combination of education and experience must be sufficient to demonstrate that the applicant possesses the knowledge, skills, and abilities required to perform work in the occupation, and comparable to that normally acquired through the completion of a four-year course of study with a major in the field.

Salary grade requirements include the following: **GS-7:** One full year of graduate education, or superior academic achievement during undergraduate studies, or a bachelor's degree and one year of specialized experience. **GS-9:** A master's degree, or two years of graduate education, or a bachelor's degree and one year of specialized experience equivalent to at least GS-7. **GS-11:** A Ph.D. or equivalent doctoral degree, or three years of graduate education, or a bachelor's degree and one year of specialized experience equivalent to at least GS-9. **GS-12:** A bachelor's degree and one year of specialized experience equivalent to GS-11. **GS-13:** A bachelor's degree and one year of specialized experience equivalent to GS-12. Tentative appointees must pass a background investigation, drug screening test, and polygraph examination, and qualify for a top-secret security clearance.

Training

FBI chemists attend various professional seminars, workshops, and courses that focus on scientific techniques used to identify various chemicals, poisons, controlled substances, explosives residues, paints, petroleum products, and many other substances. They complete ongoing training in the use and maintenance of scientific instruments, and also in computer software programs that are used in chemical analyses. The Bureau's chemists attend conferences hosted by professional organizations, and also attend classes at the FBI Academy's Forensic Science Research and Training Center.

Contact: Laboratory Division; Federal Bureau of Investigation; U.S. Department of Justice; 935 Pennsylvania Ave. NW; Washington, DC 20535; phone: (202) 324-2727; Internet: www.fbi.gov/

Document Analyst (GS-1397)
United States Secret Service, U.S. Department of Homeland Security

Document analysts in the Forensic Sciences Division of the United States Secret Service (USSS) analyze documents and paraphernalia associated with counterfeiting operations, and provide other analytical services in support of USSS investigative and protective functions worldwide. USSS document analysts combat counterfeiting and other crimes by applying their unique technical expertise and working closely with U.S. and foreign law enforcement agencies. Document analysis often focuses on counterfeit currency, identification cards, credit cards, checks, bonds, U.S. Department of Agriculture food coupons, and U.S. postage stamps. USSS document analysts also analyze threatening correspondence directed toward the president, vice president, and other persons protected by the USSS. The Secret Service has exclusive jurisdiction over investigations involving counterfeiting of U.S. obligations and securities.

Document analysts use magnifying devices, specialized lighting and energy sources, computers, energy dispersive x-ray, spectrum analyzers, and a wide range of techniques and procedures to examine, identify, and classify questioned and known documents; serve as expert analysts during crime scene investigations; use laboratory instruments and apply the principles of organic and inorganic chemistry, ink and paper chemistry, physics, and related scientific and technical areas to identify, analyze, and draw conclusions from examinations; participate in research to resolve difficult problems and issues from a variety of sources, and to analyze aspects of technological advances and their effect on USSS investigative and enforcement operations; coordinate activities and maintain liaison with federal, state, local, and foreign law enforcement agencies; prepare written reports; testify as expert witnesses in federal and state criminal court trials and hearings to present evidence pertaining to the analysis of document evidence; and maintain USSS forensic laboratories.

Qualifications and Salary Level

GS-7: One full year of graduate education, or superior academic achievement during undergraduate studies, or one year of specialized experience equivalent to at least GS-5. **GS-9:** A master's degree, or two years of graduate education, or one year of specialized experience equivalent to at least GS-7. **GS-11:** A Ph.D. or equivalent doctoral degree, or three years of graduate education, or one year of specialized experience equivalent to at least GS-9. **GS-12:** One year of specialized experience equivalent to at least GS-11. **GS-13:** One year of specialized experience equivalent to at least GS-12. Undergraduate or graduate education must have included major study in the areas of either physical science, biological science, graphic arts, criminal justice, criminology, police science, or law. The application process includes a drug screening test, a background investigation, and a top-secret security clearance determination.

Training

USSS document analysts attend in-house training, professional conferences, and workshops throughout their careers that are concerned with subjects such as handwriting and hand printing comparison, identification of machined impressions, ink analysis, obliterated writings, currency production, counterfeiting techniques, and questioned document examination methods. Training is presented by USSS staff, paper and ink manufacturers, and organizations such as the U.S. Mint, Bureau of Engraving and Printing, American Numismatic Association, Institute of Paper Science and Technology, American Society of Questioned Document Examiners, International Association for Identification, and American Academy of Forensic Sciences.

Contact: Personnel Division; United States Secret Service; U.S. Department of Homeland Security; 950 H St. NW; Washington, DC 20223; phone: (202) 406-5800; Internet: www.secretservice.gov/; e-mail: jobs@secretservice.gov

Document Analyst (GS-1397)
Bureau of Alcohol, Tobacco, Firearms and Explosives; U.S. Department of Justice

Document analysts serving with the Bureau of Alcohol, Tobacco, Firearms and Explosives (ATF) examine and analyze document evidence primarily in support of ATF enforcement operations. These activities involve detecting altered and forged documents; restoring or deciphering damaged, eradicated, obliterated, or charred documents; and otherwise providing forensic assessments of evidence in criminal investigations carried out by ATF and other law enforcement agencies. ATF document analysts are highly regarded for their research and development projects concerning the identification and analysis of document evidence, and their advancements in technology and methodology to solve crimes through expert forensic analysis.

ATF document analysts conduct examinations and comparisons of questioned and known handwriting, hand printing, typewriting, photocopies, counterfeit cigarette tax stamps, impressions made from mechanical devices and rubber stamps, and other documents to establish authenticity, alteration, or common authorship. They perform these examinations and analyses using sequential morphological, chemical, microscopic, photographic, and computer imaging techniques, as well as other scientific procedures. Their findings often are used by ATF special agents to reach positive outcomes in ATF investigations, such as confessions and criminal convictions. Document analysts frequently provide advice and assistance to United States attorneys; state prosecuting attorneys; ATF special agents; and criminal investigators from other federal, state, and local law enforcement agencies on matters relating to forensic document examination. They also prepare written reports of their findings; furnish depositions and affidavits; provide expert testimony in evidentiary hearings and criminal trials; assist with the preparation of training materials; conduct training in procedures for collecting, preserving, labeling, packaging, and submitting document evidence to ATF laboratories; and represent ATF in national and local peer group professional organizations.

Qualifications and Salary Level

GS-7: One full year of graduate education, or superior academic achievement during undergraduate studies, or one year of specialized experience equivalent to at least GS-5. **GS-9:** A master's degree, or two years of graduate education, or one year of specialized experience equivalent to at least GS-7. **GS-11:** A Ph.D. or equivalent doctoral degree, or three years of graduate education, or one year of specialized experience equivalent to at least GS-9. **GS-12:** One year of specialized experience equivalent to at least GS-11. **GS-13:** One year of specialized experience equivalent to at least GS-12. Undergraduate or graduate education must have included major study in the areas of either physical science, biological science, graphic arts, criminal justice, criminology, police science, or law. Candidates must successfully undergo a background investigation, qualify for a top-secret security clearance, and pass a drug test prior to appointment.

Training

Ongoing training for ATF document analysts includes a variety of courses, workshops, and seminars concerning questioned document examination, forensic handwriting analysis, physiology of handwriting, forensic science laboratory techniques, imaging methods, technical equipment, courtroom testimony, and other related subjects. Courses are offered by organizations such as the ATF National Academy, Federal Law Enforcement Training Center (see chapter 16), colleges and universities, American Board of Forensic Document Examiners, and other professional forensic science organizations.

Contact: Personnel Division; Bureau of Alcohol, Tobacco, Firearms and Explosives; U.S. Department of Justice; 650 Massachusetts Ave. NW—Room 4100; Washington, DC 20226; phone: (202) 927-8610; Internet: www.atf.gov/; e-mail: persdiv@atf.gov

Document Analyst (Forensic Examiner) (GS-1397)
Federal Bureau of Investigation, U.S. Department of Justice

FBI document analysts plan, coordinate, direct, and conduct a variety of forensic science activities in support of criminal investigations for the FBI and other federal, state, local, and foreign law enforcement agencies. Their skilled expertise in document analysis is used during the investigation of crimes involving fraud against the government, check fraud, forgery, counterfeiting, bank robbery, threats, homicide, kidnapping, and many other offenses. The work of FBI document analysts focuses primarily on the examination and comprehensive technical analyses of evidence seized at crime scenes or during the execution of search warrants; or obtained from individuals, government agencies, or private firms in response to subpoenas or through other investigative means.

To establish authenticity, alteration, common authorship, or other characteristics, FBI document analysts inventory, examine, and analyze evidence such as handwriting, hand printing, typewriting, typewriter ribbons, printers, photocopiers, facsimiles, check-writer impressions, dry seals, watermarks, inks, erasures, paper products, altered or obliterated writing, burned or charred paper, and counterfeit documents. FBI document analysts perform examinations using a variety of imaging techniques that utilize computers, microscopes, chemical substances, photographic equipment, infrared technology, casts, and sequential morphological analysis. They often compare their findings with information contained in several databases maintained by the FBI Questioned Document Unit, such as the Anonymous Letter File, Bank Robbery Note File, National Fraudulent Check File, Office Equipment File, Shoeprint File, and Watermark File. Document analysts prepare written reports, and present oral briefings to case agents and supervisors, assistant United States attorneys, grand juries, and law enforcement officers of other agencies. They also prepare court exhibits and testify as expert witnesses during trials and evidentiary hearings to explain forensic procedures that were followed and the results obtained.

Qualifications and Salary Level

GS-7: One full year of graduate education, or superior academic achievement during undergraduate studies, or a bachelor's degree and one year of specialized experience. **GS-9:** A master's degree, or two years of graduate education, or a bachelor's degree and one year of specialized experience equivalent to at least GS-7. **GS-11:** A Ph.D. or equivalent doctoral degree, or three years of graduate education, or a bachelor's degree and one year of specialized experience equivalent to at least GS-9, or certification by the American Board of Forensic Document Examiners. **GS-12:** A bachelor's degree and one year of specialized experience equivalent to at least GS-11. **GS-13:** A bachelor's degree and one year of specialized experience equivalent to at least GS-12. The application process includes a drug screening test, background investigation, polygraph examination, and top-secret security clearance determination.

Training

Initial training for FBI document analysts consists of a two-year apprenticeship program that includes classroom training and actual document examinations under the guidance and evaluation of experienced FBI document analysts. In addition to subjects relating to the examination and analysis of handwriting, typewriting, and other materials, document analyst trainees also participate in moot court exercises to qualify for certification as FBI forensic examiners. In-service training includes courses and professional seminars that are presented by FBI staff, academic institutions, firms associated with the ink and paper industry, and related professional organizations. Instruction focuses on subjects such as ink and paper chemistry and dating procedures, various printing processes, laboratory techniques, and other aspects of forensic document examination.

Contact: Laboratory Division; Federal Bureau of Investigation; U.S. Department of Justice; 935 Pennsylvania Ave. NW; Washington, DC 20535; phone: (202) 324-2727; Internet: www.fbi.gov/

Evidence and Seized Property Custodian (GS-1802)
United States Fish and Wildlife Service, U.S. Department of the Interior

Evidence and seized property custodians of the U.S. Fish and Wildlife Service (FWS) perform administrative functions concerning the seizure and maintenance of property and evidence in support of FWS law enforcement operations. They serve within the FWS Office of Law Enforcement, which investigates and enforces violations of wildlife protection laws in partnership with other federal, state, tribal, local, and foreign law enforcement agencies.

These personnel receive evidence and seized property from FWS special agents, wildlife inspectors, refuge law enforcement officers, and park rangers that were seized during criminal investigations, border searches, patrols, or through other enforcement operations. Evidence and seized property custodians tag property; assign storage locations; make appropriate entries into manual logs and computer systems; maintain records pertaining to evidence or property, such as chain of custody receipts, property seizure notices, sales and donation records, and property or evidence destruction records; maintain physical security of evidence storage facilities; code and enter data into computer systems relating to forfeited or abandoned property, import and export declarations, and case reports; prepare and process violation notices for federal court cases; and facilitate administrative property forfeiture proceedings, including tasks such as posting forfeiture notices in newspapers. They also conduct inventories, follow through with disposal of forfeited or abandoned property, and maintain related records. Evidence and seized property custodians wear official FWS uniforms.

Qualifications and Salary Level

GS-4: Two years of education above high school, or one year of general experience.
GS-5: Four years of education above high school, or one year of specialized experience equivalent to at least GS-4. Qualifying experience and education can be combined to meet total experience requirements. A background investigation is required.

Training

FWS evidence and seized property custodians complete ongoing on-the-job and in-house training on the subjects of evidence handling and tracking procedures, evidence chain of custody requirements, property seizure and forfeiture issues, computer system hardware and software, computer and physical security procedures, FWS policies and regulations, and other relevant topics.

Contact: Office of Law Enforcement; U.S. Fish and Wildlife Service; 4401 N. Fairfax Dr.; Arlington, VA 22203; phone: (703) 358-1949; Internet: www.fws.gov/le/

Explosives Enforcement Specialist (GS-1801)

Bureau of Alcohol, Tobacco, Firearms and Explosives; U.S. Department of Justice

Explosives enforcement specialists serving with the Bureau of Alcohol, Tobacco, Firearms and Explosives (ATF) provide direct technical support to ATF special agents and other law enforcement officers in criminal investigations involving explosives and destructive incendiary devices. ATF's national and international response teams rely on these highly trained technicians to participate in crime scene analysis and cause-and-origin investigations of fires and explosives incidents throughout the U.S. and worldwide.

ATF explosives enforcement specialists provide on-site expertise to investigations concerning criminal and accidental explosions and arson. They identify bombs and other explosive devices; examine evidence; assemble, disassemble, and test explosives and incendiary devices; use various technical procedures and equipment to determine cause and origin of explosions and fires; write reports and prepare documentation on the effects of bombs and destructive devices; make explosion and arson classifications for industry and government agencies; assist in the preparation of court cases that involve arson and explosives incidents; and testify in evidentiary hearings and criminal trials in support of their findings and expert opinions. They also conduct render-safe procedures of improvised explosive devices and perform underwater explosives recoveries. When responding to incidents involving vehicle bombs that have not detonated, ATF explosives enforcement specialists operate remote vehicle-bomb disruption systems that are designed to defeat car and truck bombs too large to overcome by traditional methods. They also travel with U.S. State Department antiterrorism personnel to assess the capabilities of foreign governments to respond to terrorist or explosives incidents.

Qualifications and Salary Level

GS-5: Completion of a four-year course of study leading to a bachelor's degree; or three years of general experience, one year of which was equivalent to at least GS-4. **GS-7:** One full year of graduate education, or superior academic achievement during undergraduate studies, or one year of specialized experience equivalent to at least GS-5. **GS-9:** A master's degree, or two years of graduate education, or one year of specialized experience equivalent to at least GS-7. **GS-11:** A Ph.D. or equivalent doctoral degree, or three years of graduate education, or one year of specialized experience equivalent to at least GS-9. **GS-12:** One year of specialized experience equivalent to at least GS-11. **GS-13:** One year of specialized experience equivalent to at least GS-12. Education can be combined with experience to meet minimum requirements for positions at GS-11 and below. The application process includes a drug screening test, background investigation, and top-secret security clearance determination.

Training

ATF explosives enforcement specialists attend courses that focus on subjects such as weapon familiarization and caches, pyrotechnics, arson and explosives investigation, search techniques, commercial and homemade explosives, radio-controlled explosive devices, car bombs, triggering devices, low-intensity conflict, booby traps, chemical and biological munitions, explosive ordnance disposal, evaluation and recovery of underwater explosives, photography, hazardous materials, terrorist attacks, and electronic devices. Many ATF explosives enforcement specialists attend the U.S. Army's

Hazardous Devices School, a five-week course conducted at Redstone Arsenal in Alabama that covers demolition procedures, search techniques, fuzing and arming, render-safe procedures, tools and equipment, and disposal of hazardous devices. They also attend training programs presented by ATF staff, the Federal Law Enforcement Training Center, the International Association of Bomb Technicians and Investigators, and other organizations.

Contact: Personnel Division; Bureau of Alcohol, Tobacco, Firearms and Explosives; U.S. Department of Justice; 650 Massachusetts Ave. NW—Room 4100; Washington, DC 20226; phone: (202) 927-8610; Internet: www.atf.gov/; e-mail: persdiv@atf.gov

Fingerprint Specialist (GS-0072)
Naval Criminal Investigative Service, U.S. Department of Defense

Naval Criminal Investigative Service (NCIS) fingerprint specialists provide expert forensic support in the investigation of major crimes such as homicide, burglary, drug trafficking, fraud, embezzlement, and other offenses. NCIS operates regional forensic laboratories and technical services detachments in support of NCIS field operations, the U.S. Marine Corps, other Defense Department investigative organizations, and other law enforcement agencies to provide rapid and accurate forensic analysis of crime scene evidence.

The primary responsibilities of NCIS fingerprint specialists include conducting visual, chemical, photographic, and other scientific and instrumental examinations of physical evidence, and developing latent impressions to form opinions regarding their identification; developing, analyzing, preserving, and identifying impressions of fingerprints and other body parts; identifying glove impressions; using special microscopic and photographic processes to examine physical evidence; performing digital image capture, image enhancement, and image retention of forensic evidence; preparing formal written reports on the results of examinations; assisting prosecuting attorneys with criminal case preparation; testifying in court; maintaining records; attending scientific conferences and symposia; and establishing and conducting formal training programs for criminal investigators. This is a civilian position and does not require active-duty military service.

Qualifications and Salary Level

GS-7: One year of specialized experience equivalent to at least GS-5 that demonstrated the ability to classify inked fingerprints by the Henry and NCIC systems. **GS-9:** One year of specialized experience equivalent to at least GS-7 that provided knowledge of the techniques for comparing and lifting latent fingerprints on evidentiary materials, in photographing latent and inked prints, and in making photographic enlargements for court demonstrations. **GS-11:** One year of specialized experience equivalent to at least GS-9 performing complex latent fingerprint examinations, preparing written laboratory reports based on examinations, and testifying as an expert witness in the area of latent fingerprint examinations. **GS-12:** One year of specialized experience equivalent to at least GS-11 analyzing complex fingerprint cases and imperfect or partial latent fingerprint impressions that contain only the minimum number of points necessary to make an identification, and conducting methods-development projects to improve latent fingerprint examination capabilities. **GS-13:** One year of specialized experience equivalent to at least GS-12. Tentative appointees must pass a drug screening test and background investigation, and qualify for a top-secret security clearance.

Training

Initial and in-service training for NCIS fingerprint specialists consists of various professional seminars, conferences, and symposia hosted by organizations such as the International Association for Identification and the American Academy of Forensic Sciences, among others. They also can attend courses at the FBI Academy, the Federal Law Enforcement Training Center (see chapter 16), and state and local training academies.

Contact: Naval Criminal Investigative Service; 716 Sicard St. SE; Washington Navy Yard; Washington, DC 20388; phone: (202) 433-8800; Internet: www.ncis.navy.mil/; e-mail: jobs@ncis.navy.mil

Fingerprint Specialist (GS-0072)
United States Secret Service, U.S. Department of Homeland Security

Fingerprint specialists serving with the Forensic Sciences Division of the U.S. Secret Service (USSS) perform various complex, delicate, and sensitive fingerprint identification assignments in support of USSS investigative and protective functions. Their expertise is crucial to the success of USSS criminal investigations involving counterfeiting, credit card fraud, computer crimes, identity theft, access device fraud, and other offenses.

USSS fingerprint specialists use advanced laboratory equipment and scientific techniques to examine of a variety of surfaces—such as counterfeit currency, credit cards, and computers—and to develop, examine, preserve, and identify latent fingerprints. They serve as members of response teams that are dispatched to crime scenes; conduct visual, chemical, photographic, and other scientific and instrumental examinations of latent impressions; use Automated Fingerprint Identification System, Live Scan, and other state-of-the-art technology to develop, enhance, and preserve latent fingerprints; prepare detailed statistical and laboratory reports regarding the examinations; conduct methods-development projects to improve latent fingerprint examination capabilities; assist prosecuting attorneys with criminal case preparation; testify in federal, state, local, and military courts as expert witnesses in the area of latent fingerprint examination; and maintain laboratory reports and records. USSS fingerprint specialists also participate in highly technical and in-depth research projects to develop new and advanced approaches to fingerprint examinations, and instruct USSS special agents and other law enforcement officers on how to obtain and preserve fingerprints.

Qualifications and Salary Level

GS-7: One year of specialized experience equivalent to at least GS-5 that demonstrated the ability to classify inked fingerprints by the Henry and NCIC systems. **GS-9:** One year of specialized experience equivalent to at least GS-7 that provided knowledge of the techniques for comparing and lifting latent fingerprints on evidentiary materials, in photographing latent and inked prints, and in making photographic enlargements for court demonstrations. **GS-11:** One year of specialized experience equivalent to at least GS-9 performing complex latent fingerprint examinations, preparing written laboratory reports based on examinations, and testifying as an expert witness in the area of latent fingerprint examinations. **GS-12:** One year of specialized experience equivalent to at least GS-11 analyzing complex fingerprint cases and imperfect or partial latent fingerprint impressions that contain only the minimum number of points necessary to make an identification, and conducting methods-development projects to improve latent fingerprint examination capabilities. **GS-13:** One year of specialized experience equivalent to at least GS-12. Tentative appointees must qualify for a top-secret security clearance and pass a background investigation and drug screening test.

Training

Throughout their careers, USSS fingerprint specialists attend professional conferences and workshops that are concerned with new technology for processing, examining, and comparing fingerprints, palm prints, and footprints; fluorescent chemicals used with examination equipment and light sources; and updates of ongoing research concerning the examination of fingerprints and other evidence. Training is presented by groups such as the International Association for Identification, the American Academy of Forensic Sciences, and other professional and scientific organizations.

Contact: Personnel Division; United States Secret Service; U.S. Department of Homeland Security; 950 H St. NW; Washington, DC 20223; phone: (202) 406-5800; Internet: www.secretservice.gov/; e-mail: jobs@secretservice.gov

Fingerprint Specialist (GS-0072)
Bureau of Alcohol, Tobacco, Firearms and Explosives; U.S. Department of Justice

Bureau of Alcohol, Tobacco, Firearms and Explosives (ATF) fingerprint specialists participate in criminal investigations that focus on domestic and international firearms trafficking, violent crimes, arson, bombings, drug trafficking, alcohol smuggling, and many other crimes. They are assigned to ATF's Office of Laboratory Services. The ATF National Laboratory—which was created by an Act of Congress in 1886—is the second oldest continuing U.S. federal laboratory. Most evidence received in ATF forensic laboratories is examined for the presence of identifiable latent prints.

The Bureau's fingerprint specialists examine and identify fingerprint evidence relating to complex, delicate, sensitive, and sensational criminal cases in support of ATF enforcement operations. They are responsible for examining evidence such as documents, component parts of bombs and incendiary devices, and firearms using dye staining, super-glue fuming, chemical developers, lasers, and traditional powder techniques. Examples of tasks carried out by these personnel include responding to major crime scenes to search for, collect, preserve, label, and package evidence; performing latent fingerprint examinations using visual, microscopic, photographic, computer image enhancement, sequential chemical, physical development, and other scientific techniques to identify latent impressions; preparing reports; assisting ATF special agents and prosecuting attorneys with criminal case preparation; testifying in court hearings and criminal trials; maintaining liaison with personnel from other law enforcement agencies; and caring for forensic laboratory instruments and equipment.

Qualifications and Salary Level

GS-7: One year of specialized experience equivalent to at least GS-5 that demonstrated the ability to classify inked fingerprints by the Henry and NCIC systems. **GS-9:** One year of specialized experience equivalent to at least GS-7 that provided knowledge of the techniques for comparing and lifting latent fingerprints on evidentiary materials, in photographing latent and inked prints, and in making photographic enlargements for court demonstrations. **GS-11:** One year of specialized experience equivalent to at least GS-9 performing complex latent fingerprint examinations, preparing written laboratory reports based on examinations, and testifying as an expert witness in the area of latent fingerprint examinations. **GS-12:** One year of specialized experience equivalent to at least GS-11 analyzing complex fingerprint cases and imperfect or partial latent fingerprint impressions that contain only the minimum number of points necessary to make an identification, and conducting methods-development projects to improve latent fingerprint examination capabilities. **GS-13:** One year of specialized experience equivalent to at least GS-12. The application process includes a drug screening test, background investigation, and top-secret security clearance determination.

Training

Training for ATF fingerprint specialists includes a wide range of courses, seminars, and workshops that focus on fingerprint classification, latent print comparison and identification, courtroom testimony, imaging methods, technical equipment, laboratory techniques, and other related subjects. ATF fingerprint examiners attend a one-week course relating to courtroom testimony; basic and advanced training in latent fingerprint identification at the FBI Academy; and various training programs presented by the ATF National Academy, the Federal Law Enforcement Training Center (see chapter 16), colleges and universities, the International Association for Identification, and other professional forensic organizations.

Contact: Personnel Division; Bureau of Alcohol, Tobacco, Firearms and Explosives; U.S. Department of Justice; 650 Massachusetts Ave. NW—Room 4100; Washington, DC 20226; Phone: (202) 927-8610; Internet: www.atf.gov/; e-mail: persdiv@atf.gov.

Fingerprint Specialist (GS-0072)
Federal Bureau of Investigation, U.S. Department of Justice

In support of investigations conducted by the FBI and other federal, state, local, and foreign law enforcement agencies, FBI fingerprint specialists classify, search, verify, and file fingerprints and other vestigial prints for identification. The FBI maintains the world's largest fingerprint repository, which has more than 200 million fingerprint cards and operates with sophisticated computer databases.

FBI fingerprint specialists examine crime scene evidence to detect, develop, analyze, and preserve latent fingerprints, palm prints, footprints, lip prints, and prints of other body parts. They compare these prints with those of known suspects or victims, or those on file in the Bureau's Automated Fingerprint Identification System database, by employing techniques that involve the use of chemicals, powders, lasers, alternative light sources, and other scientific methods. Many fingerprint specialists are members of the FBI's evidence response teams or disaster squads, which provide technical assistance worldwide in major evidence recovery operations or the identification of deceased victims of accidents or catastrophes. FBI fingerprint specialists prepare detailed reports, maintain records, testify in evidentiary hearings and criminal trials in support of their findings, and prepare charts and other exhibits for use in the courtroom. Their duties also include conducting research studies in latent fingerprint identification, and providing training in latent fingerprint work to local, state, federal, and foreign law enforcement personnel.

Qualifications and Salary Level

GS-7: One year of specialized experience equivalent to at least GS-5 that demonstrated the ability to classify inked fingerprints by the Henry and NCIC systems. **GS-9:** One year of specialized experience equivalent to at least GS-7 that provided knowledge of the techniques for comparing and lifting latent fingerprints on evidentiary materials, in photographing latent and inked prints, and in making photographic enlargements for court demonstrations. **GS-11:** One year of specialized experience equivalent to at least GS-9 performing complex latent fingerprint examinations, preparing written laboratory reports based on examinations, and testifying as an expert witness in the area of latent fingerprint examinations. **GS-12:** One year of specialized experience equivalent to at least GS-11 analyzing complex fingerprint cases and imperfect or partial latent fingerprint impressions that contain only the minimum number of points necessary to make an identification, and conducting methods-development projects to improve latent fingerprint examination capabilities. **GS-13:** One year of specialized experience equivalent to at least GS-12. The application process includes a drug screening test, background investigation, polygraph examination, and top-secret security clearance determination.

Training

Training for FBI fingerprint specialists includes an in-house training program that focuses on the examination and classification of fingerprints, fingerprint identification procedures, and FBI policies and procedures relating to fingerprint classification. They also complete a period of supervised on-the-job training and can attend courses, seminars, and conferences conducted by organizations such as the International Association for Identification or the American Academy of Forensic Sciences, academic institutions, and the FBI Academy. Fingerprint specialists assigned to the FBI disaster squad or evidence response teams attend training programs to enhance their fingerprint identification skills and assist them in carrying out responsibilities relating to these special assignments.

Contact: Laboratory Division; Federal Bureau of Investigation; U.S. Department of Justice; 935 Pennsylvania Ave. NW; Washington, DC 20535; phone: (202) 324-2727; Internet: www.fbi.gov/

Firearm and Toolmark Examiner (GS-1397)
Bureau of Alcohol, Tobacco, Firearms and Explosives; U.S. Department of Justice

Firearm and toolmark examiners serve as technical experts in ballistics and other scientific disciplines within the forensic science laboratories of the Bureau of Alcohol, Tobacco, Firearms and Explosives (ATF). These skilled technicians process and carefully examine physical evidence submitted by ATF personnel and other federal, state, and local law enforcement agencies.

ATF firearm and toolmark examiners perform a variety of firearm examinations and comparisons to determine matches of bullets, firearms, cartridge cases, firing pin impressions, breech lock markings, extractor marks, tools and tool impressions, and other items. For example, they perform weapon function testing to determine whether firearms have been altered or to identify manufacturing defects. Weapons are also test-fired and compared to bullets or cartridge cases collected at crime scenes. During investigations of shooting incidents, firearm and toolmark examiners perform projectile comparisons, bullet trajectory determinations, distance and shot pattern determinations, and crime scene reconstruction. Gunshot residue examinations enable firearm and toolmark examiners to establish the distance between a firearm and a victim at the time of discharge. By applying chemical, thermal, and magnetic techniques, firearm and toolmark examiners can restore obliterated or altered serial numbers to identify ownership of stolen weapons. Toolmark examinations commonly relate to bombing and arson crimes, and they often include comparing fractures or matching impressions caused by cutting, drilling, gripping, and prying tools. In these examinations, firearm and toolmark examiners perform microscopic comparisons to identify tools or objects used in crimes.

Firearm and toolmark examiners also respond to major crime scenes to assist in the collection, preservation, and packaging of evidence; testify in court concerning laboratory examinations; train ATF employees and personnel from other law enforcement agencies; and participate in various activities with professional organizations.

Qualifications and Salary Levels

GS-7: One full year of graduate education, or superior academic achievement during undergraduate studies, or one year of specialized experience equivalent to at least GS-5. **GS-9:** A master's degree, or two years of graduate education, or one year of specialized experience equivalent to at least GS-7. **GS-11:** A Ph.D. or equivalent doctoral degree, or three years of graduate education, or one year of specialized experience equivalent to at least GS-9. **GS-12:** One year of specialized experience equivalent to at least GS-11. **GS-13:** One year of specialized experience equivalent to at least GS-12. Undergraduate or graduate education must have included major study in the areas of either physical science, biological science, graphic arts, criminal justice, criminology, police science, or law. Candidates must successfully undergo a background investigation, qualify for a top-secret security clearance, and pass a drug test prior to appointment.

Training

Training for ATF firearm and toolmark examiners consists of various courses and seminars that cover subjects such as bullet and cartridge case comparisons, the identifying features of fired ammunition, trigger pull testing, rifling, ballistic identification systems, arson, explosives, toolmark identification and comparison, impression casting, analytical instruments and procedures, disposition of evidence, reference collections and databases, and courtroom testimony. Training in these and other related subjects is presented by ATF's National Firearms Examiner Academy (see chapter 16), the FBI Academy, the Association of Firearm and Toolmark Examiners, the International Association for Identification, state and local police academies, and other organizations.

Contact: Personnel Division; Bureau of Alcohol, Tobacco, Firearms and Explosives; U.S. Department of Justice; 650 Massachusetts Ave. NW—Room 4100; Washington, DC 20226; phone: (202) 927-8610; Internet: www.atf.gov/; e-mail: persdiv@atf.gov

Firearms Enforcement Technician (GS-0301)
Bureau of Alcohol, Tobacco, Firearms and Explosives; U.S. Department of Justice

Firearms enforcement technicians of the Bureau of Alcohol, Tobacco, Firearms and Explosives (ATF) are responsible for the receipt, custody, and initial administrative processing of evidence seized during ATF criminal investigations. These activities—particularly the accurate chain of custody—are critical to the successful prosecution of criminals and the safety of ATF personnel.

The primary responsibilities of ATF firearms enforcement technicians include receiving evidence and completing appropriate documentation; examining firearms to determine whether they are loaded; identifying various types of firearms and ammunition; recording evidence in master record books and automated database systems; assigning case numbers and preparing case jackets; maintaining the evidence chain of custody; releasing evidence to laboratory personnel and others for examination, and returning evidentiary materials upon completion of examinations; and maintaining records of the disposition of processed materials. ATF firearms enforcement technicians also participate in the coordination and administration of the Gun Control Act of 1968 by furnishing technical assistance to resolve unusual problems arising in the area of firearms enforcement; use reference materials including military manuals, foreign publications, and other firearms literature to assist in technical aspects of the position; and assist with the maintenance of the ATF Firearms Reference Library.

Qualifications and Salary Level

GS-5: Completion of a four-year course of study leading to a bachelor's degree; or three years of general experience, one year of which was equivalent to at least GS-4. **GS-7:** One full year of graduate education, or superior academic achievement during undergraduate studies, or one year of specialized experience equivalent to at least GS-5. **GS-9:** A master's degree, or two years of graduate education, or one year of specialized experience equivalent to at least GS-7. **GS-11:** A Ph.D. or equivalent doctoral degree, or three years of graduate education, or one year of specialized experience equivalent to at least GS-9. **GS-12:** One year of specialized experience equivalent to at least GS-11. Equivalent combinations of education and experience can be used to meet minimum experience requirements. Tentative appointees must pass a drug screening test and background investigation, and qualify for a top-secret security clearance.

Training

ATF firearms enforcement technicians attend various training programs throughout their careers, consisting primarily of in-house courses conducted by ATF staff, and advanced armorers schools presented by firearms manufacturers and other training organizations. This training focuses on subjects such as firearms handling, examination, and identification; gunsmith techniques; mechanical aspects of firearms; evidence processing requirements; inventory systems; and computer databases.

Contact: Personnel Division; Bureau of Alcohol, Tobacco, Firearms and Explosives; U.S. Department of Justice; 650 Massachusetts Ave. NW—Room 4100; Washington, DC 20226; phone: (202) 927-8610; Internet: www.atf.gov/; e-mail: persdiv@atf.gov

Forensic Chemist (GS-1320)
Bureau of Alcohol, Tobacco, Firearms and Explosives; U.S. Department of Justice

Forensic chemists of the Bureau of Alcohol, Tobacco, Firearms and Explosives (ATF) serve within ATF's forensic science laboratories nationwide. They are responsible for scientific analyses of physical evidence or samples pertaining to ATF criminal investigations and regulatory enforcement cases using various chemical, physical, and instrumental techniques.

The specialized tasks performed by ATF forensic chemists are geared toward determining the chemical and physical properties of alcohol and tobacco products, firearms, explosives, fire debris, and other substances. These tasks include ascertaining the specific data to be obtained; identifying the approach, methods, and procedures to be used; making adaptations and modifications of existing methods to satisfy unusual requirements and to solve specific problems; compiling data; and interpreting the results. They also prepare laboratory reports with conclusions supported by the analytical data, assist prosecuting attorneys with criminal case preparation, and testify in court in an expert witness capacity.

ATF forensic chemists assigned to the Explosives Section examine explosives, accelerants, gunshot residue, soil, hair, paint, fibers, glass, wire and other metals, plastics, and tapes in connection with criminal cases to identify suspects and the types of criminal offenses involved. Those assigned to the Alcohol and Tobacco Laboratory analyze alcoholic beverages, medicines, flavors, foods, and products made with specially denatured alcohol to monitor industry practices and ensure compliance with applicable laws and regulations. ATF forensic chemists respond to major crime scenes to assist ATF special agents and other law enforcement officers in processing physical evidence. They also conduct training programs for employees of ATF and other law enforcement agencies.

Qualifications and Salary Level

GS-5: Completion of a four-year course of study leading to a bachelor's degree, with a major in physical sciences, life sciences, or engineering that included 30 semester hours in chemistry, supplemented by coursework in mathematics and at least six semester hours of physics; or a combination of education and experience, the coursework of which was equivalent to a major as indicated above. **GS-7:** One full year of graduate education related to the position, or superior academic achievement during undergraduate studies, or one year of specialized experience equivalent to at least GS-5. **GS-9:** A master's degree, or two years of graduate education related to the position, or one year of specialized experience equivalent to at least GS-7. **GS-11:** A Ph.D. or equivalent doctoral degree, or three years of graduate education related to the position, or one year of specialized experience equivalent to at least GS-9. **GS-12:** One year of specialized experience equivalent to at least GS-11. **GS-13:** One year of specialized experience equivalent to at least GS-12. Qualifying education can be substituted for experience, and vice versa. The application process includes a drug screening test, background investigation, and top-secret security clearance determination.

Training

ATF forensic chemists attend courses, seminars, and conferences that include instruction in pyrotechnics and explosives, investigative techniques, technical equipment and instrumentation, theoretical and analytical chemistry, forensic microscopy, gas chromatography, hazardous materials, fire debris, courtroom testimony, and other related subjects. These courses are presented by organizations such as the ATF National Academy at the Federal Law Enforcement Training Center (see chapter 16), EPA National Enforcement Training Institute, International Association of Bomb Technicians and Investigators, colleges and universities, and various manufacturers and vendors of technical equipment.

Contact: Personnel Division; Bureau of Alcohol, Tobacco, Firearms and Explosives; U.S. Department of Justice; 650 Massachusetts Ave. NW—Room 4100; Washington, DC 20226; phone: (202) 927-8610; Internet: www.atf.gov/; e-mail: persdiv@atf.gov

Forensic Chemist (GS-1320)
Drug Enforcement Administration, U.S. Department of Justice

Drug Enforcement Administration (DEA) forensic chemists conduct complex analyses of samples to detect the presence of controlled substances in support of investigations concerning the illicit growing, manufacture, or distribution of controlled substances. Serving within several DEA forensic laboratories nationwide, forensic chemists provide scientific support to DEA special agents and agencies such as the FBI, U.S. Customs and Border Protection, and other federal, state, local, and foreign law enforcement agencies.

DEA forensic chemists conduct various quantitative and qualitative chemical analyses of evidence to detect, identify, and quantify controlled substances. These activities involve calibrating and operating analytical instruments; independently analyzing and identifying difficult, complex, new, unusual, and unprecedented samples of controlled substances, adulterants, and diluents; preparing written reports; conducting research and developing new methods of controlled substance analysis; and developing intelligence data used to determine trends in international trafficking of illicit drugs. Forensic chemists provide expert consultation to DEA special agents and diversion investigators, task force officers, and other law enforcement personnel engaged in criminal investigations; assist in criminal case preparation; provide expert testimony in federal and state courts against sophisticated criminal organizations; and exchange information with international, federal, state, and local academic research organizations.

Qualifications and Salary Level

GS-5: Completion of a four-year course of study leading to a bachelor's degree, with a major in physical sciences, life sciences, or engineering that included 30 semester hours in chemistry, supplemented by coursework in mathematics and at least six semester hours of physics; or a combination of education and experience, the coursework of which was equivalent to a major as indicated above. **GS-7:** One full year of graduate education related to the position, or superior academic achievement during undergraduate studies, or one year of specialized experience equivalent to at least GS-5. **GS-9:** A master's degree, or two years of graduate education related to the position, or one year of specialized experience equivalent to at least GS-7. **GS-11:** A Ph.D. or equivalent doctoral degree, or three years of graduate education related to the position, or one year of specialized experience equivalent to at least GS-9. **GS-12:** One year of specialized experience equivalent to at least GS-11. **GS-13:** One year of specialized experience equivalent to at least GS-12. Applicants can use equivalent combinations of specialized experience and education to meet total experience requirements. Tentative appointees must qualify for a security clearance and pass a background investigation and drug screening test.

Training

Initial training for DEA forensic chemists consists of a six-month on-the-job orientation to laboratory procedures, evidence-handling practices, chain-of-custody requirements, and various analytical techniques. This training is followed by a three-week DEA Forensic Chemist Basic School that focuses primarily on DEA policies, administrative paperwork, ethics, evidence processing and sampling, hazardous waste disposal, law, pharmacology, the Controlled Substances Act, and laboratory procedures. This training is followed by a one-week Basic Clandestine Laboratory Course. In-service training includes in-house instruction relating to chemical analysis, instrument maintenance and calibration, various scientific techniques, and other subjects. DEA forensic chemists also attend conferences, seminars, and workshops presented by organizations such as the American Academy of Forensic Sciences.

Contact: Recruiting information can be obtained from any DEA field office, or by contacting the Office of Personnel; Drug Enforcement Administration; U.S. Department of Justice; 2401 Jefferson Davis Hwy.; Alexandria, VA 22301; phone: (202) 307-1000; Internet: www.dea.gov/.

Investigations Specialist (GS-0301)
Office of Inspector General, Federal Deposit Insurance Corporation

Investigations specialists serving with the Federal Deposit Insurance Corporation (FDIC) Office of Inspector General (OIG) assist FDIC-OIG special agents with investigative and enforcement activities relating to FDIC programs and operations. Investigations carried out by FDIC-OIG focus on crimes such as bank fraud, money laundering, filing false bank reports, misapplication of bank funds, and other financial crimes concerning the nation's financial system.

FDIC-OIG investigations specialists perform a full range of investigative support duties, such as searching investigative databases; gathering information in criminal investigations, including evidence that can be used to obtain search warrants; monitoring and analyzing complex and highly sensitive investigations and operations to ensure that reporting and investigative requirements have been met; performing background searches of individuals and companies to determine whether the subjects of investigations have real property or other assets, liens, lawsuits, judgments, bankruptcies, or criminal convictions; and safeguarding investigative files and property. They also prepare investigative summaries, data, briefs, and status reports to OIG management officials, and assist with the preparation of FDIC-OIG's semiannual report to Congress. Investigations specialists coordinate many activities with the FBI; U.S. Secret Service; IRS Criminal Investigation Division; various OIG agencies; and other federal, state, and local law enforcement agencies.

Qualifications and Salary Levels

GS-7: One full year of graduate education, or superior academic achievement during undergraduate studies, or one year of specialized experience equivalent to at least GS-5. **GS-9:** A master's degree, or two years of graduate education, or one year of specialized experience equivalent to at least GS-7. **GS-11:** A Ph.D. or equivalent doctoral degree, or three years of graduate education, or one year of specialized experience equivalent to at least GS-9. **GS-12:** One year of specialized experience equivalent to at least GS-11.

Training

FDIC-OIG investigations specialists receive ongoing on-the-job training pertaining to computer databases; investigative strategies; public record searches; sources of information; the Bank Secrecy Act, USA PATRIOT Act, Federal Information Security Management Act, Bank Merger Act, and other laws; report writing; and other subjects. They also can attend courses and seminars offered by government agencies, educational institutions, and private firms.

Contact: Office of Investigations; FDIC Office of Inspector General; 801 17th St. NW; Washington, DC 20434; phone: (202) 416-4255; Internet: www.fdicig.gov/

Investigative Assistant (GS-1802)
United States Secret Service, U.S. Department of Homeland Security

U.S. Secret Service (USSS) investigative assistants serve the agency in a wide range of investigative and protective support capacities that enable USSS special agents to carry out their responsibilities in an efficient manner. These personnel are assigned to USSS field offices nationwide.

USSS investigative assistants provide administrative and technical assistance to special agents during protection assignments; criminal investigations pertaining to offenses such as counterfeiting, financial institution fraud, access device fraud, money laundering, forgery, and computer crimes; and the processing of asset forfeiture actions. Some of the tasks they perform include assisting with preliminary preparations for protection assignments; reviewing case referrals and conducting preliminary inquiries to determine the validity of the information received; conducting preliminary searches of computerized databases to identify criminal records, addresses, and other background information on persons under investigation; entering information into databases; maintaining liaison contacts, sharing information, and providing assistance to local, state, and federal law enforcement agencies; typing investigative reports, case reports, statements, affidavits, and correspondence; troubleshooting and performing limited computer maintenance; and serving as an alternative administrative officer on an as-needed basis. The responsibilities of USSS investigative assistants can vary widely depending on the office of assignment and initiatives underway at any given time.

Qualifications and Salary Levels

GS-5: Completion of a four-year course of study leading to a bachelor's degree; or three years of general experience, one year of which was equivalent to at least GS-4. **GS-6:** One year of specialized experience equivalent to at least GS-5. **GS-7:** One year of specialized experience equivalent to at least GS-6. **GS-8:** One year of specialized experience equivalent to at least GS-7. As a general rule, experience and education can be combined to meet total experience requirements only for positions at the GS-5 grade. However, graduate education can be substituted for experience for grades GS-6 through GS-8 if the coursework is directly related to the responsibilities of the position. Candidates must successfully undergo a background investigation, qualify for a security clearance, and pass a drug test prior to appointment.

Training

Professional development for investigative assistants consists of on-the-job training, courses, and seminars that are concerned with investigative procedures, protective operations, legal requirements, the Privacy Act, law enforcement and open-source database resources, computer hardware and software, administrative procedures, ethics, and other subjects.

Contact: Personnel Division; United States Secret Service; U.S. Department of Homeland Security; 950 H St. NW; Washington, DC 20223; phone: (202) 406-5800; Internet: www.secretservice.gov/; e-mail: jobs@secretservice.gov

Investigative Assistant (GS-1802)
Bureau of Diplomatic Security, U.S. Department of State

The Office of Investigations and Counterintelligence within the Bureau of Diplomatic Security (DS) relies on the knowledge and skills of investigative assistants for technical, administrative, and analytical support related to criminal investigations and other DS operational activities. The contributions of these personnel enable DS special agents and other staff to carry out the security of diplomatic missions, investigate passport and visa fraud, conduct personnel security investigations, protect the secretary of state and other high-ranking officials, and perform other functions more effectively and efficiently.

The primary responsibilities of DS investigative assistants include gathering and evaluating factual information associated with inspections or investigations; conducting complex searches of data files and interpreting the data; searching numerous law enforcement and open-source databases to collect information; serving as technical experts on the nature, composition, and operational features of the National Crime Information Center database and other databases used by DS; providing results of searches and other investigative activities to DS special agents and investigative analysts, police departments, and federal law enforcement agencies; reviewing law enforcement reports, credit reports, immigration records, vital statistics, and medical records; and communicating with city, county, state, and federal government agencies, as well as public and private institutions and organizations to obtain and verify information relating to terrorism investigations. DS investigative assistants also maintain an extensive database for all geographical areas of the world concerning terrorists and terrorist groups, terrorist activities and incidents, surveillance operations, terrorist threat letters and other threats, terrorist victims and witnesses, and suspicious events.

Qualifications and Salary Levels

GS-5: Completion of a four-year course of study leading to a bachelor's degree; or three years of general experience, one year of which was equivalent to at least GS-4. **GS-6:** One year of specialized experience equivalent to at least GS-5. **GS-7:** One year of specialized experience equivalent to at least GS-6. **GS-8:** One year of specialized experience equivalent to at least GS-7. As a general rule, experience and education can be combined to meet total experience requirements only for positions at the GS-5 grade. However, graduate education can be substituted for experience for grades GS-6 through GS-8 if the coursework is directly related to the responsibilities of the position. The application process includes a drug screening test, background investigation, and top-secret security clearance determination.

Training

Professional development for DS investigative specialists consists mostly of on-the-job training that varies from one specialist to another depending on experience and skill levels. Training and development could concentrate on areas such as database searches, sources of information, the functions of federal law enforcement agencies, domestic and international terrorism, legal requirements, operations security, and other topics.

Contact: Bureau of Diplomatic Security; U.S. Department of State; 2201 C St. NW; Washington, DC 20520; phone: (202) 647-4000; Internet: www.state.gov/m/ds/; e-mail: DSrecruitment@state.gov

Investigative Specialist (GS-1801)
Federal Bureau of Investigation, U.S. Department of Justice

The primary mission of the FBI in foreign counterintelligence investigations is to identify, penetrate, and neutralize the threat posed—which is where the Bureau's elite team of covert investigative specialists lends its expertise. FBI investigative specialists collect, analyze, and make use of intelligence information to assess and respond to the activities of foreign powers and their agents that could adversely affect national security. They accomplish these tasks by participating as members of teams that conduct discreet surveillance coverage in foreign counterintelligence and counterterrorism cases. The FBI is the lead foreign counterintelligence agency within the U.S. intelligence community.

FBI investigative specialists are assigned to the Bureau's Special Surveillance Group (SSG), and are known in counterespionage circles as "The G's." They perform surveillance missions in a variety of environments and circumstances, including static positions, on foot, and in vehicles. Investigative specialists document their observations through surveillance logs and detailed written reports which provide a record of the activities of those under surveillance. They also provide periodic briefings to special agents in the field and other FBI personnel on a need-to-know basis. Investigative specialists draw on a variety of resources and techniques in carrying out surveillance tasks, including the use of sophisticated video and photographic equipment to document the activities of their surveillance targets, other technical investigative devices, and radio communications equipment. The work of investigative specialists sometimes involves surveillance activities on extended shifts, at night, and on weekends and holidays.

Qualifications and Salary Levels

GS-5: Completion of a four-year course of study leading to a bachelor's degree; or three years of general experience, one year of which was equivalent to at least GS-4. Preference is given to applicants whose major field of study is in the areas of political science, history, journalism, international studies, psychology, sociology, criminology, or certain foreign languages. **GS-7:** One full year of graduate education, or superior academic achievement during undergraduate studies in the disciplines described under GS-5, or a bachelor's degree and one year of specialized experience equivalent to at least GS-5. **GS-9:** A master's degree, or two years of graduate education in the disciplines described under GS-5, or a bachelor's degree and one year of specialized experience equivalent to at least GS-7. **GS-11:** A Ph.D. or equivalent doctoral degree, or three years of graduate education in the disciplines described under GS-5, or a bachelor's degree and one year of specialized experience equivalent to at least GS-9. **GS-12:** One year of specialized experience equivalent to at least GS-11. **GS-13:** One year of specialized experience equivalent to at least GS-12.

Investigative specialists are required to be available for permanent transfers or temporary duty assignments wherever the needs of the FBI dictate. Applicants are required to sign an agreement in which they commit to remaining in the position for at least two years. The application process includes a background investigation, medical examination, drug test, polygraph examination, and top-secret security clearance determination.

Training

FBI investigative specialists attend an eight-week course at the FBI Academy that focuses on foreign counterintelligence, fundamentals of surveillance, and defensive driving techniques. Basic and in-service training for investigative specialists are likely to concentrate on subjects such as foreign counterintelligence operations, national security issues, economic espionage, terrorism, and weapons of mass destruction. Depending on the nature of assignments and expertise of individual investigative specialists, instruction in surveillance methods could focus on surveillance planning, mobile and static surveillance techniques, foot surveillance, countersurveillance, observation skills, daytime and nighttime operations, urban and rural surveillance techniques, covert photography and video techniques, technical investigative equipment, electronic surveillance countermeasures, radio communications, law enforcement computer databases, legal subjects, defensive tactics, and report writing. In-service training is available from the FBI Academy, Federal Law Enforcement Training Center (see chapter 16), other law enforcement agencies, and organizations such as the National Technical Investigators' Association.

Contact: Federal Bureau of Investigation; U.S. Department of Justice; 935 Pennsylvania Ave. NW; Washington, DC 20535; phone: (202) 324-2727; Internet: www.fbi.gov/

Investigative Technician (GS-1802)
Bureau of Land Management, U.S. Department of Interior

Bureau of Land Management (BLM) law enforcement rangers and special agents protect America's natural resources and the public on more than 260 million acres of government-owned land nationwide. Investigative technicians contribute to the mission of BLM's Office of Law Enforcement and Security by performing various investigative, technical, administrative, and intelligence-related functions while working closely with BLM law enforcement officers.

Investigative specialists perform specialized investigative and intelligence-gathering tasks in support of BLM criminal investigations. These personnel obtain background information on suspects through database searches, telephone inquiries, structured interviews, correspondence, and other means; research, compile, and analyze records, intelligence data, and other information from various sources; develop investigative leads and apply various intelligence techniques; gather evidence; and brief special agents and other appropriate personnel on investigative and intelligence data obtained. BLM investigative technicians also participate in field work, such as the execution of search warrants; coordinate logistics for these and other law enforcement operations; and handle administrative tasks such as writing reports, maintaining custody of evidence and exhibits, and maintaining BLM computer databases.

Qualifications and Salary Levels

GS-5: Completion of a four-year course of study leading to a bachelor's degree; or three years of general experience, one year of which was equivalent to at least GS-4. **GS-6:** One year of specialized experience equivalent to at least GS-5. **GS-7:** One year of specialized experience equivalent to at least GS-6. **GS-8:** One year of specialized experience equivalent to at least GS-7. As a general rule, experience and education can be combined to meet total experience requirements only for positions at the GS-5 grade. However, graduate education can be substituted for experience for grades GS-6 through GS-8 if the coursework is directly related to the responsibilities of the position. Appointment is contingent upon a satisfactory background investigation.

Training

Professional development for BLM investigative technicians consists of on-the-job training, courses, and seminars that are concerned with subjects such as interviewing techniques, intelligence operations, investigative procedures, law enforcement and open-source database resources, public records, sources of information, legal requirements, the Privacy Act, computer hardware and software, and administrative procedures.

Contact: Office of Law Enforcement and Security; Bureau of Land Management; U.S. Department of the Interior; 1849 C St. NW; Washington, DC 20240; phone: (202) 208-3269; Internet: www.blm.gov/; e-mail: woinfo@blm.gov

Photographer (GS-1060)
Bureau of Alcohol, Tobacco, Firearms and Explosives; U.S. Department of Justice

Bureau of Alcohol, Tobacco, Firearms and Explosives (ATF) photographers coordinate and provide a wide range of photographic services in support of ATF law enforcement and other Bureau activities. Their expertise is called upon to participate in sensitive and nonsensitive ATF operations nationwide, around the clock.

The primary responsibilities of ATF photographers include photographing crime scene evidence; taking surveillance photographs utilizing film and digital cameras, pinhole cameras, special lenses and filters, infrared equipment, and an assortment of other devices; operating a variety of standard and specialized cameras, complex photographic devices, and printing and processing equipment in other situations; developing technical specifications for the design and construction of new equipment to be used in forensic photography, such as equipment used in ATF criminal investigations to photograph evidence and crime scenes; developing and printing black-and-white and color prints, and 35mm slides; and carrying out other assignments relating to ATF law enforcement operations. ATF photographers also photograph special events and awards ceremonies; take training class photographs and official portraits; and photograph events or activities for public information and training purposes to be used in brochures, newsletters, multimedia presentations, training programs, and the ATF weapons catalog.

Qualifications and Salary Level

GS-7: One year of specialized experience equivalent to at least GS-6 that involved the operation of standard and specialized camera and film processing equipment. **GS-8:**

One year of specialized experience (as described above) equivalent to at least GS-7. **GS-9:** One year of specialized experience (as described above) equivalent to at least GS-8. **GS-10:** One year of specialized experience (as described above) equivalent to at least GS-9. **GS-11:** One year of specialized experience (as described above) equivalent to at least GS-10. Tentative appointees must qualify for a top-secret security clearance and pass a drug screening test, medical examination, and background investigation.

Training

ATF photographers attend courses, seminars, and workshops that cover camera systems and meters, special films, lenses, photographic equipment maintenance, flash photography, darkroom techniques, film processing, infrared photography, crime scene and arson photography, photographic surveillance equipment and techniques, night vision photography, and other topics. These training programs are conducted by ATF staff and organizations such as the Federal Law Enforcement Training Center (see chapter 16), FBI, Evidence Photographers International Council, and various photographic equipment manufacturers.

Contact: Personnel Division; Bureau of Alcohol, Tobacco, Firearms and Explosives; U.S. Department of Justice; 650 Massachusetts Ave. NW—Room 4100; Washington, DC 20226; phone: (202) 927-8610; Internet: www.atf.gov/; e-mail: persdiv@atf.gov

Seized Property Specialist (GS-1801)
United States Immigration and Customs Enforcement, U.S. Department of Homeland Security

U.S. Immigration and Customs Enforcement (ICE) seized property specialists perform a wide range of technical, administrative, and clerical functions in support of the agency's investigative and asset forfeiture programs. These personnel play an important role in ICE enforcement operations targeting the entry of illegal narcotics, restricted merchandise, and other goods into the United States, and the agency's efforts to seize and forfeit assets that are the proceeds of federal crimes or were used to facilitate criminal activity.

ICE seized property specialists are responsible for the custody, management, and disposition of seized and forfeited property—such as currency, narcotics, firearms, vehicles, jewelry, child pornography, real estate, and vehicles—and for many other collateral tasks. These responsibilities involve receiving goods from ICE special agents and other staff; maintaining a carefully monitored chain of custody; storing and ensuring the security of seized property; determining the value of property through appraisals and other means; identifying liens; maintaining an inventory of seized goods; and disposing of property through sales, destruction, or other methods. Seized property specialists provide direct support to ICE special agents by gathering data regarding individual case assignments; researching and compiling information and figures relating to arrests, property seizures, and evidence; and assisting with case research and trial preparation. They also make arrangements for the transfer of property to contractors for storage and disposition; witness or supervise the destruction of narcotics and other goods; maintain liaison with other law enforcement agencies; and perform clerical duties such as typing, filing, and screening mail.

Qualifications and Salary Levels

GS-5: Completion of a four-year course of study leading to a bachelor's degree; or three years of general experience, one year of which was equivalent to at least GS-4. **GS-6:** One year of specialized experience equivalent to at least GS-5. **GS-7:** One year of specialized experience equivalent to at least GS-6. **GS-8:** One year of specialized experience equivalent to at least GS-7.

Training

Professional development seized property specialists consists of on-the-job training, classes, and seminars that focus on subjects such as inventory systems, contractor agreements, legal requirements, the Privacy Act, hazardous materials, databases, computer software, ethics, and administrative procedures.

Contact: Office of Investigations; United States Immigration and Customs Enforcement; U.S. Department of Homeland Security; 425 I St. NW; Washington, DC 20536; phone: (202) 514-0078; Internet: www.ice.gov/

Seizure and Forfeiture Specialist (GS-0301)
United States Marshals Service, U.S. Department of Justice

The U.S. Marshals Service (USMS) administers the Department of Justice (DOJ) Asset Forfeiture Program, which encompasses the seizure and forfeiture of assets that facilitated or were the proceeds of federal crimes. USMS seizure and forfeiture specialists manage and dispose of forfeited property that was seized by federal law enforcement agencies and U.S. Attorneys' offices nationwide. Asset forfeiture has become an important component in the federal government's efforts to combat major criminal activities.

In carrying out the DOJ Asset Forfeiture Program, USMS seizure and forfeiture specialists provide technical support, information, and financial management services to coordinate the legal and administrative aspects of judicial and agency-initiated property seizures. These activities involve attending pre-seizure meetings; receiving seizure and forfeiture–related writs, court orders, and warrants, and reviewing them for accuracy; receiving administrative documents from DOJ and other government agencies involved in seizure and forfeiture actions; maintaining an automated inventory and forfeiture case tracking system; compiling data for reports and records by extracting data from legal documents, seized property records, and automated systems; performing accounting functions concerning seized assets; reviewing invoices and receipts pertaining to seizure cases; monitoring reports on seized asset–related accounts; resolving various problems and discrepancies; and providing direct support in procurement and property management efforts. USMS seizure and forfeiture specialists coordinate operations with other federal agencies that have asset forfeiture responsibilities, such as the Drug Enforcement Administration; FBI; Criminal Investigation Division of the Internal Revenue Service; Bureau of Alcohol, Tobacco, Firearms and Explosives; and U.S. Attorneys' offices.

Qualifications and Salary Level

GS-5: Completion of a four-year course of study leading to a bachelor's degree; or three years of general experience, one year of which was equivalent to at least GS-4. **GS-7:** One full year of graduate education, or superior academic achievement during undergraduate studies, or one year of specialized experience equivalent to at least

GS-5. **GS-9:** A master's degree, or two years of graduate education, or one year of specialized experience equivalent to at least GS-7. **GS-11:** A Ph.D. or equivalent doctoral degree, or three years of graduate education, or one year of specialized experience equivalent to at least GS-9. **GS-12:** One year of specialized experience equivalent to at least GS-11. Experience and education can be combined to meet specialized experience requirements. Candidates must successfully complete a background investigation and pass a drug test prior to appointment.

Training

Initial training for seizure and forfeiture specialists consists of a one-week course presented by USMS staff which focuses on agency policies, procedures, and rules; an overview of seizure and forfeiture processes; legal issues and statutes; procedures relating to the seizure of vehicles, boats, real estate, cash, and other assets; and property disposal methods. In-service training covers topics such as DOJ Asset Forfeiture Program updates, legal issues, computer database programs and other software, and problem solving. In-service training also can include courses pertaining to real estate sales and laws, including those offered by real estate brokers leading to licensing as a real estate agent.

Contact: Human Resources Division; United States Marshals Service; U.S. Department of Justice; 600 Army-Navy Dr.; Arlington, VA 22202; phone: (202) 307-9437; Internet: www.usmarshals.gov/; e-mail: us.marshals@usdoj.gov

Victim Specialist (GS-1801)
Federal Bureau of Investigation, U.S. Department of Justice

To properly address the rights and needs of those victimized by crimes investigated by the FBI, the Bureau's victim specialists ensure that victims are treated with respect, fairness, and compassion in the criminal justice system, in accordance with the law. Under the direction of the FBI Office for Victim Assistance, victim specialists are responsible for ensuring that all victims of crimes investigated by the FBI are identified, are offered assistance, and have the opportunity to receive information about case events and court hearings.

FBI victim specialists assist crime victims by providing information about available assistance and referrals to the organizations that provide these services, such as state crime victim compensation programs and homicide bereavement support groups, and groups that provide mental health counseling, rape crisis center support, and special services for child victims. FBI victim specialists also maintain contact with victims during investigations to notify them about events such as the arrest of a suspect, whether the case is declined for prosecution, or if the case is being referred to state or local authorities. When more than one federal agency is involved in an investigation, victim specialists work closely with other agencies to ensure that victims receive appropriate assistance. To further ensure that victims are afforded appropriate services and information, victim specialists maintain resource materials for use by victims and FBI staff, and conduct research studies to evaluate and enhance the FBI's victim assistance program. They also present training and information to FBI special agents, other Bureau personnel, and other law enforcement agencies to assist them in working with victims; speak to public, civic, and special-interest groups about victims' issues; and present training at regional, national, and international professional conferences. In some cases, victim specialists respond to crime scenes to provide crisis intervention and information to victims about services they may be eligible to receive.

Qualifications and Salary Levels

GS-9: A master's degree, or two years of graduate education, or a bachelor's degree and one year of specialized experience equivalent to at least GS-7. **GS-11:** A Ph.D. or equivalent doctoral degree, or three years of graduate education, or a bachelor's degree and one year of specialized experience equivalent to at least GS-9. **GS-12:** A bachelor's degree and one year of specialized experience equivalent to GS-11. Tentative appointees must qualify for a top-secret security clearance and pass a background investigation, polygraph examination, and drug screening test.

Training

FBI victim specialists attend training programs that are presented by the FBI, other government agencies, professional associations, and academic organizations. These programs focus on topics such as victimology, crisis intervention, handling cases, federal jurisdiction and initiatives, federal victim assistance programs, legal requirements, the Federal Crime Victims' Bill of Rights, victim services innovations, victim program policies, program management, research methods, report writing, and interviewing techniques. Several federal agencies offer courses and seminars to victim program personnel, such as the Federal Law Enforcement Training Center, the Drug Enforcement Administration, the U.S. Department of Defense, the Office for Victims of Crime, and various U.S. Attorneys' offices. Many academic and professional organizations also offer training, such as the National Center for Victims of Crime, the National Organization for Victim Assistance, the National Crime Victims Research and Treatment Center, and the National Victim Assistance Academy.

Contact: Federal Bureau of Investigation; U.S. Department of Justice; 935 Pennsylvania Ave. NW; Washington, DC 20535; phone: (202) 324-2727; Internet: www.fbi.gov/

CHAPTER 10

General and Compliance Investigators

"Injustice anywhere is a threat to justice everywhere."

—*Martin Luther King, Jr.*

Careers in the general and compliance investigating series revolve primarily around inspections and investigations to ensure compliance with federal laws and regulations. More specifically, general and compliance investigators gather information and follow leads to determine the character, practices, suitability, or qualifications of persons or organizations either seeking, claiming, or receiving federal benefits, permits, or employment. As a result, these inspections and investigations are used as a basis for administrative judgments, sanctions, or penalties. Although the majority of investigations carried out by these personnel are not concerned with criminal law violations, occasionally general and compliance investigators work closely with criminal investigators and assist the United States Attorney's Office with criminal prosecution or civil action.

Not surprisingly, the roles and responsibilities of general and compliance investigators vary widely, ranging from those who investigate compliance with labor laws to others who determine the causes of accidents involving aircraft, trains, marine vessels, and pipelines. General and compliance investigations also focus on federal food stamp and crop insurance programs, food safety, securities laws, pension and welfare plans, the diversion of controlled substances, civil rights, consumer products, federal elections, environmental laws, income taxes, corruption in labor unions, and provisions of other federal programs and operations.

Air Safety Investigator (GS-1815)
Federal Aviation Administration, U.S. Department of Transportation

The Federal Aviation Administration (FAA) Office of Accident Investigation is the principal organization within the FAA with respect to aircraft accident investigations and coordination of activities with the National Transportation Safety Board. FAA air safety investigators are responsible for investigating aircraft accidents and incidents in the United States, or anywhere in the world if a U.S. citizen was on board. In addition, these personnel investigate aviation accidents and incidents worldwide involving aircraft either of United States Registry, or manufactured in the United States, or built with U.S. components.

FAA air safety investigators serve in various areas of specialization that cover particular segments of aviation investigations. Depending on their particular specialty, these personnel interview witnesses; examine aircraft wreckage, structures, power plants, navigational systems, components, equipment, and records; gather information pertaining to meteorology, air traffic control, air navigation, airport communications, air carrier operations, and pilot performance; monitor laboratory tests of failed or malfunctioning parts; conduct airworthiness studies; prepare detailed reports of the facts, conditions, and circumstances relating to each accident and a determination of the probable causes; provide testimony at public hearings; make recommendations to alleviate safety hazards and prevent similar accidents in the future; and perform other related functions. FAA air safety investigators are eligible to receive Administratively Uncontrollable Overtime pay.

Qualifications and Salary Levels

GS-9: One year of specialized experience equivalent to GS-7. **GS-11:** One year of specialized experience equivalent to GS-9. **GS-12:** One year of specialized experience equivalent to GS-11. **GS-13:** One year of specialized experience equivalent to GS-12. **GS-14:** One year of specialized experience equivalent to GS-13.

Applicants must have a high school diploma or its equivalent; a current first- or second-class medical certificate in accordance with FAA regulations; a valid driver's license; fluency in the English language; and no chemical dependencies or drug abuse that could interfere with job performance. Additional eligibility requirements depend on areas of specialization, and include appropriate FAA pilot certificates or military ratings, and meeting specific flight-hour requirements. Applicants for all grades and specializations must have a Commercial Pilot Certificate with instrument rating, or an appropriate certificate or military rating that meets or exceeds requirements of the Commercial Pilot Certificate (such as an Airline Pilot Certificate). Candidates are required to undergo a personal interview and to show necessary certificates and log books.

Training

Initial training for FAA air safety investigators includes a one-week Aircraft Accident Investigation Course at the FAA Academy in Oklahoma City, Oklahoma, that covers fundamental techniques of investigations. This course includes instruction concerning working relationships with the NTSB, accident site security, analysis of wreckage, records review, evidence analysis, interviewing techniques, photography, and other topics. These personnel also attend an eight-day Rotorcraft Safety and Accident Investigation Course at the Bell Helicopter Training and Development Center that focuses on various aspects of helicopter crashes, such as design deficiencies, structural considerations, fire protection systems, counterfeit parts, and metallurgical failures. Additional in-service training is concerned with subjects such as accident investigation techniques and case studies, technical investigative equipment, forensic laboratory techniques, accident causes related to human factors, wreckage documentation, investigator safety, new technology and equipment, and related subjects.

Contact: Office of Accident Investigation; Federal Aviation Administration; U.S. Department of Transportation; 800 Independence Ave. SW—Room 838; Washington, DC 20591; phone: (202) 267-9612; Internet: www.faa.gov/

Aviation Accident Investigator (GS-1801)
Office of Aviation Safety, National Transportation Safety Board

The National Transportation Safety Board (NTSB) is an independent federal agency charged by Congress with investigating civil aviation accidents and significant accidents in other modes of transportation, and with issuing safety recommendations aimed at preventing future accidents. NTSB aviation accident investigators are responsible for the investigation of aircraft accidents and incidents throughout the United States; of aviation accidents involving American aircraft operating anywhere in the world; and of accidents involving aircraft that were either manufactured in the United States or built with major components that were manufactured in the United States.

Depending on the nature of accidents, NTSB aviation accident investigators examine aircraft wreckage, structures, systems, engines, and instruments; maintenance records; flight details; pilot performance; evidence of fires and explosions; radar data; meteorology; flight data recorder information; air traffic control information; witness accounts; and other evidence. NTSB investigations sometimes involve work at unusual hours and for long periods in remote, rugged, and hostile settings. Investigations often are accomplished with the assistance of Federal Aviation Administration (FAA) air safety investigators and specialists from regulatory agencies and other organizations outside the NTSB who provide technical expertise. Investigative results are detailed in written reports that also serve as the basis for specific recommendations for corrective action.

Qualifications and Salary Levels

GS-9: One year of specialized experience equivalent to GS-7. **GS-11:** One year of specialized experience equivalent to GS-9. **GS-12:** One year of specialized experience equivalent to GS-11. **GS-13:** One year of specialized experience equivalent to GS-12. **GS-14:** One year of specialized experience equivalent to GS-13.

Applicants must have a high school diploma or its equivalent; a current first- or second-class medical certificate in accordance with FAA regulations; a valid driver's license; fluency in the English language; and no chemical dependencies or drug abuse that could interfere with job performance. Additional eligibility requirements depend on areas of specialization, and include appropriate FAA pilot certificates or military ratings, and meeting specific flight-hour requirements. Applicants for all grades and specializations must have a Commercial Pilot Certificate with instrument rating, or an appropriate certificate or military rating that meets or exceeds requirements of the Commercial Pilot Certificate (such as an Airline Pilot Certificate). Candidates are required to undergo a personal interview and to show necessary certificates and log books.

Training

Basic training for NTSB aviation accident investigators consists of a two-week Aircraft Accident Investigation course at the NTSB Academy in Ashburn, Virginia, which is located on the campus of George Washington University. This course offers instruction in subjects such as crash site documentation and management; aircraft operations and mechanics; fire and explosions; fracture recognition; weather and radar analysis; survival factors; human performance issues; interviewing techniques; accident report writing; and case studies of midair collisions, in-flight fires, in-flight breakups, and weather-related accidents. NTSB aviation accident investigators also receive ongoing training that focuses on aviation accident investigative techniques, NTSB operating rules and legal authority, air carrier operations, turbine engines, propellers, forensic pathology and toxicology, air traffic control and radar, hazardous materials investigations, accident site photography, disaster response, safety recommendations, psychological stress management, and related subjects.

Contact: Office of Aviation Safety; National Transportation Safety Board; 490 L'Enfant Plaza SW; Washington, DC 20594; phone: (202) 314-6000; Internet: www.ntsb.gov/

Background Investigator (GS-1810)
United States Park Police, National Park Service, U.S. Department of the Interior

Background investigators employed by the United States Park Police (USPP) conduct personnel security investigations to determine suitability for positions of trust with the USPP. These investigators conduct pre-employment and other background investigations of job applicants and incumbent employees.

Some responsibilities of USPP background investigators include investigative planning; reviewing records relating to education, employment, arrest and criminal convictions, driver's license, and medical treatment; evaluating information contained in various records to determine relevance to personnel security criteria; interviewing neighbors, personal and professional references, present and former employers, and others; resolving conflicts or omissions in facts or evidence; exploring derogatory information developed through investigative interviews, records obtained, or provided by the applicant or employee; serving as a liaison with other agency applicant investigators; drafting letters and memoranda; preparing investigative reports; assisting police personnel with applicant processing, including fingerprinting and photographing of job applicants or employees, and forms processing; and maintaining pre-employment investigative case files. USPP background investigators also must testify in court and other judicial and administrative hearings concerning background investigations.

Qualifications and Salary Levels

GS-7: One full year of graduate education, or superior academic achievement during undergraduate studies, or one year of specialized experience equivalent to GS-5. **GS-9:** A master's degree, or two years of graduate education, or one year of specialized experience equivalent to GS-7. **GS-11:** A Ph.D. or equivalent doctoral degree, or three years of graduate education, or one year of specialized experience equivalent to GS-9. Qualifying education can be substituted for experience, and vice versa. Candidates must submit to a background investigation, qualify for a security clearance, and pass a drug test prior to appointment.

Training

USPP background investigators and all other National Park Service (NPS) personnel attend a two-week orientation program at the Grand Canyon National Park that provides an introduction to NPS foundations and values. This five-part program consists of computer-based and classroom instruction that focuses on the NPS mission and core values, shared stewardship, integrity, tradition, and respect. Background investigators also receive on-the-job and formal in-service training to develop and enhance job skills in areas such as report writing, legal requirements, interviewing techniques, sources of information, USPP policies and procedures, and computer software programs.

Contact: United States Park Police Headquarters; National Park Service; U.S. Department of the Interior; 1100 Ohio Dr. SW; Washington, DC 20024; phone: (202) 619-7056; Internet: www.nps.gov/uspp/

Background Investigator (GS-1810)
Federal Investigative Services Division, U.S. Office of Personnel Management

U.S. Office of Personnel Management (OPM) background investigators conduct sensitive investigations to facilitate the evaluation of individuals' trustworthiness for access to classified information, placement in federal employment, retention in the military services, or placement into sensitive positions of those already employed in federal positions.

Background investigations carried out by these personnel generally involve selecting the most efficient methods for planning, scheduling, and conducting investigations; identifying resources required for investigations; interviewing current and former employers, neighbors, teachers, personal and business associates, creditors, relatives, and other persons; obtaining copies of transcripts, diplomas, and other records from educational institutions, government agencies, and other sources; confirming the authenticity of documents and reference statements; following leads; developing information from a variety of other sources; and analyzing facts clearly, accurately, logically, and objectively. These investigations also involve sorting out and exploring allegations, hearsay information, and other vague or intangible information of an adverse nature; and engaging in dialog with managers and representatives at contractor facilities, various federal government organizations, and law enforcement agencies to gather information and to develop effective and cooperative working relationships.

OPM background investigators also prepare detailed reports of investigation in accordance with OPM guidelines and instructions, which include a summary of significant findings, conclusions, and recommendations for additional investigative actions. Although OPM maintains a large cadre of background investigators, a private contractor conducts many background investigations on behalf of OPM.

Qualifications and Salary Levels

GS-7: One full year of graduate education, or superior academic achievement during undergraduate studies, or one year of specialized experience equivalent to GS-5. **GS-9:** A master's degree, or two years of graduate education, or one year of specialized experience equivalent to GS-7. **GS-11:** A Ph.D. or equivalent doctoral degree, or three years of graduate education, or one year of specialized experience equivalent to GS-9. **GS-12:** One year of specialized experience equivalent to GS-11. Applicants can use equivalent combinations of specialized experience and education to meet total experience requirements. The application process includes a drug screening test and background investigation.

Training

Most training for OPM background investigators is of the on-the-job variety, which involves working closely with experienced OPM background investigators to develop and enhance the skills necessary to perform job tasks. Background investigators also can attend courses and seminars relating to investigative techniques, interviewing methods, report writing, sources of information, and other subjects.

Contact: Federal Investigative Services Division; U.S. Office of Personnel Management; 1900 E St. NW; Washington, DC 20415; phone: (202) 606-1800; Internet: www.opm.gov/

Civil Investigator (GS-1810)
Office of Civil Enforcement, U.S. Environmental Protection Agency

Under the Environmental Protection Agency's (EPA's) Office of Civil Enforcement, EPA civil investigators zero-in on violations of federal environmental laws to protect human health and the environment. EPA civil investigations are concerned with violations of laws that regulate businesses, individuals, and organizations; such laws include the Clean Air Act, Clean Water Act, Resource Conservation and Recovery Act, Safe Drinking Water Act, National Emissions Standards for Hazardous Air Pollutants, Toxic Substances Control Act, and many other laws.

In cooperation with multi-disciplined teams of experts, EPA civil investigators are responsible for developing evidence to prove violations; identifying, locating, and interviewing potential witnesses; identifying responsible parties and determining their ability to pay for environmental cleanup and proposed fines; developing links between various known and unknown corporate entities—such as parent corporations, subsidiaries, and successor companies—that help determine responsibility and liability for environmental violations; tracking unreported corporate or individual finances; preparing reports to support enforcement actions; and testifying in civil and criminal proceedings. Investigations often are conducted with the assistance of air, water, and solid waste pollution control officials, and legal and technical representatives of other federal, state, and local agencies. When deliberate violations are detected, the investigations are referred to EPA special agents for criminal enforcement action.

Qualifications and Salary Levels

GS-5: Completion of a four-year course of study leading to a bachelor's degree; or three years of general experience, one year of which was equivalent to GS-4. **GS-7:** One full year of graduate education, or superior academic achievement during undergraduate studies, or one year of specialized experience equivalent to GS-5. **GS-9:** A master's degree, or two years of graduate education, or one year of specialized experience equivalent to GS-7. **GS-11:** A Ph.D. or equivalent doctoral degree, or three years of graduate education, or one year of specialized experience equivalent to GS-9. **GS-12:** One year of specialized experience equivalent to GS-11. **GS-13:**

One year of specialized experience equivalent to GS-12. Experience and education can be combined to meet total experience requirements.

Training

EPA civil investigators receive an orientation to the mission, policies, procedures, and rules of the agency, as well as instruction concerning environmental laws and regulations, EPA agencies and enforcement operations, financial investigations, investigative techniques, and other relevant subjects. Throughout their careers, EPA civil investigators receive training at the EPA National Enforcement Training Institute, including courses that focus on compliance and enforcement principles, case development processes, interviewing and interrogation, evidence collection, civil penalties, and team approaches to environmental investigations, among other topics.

Contact: Office of Civil Enforcement; U.S. Environmental Protection Agency; 1200 Pennsylvania Ave.; Washington, DC 20460; phone: (202) 564-0027; Internet: www.epa.gov/compliance/civil/; e-mail: public-access@epamail.epa.gov

Compliance Investigator (GS-1801)
Risk Management Agency, U.S. Department of Agriculture

U.S. farmers have the option of purchasing federal crop insurance to protect against unexpected production losses from natural causes, such as drought, excessive moisture, hail, wind, flooding, hurricanes, tornadoes, and lightning. Compliance investigators of the U.S. Department of Agriculture (USDA) Risk Management Agency (RMA) are responsible for overseeing crop insurance program operations to ensure compliance of private insurance companies and farmers with laws and regulations related to the Crop Insurance Act of 1980, the Agricultural Risk Protection Act of 2000, and other laws and regulations.

RMA compliance investigators perform on-site reviews of insurance company records and operations to ensure compliance with insurance agreements and related policies, procedures, and guidelines; conduct farm inspections to ascertain crop production, losses, farming practices, and irregularities in claims for indemnity payments; inspect business records maintained by grain elevators, brokers, and other entities to assess crop production and marketing levels; and prepare comprehensive written investigative reports. Investigations involving fraud and criminal prosecution are conducted jointly with USDA Office of Inspector General special agents.

Qualifications and Salary Levels

GS-5: Completion of a four-year course of study leading to a bachelor's degree; or three years of general experience, one year of which was equivalent to GS-4. **GS-7:** One full year of graduate education, or superior academic achievement during undergraduate studies, or one year of specialized experience equivalent to GS-5. **GS-9:** A master's degree or two years of graduate education, or one year of specialized experience equivalent to GS-7. **GS-11:** A Ph.D. or equivalent doctoral degree, or three years of graduate education, or one year of specialized experience equivalent to GS-9. **GS-12:** One year of specialized experience equivalent to GS-11. Equivalent combinations of education and experience can be used to meet minimum experience requirements.

Training

RMA Compliance Investigators attend the two-week Introduction to Criminal Investigations Training Program at the Federal Law Enforcement Training Center in Glynco, Georgia (see chapter 16). In-service training includes specialized courses that focus on topics such as crop insurance program regulations, criminal and civil law, interviewing, investigative techniques, financial investigations, auditing methods, the Freedom of Information Act, the Privacy Act, and report writing.

Contact: Risk Management Agency; U.S. Department of Agriculture; 1400 Independence Ave. SW—Room 6092; Washington, DC 20250; phone: (202) 690-2803; Internet: www.rma.usda.gov/; e-mail: rma.mail@rma.usda.gov

Compliance Officer (GS-1801)
Food Safety and Inspection Service, U.S. Department of Agriculture

The Food Safety and Inspection Service (FSIS) of the U.S. Department of Agriculture (USDA) is responsible for ensuring that the nation's commercial supply of meat, poultry, and egg products are safe, wholesome, and correctly labeled and packaged as required by the Federal Meat Inspection Act, the Poultry Products Inspection Act, and the Egg Products Inspection Act. Compliance officers serve with the FSIS Office of Program Evaluation, Enforcement, and Review (OPEER).

FSIS compliance officers conduct compliance reviews and investigations of commercial operations, such as retail stores, restaurants, cold-storage warehouses, distributors, salvage operators, renderers, brokers, animal food manufacturers, and other handlers or processors of meat, poultry, and egg products. These reviews and investigations often support administrative actions, civil litigation, and referral for criminal prosecution pertaining to the sale of uninspected, adulterated, unwholesome, contaminated, misbranded, or falsely labeled products; insanitary conditions in meat and poultry slaughter and processing facilities; and the slaughter, processing, and sale of products from diseased or injured animals. Minor violations of law that are not referred to United States attorneys for prosecution are handled through FSIS Notice of Warning procedures. Complex criminal investigations normally are conducted jointly with special agents of the USDA Office of Inspector General. FSIS compliance officers also promote and facilitate the efforts of the FSIS Compliance and Investigations Division through contacts with government officials, private industry, and the public.

Qualifications and Salary Levels

GS-5: Completion of a four-year course of study leading to a bachelor's degree; or three years of general experience, one year of which was equivalent to GS-4. **GS-7:** One full year of graduate education, or superior academic achievement during undergraduate studies, or one year of specialized experience equivalent to GS-5. **GS-9:** A master's degree, or two years of graduate education, or one year of specialized experience equivalent to GS-7. **GS-11:** A Ph.D. or equivalent doctoral degree, or three years of graduate education, or one year of specialized experience equivalent to GS-9. **GS-12:** One year of specialized experience equivalent to GS-11. Qualifying education can be substituted for experience, and vice versa. Applicants must pass a background investigation and qualify for a security clearance.

Training

Training for FSIS compliance officers consists of structured basic, intermediate, and advanced Compliance Officer Training courses that cover fundamentals and advanced techniques relating to various responsibilities of the position. These courses are concerned with provisions of the Federal Meat Inspection Act, the Poultry Products Inspection Act, and the Egg Products Inspection Act; compliance review, inspection, and investigative techniques; FSIS personnel policies, procedures, and regulations; criminal, civil, and administrative actions; and cooperation with government and law enforcement agencies. FSIS compliance officers also attend a variety of in-service programs at the Federal Law Enforcement Training Center (FLETC), of which some are taught by FSIS personnel and others by FLETC staff. These include a one-week basic officer safety course, an expanded three-week officer safety course, and conflict resolution training, among other programs. Additional in-service training focuses on investigative techniques, updates of laws and regulations, and other subjects related to compliance reviews and investigative operations.

Contact: Office of Program Evaluation, Enforcement and Review; Food Safety and Inspection Service; 1400 Independence Ave. SW—Room 3133; U.S. Department of Agriculture; Washington, DC 20250; phone: (202) 418-8874; Internet: www.fsis.usda.gov/

Diversion Investigator (GS-1801)
Drug Enforcement Administration, U.S. Department of Justice

Diversion investigators of the Drug Enforcement Administration (DEA) are charged with preventing and eliminating the diversion of and illicit trafficking in legitimate pharmaceutical drugs and chemicals throughout the United States. The duties of diversion investigators encompass all front-line aspects of the DEA's responsibilities under both the Controlled Substances Act and the Chemical Diversion and Trafficking Act concerning the diversion of controlled drugs and related substances from legitimate channels. The primary subjects of inspection or investigation are medical practitioners and their staff; pharmacies; and companies engaged in the manufacturing, distributing, importing, or exporting of legitimately produced controlled substances and chemicals; and narcotic treatment programs.

The responsibilities of these investigators include planning, organizing, and conducting investigations; examining books and records of registrants, such as physicians and pharmacists, to ascertain receipt and disposition of controlled drugs; evaluating security controls over controlled substances; conducting interviews; recognizing, collecting, and preserving evidence; supporting DEA criminal investigative programs as intelligence is encountered related to diversion and excessive purchases of controlled drugs and diluents; and preparing detailed reports that support administrative, civil, and criminal proceedings. In many investigations, diversion investigators work closely with DEA special agents in undercover operations and the execution of search warrants. They also work with the United States Attorneys Office and prosecutors at state and local levels, present evidence to grand juries, and testify during criminal trials and administrative hearings. Diversion investigators are stationed at more than 80 DEA offices nationwide and overseas.

Qualifications and Salary Levels

GS-7: One full year of graduate education, or superior academic achievement during undergraduate studies, or one year of specialized experience equivalent to GS-5.

GS-9: A master's degree or two years of graduate education, or one year of specialized experience equivalent to GS-7. **GS-11:** A Ph.D. or equivalent doctoral degree, or three years of graduate education, or one year of specialized experience equivalent to GS-9. **GS-12:** One year of specialized experience equivalent to GS-11.

Applicants can use equivalent combinations of specialized experience and education to meet total experience requirements. Tentative appointees must qualify for a security clearance, and pass a background investigation, polygraph exam, drug screening test, and physical exam. Applicants must be willing to accept assignments and relocate anywhere in the United States. Eyesight requirements include distant vision of at least 20/40 (Snellen), near vision of at least 20/25, the ability to read Jaeger Type #2 characters at 14 inches, and the ability to distinguish basic colors. (Glasses and contact lenses are permitted.) Hearing requirements include the ability to hear conversational voice at a distance of 20 feet with both ears. (Hearing aids are permitted.)

Candidates with certain experience, skills, or education may be given special consideration in the hiring process. For example, the DEA is especially interested in candidates that have investigative experience, proficiency in a foreign language, accounting experience or an accounting degree, chemistry experience or a degree in chemistry, pharmacology experience or a degree in pharmacology, computer skills or experience, military service, law enforcement experience, or a criminal justice degree.

Training

DEA diversion investigators attend a 12-week Diversion Investigator Basic Training School at the DEA training academy in Quantico, Virginia. This course provides an overview of drug diversion methods and the pharmaceutical and chemical industries. Some topics covered during the program include controlled substance laws and regulations, pharmaceutical drug identification, drug manufacturing and distribution processes, pharmacy records auditing, drug diversion methods, case studies, interviewing and investigative techniques, courtroom procedures and testimony, clandestine laboratory operations, auditing techniques, report writing, and computer software tools. Approximately every two years thereafter, diversion investigators attend a one-week refresher training course that covers legal updates, ethics and integrity, computer systems, and agency operational issues. Periodic in-service training is concerned with asset forfeiture, money laundering, legal updates, auditing and investigative techniques, and other specialized courses and updates as needed.

Contact: Recruiting information can be obtained from any DEA field office, or by contacting Diversion Investigator Recruitment; Drug Enforcement Administration; U.S. Department of Justice; Washington, DC 20537; phone: (202) 307-8846; Internet: www.deadiversion.usdoj.gov/.

Field Investigator
Enforcement Division, National Indian Gaming Commission

The National Indian Gaming Commission (NIGC) is an independent federal regulatory agency that is responsible for regulating and monitoring certain gaming activities conducted on Native American lands. The Commission was created by Congress in 1988 to shield Indian gaming from organized crime and other corrupting influences; to ensure that Native American tribes are the primary beneficiaries of gaming operations; and to assure that gaming is conducted fairly and honestly by gaming operators and players. In furtherance of these goals, NIGC field investigators monitor the gaming activities of Native American tribes to ensure compliance with tribal, state, and federal gaming laws and regulations.

To achieve this mission, these personnel conduct investigations of violations of the Indian Gaming Regulatory Act, NIGC regulations, and tribal ordinances; analyze investigative data; prepare reports; testify in administrative hearings and other proceedings; conduct background investigations of Indian gaming operation employees; provide training and assistance to tribal agencies and gaming management contractors; maintain working relationships with tribal, local, state, and federal law enforcement and regulatory agencies; and serve as a liaison between the NIGC and tribal governments. They also attend staff meetings to keep the Commission advised of developments in the Indian gaming industry.

Qualifications and Salary Levels

NIGC field investigators are appointed through excepted service hiring processes. The qualifications and salaries of field investigators are similar to general and compliance investigator positions at the GS-9, GS-11, GS-12, and GS-13 levels with other federal agencies. NIGC seeks candidates with strong oral and written communication skills; work experience with a tribal, local, state, or federal law enforcement or regulatory agency; and skill in gathering and analyzing information and conducting complex investigations. In addition, an undergraduate degree in criminal justice, public administration, business, or related disciplines is preferred, as is knowledge of or experience in gaming operations.

Training

Throughout their careers, NIGC Field Investigators attend various training courses, seminars, and conferences pertaining to Indian gaming laws and regulations, illegal gambling operations, gaming investigative techniques, federal and Native American tax laws, regulatory authority, investigative jurisdiction, interviewing techniques, Native American cultural sensitivity, and other related subjects. Training is presented by NIGC staff, the FBI, other law enforcement agencies, companies that manufacture gaming equipment and devices, and other organizations.

Contact: Personnel Office; National Indian Gaming Commission; 1441 L St. NW—Ste. 9100; Washington, DC 20005; phone: (202) 632-7003; Internet: www.nigc.gov/; e-mail: info@nigc.gov

Futures Trading Investigator
Division of Enforcement, Commodity Futures Trading Commission

The Commodity Futures Trading Commission (CFTC) regulates trading on 11 U.S. futures exchanges that offer active futures and options contracts, as well as the activities of numerous commodity exchange members, public brokerage houses, futures industry sales personnel, commodity trading advisers, and commodity pool operators. The Division of Enforcement is the law enforcement arm of CFTC, with responsibility for the investigation and prosecution of violations of the Commodity Exchange Act and the Commission's regulations. Investigations carried out by CFTC futures trading investigators are concerned with offenses such as price manipulations and illegal trade practices on contract markets regulated by the Commission; and fraud against customers involved in the trading of futures contracts, leverage contracts, and options.

These investigators detect patterns of trading activity that suggest potential violations; conduct interviews; serve subpoenas; review and analyze detailed financial, business, and accounting records obtained through subpoenas and inspections; draft memoranda and detailed investigative reports recommending legal actions; prepare charts, summaries, and affidavits used in hearings and trials, and testify as to their content; provide technical assistance to CFTC attorneys in criminal prosecutions and administrative or civil enforcement actions; and work with other investigators, attorneys, and auditors in task force operations. CFTC investigations result in various civil and administrative actions, such as temporary statutory restraining orders; preliminary and permanent injunctions to halt ongoing violations; civil monetary penalties; the freezing of assets; restitution to customers; disgorgement of unlawfully acquired benefits; orders suspending, denying, revoking, or restricting registration; and criminal convictions.

Qualifications and Salary Levels

CFTC futures trading investigators are appointed through excepted service hiring processes. The qualifications and salaries of these personnel are similar to general and compliance investigator positions at the GS-7, GS-9, GS-11, GS-12, and GS-13 levels with other federal agencies. The CFTC Division of Enforcement seeks candidates with knowledge of investigative principles and techniques concerning investment businesses, financial fraud, and consumer fraud; the ability to conduct interviews, review financial records, prepare reports, and advise and negotiate with persons and organizations subject to CFTC regulation; and skill in computer applications such as word processing, database, and spreadsheet programs.

Training

Initial training for CFTC investigators includes an orientation program that covers the mission, policies, procedures, and rules of the agency; evidence-gathering techniques; as well as an introduction to the varieties of investigations carried out by the Division of Enforcement. In-service training includes courses, seminars, and workshops pertaining to various aspects of futures and options trading, such as commodity exchanges, trading floor activities, trading abuses, fraud investigation, case studies, surveillance of electronic markets, sharing of investigative information and resources, money laundering, international investigations, interviewing and taking testimony from witnesses, organizing and presenting evidence for trial, and ethics.

Contact: Division of Enforcement; Commodity Futures Trading Commission; 1155 21st St. NW; Washington, DC 20581; phone: (202) 418-5320; Internet: www.cftc.gov/anr/anrenf98.htm; e-mail: enforcement@cftc.gov

Industry Operations Investigator (GS-1801)
Bureau of Alcohol, Tobacco, Firearms and Explosives, U.S. Department of Justice

The Bureau of Alcohol, Tobacco, Firearms and Explosives (ATF) employs industry operations investigators in furtherance of ATF's regulatory mission to ensure consumer and industry compliance with laws and regulations relating to the firearms and explosives industries in the United States. The work of industry operations investigators revolves around investigations and inspections of firearms and explosives dealers, importers, exporters, manufacturers, wholesalers, and users that are under the jurisdiction of the Gun Control Act, the National Firearms Act, the Arms Export Control Act, the Organized Crime Control Act, and other federal firearms and explosives laws and regulations.

Examples of responsibilities carried out by these personnel include conducting inspections, examinations, and investigations of firearms and explosives manufacturing facilities; examining buildings, equipment, and finished products; taking inventory; analyzing records and reports; evaluating the reliability of recordkeeping systems; determining whether operations are in accordance with laws and regulations; examining documentation of firearms and explosives transactions; conducting interviews of persons associated with industries regulated by ATF; and determining whether persons hoping to enter business in regulated industries meet established legal requirements for obtaining federal permits or licenses to conduct operations. Investigations often uncover fraudulent records, firearms and explosives thefts, and willful noncompliance with federal regulations by firearms and explosives licensees. Industry operations investigators also assist ATF special agents with criminal investigations, intelligence gathering, task force activities, and the execution of search warrants concerning the diversion of firearms, explosives, alcohol, and tobacco products from legitimate channels to illegal commerce.

Qualifications and Salary Levels

GS-5: Completion of a four-year course of study leading to a bachelor's degree; or three years of general experience, one year of which was equivalent to GS-4. **GS-7:** One full year of graduate education, or superior academic achievement during undergraduate studies, or one year of specialized experience equivalent to GS-5. **GS-9:** A master's degree, or two years of graduate education, or one year of specialized experience equivalent to GS-7. **GS-11:** A Ph.D. or equivalent doctoral degree, or three years of graduate education, or one year of specialized experience equivalent to GS-9. **GS-12:** One year of specialized experience equivalent to GS-11. Qualifying education can be substituted for experience, and vice versa. Candidates must successfully complete a background investigation, qualify for a top-secret security clearance, and pass a drug test prior to appointment.

Training

ATF industry operations investigators attend a five-week basic training course at the Federal Law Enforcement Training Center in Glynco, Georgia. This program includes instruction in areas such as firearms laws and regulations; firearms importing and exporting procedures; inspection of firearms and explosives manufacturing facilities; firearm tracing techniques; licensed firearms and explosives dealer operations; identification of firearms and explosives; ATF laboratory operations; and interviewing techniques. On-the-job and in-service training are concerned with firearms trafficking; diversions of alcohol, tobacco, firearms, and explosives; industry and legal updates; explosive devices; and other relevant topics.

Contact: Personnel Division; Bureau of Alcohol, Tobacco, Firearms and Explosives; U.S. Department of Justice; 650 Massachusetts Ave. NW—Room 4100; Washington, DC 20226; phone: (202) 927-8610; Internet: www.atf.gov/; e-mail: persdiv@atf.gov

Investigator (GS-1810)
Animal and Plant Health Inspection Service, U.S. Department of Agriculture

The Animal and Plant Health Inspection Service (APHIS) of the Department of Agriculture (USDA) was established to conduct regulatory programs to protect and improve animal and plant health nationwide. APHIS administers and enforces federal laws and regulations pertaining to animal and plant health and quarantine, humane treatment of animals, and the control and eradication of pests and diseases.

Under the Investigative and Enforcement Services (IES) division, APHIS investigators conduct investigations of alleged violations of federal laws and regulations governing the interstate and international movement of plant materials and livestock; the welfare and treatment of animals, including provisions of the Animal Welfare Act and the Horse Protection Act; the manufacture and distribution of veterinary biological products; the transportation and interstate shipment of organisms; quarantine rules that restrict the interstate movement of certain animals, plants, and agricultural products; standards established for accredited veterinarians working in federal or state cooperative programs; standards that control the quality of veterinary biological products; unauthorized release of genetically engineered organisms; and standards for garbage and food that is fed to swine.

APHIS investigators also are responsible for meeting with individuals or groups representing the agriculture industry, animal dealers and exhibitors, civic groups, and federal and state regulatory agencies to explain federal programs and regulatory requirements. Their duties also include training other APHIS employees in techniques for collecting evidence, conducting interviews, and enforcing APHIS regulations. Investigations are often conducted jointly with agencies such as the USDA Office of Inspector General, U.S. Immigration and Customs Enforcement, IRS Criminal Investigation Division, U.S. Fish and Wildlife Service, Food and Drug Administration, and other law enforcement or regulatory agencies.

Qualifications and Salary Levels

GS-5: Completion of a four-year course of study leading to a bachelor's degree; or three years of general experience, one year of which was equivalent to GS-4. **GS-7:** One full year of graduate education, or superior academic achievement during undergraduate studies, or one year of specialized experience equivalent to GS-5. **GS-9:** A master's degree, or two years of graduate education, or one year of specialized experience equivalent to GS-7. **GS-11:** A Ph.D. or equivalent doctoral degree, or three years of graduate education, or one year of specialized experience equivalent to GS-9. **GS-12:** One year of specialized experience equivalent to GS-11. Applicants can use equivalent combinations of specialized experience and education to meet total experience requirements. The application process includes a background investigation and security clearance determination.

Training

APHIS investigators attend the two-week Introduction to Criminal Investigations Training Program at the Federal Law Enforcement Training Center in Glynco, Georgia (see chapter 16), as well as an in-house orientation to the mission and rules of APHIS and the IES. Ongoing in-service training for these personnel includes specialized courses and in-house training programs concerning APHIS program regulations and investigations, interviewing techniques, photography, white-collar crime, legal issues and updates, evidence-collection techniques, and other subjects.

Contact: Investigative and Enforcement Services; Animal and Plant Health Inspection Service; U.S. Department of Agriculture; 4700 River Rd.—Unit 85; Riverdale, MD 20737; phone: (301) 734-8684; Internet: www.aphis.usda.gov/ies/

Investigator (GS-1810)
Food and Nutrition Service, U.S. Department of Agriculture

The Food and Nutrition Service (FNS) administers the nutrition assistance programs of the U.S. Department of Agriculture (USDA). Under the authority and direction of the FNS Retailer Investigations Branch, FNS investigators plan and conduct investigations of retail firms that are authorized to participate in the USDA Food Stamp Program (FSP) and are suspected of unlawfully selling products or services in exchange for food stamps.

Tasks performed by these personnel include evaluating investigative priorities, plans, alternatives, and data to develop appropriate investigative strategies; examining records of program participation by retailers including food stamp redemption history, complaints, observed violations, and previous investigations to detect clues or links in evidence that are most likely to result in successful investigations; interacting with informants and law enforcement officers for undercover and investigative support; working in an undercover capacity and attempting to conduct violative food stamp transactions to obtain firsthand evidence; conducting interviews and preparing written investigative reports with the intent of justifying future criminal investigations by the USDA Office of Inspector General (USDA-OIG); participating in task force operations; and providing technical assistance to FNS regional offices, the USDA Office of General Counsel, and USDA-OIG relating to administrative hearings and judicial reviews.

Senior investigators also verify food stamp redemptions and subpoenaed sales records of firms with high redemptions; scrutinize firms that are authorized to participate in the FSP as retailers, but also conduct wholesale operations; and investigate authorized retailers that unlawfully acquire food stamps from firms not authorized to participate in the FSP. Investigations often are conducted jointly with USDA-OIG special agents and other law enforcement agencies.

Qualifications and Salary Levels

GS-5: Completion of a four-year course of study leading to a bachelor's degree; or three years of general experience, one year of which was equivalent to GS-4. **GS-7:** One full year of graduate education, or superior academic achievement during undergraduate studies, or one year of specialized experience equivalent to GS-5. **GS-9:** A master's degree, or two years of graduate education, or one year of specialized experience equivalent to GS-7. **GS-11:** A Ph.D. or equivalent doctoral degree, or three years of graduate education, or one year of specialized experience equivalent to GS-9. **GS-12:** One year of specialized experience equivalent to GS-11. Experience and education can be combined to meet total experience requirements. FNS investigator candidates must pass a background investigation.

Training

FNS investigators attend the two-week Introduction to Criminal Investigations Training Program at the Federal Law Enforcement Training Center in Glynco, Georgia (see chapter 16). In-service training includes instruction concerning topics such as Food Stamp Program regulations and investigations; informant development; criminal, civil, and administrative law; report writing; interviewing techniques; case management; and other subjects. In-service training consists of various courses at the Federal Law Enforcement Training Center, seminars, conferences, and other programs.

Contact: Personnel Division; Food and Nutrition Service; U.S. Department of Agriculture; 3101 Park Center Dr.—Room 620; Alexandria, VA 22302; phone: (703) 305-2062; Internet: www.fns.usda.gov/

Investigator (GS-1810)
Defense Security Service, U.S. Department of Defense

The Defense Security Service (DSS)—formerly known as the Defense Investigative Service—provides security services to the Department of Defense (DoD) through the integration of personnel security, industrial security, information systems security, and counterintelligence. DSS administers the National Industrial Security Program on behalf of the DoD and 22 other executive branch departments and agencies, and provides oversight to more than 11,000 cleared contractor facilities performing on classified contracts.

DSS investigators conduct security background investigations of civilian, military, and contractor personnel being considered for assignments to positions requiring access to classified DoD information or highly sensitive DoD areas. Investigations carried out by these personnel focus on allegations of subversive affiliations, adverse suitability information, or any other situation that requires resolution to complete personnel security investigations. The majority of investigative activity consists of reviewing records and interviewing neighbors and employers of the subject of the investigation to verify education and employment; locating, analyzing, and summarizing information; submitting factual data necessary to prove or disapprove a variety of developed allegations; completing and transmitting correspondence and written reports of investigative findings; and developing working relationships with individuals both within and outside of DSS.

Qualifications and Salary Levels

GS-5: Completion of a four-year course of study leading to a bachelor's degree; or three years of general experience, one year of which was equivalent to GS-4. **GS-7:** One full year of graduate education, or superior academic achievement during undergraduate studies, or one year of specialized experience equivalent to GS-5. **GS-9:** A master's degree, or two years of graduate education, or one year of specialized experience equivalent to GS-7. **GS-11:** A Ph.D. or equivalent doctoral degree, or three years of graduate education, or one year of specialized experience equivalent to GS-9. **GS-12:** One year of specialized experience equivalent to GS-11. Qualifying education can be substituted for experience, and vice versa. Tentative appointees must pass a drug screening test and background investigation, and qualify for a security clearance.

Training

Training for DSS investigators consists of courses that focus on the elements of personnel security investigations; the DSS Investigative Handbook (Manual for Personnel Security Investigations); case management; record reviews; investigative leads; interviewing techniques; issue resolution; report writing; adjudicative procedures; polygraph examinations; DSS policies, procedures, regulations, and requirements; and other subjects. Instruction is presented through classroom lectures and practical exercises offered by the Defense Security Service Academy in Linthicum, Maryland, and by other training providers.

Contact: Defense Security Service; U.S. Department of Defense; 1340 Braddock Place; Alexandria, VA 22314; phone: (703) 325-9471; Internet: www.dss.mil/; e-mail: cpao@dss.mil

Investigator (GS-1810)
Office for Civil Rights, U.S. Department of Education

The Department of Education (ED) Office for Civil Rights (OCR) is responsible for enforcing federal statutes that prohibit discrimination on the basis of race, color, national origin, gender, disability, or age in education programs and activities that receive federal financial assistance. Civil rights laws enforced by ED-OCR extend to all state education agencies, elementary and secondary school systems, colleges and universities, vocational schools, proprietary schools, state vocational rehabilitation agencies, libraries, and museums that receive ED funds.

ED-OCR investigators plan and conduct a range of investigative functions in support of civil rights compliance activities. Their specific responsibilities include identifying allegations, issues, applicable theories of law, pertinent data, potential sources of evidence, investigative techniques to be employed, and the scope of cases under investigation; reviewing records and data; interviewing witnesses; drafting written reports of investigation; assisting in complaint resolution through mediation to secure voluntary compliance with civil rights laws and ED regulations; and providing technical assistance, information, and related services to education program recipients and other parties regarding their civil rights and responsibilities. ED-OCR investigators are based in 12 offices located throughout the United States.

Qualifications and Salary Levels

GS-5: Completion of a four-year course of study leading to a bachelor's degree; or three years of general experience, one year of which was equivalent to GS-4. **GS-7:** One full year of graduate education, or superior academic achievement during undergraduate studies, or one year of specialized experience equivalent to GS-5. **GS-9:** A master's degree, or two years of graduate education, or one year of specialized experience equivalent to GS-7. **GS-11:** A Ph.D. or equivalent doctoral degree, or three years of graduate education, or one year of specialized experience equivalent to GS-9. **GS-12:** One year of specialized experience equivalent to GS-11. Applicants can use equivalent combinations of specialized experience and education to meet total experience requirements. A background investigation is required. Applicants are subject to verification that they have not defaulted on any loan funded or guaranteed by the U.S. Department of Education.

Training

Training and development for ED-OCR investigators includes an orientation program that covers the mission, policies, procedures, and rules of the agency, followed by courses in report writing, interviewing techniques, and various investigative methods. On-the-job training and guidance are provided by senior Equal Employment Opportunity (EEO) specialists and staff attorneys on a variety of investigative functions and skills. In-service training includes courses in subjects such as EEO regulations, diversity, computer hardware and software, computer Local Area Network (LAN) functions, and other pertinent topics.

Contact: Office for Civil Rights; U.S. Department of Education; 550 12th St. SW; Washington, DC 20202; phone: (800) 421-3481; Internet: www.ed.gov/ocr/; e-mail: ocr@ed.gov

Investigator (GS-1810)
Office of Superfund Remediation and Technology Innovation, U.S. Environmental Protection Agency

The Office of Superfund Remediation and Technology Innovation (OSRTI) of the Environmental Protection Agency (EPA) manages the EPA Superfund Program, which was created by Congress to protect citizens from the dangers posed by abandoned or uncontrolled hazardous waste sites, and to develop long-term solutions for the nation's most serious hazardous waste problems. The EPA seeks to achieve prompt hazardous waste site cleanup and maximum liable party participation in performing and paying for cleanup.

EPA-OSRTI investigators plan and conduct investigations pertaining to Superfund sites in support of enforcement or civil actions under the Comprehensive Environmental Response, Compensation, and Liability Act of 1980. The primary responsibilities of these investigators include assembling documentation necessary to support enforcement proceedings; conducting searches to identify liable parties that caused contamination; obtaining and analyzing financial records and information relating to liable parties to determine their financial status, viability, and ability to pay for cleanup; coordinating investigations and activities with other federal, state, or local agencies; preparing investigative reports; providing information to the EPA Criminal Investigation Division for criminal enforcement actions; testifying in enforcement actions and assisting the United States Attorney and EPA legal staff in preparing cases for negotiations or litigation; and training state and local hazardous waste enforcement staff on interviewing and investigative techniques.

Qualifications and Salary Levels

GS-5: Completion of a four-year course of study leading to a bachelor's degree; or three years of general experience, one year of which was equivalent to GS-4. **GS-7:** One full year of graduate education, or superior academic achievement during undergraduate studies, or one year of specialized experience equivalent to GS-5. **GS-9:** A master's degree, or two years of graduate education, or one year of specialized experience equivalent to GS-7. **GS-11:** A Ph.D. or equivalent doctoral degree, or three years of graduate education, or one year of specialized experience equivalent to GS-9. **GS-12:** One year of specialized experience equivalent to GS-11. **GS-13:** One year of specialized experience equivalent to GS-12. Equivalent combinations of education and experience can be used to meet minimum experience requirements.

Training

Initial training for EPA-OSRTI investigators includes an orientation to the mission, policies, procedures, and rules of the agency, followed by instruction relating to EPA programs and operations, Superfund laws and regulations, and EPA enforcement actions. In-service training is concerned with interviewing techniques, legal issues and updates, computer databases, financial investigations, money laundering, and other courses conducted by staff at the EPA, Federal Law Enforcement Training Center, and other organizations.

Contact: Office of Superfund Remediation and Technology Innovation; U.S. Environmental Protection Agency; 1200 Pennsylvania Ave. NW; Washington, DC 20460; phone: (202) 272-0167; Internet: www.epa.gov/superfund/; e-mail: public-access@epamail.epa.gov

Investigator (GS-1810)
Office of General Counsel, Federal Election Commission

The Federal Election Commission (FEC) has exclusive jurisdiction in the administration and civil enforcement of laws regulating the acquisition and expenditure of campaign funds to ensure compliance by participants in the federal election campaign process. Investigators of the FEC Office of General Counsel (OGC) plan and conduct investigations concerning violations of the Federal Election Campaign Act (FECA), the Presidential Election Campaign Fund Act, and the Presidential Primary Matching Payment Account Act. These laws are concerned with public funding of presidential elections, public disclosure of the financial activities of political committees involved in federal elections, and limitations and prohibitions on contributions and expenditures made to influence federal elections.

FEC investigators are responsible for reviewing complaints of FECA violations; locating records, individuals, and entities; employing skip-tracing tactics and other search strategies to obtain information, locate assets, and identify personal and business affiliations; interviewing witnesses and preparing affidavits; examining financial reports and documents; identifying money-laundering activities; analyzing and summarizing results of investigations; preparing written investigative reports; conducting follow-up investigations to obtain supplemental evidence in cases being considered for litigation; assisting attorneys in settlement discussions in an attempt to obtain conciliation agreements that are mutually satisfactory and consistent with agency policy and authority; and participating in pretrial and trial proceedings.

Qualifications and Salary Levels

GS-5: Completion of a four-year course of study leading to a bachelor's degree; or three years of general experience, one year of which was equivalent to GS-4. **GS-7:** One full year of graduate education, or superior academic achievement during undergraduate studies, or one year of specialized experience equivalent to GS-5. **GS-9:** A master's degree, or two years of graduate education, or one year of specialized experience equivalent to GS-7. **GS-11:** A Ph.D. or equivalent doctoral degree, or three years of graduate education, or one year of specialized experience equivalent to GS-9. **GS-12:** One year of specialized experience equivalent to GS-11. **GS-13:** One year of specialized experience equivalent to GS-12. Applicants can use equivalent combinations of specialized experience and education to meet total experience requirements.

Training

The FEC-OGC actively recruits candidates to fill investigator positions that are fully trained and experienced in white-collar investigations. Initial and in-service training for FEC-OGC investigators includes an orientation that covers the mission, policies, procedures, and rules of the agency, and periodic instruction related to specific responsibilities of the position. This training could include instruction in areas such as money-laundering investigation, campaign finance law, interviewing techniques, legal updates, and report writing.

Contact: Office of General Counsel; Federal Election Commission; 999 E St. NW; Washington, DC 20463; phone: (202) 694-1100 or (800) 424-9530; Internet: www.fec.gov/; e-mail: personnel@fec.gov

Investigator (GS-1810)
United States Attorney's Office, U.S. Department of Justice

United States attorneys serve as the nation's principal litigators under the direction of the Attorney General, with responsibility for prosecuting criminal cases brought by the federal government, prosecuting and defending civil cases in which the United States is a party, and collecting debts owed the federal government that are administratively uncollectible. United States Attorney's offices employ investigators to perform investigative and support functions pertaining to Affirmative Civil Enforcement (ACE) litigation, healthcare fraud, and other matters. Investigations generally focus on fraud, waste, and abuse in government programs and operations, including Medicare and Medicaid fraud, procurement fraud relating to Defense Department contracts, controlled substance violations, financial institution fraud, and other violations. Investigations tend to be highly complex and sensitive in nature, often relating to civil and criminal violations committed by prominent individuals and corporations.

The primary responsibilities of these investigators include determining applicable regulatory and statutory laws; interviewing witnesses; planning and conducting surveillance of suspects; reviewing various business and financial records; devising methods for obtaining, preserving, and presenting evidence; using laboratories and other forensic services to identify handwriting, fingerprints, questioned documents and substances, sound and video recordings, and other evidence; coordinating investigative activities with law enforcement officers, auditors, and legal staff from federal, state, and local agencies; and preparing interim and final reports on the progress of investigations.

Qualifications and Salary Levels

GS-9: A master's degree, or two years of graduate education, or one year of specialized experience equivalent to GS-7. **GS-11:** A Ph.D. or equivalent doctoral degree, or three years of graduate education, or one year of specialized experience equivalent to GS-9. **GS-12:** One year of specialized experience equivalent to GS-11. **GS-13:** One year of specialized experience equivalent to GS-12. Qualifying education can be substituted for experience, and vice versa. The application process includes a drug screening test, background investigation, credit check, and security clearance determination.

Training

United States Attorney's Office investigators attend periodic in-service training courses that are presented by Justice Department staff relating to subjects such as ACE litigation, healthcare fraud issues, procurement and program fraud, coordinating civil and criminal intake proceedings, investigative resources, task force operations, and other topics. Additional training opportunities include courses, seminars, and distance-learning programs presented by a variety of training providers.

Contact: Direct inquiries to the United States Attorney's Office where employment is sought, or to Executive Office for United States Attorneys; U.S. Department of Justice; 950 Pennsylvania Ave. NW; Washington, DC 20530; phone: (202) 616-6900; Internet: www.usdoj.gov/usao/eousa/.

Investigator (GS-1810)
Investigation and Prosecution Division, U.S. Office of Special Counsel

The United States Office of Special Counsel (OSC) is an independent federal investigative and prosecutorial agency whose enforcement authority includes investigating alleged prohibited personnel practices and Hatch Act violations in the federal government, as well as litigating cases arising out of investigations before the U.S. Merit Systems Protection Board. OSC investigations conducted by the Investigation and Prosecution Division typically focus on personnel practices and other activities prohibited by civil service law, rule, or regulation, including provisions of the Civil Service Reform Act; violations of Hatch Act provisions relating to prohibited political activity by federal, state, and local government employees; violations of the Whistleblower Protection Act; and certain cases involving the denial of federal employment or re-employment rights to veterans and military reservists seeking to return to the federal workplace following active duty with the armed services.

OSC investigators are responsible for investigative planning and coordinating with OSC attorneys; conducting interviews of witnesses and subjects of investigation; obtaining evidence by following up with pertinent leads; obtaining and reviewing documents and official records; preparing comprehensive summaries, memoranda, and reports of investigation; making recommendations concerning prosecution or resolution of matters through other means; and handling settlement negotiations. OSC investigators are based in the headquarters office in Washington, DC, as well as field offices located in Dallas, Detroit, and San Francisco.

Qualifications and Salary Levels

GS-9: A master's degree, or two years of graduate education, or one year of specialized experience equivalent to GS-7. **GS-11:** A Ph.D. or equivalent doctoral degree, or three years of graduate education, or one year of specialized experience equivalent to GS-9. **GS-12:** One year of specialized experience equivalent to GS-11. **GS-13:** One year of specialized experience equivalent to GS-12. Experience and education can be combined to meet total experience requirements. Candidates must pass a background investigation.

Training

OSC Investigators receive on-the-job and periodic in-service training that focuses on personnel matters, agency adverse action procedures, personnel action requirements, position classifications, personnel investigations, interviewing techniques, legal updates, employee information programs, prohibited personnel practices, alternative dispute resolution, Equal Employment Opportunity provisions, and other relevant topics. Training is presented by Investigation and Prosecution Division staff, other OSC personnel, the Federal Law Enforcement training Center, and representatives of other government agencies and training providers.

Contact: Investigation and Prosecution Division; U.S. Office of Special Counsel; 1730 M St. NW—Ste. 218; Washington, DC 20036; phone: (202) 254-3600; Internet: www.osc.gov/

Labor Investigator (GS-1801)
Office of Labor-Management Standards, Employment Standards Administration, U.S. Department of Labor

The Office of Labor-Management Standards (OLMS) is responsible for administering and enforcing provisions of the Labor-Management Reporting and Disclosure Act of 1959 (LMRDA) to ensure basic standards of democracy and fiscal responsibility in labor organizations representing employees in private industry and the U.S. Postal Service. The Office also administers provisions of the Civil Service Reform Act of 1978 and the Foreign Service Act of 1980 concerned with standards of conduct for federal employee organizations.

OLMS labor investigators are responsible for conducting investigations and audits relating to improper or corrupt practices by labor unions and their officers and representatives, including violations of LMRDA provisions and related statutes. In order to protect and safeguard union funds and assets, criminal investigations often focus on allegations of embezzlement and other financial fraud by union officers or employees. Civil investigations include violations of the LMRDA that could have affected the outcome of labor union officer elections.

The primary duties of OLMS labor investigators include reviewing financial reports, union constitutions, and other documents; examining union operations and financial practices; meeting with union officials and their attorneys to observe and discuss union practices and techniques; negotiating for voluntary compliance with LMRDA provisions; supervising union elections; preparing investigative reports; referring investigative findings to the United States Attorney for possible criminal prosecution; and testifying as a witness before grand juries and in criminal and civil trials.

Qualifications and Salary Levels

GS-5: Completion of a four-year course of study leading to a bachelor's degree; or three years of general experience, one year of which was equivalent to GS-4. **GS-7:** One full year of graduate education, or superior academic achievement during undergraduate studies, or one year of specialized experience equivalent to GS-5. **GS-9:** A master's degree, or two years of graduate education, or one year of specialized experience equivalent to GS-7. **GS-11:** A Ph.D. or equivalent doctoral degree, or three years of graduate education, or one year of specialized experience equivalent to GS-9. **GS-12:** One year of specialized experience equivalent to GS-11. **GS-13:**

One year of specialized experience equivalent to GS-12. Qualifying education can be substituted for experience, and vice versa. Candidates must successfully complete a background investigation and qualify for a security clearance.

Training

Initial and in-service training for OLMS labor investigators includes an orientation to the mission, policies, procedures, and rules of the agency, as well as courses provided by Labor Department staff and outside organizations that focus on the investigation of union officer elections, white-collar fraud, embezzlement, financial disclosure reports, compliance auditing techniques, provisions of the LMRDA, financial investigations, legal issues and updates, interviewing techniques, report writing, and other subjects.

Contact: Office of Labor-Management Standards; Employment Standards Administration; U.S. Department of Labor; 200 Constitution Ave. NW; Washington, DC 20210; phone: (202) 693-0123; Internet: www.dol.gov/esa/olms_org.htm; e-mail: olms-public@dol.gov

Marine Accident Investigator (GS-1801)
Office of Marine Safety, National Transportation Safety Board

Marine accident investigators of the National Transportation Safety Board (NTSB) are responsible for organizing, managing, and coordinating the investigation of major marine accidents, and also for developing and presenting reports with safety recommendations for adoption by the NTSB. These investigations are conducted to determine the facts, conditions, circumstances, and causes of marine accidents, and the results are used to ascertain measures to prevent similar accidents or incidents in the future.

Among accidents investigated are those involving the loss of six or more lives, the loss of vessels over 100 gross tons, or where damage exceeds $500,000; public and nonpublic vessel collisions with fatalities or at least $75,000 damage; small passenger vessels carrying more than six passengers; large passenger vessels, such as ocean cruise ships, excursion vessels, and ferries; tank ships and tank barges, commercial fishing vessels, oceangoing vessels, and inland tow vessels; and those involving serious hazardous material threats to life, property, or the environment. Results of these investigations serve as the basis for specific recommendations for corrective action.

NTSB marine accident investigators examine safety issues relating to the adequacy of shipboard communications; design, installation, and testing of navigational and integrated bridge systems; bridge resource management; adequacy of emergency preparedness and evacuation plans; adequacy of fire prevention, detection, and control measures; boating safety standards; vessel towing procedures; port safety; human fatigue and performance; drug and alcohol use by marine personnel; and marine personnel training standards, among other issues. NTSB marine accident investigators are required to remain on call and to respond to accident sites outside of normal work hours.

Qualifications and Salary Levels

GS-9: A master's degree, or two years of graduate education, or one year of specialized experience equivalent to GS-7. **GS-11:** A Ph.D. or equivalent doctoral degree, or three years of graduate education, or one year of specialized experience equivalent to GS-9. **GS-12:** One year of specialized experience equivalent to GS-11. **GS-13:** One year of specialized experience equivalent to GS-12. **GS-14:** One year of specialized experience equivalent to GS-13. Candidates must possess knowledge and experience relating to areas such as marine engineering, steam or diesel propulsion plants, human performance, or other aspects of marine operations or accident investigation. Tentative appointees must pass a personal interview, background investigation, and drug screening test.

Training

NTSB marine accident investigators attend training programs throughout their careers that are presented at the NTSB Academy in Ashburn, Virginia. Additional training is offered by organizations such as the United States Coast Guard, Maritime Institute of Technology and Graduate Studies, United States Merchant Marine Academy, Transportation Safety Institute, RTM Simulation Training and Research Center, National Fire Academy, and the FBI. Some of the training topics include marine accident investigation, accident photography, evidence preservation, arson investigation, interviewing techniques, tanker safety, bridge resource management, radar plotting, crude oil washing, public speaking, and many other subjects.

Contact: Office of Marine Safety; National Transportation Safety Board; 490 L'Enfant Plaza SW; Washington, DC 20594; phone: (202) 314-6000; Internet: www.ntsb.gov/

Market Surveillance Specialist
Division of Enforcement, U.S. Securities and Exchange Commission

The U.S. Securities and Exchange Commission (SEC) administers and enforces federal securities laws and SEC regulations to provide protection for investors and to ensure that securities markets are fair and honest. Market surveillance specialists of the SEC Division of Enforcement, Office of Market Surveillance, conduct investigations into possible violations of federal securities laws, and prosecute the Commission's civil suits in the federal courts as well as its administrative proceedings.

Tasks performed by these personnel include investigative planning and theory development; analyzing market trading data, brokerage records, and formal filings; selecting actively traded stocks to review for possible fraudulent or manipulative activity; reviewing exemptive applications, orders, and no-action requests; interviewing witnesses; interrogating suspects; taking testimony or obtaining written statements; preparing investigative reports, including detailed charts and schedules; and making recommendations on further courses of action to follow. SEC market surveillance specialists also provide technical advice to staff on matters such as methods and practices involved in entering and executing orders for securities, the conduct of trading specialists and floor traders, activities of exchange members, and related technical and financial matters. Investigations often result in civil money penalties, the disgorgement of illegal profits, and court actions barring or suspending individuals from acting as corporate officers or directors.

Qualifications and Salary Levels

SEC market surveillance specialists are appointed through excepted service hiring processes. The qualifications and salaries of these investigators are similar to general and compliance investigator positions at the GS-9, GS-11, GS-12, and GS-13 levels with other federal agencies. The SEC seeks candidates with experience that demonstrates the ability to interpret financial data; knowledge of the rules and regulations of the national securities exchanges and the National Association of Securities Dealers; knowledge of securities industry operations, trading, underwriting, record-keeping, and compliance practices; and an understanding of SEC enforcement processes. Education can be substituted for experience if it demonstrates the knowledge, skills, and abilities necessary to perform the job tasks of SEC market surveillance specialists.

Training

The SEC actively recruits candidates to fill market surveillance specialist positions who are fully trained and experienced in securities industry processes and functions. Initial training includes an in-house orientation that covers the mission, policies, procedures, and rules of the agency. Market surveillance specialists also can attend seminars that cover updates of federal securities laws and regulations, market trading dynamics, financial investigations, other investigative techniques, fraud schemes, and other subjects pertaining to specific responsibilities.

Contact: Office of Market Surveillance; Division of Enforcement; U.S. Securities and Exchange Commission; 100 F St. NE; Washington, DC 20549; phone: (202) 551-4120; Internet: www.sec.gov/divisions/enforce.shtml; e-mail: enforcement@sec.gov

Pension Investigator (GS-1801)
Employee Benefits Security Administration, U.S. Department of Labor

As the national guardian of a vast private retirement and welfare benefit system, the Employee Benefits Security Administration (EBSA)—formerly known as the Pension and Welfare Benefits Administration—is charged with assuring responsible management of about 700,000 pension plans and six million private health and welfare plans in the United States. Working within the Office of Enforcement, EBSA pension investigators conduct civil and criminal investigations involving fiduciary breaches, benefits disputes, participants' rights, and reporting and disclosure provisions of Title I of the Employee Retirement Income Security Act of 1974 (ERISA).

Examples of responsibilities carried out by these personnel include identifying issues under investigation; case planning; examining records involving financing and investment activity relating to employee benefits plans; locating pension and welfare plan participants and beneficiaries; conducting interviews; negotiating compliance with plan administrators, trustees, and attorneys; assembling and identifying exhibits for investigative reports, civil litigation, and criminal prosecutions; preparing investigative reports; making recommendations as to appropriate civil or criminal action; and conducting technical assistance sessions with plan administrators, employer and employee organizations, labor organizations, colleges and universities, and civic groups to promote understanding of ERISA.

The Office of Enforcement is composed of the Division of Field Operations, which coordinates national civil enforcement policy with EBSA field offices and government agencies; the Division of Enforcement Support, which oversees national targeting efforts and provides technical and administrative assistance to EBSA field offices; and the Deputy Director for Criminal Enforcement, who coordinates national criminal enforcement policy with EBSA field offices and with other government departments and agencies, such as the U.S. Department of Justice.

Qualifications and Salary Levels

GS-7: One full year of graduate education, or superior academic achievement during undergraduate studies, or one year of specialized experience equivalent to GS-5. **GS-9:** A master's degree, or two years of graduate education, or one year of specialized experience equivalent to GS-7. **GS-11:** A Ph.D. or equivalent doctoral degree, or three years of graduate education, or one year of specialized experience equivalent to GS-9. **GS-12:** One year of specialized experience equivalent to GS-11. **GS-13:** One year of specialized experience equivalent to GS-12. Applicants can use equivalent combinations of specialized experience and education to meet total experience requirements.

Training

Initial training for pension investigators consists of a three-week course presented by EBSA staff that focuses on ERISA provisions, Labor Department regulations, criminal laws concerning employee benefit plans, and investigative techniques. This training is followed by a two-week course pertaining to the operations of financial institutions; a two-week criminal enforcement course that covers criminal statutes and regulations concerning pension and health plans; and a two-week program that focuses on accounting methods. In-service training includes courses relating to investigations in an automated environment, forensic accounting, pension and welfare benefit program regulations, advanced interviewing techniques, white-collar crime, financial investigations, collection and preservation of evidence, and other subjects.

Contact: Office of Enforcement; Employee Benefits Security Administration; U.S. Department of Labor; 200 Constitution Ave. NW; Washington, DC 20210; phone: (202) 693-8440; Internet: www.dol.gov/ebsa/

Pipeline Accident Investigator (GS-1801)
Office of Railroad, Pipeline, and Hazardous Materials Safety, National Transportation Safety Board

National Transportation Safety Board (NTSB) pipeline accident investigators are responsible for a variety of tasks associated with the investigation of pipeline transportation accidents in the United States. These personnel are responsible for investigating accidents that involve the release of substances such as natural gas, propane, crude petroleum and petroleum products, or other highly volatile liquids; significant damage to the environment; fatalities or severe personal injuries; or extensive property damage.

NTSB pipeline accident investigators also conduct and review special pipeline transportation safety studies and investigations; evaluate pipeline transportation safety programs; exchange information with other organizations concerned with pipeline transportation safety; and report their conclusions and findings in writing to the NTSB and other organizations. The results of these investigations serve as the basis for specific recommendations for corrective action. Among the safety issues examined are the inspection and testing of pipelines; control of pipeline corrosion damage; vulnerability to premature failure of plastic piping used to transport natural gas; adequacy of federal and industry standards on pipeline design; damage to pipelines caused by excavation or construction activities; preparedness of pipeline operators to respond to threats to their pipelines and to minimize the potential for product releases; adequacy of gas company employee training programs; and safety performance of pipeline companies. Pipeline accident investigations sometimes involve work at unusual hours and for long periods of time in remote, rugged, and hostile settings. In addition, investigators can be exposed to hazardous materials and bloodborne pathogens.

Qualifications and Salary Levels

GS-9: A master's degree, or two years of graduate education, or one year of specialized experience equivalent to GS-7. **GS-11:** A Ph.D. or equivalent doctoral degree, or three years of graduate education, or one year of specialized experience equivalent to GS-9. **GS-12:** One year of specialized experience equivalent to GS-11. **GS-13:** One year of specialized experience equivalent to GS-12. **GS-14:** One year of specialized experience equivalent to GS-13. Candidates must possess technical writing skills; technical experience concerned with pipeline distribution and transmission; and knowledge of liquid pipeline systems. Tentative appointees must pass a personal interview, background investigation, and drug screening test.

Training

Initial and in-service training for pipeline accident investigators includes courses that focus on the inspection and safety evaluation of gas and liquid pipeline systems, risk assessment and management, odor and leak detection, gas pressure regulation, joining of pipeline materials, metallurgy and plastics, emergency response and preparedness, fault tree analysis, interviewing techniques, and other subjects. Training is presented by NTSB staff and organizations such as the Transportation Safety Institute and the Federal Law Enforcement Training Center, as well as pipeline system operators, utility companies, and private consultants.

Contact: Office of Railroad, Pipeline, and Hazardous Materials Safety; National Transportation Safety Board; 490 L'Enfant Plaza SW; Washington, DC 20594; phone: (202) 314-6000; Internet: www.ntsb.gov/

Product Safety Investigator (GS-1801)
Directorate for Field Operations, U.S. Consumer Product Safety Commission

The United States Consumer Product Safety Commission (CPSC) is an independent federal agency responsible for administering laws to protect the public against unreasonable risks of injury from consumer products, including the Consumer Product Safety Act, Flammable Fabrics Act, Federal Hazardous Substances Act, Labeling of Hazardous Art Materials Act, Child Safety Protection Act, Poison Prevention Packaging Act, and Refrigerator Safety Act. To ensure compliance with

CPSC regulations, laws, and product standards, CPSC product safety investigators conduct inspections of manufacturers, distributors, wholesalers, and retailers that produce, assemble, distribute, and sell consumer products.

Primary responsibilities include examining copies of consumer complaints; conducting site visits of production plants, company offices, distribution centers, and other facilities; examining production methods, product specifications, firm testing methods, quality control procedures, product certification, and labeling operations; and inspecting plant assembly processes and records. Other tasks include field testing and evaluating products to determine compliance with applicable standards; identifying potential, substantial, and imminent product hazards; interviewing consumers, police and fire officials, medical examiners, and witnesses; obtaining affidavits and documents; preparing written reports reflecting significant observations and describing evidence collected; and advising business firms of their responsibilities under CPSC regulations and laws. These personnel also respond to media inquiries, participate in media interviews, maintain contact with Congressional offices, and conduct information and education campaigns that inform the public and promote consumer safety.

Qualifications and Salary Levels

GS-7: One full year of graduate education, or superior academic achievement during undergraduate studies, or one year of specialized experience equivalent to GS-5. **GS-9:** A master's degree, or two years of graduate education, or one year of specialized experience equivalent to GS-7. **GS-11:** A Ph.D. or equivalent doctoral degree, or three years of graduate education, or one year of specialized experience equivalent to GS-9. **GS-12:** One year of specialized experience equivalent to GS-11. Experience and education can be combined to meet total experience requirements. Candidates must be capable of moderate physical exertion, including lifting and carrying objects up to 44 pounds, climbing ladders, crawling, kneeling, and bending.

Training

CPSC Investigators attend a one-week New Investigator Training Course conducted by Commission staff, which includes instruction pertaining to CPSC operations; general investigative techniques; the inspection and investigation of manufacturers, distributors, wholesalers, and retailers; product quality control; collection of product samples and evidence; investigation of injuries and deaths; interviewing techniques; and CPSC laboratory operations. In-service training includes courses relating to matters such as complaint processing; infant suffocation; fire investigations; legal issues and updates; product testing and quality control; report writing; and computer hardware, software, and electronic mail.

Contact: Office of Human Resources Management; Consumer Product Safety Commission; 4330 East West Hwy.—Room 523; Bethesda, MD 20814; phone: (301) 504-7925; Internet: www.cpsc.gov/; e-mail: recruitapps@cpsc.gov

Railroad Accident Investigator (GS-2121),
Office of Railroad, Pipeline, and Hazardous Materials Safety; National Transportation Safety Board

Railroad accident investigators of the National Transportation Safety Board (NTSB) are responsible for investigating accidents involving passenger, freight, rail transit, and commuter trains throughout the United States, and also for promoting railroad safety and eliminating safety hazards, improving investigative methods, and preventing railroad accidents.

Tasks performed by these personnel include examining train wreckage, track, and signals for evidence of structural failure, tampering, or equipment malfunction; reconstructing components involved in accidents; conducting or observing equipment tests or crash simulations; examining train orders, operating rules, and other records that provide information about causes of accidents; arranging for metallurgical or chemical analyses of wreckage; interviewing witnesses; applying knowledge of the interrelationships between railroad signals and train control, railroad track, locomotive power and equipment, railroad operating practices, and hazardous materials; and preparing written reports including findings as to the probable causes of accidents. The results of investigations also serve as the basis for specific recommendations for corrective action. Major safety issues examined by NTSB railroad accident investigators include the adequacy of medical standards and examinations for locomotive engineers, railroad dispatching operations, train control systems, crash-worthiness of locomotives and components, inspection and maintenance of equipment, and emergency response procedures, among others.

Qualifications and Salary Levels

GS-9: A master's degree, or two years of graduate education, or one year of specialized experience equivalent to GS-7. **GS-11:** A Ph.D. or equivalent doctoral degree, or three years of graduate education, or one year of specialized experience equivalent to GS-9. **GS-12:** One year of specialized experience equivalent to GS-11. **GS-13:** One year of specialized experience equivalent to GS-12. **GS-14:** One year of specialized experience equivalent to GS-13.

Candidates must have experience that demonstrated knowledge of the railroad industry, including economic and operating considerations and equipment; general safety and health principles and practices applicable to the industry; railroad accident investigation techniques; technical aspects concerned with railroad mechanical or operating systems; skill in written and oral communication, and the ability to write technical reports; and proficiency in the use of personal computers. Tentative appointees must pass a personal interview, background investigation, and drug screening test.

Training

Initial and in-service training for railroad accident investigators includes a variety of courses that are presented by the NTSB and outside organizations such as railroad companies, locomotive manufacturers, and equipment suppliers. Training focuses on various accident reconstruction and investigative techniques, new technology, track structures and engineering, photography techniques, accident report writing, NTSB policies and procedures, and other subjects.

Contact: Office of Railroad, Pipeline, and Hazardous Materials Safety; National Transportation Safety Board; 490 L'Enfant Plaza SW; Washington, DC 20594; phone: (202) 314-6000; Internet: www.ntsb.gov/

Revenue Officer (GS-1169)
Internal Revenue Service Collection Division, U.S. Department of the Treasury

Revenue Officers of the Internal Revenue Service (IRS) are responsible for collecting delinquent tax accounts and securing delinquent tax returns in order to protect the interests of the taxpaying public by obtaining maximum compliance with U.S. tax laws. Collecting taxpayer delinquent accounts requires revenue officers to review the accounts, compute the amount of tax and interest owed, and determine which penalties should be assessed.

Examples of responsibilities carried out by these personnel include planning and conducting investigations and research; tracing the whereabouts of delinquent taxpayers; following leads and contacting third parties for information; interviewing taxpayers, accountants, attorneys, and witnesses; obtaining and analyzing financial statements and records; issuing summonses, liens, levies, seizures, and referrals that legally require taxpayers to present various books and records; placing on public record evidence of tax liabilities; attaching bank accounts and payroll checks; seizing and selling private property; determining the accuracy of assessed liabilities, and adjusting or abating erroneous liabilities; testifying in court; and helping taxpayers to understand their tax obligations. When voluntary payment of the tax is not made, revenue officers can impose penalties or invoke administrative and judicial remedies. Revenue officers also can recommend accepting an offer in compromise or arrange for installment payments. When efforts to reach payment agreements fail, revenue officers can levy salaries or wages, bank accounts, and other assets; file a nominee lien or an administrative transfer of assessment; or seize and sell taxpayers' property.

Revenue officers are assigned to field offices located in seven regions throughout the country. Much of their field work is conducted outside of office settings in meetings with taxpayers in varied environments.

Qualifications and Salary Levels

GS-5: Completion of a four-year course of study leading to a bachelor's degree; or three years of general experience, one year of which was equivalent to GS-4. **GS-7:** One full year of graduate education, or superior academic achievement during undergraduate studies, or one year of specialized experience equivalent to GS-5. **GS-9:** A master's degree, or two years of graduate education, or one year of specialized experience equivalent to GS-7. **GS-11:** A Ph.D. or equivalent doctoral degree, or three years of graduate education, or one year of specialized experience equivalent to GS-9. **GS-12:** One year of specialized experience equivalent to GS-11. Equivalent combinations of education and experience can be used to meet minimum experience requirements. Appointment is contingent upon a satisfactory background investigation, including a tax audit.

Training

Initial training for IRS revenue officers includes classroom and on-the-job training in areas such as business law, tax law, financial statement analysis, investigative techniques, and collection enforcement procedures. During the on-the-job training phase, senior IRS revenue officers assist new officers with the application of skills and techniques learned in the classroom with actual work assignments. Training is designed to prepare new officers as rapidly as possible for independent performance and the responsibilities of the position. In-service training also is available to enhance advancement to higher-level positions.

Contact: Internal Revenue Service; U.S. Department of the Treasury; 1111 Constitution Ave. NW; Washington, DC 20224; phone: (202) 622-5000; Internet: www.irs.treas.gov/

Safety Investigator (GS-2123)
Federal Motor Carrier Safety Administration, U.S. Department of Transportation

The Federal Motor Carrier Safety Administration (FMCSA) was established within the U.S. Department of Transportation in an effort to reduce crashes, injuries, and fatalities involving large trucks and buses. In furtherance of this mission, FMCSA safety investigators conduct investigations and inspections to promote and enforce compliance with federal motor carrier safety and hazardous materials laws and regulations to ensure the safe operation of commercial vehicles and motor carriers.

Some examples of responsibilities carried out by these personnel include planning and conducting unannounced roadside inspections of interstate commercial motor vehicle and driver documentation to determine carrier or driver compliance with government regulations; conducting investigations into alleged violations either as follow-up to inspections or in response to complaints; conducting safety, security, and hazardous materials investigations of motor carrier and shipper operations; preparing written investigative reports; and maintaining liaison with federal, state, and local law enforcement agencies. Additional tasks performed by FMCSA safety investigators include analyzing compliance review, enforcement, and inspection results; accident and incident reports; complaints; and other information to identify safety and compliance problems or trends among motor carriers and shippers. These personnel also provide technical assistance and information on federal programs, motor carrier safety, hazardous materials, transportation safety, and other topics to motor carrier officials and employees, industry representatives, state and local law enforcement and emergency response personnel, and others interested in highway safety.

Qualifications and Salary Levels

GS-7: One full year of graduate education, or superior academic achievement during undergraduate studies, or one year of specialized experience equivalent to GS-5. **GS-9:** A master's degree, or two years of graduate education, or one year of specialized experience equivalent to GS-7. **GS-11:** A Ph.D. or equivalent doctoral degree, or three years of graduate education, or one year of specialized experience equivalent to GS-9. **GS-12:** One year of specialized experience equivalent to GS-11. Experience and education can be combined to meet total experience requirements. Applicants must successfully complete a background investigation, pass a drug test, and submit a statement of financial interests prior to appointment.

Training

Initial training includes a nine-week FMCSA Safety Investigator Academy training program at the FMCSA National Training Center in Arlington, Virginia. The Academy training program and in-service courses are concerned with topics such as the FMCSA Field Operations Training Manual; investigative techniques; motor carrier laws and regulations; enforcement and compliance procedures; highway safety; motor carrier roadside inspections; logbooks, medical certificates, commercial driver's licenses, shipping documents, and other paperwork; compliance reviews; crash profiles; crash statistics; traffic enforcement; cargo tanks and other bulk packaging; explosives, radioactive materials, and other hazardous cargo; motor carrier safety management systems; communication with motor carrier associations, shippers, and insurers; and liaison with law enforcement and other government agencies. Safety investigators also can attend commercial vehicle drug interdiction training that is presented by FMCSA, the Drug Enforcement Administration, and the El Paso Intelligence Center. This training includes instruction concerning interstate transportation of illegal drugs, bulk drug movement indicators, detection methods, drug trafficking trends, interviewing techniques, and related subjects.

Contact: Federal Motor Carrier Safety Administration; U.S. Department of Transportation; 400 Seventh St. SW; Washington, DC 20590; phone: (202) 366-2519; Internet: www.fmcsa.dot.gov/

Chapter 11

Compliance Inspectors and Specialists

"Adam was but human—this explains it all. He did not want the apple for the apple's sake; he wanted it only because it was forbidden."

—Mark Twain

Careers that involve compliance inspection and examination are concerned with the enforcement of laws, regulations, and standards that are geared toward particular industries, organizations, or activities regulated by the federal government. These careers are highly specialized and involve tasks such as preventing railroad accidents, obtaining compliance with wage and hour laws, inspecting underground and surface mining operations, detecting and controlling plant pests, inspecting establishments that produce alcohol and tobacco products, ensuring compliance with wildlife laws and treaties, determining tariff classifications and the admissibility of merchandise, enforcing marine safety laws and regulations, and carrying out deportation proceedings.

The work of compliance inspectors and specialists requires a thorough knowledge of inspection and investigation techniques, and of the standards, laws, and regulations enforced. Inspectors and specialists must also have the ability to apply varied techniques to gain compliance, including investigation, analysis, negotiation, conciliation, education, persuasion, and litigation. In addition, a thorough understanding of business organization, recordkeeping systems, and practices related to the laws and regulations administered are crucial.

Agriculture Specialist (GS-0401)
United States Customs and Border Protection, U.S. Department of Homeland Security

U.S. Customs and Border Protection (CBP) agriculture specialists play a critical role in homeland security and the protection of America's food supply and agricultural resources by examining and determining the admissibility of agriculture commodities into the United States. In carrying out CBP's mission to prevent agroterrorism and bioterrorism, CBP agriculture specialists stationed at U.S. ports of entry—including land borders, airports, seaports, and pre-clearance stations—apply border inspections, analysis, and intelligence to prevent the introduction of harmful pests, diseases, and

321

pathogens that could cause serious damage to America's crops, livestock, pets, and the environment.

Specific tasks carried out by CBP agriculture specialists include collecting and analyzing information relating to the importation of agricultural goods; identifying high-risk targets; conducting visual and physical inspections of cargo, conveyances, and passenger baggage entering the United States; examining shipping manifests and other documents; treating, disinfecting, and decontaminating prohibited commodities, conveyances, contaminants, or agricultural materials; and enforcing various laws and agency regulations.

Qualifications and Salary Levels

GS-5: Completion of a four-year course of study leading to a bachelor's degree in biological sciences, agriculture, natural resource management, chemistry, or a closely related field such as botany or entomology; or a combination of experience and education that includes 24 semester hours in the disciplines listed above and job experience in areas such as pest control, pesticide application, inspecting aircraft or passengers, x-ray or environmental monitoring, or farm management related to disease control, insect detection and eradication, or pest control. **GS-7:** All requirements for GS-5, plus either superior academic achievement during undergraduate studies or one year of graduate education in a field of study discussed under GS-5, or one full year of specialized experience equivalent to GS-5. Examples of qualifying experience include inspecting vessels, vehicles, aircraft, and baggage for the presence of restricted plant material, pests, or diseases; and reviewing or analyzing passenger or commodity documents to assess the agricultural risk of their entry into the United States. **GS-9:** All requirements for GS-5, plus either a master's degree or two years of graduate education in a field of study discussed under GS-5, or one year of specialized experience equivalent to GS-7. **GS-11:** All requirements for GS-5, plus either a Ph.D. or equivalent doctoral degree, or three years of graduate education in a field of study discussed under GS-5, or one year of specialized experience equivalent to GS-9. **GS-12:** One year of specialized experience equivalent to GS-11. **GS-13:** One year of specialized experience equivalent to GS-12. CBP agriculture specialist candidates must successfully complete a background investigation and pass a drug test prior to appointment.

Training

Newly appointed CBP agriculture specialists complete "pre-academy" orientation training at their respective duty stations, which covers the missions of the Department of Homeland Security, CBP, U.S. Citizenship and Immigration Services, and U.S. Immigration and Customs Enforcement. Initial basic training consists of a nine-week agriculture specialist training program at the U.S. Department of Agriculture Professional Development Center in Frederick, Maryland. This course includes instruction concerning laws and regulations, pest identification, pesticide certification, detection of agroterrorism and bioterrorism, cargo and passenger processing, detection of fraudulent documents, defensive driving, stress and lifestyle management, integrity, professionalism, and other topics. Ongoing in-service training focuses on subjects such as contraband concealment methods, identifying high-risk shipments, document analysis, interviewing techniques, terrorism awareness, hazardous materials, officer safety, animal diseases, and report writing.

Contact: United States Customs and Border Protection; U.S. Department of Homeland Security; 1300 Pennsylvania Ave. NW; Washington, DC 20229; phone: (202) 344-1250; Internet: www.cbp.gov/

Commercial Fishing Vessel Examiner
(GS-1801) United States Coast Guard, U.S. Department of Homeland Security

Commercial fishing vessel examiners of the United States Coast Guard (USCG), U.S. Department of Homeland Security, are responsible for providing technical expertise, advanced training, and project leadership in the enforcement of marine safety, pollution prevention, and various vessel-occupant laws, regulations, treaties, and international conventions. To carry out their mission, these personnel conduct technical inspections of fishing vessels in accordance with the USCG commercial fishing vessel safety program.

Their primary responsibilities include determining that vessels have proper documentation and certification; examining vessel navigation, communication, alarm, lifesaving, and pollution prevention systems, and machinery to ensure proper operation and compliance with standards and regulations; inspecting vessel hulls, internal structural members, fittings, tanks, holding areas, and structural fire protection systems to ensure that they are sound; conducting training for vessel owners and others to explain the intent and interpretation of regulations; drafting public affairs announcements; writing analytical reports; and working with commercial fishing industry personnel to ensure that vessels are operated safely, but without undue negative impact on the fishing community.

Qualifications and Salary Levels

GS-7: One full year of graduate education, or superior academic achievement during undergraduate studies, or one year of specialized experience equivalent to GS-5. **GS-9:** A master's degree or two years of graduate education, or one year of specialized experience equivalent to GS-7. **GS-11:** A Ph.D. or equivalent doctoral degree, or three years of graduate education, or one year of specialized experience equivalent to GS-9. **GS-12:** One year of specialized experience equivalent to GS-11. Qualifying education can be substituted for experience, and vice versa. The application process includes a drug screening test and background investigation.

Training

Initial and in-service training for USCG commercial fishing vessel examiners includes courses in subjects such as vessel stability, construction, and structural systems; maritime laws and regulations; safety equipment; visual distress signals; vessel fire-fighting and fuel systems; wooden boat inspections; Electronic Position Indicating Radio Beacons; vessel documentation and registration; enforcement operations; and other topics. Instruction is presented by USCG staff and representatives of other agencies and organizations.

Contact: United States Coast Guard; 2100 Second St. SW; Washington, DC 20593; Phone: (202) 267-1587; Internet: www.uscg.mil/

Deportation Officer (GS-1801)
United States Immigration and Customs Enforcement, U.S. Department of Homeland Security

United States Immigration and Customs Enforcement (ICE) deportation officers are involved in formal processes for the deportation of certain criminal and noncriminal aliens found in violation of federal laws pertaining to immigration and nationality matters. The mission of ICE deportation officers is to provide for the control and removal of persons who have been ordered deported or are otherwise required to depart from the United States.

Deportation officers must closely monitor deportation proceedings from initiation to conclusion; assist ICE personnel and assistant United States attorneys with case processing; conduct legal research to support decisions on deportation and exclusion cases; maintain close liaison with foreign consulates and embassies to facilitate the timely issuance of passports and travel documents required for deportation; conduct investigations and surveillance; locate and apprehend aliens who have absconded, and provide an armed escort where necessary; prepare written investigative reports; and respond to congressional inquiries. ICE deportation officers are authorized to carry firearms.

This position is covered under special retirement provisions for law enforcement officers.

Qualifications and Salary

GS-5: Completion of a four-year course of study leading to a bachelor's degree; or three years of general experience, one year of which was equivalent to GS-4. **GS-7:** One full year of graduate-level education, or superior academic achievement during undergraduate studies, or one year of specialized experience equivalent to GS-5. **GS-9:** A master's degree, or two years of graduate-level education, or one year of specialized experience equivalent to GS-7. **GS-11:** A Ph.D. or equivalent doctoral degree, or three years of graduate-level education, or one year of specialized experience equivalent to GS-9. **GS-12:** One year of specialized experience equivalent to GS-11. Equivalent combinations of education and experience can be used to meet minimum experience requirements. Tentative appointees must qualify for a security clearance and pass a background investigation, drug screening test, and physical exam. Applicants must be at least 21 years of age and under age 37. Candidates over age 37 who have previous service creditable under special law enforcement retirement provisions also may be eligible.

Training

Initial basic training for ICE deportation officers consists of a 13-week program at the Federal Law Enforcement Training Center in Glynco, Georgia (see chapter 16). This course includes instruction on immigration and nationality law, detention and removal operation procedures, statutory authority, fingerprinting, interviewing, cross-cultural communications, civil liability, arrest techniques, defensive tactics, baton techniques, search and seizure, detection of contraband, firearms qualification, defensive driving techniques, and other topics. In-service training includes specialized courses in subjects such as deportation processing, arrest and detention law, immigration law, first aid, firearms proficiency, arrest techniques, and defensive tactics.

Contact: Office of Detention and Removal; United States Immigration and Customs Enforcement; U.S. Department of Homeland Security; 801 I St. NW—Ste. 900; Washington, DC 20536; phone: (202) 305-2734; Internet: www.ice.gov/

Import Specialist (GS-1889)
United States Customs and Border Protection, U.S. Department of Homeland Security

Import specialists with United States Customs and Border Protection determine the admissibility, classification, appraisal value, and duty on the commercial importation of goods into the United States in accordance with tariff schedules and applicable laws.

Examples of responsibilities carried out by these personnel include reviewing entry documents submitted by importers or their representatives; examining samples of imported merchandise; determining the admissibility of merchandise and the accuracy of tariff classification and value declarations; interviewing importers and examining their business records; consulting with individuals who are knowledgeable about the physical characteristics or trade practices associated with particular varieties of imported merchandise and goods; examining and analyzing the results of Customs and Border Protection laboratory analyses; advising importers on probable or binding tariff classifications and rates of duty applicable to merchandise prior to its actual importation, and on the implications of various proposed changes in articles or business arrangements; and participating in operations with enforcement teams that investigate fraud, counterfeiting, and copyright violations.

Qualifications and Salary Levels

GS-5: Completion of a four-year course of study leading to a bachelor's degree; or three years of general experience, one year of which was equivalent to GS-4. **GS-7:** One full year of graduate education, or superior academic achievement during undergraduate studies, or one year of specialized experience equivalent to GS-5. **GS-9:** A master's degree, or two years of graduate education, or one year of specialized experience equivalent to GS-7. **GS-11:** A Ph.D. or equivalent doctoral degree, or three years of graduate education, or one year of specialized experience equivalent to GS-9. Experience and education can be combined to meet total experience requirements. Candidates must successfully complete a background investigation, qualify for a security clearance, and pass a drug test prior to appointment.

Training

Import specialists attend a five-week Basic Import Specialist training program at the Federal Law Enforcement Training Center (FLETC) in Glynco, Georgia, that covers laws and regulations concerning the classification and appraisement of merchandise, customs duties, identification of merchandise country-of-origin, textile quota limitations, merchandise antidumping, entry documents, and other related subjects. In-service training includes a two-week course at FLETC that focuses on customs laws, examination of import entity books and records, money laundering, commercial fraud, antiterrorism, interviewing techniques, report writing, computer databases, and public speaking. Additional in-service courses also are provided concerning specific responsibilities.

Contact: United States Customs and Border Protection; U.S. Department of Homeland Security; 1300 Pennsylvania Ave. NW; Washington, DC 20229; phone: (202) 344-1250; Internet: www.cbp.gov/

Mine Safety and Health Inspector (GS-1822)
Mine Safety and Health Administration, U.S. Department of Labor

The Mine Safety and Health Administration (MSHA) administers provisions of the Federal Mine Safety and Health Act of 1977. MSHA inspectors enforce this law and ensure compliance with mandatory safety and health standards as a means to eliminate fatal accidents, reduce the frequency and severity of nonfatal accidents, minimize health hazards, and promote improved safety and health conditions in the nation's mines regardless of size, number of employees, commodity mined, or method of extraction.

The primary responsibilities of MSHA mine safety and health inspectors include conducting inspections of metal and nonmetal underground and surface mines, mills, and quarries to identify hazardous conditions; inspecting unknown mining operations or those that present unusual or unyielding safety or health problems; examining mining practices for conformance with safety and health laws and regulations; issuing citations when violations and hazards are identified; ensuring that mining equipment is used and maintained properly; conducting investigations of mine accidents, disasters, and complaints of health and safety violations received from labor union officials, mine employees, and the public; preparing reports of inspections and investigations, including citations and orders; promoting safety by participating in safety meetings, providing instruction and demonstration in first aid and mine rescue, and conducting other training courses; and testifying at judicial hearings regarding notices of violations and orders of withdrawal. Mine safety and health inspectors also assist with rescue and firefighting operations in the aftermath of fires or explosions.

Qualifications and Salary Levels

GS-5: Completion of a four-year course of study above high school in any field; or three years of general experience related to mining operations, construction, excavation, electrical equipment or systems, heavy or engine-driven equipment, or heath and safety inspection or investigation in an industrial setting. **GS-7:** One full year of graduate education in fields related to responsibilities of the position, or one year of specialized experience equivalent to GS-5. **GS-9:** Two full years of graduate education or a master's degree in fields related to responsibilities of the position, or one year of specialized experience equivalent to GS-7. **GS-11:** One year of specialized experience equivalent to GS-9. **GS-12:** One year of specialized experience equivalent to GS-11.

Equivalent combinations of education and experience are qualifying for positions at grades GS-5 through GS-9. Uncorrected distant vision must be at least 20/50 (Snellen) in one eye and 20/70 in the other, correctable with eyeglasses (contact lenses are not acceptable) to at least 20/40 in one eye and 20/50 in the other. Near vision must be sufficient to read printed material the size of typewritten characters. Normal depth perception and field of vision are required, as is the ability to distinguish basic colors. Applicants, with or without the use of a hearing aid, must have no hearing loss in either ear of more than 40 decibels in the 500, 1000, or 2000 Hertz range. Tentative appointees must pass a medical examination, drug screening test, and background investigation.

Training

Initial basic training consists of a 16-week Entry Level Mine Safety and Health Inspector Training Program at the National Mine Health and Safety Academy in Beckley, West Virginia. This program is offered in four modules over a one-year period. The entry-level training program consists of courses in the MSHA mission, laws and regulations, accident reporting, inspection procedures, citations, interviewing techniques, fire protection, personal protective equipment, drilling and blasting, storage of materials, mine emergencies, gas detection devices, and other topics. Mine safety and health inspectors also attend intermediate and advanced courses throughout their careers. These focus on subjects such as accident investigation, evacuation procedures, underground ventilation, courtroom procedures, safety and inspection procedures, accident prevention, industrial hygiene, mine emergency procedures, mining technology, and other subjects.

Contact: Mine Safety and Health Administration; U.S. Department of Labor; 1100 Wilson Blvd.—21st Floor; Arlington, VA 22209; phone: (202) 693-9400; Internet: www.msha.gov/

Plant Health Safeguarding Specialist (GS-0436)

Animal and Plant Health Inspection Service, U.S. Department of Agriculture

The Plant Protection and Quarantine division of the U.S. Department of Agriculture (USDA) Animal and Plant Health Inspection Service (APHIS) is responsible for programs pertaining to the control and eradication of plant pests and diseases in the United States. APHIS plant health safeguarding specialists—known also as plant protection and quarantine officers—enforce federal laws and regulations that prohibit or restrict the entry of foreign pests and plants, plant products, animal products and byproducts, soil, and other materials that could harbor crop-destroying pests or diseases.

In furtherance of this mission, these personnel perform a variety of tasks at plant inspection stations and international ports of entry, in rural areas, and at other locations nationwide that concern importing and exporting operations, the exclusion of plant and soil materials, permits and compliance, and pest detection activities. These tasks include inspection operations, post-entry quarantine and safeguarding of seized or forfeited property, trade facilitation and export certification tasks, regulation and clearance of high-risk propagative plant material, pest diagnostic identification, disinfection and sterilization of goods, irradiation of regulated articles for plant and animal pests and diseases, a variety of tasks in accordance with the Convention on International Trade in Endangered Species (CITES), and other activities.

Qualifications and Salary Levels

GS-5: Basic eligibility requirements for GS-5 and all other levels include a bachelor's degree with a major in biology, agriculture, or a closely related field that included 24 semester hours of study in agronomy, cell biology, botany, entomology, forestry, horticulture, mycology, nematology, plant pathology, soil science, or related courses; or a combination of education (as described above) and experience related to the position.
GS-7: All requirements for GS-5, plus one year of graduate-level education, or superior

academic achievement during undergraduate studies, or one year of specialized experience equivalent to at least GS-5. **GS-9:** All requirements for GS-5, plus a master's degree, or two years of graduate-level education, or one year of specialized experience equivalent to at least GS-7. **GS-11:** All requirements for GS-5, plus a Ph.D. or equivalent doctoral degree, or three years of graduate-level education, or one year of specialized experience equivalent to at least GS-9. Applicants can use equivalent combinations of specialized experience and education to meet total experience requirements. Tentative appointees must pass a background investigation and qualify for a security clearance.

Training

Newly appointed APHIS plant health safeguarding specialists attend a 10-week Basic Agricultural Safeguarding Training Program that consists of technical instruction relating to specific duties of the position. Topics of instruction focus on laws and regulations, exclusion of imported goods, quarantine procedures, export certification, plant diseases, pest identification, pesticide application, safeguarding procedures, biosecurity, CITES provisions, and other subjects. Portions of this training program are conducted at the USDA Professional Development Center in Frederick, Maryland, while remaining segments are completed in the field. Plant health safeguarding specialists must also complete a prescribed in-service training program concerned with the essential skills of the position, and pass an examination to become certified as a Regulatory Pest Control Applicator.

Contact: Inquiries should be directed to the office where employment is sought, or to Animal and Plant Health Inspection Service; U.S. Department of Agriculture; Washington, DC 20250; phone: (202) 720-2511; Internet: www.aphis.usda.gov/ppq/.

Railroad Safety Inspector (GS-2121)
Federal Railroad Administration, U.S. Department of Transportation

The Federal Railroad Administration (FRA) is responsible for ensuring the safety of the nation's railroad system, which consists of more than 600 passenger, freight, and commuter railroads; 230,000 miles of railroad track; 89,000 track miles of signal and train control systems; 1.2 million freight cars; and 20,000 locomotives operating nationwide. FRA railroad safety inspectors conduct inspections and accident investigations to ensure compliance with federal laws and railroad safety regulations. Inspection operations are divided into five areas of specialization including Track Inspection, Signals and Train Control, Motive Power and Equipment, Hazardous Materials, and Operating Practices.

The responsibilities of the position depend on the area of specialization, although they generally involve planning and conducting inspections of rail facilities, equipment, rolling stock, operations, and pertinent records; reviewing carrier records to ensure compliance with occupational safety and health standards; investigating complaints from railroad employees, legislative and governmental representatives, and the general public; conducting investigations of railroad collisions, derailments, and other accidents resulting in serious injury or property damage; applying technical and regulatory standards; applying knowledge of methods used in the installation, operation, maintenance, and manufacturing of railroad equipment and systems; preparing investigative and accident reports; seeking correction of unsafe conditions; conducting safety meetings and training sessions relating to areas of specialization; and providing expert testimony during the course of civil litigation.

Qualifications and Salary Levels

GS-5: Completion of a four-year course of study above high school leading to a bachelor's degree, with a major in engineering, electronics, physics, occupational or industrial safety, or other fields related to the position; or three years of general experience, one year of which was equivalent to at least GS-4, that provided knowledge of the construction, operation, overhaul, maintenance, repair, or installation of mechanical or electronic equipment used in an industrial setting; and the ability to read and understand written material, blueprints, specifications, or related technical material. **GS-7:** One year of specialized experience equivalent to GS-5 that demonstrated knowledge of basic inspection techniques and safety practices related to the railroad industry. **GS-9:** One year of specialized experience equivalent to GS-7 that demonstrated knowledge of the railroad industry, including economic and operating considerations and equipment, general safety and health principles and practices applicable to the industry, and railroad accident investigation techniques. **GS-11:** One year of specialized experience equivalent to GS-9 that demonstrated knowledge of the railroad industry, including economic and operating considerations and equipment, general safety and health principles and practices applicable to the industry, and railroad accident investigation techniques. **GS-12:** One year of specialized experience equivalent to GS-11 that demonstrated knowledge of the railroad industry, including economic and operating considerations and equipment, general safety and health principles and practices applicable to the industry, and railroad accident investigation techniques.

Candidates must successfully complete a background investigation and pass a drug test prior to appointment.

Training

Initial training for FRA railroad safety inspectors includes an orientation to the mission, policies, procedures, and rules of the agency. During the first two years of service, these personnel also attend a variety of one- to two-week courses relating to each of the five areas of specialization, as well as courses concerning the inspection of bridges and steam engines, railroad safety inspections, and investigation procedures. Additional in-service training courses presented by FRA staff and railroad industry firms are attended recurrently once specialization is achieved.

Contact: Federal Railroad Administration; U.S. Department of Transportation; 400 Seventh St. SW; Washington, DC 20590; phone: (202) 632-3124; Internet: www.fra.dot.gov/

Wage and Hour Compliance Specialist (GS-0249)
Employment Standards Administration, U.S. Department of Labor

Wage and hour compliance specialists of the Employment Standards Administration, U.S. Department of Labor, conduct investigations of commercial, industrial, agricultural, and other business enterprises and public institutions to monitor and ensure compliance with a variety of federal labor laws. Investigations often are conducted to substantiate violations pertaining to minimum or prevailing wage rates, overtime pay requirements, child labor restrictions, wage garnishments, domestic service in house-holds, employment eligibility, migrant safety and health protection, certain forms of employment discrimination, and similar matters related to conditions of employment, wages, and hours worked.

The primary responsibilities of wage and hour compliance specialists include conduct-ing site visits of business establishments; interviewing employers or their representa-tives; observing work operations; reviewing business records; interviewing current or former employees to determine compliance with laws and regulations enforced, and to substantiate violations; educating employers regarding requirements for compliance; and persuading employers to recognize violations and take appropriate corrective action for future compliance, including payment of back wages or civil money penalties. Where voluntary compliance is not achieved, wage and hour compliance specialists recommend civil action to compel compliance, and in some cases work with government attorneys to develop evidence and prosecute willful violators.

Qualifications and Salary Levels

GS-5: Completion of a four-year course of study leading to a bachelor's degree; or three years of general experience, one year of which was equivalent to GS-4. **GS-7:** One full year of graduate education, or superior academic achievement during under-graduate studies, or one year of specialized experience equivalent to GS-5. **GS-9:** A master's degree, or two years of graduate education, or one year of specialized experi-ence equivalent to GS-7. **GS-11:** A Ph.D. or equivalent doctoral degree, or three years of graduate education, or one year of specialized experience equivalent to GS-9. **GS-12:** One year of specialized experience equivalent to GS-11. Equivalent combinations of education and experience can be used to meet minimum experience requirements.

Training

Initial and in-service training for wage and hour compliance specialists includes instruction conducted by Labor Department staff relating primarily to provisions of the Fair Labor Standards Act, Migrant and Seasonal Agricultural Worker Protection Act, Employee Polygraph Protection Act, Family and Medical Leave Act, Davis Bacon Act, Service Contract Act, wage garnishment provisions of the Consumer Credit Protection Act, and a number of employment standards and worker protections as provided in several immigration-related statutes.

Contact: Wage and Hour Division; Employment Standards Administration; U.S. Department of Labor; 200 Constitution Ave. NW; Washington, DC 20210; phone: (866) 487-9243; Internet: www.dol.gov/esa/whd/

Wildlife Inspector (GS-1801)
United States Fish and Wildlife Service, U.S. Department of the Interior

The United States Fish and Wildlife Service (FWS) maintains a force of uniformed wildlife inspectors to ensure that wildlife shipments entering or leaving the United States comply with federal wildlife trade laws and international treaties, and to inter-cept illegal shipments of federally protected wildlife. FWS wildlife inspectors are stationed at ports of entry and other locations throughout the United States and its territories where wildlife import and export shipments occur—such as U.S. international airports and sea or land border points of entry—where they examine wild animals, packages, crates, and other containers that are transported by air, sea, and land carriers, carried by individuals, or delivered through the mail.

Examples of responsibilities carried out by wildlife inspectors include examining documentation that accompanies shipments; physically inspecting the contents of shipments; seizing animals and wildlife products; participating in investigations; providing expertise to other agencies in wildlife law and species identification; testifying in court; and fulfilling administrative duties associated with the inspection and clearance of wildlife imports and exports. Inspections and investigations often are coordinated with FWS special agents, as well as investigative and compliance personnel of U.S. Customs and Border Protection, U.S. Department of Agriculture Animal and Plant Health Inspection Service, National Marine Fisheries Service, U.S. Immigration and Customs Enforcement, and U.S. Coast Guard.

Qualifications and Salary Levels

GS-5: Completion of a four-year course of study leading to a bachelor's degree; or three years of general experience, one year of which was equivalent to GS-4. **GS-7:** One full year of graduate education, or superior academic achievement during undergraduate studies, or one year of specialized experience equivalent to GS-5. **GS-9:** A master's degree, or two years of graduate education, or one year of specialized experience equivalent to GS-7. **GS-11:** A Ph.D. or equivalent doctoral degree, or three years of graduate education, or one year of specialized experience equivalent to GS-9. **GS-12:** One year of specialized experience equivalent to GS-11. Applicants can use equivalent combinations of specialized experience and education to meet total experience requirements. Conditions of employment include the ability to crawl into shipping containers and other small spaces, stand for long periods of time, lift up to 50 pounds without assistance, and climb ladders. The application process includes a background investigation and physical examination.

Training

Wildlife inspectors attend a four-week Wildlife Inspector Basic Training Program at the Federal Law Enforcement Training Center in Glynco, Georgia. This course, which is conducted by FWS personnel, includes instruction pertaining to wildlife laws and treaties; FWS operational policies and port procedures; mammal, reptile, and amphibian identification; fish and wildlife handling and inspection techniques; identification of wildlife parts and manufactured wildlife products; and cooperative enforcement activities with the Department of Homeland Security, the Department of Agriculture, and the Canadian Wildlife Service. Annual in-service training includes instruction concerning problems and trends associated with the illegal importation of wildlife parts and products; legal updates and issues regarding the importing, exporting, and inspection of fish and wildlife; officer safety techniques; and related subjects.

Contact: Office of Law Enforcement; U.S. Fish and Wildlife Service; 4401 N. Fairfax Dr.; Arlington, VA 22203; phone: (703) 358-1949; Internet: www.fws.gov/le/

CHAPTER 12

Security Specialists

"When a man assumes a public trust, he should consider himself as public property."

—Thomas Jefferson

Federal security specialists perform a broad range of tasks associated with the identification and protection of information, personnel, property, facilities, operations, and material from unauthorized disclosure, misuse, theft, fraud, assault, vandalism, espionage, sabotage, or loss. The majority of security specialists in the competitive service are classified in the GS-0080 occupational series.

Among the most common careers in this series are physical security specialists and personnel security specialists. Generally speaking, physical security specialists design, install, operate, and monitor devices and systems that are used to protect against fire, theft, vandalism, and illegal entry in order to safeguard personnel, property, and information. These professionals are employed by agencies that include the Secret Service, U.S. Capitol Police, Agricultural Research Service, Federal Protective Service, and U.S. Marshals Service, among others. Agencies such as the Bureau of Engraving and Printing, Drug Enforcement Administration, Comptroller of the Currency, Defense Security Service, and Federal Emergency Management Agency employ personnel security specialists to analyze and evaluate the character and background of employees, candidates for employment, federal contractor personnel, and other persons having or proposed to be granted access to classified or other sensitive information, materials, or work sites.

Crime Prevention Specialist (GS-0301)
National Institutes of Health, U.S. Department of Health and Human Services

The Division of Physical Security Management of the National Institutes of Health (NIH) ensures that security operations at all NIH facilities operate as effectively and efficiently as possible. To ensure the safety of NIH staff, patients, visitors, and property, the Division of Physical Security Management takes a proactive approach to physical security, access control, and crime prevention services that are tailored to the unique environment of the NIH enclave.

In furtherance of this goal, crime prevention specialists conduct security assessments throughout the NIH campus, which consists of 75 buildings on more than 300 acres.

These include a research hospital, outpatient clinic, pediatric treatment center, numerous research and education facilities, and the National Library of Medicine. Crime prevention specialists conduct comprehensive physical security surveys of NIH buildings and grounds to determine the effectiveness of security systems and ensure the protection of government equipment and experiments, NIH personnel, and visitors. They are responsible for developing, reviewing, and managing the physical security requirements at all NIH facilities; for ensuring that NIH is using the most advanced equipment in the field of physical security, especially electronic locking devices and security systems, closed-circuit television surveillance systems, and similar instrumentation and equipment; for reviewing proposed new construction and renovation plans for NIH facilities to ensure that adequate security measures are incorporated; and for developing and maintaining close liaison with security professional groups, the NIH Division of Police, and other law enforcement and government agencies.

Qualifications and Salary

GS-7: One full year of graduate education, or superior academic achievement during undergraduate studies, or one year of specialized experience equivalent to GS-5. **GS-9:** A master's degree, or two years of graduate education, or one year of specialized experience equivalent to GS-7. **GS-11:** A Ph.D. or equivalent doctoral degree, or three years of graduate education, or one year of specialized experience equivalent to GS-9. **GS-12:** One year of specialized experience equivalent to GS-11. Experience and education can be combined to meet total experience requirements.

Training

Initial training for NIH crime prevention specialists depends upon the experience and prior training of individual personnel, although it could include formal security or crime prevention training at the Federal Law Enforcement Training Center in Glynco, Georgia, or the National Crime Prevention Institute in Louisville, Kentucky. In-service training could include courses or seminars offered by the American Society for Industrial Security, colleges or universities, or private training organizations in subjects such as closed-circuit television systems, electronic and mechanical locking hardware, keying and access control systems, environmental security design, or other subjects related to physical security and crime prevention.

Contact: Division of Physical Security Management; National Institutes of Health; U.S. Department of Health and Human Services; 31 Center Dr.—Building 31; Bethesda, MD 20892; phone: (301) 496-9109; Internet: www.ser.ors.od.nih.gov/physical_security.htm

Federal Air Marshal
Transportation Security Administration, U.S. Department of Homeland Security

The mission of the Federal Air Marshal Service (FAMS) is to promote confidence in the Nation's civil aviation system through the effective deployment of federal air marshals to detect, deter, and defeat hostile acts targeting U.S. air carriers, airports, passengers, and crews. Federal air marshals are deployed worldwide on passenger flights of U.S. air carriers to counter the risk of criminal or terrorist violence, including aircraft piracy and threats to national security.

Their responsibilities include a variety of investigative, security, and law enforcement tasks, such as identifying individuals or events that could pose a risk of terrorism or a threat to airline or passenger safety; conducting surveillance and counter-surveillance, interviews, interrogations, and background checks; performing undercover and other covert assignments; planning and coordinating operations with federal, state, county, local, and foreign law enforcement officers and other government officials; participating in multi-agency task force operations; conducting intelligence activities; making arrests; executing search warrants; writing reports; preparing cases for legal action in cooperation with the United States Attorney's Office; and testifying in court. Federal air marshals are based at field offices in Atlanta, Boston, Charlotte, Chicago, Cincinnati, Cleveland, Dallas, Denver, Detroit, Houston, Las Vegas, Los Angeles, Miami, Minneapolis–St. Paul, Newark, Orlando, Philadelphia, Pittsburgh, and Seattle. Federal air marshals are required to work shifts around the clock, including weekends and holidays; to incur overnight travel on a regular basis; and to participate in a mandatory physical fitness program. They are authorized to carry firearms.

Federal air marshals are covered under special retirement provisions for federal law enforcement officers.

Qualifications and Salary

The Transportation Security Administration (TSA) is an excepted service agency and does not follow competitive service hiring processes or the General Schedule pay system. Job qualifications and salaries for federal air marshals are similar to those of security specialists with other federal agencies at the GS-5 through GS-13 levels in the competitive service. Specifically, the requirements and salary for TSA Pay Band G are similar to those for GS-5 through GS-7; Pay Band H is about the same as GS-9 through GS-12; and Pay Band I is similar to GS-13. Experience and education can be combined to meet total experience requirements for Pay Bands G and H. TSA prefers candidates with effective oral and written communication skills; knowledge of investigative techniques; ability to effectively solve problems; ability to function effectively in a team environment; knowledge of law enforcement functions, laws, policies, and procedures; and ability to function effectively in a stressful environment. The application process includes a physical examination, drug and alcohol screening, background investigation, and top-secret security clearance determination. Appointees are required to relocate to different geographic duty locations according to the needs of FAMS, and to sign a mobility agreement as a condition of employment.

Training

Training for federal air marshals begins with a seven-week basic training program at the Federal Law Enforcement Training Center (FLETC) in Artesia, New Mexico. Basic training is followed by a seven-week specialized follow-on course at the FAMS Training Academy in Atlantic City, New Jersey. Basic, follow-on, and in-service training consists of scenario-based instruction that focuses on responses to hijacking situations; terrorist threats; intoxicated, disruptive, or disorderly passengers; interference with flight crew members; suspicious activities and persons; security breaches; medical emergencies; flight simulator training; and other matters. Federal air marshals also are trained in basic and advanced marksmanship, emergency evacuation procedures, aircraft configurations, vital aircraft systems, operational tactics, surveillance detection, weapons of mass destruction, identification of explosives, legal subjects, FAA regulations, physical fitness, defensive tactics, arrest techniques, use of force, emergency medicine, psychology of survival, and other topics. Federal air marshal training at

FLETC Artesia and the FAMS Training Academy is carried out in facilities that are specifically geared to the unique environment and circumstances faced by federal air marshals, including environmentally controlled commercial passenger jets that are used for tactical training simulation.

Contact: Federal Air Marshal Service; Transportation Security Administration; U.S. Department of Homeland Security; 601 S. 12th St.; Arlington, VA 22202; phone: (800) 887-1895; Internet: www.tsa.gov/

Industrial Security Specialist (GS-0080)
Missile Defense Agency, U.S. Department of Defense

The mission of the Missile Defense Agency (MDA)—formerly known as the Ballistic Missile Defense Organization—is to develop, test, and prepare for deployment a layered national missile defense system to intercept missiles in all phases of flight and against all ranges of threats. Missile Defense Agency industrial security specialists advise and assist in implementing the MDA Foreign Disclosure Guidance.

Their responsibilities include oversight of the development, establishment, and management of the Joint National Test Facility (JNTF) Foreign Disclosure information program in support of MDA and JNTF personnel, contacts, visitors, international conferences, multi-national war games, and assigned foreign exchange personnel. Some of the tasks carried out by these personnel include identifying potential information disclosure problems and developing approaches for avoiding problems; identifying and assisting investigative personnel in the event of unauthorized disclosure of data and items to foreign nationals; and planning and developing foreign disclosure processes, instructions, and guidance regarding national and agency principles, programs, policies, directives, and regulations pertaining to national disclosure policy, foreign military sales, security assistance, technology transfer, and Export Control Act provisions. This is a civilian position and does not require active duty military service.

Qualifications and Salary

GS-7: One full year of graduate education, or superior academic achievement during undergraduate studies, or one year of specialized experience equivalent to GS-5. **GS-9:** A master's degree, or two years of graduate education, or one year of specialized experience equivalent to GS-7. **GS-11:** A Ph.D. or equivalent doctoral degree, or three years of graduate education, or one year of specialized experience equivalent to GS-9. **GS-12:** One year of specialized experience equivalent to GS-11. **GS-13:** One year of specialized experience equivalent to GS-12. Equivalent combinations of education and experience can be used to meet minimum experience requirements. Tentative appointees must undergo a background investigation, qualify for a security clearance, and pass a drug screening test.

Training

Training for MDA industrial security specialists depends on the experience of individual personnel and nature of assignments. Initial and in-service training could focus on the principles of personnel, physical, and information security; security classifications and clearance levels; storage of classified or sensitive information; access controls; intrusion detection devices; espionage and sabotage; security plans and surveys; applicable laws and regulations; legal updates; report writing; and agency-specific issues and instructions.

Contact: Missile Defense Agency; U.S. Department of Defense; The Pentagon; Washington, DC 20301; phone: (703) 695-6420; Internet: www.mda.mil/; e-mail: mda.info@mda.mil

Information Security Specialist (GS-0080)
El Paso Intelligence Center, Drug Enforcement Administration, U.S. Department of Justice

Information security specialists assigned to the El Paso Intelligence Center (EPIC) in El Paso, Texas, are responsible for administering the Drug Enforcement Administration (DEA) sensitive compartmented information (SCI) program. EPIC—which is staffed by more than a dozen agencies and led by the DEA—is a clearinghouse for tactical intelligence and the collection, analysis, and dissemination of information related to worldwide drug movement and alien smuggling.

The primary responsibilities of DEA information security specialists assigned to EPIC include ensuring that all SCI is properly accounted for, controlled, transmitted, packaged, and safeguarded; maintaining all applicable SCI directives, regulations, and manuals; enforcing and supporting related Executive Orders and Presidential Directives; directing SCI physical and technical security actions, procedures, and personnel access; serving as the point-of-contact for SCI material control and accountability; ensuring that SCI is disseminated only to authorized persons, and that material is destroyed in authorized destruction facilities; providing SCI support to appropriately cleared Defense Department contractors; conducting a continuing security education training program; and maintaining listings of available SCI electronic and hard-copy products and interfaces with other telecommunications centers. Information security specialists also are assigned to DEA headquarters and the agency's field offices, where they protect the data security infrastructure and prevent the compromise or destruction of information systems; ensure compliance with federal regulations and accreditation requirements; manage DEA user accounts, including intrusion detection and response measures; conduct compliance reviews and security awareness training; and manage information encryption systems.

Qualifications and Salary

GS-5: Completion of a four-year course of study leading to a bachelor's degree; or three years of general experience, one year of which was equivalent to GS-4. **GS-7:** One full year of graduate education, or superior academic achievement during undergraduate studies, or one year of specialized experience equivalent to GS-5. **GS-9:** A master's degree, or two years of graduate education, or one year of specialized experience equivalent to GS-7. **GS-11:** A Ph.D. or equivalent doctoral degree, or three years of graduate education, or one year of specialized experience equivalent to GS-9. **GS-12:** One year of specialized experience equivalent to GS-11. **GS-13:** One year of specialized experience equivalent to GS-12. Experience and education can be combined to meet total experience requirements. Appointees must qualify for a security clearance and pass a background investigation and drug screening test.

Training

DEA information security specialists receive ongoing on-the-job and formal training relating to SCI requirements, directives, best practices, access restrictions, control channels, classification, sensitive information compartments and subcompartments, and special access programs. Depending on the expertise of individual personnel and the nature of their responsibilities, additional training could include instruction in areas such as information security hardware and software, certificate authorities, tokens, firewalls, and encryption techniques for secure communications applications; identifying information security vulnerabilities; electronic crimes; data encryption technology; and other topics. Training is presented by DEA staff, and also is available from recognized experts of organizations such as the National Institute of Standards and Technology, National Security Agency, U.S. Department of Energy, FBI, Computer Sciences Corporation, Cisco Systems, IBM Corporation, various colleges and universities, and other training providers.

Contact: Recruiting information can be obtained from any DEA field office, or by contacting the Office of Personnel; Drug Enforcement Administration; U.S. Department of Justice; 2401 Jefferson Davis Highway; Alexandria, VA 22301; phone: (202) 307-1000; Internet: www.dea.gov/.

Information Security Specialist
Office of Nuclear Security and Incident Response, U.S. Nuclear Regulatory Commission

The United States Nuclear Regulatory Commission (NRC) is an independent agency that was established by Congress to ensure adequate protection of the public health and safety, the environment, and the common defense and security in the use of nuclear materials in the United States. Under the Office of Nuclear Security and Incident Response, Information Security Section, NRC information security specialists perform tasks associated with a number of programs pertaining to information and technical security, counterintelligence, communications, and foreign disclosure of information to protect classified and sensitive unclassified information and telecommunications.

NRC information security specialists are responsible for transmitting and protecting intelligence information; recommending security measures and implementing policy for sensitive compartmented information (SCI) and special access program (SAP) information received and used within the NRC and the agency's contractor facilities; disseminating SCI and SAP information to appropriate persons; maintaining all facilities that receive, process, or store SCI and SAP information within the NRC in accordance with national directives and agency policies; preparing daily intelligence briefings for senior NRC officials, commissioners, and staff; and conducting liaison activities with various agencies and organizations in the U.S. intelligence community. Information security specialists also receive communications and reports concerning requirements in the Code of Federal Regulations pertaining to "Facility Security Clearance and Safeguarding of National Security Information and Restricted Data." The NRC Office of Nuclear Security and Incident Response works with the Department of Homeland Security, Central Intelligence Agency, FBI, and other agencies concerned with terrorism to assess and respond to potential threats to national security.

Qualifications and Salary

NRC information security specialists are appointed through excepted service hiring procedures. The qualifications and salaries of this position are similar to information security specialists at the GS-9, GS-11, GS-12, and GS-13 levels with other federal agencies. When filling vacancies for this position, the Nuclear Regulatory Commission seeks candidates who possess knowledge of the principles and techniques for protecting SCI and SAP material; knowledge of global proliferation, nonproliferation, and other legal issues; experience in the transmission and protection of intelligence information; knowledge of the U.S. intelligence community; and strong written and oral communication skills. Candidates must successfully undergo a background investigation, qualify for a top-secret security clearance, and pass a drug test prior to appointment.

Training

In-service and on-the-job training for NRC information security specialists depends largely on the level of experience and nature of assignments of individual personnel. Generally speaking, training for these professionals focuses on areas such as U.S. intelligence community operations; NRC policies and federal requirements pertaining to SCI and SAP programs; the collection, analysis, classification, dissemination, and destruction of sensitive information and intelligence; access controls; report writing; technical security procedures; computer hardware systems and software programs; applicable laws and regulations; and additional agency-specific issues and instructions. Training consists of instruction presented by NRC staff, other government agencies, colleges and universities, and private companies.

Contact: Information Security Section; Office of Nuclear Security and Incident Response; U.S. Nuclear Regulatory Commission; Washington, DC 20555; phone: (301) 415-7000; Internet: www.nrc.gov/; e-mail: opa@nrc.gov

Museum Security Specialist (GS-1801)
Office of Protection Services, Smithsonian Institution

Smithsonian Institution museum security specialists are responsible for protecting the world's largest museum complex, which includes 18 museums; the National Gallery of Art and eight other galleries; the Kennedy Center for the Performing Arts; the National Zoo; nine research facilities located in several states; and more than 140 million objects, artworks, treasures, and specimens.

Some examples of responsibilities carried out by these personnel include the investigation of criminal incidents involving theft of Smithsonian artifacts and property, vandalism, shoplifting violations that occur in museum shops, pickpocketing, purse snatching, sex offenses, assaults, homicides, armed robberies, narcotics crimes, and accidents where potential tort claims are likely. These investigations often require collecting evidence; interviewing victims, witnesses, and complainants; interrogating suspects; preparing detailed written reports; and testifying in court or other hearings. Additional responsibilities of these personnel include conducting surveillance and gathering intelligence concerning criminal activity and threats; advising museum managers on collections control and physical security matters; conducting security surveys and inspections; protecting dignitaries and other VIPs; supervising the construction of alarm systems and control centers; and participating in the intrastate and interstate security escort of valuable artifacts in transit to or from Smithsonian facilities. Smithsonian museum security specialists are authorized to carry firearms.

Qualifications and Salary

GS-5: Completion of a four-year course of study leading to a bachelor's degree; or three years of general experience, one year of which was equivalent to GS-4. **GS-7:** One full year of graduate education, or superior academic achievement during

undergraduate studies, or one year of specialized experience equivalent to GS-5.
GS-9: A master's degree, or two years of graduate education, or one year of specialized experience equivalent to GS-7. **GS-11:** A Ph.D. or equivalent doctoral degree, or three years of graduate education, or one year of specialized experience equivalent to GS-9. **GS-12:** One year of specialized experience equivalent to GS-11. Equivalent combinations of education and experience can be used to meet minimum experience requirements. Tentative appointees must pass a background investigation.

Training

Smithsonian museum security specialists attend a wide range of introductory and in-service training courses and seminars, including a three-week museum security training program that focuses on physical security principles, Smithsonian policies and procedures, and the diverse set of security challenges within Smithsonian facilities. Museum security specialists are trained with the aid of Firearms Training Simulators, and receive instruction in control-room operations, human relations, confrontation management, security awareness, crime prevention, firearms proficiency, and other subjects relating to specific responsibilities of the position.

Contact: Office of Protection Services; Smithsonian Institution; 1000 Jefferson Dr. SW; Washington, DC 20560; phone: (202) 633-1000; Internet: www.si.edu/; e-mail: info@si.edu

Nuclear Materials Courier (GS-0084)
National Nuclear Security Administration, U.S. Department of Energy

The National Nuclear Security Administration (NNSA) is responsible under law for safeguarding and transporting nuclear weapons, components, and other highly sensitive nuclear materials from points of manufacture or origin to authorized destinations. Nuclear materials couriers employed by the NNSA Office of Secure Transportation are responsible for protecting, moving, and delivering nuclear weapons, components, and materials owned or controlled by the U.S. Department of Energy to military or civilian recipients for appropriate use, storage, or disposal. These armed personnel spend about three weeks each month traveling on mission assignments throughout the contiguous 48 states in convoys of armored 18-wheel tractor-trailer trucks and escort vehicles, or accompanying shipments by air or rail.

The primary mission of nuclear materials couriers is to protect nuclear shipments from theft or sabotage. They are authorized under the Atomic Energy Act to use tactical weapons, make arrests, or use deadly force to accomplish this mission, if necessary. In carrying out their responsibilities, nuclear materials couriers operate specially equipped tractor-trailers that are designed and constructed to deter and prevent unauthorized removal of cargo, protect the cargo against damage in the event of an accident or fire, and protect the occupants against an attack. Nuclear materials couriers also operate communications, electronic, and other equipment in transit to further enhance the safety and security of convoy personnel, their cargo, and the public. In other words, NNSA convoys are essentially special response teams on the move. Nuclear materials couriers are permanently assigned to one of three duty stations: Albuquerque, New Mexico; Amarillo, Texas; or Oak Ridge, Tennessee.

This position is covered under special retirement provisions for federal law enforcement officers.

Qualifications and Salary

GS-8: One year of experience equivalent to at least the GS-7 level that demonstrated the ability to learn, comprehend, and apply courier rules, regulations, laws, general and special orders, and administrative procedures relating to protection and security systems; and to communicate effectively in person-to-person contacts. **GS-9:** One year of experience (as described under GS-8) equivalent to at least the GS-8 level. **GS-10:** One year of experience (as described under GS-8) equivalent to at least the GS-9 level. **GS-11:** One year of experience (as described under GS-8) equivalent to at least the GS-10 level. **GS-12:** One year of experience (as described under GS-8) equivalent to at least the GS-11 level. **GS-13:** One year of experience (as described under GS-8) equivalent to at least the GS-12 level.

Appointees must be at least 21 years of age and under age 37. However, candidates over age 37 who have previous service creditable under special law enforcement retirement provisions also may be eligible. Some examples of qualifying experience include work as an armed guard, security officer, or law enforcement officer, or experience in the U.S. Coast Guard or military. Such experience must have involved protecting property against the hazards of fire, theft, damage, accident, sabotage, or trespass; maintaining law and order; protecting lives; or similar duties. Medical requirements include the following:

- Distant visual acuity less than 20/70 uncorrected in each eye, correctable to 20/20 with contact lenses or eyeglasses.

- Ability to distinguish colors as determined by an Ishihara color-screening test.

- No hearing loss greater than 30 decibels at 500, 1000, and 2000 Hertz in either ear. (Hearing aids are not permitted.)

- No conditions that interfere with distinct speech.

- Blood pressure readings below 150/90 without medication.

- No clinical diagnosis of cardiovascular disease, diabetes, chronic lung disease, genitourinary disease, or glaucoma.

- No mental, nervous, organic, or functional psychiatric disorder.

- No history or clinical diagnosis of seizure disorder or other form of disease of the nervous system.

- No physical limitations, disease, or mental impairment or condition, which in the opinion of NNSA medical authorities would render candidates unable to perform the duties of the position and meet job requirements.

The application process includes a polygraph examination, psychological assessment, background investigation, security clearance determination, drug and alcohol screening, and medical evaluation.

Training

All candidates selected will initially attend a 20-week basic training academy at Ft. Chaffee in Fort Smith, Arkansas. Basic training consists of instruction relating to tractor-trailer operations; commercial driver's license certification; communications systems operation; defensive driving; firearms; preparation for armed attacks, and other law enforcement tactics; use of force; physical fitness; first-aid; and other subjects.

Candidates are required to run one mile in eight and one-half minutes or less, and to complete a 40-yard dash (beginning in a prone position) in eight seconds or less. Following recruit training, nuclear materials couriers spend about seven months in on-the-job training. In-service training is ongoing and is designed primarily to update instruction taught during basic training. Examples of in-service training topics include team tactics, terrorist tactics, new adversary technology, physical fitness, defensive tactics, firearms, and driving proficiency.

Contact: National Nuclear Security Administration; United States Department of Energy; P.O. Box 5400; Albuquerque, NM 87185; phone: (505) 845-6202; Internet: www.nnsa.doe.gov/

Personnel Security Specialist (GS-0080)
Defense Security Service, U.S. Department of Defense

Defense Security Service (DSS) personnel security specialists conduct highly complex and sensitive personnel security investigations of employees who require access to classified and sensitive Department of Defense (DoD) information or highly sensitive DoD areas. Subjects of investigations include military and civilian personnel of the DoD, Air Force, Army, and Navy; DoD contractors; and employees of facilities in private industry requiring a security clearance in accordance with the National Industrial Security Program (NISP).

DSS personnel security specialists are responsible for a variety of tasks associated with DoD security clearance determinations, such as conducting in-depth reviews of investigative reports and related application documents for industrial security clearances; reviewing information relating to individuals' loyalty, character, trustworthiness, and reliability to ensure that he or she is eligible to access classified information or for appointment to a sensitive position or position of trust; evaluating adverse information reports for DoD contractors and government agencies in accordance with the NISP Operating Manual; reviewing security violations reported by DSS field offices and other executive department security offices; evaluating personnel security questionnaires that indicate possible foreign representation on an individual; determining the degree and extent of investigative inquiry that is required in resolving allegations of adverse information. DSS personnel security specialists also identify and review cases that contain major adverse information to determine whether suspension of a security clearance is warranted, and prepare written recommendations for security clearance suspension actions.

Qualifications and Salary

GS-5: Completion of a four-year course of study leading to a bachelor's degree; or three years of general experience, one year of which was equivalent to GS-4. **GS-7:** One full year of graduate education, or superior academic achievement during undergraduate studies, or one year of specialized experience equivalent to GS-5. **GS-9:** A master's degree, or two years of graduate education, or one year of specialized experience equivalent to GS-7. **GS-11:** A Ph.D. or equivalent doctoral degree, or three years of graduate education, or one year of specialized experience equivalent to GS-9. **GS-12:** One year of specialized experience equivalent to GS-11. Qualifying education can be substituted for experience, and vice versa. Tentative appointees must qualify for a security clearance and pass a background investigation and drug screening test.

Training

Training for DSS personnel security specialists includes an overview of the NISP as implemented by the DoD; the NISP Operating Manual; the government acquisition cycle; communications security; international transfer of classified information; and personnel security clearances, facility clearances, and safeguarding of classified materials as they relate to the Government Contracting Activity and civilian contractors. Personnel security specialists also can complete job-specific formal classroom training, computer-based training, and distance learning training throughout their careers at the DSS Academy in Linthicum, Maryland, and at other locations.

Contact: Defense Security Service; 1340 Braddock Place; Alexandria, VA 22314; phone: (703) 325-9471; Internet: www.dss.mil/; e-mail: occ.cust.serv@dss.mil

Personnel Security Specialist (GS-0080)
Federal Emergency Management Agency, U.S. Department of Homeland Security

The Federal Emergency Management Agency (FEMA) is responsible for emergency planning, preparedness, mitigation, response, and recovery relating to catastrophic disasters, and for programs providing recovery assistance and the protection of life and property. FEMA personnel security specialists conduct investigations into the suitability, integrity, and loyalty of FEMA employees, as well as applicants for employment, contractors, and other designated personnel.

Some of their responsibilities include preparing, reviewing, and evaluating investigative reports to determine whether current or prospective employees meet FEMA personnel security standards; processing requests concerning access to special access program and sensitive compartmented information, including restricted data pertaining to North Atlantic Treaty Organization (NATO) and Department of Energy operations; processing clearance applications for national security and public trust positions; conducting pre-employment interviews, subject interviews, record checks, and other investigative functions; preparing recommendations for interim suspension of security clearances of cleared personnel on whom significant derogatory information becomes known; and conducting security briefings involving SAP information, foreign contacts, and counterintelligence. Personnel security specialists and other FEMA personnel are required to respond to emergencies on a 24-hour on-call basis.

Qualifications and Salary

GS-5: Completion of a four-year course of study leading to a bachelor's degree; or three years of general experience, one year of which was equivalent to GS-4. **GS-7:** One full year of graduate education, or superior academic achievement during undergraduate studies, or one year of specialized experience equivalent to GS-5. **GS-9:** A master's degree, or two years of graduate education, or one year of specialized experience equivalent to GS-7. **GS-11:** A Ph.D. or equivalent doctoral degree, or three years of graduate education, or one year of specialized experience equivalent to GS-9. **GS-12:** One year of specialized experience equivalent to GS-11. Experience and education can be combined to meet total experience requirements. Candidates must successfully undergo a background investigation, qualify for a security clearance, and pass a drug test prior to appointment.

Training

Training and development for personnel security specialists ordinarily consists of instruction in areas such as FEMA personnel standards, security clearance eligibility requirements, position sensitivity and security suitability determinations, adverse personnel action and derogatory information, interviewing techniques, report writing, applicable laws and regulations, legal updates, agency policies and procedures, and other agency-specific training. Basic and in-service training can include job-specific courses that are presented by FEMA staff; federal, state, or local law enforcement training programs or academies; colleges or universities; and other organizations.

Contact: Personnel and Information Security Division; Federal Emergency Management Agency; 500 C St. SW; Washington, DC 20472; phone: (202) 566-1600; Internet: www.fema.gov/

Personnel Security Specialist (GS-0080)
Drug Enforcement Administration, U.S. Department of Justice

Drug Enforcement Administration (DEA) personnel security specialists conduct inquiries to determine whether DEA personnel or persons seeking employment in sensitive positions meet the agency's personnel security standards to the extent that their retention, hiring, or access to classified information is consistent with DEA integrity standards and national security.

The primary responsibilities of DEA personnel security specialists include reviewing and evaluating investigative reports and collateral information; determining the adequacy of personnel security investigations; conducting interviews of employees concerning minor derogatory allegations against them; determining the degree and extent of investigative inquiry that is required in resolving allegations of adverse information; examining the relationships of facts to provisions of applicable laws and regulations, and their relevancy to the issues involved; developing detailed and objective summaries of the information considered; and recommending approval or denial of clearances for access to classified information based on the results of inquiries and knowledge of subversive activities and other factors pertinent to the administration of personnel security. DEA personnel security specialists also are responsible for initiating investigative action for updating or processing documentation for special access program clearances or recertification of clearances through appropriate agencies.

Qualifications and Salary

GS-5: Completion of a four-year course of study leading to a bachelor's degree; or three years of general experience, one year of which was equivalent to GS-4. **GS-7:** One full year of graduate education, or superior academic achievement during undergraduate studies, or one year of specialized experience equivalent to GS-5. **GS-9:** A master's degree, or two years of graduate education, or one year of specialized experience equivalent to GS-7. **GS-11:** A Ph.D. or equivalent doctoral degree, or three years of graduate education, or one year of specialized experience equivalent to GS-9. **GS-12:** One year of specialized experience equivalent to GS-11. Equivalent combinations of education and experience can be used to meet minimum experience requirements. The application process includes a drug screening test, background investigation, and security clearance determination.

Training

Basic, in-service, and on-the-job training for these personnel focuses on topics such as DEA personnel security policies, procedures, eligibility standards, and forms; personnel security investigations tracking; employment suitability determinations and issues; special access program requirements; interviewing techniques; personnel security investigative reports; report writing; adjudication of personnel security investigation results; databases and other information systems; legal updates; and other subjects.

Contact: Recruiting information can be obtained from any DEA field office, or by contacting the Office of Personnel; Drug Enforcement Administration; U.S. Department of Justice; 2401 Jefferson Davis Hwy.; Alexandria, VA 22301; phone: (202) 307-1000; Internet: www.dea.gov/

Personnel Security Specialist (GS-0080)
Bureau of Engraving and Printing, U.S. Department of the Treasury

Personnel security specialists of the Bureau of Engraving and Printing (BEP) participate in a continuing program of personnel security controls, with responsibility for conducting comprehensive investigations concerned with the security suitability of individuals serving in sensitive positions or with access to classified information. Personnel security investigations focus on BEP job applicants, nongovernment personnel assigned at the BEP, and incumbents for promotion or retention in BEP positions.

Some of the primary responsibilities of BEP personnel security specialists include collecting information from persons such as co-workers, neighbors, supervisors, and others to determine suitability for employment; analyzing results of investigative findings and making recommendations that could result in the granting of employment, denial or termination of employment, initiation of corrective measures, or criminal prosecution; conducting surveys and inspections of personnel security programs and systems, and preparing comprehensive reports of deficiencies and violations observed; tracking, monitoring, and reporting on the status of personnel security investigations; administering classified document accountability and storage controls; and making recommendations for corrective actions and for enhancing overall personnel security controls. BEP personnel security specialists also serve as a security liaison with representatives of other Treasury bureaus, other federal and municipal government agencies, and various law enforcement agencies. BEP physical security specialists are authorized to carry firearms and they occasionally perform armed escort services.

Qualifications and Salary

GS-5: Completion of a four-year course of study leading to a bachelor's degree; or three years of general experience, one year of which was equivalent to GS-4. **GS-7:** One full year of graduate education, or superior academic achievement during undergraduate studies, or one year of specialized experience equivalent to GS-5. **GS-9:** A master's degree, or two years of graduate education, or one year of specialized experience equivalent to GS-7. **GS-11:** A Ph.D. or equivalent doctoral degree, or three years of graduate education, or one year of specialized experience equivalent to GS-9. **GS-12:** One year of specialized experience equivalent to GS-11. **GS-13:** One year of specialized experience equivalent to GS-12. Qualifying education can be substituted for experience, and vice versa. Tentative appointees must qualify for a security clearance, and pass a background investigation and drug screening test.

Training

BEP personnel security specialists attend the 11-week Criminal Investigator Training Program at the Federal Law Enforcement Training Center in Glynco, Georgia (see chapter 16). In-service training includes specialized courses relating to various aspects of personnel security investigations, including areas such as interviewing techniques, sources of information, security controls and systems, security clearance determinations, criminal and civil law updates, report writing, defensive tactics, firearms proficiency, officer safety, document classification and storage requirements, and other relevant topics.

Contact: Office of Human Resources; Bureau of Engraving and Printing; U.S. Department of the Treasury; 14th and C Sts. SW; Washington, DC 20228; phone: (202) 874-2545; Internet: www.moneyfactory.gov; e-mail: BEPjobs@bep.treas.gov

Personnel Security Specialist (GS-0080)
Office of the Comptroller of the Currency, U.S. Department of the Treasury

The Office of the Comptroller of the Currency (OCC) charters, regulates, and supervises national banks to ensure a safe, sound, and competitive national banking system that supports the citizens, communities, and economy of the United States. OCC personnel security specialists are responsible for implementing policies and procedures for the OCC personnel suitability and security program to ensure the continuous security evaluation of OCC employees and contractors.

Examples of responsibilities carried out by these personnel include determining the suitability and security eligibility of individuals for entry and retention in sensitive and nonsensitive positions; conducting evaluations and recommending revisions to sensitivity level determinations for various positions; reviewing investigative reports and making recommendations to grant, deny, revoke, suspend, or restrict security clearances; administering those portions of the federal government's National Industrial Security Program (NISP) that are concerned with personnel security; coordinating with OCC contracting officers and representatives in the management of contracts requiring cleared personnel with access to classified information; and otherwise ensuring that the OCC personnel suitability and security program operates in compliance with U.S. Treasury Department and other federal requirements. OCC personnel security specialists also provide information and guidance on personnel security policies and procedures for adverse security determinations and related matters.

Qualifications and Salary

GS-5: Completion of a four-year course of study leading to a bachelor's degree; or three years of general experience, one year of which was equivalent to GS-4. **GS-7:** One full year of graduate education, or superior academic achievement during undergraduate studies, or one year of specialized experience equivalent to GS-5. **GS-9:** A master's degree, or two years of graduate education, or one year of specializedexperience equivalent to GS-7. **GS-11:** A Ph.D. or equivalent doctoral degree, or three years of graduate education, or one year of specialized experience equivalent to GS-9. **GS-12:** One year of specialized experience equivalent to GS-11. Applicants can use equivalent combinations of specialized experience and education to meet total experience requirements. Tentative appointees must pass a background investigation.

Training

OCC personnel security specialists attend various courses, seminars, conferences, and workshops throughout their careers to develop knowledge of the OCC personnel suitability and security program and specific responsibilities of the position. Depending on the level of experience of each individual and the nature of assignments, this training could cover topics such as personnel security file maintenance and information management, suitability adjudication documentation, the NISP, security violations, disciplinary actions, computer software programs, agency policies and procedures, and personnel security forms, among other subjects.

Contact: Office of the Comptroller of the Currency; U.S. Department of the Treasury; 250 E St. SW; Washington, DC 20219; phone: (202) 874-5000; Internet: www.occ.treas.gov/; e-mail: careers@occ.treas.gov

Physical Security Specialist (GS-0080)
Agricultural Research Service, U.S. Department of Agriculture

The Agricultural Research Service (ARS) of the U.S. Department of Agriculture (USDA) conducts research to develop new knowledge and technology needed to solve technical agricultural problems of broad scope and high national priority. Included among ARS research programs is support for the National Drug Control Strategy, for which it provides scientific expertise in the areas of illicit crop eradication and drug crop estimates. ARS physical security specialists support the USDA Beltsville Agricultural Research Center (BARC), which includes more than 500 buildings located on 6,800 acres in Beltsville, Maryland.

Some of the tasks performed by these personnel include conducting on-site surveys, analyses, and evaluation of the adequacy and performance of physical security structures and devices such as fences, barriers, lighting, intrusion detection systems, locks, and access controls; preparing written reports describing actions taken to correct security deficiencies; oversight and coordination of contracts for the monitoring and maintenance of more than 70 intrusion alarm and access control systems and devices; reviewing access control data to determine whether systems are operating properly; assisting with the maintenance and repair of electronic security and access control systems; ensuring that security and access codes are issued to new employees, and that codes assigned to former employees are removed; and serving as liaison with other BARC organizations regarding physical security and fire alarm matters.

Qualifications and Salary

GS-5: Completion of a four-year course of study leading to a bachelor's degree; or three years of general experience, one year of which was equivalent to GS-4. **GS-7:** One full year of graduate education, or superior academic achievement during undergraduate studies, or one year of specialized experience equivalent to GS-5. **GS-9:** A master's degree, or two years of graduate education, or one year of specialized experience equivalent to GS-7. **GS-11:** A Ph.D. or equivalent doctoral degree, or three years of graduate education, or one year of specialized experience equivalent to GS-9. **GS-12:** One year of specialized experience equivalent to GS-11. Experience and education can be combined to meet total experience requirements. Appointment is contingent upon a satisfactory background investigation.

Training

ARS physical security specialists have opportunities to attend a variety of basic and advanced training programs throughout their careers. These could focus on alarm and intrusion detection systems, access control systems and locking devices, report writing, physical security surveys, crime prevention, applicable laws and regulations, legal updates, and various agency-specific issues and instructions. Training in these subjects is presented by USDA or ARS staff; federal, state, or local law enforcement training programs or academies; colleges or universities; or other organizations.

Contact: Human Resources Division; Agricultural Research Service; U.S. Department of Agriculture; 5601 Sunnyside Ave.; Beltsville, MD 20705; phone: (301) 504-1400; Internet: www.ars.usda.gov/

Physical Security Specialist (GS-0080)
Physical Security Division, U.S. Capitol Police

Created by Congress in 1828, the original duty of the United States Capitol Police (USCP) department was to provide security for the United States Capitol Building. Expanding on this original mission, USCP physical security specialists presently are responsible for the design and installation of various electronic security systems used for protecting the Capitol Building and a large complex of congressional buildings in the Washington, D.C. area.

Their primary responsibilities revolve around designing, evaluating, installing, and calibrating components and assemblies of electronic security systems, which includes testing and aligning digital circuits and replacing defective parts and devices; adapting security equipment to perform new or different functions depending on the application or assignment; designing and assembling certain electronic equipment that is not available commercially; overseeing the installation of security equipment and systems by government contractors; training USCP personnel in the operation of monitoring equipment and various security devices; developing and designing engineering specifications for new electronic equipment and systems; assisting with the operation and maintenance of an electronics laboratory, including the establishment of test procedures for bench operation and the inspection of equipment; and maintaining records of installations and related field tests. USCP physical security specialists are non-sworn civilian personnel.

Qualifications and Salary

GS-5: Completion of a four-year course of study leading to a bachelor's degree; or three years of general experience, one year of which was equivalent to GS-4. **GS-7:** One full year of graduate education, or superior academic achievement during undergraduate studies, or one year of specialized experience equivalent to GS-5. **GS-9:** A master's degree, or two years of graduate education, or one year of specialized experience equivalent to GS-7. **GS-11:** A Ph.D. or equivalent doctoral degree, or three years of graduate education, or one year of specialized experience equivalent to GS-9. **GS-12:** One year of specialized experience equivalent to GS-11. Equivalent combinations of education and experience can be used to meet minimum experience requirements. Tentative appointees must qualify for a top-secret security clearance and pass a background investigation.

Training

USCP physical security specialists receive on-the-job and periodic in-service training that covers agency policies and directives and areas such as access control systems and technology, intrusion detection systems and devices, closed-circuit television systems, electronics troubleshooting and repair, installation of security equipment and systems, emerging technologies, threat and vulnerability assessments, and related topics.

Contact: Security Services Bureau; United States Capitol Police; 119 D St. NE; Washington, DC 20510; phone: (202) 225-7053; Internet: www.uscapitolpolice.gov/; e-mail: recruiting@cap-police.senate.gov

Physical Security Specialist (GS-0080)
Federal Protective Service, United States Immigration and Customs Enforcement, U.S. Department of Homeland Security

Prior to realignment of federal law enforcement agencies in the wake of the terrorist attacks of September 11, 2001, the Federal Protective Service (FPS) served as the law enforcement and security arm of the Public Buildings Service, a division of the U.S. General Services Administration (GSA). Presently, FPS is a division of U.S. Immigration and Customs Enforcement of the Department of Homeland Security. FPS physical security specialists determine security needs in federal office buildings and facilities, including specific devices, systems, or services that would most effectively mitigate security risks to tenants and visitors.

Examples of responsibilities carried out by these personnel include developing security plans, which include provisions for safes, alarms, locks, fences, intrusion detection, and other devices; developing detailed reports on security surveys, crime assessments, agency consultations, crime awareness training, and security system design; recommending appropriate action where security requirements are not being observed; training building occupants concerning office security, sexual assault, crime prevention, and Occupant Emergency Plans; conducting inspections of security systems to ensure proper fulfillment of security systems contracts; coordinating security, parking, traffic control, investigative, and intelligence support functions with federal, state, and local law enforcement agencies; and enforcing federal laws, building rules, and regulations during emergencies and special investigative situations. FPS physical security specialists also serve as members of federal building security committees, through which they assist with security vulnerability assessments to ensure that security systems in federal facilities meet U.S. Department of Justice standards. FPS physical security specialists are authorized to carry firearms and make arrests.

Qualifications and Salary

GS-7: One full year of graduate education, or superior academic achievement during undergraduate studies, or one year of specialized experience equivalent to GS-5. **GS-9:** A master's degree, or two years of graduate education, or one year of specialized experience equivalent to GS-7. **GS-11:** A Ph.D. or equivalent doctoral degree, or three years of graduate education, or one year of specialized experience equivalent to GS-9. **GS-12:** One year of specialized experience equivalent to GS-11. Qualifying education can be substituted for experience, and vice versa. Candidates must successfully undergo a background investigation, qualify for a security clearance, and pass a drug screening test prior to appointment.

Training

Initial training for FPS physical security specialists consists of three programs that are presented over a period of about three months. These include a general orientation to physical security principles and an overview of the basic responsibilities of the position, followed by the 10-week Mixed Basic Police Training Program at the Federal Law Enforcement Training Center (FLETC) in Glynco, Georgia (see chapter 16), which is followed by the FPS Physical Security Academy at FLETC. These programs introduce FPS physical security specialists to the fundamentals of FPS police and security operations, and include instruction in subjects such as federal criminal law, Constitutional law, arrest techniques, defensive tactics, firearms proficiency, driving skills, terrorism, bombs and explosives, intrusion detection systems, risk assessment, crime prevention, and other topics. FPS physical security specialists also receive on-the-job training and attend various in-service courses throughout their careers.

Contact: Federal Protective Service; United States Immigration and Customs Enforcement; U.S. Department of Homeland Security; 801 I St. NW—Ste. 900; Washington, DC 20536; phone: (202) 514-2648; Internet: www.ice.gov/fps/

Physical Security Specialist (GS-0080)
United States Secret Service, U.S. Department of Homeland Security

Serving with the Technical Security Division in support of United States Secret Service (USSS) protective and investigative missions, USSS physical security specialists provide technical expertise and hands-on support in the areas of physical security; technical surveillance; explosives countermeasures; fire safety; and chemical, biological, and radiological (CBR) countermeasures.

Some examples of responsibilities carried out by these personnel include conducting physical security surveys; installing and maintaining intrusion prevention and detection, video assessment, and access control systems; conducting countermeasures in support of criminal investigations; installing, maintaining, and operating technical surveillance equipment; conducting fire safety surveys, evaluating fire protection systems, and implementing personnel evacuation plans; developing and implementing countermeasures to explosive and CBR threats against protected persons and facilities; testing, troubleshooting, and modifying electronic equipment; and analyzing technical problems and developing solutions pertaining to physical security equipment and systems. Although USSS physical security specialists are assigned to the Washington, D.C. area, they travel frequently throughout the United States and to foreign countries to perform liaison assignments. USSS physical security specialists are authorized to carry firearms.

This position is covered under special retirement provisions for law enforcement officers.

Qualifications and Salary

GS-7: One full year of graduate education, or superior academic achievement during undergraduate studies, or one year of specialized experience equivalent to GS-5. **GS-9:** A master's degree, or two years of graduate education, or one year of specialized experience equivalent to GS-7. **GS-11:** A Ph.D. or equivalent doctoral degree, or three years of graduate education, or one year of specialized experience equivalent to GS-9.

GS-12: One year of specialized experience equivalent to GS-11. **GS-13:** One year of specialized experience equivalent to GS-12.

Appointees must be at least 21 years of age and under age 37. However, candidates over age 37 who have previous service creditable under special law enforcement retirement provisions also may be eligible. Qualifying education can be substituted for experience, and vice versa. Tentative appointees must qualify for a top-secret security clearance and pass a background investigation, polygraph exam, physical exam, and drug screening test. Eyesight must be correctable to 20/20 in each eye. Weight must be proportionate to height.

Training

During the first year of assignment, USSS physical security specialists receive formal classroom and on-the-job training in areas such as terrorism awareness, protective operations, bombs and explosives, physical security fundamentals, fire safety, firearms, defensive tactics, and first aid. Afterward, they complete specialized in-service courses, seminars, and other training programs on an ongoing basis.

Contact: Personnel Division; United States Secret Service; U.S. Department of Homeland Security; 245 Murray Dr.—Bldg. 410; Washington, DC 20223; phone: (202) 406-5800 or (888) 813-8777; Internet: www.secretservice.gov/; e-mail: tsdjobs@secretservice.gov

Physical Security Specialist (GS-0080)
United States Marshals Service, U.S. Department of Justice

The United States Marshals Service (USMS) is the law enforcement and security arm of the U.S. federal court system. In furtherance of this role, USMS physical security specialists administer security programs to protect federal court facilities and property, judges, United States attorneys, law enforcement and court personnel, and court visitors.

Examples of responsibilities carried out by these personnel include conducting continuous on-site inspections of federal court buildings and grounds to determine security system requirements and assess the condition of existing devices and measures; evaluating, planning, and creating specifications for security systems, including intrusion detection devices, automated access control equipment, closed-circuit television monitoring devices, and duress systems; coordinating the installation, upgrading, and maintenance of all interior and exterior physical security devices; using technical knowledge and skills to ensure that security devices operate properly and are resistant to false activations by human-made causes and naturally occurring phenomena; and analyzing, testing, and recommending experimental projects for security system modifications and enhancements. USMS physical security specialists also provide expertise in negotiating the technical aspects of physical security systems and equipment contracts, and perform technical evaluations of multi-phase contractor proposals and design plans.

Qualifications and Salary

GS-5: Completion of a four-year course of study leading to a bachelor's degree; or three years of general experience, one year of which was equivalent to GS-4. **GS-7:** One full year of graduate education, or superior academic achievement during undergraduate studies, or one year of specialized experience equivalent to GS-5. **GS-9:** A master's degree, or two years of graduate education, or one year of specialized experience equivalent to GS-7. **GS-11:** A Ph.D. or equivalent doctoral degree, or three years of graduate education, or one year of specialized experience equivalent to GS-9. **GS-12:** One year of specialized experience equivalent to GS-11. Equivalent combinations of education and experience can be used to meet minimumexperience requirements. USMS physical security specialist candidates must pass a background investigation and qualify for a security clearance prior to appointment.

Training

USMS physical security specialists attend various courses, seminars, and workshops throughout their careers relating to physical security planning, implementation, and evaluation. Some of these training programs are presented by USMS staff, while others are offered by government agencies such as the United States Army Corps of Engineers and the U.S. Secret Service, and manufacturers of security systems and equipment such as Diebold, Mosler Corporation, and ADT Services, among others.

Contact: Human Resources Division; United States Marshals Service; U.S. Department of Justice; 600 Army-Navy Dr.; Arlington, VA 22202; phone: (202) 307-9437; Internet: www.usmarshals.gov/; e-mail: us.marshals@usdoj.gov

Physical Security Specialist (GS-0080)
Bureau of Engraving and Printing, U.S. Department of the Treasury

The Bureau of Engraving and Printing (BEP) designs, prints, and finishes all of the nation's paper currency, as well as U.S. postage stamps, U.S. Treasury securities, naturalization certificates, U.S. Coast Guard water use licenses, presidential appointment certificates, White House invitations, military identification cards, and other security documents. Physical security specialists protect BEP operations through the development of security policy and the design, development, installation, and evaluation of security systems and devices at the headquarters facility in Washington, D.C.; a currency manufacturing plant in Fort Worth, Texas; and at BEP contract sites.

Some of their primary responsibilities revolve around planning and implementing protective systems and security procedures; operating state-of-the-art physical security equipment, including closed-circuit television systems, access control alarm monitoring systems, video badging systems, digital video recording systems, and visitor access control systems; operating intrusion detection devices, lock and key systems, and access control devices; conducting physical security inspections and surveys of facilities, evaluating findings, and recommending appropriate actions to correct deficiencies; resolving complex security problems; analyzing security accountability discrepancies, security violations, and criminal activity; preparing inspection and investigation reports; and assisting federal law enforcement agencies with investigative and other analytical activities involving the accountability or theft of Bureau products. Experienced physical security specialists serve with interagency working groups to share information on terrorist activities or other security threats, protective systems, equipment, and techniques developed by other Federal agencies, private industry, and foreign businesses and governments. BEP physical security specialists are authorized to carry firearms.

Qualifications and Salary

GS-7: One full year of graduate education, or superior academic achievement during undergraduate studies, or one year of specialized experience equivalent to GS-5. **GS-9:** A master's degree, or two years of graduate education, or one year of specialized experience equivalent to GS-7. **GS-11:** A Ph.D. or equivalent doctoral degree, or three years of graduate education, or one year of specialized experience equivalent to GS-9. **GS-12:** One year of specialized experience equivalent to GS-11. **GS-13:** One year of specialized experience equivalent to GS-12. Qualifying education can be substituted for experience, and vice versa. Tentative appointees must qualify for a security clearance and pass a background investigation and drug screening test.

Training

Initial training for BEP physical security specialists consists of a two-week in-house program followed by the 11-week Criminal Investigator Training Program at the Federal Law Enforcement Training Center in Glynco, Georgia (see chapter 16). These personnel also complete various in-service training programs that include specialized instruction in security equipment and systems, new technology, counterterrorism, vulnerability assessments, investigative techniques, criminal and civil law, firearms proficiency, and other subjects.

Contact: Office of Human Resources; Bureau of Engraving and Printing; U.S. Department of the Treasury; 14th and C Sts. SW; Washington, DC 20228; phone: (202) 874-2545; Internet: www.moneyfactory.gov; e-mail: BEPjobs@bep.treas.gov

Regional Security Officer
Bureau of Diplomatic Security, U.S. Department of State

Many State Department Bureau of Diplomatic Security (DS) special agents serve overseas as regional security officers at U.S. diplomatic or consular posts, where they are responsible for administering a broad range of security services to protect Foreign Service personnel and their families, State Department facilities and operations, and information against hostile intelligence, criminal, and terrorist activities.

DS regional security officers safeguard classified and sensitive information and materials in accordance with presidential directives or executive orders; implement security- or safety-related aspects of new office building construction, architectural security related design, counter-terrorist access controls, or design of anti-intrusion devices; maintain an effective security program against terrorist, espionage, and criminal threats of U.S. interests, diplomatic installations, and personnel abroad; detect and investigate attempts by hostile intelligence to subvert U.S. personnel and interests overseas; conduct overseas investigations for the State Department and other federal agencies; and conduct security-related training for personnel of U.S. foreign affairs agencies and law enforcement officials of friendly foreign governments. DS regional security officers also serve as the advisor to the U.S. ambassador on all security-related matters, and as the U.S. liaison with the host country's law enforcement agencies. These personnel are authorized to conduct surveillance and undercover operations and carry firearms. Individual assignments often involve frequent travel between Foreign Service posts in various countries.

Qualifications and Salary

Appointees must be at least age 21 and under age 37, although candidates over age 37 who have previous service creditable under special law enforcement retirement provisions also may be eligible. Basic requirements include a bachelor's degree and one year of specialized experience, although graduate education or academic achievements during undergraduate studies can be substituted for experience. Foreign language ability is preferred, but not required. Eyesight requirements include uncorrected distant vision of at least 20/100 in each eye, corrected to 20/20 in one eye and 20/30 in the other eye, and ability to pass color vision and depth perception tests. Hearing loss must not exceed 30 decibels at 500, 1000, and 2000 cycles per second in either ear. (Hearing aids are not permitted.) The application process includes a writing exam that is evaluated for mastery of grammar, spelling, logic, organization, vocabulary, and word selection; a medical examination; a panel interview; and a background investigation. Tentative appointees must qualify for a top-secret security clearance. Salary for this position does not fall under the General Schedule pay system, although it is similar to GS-1811 special agent positions of other federal law enforcement agencies. Overseas salaries can be adjusted to include cost-of-living allowances, post differentials, danger pay, or other allowances specific to posts of assignment.

Training

Initial training for DS regional security officers consists of a rigorous six-month program. This training begins with an orientation in Washington, D.C., which is followed by the 11-week Criminal Investigator Training Program at the Federal Law Enforcement Training Center in Glynco, Georgia (see chapter 16). Regional security officers then receive approximately three months of specialized training at various sites in the Washington, D. C. area, consisting of courses in passport and visa fraud, investigative techniques, officer safety, defensive tactics, firearms proficiency, emergency medical techniques, driver training, and other subjects.

Contact: Bureau of Diplomatic Security; U.S. Department of State; 2201 C St. NW; Washington, DC 20520; phone: (202) 647-4000; Internet: www.state.gov/m/ds/; e-mail: DSrecruitment@state.gov

Security Specialist (GS-0080)
United States Bureau of the Census, U.S. Department of Commerce

Security specialists of the United States Bureau of the Census participate in the enhancement and administration of the Bureau's security program to ensure the protection and safeguarding of personnel, information, and property.

Some of the tasks performed by these personnel include designing, installing, and maintaining electronic security systems, such as intrusion detection alarms, access control devices, and closed-circuit television equipment; monitoring security alarm systems and arranging for maintenance and adjustments of equipment; conducting site visits to evaluate the performance of security systems; responding to emergencies and incidents such as assaults, robberies, and suspicious persons; conducting follow-up investigations involving crimes and various incidents; participating with the contract guard force, Federal Protective Service (FPS), United States Secret Service, FBI, and other law enforcement personnel during emergencies, civil disturbances, and bomb threat incidents; maintaining liaison with the FPS with respect to building security, intelligence gathering, and terrorist threats; assisting in determining access requirements pertaining to national security information; reviewing security clearance determinations for Bureau employees and other persons with access to sensitive information, resources, material, or works sites; and implementing the Bureau's security awareness program to protect property, restricted information, and national security material.

Qualifications and Salary

GS-7: One full year of graduate education, or superior academic achievement during undergraduate studies, or one year of specialized experience equivalent to GS-5. **GS-9:** A master's degree, or two years of graduate education, or one year of specialized experience equivalent to GS-7. **GS-11:** A Ph.D. or equivalent doctoral degree, or three years of graduate education, or one year of specialized experience equivalent to GS-9. **GS-12:** One year of specialized experience equivalent to GS-11. Equivalent combinations of education and experience can be used to meet minimum experience requirements. Candidates must qualify for a security clearance and pass a background investigation.

Training

Training for Census Bureau security specialists focuses on various aspects of personnel, physical, and information security; security administration; access control systems; security awareness; security clearance and suitability determinations; computer hardware systems and software programs; applicable laws and regulations; legal updates; and other agency-specific training. These professionals attend courses that are presented by agency staff; federal, state, or local law enforcement training programs or academies; colleges or universities; and other organizations.

Contact: Human Resources Division; Bureau of the Census; U.S. Department of Commerce; 4700 Silver Hill Rd.; Washington, DC 20233; phone: (301) 763-4748; Internet: www.census.gov/; e-mail: recruiter@census.gov

Security Specialist (GS-0080)
Office of Administration, Executive Office of the President

The Office of Administration (OA) provides administrative support services to all units within the Executive Office of the President (EOP), including direct support to the president of the United States; information, personnel, and financial management; data processing; library services; records maintenance; and general office operations such as mail, messenger, printing, procurement, and supply services. EOP security specialists perform a variety of administrative duties pertaining to personnel security and investigations in direct support of the OA Security Office.

Examples of responsibilities carried out by these personnel include maintaining an effective personnel security program, which is primarily concerned with making suitability-for-employment determinations regarding employees and job applicants; conducting interviews and reviewing reports of investigations and other data to determine whether employees or job applicants meet national security standards; determining the adequacy of personnel security investigations; determining whether security clearances should be granted, suspended, revoked, or denied; conducting security indoctrinations and debriefings for newly assigned and departing personnel; conducting monthly security briefings for all new employees in coordination with the United

States Secret Service; performing tasks concerned with the physical protection of classified material to ensure that the material is not compromised or sabotaged; and implementing controls to ensure that only authorized personnel are granted access to sensitive information. EOP security specialists also review security files for all EOP employees in critical-sensitive positions, and recommend appropriate action for upgrading their access to classified information.

Qualifications and Salary

GS-7: One full year of graduate education, or superior academic achievement during undergraduate studies, or one year of specialized experience equivalent to GS-5. **GS-9:** A master's degree, or two years of graduate education, or one year of specialized experience equivalent to GS-7. **GS-11:** A Ph.D. or equivalent doctoral degree, or three years of graduate education, or one year of specialized experience equivalent to GS-9. **GS-12:** One year of specialized experience equivalent to GS-11. Applicants can use equivalent combinations of specialized experience and education to meet total experience requirements. Candidates must qualify for a security clearance and pass a background investigation and drug screening test.

Training

EOP security specialists receive ongoing training to develop their knowledge, skills, and abilities in areas such as sensitive compartmented information and special access program requirements, personnel standards, security clearance eligibility requirements, adverse personnel action and derogatory information, position sensitivity and security suitability determinations, interviewing techniques, report writing, applicable laws and regulations, legal updates, agency policies and procedures, and other agency-specific training.

Contact: Human Resources Management Division; Office of Administration; Executive Office of the President; 725 17th St. NW; Washington, DC 20503; phone: (202) 395-5892; Internet: www.whitehouse.gov/oa/

Security Specialist (GS-0080)
United States Geological Survey, U.S. Department of the Interior

The United States Geological Survey (USGS) is the nation's primary provider of earth and biological science information related to classification of public lands, topographic mapping, natural hazards, certain aspects of the environment, and mineral, energy, water, and biological resources. USGS security specialists are responsible for planning, developing, and implementing programs pertaining to the protection of sensitive compartmented information (SCI) and related information storage and processing facilities.

Their responsibilities focus primarily on the coordination of SCI security operations; conducting periodic inspections of automated information systems security procedures to ensure that sensitive information, equipment, and material are not compromised; inspecting security hardware and devices; investigating security violations; monitoring operating procedures for inventory control accountability of classified information; managing the issuance, control, and accountability of security badges, access key cards, locks, and keys; initiating, reviewing, and analyzing security clearance documents to ensure that all required information is provided, and screening for any derogatory information and assessing the impact of the information; identifying security training needs; and administering security briefings and education programs for USGS personnel, other government agencies, and contractors.

Qualifications and Salary

GS-7: One full year of graduate education, or superior academic achievement during undergraduate studies, or one year of specialized experience equivalent to GS-5. **GS-9:** A master's degree, or two years of graduate education, or one year of specialized experience equivalent to GS-7. **GS-11:** A Ph.D. or equivalent doctoral degree, or three years of graduate education, or one year of specialized experience equivalent to GS-9. **GS-12:** One year of specialized experience equivalent to GS-11. Experience and education can be combined to meet total experience requirements. The application process includes a background investigation and security clearance determination.

Training

Training for USGS security specialists depends largely on the experience, expertise, and nature of assignments of individual personnel, although it could include instruction relating to the control and processing of SCI and other classified materials, the identification and investigation of security violations, security awareness, legal updates, and other topics relating to specific responsibilities.

Contact: Personnel Office; United States Geological Survey; U.S. Department of the Interior; 12201 Sunrise Valley Dr.; Reston, VA 20192; phone: (703) 648-6131; Internet: www.usgs.gov/

Security Specialist (GS-0080)
Criminal Division, U.S. Department of Justice

The Criminal Division of the Department of Justice employs security specialists to participate in the implementation of the Federal Witness Security Program, which is operated for the protection of government witnesses whose lives are in danger as a result of their testimony against organized crime figures, drug traffickers, terrorists, or other major criminals.

Their principal responsibilities include preparing Program manuals and regulations; maintaining liaison and coordinating activities with the United States Attorney's Office, United States Marshals Service (USMS), Federal Bureau of Prisons, FBI, and other law enforcement agencies; arranging USMS interviews of prospective witnesses prepared for relocation to determine suitability for participation in the Program; making recommendations to approve or deny requests for Program participation; coordinating debriefing of witnesses after entry into the Program; inspecting special prison sites where prisoner-witnesses are housed; monitoring and coordinating investigations resulting from threats or attacks directed at relocated witnesses; establishing guidelines on travel by protected witnesses; and resolving disputes among witnesses, prosecutors, and investigative agencies concerning job assistance, area of relocation, and termination of subsistence. Criminal Division security specialists also conduct conferences and seminars for investigators and prosecutors to facilitate dissemination of Program information, and prepare responses to inquiries from the White House, Congress, the media, and the public.

Qualifications and Salary

GS-7: One full year of graduate education, or superior academic achievement during undergraduate studies, or one year of specialized experience equivalent to GS-5. **GS-9:** A master's degree, or two years of graduate education, or one year of specialized experience equivalent to GS-7. **GS-11:** A Ph.D. or equivalent doctoral degree, or three years of graduate education, or one year of specialized experience equivalent to GS-9. **GS-12:** One year of specialized experience equivalent to GS-11. Equivalent combinations of education and experience can be used to meet minimum experience requirements. Those tentatively selected must pass a background investigation and qualify for a security clearance.

Training

Initial training for security specialists of the Criminal Division consists of an orientation to the mission, policies, procedures, and rules of the agency, as well as an overview of the Federal Witness Security Program. Ongoing in-service training includes instruction on subjects such as report writing, computer security, information security, and other topics pertaining to specific responsibilities of the position. The majority of in-service training is provided by Justice Department staff, although some training is presented by outside organizations.

Contact: Criminal Division; U.S. Department of Justice; 950 Pennsylvania Ave.; Washington, DC 20530; phone: (202) 514-2601; Internet: www.usdoj.gov/criminal/ criminal-home.html; e-mail: Criminal.Division@usdoj.gov

Security Specialist (GS-0080)
Justice Management Division, U.S. Department of Justice

The Justice Management Division (JMD) provides assistance to senior Department of Justice (DOJ) management officials relating to DOJ policies for budget and financial management, personnel management and training, equal opportunity programs, ethics training and advice, automatic data processing, telecommunications, security, records management, procurement, real property, and material management, and for all other matters pertaining to DOJ management and administration. Security specialists serving in the JMD Personnel Security Group conduct investigations into the suitability of DOJ employees and contractor personnel for employment, sensitive positions, or positions of trust.

Some examples of responsibilities carried out by these personnel include conducting and directing investigations; assisting in the preparation of reviews and evaluations of investigative reports to determine whether current or prospective employees or contractors meet national security and employment suitability standards appropriate to the position sensitivity level; evaluating investigative reports to determine eligibility for granting access to national security information or sensitive compartmented information (SCI); responding to inquiries for verification of security clearances; maintaining computerized personnel security records; assisting in the preparation of policies, orders, directives, and manuals concerning personnel security and associated programs; reviewing component security program activities to determine the adequacy of compliance with the DOJ personnel security program; and generating reports and statistical information.

Qualifications and Salary

GS-7: One full year of graduate education, or superior academic achievement during undergraduate studies, or one year of specialized experience equivalent to GS-5. **GS-9:** A master's degree, or two years of graduate education, or one year of specialized experience equivalent to GS-7. **GS-11:** A Ph.D. or equivalent doctoral degree, or three years of graduate education, or one year of specialized experience equivalent to GS-9. **GS-12:** One year of specialized experience equivalent to GS-11. Applicants can use equivalent combinations of specialized experience and education to meet total experience requirements. Tentative appointees must pass a background investigation and drug screening test.

Training

Career development for JMD security specialists consists of on-the-job and in-service instruction that includes an orientation to the mission, policies, procedures, and rules of the JMD and DOJ, as well as other job-specific training. These include seminars or courses relating to employee and contractor suitability determinations, requirements for access to national security or SCI, adjudications guidelines and processes, alcohol and drug addition, indebtedness, derogatory information, and other topics.

Contact: Justice Management Division; U.S. Department of Justice; 950 Pennsylvania Ave.; Washington, DC 20530; phone: (202) 514-2000; Internet: www.usdoj.gov/jmd/

Transportation Security Officer
Transportation Security Administration, U.S. Department of Homeland Security

Transportation security officers—formerly known as transportation security screeners—serve on the front lines of the civil aviation industry to provide protection of air travelers, aircraft, air carriers, and airports. These personnel are responsible for identifying dangerous and potentially life-threatening objects in baggage and cargo, and on passengers, and preventing the objects from being transported onto aircraft. For example, some of the prohibited items seized by transportation security officers have included knives and other cutting instruments, firearms and ammunition, explosives, flammable liquids and other incendiary devices, pepper spray, and clubs.

Some of the tasks carried out by transportation security officers include controlling airport terminal entry and exit points; screening passenger tickets; examining checked baggage and carry-on items; operating alarm systems, magnetometers, handheld security wand metal detectors, x-ray machines, explosives detection machines and portals, and other electronic imaging and detection devices; conducting pat-down searches of persons seeking to board aircraft; monitoring the flow of passengers through screening checkpoints to facilitate the orderly and efficient processing of passengers; and responding to inquiries and crisis situations. Transportation security officers also participate in information briefings to discuss security issues and sensitive or classified information relating to potential threats to aviation operations.

Qualifications and Salary

The Transportation Security Administration (TSA) is an excepted service agency and does not follow competitive service hiring processes or the General Schedule pay system. Job qualifications and salaries for TSA transportation security officers are similar to those of security guard positions with federal agencies at the GS-4 to GS-5 levels in the competitive service. Minimum qualifications for TSA transportation security officers include either a high school diploma, GED certificate, or equivalent; or at least one year of full-time work experience in security, aviation screener, or x-ray technician work; proficiency in the English language, including reading, writing, speaking, and listening; interpersonal skills; and the ability to repeatedly lift and carry baggage weighing at least 70 pounds. Eyesight requirements include distant vision correctable to at least 20/30 in one eye and 20/100 or better in the other eye, near vision correctable to at least 20/40 with both eyes, and color perception. Hearing loss cannot exceed 25 decibels at 500, 1000, 2000, and 3000 Hertz in each ear, and a single reading of 45 decibels at 4000 Hertz and 6000 Hertz in each ear. Candidates also must have adequate joint mobility, dexterity, and range of motion. The application process includes a drug and alcohol screening test, a background investigation, and a medical evaluation.

Training

Basic training for TSA transportation security officers consists of a 200-hour program that includes 72 hours of classroom instruction, 128 hours of on-the-job training, and a certification examination. The training curriculum focuses on screening functions and security checkpoint operations; the equipment, tools, and skills used to identify prohibited items in baggage and cargo and carried by passengers; observing passenger behavior; terrorist operations; intelligence information; customer service principles; interpersonal skills; teamwork; federal regulations; TSA rules, standard operating procedures, and directives; and other related subjects. This training includes classroom lectures, videotaped presentations, practical exercises, materials on CD-ROM, and online instruction. TSA policies require transportation security officers to complete at least three hours of skills refresher training per week, averaged over each quarter, in areas such as x-ray image interpretation, screening techniques, standard operating procedures, ethics, and federal Privacy Act issues. Recurrent training is presented through TSA's Online Learning Center and by TSA instructors and contractor personnel.

Contact: Transportation Security Administration; U.S. Department of Homeland Security; 601 S. 12th St.; Arlington, VA 22202; phone: (800) 887-1895; Internet: www.tsa.gov/

CHAPTER 13

Correctional Officers and Specialists

"If you want total security, go to prison. There you're fed, clothed, given medical care and so on. The only thing lacking is freedom."

—*Dwight D. Eisenhower*

This chapter features 10 careers associated with the federal correctional system—of which one-half are with the Federal Bureau of Prisons (BOP). Careers that are profiled in this chapter include clinical psychologists, correctional officers, correctional program specialists, correctional treatment specialists, detention enforcement officers, drug treatment specialists, and inmate systems specialists. Each of these personnel plays a vital role in a coordinated effort to operate correctional facilities that are safe, humane, and secure, and which provide work, counseling, and other opportunities to assist offenders in becoming law-abiding citizens.

Correctional officers are stationed on the front lines of the correctional system by agencies such as the BOP, Bureau of Indian Affairs, and National Park Service. These federal officers are responsible for the confinement, supervision, safety, health, and protection of inmates, and for the overall operation of correctional facilities and programs. Detention enforcement officers of the U.S. Marshals Service also are responsible for correctional supervision of prisoners.

Clinical psychologists, correctional treatment specialists, and drug treatment specialists assess, evaluate, and treat prisoners with a variety of problems and disorders through group and individual counseling, education, and other techniques. Correctional program specialists are employed by the BOP and the Navy to develop, implement, and coordinate various programs relating to the treatment and rehabilitation of inmates. Inmate systems specialists ensure that new federal prisoners are processed appropriately, and also that inmates' mail is handled according to BOP and Postal Service regulations.

Settings in which federal correctional officers and specialists perform their duties include federal correctional institutions, military and community-based facilities, camps, jails, medical facilities, and a national park. All institution-based correctional personnel are covered under special retirement provisions for law enforcement officers, and most are authorized to carry firearms and make arrests.

Clinical Psychologist (GS-0180)
Federal Bureau of Prisons, U.S. Department of Justice

With a team of more than 400 psychologists, the Federal Bureau of Prisons (BOP) is one of the largest employers of psychologists in the United States. In most BOP institutions, doctoral-level psychologists function as front-line providers of mental health services to inmates. BOP clinical psychologists are responsible for the assessment, evaluation, and treatment of prisoners with a variety of problems of personality, emotional adjustment, mental illness, or other disorders.

Using professional knowledge of psychological principles, theories, methods, and techniques, BOP clinical psychologists administer and interpret psychological tests that are used for diagnosing mental and personality disorders; apply data derived from these tests to determine physical and psychological diagnoses; assist in developing appropriate courses of treatment; develop and organize individual and group psychotherapy sessions and other rehabilitative programs; and prepare comprehensive written reports. They also provide mental health consultation to BOP hostage negotiation and crisis support teams, and conduct Employee Assistance Program counseling to BOP personnel. Most inmates are self-referred, although some are referred either by prison staff, the federal courts, or parole boards. BOP clinical psychologists are authorized to carry firearms and make arrests.

This position is covered under special retirement provisions for law enforcement officers. Similar BOP positions are filled under the GS-0180 Counseling Psychologist series.

Qualifications and Salary Levels

GS-11: Completion of all requirements for a Ph.D. or equivalent doctoral degree directly related to clinical psychology. **GS-12:** Completion of all requirements for a Ph.D. or equivalent doctoral degree directly related to clinical psychology, and one year of specialized experience equivalent to GS-11. **GS-13:** Completion of all requirements for a Ph.D. or equivalent doctoral degree directly related to clinical psychology, and one year of specialized experience equivalent to GS-12. Applicants must be at least 21 years of age and under age 37. However, candidates over age 37 who have previous service creditable under special law enforcement retirement provisions also may be eligible. If a shortage of applicants exists, highly qualified clinical psychologist candidates can receive a waiver that allows them to be hired prior to reaching age 40. Tentative appointees must qualify for a security clearance and pass a background investigation, personal interview, drug screening test, and physical exam.

Training

Clinical psychologists attend the three-week Introduction to Correctional Techniques training program presented by the BOP Staff Training Academy at the Federal Law Enforcement Training Center in Glynco, Georgia (see chapter 16), followed by a two-week correctional institution familiarization course. BOP sponsors an extensive Continuing Professional Education program that is endorsed by the American Psychological Association. This program includes courses concerned with correctional psychology, hostage negotiation, Crisis Support Team activities, drug abuse treatment, correctional supervision, therapeutic environments, group treatment processes, inmate suicide, legal issues and updates, inmate profiles, inmate and staff diversity, interpersonal skills, and other subjects. BOP also provides funding to each clinical psychologist so they can take advantage of professional training opportunities offered nationwide.

Clinical psychologists regularly present papers at national conferences and publish research in psychological and criminal justice journals.

Contact: Federal Bureau of Prisons; U.S. Department of Justice; 320 First St. NW—Ste. 460; Washington, DC 20534; phone: (202) 307-3198 or (800) 347-7744; Internet: www.bop.gov/

Correctional Officer (GS-0007)
Bureau of Indian Affairs, U.S. Department of the Interior

Bureau of Indian Affairs (BIA) correctional officers are responsible for the confinement, safety, health, and protection of criminal offenders in BIA custody, and for the overall operation of correctional facilities and programs.

These personnel conduct preliminary interviews for physical and mental health classification assessments; conduct inmate supervision and counts; provide for facility safety and security, key control, inmate transportation, and perimeter security; perform inmate and cell searches; ensure compliance with correctional facility rules and regulations; coordinate and supervise services, activities, and programs relating to areas such as medical care, food service, laundry, recreation, library usage, counseling, religious services, and work programs; maintain fire safety; and prepare written reports. BIA correctional officers work closely with other criminal justice personnel, government and community officials, medical staff, and mental health professionals to ensure that inmate treatment plans are implemented according to correctional program standards and legal requirements.

This position is covered under special retirement provisions for law enforcement officers.

Qualifications and Salary Levels

GS-3: One year of education above high school, or six months of general experience.
GS-4: Two years of education above high school, or one year of general experience.
GS-5: Completion of a four-year course of study leading to a bachelor's degree; or three years of general experience, one year of which was equivalent to GS-4. **GS-6:** One half year of graduate-level education with major study in criminal justice, social science, or other fields related to the position; or one year of specialized experience equivalent to GS-5. **GS-7:** One full year of graduate-level education (in the fields listed under GS-6), or one year of specialized experience equivalent to GS-6. **GS-8:** One year of specialized experience equivalent to GS-7. **GS-9:** One year of specialized experience equivalent to GS-8.

Experience and education can be combined to meet total experience requirements. Applicants must be at least 21 years of age and under age 37. Candidates over age 37 who have previous service creditable under special law enforcement retirement provisions also may be eligible. Eyesight requirements include distant vision of at least 20/100 (Snellen) in each eye without correction, and at least 20/30 in each eye with correction. Normal hearing is required, including ability to hear the conversational voice and whispered speech without the use of a hearing aid. Those tentatively selected must pass a background investigation and drug screening test. Under the Indian Reorganization Act of 1934, qualified Native American applicants are given hiring preference for BIA positions, although applications from non–Native American candidates are encouraged.

Training

Initial training for BIA correctional officers includes the five-week Basic Corrections Officer Training Program within the Indian Police Academy at the Federal Law Enforcement Training Center in Artesia, New Mexico. This program—which is designed exclusively for BIA and tribal correctional officers—provides instruction on Indian Country jurisdiction, constitutional law, the civil rights of inmates, jail operations, fire safety, alcohol and substance abuse, contraband control, cell searches, inmate health screening, crisis intervention, disturbance control, bookings and admissions, jail security, environmental health inspections, record keeping, suicide prevention, inmate management, community policing, special inmate problems, and physical conditioning. BIA correctional officers also attend various in-service courses throughout their careers.

Contact: Direct inquiries to the personnel office where employment is sought, or to Office of Personnel; Bureau of Indian Affairs; Department of the Interior; 1849 C St. NW; Washington, DC 20240; phone: (202) 208-3710; Internet: www.doi.gov/bureau-indian-affairs.html/.

Correctional Officer (GS-0007)
National Park Service, U.S. Department of the Interior

The National Park Service (NPS) employs correctional officers at Yosemite National Park to receive and process persons arrested on Park property, and to perform a variety of functions related to the detention, custody, security, counseling, care, and treatment of prisoners.

The primary responsibilities of these officers include prisoner processing and fingerprinting; ensuring that security and custody procedures are followed relating to prisoner transportation, movement, detention, protection, and separation; informing prisoners of and ensuring compliance with NPS rules and regulations; performing regular shakedowns of cells; and serving as a court bailiff. As fully commissioned law enforcement officers who are deputized as special deputy United States marshals, NPS correctional officers occasionally participate in Park patrol and emergency operations, and are authorized to carry firearms and make arrests.

Yosemite National Park is the only NPS location where correctional officers are employed. This position is covered under special retirement provisions for law enforcement officers.

Qualifications and Salary Levels

GS-5: Completion of a four-year course of study leading to a bachelor's degree; or three years of general experience, one year of which was equivalent to GS-4. **GS-6:** One half year of graduate-level education with major study in criminal justice, social science, or other fields related to the position; or one year of specialized experience equivalent to GS-5. **GS-7:** One full year of graduate-level education (in the fields listed under GS-6), or one year of specialized experience equivalent to GS-6. **GS-8:** One year of specialized experience equivalent to GS-7. **GS-9:** One year of specialized experience equivalent to GS-8.

Equivalent combinations of education and experience can be used to meet minimum experience requirements. Tentative appointees must qualify for a security clearance and pass a personal interview, background investigation, drug screening test, and physical exam. Applicants must be at least 21 years of age and under age 37.

Candidates over age 37 who have previous service creditable under special law enforcement retirement provisions also may be eligible. Eyesight requirements include distant vision of at least 20/100 (Snellen) in each eye without correction, and at least 20/30 in each eye with correction. Normal hearing is required, including ability to hear the conversational voice and whispered speech without the use of a hearing aid.

Training

Those appointed to NPS correctional officer positions typically are fully commissioned law enforcement officers who have already completed either state-certified police academy training or the 16-week Natural Resources Police Training Program at the Federal Law Enforcement Training Center in Glynco, Georgia. NPS correctional officers also receive a minimum of 40 hours of in-service training annually, including courses in subjects such as criminal law, laws of arrest, civil liability, patrol techniques, firearms proficiency, defensive tactics, and first aid.

Contact: Division of Personnel Management; National Park Service; Department of the Interior; 1849 C St. NW; Washington, DC 20240; phone: (202) 208-6843; Internet: www.nps.gov/

Correctional Officer (GS-0007)
Federal Bureau of Prisons, U.S. Department of Justice

Correctional officers of the Federal Bureau of Prisons (BOP) perform a wide range of tasks concerning the custody, treatment, supervision, safety, and well-being of inmates in federal correctional institutions, camps, jails, and medical facilities.

Their primary responsibilities include guiding inmate conduct; monitoring activities such as exercise, dining, and showering; supervising work details; searching inmates and their living quarters for weapons, drugs, and contraband; inspecting locks, window bars, doors, and gates for signs of tampering; maintaining control room posts; and monitoring closed-circuit television cameras and computerized tracking and detection systems. They also escort inmates to and from visits with medical staff, other correctional personnel, and visitors; inspect mail and visitors for prohibited items; carry out plans for the treatment and modification of inmates' attitudes; instruct and counsel inmates on institutional and personal problems; and assist with investigations involving crimes committed within correctional facilities. BOP correctional officers are authorized to carry firearms and make arrests.

This position is covered under special retirement provisions for law enforcement officers.

Qualifications and Salary Levels

GS-5: Completion of a four-year course of study leading to a bachelor's degree; or three years of general experience, one year of which was equivalent to GS-4. **GS-6:** One half year of graduate-level education with major study in criminal justice, social science, or other fields related to the position; or one year of specialized experience equivalent to GS-5. **GS-7:** One full year of graduate-level education (in the fields listed under GS-6), or one year of specialized experience equivalent to GS-6. **GS-8:** One year of specialized experience equivalent to GS-7. **GS-9:** One year of specialized experience equivalent to GS-8.

Qualifying education can be substituted for experience, and vice versa. Candidates must qualify for a security clearance and pass a personal interview, background investigation, drug screening test, and physical exam. Applicants must be at least 21 years of age and under age 37. Candidates over age 37 who have previous service creditable under special law enforcement retirement provisions also may be eligible. Eyesight requirements include distant vision of at least 20/100 (Snellen) in each eye without correction, and at least 20/30 in each eye with correction. Normal hearing is required, including ability to hear the conversational voice and whispered speech without the use of a hearing aid.

Training

Correctional officers attend the three-week Introduction to Correctional Techniques training program presented by the BOP Staff Training Academy at the Federal Law Enforcement Training Center in Glynco, Georgia (see chapter 16), followed by a two-week correctional institution familiarization course conducted by BOP staff. In-service training includes a minimum of 40 hours of courses annually, encompassing subjects such as correctional supervision, inmate suicide, hostage situations, interpersonal skills, use of force, legal issues and updates, inmate and staff diversity, and other topics related to specific duties.

Contact: Federal Bureau of Prisons; U.S. Department of Justice; 320 First St. NW—Ste. 460; Washington, DC 20534; phone: (202) 307-3198 or (800) 347-7744; Internet: www.bop.gov/

Correctional Program Specialist (GS-0006)
United States Navy, U.S. Department of Defense

United States Navy correctional program specialists are responsible for developing, examining, and analyzing a wide range of programs concerning the treatment and rehabilitation of prisoners incarcerated in Navy correctional facilities.

Tasks performed by these personnel include developing programs and determining levels of staff expertise needed to meet program goals and prisoner needs; implementing, coordinating, and monitoring prisoner treatment efforts and initiating necessary changes; arranging for facilities, materials, instructors, and security; drafting policies concerning program procedures and operations; monitoring prisoners to determine their suitability for participation in programs and making recommendations for their release; participating as a member of various boards and panels to assess the effectiveness of program components and implementation strategies, and to assess prisoners' progress in rehabilitation; implementing corrections policies and regulations; and communicating with high-level Navy officials and personnel from other agencies and organizations.

Navy correctional program specialists are covered under special retirement provisions for law enforcement officers. This is a civilian position and does not require active duty military service.

Qualifications and Salary Levels

GS-5: Completion of a four-year course of study leading to a bachelor's degree; or three years of general experience, one year of which was equivalent to GS-4. **GS-7:** One full year of graduate-level education, or superior academic achievement during undergraduate studies, or one year of specialized experience equivalent to GS-5. **GS-9:** A master's degree, or two years of graduate-level education, or one year of specialized experience equivalent to GS-7. **GS-11:** A Ph.D. or equivalent doctoral degree, or three years of graduate-level education, or one year of specialized experience equivalent to GS-9. **GS-12:** One year of specialized experience equivalent to GS-11.

Experience and education can be combined to meet total experience requirements. Candidates must successfully complete a background investigation, qualify for a security clearance, and pass a drug test, personal interview, and physical exam prior to appointment. Applicants must be at least 21 years of age and under age 37. Candidates over age 37 who have previous service creditable under special law enforcement retirement provisions also may be eligible. Eyesight requirements include distant vision of at least 20/100 (Snellen) in each eye without correction, and at least 20/30 in each eye with correction. Normal hearing is required, including ability to hear the conversational voice and whispered speech without the use of a hearing aid.

Training

Initial training for Navy correctional program specialists is conducted by Navy personnel, and includes a 140-hour Correctional Specialist Course and a 40-hour pre-service course. These in-house programs focus on Navy policies and procedures, an overview of the correctional system, correctional issues, military law, civil liability, and other subjects. Additional training includes a four-week program that covers group and individual counseling methods, as well as various courses and workshops pertaining to correctional program development, interpersonal communication, interviewing techniques, hostage negotiation, self-defense, and other tasks. In-service training is presented by organizations such as the American Correctional Association, American Jail Association, and the FBI.

Contact: Direct inquiries to the Human Resources Office where employment is sought, or contact United States Navy; 614 Sicard St. SE—Ste. 100; Washington, DC 20374; phone: (703) 614-1271; Internet: www.navy.mil/; e-mail: help@chinfo.navy.mil.

Correctional Program Specialist (GS-0006)
Federal Bureau of Prisons, U.S. Department of Justice

Although specific responsibilities vary widely among positions in this occupational series, correctional program specialists of the Federal Bureau of Prisons (BOP) are responsible for coordinating training programs that promote the health, spirituality, and well-being of prison inmates. Under the supervision of BOP correctional program officers, chief psychologists, chaplains, or administrators, correctional program specialists coordinate programs pertaining to recreation, religion, disease prevention, health education, physical fitness, rational thinking, criminal lifestyle confrontation, anger management, drug eradication, peer influences, ethics, relapse prevention, victim impact, and a variety of other subjects.

Examples of responsibilities carried out by these personnel include assisting with needs assessments and task analysis functions; developing program content; selecting and expelling inmates; scheduling; providing group counseling regarding BOP policies; preparing reports relevant to inmate histories and their progress in treatment; entering and retrieving data from computer systems; coordinating psychology services activities; purchasing equipment, materials, and supplies; and other tasks relating to the overall operation of BOP programs. Correctional program specialists are authorized to carry firearms and make arrests.

This position is covered under special retirement provisions for law enforcement officers.

Qualifications and Salary Levels

GS-5: Completion of a four-year course of study leading to a bachelor's degree; or three years of general experience, one year of which was equivalent to GS-4. **GS-7:** One full year of graduate-level education, or superior academic achievement during undergraduate studies, or one year of specialized experience equivalent to GS-5. **GS-9:** A master's degree, or two years of graduate-level education, or one year of specialized experience equivalent to GS-7. **GS-11:** A Ph.D. or equivalent doctoral degree, or three years of graduate-level education, or one year of specialized experience equivalent to GS-9. **GS-12:** One year of specialized experience equivalent to GS-11.

Equivalent combinations of education and experience can be used to meet minimum experience requirements. Successful completion of a background investigation, drug test, physical exam, personal interview, and security clearance process also is required. Candidates must be at least 21 years of age, and under age 37. Candidates over age 37 who have previous service creditable under special law enforcement retirement provisions also may be eligible.

Training

Correctional program specialists attend the three-week Introduction to Correctional Techniques training program presented by the BOP Staff Training Academy at the Federal Law Enforcement Training Center in Glynco, Georgia (see chapter 16), followed by a two-week correctional institution familiarization course conducted by BOP staff. In-service training includes a minimum of 40 hours of coursework annually, pertaining to subjects such as communicable diseases, drug and alcohol testing, correctional supervision, inmate suicide, interpersonal skills, interviewing techniques, legal issues and updates, inmate profiles, inmate and staff diversity, and other topics related to specific duties.

Contact: Federal Bureau of Prisons; U.S. Department of Justice; 320 First St. NW—Ste. 460; Washington, DC 20534; phone: (202) 307-3198 or (800) 347-7744; Internet: www.bop.gov/

Correctional Treatment Specialist (GS-0101)
United States Parole Commission, U.S. Department of Justice

The United States Parole Commission (USPC) is responsible for parole functions pertaining to eligible federal and District of Columbia (DC) prisoners and parolees. The USPC maintains the sole authority to grant, modify, or revoke parole; to conduct supervision of parolees and prisoners released upon the expiration of their sentences; and to determine parole supervisory conditions and terms.

Serving in the capacity of hearing examiner, USPC correctional treatment specialists conduct a wide range of parole hearings that involve eligible federal and DC prisoners, military prisoners confined in federal institutions, alleged parole or mandatory release violators, State Witness Protection cases, and Foreign Transfer Treaty cases. As a result of these hearings, correctional treatment specialists prepare case summaries and make recommendations for granting or denying parole, early discharge from supervision, issuance of a warrant or summons for violation of the conditions of supervision, and revocation of parole. In arriving at decisions concerning these issues, USPC correctional treatment specialists must take into account a number of factors, such as the severity of the offense committed, the need for just punishment, the offender's criminal history, the offender's risk of recidivism, and the offender's conduct in the institution.

This position is covered under special retirement provisions for law enforcement officers.

Qualifications and Salary Levels

GS-5: A bachelor's degree that included at least 24 semester hours of coursework in the behavioral or social sciences; or a combination of education and experience that included at least 24 semester hours of coursework in the behavioral or social sciences, and that provided the applicant with knowledge of one or more of the behavioral or social sciences equivalent to a bachelor's degree. **GS-7:** One full year of graduate-level education, or superior academic achievement during undergraduate studies, or one year of specialized experience equivalent to GS-5. **GS-9:** A master's degree, or two years of graduate-level education, or one year of specialized experience equivalent to GS-7. **GS-11:** A Ph.D. or equivalent doctoral degree, or three years of graduate-level education, or one year of specialized experience equivalent to GS-9. **GS-12:** One year of specialized experience equivalent to GS-11.

Graduate education must have been in corrections or a related field such as criminal justice, sociology, psychology, counseling, social work, or other coursework related to the position. Qualifying education can be substituted for experience, and vice versa. Tentative appointees must qualify for a security clearance and pass a background investigation, personal interview, drug screening test, and physical exam. Applicants must be at least 21 years of age and under age 37. Candidates over age 37 who have previous service creditable under special law enforcement retirement provisions also may be eligible.

Training

Newly appointed USPC correctional treatment specialists are given an orientation to the mission, policies, procedures, and rules of the agency, as well as an overview of the parole process, parole laws and regulations, and professional contacts. The orientation also includes an introduction to Federal Bureau of Prisons and United States Probation operations. In-service training could include courses and participation in criminal justice conferences pertaining to the parole process, legal issues and updates, parole case studies, and other pertinent matters relating to the position.

Contact: United States Parole Commission; U.S. Department of Justice; 5550 Friendship Blvd.—Ste. 420; Chevy Chase, MD 20815; phone: (301) 492-5990; Internet: www.usdoj/gov/uspc/

Detention Enforcement Officer (GS-1802)
United States Marshals Service, U.S. Department of Justice

The United States Marshals Service (USMS) assumes custody of individuals arrested by all federal law enforcement agencies, and is responsible for housing and transporting prisoners from the time they are in federal custody until they are either acquitted or sentenced.

In furtherance of the USMS mission, detention enforcement officers are responsible for the receiving, processing, detaining, tracking, and security of prisoners in USMS custody. Some of the tasks they perform include supervising prisoners; searching prisoners for concealed weapons, contraband, and other prohibited items; taking inventories of personal property; interviewing prisoners to obtain personal history information; entering personal data into automated database systems; taking photographs and fingerprints; operating busses or large passenger vans; transporting prisoners to and from federal or state detention facilities, cellblocks, and courtrooms; and maintaining courtroom discipline. In applying the expertise of detention enforcement officers, the USMS completes more than 160,000 prisoner movements annually via coordinated air and ground systems. USMS detention enforcement officers are authorized to carry firearms.

This position is covered under special retirement provisions for law enforcement officers.

Qualifications and Salary Levels

GS-5: Completion of a four-year course of study leading to a bachelor's degree; or three years of general experience, one year of which was equivalent to GS-4. **GS-6:** One half year of graduate-level education with major study in criminal justice, social science, or other fields related to the position; or one year of specialized experience equivalent to GS-5. **GS-7:** One full year of graduate-level education (in the fields listed under GS-6), or one year of specialized experience equivalent to GS-6. **GS-8:** One year of specialized experience equivalent to GS-7.

Experience and education can be combined to meet total experience requirements for positions at grade GS-5. Applicants must be at least 21 years of age and under age 37. Candidates over age 37 who have previous service creditable under special law enforcement retirement provisions also may be eligible. Candidates must successfully complete a background investigation, qualify for a security clearance, and pass a drug test and physical exam prior to appointment.

Training

Training for USMS detention enforcement officers includes an orientation to the mission, policies, procedures, and rules of the agency, followed by in-house instruction that focuses on prisoner processing, detention and prisoner movement procedures, officer safety, the USMS Prisoner Tracking System computer program, and other subjects. These personnel also receive periodic in-service training related to specific responsibilities of the position, depending on the experience and needs of each officer.

Contact: Human Resources Division; United States Marshals Service; U.S. Department of Justice; 600 Army Navy Dr.; Arlington, VA 22202; phone: (202) 307-9437; Internet: www.usmarshals.gov/; e-mail: us.marshals@usdoj.gov

Drug Treatment Specialist (GS-0101)
Federal Bureau of Prisons, U.S. Department of Justice

Drug treatment specialists of the Federal Bureau of Prisons (BOP) provide substance abuse counseling and education to inmates of BOP correctional institutions.

Drug treatment specialists are responsible for developing and evaluating substance abuse programs; managing assigned caseloads of offenders who have histories of substance abuse; coordinating inmate training programs; developing social histories; identifying deficiencies and excesses in inmates' patterns of thought and behavior, and recommending or devising corrective measures; providing group and individual counseling; applying assessment and treatment techniques to help inmates overcome criminal lifestyle and drug abuse problems; evaluating the progress of program participants; planning aftercare programs; working with prisoners, their families, and interested persons in developing parole and release plans; completing progress reports and administrative paperwork; providing case reports to the U.S. Parole Commission; and interacting with U.S. probation officers and other agencies in developing and implementing release plans or programs. Drug treatment specialists are authorized to carry firearms and make arrests.

This position is covered under special retirement provisions for law enforcement officers.

Qualifications and Salary Levels

GS-5: A bachelor's degree that included at least 24 semester hours of coursework in the behavioral or social sciences, or a combination of education and experience that included at least 24 semester hours of coursework in these subjects and that provided knowledge of one or more of the behavioral or social sciences equivalent to a bachelor's degree. **GS-7:** One full year of graduate-level education, or superior academic achievement during undergraduate studies, or one year of specialized experience equivalent to GS-5. **GS-9:** A master's degree, or two years of graduate-level education, or one year of specialized experience equivalent to GS-7. **GS-11:** A Ph.D. or equivalent doctoral degree, or three years of graduate-level education, or one year of specialized experience equivalent to GS-9. **GS-12:** One year of specialized experience equivalent to GS-11.

Applicants must have completed three semester hours of undergraduate coursework or 50 hours of training in alcohol or drug abuse, or have six months of experience counseling drug or alcohol abusers. Tentative appointees must qualify for a security clearance and pass a background investigation, personal interview, drug screening test, and physical exam. Applicants must be at least 21 years of age and under age 37. Candidates over age 37 who have previous service creditable under special law enforcement retirement provisions also may be eligible.

Training

Drug treatment specialists attend the three-week Introduction to Correctional Techniques training program presented by the BOP Staff Training Academy at the Federal Law Enforcement Training Center in Glynco, Georgia (see chapter 16), as well as a two-week correctional institution familiarization course conducted by BOP staff. This training is followed by a two-week Drug Abuse Treatment Specialist course that covers drug abuse program policies and procedures, group treatment processes, and other clinical issues. In-service training includes a minimum of 40 hours of coursework annually, pertaining to subjects such as cognitive skill building, creating therapeutic environments, group treatment processes, inmate suicide, interpersonal skills, inmate profiles, inmate and staff diversity, and other topics.

Contact: Federal Bureau of Prisons; U.S. Department of Justice; 320 First St. NW—Ste. 460; Washington, DC 20534; phone: (202) 307-3198 or (800) 347-7744; Internet: www.bop.gov/

Inmate Systems Specialist (GS-0007)
Federal Bureau of Prisons, U.S. Department of Justice

Inmate systems specialists serving with the Federal Bureau of Prisons (BOP) perform many tasks relating to the intake and oversight of BOP prisoners.

They screen newly committed prisoners to ensure that they have proper identification; determine potential medical and social problems, assaultive behavior, psychological well-being, and anxieties associated with confinement and separation needs; ensure proper accountability for personal property; issue hygiene items; coordinate necessary medical and psychological treatment; and enforce prison rules. Upon completion of initial processing, inmate systems specialists escort prisoners to their assigned housing units. They are also responsible for management of the mail room, inmate property room, and receiving and discharge areas. These functions involve tasks associated with inmate admission and release systems, the prevention of contraband introduction, adherence to postal regulations, delivery and processing of mail and packages, compliance with court directives, safeguarding and disbursing of personal property, and coordination of prisoner transfers to other institutions and facilities. Inmate systems specialists are authorized to carry firearms.

This position is covered under special retirement provisions for law enforcement officers.

Qualifications and Salary Levels

GS-5: Completion of a four-year course of study leading to a bachelor's degree; or three years of general experience, one year of which was equivalent to GS-4. **GS-6:** One half year of graduate-level education with major study in criminal justice, social science, or other fields related to the position; or one year of specialized experience equivalent to GS-5. **GS-7:** One full year of graduate-level education (in the fields listed under GS-6), or one year of specialized experience equivalent to GS-6. **GS-8:** One year of specialized experience equivalent to GS-7.

Equivalent combinations of education and experience can be used to meet minimum experience requirements. Applicants must be at least 21 years of age and under age 37. Candidates over age 37 who have previous service creditable under special law enforcement retirement provisions also may be eligible. Tentative appointees must qualify for a security clearance and pass a background investigation, personal interview, drug screening test, and physical exam.

Training

Inmate systems specialists attend the three-week Introduction to Correctional Techniques training program presented by the BOP Staff Training Academy at the Federal Law Enforcement Training Center in Glynco, Georgia (see chapter 16), as well as a two-week correctional institution familiarization course conducted by BOP staff. This training is followed by an orientation to administrative procedures and other protocol at the duty station. In-service training includes a minimum of 40 hours of coursework annually, and could include instruction concerning BOP computer database programs, security practices, inmate supervision techniques, inventory control, postal regulations, and other subjects.

Contact: Federal Bureau of Prisons; U.S. Department of Justice; 320 First St. NW—Ste. 460; Washington, DC 20534; phone: (202) 307-3198 or (800) 347-7744; Internet: www.bop.gov/

CHAPTER 14

Federal Court Personnel and Prosecutors

"There are a thousand hacking at the branches of evil to one who is striking at the root."

—Henry David Thoreau

T he United States Constitution established the judicial branch as one of three branches of the federal government. Agencies of the judicial branch protect rights and liberties guaranteed by the Constitution by interpreting and applying the law through fair and impartial judgments. Although careers with judicial branch agencies technically are not enforcement oriented—inasmuch as the responsibility for law enforcement rests with the executive branch—their role is crucial to the administration of justice. Indeed, many of the most important personnel in the federal criminal justice system serve honorably in positions associated with judicial branch agencies.

Situated at the heart of the judicial branch, the United States district courts are the trial courts of the federal system. Within limits set by Congress and the Constitution, these courts have jurisdiction to hear nearly all categories of federal cases, including both civil and criminal matters. There are 94 federal judicial districts, including at least one district in each state, the District of Columbia, and Puerto Rico. In addition, three territories of the United States—the Virgin Islands, Guam, and the Northern Mariana Islands—have district courts that handle federal cases.

Most of the positions discussed in this chapter are in the excepted service and are not covered under the General Schedule pay system. For these positions, similar or equivalent salaries to those of the General Schedule pay system are provided.

Assistant Federal Public Defender
Federal Public Defender's Office, U.S. District Court

One of the fundamental principles of the American criminal justice system is that indigent defendants—those who cannot afford a private attorney—are provided with court-appointed legal representation to ensure that they receive an adequate defense. Assistant federal public defenders represent persons accused of criminal law violations that are adjudicated in the United States district courts. In accordance with the Sixth Amendment to the United States Constitution and the Criminal Justice Act of 1964, they handle caseloads composed of federal misdemeanors, felonies, parole and probation violations, habeas corpus proceedings, and grand jury matters. They also manage direct appeals to the U.S. Circuit Court of Appeals and petitions for a writ of certiorari to the U.S. Supreme Court.

The criminal charges defended by assistant federal public defenders are diverse, including drug crimes, white-collar offenses, tax law violations, crop insurance fraud, firearms offenses, bank robbery, homicide, racketeering, bank fraud, environmental crimes, computer-based offenses, and many other crimes. Assistant federal public defenders represent adults and juveniles at every stage of legal proceedings from the initial appearance before a United States Magistrate Judge through appellate proceedings. These include processes such as extradition and treaty transfer proceedings, arraignment, bail and detention hearings, motions, interviews and conferences, plea negotiation, trial, sentencing hearings, and appeal proceedings. Their responsibilities also include tasks such as obtaining and reviewing records, conducting legal research, writing legal briefs, and conducting investigations. The work of federal public defenders in many judicial districts involves extensive travel.

Qualifications and Salary Levels

The qualifications for assistant federal public defenders can vary somewhat from one judicial district to another, although they generally include a Juris Doctorate degree from a law school accredited by the American Bar Association; membership in good standing of the state bar where the position will be held; at least three years of litigation experience, clerkship experience, or a combination of the two; proficiency in research techniques; and effective written and oral communication abilities. Qualification requirements also could include proficiency in computer-assisted legal research methods, word processing capabilities, and time management skills.

Candidates must successfully complete a background investigation and pass a drug test prior to appointment. Salary is commensurate with experience and education, although generally it is about the same as salaries for assistant U.S. attorneys with similar experience.

Training

Assistant federal public defenders receive an orientation that focuses on court policies and procedures, administrative matters, and other relevant information. Ongoing training is coordinated through or offered by organizations such as the Office of Defender Services within the Administrative Office of the U.S. Courts, the Federal Judicial Center, National Legal Aid and Defender Association, American Bar Association, National Association of Criminal Defense Lawyers, and various college and university law schools. Training focuses on a variety of criminal defense strategies and advocacy skills, including topics such as search and seizure, criminal law, pretrial processes, discovery issues, jury selection, opening statements, cross examination, direct examination, litigating false confessions, closing statements, economic crimes, Native American law, welfare advocacy, United States Sentencing Commission guidelines, courtroom technology, joint defense agreements, ethics, and cost containment.

Contact: Inquiries should be directed to the U.S. district court where employment is sought, or to the Administrative Office of the U.S. Courts; One Columbus Circle NE; Washington, DC 20544; phone: (202) 502-2600; Internet: www.uscourts.gov/.

Assistant United States Attorney
United States Attorney's Office, U.S. Department of Justice

The U.S. Department of Justice (DOJ) is the law firm of the federal government—and the world's largest legal employer. Although DOJ operations require the talents of personnel serving in a wide range of occupations, much of the Department's mission to enforce federal laws and defend the interests of the United States according to the law is carried out by assistant United States attorneys (AUSAs). These personnel serve under the direction of the United States Attorney of each judicial district. The United States attorneys are presidential appointees who serve under the direction of the United States Attorney General as the chief federal law enforcement officer within their particular districts.

AUSAs carry out three primary responsibilities afforded under the U.S. Code: the prosecution of criminal cases brought by the federal government, the prosecution and defense of civil cases in which the United States is a party, and the collection of debts owed the federal government that are administratively uncollectible. Although the distribution of caseload varies between districts, each AUSA handles a mixture of simple and complex litigation—primarily through the Criminal and Civil divisions—depending on the resources and priorities of the districts served.

AUSAs perform a variety of tasks associated with criminal and civil litigation, such as working with federal law enforcement officers and others during investigations, and representing the United States during arraignments, bail and detention hearings, motions, trials, sentencing hearings, and appeal proceedings. AUSAs assigned to the Criminal Division enforce federal criminal laws that protect life, liberty, and property of citizens at both the trial and appellate level. These include crimes such as drug trafficking, terrorism, firearms offenses, gang violence, organized crime, bank robbery, public corruption, immigration violations, white collar crime, money laundering, child pornography, postal theft, credit card fraud, murder for hire, counterfeiting, environmental crimes, healthcare fraud, and computer crimes.

In addition to defending the United States and its agencies in civil lawsuits, AUSAs assigned to the Civil Division handle cases at both the trial and appellate level concerned with the False Claims Act and the Federal Tort Claims Act, employment discrimination, medical malpractice, civil rights, land condemnations, contract disputes, mortgage foreclosures, bankruptcies, Affirmative Civil Enforcement, antitrust laws, and the collection of federal penalties and restitution, among other matters. In doing so, they determine strategy and tactics, work with federal law enforcement officers and other personnel, prepare pleadings and briefs, and manage discovery and trial proceedings.

Qualifications and Salary Levels

Basic qualifications for AUSAs generally include a Juris Doctorate degree from a law school accredited by the American Bar Association, membership in good standing of the state bar where the position will be held, at least one year of professional legal experience, and excellent written and oral communication skills. Other requirements often vary from one office to another, and could include additional professional legal experience; trial experience; experience in the prosecution or litigation of matters concerned with the division or section where the selectee will be assigned; experience in the preparation of appellate briefs and presentation of appellate arguments; proficiency in research techniques; experience with task force investigations; foreign language proficiency; and computer skills.

Candidates must successfully complete a background investigation and pass a drug test prior to appointment. Salary is commensurate with experience and education, although generally it is similar to GS-12 to GS-15 (can be higher or lower).

Training

The nature of training for AUSAs is based largely on the division of assignment and nature of specialization of each individual. The Executive Office for United States Attorneys, the National Advocacy Center, and the American Bar Association offer a wide variety of training programs that AUSAs can take advantage of. Many professional organizations and law schools also hold conferences and seminars that AUSAs attend. Overall, AUSAs receive training in areas such as criminal and civil law, environmental law, trial advocacy skills, grand jury practices, evidence, sentencing guidelines, asset forfeiture, money laundering, Affirmative Civil Enforcement, public corruption, cybercrimes and computer forensics, terrorism, child exploitation cases, intellectual property crimes, bankruptcy fraud, civil rights violations, Native American issues, securities fraud, financial litigation, and healthcare fraud.

Contact: Inquiries should be directed to the U.S. Attorney's office where employment is sought, or to the Executive Office for United States Attorneys; U.S. Department of Justice; 950 Pennsylvania Ave. NW; Washington, DC 20530; phone: (202) 616-6900; Internet: www.usdoj.gov/usao/eousa/.

Assistant United States Trustee
Office of the United States Trustee, U.S. Department of Justice

The United States Trustee Program is the component of the U.S. Department of Justice (DOJ) that is responsible for overseeing the administration of bankruptcy cases and private trustees under the United States Code. It consists of 21 regional U.S. Trustee offices nationwide and an Executive Office for U.S. Trustees in Washington, D.C. Assistant U.S. trustees are attorneys whose responsibilities involve promoting the efficiency and protecting the integrity of the federal bankruptcy system.

As "watchdogs" over the bankruptcy process, these personnel monitor the administration of cases filed under chapters 7, 11, 12, and 13 of the Bankruptcy Code, and oversee the conduct of bankruptcy parties and private estate trustees to ensure compliance with applicable laws and procedures. Their responsibilities include tasks such as reviewing bankruptcy cases; overseeing reorganization filings by businesses, farms, and individuals; drafting motions, pleadings, and briefs; handling other litigation matters; legal research; supervising liquidation proceedings; and trying cases in the bankruptcy courts and U.S. district courts. Assistant U.S. trustees also are responsible for identifying and investigating bankruptcy fraud and abuse in coordination with assistant United States attorneys, the FBI, and other law enforcement agencies. These matters involve detecting concealment of assets, crimes by attorneys and bankruptcy petition preparers, credit card fraud schemes, identity fraud, the creation of false documents, and other related crimes.

Another top priority of assistant U.S. trustees is to combat fraud and abuse in the bankruptcy system through civil enforcement. This involves seeking civil remedies against those who engage in bankruptcy fraud or abuse, such as debtors and their attorneys, bankruptcy petition preparers, creditors, and others who attempt to take advantage of debtors' financial difficulties.

Qualifications and Salary Levels

The general qualifications for assistant U.S. trustees include a Juris doctorate degree from a law school accredited by the American Bar Association, membership in good standing of the state bar where the position will be held, excellent written and oral communication skills, and at least one year of professional legal experience. However, depending on requirements from one office to another or the level of positions being filled, additional qualifications could include two or more years of legal experience; trial experience; knowledge of accounting principles; experience in the preparation of appellate briefs and presentation of appellate arguments; proficiency in research techniques; foreign language proficiency; computer skills; or other requirements.

Candidates must successfully complete a background investigation and pass a drug test prior to appointment. Salary is commensurate with experience and education, although generally it is similar to GS-12 to GS-15 (can be higher or lower).

Training

Much of the training for assistant U.S. trustees is held at the National Bankruptcy Training Institute (NBTI), which offers various courses that enhance professional, technical, and management skills. NBTI is a component of the National Advocacy Center, which is a cooperative partnership of the U.S. Attorney's Office of Legal Education, the National District Attorneys Association, and NBTI. Training through NBTI and other providers focuses on subjects such as the Bankruptcy Abuse and Consumer Protection Act of 2005, other bankruptcy statutes, case law, bankruptcy fraud, civil enforcement strategies, accounting and finance fundamentals, litigation principles, liquidation proceedings, case monitoring and administration, and negotiation skills.

Contact: Inquiries should be directed to the U.S. Trustee's office where employment is sought, or to the Executive Office for United States Trustees; U.S. Department of Justice; 20 Massachusetts Ave. NW; Washington, DC 20530; phone: (202) 307-1391; Internet: www.usdoj.gov/ust/.

Federal Court Interpreter
Office of the Clerk of Court, U.S. District Court

Court interpreters provide a vital service to the federal courts in cases that involve witnesses or other persons who do not understand or speak English. The work of federal court interpreters is critical to ensure that justice is carried out fairly for defendants and others. The Court Interpreters Act of 1978 requires the courts to use an interpreter when a "…party, including a defendant in a criminal case, or a witness…speaks only or primarily a language other than the English language…so as to inhibit such party's comprehension of the proceedings or communication with counsel…" Spanish is the language most commonly encountered by federal court interpreters—typically accounting for more than 90 percent of all interpreting events nationwide—followed by Mandarin, Arabic, Russian, Vietnamese, Portuguese, Cantonese, Korean, French, and Haitian-Creole. The need for interpretation of a specific language is determined by the local U.S. district courts. However, in accordance with the Court Interpreters Act, the Administrative Office of the U.S. Courts (AOUSC) prescribes the standards and guidelines for selecting and using interpreters in federal court proceedings.

Federal court interpreters present a verbatim rendition of court testimony, and the English rendition by the interpreter becomes part of the official court record. In accordance with Federal Rule of Evidence 604, federal court interpreters are required to take an oath to faithfully and impartially interpret the speech of the witness or defendant. They must interpret exactly what the witness or defendant says, without commenting on it, even if the interpreter believes the person is lying. Furthermore, they must be able to do so without any additions, omissions, or other misleading factors that could alter the intended meaning of the message. In addition to interpreting courtroom testimony, federal court interpreters also translate speech outside of the courtroom so that a proper defense can be prepared, as well as the text of documents submitted into evidence, recordings of conversations produced through wiretap operations, and correspondence to and from the court. The AOUSC classifies three categories of interpreters: Certified Interpreters, Professionally-Qualified Interpreters, and Language-Skilled Interpreters.

Qualifications and Salary Levels

The qualifications for federal court interpreters depend on the category of expertise sought. To qualify as a Certified Interpreter, candidates must have passed the AOUSC certification examination in either Spanish, Navajo, or Haitian-Creole. These are the only languages for which this certification presently is offered.

In other languages, interpreters are designated as Professionally-Qualified or Language-Skilled. Professionally-Qualified interpreters must have passed a recognized interpreter examination and have experience as a conference or seminar interpreter with any United States agency, the United Nations, or a similar entity; or have membership in a professional interpreter association and at least 50 hours of conference interpreting experience. Language-skilled interpreters are those who otherwise can demonstrate to the satisfaction of the court their ability to interpret from the foreign language into English and vice versa in court proceedings. Prior experience in state or federal courtrooms is preferred, although typically it is not required. Impartiality and the ability to communicate professionally with educated and uneducated persons who appear in the courtroom—as well as their counsel—also are required. Candidates must have the ability to translate complex written documents for court use.

Successful completion of a background investigation is required. Salary is commensurate with the category of expertise. The salary range for Certified and Professionally-Qualified interpreters is similar to GS-9 to GS-13. Language-skilled interpreters are hired primarily on a part-time (contract) basis, for which they are paid a daily rate that is similar to starting salary at GS-9.

Training

Many professional associations offer training seminars and conferences that are attended by federal court interpreters, such as the National Association of Judiciary Interpreters and Translators, American Translators Association, American Translation and Interpretation Studies Association, and other organizations. In addition, many colleges and universities offer courses and seminars, such as Boston University, California State University, Georgetown University, City University of New York, Kent State University, New York University, University of Arizona, University of Charleston, University of North Carolina, and University of Wisconsin-Milwaukee. Conferences, seminars, workshops, and courses focus on subjects such as dialectal variations, verbatim vs. cultural interpreting, cultural interference, confidentiality and privileged communications, case law, ethics, translation of medical materials, Internet research, and computer software.

Contact: Inquiries should be directed to the U.S. district court where employment is sought, or to the Administrative Office of the U.S. Courts; One Columbus Circle NE; Washington, DC 20544; phone: (202) 502-2600; Internet: www.uscourts.gov/.

Federal Criminal Defense Investigator

Federal Public Defender's Office, U.S. District Court

Although indigent defendants are entitled to court-appointed legal representation to ensure that they receive an adequate defense, the ability of assistant federal defenders to provide an adequate defense often is limited by the availability of investigative resources. To ensure that indigent persons receive equal justice under the law, federal criminal defense investigators work with assistant federal public defenders in providing a criminal defense for those charged with crimes that are adjudicated in the United States district courts.

Although the tasks performed by federal criminal defense investigators vary from one case to another, their responsibilities generally include interviewing defendants; locating and interviewing victims, witnesses, experts, and law enforcement personnel; locating, obtaining, and reviewing records, reports, transcripts, and other documents; locating and retrieving tangible evidence and personal property; reviewing and analyzing documents and other materials obtained during court discovery processes; establishing and maintaining good working relationships with individuals and agencies that interact with the federal public defender's office; following leads; and serving subpoenas. In many cases, federal criminal defense investigators must also visit, photograph, and re-create crime scenes; prepare comprehensive written reports; and testify in court concerning their actions and findings.

Qualifications and Salary Levels

The qualification requirements for the federal criminal defense investigator position often vary somewhat from one federal defender's office to another. However, requirements generally include at least a high school education or equivalent; at least one year of criminal investigative experience or comparable experience in information gathering; the ability to analyze and evaluate facts, evidence, and related information; and the ability to communicate effectively orally and in writing. Oftentimes education can be substituted for investigative experience. Competitive candidates will have a record of considerable resourcefulness, creativity, initiative, drive, tact, and discretion; computer skills, including knowledge of word processing and spreadsheet programs, and the Internet; and knowledge of cameras, tape recorders, and other technical investigative equipment. Foreign language abilities also can be a plus.

Candidates must pass a background investigation. Salary is commensurate with experience, although typically it is similar to the GS-9 to GS-13 levels.

Training

Many federal criminal defense investigators attend conferences, seminars, and other training programs offered by organizations such as the National Legal Aid and Defender Association, National Association of Criminal Defense Lawyers, National Defender Investigator Association, National Association of Legal Investigators, and Criminal Defense Investigation Training Council. These programs include instruction on topics such as investigative techniques, legal matters, forensic sciences, police procedures, eyewitness identification, testimonial evidence, records chronology, personality disorders, interviewing, death investigations, surveillance, process service, demonstrative evidence, courtroom testimony, death penalty defense, team building, ethics, and sources of information. The National Association of Legal Investigators and the Criminal Defense Investigation Training Council offer professional certification programs for criminal defense investigators.

Contact: Inquiries should be directed to the federal public defender's office where employment is sought, or to the Administrative Office of the U.S. Courts; One Columbus Circle NE; Washington, DC 20544; phone: (202) 502-2600; Internet: www.uscourts.gov/

Official Court Reporter
Office of the Clerk of Court, U.S. District Court

Official court reporters are responsible for recording verbatim testimony—often with the aid of computer-assisted technology—for civil and criminal court proceedings and for any other purpose designated by rule or order of the court, or by a district court judge or magistrate judge.

Two primary methods of court reporting are used by these personnel. The majority of official court reporters use a stenographic machine that translates keystrokes into symbols that correspond to the spoken word. These symbols are recorded on computer disks or CD-ROM, which are then translated and displayed as text in a process called computer-aided transcription (CAT). Machines used for realtime captioning display text instantly on a computer monitor in a process known as communications access realtime translation (CART). The other primary method is known as voice writing, through which an official court reporter speaks directly into a hand-held mask containing a microphone with a voice silencer. Voice writers report verbatim everything that is said by judges, witnesses, attorneys, and other parties to proceedings. Some voice writers produce a transcript in realtime, using computer speech recognition technology. Otherwise, the official court reporter must translate the voice files into text after the proceeding has ended. Electronic sound recording equipment often is used to augment these primary methods of reporting.

Regardless of the method used, official court reporters are responsible for ensuring a complete, accurate, and secure legal record. At the request of the court or a party to the proceedings, official court reporters prepare transcripts within required formats, time frames, and cost requirements established by the Judicial Conference of the United States. In addition to preparing and protecting the legal record, many court reporters assist judges and trial attorneys in a variety of ways, such as organizing and searching for information in the official record or making suggestions to judges and attorneys regarding courtroom administration and procedure.

Qualifications and Salary Levels

Minimum requirements for the official court reporter position vary somewhat from one court to another. There are five qualification levels that correspond to experience and certification, and salary is determined accordingly. To qualify for Level 1, candidates must be certified as a Registered Professional Reporter by the National Court Reporters Association or have passed an equivalent qualifying examination. Level 2 applicants must have a Certificate of Merit from the National Court Reporters Association (or an equivalent certification), or have satisfactorily served the U. S. district court as an official court reporter for 10 years. To qualify for Level 3, applicants must meet all the criteria for levels 1 and 2, or meet the criteria for Level 1 and also possess Realtime Certification. To qualify for Level 4, applicants must meet the criteria for Level 2, plus Realtime Certification. Level 5 candidates must meet the criteria for Level 3, plus Realtime Certification.

Salary ranges from Level 1, which is similar to GS-12, to Level 5, which is similar to GS-13. Official court reporters also earn fees for transcripts sold. Inasmuch as court reporting requires the use of computerized stenography or speech recognition equipment, court reporters must be knowledgeable about computer hardware and software applications. Excellent oral and written communication skills also are required. Candidates must pass a background investigation.

Training

The nature of training for official court reporters depends on the experience level of each individual and the needs of each court served. Training is offered by more than 80 technical schools and colleges that are approved by the National Court Reporters Association—all of which require students to capture a minimum of 225 words per minute. Many organizations hold conferences and seminars attended by official court reporters, including the National Court Reporters Association, United States Court Reporters Association, National Verbatim Reporters Association, Society for the Technological Advancement of Reporting, and many associations on the state and local levels. These focus on subjects such as computer-aided transcription, communications access realtime translation, software programs, computer data security, grammar and punctuation, editing techniques, preventing hand and wrist injuries, employment issues, tax planning, and time management.

Contact: Inquiries should be directed to the U.S. district court where employment is sought, or to the Administrative Office of the U.S. Courts; One Columbus Circle NE; Washington, DC 20544; phone: (202) 502-2600; Internet: www.uscourts.gov/.

Paralegal Specialist (GS-0950)
United States Attorney's Office, U.S. Department of Justice

Although federal prosecutors assume ultimate responsibility for the work performed by the United States Attorney's Office, they often delegate many of their tasks to paralegals. Paralegal specialists serve in a variety of roles in support of assistant United States attorneys, although the nature of these roles can vary depending on whether they are assigned to the Criminal or Civil Division and the variety of cases handled in each office. Nonetheless, there are more similarities than differences in the work performed from one division or office to another.

Generally speaking, paralegal specialists execute a multitude of complex tasks relating to criminal prosecutions and civil litigation, such as performing detailed legal research;

analyzing legal decisions; compiling substantive information on legal subjects; researching issues and legislative history; and collecting, analyzing, and evaluating evidence associated with hearings, appeals, and litigation. They also prepare legal documents, such as extradition requests, letters, immunity requests, writs of habeas corpus, grand jury and trial subpoenas, discovery letters, answers, motions, trial briefs, exhibit lists, jury instructions, appellate briefs, spreadsheets, and other technical documents concerning the acquisition of evidence or testimony for criminal investigations and trials. In many cases, paralegal specialists interview witnesses in support of assistant U.S. attorneys in preparation for grand jury or trials; collect, analyze and evaluate evidentiary materials, including deposition and trial transcripts, written discovery materials, medical records, employment records, administrative records, and witness statements; prepare narrative summaries, charts, tables, graphs, and other visual aids to be used at trial; compile, organize, and index discovery materials and trial exhibits; and otherwise support assistant U.S. attorneys at trials, hearings, and depositions. Paralegal specialists also are responsible for monitoring the progress of pending cases; initiating action to ensure that legal pleadings, forms, reports, correspondence, and other documents are prepared and submitted within established deadlines; and maintaining contact with law enforcement agencies to ensure cooperation in all aspects of cases.

Qualifications and Salary Levels

GS-7: One full year of graduate education, or superior academic achievement during undergraduate studies; or one year of specialized experience equivalent to GS-5. **GS-9:** A master's degree, or two years of graduate education, or one year of specialized experience equivalent to GS-7. **GS-11:** A Ph.D. or equivalent doctoral degree, or three years of graduate education, or one year of specialized experience equivalent to GS-9. **GS-12:** One year of specialized experience equivalent to GS-11. Equivalent combinations of education and experience can be used to meet minimum experience requirements. The application process includes a drug screening test, background investigation, and security clearance determination.

Training

The National Advocacy Center, National Federation of Paralegal Associations, American Association for Paralegal Education, National Association of Legal Assistants, and other organizations offer conferences, online seminars, other distance learning programs, and various courses for paralegal specialists. In addition, training is offered at more than 250 paralegal programs nationwide that are approved by the American Bar Association. Some of the subjects covered in these training programs include topics such as Affirmative Civil Enforcement, legal writing, legal citations and research, databases and sources of information, asset forfeiture, bankruptcy proceedings, criminal debt collection, financial litigation, grand jury coordination, the Freedom of Information Act, violent crime, white collar crime, trial preparation, appellate processes, computer hardware and software, ethics and professional responsibility, conflicts of interest, and confidentiality.

Contact: Inquiries should be directed to the U.S. Attorney's office where employment is sought, or to the Executive Office for United States Attorneys; U.S. Department of Justice; 950 Pennsylvania Ave. NW; Washington, DC 20530; phone: (202) 616-6900; Internet: www.usdoj.gov/usao/eousa/.

U.S. Pretrial Services Officer

Division of Probation and Pretrial Services, United States District Court

United States pretrial services officers are based at every U.S. district court, where they gather information and prepare reports for judges who must decide whether arrested persons should be released before trial in the federal court system. These personnel are responsible for investigating defendants charged with federal criminal offenses, assessing potential risk to the public posed by pretrial release of arrested persons, and for making recommendations on the amount of bail and the conditions to be met by defendants if released.

Inquiries typically examine defendants' character, family ties, mental condition, length of residence, and history of drug or alcohol abuse. This process involves interviewing defendants, arresting authorities, the United States Attorney's Office, and family and community members; examining data of law enforcement automated criminal records systems; and developing a supervision plan. U.S. pretrial services officers also supervise defendants released on bail to monitor compliance with the conditions of release; enforce court-imposed conditions of release, including drug testing and mental health treatment, curfew, home confinement with electronic monitoring, and restrictions on personal association, place of abode, and travel; and maintain detailed records of case activity. They also assist with pretrial diversion cases, which involve court supervision agreements as an alternative to prosecution; assist defendants needing medical care, food, clothing, shelter, and other assistance by referring them to appropriate community service or government agencies; notify the court and the United States Attorney's Office of pretrial release violations; and prepare petitions or reports to the court recommending revocation or modification of conditions of release. As fully commissioned law enforcement personnel, U.S. pretrial services officers are authorized to carry firearms.

This position is covered under special retirement provisions for law enforcement officers.

Qualifications and Salary Levels

Applicants must be at least 21 years of age and under the age of 37. Candidates over age 37 who have previous service creditable under special law enforcement retirement provisions also may be eligible. Requirements include a bachelor's degree from an accredited college or university in a field such as criminal justice, criminology, psychology, sociology, human relations, business, or public administration; and at least one year of specialized experience relating to probation, pretrial services, parole, corrections, criminal investigation, or work in substance abuse treatment. (Experience as a police patrol officer or security officer is not acceptable.) Qualifying specialized experience can be substituted by superior academic achievement during undergraduate studies, or completion of a master's or Juris doctorate degree, or one year of graduate education in a closely related field of study. Candidates also must be in good physical health, possess good writing and communication skills, and pass a background investigation.

Salary for this position does not fall under the General Schedule pay system. Starting salary is similar to GS-7, and salary for journeyman grade is similar to GS-13.

Training

U.S. pretrial services officers attend an orientation training program at their duty station, followed by an intensive six-day seminar at the Federal Judicial Center in Washington, D.C. These programs provide an overview of federal court operations, safety and security, the Probation and Pretrial Services Automated Case Tracking System, sentencing guidelines, pre-sentence reports, Agency forms and standards, and terminology. In-service training could include courses relating to pretrial diversion programs, financial investigations, substance abuse, gangs in the penal system, ethnic sensitivity, report writing, law, court operations, computer automation, critical incident stress management, defensive tactics, firearms proficiency, and other subjects. Intermediate and advanced training is offered at the Federal Judicial Center, the Federal Law Enforcement Training Center, and other training academies and schools.

Contact: Inquiries should be directed to the office where employment is sought, or to Probation and Pretrial Services; Administrative Office of the U.S. Courts; One Columbus Circle NE; Washington, DC 20544; phone: (202) 273-1120; Internet: www.uscourts.gov/.

U.S. Probation Officer
Division of Probation and Pretrial Services, United States District Court

As fully commissioned law enforcement officers under the Division of Probation and Pretrial Services, United States probation officers are responsible for the investigation and supervision of criminal offenders on probation, parole, or supervised release in each of the 94 district courts of the federal court system. All U.S. probation officers are appointed by a specific district court, which is administered by a Chief Judge. In accordance with the Federal Rules of Criminal Procedure, U.S. probation officers conduct investigations and prepare reports for the court with recommendations for sentencing of individuals convicted of federal offenses.

Primary responsibilities include investigating offenders' backgrounds; preparing pre-sentence reports that include recommendations for sentencing; providing court testimony in support of investigative findings and the application of sentencing guidelines; and monitoring offenders under court supervision. The preparation of these reports requires interviewing offenders and their families; investigating the offense, prior record, and financial status of the offender; contacting law enforcement agencies, attorneys, crime victims, schools, churches, and civic organizations; and other activities, depending on the nature of each case. To reduce risk to the community and maximize adherence to court-imposed conditions, U.S. probation officers supervise and maintain contact with offenders, and investigate offenders' employment, sources of income, lifestyles, substance abuse, and associates. Their findings often result in referrals to outside agencies such as medical facilities, counseling and drug treatment programs, and employment and training sources. Investigations and supervision require frequent contact with the U.S. Parole Commission, Federal Bureau of Prisons, military authorities, and attorneys. U.S. probation officers are authorized to carry firearms.

This position is covered under special retirement provisions for law enforcement officers.

Qualifications and Salary Levels

Applicants must be at least 21 years of age and under the age of 37. Candidates over age 37 who have previous service creditable under special law enforcement retirement provisions could also be eligible. Requirements include a bachelor's degree from an accredited college or university in a field such as criminal justice, criminology, psychology, sociology, human relations, business, or public administration; and at least one year of specialized experience relating to probation, pretrial services, parole, corrections, criminal investigation, or work in substance abuse treatment. (Experience as a police patrol officer or security officer is not acceptable.) Qualifying specialized experience can be substituted by superior academic achievement during undergraduate studies, completion of a master's or Juris doctorate degree, or one year of graduate education in a closely related field of study. Candidates must also be in good physical health, possess good writing and communication skills, and pass a background investigation.

Salary for this position does not fall under the General Schedule pay system. Starting salary is similar to GS-7, and salary for journeyman grade is similar to GS-13.

Training

U.S. probation officers attend an orientation training program at their duty station, followed by an intensive six-day seminar at the Federal Judicial Center in Washington, D.C. Training subjects include an overview of federal court operations, safety and security, sentencing guidelines, pre-sentence reports, Agency forms and standards, and terminology. In-service training could include courses that focus on the Probation and Pretrial Services Automated Case Tracking System, case management and investigation techniques, supervision of offenders, substance abuse and mental health treatment options, report writing, law, sentencing guidelines, court operations, computer automation, firearms proficiency, defensive tactics, and other subjects. Intermediate and advanced training is offered at the Federal Judicial Center, the Federal Law Enforcement Training Center, and other training academies and schools.

Contact: Inquiries should be directed to the office where employment is sought, or to Probation and Pretrial Services; Administrative Office of the U.S. Courts; One Columbus Circle NE; Washington, DC 20544; phone: (202) 273-1120; Internet: www.uscourts.gov/.

CHAPTER 15

Communications and Electronics Personnel

"Never doubt that a small group of thoughtful, committed citizens can change the world. Indeed, it's the only thing that ever has."

—*Margaret Mead*

Effective communication is the lifeblood of any successful organization, and law enforcement agencies are no exception. Indeed, law enforcement officers rely heavily on communications personnel and equipment to carry out their responsibilities safely and efficiently, around the clock. In support of operations at every level, law enforcement communications equipment operators, telecommunications specialists, and electronics technicians are responsible for operating and maintaining radio telecommunication systems, telephones and telephone switching equipment, law enforcement computer database systems, and other electronic communication devices that are used in law enforcement, fire suppression, and other emergency response operations.

Careers that involve the relay of radio communication traffic and critical data to law enforcement and other emergency personnel include communications equipment operators, emergency communication dispatchers, emergency vehicle dispatchers, law enforcement communications assistants, public safety dispatchers, radio telecommunications equipment operators, and telecommunications equipment operators. These personnel provide vital support to field operations of agencies such as the Drug Enforcement Administration, United States Army, United States Navy, National Park Service, Secret Service, Bureau of Indian Affairs, and United States Marshals Service.

Communications Equipment Operator (GS-0392)
Drug Enforcement Administration, U.S. Department of Justice

Drug Enforcement Administration (DEA) communications equipment operators perform a wide range of communications functions in support of field operations and the administration of DEA programs.

Primary responsibilities include operating UHF multi-frequency radio communication equipment; monitoring radios for DEA field traffic carried out by DEA agents and law enforcement officers working jointly with the agency on task force operations or other initiatives; responding to radio requests and researching information contained in automated law enforcement database systems relating to vehicle registrations, driver's license information, and criminal records; providing coordination and law enforcement data to DEA units and other agencies during land, sea, and air pursuits, interceptions, and surveillance operations; handling city-to-city and car-to-base "patching" communications; dispatching emergency personnel; receiving, encoding, and transmitting messages on cryptographic equipment; maintaining logs of radio, telephone, or other communications; monitoring building security through closed-circuit television surveillance and audio systems; taking incoming telephone calls from the public; and responding to inquiries from DEA management, special agents, and other personnel.

Qualifications and Salary

GS-4: Two years of education above high school, or one year of general experience.
GS-5: Four years of education above high school, or one year of specialized experience equivalent to at least GS-4. **GS-6:** One year of specialized experience equivalent to GS-5. **GS-7:** One year of specialized experience equivalent to GS-6. **GS-8:** One year of specialized experience equivalent to GS-7.

Experience and education can be combined to meet total experience requirements for positions at grades GS-5 and below. Those tentatively selected must qualify for a security clearance and pass a background investigation and drug screening test.

Training

Communications equipment operators typically receive on-the-job training and attend courses relating to automated law enforcement database systems, radio communication equipment, dispatching procedures, computer hardware and software, agency policies and directives, administrative paperwork, and agency-specific procedures. Training programs are conducted by DEA staff; federal, state, or local law enforcement training programs or academies; colleges or universities; or other organizations.

Contact: Direct inquiries to the DEA field office where employment is sought, or to Office of Personnel Drug Enforcement Administration; U.S. Department of Justice; 2401 Jefferson Davis Hwy.; Alexandria, VA 22301; phone: (202) 307-7977; Internet: www.dea.gov/.

Dispatcher (GS-1802)
United States Secret Service, U.S. Department of Homeland Security

Secret Service dispatchers fill a critical role in the Agency's protective operations and criminal investigation missions—including efforts to protect the president and vice president of the United States, former U.S. presidents, and other important persons.

In carrying out their responsibilities, Secret Service dispatchers operate multi-frequency radio communication console units to maintain ongoing contact with Secret Service special agents and Uniformed Division officers in the field. They perform these tasks within mobile, base station, and portable units located in Secret Service field offices and subordinate offices. Some of their responsibilities include transmitting and receiving messages using complex telecommunications equipment; communicating with various federal, state, local, and foreign law enforcement agencies to exchange investigative information; conducting research and developing investigative leads as circumstances unfold; monitoring law enforcement radio frequencies; and receiving information by telephone from law enforcement officers, informants, and members of the public who provide information of value to Secret Service operations. Other tasks include preparing routine incident forms; maintaining a log of unusual incidents; using special procedures in cases of bomb threats, criminal surveillance, and protective movements and activities; accessing computer networks and database systems to obtain information; and serving at command posts.

Qualifications and Salary

GS-4: Two years of education above high school, or one year of general experience. **GS-5:** Four years of education above high school, or one year of specialized experience equivalent to at least GS-4. **GS-6:** One year of specialized experience equivalent to GS-5. **GS-7:** One year of specialized experience equivalent to GS-6. **GS-8:** One year of specialized experience equivalent to GS-7. Equivalent combinations of education and experience can be used to meet minimum experience requirements for positions at grades GS-5 and below. Those tentatively selected must qualify for a security clearance and pass a background investigation and drug screening test.

Training

Secret Service dispatchers typically receive a combination of on-the-job training and classroom instruction that covers topics such as message handling, radio discipline, dispatching procedures, radio communication equipment and technology, automated law enforcement database systems, handling critical incidents and crisis intervention, interviewing techniques, caller confidentiality, computer hardware and software, administrative tasks, legal aspects of dispatch operations, and agency policies and procedures. Ongoing training is provided by the Secret Service, and also is available from other law enforcement agencies, training academies, and other recognized authorities.

Contact: United States Secret Service; U.S. Department of Homeland Security; 800 G St. NW—Room 912; Washington, DC 20223; phone: (202) 406-5800; Internet: www.secretservice.gov

Electronics Technician (GS-0856)
Forest Service U.S. Department of Agriculture

Communicating within the U.S. National Forest System—which encompasses nearly 200 million acres—presents unique challenges. To meet these challenges, Forest Service (FS) electronics technicians install, test, maintain, and repair all fixed-station and mobile radio equipment used in FS law enforcement, fire suppression, and emergency operations, as well as in other applications.

The primary responsibilities of FS electronics technicians include identifying and analyzing telecommunications system requirements for both voice and data telecommunication systems; performing scheduled preventive maintenance checks, routine service work, and necessary technical corrections to ensure reliable technical and operational performance; making emergency and nonscheduled equipment repairs; operating and maintaining electronic testing equipment; maintaining a communications parts inventory; providing assistance with the implementation of FS communications plans; performing technical inspection of new equipment prior to installation to ensure compliance with FS specifications; assisting with the inspection of special use electronic sites and permits for compliance with regulations; training FS personnel in correct radio operating procedures, proper radio discipline, and minor servicing of equipment; and performing technical duties in establishing communications facilities for law enforcement, fire suppression, and other communications.

FS electronics technicians also perform work involved with the acquisition, evaluation, support, and implementation of wide area network (WAN) computer systems and applications. In doing so, they provide a broad range of technical expertise to implement WANs, including systemwide design, documentation, debugging, and maintenance in accordance with FS Office of Information Resources Management regulations, policies, and directives.

Qualifications and Salary

GS-5: A four-year course of study leading to a bachelor's degree in electrical engineering, electronics engineering, or electronics technology; or three years of study in an accredited curriculum in electronics; or a four-year course of study leading to a bachelor's degree that included major study or at least 24 semester hours in any combination of courses in engineering, physical science, technology, or mathematics, of which at least 12 semester hours included electronics courses; or one year of specialized experience equivalent to GS-4 as either an electronics technician, inspector, or mechanic, or as a television or radio repair technician in a commercial shop. **GS-7:** One full year of graduate education directly related to the position, or one year of specialized experience (as described under GS-5) equivalent to GS-5. **GS-9:** Two full years of graduate education directly related to the position, or one year of specialized experience (as described under GS-5) equivalent to GS-7. **GS-10:** One year of specialized experience (as described under GS-5) equivalent to GS-9. **GS-11:** One year of specialized experience (as described under GS-5) equivalent to GS-10. **GS-12:** One year of specialized experience (as described under GS-5) equivalent to GS-11. Equivalent combinations of education and experience can be used to meet minimum experience requirements. Candidates also must pass a background investigation.

Training

Training and development opportunities for FS electronics technicians focus on theories and techniques concerning the design, development, evaluation, testing, installation, use, and maintenance of electronic equipment used in law enforcement and public safety operations. Various courses, seminars, conferences, and informal instruction are presented by FS staff, other agencies, the Federal Law Enforcement Training Center, and state and local law enforcement training academies. Training also is available from electronics industry associations such as the National Technical Investigators Association, the Institute of Electrical and Electronics Engineers, and other organizations. The nature of training often depends on the needs of individual personnel, agency requirements, and availability of courses.

Contact: Direct inquiries to the regional or local FS office where employment is sought, or Forest Service; U.S. Department of Agriculture; 1400 Independence Ave. SW; Washington, DC 20250; phone: (202) 205-8333; Internet: www.fs.fed.us; e-mail: mailroom_wo@fs.fed.us.

Electronics Technician (GS-0856)
Bureau of Land Management, U.S. Department of the Interior

Electronics technicians serving with the Bureau of Land Management (BLM) maintain and repair all mobile and portable radio equipment used in law enforcement, fire suppression, emergency, and other communications.

Primary responsibilities include maintaining two-way radios, telephone systems, and data communications equipment; setting up and testing equipment; repairing, modifying, and programming mobile, base station, repeater and portable VHF, UHF, FM, and AM radio systems; maintaining various power sources used in remote locations, including AC power supplies and battery chargers, solar panel charge regulators, and rechargeable batteries; installing and removing mobile radios, cellular telephones, and associated antenna systems and accessories in vehicles; reviewing manufacturers' specifications and schematics to evaluate radio performance; executing initial acceptance checks on new radio equipment to ensure that equipment meets contracting specifications; maintaining records of repairs and inventory of equipment; providing radio training to BLM personnel; and assisting telecommunications specialists on various projects.

Due to the diverse nature of land managed by BLM, electronics technicians often carry out their responsibilities over remote or rugged terrain, in conservation or wilderness areas, and at high altitudes where climatic conditions are variable and extreme.

Qualifications and Salary

GS-5: A four-year course of study leading to a bachelor's degree in electrical engineering, electronics engineering, or electronics technology; or three years of study in an accredited curriculum in electronics; or a four-year course of study leading to a bachelor's degree that included major study or at least 24 semester hours in any combination of courses in engineering, physical science, technology, or mathematics, of which at least 12 semester hours included electronics courses; or one year of specialized experience equivalent to GS-4 as either an electronics technician, inspector, or mechanic, or as a television or radio repair technician in a commercial shop. **GS-7:** One full year of graduate education directly related to the position, or one year of specialized experience (as described under GS-5) equivalent to GS-5. **GS-9:** Two full years of graduate education directly related to the position, or one year of specialized experience (as described under GS-5) equivalent to GS-7. **GS-10:** One year of specialized experience (as described under GS-5) equivalent to GS-9. **GS-11:** One year of specialized experience (as described under GS-5) equivalent to GS-10. **GS-12:** One year of specialized experience (as described under GS-5) equivalent to GS-11. Qualifying education can be substituted for experience, and vice versa. Successful completion of a background investigation also is required.

Training

Professional development for BLM electronics technicians is concerned with various communication devices and other equipment. Depending on their expertise and area of specialty, electronics technicians receive ongoing training that is geared to areas such as troubleshooting, equipment testing and maintenance, installation techniques, alternating-current and direct-current circuits, circuit boards, circuit protection, power supplies, antennas, and other topics. BLM electronics technicians can attend a variety of courses at the BLM National Training Center in Phoenix, Arizona. In addition, they can take advantage of training offered by universities, community colleges, and technical schools nationwide, such as courses offered at Boise State University, Cleveland Institute of Electronics, Texas State Technical College, University of Hawaii, Salt Lake Community College, and Pittsburgh Technical Institute.

Contact: Office of Law Enforcement and Security; Bureau of Land Management; U.S. Department of the Interior; 1849 C St. NW; Washington, DC 20240; phone: (202) 452-5125; Internet: www.blm.gov/

Electronics Technician (GS-0856)
Bureau of Alcohol, Tobacco, Firearms and Explosives; U.S. Department of Justice

Bureau of Alcohol, Tobacco, Firearms and Explosives (ATF) electronics technicians provide support to ATF surveillance, undercover, and general field operations by ensuring that technical investigative equipment is maintained and used at optimum operational performance levels. By applying knowledge of the capabilities, limitations, operations, design characteristics, and functional use of a variety of technical investigative devices and systems, ATF electronics technicians design, modify, repair, and test electronics systems and devices used in covert electronic surveillance applications.

Responsibilities include ensuring that electronic audio and video surveillance devices and other technical investigative equipment functions properly and remains state-of-the-art; operating a wide range of electronics maintenance and repair equipment, as well as hand and power tools and machine shop equipment; providing operational and troubleshooting expertise to the ATF Criminal Enforcement Branch as well as field investigative personnel; preparing reports, technical documentation, and diagrams; and reviewing technical publications to stay abreast of electronic technological improvements.

Qualifications and Salary

GS-5: Completion of a four-year course of study leading to a bachelor's degree in electrical engineering, electronics engineering, or electronics technology; or three years of study in an accredited curriculum in electronics; or a four-year course of study leading to a bachelor's degree that included major study or at least 24 semester hours in any combination of courses in engineering, physical science, technology, or mathematics, of which at least 12 semester hours included electronics courses; or one year of specialized experience equivalent to GS-4 as either an electronics technician, inspector, or mechanic, or as a television or radio repair technician in a commercial shop. **GS-7:** One full year of graduate education directly related to the position, or one year of specialized experience (as described under GS-5) equivalent to GS-5. **GS-9:** Two full years of graduate education directly related to the position, or one year of specialized experience (as described under GS-5) equivalent to GS-7 **GS-11:** One year of specialized experience (as described under GS-5) equivalent to GS-9. **GS-12:** One year of specialized experience (as described under GS-5) equivalent to GS-11. Equivalent combinations of education and experience can be used to meet minimum experience requirements. Candidates also must pass a background investigation.

Training

ATF electronics technicians attend training programs, seminars, and conferences throughout their careers that focus on the assembly, installation, disguising, application, and repair of technical investigative equipment. Training also includes instruction pertaining to the development and advancement of new technical surveillance techniques, electronic audio and video surveillance devices, and other technical investigative equipment. Training is conducted by the ATF Criminal Enforcement Branch in Washington, D.C.; various organizations that manufacture, sell, or service electronic surveillance devices; organizations such as the National Technical Investigators Association; and other recognized authorities.

Contact: Personnel Division; Bureau of Alcohol, Tobacco, Firearms and Explosives; U.S. Department of Justice; 650 Massachusetts Ave. NW—Room 4100; Washington, DC 20226; phone: (202) 927-8423; Internet: www.atf.gov/; e-mail: persdiv@atf.gov

Electronics Technician (GS-0856)
Federal Bureau of Prisons, U.S. Department of Justice

The primary functions of Federal Bureau of Prisons (BOP) electronics technicians revolve around the installation, maintenance, and repair of communications and technical equipment to ensure the safety and well-being of inmates, visitors, and BOP personnel on the grounds of federal correctional institutions, penitentiaries, camps, jails, and medical facilities.

Primary responsibilities include planning, organizing, and executing projects for the installation, maintenance, and repair of communications systems, security systems, and auxiliary equipment. Examples of responsibilities carried out by these personnel include troubleshooting, testing, installing, and repairing electronic and electro-mechanical equipment and systems; performing routine service work and necessary technical corrections to ensure reliable technical and operational performance; and interpreting and applying plans, specifications, blueprints, and sketches for electronic projects. As sworn federal officers, their secondary responsibilities include maintaining security during emergency situations, staff shortages, and training exercises. BOP electronics technicians are authorized to enforce criminal statutes and judicial sanctions, conduct investigations, carry firearms, and make arrests.

This position is covered under special retirement provisions for law enforcement officers.

Qualifications and Salary

GS-5: Completion of a four-year course of study leading to a bachelor's degree in electrical engineering, electronics engineering, or electronics technology; or three years of study in an accredited curriculum in electronics; or a four-year course of study leading to a bachelor's degree that included major study or at least 24 semester hours in any combination of courses in engineering, physical science, technology, or mathematics, of which at least 12 semester hours included electronics courses; or one year of specialized experience equivalent to GS-4 as either an electronics technician, inspector, or mechanic, or as a television or radio repair technician in a commercial shop. **GS-7:** One full year of graduate education directly related to the position, or one year of specialized experience (as described under GS-5) equivalent to GS-5. **GS-9:** Two full years of graduate education directly related to the position, or one year of specialized experience (as described under GS-5) equivalent to GS-7. **GS-11:** One year of specialized experience (as described under GS-5) equivalent to GS-9. **GS-12:** One year of specialized experience (as described under GS-5) equivalent to GS-11. Experience and education can be combined to meet total experience requirements for positions at grades GS-5 and below. Tentative appointees must qualify for a security clearance and pass a background investigation, personal interview, drug screening test, and physical exam.

Training

BOP electronics technicians attend the three-week Introduction to Correctional Techniques training program presented by the BOP Staff Training Academy at the Federal Law Enforcement Training Center in Glynco, Georgia (see chapter 16), as well as a two-week correctional institution familiarization course conducted by BOP staff. In-service professional development includes a minimum of 40 hours of training annually pertaining to correctional issues and techniques, as well as training related to the assembly, installation, operation, maintenance, and repair of communications and technical equipment.

Contact: Federal Bureau of Prisons; U.S. Department of Justice; 320 First St. NW—Ste. 460; Washington, DC 20534; phone: (202) 307-3198 or (800) 347-7744; Internet: www.bop.gov/

Emergency Communication Dispatcher (GS-0303)
United States Army, U.S. Department of Defense

Emergency communication dispatchers of the United States Army are responsible for the control of all police, fire, and ambulance emergency response calls at Army installations.

Primary responsibilities of these personnel include receiving emergency and nonemergency calls for service and determining their nature; dealing with members of the public requiring emergency services, including those who are in an emotional, agitated, or excited state of mind; dispatching, rendering assistance and guidance, and supplying critical information to police, fire, ambulance, and other emergency units; operating a variety of state-of-the-art radio transmitters and receivers, automated communication information and database systems, tape and digital recording devices, telephone systems, commercial and Defense Department security alarm system controls, and enhanced 911 emergency and nonemergency networks; preparing radio dispatch reports, police blotters, and other associated police and emergency response reports; filing documents and performing other administrative duties; and monitoring detention cell operations when cells are occupied by detained persons.

This is a civilian position and does not require active duty military service.

Qualifications and Salary

GS-4: Two years of education above high school, or one year of general experience. **GS-5:** Four years of education above high school, or one year of specialized experience equivalent to at least GS-4. **GS-6:** One year of specialized experience equivalent to GS-5. **GS-7:** One year of specialized experience equivalent to GS-6. **GS-8:** One year of specialized experience equivalent to GS-7. Education and experience can be combined to meet total experience requirements for positions at grades GS-5 and below. Tentative appointees must pass a background investigation, drug screening test, and medical exam; obtain and maintain certification in first aid; and qualify for a security clearance.

Training

Emergency communication dispatchers typically receive a combination of on-the-job training and classroom instruction that focuses on radio communication equipment, dispatching procedures, telephone techniques, pre-arrival instructions for providing CPR and other aid, automated law enforcement database systems, computer hardware and software, clerical tasks, and agency policies and procedures. This training and other related instruction are presented by agency staff; federal, state, or local law enforcement training programs or academies; colleges or universities; and other organizations.

Contact: Apply directly to the Army installation where employment is sought, or contact Army Personnel and Employment Service; The Pentagon; Washington, DC 20310; phone: (703) 695-3383; Internet: www.army.mil/.

Emergency Vehicle Dispatcher (GS-2151)
United States Naval Academy, U.S. Department of Defense

United States Naval Academy (USNA) emergency vehicle dispatchers are responsible for radio communication functions in support of law enforcement and security operations on the grounds of the USNA in Annapolis, Maryland, a 338-acre campus located 33 miles east of Washington, D.C.

The primary responsibilities of these personnel include receiving emergency and non-emergency telephone calls; monitoring radio transmissions of USNA police patrol units; receiving requests for police, fire, and emergency medical services, and dispatching the appropriate response units; operating computer-aided multi-frequency radio communication equipment, radio control panels, portable radios, alert tone pagers, and base intercom systems; processing inquiries through the Criminal Justice Information System, which is an interagency computer network that includes the Maryland Interagency Law Enforcement System and the National Crime Information Center; monitoring automated alarm systems that receive fire, burglary, bank, and intruder alarms from more than 300 locations throughout the USNA complex; and maintaining communications with police and fire department officials on the scenes of accidents, medical emergencies, crimes, and other incidents.

This is a civilian position and does not require active duty military service.

Qualifications and Salary

GS-4: Two years of education above high school, or one year of general experience. **GS-5:** Four years of education above high school, or one year of specialized experience equivalent to at least GS-4. **GS-6:** One year of specialized experience equivalent to GS-5. **GS-7:** One year of specialized experience equivalent to GS-6. **GS-8:** One year of specialized experience equivalent to GS-7. Experience and education can be combined to meet total experience requirements for positions at grades GS-5 and below. Tentative appointees must pass a background investigation, drug screening test, and medical exam; obtain and maintain certification in first aid; and qualify for a security clearance.

Training

USNA emergency vehicle dispatchers receive on-the-job training and attend courses relating to prioritization of calls for service, communication skills, crisis intervention, information gathering, suicide calls, liability issues, dispatching procedures associated with crimes in progress, alarm panel operation, and automated law enforcement database systems. These personnel also receive training leading to EMD (Emergency Medical Dispatch) certification, which focuses on subjects such as listening skills, telephone techniques, pre-arrival instructions for CPR and other aid, dealing with child and elderly callers, pediatric considerations, disaster preparedness, and legal issues. Training is available from USNA personnel and organizations such as the Association of Public Safety Communications Officials.

Contact: Office of Human Resources; United States Naval Academy; 121 Blake Rd.; Annapolis, MD 21402; phone: (410) 293-3822; Internet: www.usna.edu/; e-mail: info@usna.edu

Law Enforcement Communications Assistant (GS-1802)
United States Customs and Border Protection, U.S. Department of Homeland Security

Law enforcement communications assistants serving with United States Customs and Border Protection (CBP) perform a variety of crucial communications functions in support of CBP field operations to ensure the safety and efficiency of CBP personnel nationwide.

These personnel are responsible for monitoring radio communications transmitted by CBP officers that are engaged in detaining, apprehending, and deporting illegal aliens from the United States; receiving and relaying information pertaining to the location of illegal aliens; operating automated law enforcement database systems, such as the National Crime Information Center, National Law Enforcement Telecommunications System, and Master Index Remote Access System; and transmitting details obtained from automated database systems concerning driver's license and vehicle registration information, criminal record data, and immigration status information. These personnel also decode and intercept electronic border intrusion sensor devices using knowledge of terrain, local conditions, and traffic patterns; coordinate and maintain communications during emergency situations; relay information by radio or telephone to other law enforcement agencies; provide telephone coverage for anti-smuggling units; and perform daily inspections of equipment to ensure working order.

Qualifications and Salary

GS-4: Two years of education above high school, or one year of general experience.
GS-5: Four years of education above high school, or one year of specialized experience equivalent to at least GS-4. **GS-6:** One year of specialized experience equivalent to GS-5. **GS-7:** One year of specialized experience equivalent to GS-6. **GS-8:** One year of specialized experience equivalent to GS-7. Equivalent combinations of education and experience can be used to meet minimum experience requirements for positions at grades GS-5 and below. Those tentatively selected must pass a background investigation and drug screening test.

Training

The nature of training for CBP law enforcement communications assistants depends on the experience level of each individual and the needs of each office served. These personnel typically receive on-the-job training and attend courses relating to automated law enforcement database systems, interpersonal communication, dispatching procedures, radio communication equipment, telephone systems and procedures, border intrusion detection systems, computer hardware and software, administrative records and reports, and agency policies and procedures. Training programs are conducted by CBP and other law enforcement agencies, various law enforcement training academies, and other organizations.

Contact: United States Customs and Border Protection; U.S. Department of Homeland Security; 1300 Pennsylvania Ave. NW; Washington, DC 20229; phone: (202) 344-1250; Internet: www.cbp.gov/

Public Safety Dispatcher (GS-2151)
United States Navy, U.S. Department of Defense

United States Navy (USN) public safety dispatchers are responsible for radio communication functions in support of law enforcement and security operations on the grounds of USN installations, such as shipyards, airfields, supply centers, hospitals, and communication facilities.

The responsibilities of these personnel include dispatching public safety personnel, vehicles, equipment, and supplies to routine and emergency situations via internal radio communication systems; performing data entry into computer-aided dispatch and local computer systems; retrieving information from automated law enforcement database systems, such as the National Law Enforcement Telecommunications System and the National Crime Information Center; monitoring and operating emergency fire alarm and enhanced 911 telephone systems; and summoning mutual aid from outside agencies to provide for support during major fires, multiple alarms, natural disasters, medical emergencies, and other incidents. USN public safety dispatchers also maintain records of dispatched units, personnel, and equipment; prepare shift activity logs and related reports; monitor closed-circuit television equipment and intrusion detection devices; identify equipment malfunctions; and initiate appropriate action to correct equipment problems.

Similar Navy positions are filled under the GS-0392 Police Dispatcher series. This is a civilian position and does not require active duty military service.

Qualifications and Salary

GS-4: Two years of education above high school, or one year of general experience. **GS-5:** Four years of education above high school, or one year of specialized experience equivalent to at least GS-4. **GS-6:** One year of specialized experience equivalent to GS-5. **GS-7:** One year of specialized experience equivalent to GS-6. **GS-8:** One year of specialized experience equivalent to GS-7. Education and experience can be combined to meet total experience requirements for positions at grades GS-5 and below. The application process includes a drug screening test, background investigation, and security clearance determination.

Training

USN public safety dispatchers participate in a variety of training exercises and programs that are designed to maintain and enhance their emergency communication and emergency management skills. These are concerned with topics such as EMD

(Emergency Medical Dispatch) procedures, cross-command and cross-agency emergency response procedures, stress management, automated law enforcement database systems, first aid and CPR, telephone systems and procedures, dealing with distraught callers, agency policies and directives, and other subjects. Training is presented by USN personnel and representatives of other agencies and organizations, such as the Association of Public Safety Communications Officials.

Contact: Direct inquiries to the Human Resources Office where employment is sought, or contact Office of Civilian Human Resources; United States Navy; 614 Sicard St. SE—Ste. 100; Washington, DC 20374; phone: (703) 614-1271; Internet: www.navy.mil/; e-mail: help@chinfo.navy.mil.

Public Safety Dispatcher (GS-2151)
National Park Service, U.S. Department of the Interior

Public safety dispatchers of the National Park Service (NPS) are responsible for radio communication functions in support of law enforcement and security operations at locations managed by the NPS, such as national parks and monuments, trails, preserves, campgrounds, battlefields, seashores, lakeshores, recreational areas, and historic sites. NPS public safety dispatchers serve as a point-of-contact between the public, the NPS Communications Control Center, and operations personnel.

Responsibilities include relaying information on multi-frequency park radio and multi-line telephone systems during routine and emergency situations; receiving reports and coordinating responses to law enforcement incidents, search-and-rescue operations, emergency medical situations, fires, air support operations, natural disasters, downed aircraft, and special events; analyzing situations and establishing priorities during concurrent incidents; coordinating operations with other law enforcement agencies, fire departments, and rescue organizations; operating law enforcement telecommunications computer systems tied in with the National Law Enforcement Telecommunications System, National Crime Information Center, and other law enforcement databases; monitoring fire alarm systems and intrusion detection devices; maintaining logs and confidential records pertaining to all law enforcement activities and communications transactions; and operating personal computers for word processing and data entry.

Similar NPS positions are filled under series that include GS-0390 Communications Operator, GS-0390 Telecommunications Equipment Operator, GS-0392 Public Safety Communications Technician, and GS-0392 Telecommunications Technician.

Qualifications and Salary

GS-4: Two years of education above high school, or one year of general experience. **GS-5:** Four years of education above high school, or one year of specialized experience equivalent to at least GS-4. **GS-6:** One year of specialized experience equivalent to GS-5. **GS-7:** One year of specialized experience equivalent to GS-6. **GS-8:** One year of specialized experience equivalent to GS-7. Education and experience can be combined to meet total experience requirements for positions at grades GS-5 and below. Tentative appointees must pass a background investigation.

Training

Orientation and ongoing in-service training for NPS public safety dispatchers focus on topics such as information-gathering techniques, communications terminology, radio communications equipment, call classification, dispatching procedures, automated law enforcement database systems, alarm panel controls, telephone systems and procedures, pre-arrival instructions, crisis intervention, liability and accountability, Good Samaritan statutes, administrative records and reports, agency policies and procedures, and other subjects.

Contact: Direct inquiries to the personnel office where employment is sought, or to Division of Personnel Management; National Park Service; Department of the Interior; 1849 C St. NW; Washington, DC 20240; phone: (202) 208-6843; Internet: www.nps.gov/.

Radio Telecommunications Equipment Operator (GS-0390)

Bureau of Indian Affairs, U.S. Department of the Interior

Bureau of Indian Affairs (BIA) radio telecommunications equipment operators perform a wide range of data processing and dispatching functions in support of BIA law enforcement operations on Indian lands, reservations, allotments, and communities throughout Indian Country.

Working under the direction of Supervisory BIA police officers, radio telecommunications equipment operators receive reports and dispatch appropriate police personnel to calls for service, crimes in progress, disturbances, traffic accidents, emergency medical situations, fires, search-and-rescue operations, special events, and other incidents; monitor police radio frequencies; and respond to requests for telecommunication services. These tasks involve operating various automated law enforcement database and communications systems; relaying results of inquiries to BIA police personnel in the field; receiving telephone inquiries; communicating information to field units using police radio codes; operating the law enforcement Crime Reporting Information System (CRIS), a computerized network consisting of law enforcement statistical data; and maintaining confidential records, logs, and files pertaining to law enforcement activities, incoming and outgoing calls, and related communications.

Similar BIA positions are filled under the GS-0390 Telecommunications Equipment Operator designation.

Qualifications and Salary

GS-3: One year of education above high school, or six months of general experience.
GS-4: Two years of education above high school, or one year of general experience.
GS-5: Four years of education above high school, or one year of specialized experience equivalent to at least GS-4. **GS-6:** One year of specialized experience equivalent to GS-5. **GS-7:** One year of specialized experience equivalent to GS-6. **GS-8:** One year of specialized experience equivalent to GS-7.

Under the Indian Reorganization Act of 1934, qualified Native American applicants are given hiring preference for BIA positions, although applications from non–Native American candidates are encouraged. Education and experience can be combined to meet total experience requirements for positions at grades GS-5 and below. Successful completion of a background investigation is required.

Training

BIA radio telecommunications equipment operators attend the Basic Telecommunications Officer Training Program within the Federal Law Enforcement Training Center's Indian Police Academy in Artesia, New Mexico. This two-week program is designed to familiarize new BIA and tribal telecommunications personnel with the terminology, technology, procedures, situations, and challenges they will face on the job. BIA radio telecommunications equipment operators also complete on-the-job training and other programs throughout their careers in order to maintain and enhance their skills.

Contact: Direct inquiries to the personnel office where employment is sought, or to Office of Personnel; Bureau of Indian Affairs; Department of the Interior; 1849 C St. NW; Washington, DC 20240; phone: (202) 208-3710; Internet: www.doi.gov/bureau-indian-affairs.html.

Technical Enforcement Officer (GS-1801)
United States Immigration and Customs Enforcement, U.S. Department of Homeland Security

Technical enforcement officers serving with U.S. Immigration and Customs Enforcement (ICE) are responsible for installing, operating, and maintaining covert electronic and technical surveillance devices that are used to provide intelligence and evidence in ongoing criminal investigations. These highly skilled personnel provide technical support to ICE special agents and other law enforcement officers in major operations that require the use of covert audio and video recording devices, cameras, electronic tracking devices, telephone surveillance equipment, transmitters and receivers, tactical radio communications systems, courtroom playback systems, and other related equipment.

Primary responsibilities include attending briefings and assisting with the planning of enforcement operations; conducting site surveys to evaluate available applications; testing and evaluating electronic surveillance, tagging, and detecting equipment under laboratory and field conditions; installing, operating, adjusting, and repairing covert monitoring devices; operating special-purpose surveillance vehicles and electronic diagnostic equipment; resolving complex problems relating to electronic equipment; completing surveillance logs and inventories; participating in the execution of search warrants; and maintaining liaison with law enforcement personnel and agencies.

Technical enforcement officers qualify for Administratively Uncontrollable Overtime (AUO), and are authorized to carry firearms and make arrests. This position is covered under special retirement provisions for law enforcement officers.

Qualifications and Salary

GS-5: Completion of a four-year course of study leading to a bachelor's degree; or three years of general experience, one year of which was equivalent to GS-4. **GS-7:** One full year of graduate education, or superior academic achievement during undergraduate studies, or one year of specialized experience equivalent to GS-5. **GS-9:** A master's degree, or two years of graduate education, or one year of specialized experience equivalent to GS-7. **GS-11:** A Ph.D. or equivalent doctoral degree, or three years of graduate education, or one year of specialized experience equivalent to GS-9. **GS-12:** One year of specialized experience equivalent to GS-11. **GS-13:** One year of specialized experience equivalent to GS-12. Equivalent combinations of education and experience can be used to meet minimum experience requirements. Tentative appointees must qualify for a security clearance and pass a background investigation, personal interview, drug screening test, and physical exam.

Training

Initial training includes a three-week Technical Enforcement Officer School at the Federal Law Enforcement Training Center in Glynco, Georgia. This course includes lecture, laboratory applications, and practical exercises that are concerned with electronic surveillance laws, search and seizure, audio recorders, surveillance receivers and transmitters, antennas, electronic tracking devices, video applications, covert installations, site planning, and electronics troubleshooting. In-service training includes various courses pertaining to federal criminal laws, search and seizure, technical investigative equipment updates, computer database programs, firearms proficiency, use of force, laws of arrest, and other subjects related to various aspects of technical investigative equipment and law enforcement operations.

Contact: Office of Investigations; United States Immigration and Customs Enforcement; U.S. Department of Homeland Security; 425 I St. NW; Washington, DC 20536; phone: (202) 514-0078; Internet: www.ice.gov/

Telecommunications Equipment Operator (GS-0390)
United States Marshals Service, U.S. Department of Justice

Telecommunications Equipment Operators of the United States Marshals Service (USMS) operate technical communications equipment and automated systems in support of USMS law enforcement and security operations nationwide. The responsibilities of these personnel include operating telecommunication terminals linked to the National Crime Information Center (NCIC), the National Law Enforcement Telecommunications System (NLETS), and the Justice Telecommunications System; entering data into Warrant Information Network databases and forwarding data to NCIC; receiving outstanding arrest warrant information, verifying that the data is in the proper format, and converting data into the proper format, as needed; receiving fugitive apprehension information from other agencies; coordinating the arrest and detention of wanted persons via NLETS; processing teletype communications; handling telephone inquiries; monitoring closed-circuit television equipment and alarm systems to ensure building security; establishing and maintaining subject matter files; and receiving incoming messages and routing them to appropriate personnel.

Qualifications and Salary

GS-5: Four years of education above high school, or one year of specialized experience equivalent to at least GS-4. **GS-6:** One year of specialized experience equivalent to GS-5. **GS-7:** One year of specialized experience equivalent to GS-6. **GS-8:** One year of specialized experience equivalent to GS-7. Experience and education can be combined to meet total experience requirements for positions at the GS-5 level. Candidates must successfully complete a background investigation, qualify for a top-secret security clearance, and pass a drug test prior to appointment.

Training

USMS telecommunications equipment operators attend courses and receive continuous on-the-job training relating to the operation of various national and state law enforcement databases and telecommunications systems. This training is conducted by USMS staff and police agencies nationwide, and often leads to database operator certification by state police agencies. Additional training focuses on computer literacy and troubleshooting, word processing software, e-mail programs, telephone call handling procedures, and other relevant subjects.

Contact: Human Resources Division; United States Marshals Service; U.S. Department of Justice; 600 Army-Navy Dr.; Arlington, VA 22202; phone: (202) 307-9437; Internet: www.usmarshals.gov/; e-mail: us.marshals@usdoj.gov

Telecommunications Specialist (GS-0391)
Naval Criminal Investigative Service, U.S. Department of Defense

Telecommunications specialists of the Naval Criminal Investigative Service (NCIS) are responsible for installing, maintaining, repairing, and operating communication equipment in support of NCIS criminal investigative, information security, law enforcement, physical and personnel security, and counterintelligence operations worldwide.

Some of the tasks these personnel perform include evaluating radio frequency requirements; conducting site surveys, inspections, and special studies on radio frequency communication needs; testing and evaluating new equipment for the purpose of identifying required resources through which procurement decisions are made; and recommending the implementation of projects designed to fulfill radio frequency mission requirements. Other responsibilities include maintaining close working relationships with Defense Department counterpart units and other federal, state, and local law enforcement agencies; working with industry representatives to ensure that NCIS is kept abreast of advances in technology and plans that could have an impact on the NCIS communication system; and conducting training to facilitate the successful use of radio communications equipment and systems to improve the investigative, counterintelligence, and security capabilities of NCIS personnel.

This is a civilian position and does not require active duty military service.

Qualifications and Salary

GS-5: Completion of a four-year course of study leading to a bachelor's degree; or three years of general experience, one year of which was equivalent to GS-4. **GS-7:** One full year of graduate education, or superior academic achievement during undergraduate studies, or one year of specialized experience equivalent to GS-5. **GS-9:** A master's degree, or two years of graduate education, or one year of specialized experience equivalent to GS-7. **GS-11:** A Ph.D. or equivalent doctoral degree, or three years of graduate education, or one year of specialized experience equivalent to GS-9. **GS-12:** One year of specialized experience equivalent to GS-11. **GS-13:** One year of specialized experience equivalent to GS-12.

Undergraduate and graduate education must have included a major in either electrical or electronic engineering, mathematics, physics, public utilities, statistics, computer science, telecommunications or information systems management, business administration, industrial management, or other fields related to the position. Equivalent combinations of education and experience can be used to meet minimum experience requirements. Candidates must successfully complete a background investigation, qualify for a security clearance, and pass a drug test prior to appointment.

Training

NCIS telecommunications specialists receive ongoing in-house classroom instruction and on-the-job training concerned with communications equipment, transmission media, information security requirements, physical and personnel security issues, and the latest communications technology. They also attend advanced courses and seminars, conferences, and symposia hosted by various professional organizations, colleges, and universities.

Contact: Naval Criminal Investigative Service; 716 E. Sicard St. SE; Washington Navy Yard; Washington, DC 20388; phone: (202) 433-9162; Internet: www.ncis.navy.mil/

Telecommunications Specialist (GS-0391)
United States Secret Service, U.S. Department of Homeland Security

United States Secret Service (USSS) telecommunications specialists perform a range of functions associated with the planning, development, implementation, and administration of all aspects of USSS radio, telephone, and other communications systems and facilities.

In carrying out these tasks, telecommunications specialists are involved in surveying, studying, and evaluating divisions, field offices, and resident agencies to determine radio communication requirements; locating contractors to perform the installation of antenna systems, electrical power, and related equipment; installing, maintaining, and repairing complex multi-frequency, multi-site radio communications systems; installing and maintaining integrated mobile radio systems consisting of voice privacy VHF and UHF mobile radios, cellular telephones, radio scanners, and warning lights; serving as a team leader or member on protective communications support missions throughout the United States or abroad; preparing written reports; and explaining system changes, proposals, and services provided for temporary communications. USSS telecommunications specialists also are involved in the planning, design, development, and implementation of a nationwide data telecommunications network that integrates highly sensitive and technical automated data processing functions, electronic mail, facsimile, and office automation functions.

Qualifications and Salary

GS-5: Completion of a four-year course of study leading to a bachelor's degree; or three years of general experience, one year of which was equivalent to GS-4. **GS-7:** One full year of graduate education, or superior academic achievement during undergraduate studies, or one year of specialized experience equivalent to GS-5. **GS-9:** A master's degree, or two years of graduate education, or one year of specialized experience equivalent to GS-7. **GS-11:** A Ph.D. or equivalent doctoral degree, or three years of graduate education, or one year of specialized experience equivalent to GS-9. **GS-12:** One year of specialized experience equivalent to GS-11. **GS-13:** One year of specialized experience equivalent to GS-12.

Undergraduate and graduate education must have included a major in either electrical or electronic engineering, mathematics, physics, public utilities, statistics, computer science, telecommunications or information systems management, business administration, industrial management, or other fields related to the position. Qualifying education can be substituted for experience, and vice versa. Tentative appointees must qualify for a top-secret security clearance, and pass a background investigation and drug screening test.

Training

The nature of training for Secret Service telecommunications specialists is based largely on the experience and area of expertise of each individual. Generally speaking, training for these personnel focuses on technical and analytical functions pertaining to the planning, development, acquisition, testing, integration, installation, use, modification, and repair of telecommunications systems, technical investigative equipment, and security devices used in Secret Service law enforcement, investigative, and protective operations.

Contact: United States Secret Service; U.S. Department of Homeland Security; 800 G St. NW—Room 912; Washington, DC 20223; phone: (202) 406-5800; Internet: www.secretservice.gov

Telecommunications Specialist (GS-0391)
Bureau of Alcohol, Tobacco, Firearms and Explosives; U.S. Department of Justice

Telecommunications specialists of the Bureau of Alcohol, Tobacco, Firearms and Explosives (ATF) are divided between voice and radio communications systems.

Voice telecommunications specialists are responsible for designing and maintaining systems that include telephones, switchboards, switching equipment, key systems, and data or radio interfaces. These personnel perform technical and analytical work to develop and enhance ATF's telecommunications equipment and services, which cover a broad range of state-of-the-art components.

Radio telecommunications specialists plan and implement the application of radio communication systems and electronic surveillance equipment, including equipment installations in vehicles, aircraft, and fixed station sites. Radio personnel are directly involved in field enforcement activities as they relate to the operation of multi-frequency mobile and base radio systems, repeaters, antennas, concealed miniature radio transmitters, electronic listening devices, video surveillance cameras, audio and video recording devices, and other technical investigative equipment.

ATF telecommunications specialists also explore emerging technologies; conduct site surveys to determine communications needs; coordinate the purchasing, testing, installation, operation, and maintenance of equipment; adapt advanced techniques and develop innovative procedures and equipment applications to meet unique needs which cannot be satisfied through conventional means; conduct training and orientation programs for user groups; and maintain liaison with communications equipment manufacturers, suppliers, and other experts in the field.

Qualifications and Salary

GS-5: Completion of a four-year course of study leading to a bachelor's degree; or three years of general experience, one year of which was equivalent to GS-4. **GS-7:** One full year of graduate education, or superior academic achievement during undergraduate studies, or one year of specialized experience equivalent to GS-5. **GS-9:** A master's degree, or two years of graduate education, or one year of specialized experience equivalent to GS-7. **GS-11:** A Ph.D. or equivalent doctoral degree, or three years of graduate education, or one year of specialized experience equivalent to GS-9. **GS-12:** One year of specialized experience equivalent to GS-11. **GS-13:** One year of specialized experience equivalent to GS-12.

Undergraduate and graduate education must have included a major in either electrical or electronic engineering, mathematics, physics, public utilities, statistics, computer science, telecommunications or information systems management, business administration, industrial management, or other fields related to the position. Experience and education can be combined to meet total experience requirements for positions at grades GS-5 and below. Tentative appointees must qualify for a security clearance and pass a background investigation.

Training

Training for ATF telecommunications specialists includes a wide range of courses that are concerned with the design, installation, operation, maintenance, and repair of telephone and radio equipment and technical investigative devices. Many of these courses are conducted by experienced ATF telecommunications personnel, technicians from telecommunications equipment manufacturers and suppliers, technical personnel from other law enforcement agencies, or other recognized authorities.

Contact: Personnel Division; Bureau of Alcohol, Tobacco, Firearms and Explosives; U.S. Department of Justice; 50 Massachusetts Ave. NW—Room 4100; Washington, DC 20226; phone: (202) 927-8423; Internet: www.atf.gov/; e-mail: persdiv@atf.gov

Telecommunications Specialist (GS-0391)
Drug Enforcement Administration, U.S. Department of Justice

Telecommunications specialists serving with the Drug Enforcement Administration (DEA) originate and develop concepts, equipment, and planning for the use of radio communications and technical investigative equipment and systems to improve the investigative capabilities and safety of DEA special agents. Their efforts provide special technical expertise to the DEA and other domestic and foreign law enforcement agencies in a coordinated effort to reduce the flow of illicit drugs into the United States and worldwide.

Some of their primary responsibilities include participating in the planning of law enforcement operations; conducting site surveys to evaluate the possibility for communications and covert surveillance utilizing electronic devices; and installing phone intercepts, video cameras, microphones, pen registers, microwave transmitters, transponders, and other communication and covert electronic devices. They also coordinate the design, purchase, testing, integration, modification, installation, and repair of many types of technical investigative equipment used in DEA enforcement operations.

In addition to operating in DEA field offices, telecommunications specialists also are assigned to the DEA El Paso Intelligence Center, which is a clearinghouse for tactical intelligence and the collection, analysis, and dissemination of information related to worldwide drug movement and alien smuggling activities.

Qualifications and Salary

GS-5: Completion of a four-year course of study leading to a bachelor's degree; or three years of general experience, one year of which was equivalent to GS-4. **GS-7:** One full year of graduate education, or superior academic achievement during undergraduate studies, or one year of specialized experience equivalent to GS-5. **GS-9:** A master's degree, or two years of graduate education, or one year of specialized experience equivalent to GS-7. **GS-11:** A Ph.D. or equivalent doctoral degree, or three years of graduate education, or one year of specialized experience equivalent to GS-9. **GS-12:** One year of specialized experience equivalent to GS-11. **GS-13:** One year of specialized experience equivalent to GS-12.

Undergraduate or graduate education must have included a major in either electrical or electronic engineering, mathematics, physics, public utilities, statistics, computer science, telecommunications or information systems management, business administration, industrial management, or other related fields. Equivalent combinations of education and experience can be used to meet minimum experience requirements. Those tentatively selected must qualify for a security clearance and pass a background investigation and drug screening test.

Training

Telecommunications specialists attend training programs, seminars, and conferences throughout their careers that focus on the design and capabilities of various types of technical investigative equipment; techniques for the disguise and placement of audio and video surveillance devices; legal requirements associated with the use of telecommunications systems and technical investigative equipment; and the planning, development, acquisition, testing, integration, installation, use, modification, and repair of electronic devices and systems. Training is presented by DEA personnel, representatives of other law enforcement agencies, the National Technical Investigators Association, and other organizations.

Contact: Direct inquiries to the DEA Field Office where employment is sought, or to Office of Personnel; Drug Enforcement Administration; U.S. Department of Justice; 2401 Jefferson Davis Hwy.; Alexandria, VA 22301; phone: (202) 307-7977; Internet: www.dea.gov/.

PART 3

FEDERAL LAW ENFORCEMENT TRAINING

Chapter 16: Federal Training Programs and Facilities

Federal Training Programs and Facilities

"Education has for its object the formation of character."

—Herbert Spencer

Training that provides up-to-date information and practical application of the latest techniques and technology is essential to prepare law enforcement officers to carry out their responsibilities safely and effectively. Many prominent training facilities offer innovative and specialized programs to address the demands and challenges these officers and support personnel must face.

The majority of federal criminal investigators and uniformed police officers attend basic and in-service training at the Federal Law Enforcement Training Center (FLETC) in Glynco, Georgia, or at FLETC's satellite campuses in New Mexico, South Carolina, or Maryland. Many federal law enforcement technicians, specialists, inspectors, and other support staff also complete introductory and advanced courses at FLETC throughout their careers. Most federal agencies also take advantage of in-house training programs, online courses, and other training presented by state and local police academies, colleges and universities, and privately owned training organizations.

A few federal law enforcement agencies, such as the FBI, Drug Enforcement Administration (DEA), and Postal Inspection Service, operate substantial in-house academies that provide agency-specific training for new recruits and veteran personnel alike. These agencies also present a variety of training programs to other federal, state, local, and international law enforcement agencies. Some federal police departments operate in-house programs to train new recruits in lieu of sending them to FLETC; Federal Reserve Bank police officers, Department of Veterans Affairs police officers, and Postal Service police officers are trained in this fashion. Interestingly enough, although the FBI Academy is one of the most respected law enforcement training organizations in the world, the Bureau sends its police officer recruits to FLETC instead of training them in-house. On the other hand, FLETC managers routinely attend courses at the FBI academy.

This chapter provides an overview of the most widely attended training facilities and programs for federal law enforcement officers, investigators, intelligence analysts, and other personnel.

The Federal Law Enforcement Training Center (FLETC)

FLETC conducts state-of-the-art basic, advanced, specialized, and refresher courses for the majority of the federal government's law enforcement officers, who represent more than 80 federal agencies. More than 300 separate training programs are offered, each presented by a cadre of FLETC staff instructors and instructors from "partner" organizations—law enforcement agencies that maintain permanent staff and training offices at FLETC's main campus or satellite campuses. FLETC conducts more than 50 training programs for state, local, campus, and tribal law enforcement agencies, and more than 200 agency-specific programs that are taught mostly by instructors from partner agencies. FLETC trains more than 30,000 students annually at its campuses and through programs presented off-site. Details concerning the Center's basic, advanced, state and local, and international training programs are provided later in this chapter.

FLETC training programs are divided among several instructional areas, including behavioral sciences, computer and financial investigations, counterterrorism, driver and marine enforcement operations, firearms, forensics, investigative technologies, legal support, physical techniques, victim and witness programs, and law enforcement leadership, among others. Instruction is presented primarily during daytime hours on weekdays, although practical exercises often are conducted during evenings and on weekends. Many programs use professional role players during practical exercises to provide a realistic and challenging atmosphere, including training that focuses on interviewing, arrest techniques, defensive tactics, undercover transactions, and other matters. Videotaped replays also are used to critique student performance. Although many agencies design and conduct agency-specific training programs at the Center, the majority of FLETC courses are composed of personnel representing many different agencies.

Training Facilities

FLETC operates four permanent campuses, including the Glynco facility and campuses in Artesia, New Mexico; Charleston, South Carolina; and Cheltenham, Maryland. In addition, FLETC has oversight and program management responsibility for the International Law Enforcement Academies in Botswana and Costa Rica, and provides support to law enforcement training academies in Hungary and Thailand.

Glynco Main Campus and Headquarters

The main campus is located near Brunswick, Georgia. This facility is situated on more than 1,500 acres, and it accounts for about 75 percent of FLETC training activities. The Glynco campus has been updated and expanded on an ongoing basis to enhance its capabilities.

Glynco's specialized facilities include classroom buildings, computer laboratories, driver training ranges, marine facilities, computerized indoor and outdoor firearms ranges, automated judgment pistol shooting facilities, criminalistics teaching laboratories, raid houses, an explosives range, a mock international port of entry, interviewing suites, mock courtrooms, a narcotics identification laboratory, a library, office and warehouse space, and various administrative and logistical support structures. Many practical exercises are carried out within a 34-building complex that is equipped with video cameras and recording equipment used for post-exercise critiques. The physical techniques complex encompasses more than three acres and includes a gymnasium, mat rooms, weight rooms, an indoor swimming pool, a one-quarter-mile track, an obstacle course, classrooms, and other fitness and training facilities. Facilities that will accommodate a wide variety of Homeland Security training programs are under construction. Accommodations and amenities include dormitories and townhouses, dining hall, recreation areas, outdoor swimming pool, health unit, post office, convenience store, credit union, tavern, and laundry facilities.

Artesia Campus

The Artesia campus is situated on a 2,540-acre site in southwestern New Mexico near Roswell. It offers similar facilities to those at Glynco, although on a smaller scale, and is used largely for meeting the basic training needs of Bureau of Indian Affairs police officers, Border Patrol agents, and federal air marshals, and for the advanced training needs of agencies located principally in the Western region of the United States. The Artesia campus has housing and associated support capacity for more than 700 students. The campus has grown significantly over the years—especially since the attacks of September 11, 2001—in response to increases in federal law enforcement agency staffing and associated training needs.

Artesia training facilities include firearms ranges, a physical techniques complex, driver-training ranges, classrooms, computer laboratories, interview suites, a mock courtroom, drug laboratories, fingerprint laboratories, mat rooms, a gymnasium, weight rooms, office space, and a dining hall. Firearms training facilities are extensive, encompassing indoor and outdoor shooting ranges, live-fire shooting houses, three Boeing 727 aircraft used for shooting simulation exercises, a cover and concealment course, a skeet range, and judgment shooting simulators. Driving courses include high-speed pursuit ranges, non-emergency vehicle operation courses, and facilities for skid-control training. Accommodations and amenities include dormitories; a cafeteria; recreation facilities; a theater that includes DVD equipment, a Surround-Sound system, and satellite reception; a game room; a health unit; and a student center that has a tavern, bank, post office, and convenience store.

Charleston Campus

Originally, this facility—which is on the grounds of the former Charleston Naval Weapons Station—was used primarily for training immigration officers and Border Patrol agents. Today, the Charleston campus is a permanent residential training site that is home to the U.S. Coast Guard Maritime Law Enforcement Academy, the Federal Probation and Pretrial Services Academy, and other training programs.

The Charleston campus can accommodate more than 800 students. Training facilities and accommodations at this site include boat boarding platforms, shipboard simulators, an emergency-response driver-training range, skid control and non-emergency vehicle operations driver-training ranges, a commercial vehicle inspection facility, classrooms, firearms ranges, computer laboratories, forensics laboratories, mat rooms, running tracks, an obstacle course, weight rooms, a health unit, tennis courts, and softball fields. Ongoing expansion and upgrading are underway at this campus to accommodate additional students and training programs.

Cheltenham Campus

The 372-acre Cheltenham campus is used primarily for advanced training of the 19,000 federal law enforcement officers who represent more than 70 agencies in the Washington, DC, metropolitan area. The majority of programs presented at this site are geared toward firearms proficiency and firearms instructor training, driving techniques, leadership and management training, and specialized computer training. Other programs focus on bicycle patrol, vehicle ambush countermeasures, motor vehicle accident reporting and investigation, all-terrain vehicle operations, and other subjects. FLETC Cheltenham staff also are developing courses in areas such as hostage negotiation, high-risk warrant execution, raid planning and execution, canine operations, crowd control, and responses to man-made and natural disasters. The Cheltenham campus also houses the U.S. Capitol Police Training Academy, which is used for in-service training. In addition, the Washington, DC, Metropolitan Police Department and the Prince Georges County, Maryland, Police Department conduct training at the Cheltenham campus.

The Cheltenham campus is located 14 miles southeast of downtown Washington, DC, on the grounds of the former U.S. Navy Communications Detachment, which FLETC acquired in May 2001. Facilities at this site include multipurpose classrooms, firearms simulators, a 13-building tactical training village, practical exercise facilities and simulators, conference facilities, a 200-seat auditorium, a dining hall, a vehicle storage and repair facility, warehouse space for shipping and receiving, and other support structures. The Cheltenham campus has one of the largest indoor firearms ranges in the world, which includes 108 firing points. The driver-training range encompasses a skid-control pad, a non-emergency vehicle operation grid, a pursuit driving course, a vehicle maintenance facility, and a classroom building. Presently, there are no dormitory facilities on-site.

Basic Training Programs

FLETC offers three types of basic training: Center Basic, Center Integrated, and Agency-Specific.

Center Basic programs consist of entry-level recruit training that meets the needs of multiple agencies. Each class is composed of students from many agencies. Examples of Center Basic training include three of FLETC's flagship courses: the Criminal Investigator Training Program, the Mixed Basic Police Training Program, and the Natural Resources Police Training Program. *Center Integrated* Basic programs meet the mission-specific or unique requirements of a single agency, and are attended only by members of the agency. These include the Border Patrol Integrated, United States Park Police Integrated, and United States Marshals Service Integrated training programs. *Agency-Specific Basic* programs consist of entry-level training for individual agencies, which follows and supplements Center Basic training. For example, after completing the Natural Resources Police Training Program (NRPTP), Forest Service law enforcement officers attend a two-week Forest Service Basic Law Enforcement Officer Training Program at FLETC that covers agency-specific operations not addressed in the NRPTP course.

This section provides an overview of several FLETC basic training programs for federal law enforcement, intelligence, compliance, corrections, and security personnel.

Criminal Investigator Training Program

The 11-week Criminal Investigator Training Program (CITP) provides federal agents in the GS-1811 and GS-1812 occupational classifications with an in-depth study of criminal investigative and law enforcement operations. This program focuses on the fundamental techniques, concepts, and methodologies that equip criminal investigators with the knowledge and skills needed to carry out various investigative tasks, undercover and surveillance assignments, law enforcement procedures, and other functions safely and effectively. The CITP—one of FLETC's best-known training programs—is attended by agents representing more than 50 agencies.

Academic instruction in the CITP focuses on subjects such as criminal and constitutional law, search and seizure, rules of evidence, self-incrimination, laws relating to flying on aircraft while armed, detention and arrest law, use of force, informants, sources of information, orientation to federal law enforcement agencies, drugs of abuse, questioned documents, organized crime, terrorism, bombs and explosives, financial investigations, federal firearms violations, federal court procedures, ethics, and cultural diversity. Training in these and other topics provides a foundation upon which students build an understanding of criminal investigation and law enforcement fundamentals.

Classroom lectures are supplemented by practical exercises and other hands-on training in areas such as crime scene investigation, evidence collection, interviewing techniques, surveillance, photography, undercover operations, high-risk vehicle stops, fingerprinting, report writing, search warrant execution, rapid building entry, tactical procedures, searching computers, trial preparation, courtroom testimony, firearms safety, marksmanship, judgment pistol shooting, reduced light shooting, non-lethal subject control techniques, CPR, physical conditioning, emergency response driving and skid control, and other topics.

In addition, each CITP student participates throughout the program as a member of a Continuing Case Investigation (CCI) task force team. This sequentially structured investigation enables trainees to gather information, interview witnesses, plan and conduct surveillance and undercover operations, prepare search warrant affidavits, execute search warrants, seize evidence, write a criminal complaint, obtain an indictment, make arrests, and testify in court. These activities are facilitated by CCI coordinators who discuss investigative plans with students, review investigative progress, coordinate enforcement actions, and serve as first-line field supervisors during practical exercises.

Mixed Basic Police Training Program

The nine-week Mixed Basic Police Training Program (MBPTP) presents a broad range of basic law enforcement concepts and techniques that new federal police officers must grasp and be able to perform to carry out their duties. This program is attended by police officer recruits from agencies such as the FBI, AMTRAK, Bureau of Engraving and Printing, National Security Agency, Central Intelligence Agency, U.S. Capitol Police, Pentagon Force Protection Agency, Government Printing Office, Federal Protective Service, Library of Congress, U.S. Mint, National Institutes of Health, National Institute of Standards and Technology, National Zoological Park Police, U.S. Secret Service Uniformed Division, Supreme Court Police, and others.

MBPTP coursework provides a core of knowledge that prepares federal police officer recruits to handle emergencies and other demands and challenges of police work. The course covers a wide range of topics relating to the knowledge and skills required of uniformed law enforcement officers in a federal policing environment. Some of the subjects covered in this program include patrol procedures, emergency response driving, high-risk vehicle stops, violent groups, crowd control, hostage situations, critical incident response, handling abnormal persons, federal criminal law, constitutional law, vehicle searches, detention and arrest, crime scene preservation, interviewing techniques, narcotics, terrorism, criminal intelligence, federal firearms violations, courtroom testimony, VIP protection, bombs and explosives, firearms safety and marksmanship, weapons detection, non-lethal subject control techniques, and impact weapons. Students are evaluated through a series of written examinations and practical exercises that are concerned with typical situations encountered on the job.

Natural Resources Police Training Program

Federal land management agencies whose officers perform law enforcement duties in urban, rural, or isolated areas attend the 16-week Natural Resources Police Training Program (NRPTP). This course is geared toward the training needs of cultural and natural resource protectors engaged in professional law enforcement and visitor use management activities. Students in this program learn and develop the skills required of officers responsible for policing in unique environments not normally encountered by most other federal police agencies. NRPTP training is presented by FLETC staff and instructors from FLETC partner agencies, such as the USDA Forest Service, Tennessee Valley Authority, National Park Service, U.S. Fish and Wildlife Service, National Marine Fisheries Service, Bureau of Land Management, and Bureau of Reclamation. The majority of NRPTP trainees are employed by these agencies.

Lectures, laboratory sessions, and practical exercises of the NRPTP are concerned with subjects such as rural surveillance, emergency response and pursuit driving, high-risk vehicle stops, automobile and motor home search tactics, surveillance, critical incident stress, motorcycle gangs, environmental and animal rights extremist groups, officer safety and survival, archaeological and natural resources crimes, fingerprinting, federal court procedures, courtroom testimony, death investigation, drug investigations, marijuana eradication, booby traps, bombs and explosives, judgment pistol shooting, and reduced-light shooting.

U.S. Customs and Border Protection Integrated Training Program

The 14-week CBPI course is presented by the CBP Academy at the FLETC Glynco campus. This program provides newly hired CBP officers and CBP canine officers with classroom training and practical experience in areas formerly covered during INS and USCS inspector training, as well as instruction relating to the inspection of agricultural goods. CBPI training subjects focus on passenger processing, interviewing techniques, cross-cultural communication, immigration and naturalization laws, fraudulent documents, federal export and import laws, prohibited goods, agriculture inspection matters, trade processing, border search laws, antiterrorism, radiation isotope identifiers, fiberoptic scopes, x-ray equipment, firearms qualification, defensive tactics, arrest techniques, baton techniques, and violent groups.

Border inspection practical training is conducted primarily at the CBP Academy's mock port of entry, a 22,000-square-foot facility that simulates a land border, airport, and seaport. This facility is outfitted with CBP computer systems, mock entry stations with primary and secondary inspection points for pedestrian and vehicular traffic, license plate readers, radiation monitors, and other inspection tools and equipment.

Border Patrol Integrated Training Program

All Border Patrol agent recruits attend the 19-week Border Patrol Integrated Training Program (BPITP) at the FLETC campus in Artesia, New Mexico. This program is operated by CBP's Border Patrol Academy, a training program that was known originally as the El Paso District Training School in 1934. The name of the program was changed to Border Patrol Academy in 1956. All of the subjects presented in the original curriculum are included in the current BPITP course. Classes are taught by FLETC personnel and Border Patrol staff instructors.

This course includes instruction concerning patrol techniques; drug enforcement; counterterrorism; chemical, biological, and radiological weapons; Spanish language; immigration and nationality law; fraudulent documents; drug smuggling operations; behavioral sciences; confrontation management; interviewing; forensics; firearms, range safety, survival shooting techniques, and judgment pistol shooting; emergency response driving; high-risk vehicle stops; physical fitness; defensive tactics; arrest techniques; fingerprinting; and other subjects.

The BPITP is known as one of the most rigorous and demanding law enforcement training programs in the nation. In addition to strict discipline, the BPITP curriculum consists of intensive physical training, difficult legal subjects, extensive firearms training, and 222 hours of instruction focusing on Spanish grammar and conversational Spanish.

Immigration and Customs Enforcement Detention and Removal Operations Training Program

Newly hired U.S. Immigration and Customs Enforcement (ICE) immigration enforcement agents (IEAs) attend the ICE Detention and Removal Operations Training Program (ICE-DRO) to prepare for their responsibilities involving the processing, deporting, and removal of illegal aliens from the United States.

The 12-week ICE-DRO training program includes instruction in subjects such as immigration law, naturalization law, federal criminal law, statutory authority of immigration enforcement agents, civil liability, search and seizure, detention and removal operation procedures, interviewing and interrogation techniques, cross-cultural communications, terrorism operations, detection and discovery of contraband, arrest techniques, fingerprinting, defensive tactics, use of force policy, baton techniques, firearms handling and qualification, physical fitness, and driving techniques.

Intelligence Analyst Training Program

Entry-level intelligence analysts attend the two-week Intelligence Analyst Training Program (IATP) to acquire and develop basic skills and techniques to perform analytical processes associated with intelligence research projects. This program provides familiarity with the intelligence cycle, core competencies, data retrieval and analysis techniques, online research methods, and commercial databases. Trainees also learn about law enforcement information resources such as the National Crime Information Center, National Law Enforcement Telecommunications System, El Paso Intelligence Center, Financial Crimes Enforcement Network, Currency and Banking Retrieval System, and Joint Regional Information Exchange System. Learning methodologies include lectures and demonstrations presented by FLETC instructors and guest speakers, and practical exercises that enhance and reinforce students' knowledge and understanding of the subject matter.

415

Some of the subjects covered in this program include the intelligence cycle, operational planning, analytical methods and techniques, link analysis, legal aspects of intelligence, operations security, electronic sources of information, fraudulent documents, electronic worksheets and graphs, relational graphics, financial aspects of criminal investigations, geographic information systems, geographical profiling, intelligence dissemination, oral briefings, report writing, trial preparation, and courtroom testimony.

Introduction to Criminal Investigations Training Program

The two-week Introduction to Criminal Investigations Training Program (ICITP) provides an overview of the procedures, techniques, legal concerns, and general problems associated with criminal investigations. This course is designed for non-criminal investigators, such as regulatory and compliance investigators, inspectors, paralegals, auditors, technical personnel, and others who assist in criminal investigations or testify in court relating to criminal matters. The topics covered in this course enable trainees to identify and respond appropriately to criminal wrong-doing discovered through compliance inspections, noncriminal investigations, or audits, or while carrying out other activities. Instruction consists of classroom lectures and practical exercises that examine the role of the criminal investigator, with particular emphasis on interviewing skills and legal requirements.

Topics covered in the ICITP course include introduction to criminal investigations, federal court procedures, federal criminal law, the Fourth Amendment to the Constitution, administrative law, civil liability, the Privacy Act, the Freedom of Information Act, investigative techniques, informants, questioned documents, interviewing, government employee rights, description and identification, money laundering, report writing, case management, victim and witness awareness, courtroom evidence, and courtroom testimony.

Introduction to Correctional Techniques Training Program

All institution-based Federal Bureau of Prisons (BOP) employees—from cooks to surgeons—are required to complete the three-week Introduction to Correctional Techniques Training Program (known as "BOP Basic"), which is presented by the BOP Staff Training Academy at the FLETC Glynco campus. This program provides a common foundation of agency-specific training that addresses the unique requirements, demands, and challenges faced by BOP personnel employed in federal correctional institutions. The instructors—all experienced BOP personnel detailed to FLETC—present lectures, share their experiences in the field, coordinate group discussions, present videotaped case studies, and oversee practical exercises. This course is accredited by Eastern Kentucky University.

Instruction in the BOP Basic curriculum focuses on subjects such as inmate profiles, correctional law, correctional supervision, sexuality in prisons, inmate workforce, managing diversity, inmate drug and alcohol abuse, situation assessment, suicide prevention, hostage situations, prison gangs, use of force, use of restraints, interpersonal communications, stress management, firearms qualification, physical fitness, and self-defense.

Physical Security Training Program

The two-week Physical Security Training Program (PSTP) provides full-time physical security specialists, law enforcement officers, investigators, and military personnel with in-depth theoretical and practical knowledge of physical security systems and procedures. Training modules are presented systematically and cover various aspects of conceptual security considerations, vulnerability assessments, security hardware and procedures, and security surveys. The facility in which this course is held is geared toward antiterrorism and physical security, providing both a classroom and working laboratory in a hands-on training environment. For the final practical exercise, students develop a security survey, provide a briefing to the class, and undergo a critique.

Classroom lectures and practical exercises in this program focus on risk assessment, theory of physical security and crime prevention, contingency planning, security design, security survey procedures, locks and locking devices, access control, closed-circuit television systems, intrusion detection systems, computer security, perimeter security, protective lighting, fire safety, bombs and explosives, weapons and explosives detection, operations security, special events security planning and equipment, domestic and international terrorism, security legal considerations, security information resources, guard force operations, and violence in the workplace.

Advanced Training Programs

In addition to basic training programs that make up the core of FLETC instruction, the Center's partner agencies provide *Agency Advanced* training, which addresses the special requirements of the agencies. Some examples of courses include "Economic and Environmental Crimes," taught by the Air Force Office of Special Investigations; "Arson for Profit," presented by the Bureau of Alcohol, Tobacco, Firearms and Explosives; "Witness Escort Procedures," presented by the BOP; and "Advanced Antiterrorism," taught by the CBP. Agency Advanced courses typically are presented to experienced law enforcement personnel, often by instructors who are detailed to FLETC from various agencies. For this purpose, more than 20 partner agencies have training offices and full-time staff at FLETC to conduct and support Agency Advanced training. For these programs, the Center provides logistical support, facilitates the training, and schedules training facilities; feeds, houses, and transports the students; and provides instructional support upon request.

FLETC also develops and offers dozens of advanced and specialized training programs in subjects that are common to two or more agencies. These programs—known as *Center Advanced* training programs—are presented by FLETC staff instructors to address the specialized and instructor needs of federal agencies, and in many instances the needs of state and local agencies. Examples of these programs include International Banking Money Laundering, Vehicle Ambush Countermeasures, Technical Investigative Equipment, Law Enforcement Photography, Marine Tactical Operations, Police Bicycle, Fundamentals of Terrorism, Crisis Management, Defensive Tactics Instructor, and Physical Fitness Coordinator. Three highly regarded Center Advanced courses—the Weapons of Mass Destruction Training Program, Covert Electronic Surveillance Program, and Firearms Instructor Training Program—are discussed in this section.

Weapons of Mass Destruction Training Program

The Weapons of Mass Destruction Training Program (WMDTP) provides basic operational and tactical training for law enforcement personnel and others who would serve as first-responders to chemical, biological, or radiological (CBR) weapons of mass destruction (WMD) threats or incidents. This one-week program is presented by staff instructors from the FLETC Counterterrorism Division and guest speakers who are recognized authorities on WMD matters. The program is open to federal law enforcement officers, state and local police officers, fire department and rescue personnel, and others who are responsible for responding to WMD or hazardous materials incidents.

Lectures and a series of practical exercises focus on subjects such as planning for WMD incidents, CBR weapons and dispersal devices, conventional explosives as WMD, explosives and dissemination demonstration, detection and identification of CBR agents, physiological effects of chemical and biological agents, bomb and WMD threat management, downwind hazard analysis, personal protection equipment and related Occupational Safety and Health Administration Requirements, manned portable air defense systems, WMD scene management and tactical considerations, role of first responders in managing a WMD attack, medical management of WMD incidents, and principles of decontamination. Practical exercises enable students to respond to realistic problem-solving issues surrounding a WMD incident, such as wearing an assortment of personal protective equipment, firing pistols and shoulder weapons while wearing personal protective equipment, and participating in decontamination processes.

Covert Electronic Surveillance Program

The two-week Covert Electronic Surveillance Program (CESP) provides training to experienced law enforcement personnel in the use of technical investigative equipment in a variety of situations and environments. The CESP curriculum focuses on techniques for the installation, operation, and maintenance of technical electronic surveillance devices, such as body-worn microphones, transmitters and receivers, video cameras, and various audio and video recording systems. This program is open to full-time federal, state, and local law enforcement personnel who are responsible for technical surveillance activities.

The CESP course includes lectures, electronics laboratory projects, and both daytime and nighttime practical exercises that focus on federal laws for audio and video surveillance, basic electronics, site surveys, radio frequencies and antennas, microphones, audio body wire device installation and operation, audio recorders, receivers and transmitters, body-worn video, concealment techniques, covert video installations, video board cameras, closed-circuit television applications, night-vision systems, batteries and power packs, field repairs, troubleshooting, equipment maintenance and inventory, and electronic surveillance countermeasures.

Firearms Instructor Training Program

Federal, state, and local law enforcement officers who are assigned to firearms instructor responsibilities can attend the two-week Firearms Instructor Training program (FITP). This course provides familiarization with various firearms, introduces teaching techniques, and focuses on identifying and resolving shooting errors and other problems. Many instructional methodologies are used in this program, including classroom lectures, role playing, demonstrations, discussions, and practical exercises. FITP instructors include FLETC staff and law enforcement officers who are detailed to the Center.

Instruction in the FITP course includes topics such as firearms safety, instructional techniques, target analysis, basic and advanced handgun and shotgun stress, instinctive reaction, semiautomatic handguns, rifle lecture and laboratory, advanced shotgun techniques, submachine gun familiarization, reduced-light shooting, judgment pistol shooting, situation response, survival shooting techniques, downed or disabled officer situations, dual-assailant situations, trauma management, use of cover, and instructor liabilities.

State and Local Training Programs

The Office of State and Local Training (OSL) designs and presents training to state, local, campus, and tribal law enforcement agencies at FLETC facilities and other sites nationwide—often at state and local law enforcement training academies and police department facilities. FLETC collaborates with these agencies to train law enforcement personnel in a variety of subjects at minimal cost or no cost to the agencies. These programs are designed to develop specialized law enforcement skills, frequently in subjects not generally available from state and local police academies, colleges, or universities. For example, OSL training programs focus on topics such as crisis management, fraud and financial investigations, explosives investigative techniques, environmental crimes, antiterrorism intelligence awareness, domestic violence in Indian Country, domestic violence instructor training, drug enforcement for patrol officers, drug task force supervision, hate and bias crimes, and gangs. Overviews of three tuition-free OSL programs are provided below.

Anti-Terrorism Intelligence Awareness Training Program

The Anti-Terrorism Intelligence Awareness Training Program is an introductory course that provides line officers and first-line supervisors with a working knowledge of the criminal intelligence process, applicable laws, guidelines, policies, tools, and techniques related to terrorism intelligence activities. This one-day course teaches law enforcement officers various methods to identify pre-incident indicators related to terrorist activity in the community that could be encountered during police patrol and other operations. Instruction in this course includes an overview of terrorism, information concerning use of the Internet by terrorists, and an update on terrorist activity within the region in which the course is presented.

Drug Law Enforcement School for Patrol Officers

The two-day Drug Law Enforcement School for Patrol Officers program offers updated training to police officers to assist them in detecting drug-related criminal activity in the community. This course trains patrol officers in techniques for developing reasonable suspicion and probable cause and offers suggestions for enforcement options. Some of the topics covered include drug recognition and field testing, methods of concealment, roadside interviewing, "raves" and club drugs, indoor marijuana cultivation, developing reasonable suspicion, and clandestine laboratories.

Hate Bias Crime Training Program

The Hate Bias Crime Training Program is a four-day train-the-trainer course that provides all the necessary training aids and materials to train police officers to recognize, report, investigate, and prosecute hate crimes. This course examines hate crimes on a local, national, and international level. Instruction focuses on international terrorism, recognizing organized hate groups, investigating hate crimes, and proactive measures. This program is designed so that graduates will be able to deliver hate bias crime training to personnel within their agencies. The course is open to employees of federal, state, or local criminal justice, law enforcement, or correctional agencies, or other professionals in the criminal justice community.

International Training

The International Programs Division (IPD) presents training programs to foreign law enforcement agencies that are designed to combat global crime and protect U.S.

interests abroad. These programs are based primarily on three initiatives, including the United States Law and Democracy Program, the State Department's Antiterrorism Assistance Program, and International Law Enforcement Academy (ILEA) operations in Europe, Asia, Africa, and other regions of the world.

FLETC's participation in the United States Law and Democracy Program has enabled law enforcement personnel in Russia, Ukraine, and other Eastern European and Central Asian countries to receive training on subjects such as white-collar crime, financial and computer crimes, and illegal narcotics trafficking. Through the Antiterrorism Assistance Program, FLETC has provided technical assistance and training to foreign law enforcement agencies from the Middle East, Africa, Central and South America, and Asia to combat world terrorism. FLETC routinely supports the efforts of all ILEA locations, and has the lead responsibility for conducting operations both in Botswana and Costa Rica. In addition, FLETC instructors routinely travel to the ILEAs in Thailand and Hungary to conduct courses in management, leadership, financial fraud, and other subjects.

The FLETC College Intern Program

The FLETC College Intern Program (FCIP) enables students to gain firsthand experience by participating in federal law enforcement training. The FCIP is offered during three periods annually at both the main campus in Glynco, Georgia, and the campus in Artesia, New Mexico. Each session is 12 weeks in length. Interns receive a daily allowance to help defray the cost of meals, incidental expenses, and travel costs, and are provided dormitory accommodations on-site at no cost.

Intern Assignments

FCIP interns are assigned a mentor from a FLETC training division or a partner agency located on-site. They devote about one-half of their time to attending classroom lectures and participating in practical training exercises, and the other half to various administrative assignments. Assignments vary depending on the needs of the Center and projects underway at the time, although they could involve tasks such as conducting research pertaining to law enforcement, corrections, or security issues to supplement classroom and practical training; creating computer databases and examining operational issues and trends; updating and revising lesson plans, handouts, and course materials; grading examinations; or assisting with other administrative assignments associated with various FLETC programs, operations, and partner agencies. Interns also observe a variety of classroom lectures and participate in virtually every aspect of practical training exercises, such as firearms qualification, search- and arrest-warrant execution, arrest techniques, undercover and surveillance operations, and physical techniques. Interns are issued uniforms for training and physical conditioning.

College Majors

Internship opportunities are available primarily to students obtaining undergraduate or graduate degrees in criminal justice, forensic sciences, psychology, computer forensics, or law. However, students enrolled in other degree programs—such as adult education, business administration, communications, computer science, journalism, recreation, graphic design, and sports medicine—also have been selected for the FCIP in the past.

Internship Qualifications

Internship applicants must be either a college senior enrolled in a baccalaureate program or a graduate student at the time of application and at the time the internship will be served. Seniors must have completed 135 quarter hours or 90 semester hours, and they must be in the upper third of their class in academic standing. The internship must be completed as part of the student's academic requirements and prior to graduation. Applicants must intend to pursue a career in federal law enforcement.

Selection is highly competitive and is based on grade-point average (major and overall), leadership, community participation, work experience, experience related to the academic major, an essay prepared by the applicant, an Intern Nomination Form completed by the applicant's school, a recommendation letter submitted by a school faculty member, and a telephone interview. U.S. citizenship is required. A background investigation is performed prior to appointment.

Application Process

Applicants must submit an Application for Federal Employment (OF-612) or a resume; an FCIP Application; academic transcripts for all colleges attended; an Intern Nomination Form completed by a school faculty member, advisor, internship coordinator, or department chairperson; a letter prepared by the nominating school official; and an essay. The essay must address the reason for applying for the internship, career motivation and goals, knowledge of the FCIP, skills that can be applied during the internship, and preference for the FLETC division or partner agency in which to be placed.

All application materials must be submitted in one package via U.S. mail or a courier service (such as FedEx or UPS) during a two-week application period, usually about four months prior to the targeted internship. Selections usually occur within one month after the closing of the application period. Application materials must be sent to the Human Resources Division; Federal Law Enforcement Training Center; Building 46; 1131 Chapel Crossing Rd.; Glynco, GA 31524. FLETC personnel staffing specialists and internship coordinators can provide additional information or answer questions concerning the FCIP, application forms, application procedures, or other internship matters. They can be reached by telephone at (912) 267-3376.

The Inspector General Criminal Investigator Academy

The Inspector General Criminal Investigator Academy (IG Academy) provides training primarily to federal agents in the Office of Inspector General (OIG) community to assist them in carrying out their specialized missions to investigate fraud and other crimes in government programs and operations. OIG special agents—representing dozens of federal departments and agencies—are among the brightest and most respected personnel in federal law enforcement. Special agents serving with highly regarded federal law enforcement agencies—such as the Department of Agriculture OIG, Treasury Inspector General for Tax Administration, Department of Health and Human Services OIG, Department of Housing and Urban Development OIG, Defense Criminal Investigative Service, Social Security Administration OIG, and Department of Transportation OIG—attend state-of-the-art training programs at the IG Academy to learn new techniques and hone their specialized investigative skills in many areas of expertise. The IG Academy also offers courses for OIG professional support personnel.

IG Academy Training Facilities

The IG Academy is based in two locations. The primary facility is located at the FLETC Glynco campus. Students enrolled in IG Academy courses at this site are housed in dormitories and complete coursework within classrooms, mat rooms, computer laboratories, firearms ranges, raid houses, and other practical training facilities. To better serve OIG agents based in the Washington, DC, area, in 2003 the IG Academy opened a facility in Arlington, Virginia. This training site—which is located on the ground floor of the U.S. Postal Service OIG headquarters building—contains classrooms, breakout rooms, meeting rooms, staff offices, and a lunch room. All classrooms have Internet access and are equipped with contemporary audiovisual components.

Basic Training Programs

The IG Academy conducts several basic courses for entry-level or relatively inexperienced personnel, such as the Inspector General Investigator Training Program, the Inspector General Basic Non-Criminal Investigator Training Program, the Inspector General Search Warrant Execution Training Program, and the Inspector General Transitional Training program. Details concerning two of the IG Academy's most widely attended basic programs are presented below.

The Inspector General Investigator Training Program

The flagship training program of the IG Academy is the Inspector General Investigator Training Program (IGITP)—known commonly as "IG Basic"—a three-week course that develops the law enforcement and investigative skills of OIG special agents. Typically it is attended by agents as a supplement to the 11-week Criminal Investigator Training Program. Much of this hands-on course is presented through individual, small-group, and large-group investigative practical exercises, of which some are held at night.

Instruction in this program focuses on the Inspector General Act of 1978, Department of Justice guidelines for statutory law enforcement authority, investigative planning and case development, advanced investigative interviewing techniques, financial investigations, money laundering, sworn statements, Whistleblower Act, contract and grant fraud investigations, program fraud investigations, electronic sources of information, administrative subpoenas, employee misconduct investigations, employee rights and obligations, workplace searches, legal subjects, non-lethal subject control techniques, use of force, and advanced firearms training.

Inspector General Search Warrant Execution Training Program

OIG special agents without extensive experience in search warrant operations can attend the IG Academy's one-week Inspector General Search Warrant Execution Training Program. This program provides an overview of legal requirements, officer safety concerns, and challenges faced in the execution of search warrants, and teaches OIG special agents how to execute search warrants at single or multiple sites, techniques for managing large evidence seizures, and strategies for executing search warrants through multi-agency, task force, and undercover operations. Topics of instruction include basic search mechanics, risk assessment, preparation of search warrant affidavits, operational security, search and seizure methods, federal rules of evidence, problems associated with search warrant execution, and computerized search warrant inventories.

Advanced Training Programs

Many advanced in-service courses are presented to OIG special agents at the IG Academy. These programs are reviewed and updated regularly so that only the most up-to-date information and techniques are included in the curricula. IG Academy advanced training programs are concerned with subjects such as undercover operations, public corruption and employee integrity investigations, OIG Hotline operations, preservation and processing of computer-based evidence, and the investigation of procurement, contract, and grant fraud. The IG Academy also offers a Periodic Refresher Program that covers legal principles, legal updates, trial preparation, and other matters. Two highly regarded advanced IG Academy programs are discussed in this section.

Inspector General Undercover Operations Training Program

Experienced OIG special agents attend the Inspector General Undercover Operations Training Program (IGUOTP) to learn new techniques relating to stand-alone and multi-agency undercover operations. This two-week course focuses on the operational elements and administrative requirements surrounding undercover operations, such as evidence-gathering considerations, responsibilities of case agents and undercover agents, case planning, officer safety, stress management, and technical support.

Additional subjects covered in this program are concerned with undercover operations planning, Attorney General Guidelines for Undercover Operations, undercover proposals, operational considerations, aliases and cover stories, safety issues, approaching the target, informants, technical support, legal issues, problems in undercover operations, funding accountability, memorandums of understanding for joint agency investigations, spin-off cases to control work assignments, and other topics. Students attending this course complete undercover proposals that are in compliance with Attorney General Guidelines, and also participate in undercover practical exercises.

Inspector General Public Corruption and Integrity Investigations Training Program

The one-week Inspector General Public Corruption and Integrity Investigations Training Program (IGPCIITP) prepares OIG special agents to conduct corruption and employee misconduct investigations. The primary emphasis in this course is on the techniques, concerns, and common problems associated with these investigations, and on the various types of investigations OIG special agents are commonly faced with. Subjects covered during this course include the role and responsibilities of the internal investigator, types of criminal and noncriminal investigations, components of an employee misconduct investigation, considerations for the employee interview, referral of cases for criminal prosecution or administrative adjudication, referral of criminal violations to state and local prosecutors or law enforcement agencies, and other topics.

The FBI Academy

The FBI Academy is widely recognized as one of the world's finest law enforcement training centers. The FBI Training Division manages the Academy and trains FBI special agents and professional support staff, as well as local, state, federal, and international law enforcement personnel. Since its opening in 1972, the FBI Academy has remained on the cutting edge of law enforcement training, assistance, and research.

Training programs for Bureau personnel include New Agents' Training and a wide range of in-service and specialized courses for FBI special agents and support staff. Police training programs include the FBI National Academy, a 10-week multidisciplinary program for law enforcement agency managers; the Executive Training program, attended by Chief Executive Officers of America's largest law enforcement organizations; and Operational Assistance, which trains law enforcement personnel in how to respond to various emergency situations. FBI Academy instructors also conduct research projects and provide technical assistance to federal, state, local, and international law enforcement agencies on investigative techniques and other matters.

Among the instructional components of the Training Division at the FBI Academy is the world-renowned FBI Behavioral Science Unit. FBI Academy instructors, supervisory special agents, and veteran police officers assigned to this unit conduct specialized and applied training for the New Agents' Training program, the FBI National Academy, international police training programs, field police schools, FBI in-service courses, and other international courses and symposia. Behavioral Science Unit staff teach courses on a variety of topics that focus on applied criminal psychology, clinical forensic psychology, community policing and problem-solving strategies, crime analysis, death investigation, gang behavior, law enforcement officers killed and assaulted in the line of duty, research methodologies, stress management in law enforcement, violent crime, and other subjects.

Training Facilities

The FBI Academy is located on the United States Marine Corps Base at Quantico, Virginia, about 40 miles southwest of Washington, DC. The Academy grounds encompass nearly 400 wooded acres of land and more than 20 buildings. The primary training complex includes a classroom building, audiovisual facilities, administrative offices, three dormitory buildings, dining hall, library, forensic science research facilities, 1,000-seat auditorium, chapel, gymnasium, outdoor track, indoor and outdoor firearms ranges, 1.1-mile pursuit and defensive driving track, and fully equipped garage. The DEA training academy also is located on-site and shares the FBI's facilities.

Many practical exercises are conducted in the Academy's Hogan's Alley complex, where students incorporate academics, firearms, defensive tactics, communications skills, and legal knowledge. Hogan's Alley consists of facades and buildings replicating a small town, including a bank, movie theater, drug store, post office, courthouse, used car lot, and other facilities. Behind the facades are fully functioning classrooms, audiovisual facilities, storage areas, and administrative and maintenance offices. Practical exercises carried out in the Hogan's Alley complex focus on surveillance techniques, arrest procedures, tactical skills, and other competencies. For example, New Agents' Training program students participate in scenarios involving bank robberies, assaults, kidnapping incidents, hostage situations, illegal drug transactions, daytime and nighttime surveillance, felony traffic stops, the execution of search and arrest warrants, and other situations. Vehicles, radios, and other equipment are provided to scenario participants, and professional role players confront the trainees with a variety of situations.

Basic Training Programs

The FBI Academy conducts basic training for all newly appointed special agents and many professional support personnel. Special agent recruits are required to complete the FBI New Agents' Training program regardless of their previous experience, education, or training. Newly hired FBI intelligence analysts and investigative specialists also attend formal basic training programs at the Academy, and personnel serving in many other positions attend introductory courses at this facility early in their careers. All FBI employees receive on-the-job training, and many personnel complete periodic professional-development training such as conferences, seminars, Internet-based applications, satellite teleconferences, interactive video programs, and courses on CD-ROM.

This section provides overviews of basic training programs conducted at the FBI Academy for special agents, intelligence analysts, and investigative specialists.

FBI New Agents' Training Program

The FBI New Agents' Training (NAT) program consists of intensive instruction over an 18-week period that focuses on investigative and tactical training, non-investigative training, and administrative matters. The program provides special agent recruits with the basic knowledge and skills they will need to effectively carry out their responsibilities in the field. The NAT curriculum encompasses classroom and practical instruction that are spread over four major concentrations, including academics, firearms, physical training and defensive tactics, and practical applications. The program uses a building-block approach, in which lessons and practical exercises are presented in a carefully planned sequence.

Most of the 708-hour curriculum is dedicated to investigative and tactical training, including subjects such as interviewing and interrogation, counterterrorism, national security, criminal law, search and seizure, forensic sciences, information security, financial investigations, surveillance, behavioral sciences, sources of information, consensual monitoring and Title III wiretaps, espionage, background investigations, command post operations, international investigations, investigative technology, telephone records analysis, undercover operations, arrest techniques, firearms training, and defensive tactics. Non-investigative subjects focus on ethics, first aid and CPR, bloodborne pathogens, cultural diversity, equal employment opportunity, victim witness assistance programs, and other topics. Administrative subjects are concerned with topics such as relocation management, the FBI transfer policy, the Federal Employees Retirement System, and various personnel matters.

FBI Intelligence Analyst Basic Training Program

FBI intelligence analysts attend a seven-week Analytical Cadre Education Strategy (ACES) course at the FBI Academy to learn the core elements of intelligence analysis. The ACES course is designed to expose new intelligence analysts to the intelligence cycle—which is concerned with intelligence requirements, collection, analysis, reporting, and dissemination—and teach them how intelligence advances national security goals. This course also includes instruction on effective use of strategic and tactical analysis, asset vetting, report writing, the Intelligence

Community, various analytical methodologies, and other information on the latest analytic resources and techniques.

FBI Investigative Specialist Basic Training Program

Newly hired FBI investigative specialists complete an eight-week basic training course at the FBI Academy that covers fundamentals of surveillance, foreign counterintelligence, and defensive-driving techniques. This program and in-service training for investigative specialists at the FBI Academy focuses on topics such as foreign counterintelligence operations, national security issues, economic espionage, terrorism, weapons of mass destruction, surveillance techniques, countersurveillance, daytime and nighttime operations, urban and rural surveillance techniques, covert photography and video, technical investigative equipment, electronic surveillance countermeasures, radio communications, computer databases, legal subjects, defensive tactics, and report writing.

Advanced Training Programs

The FBI Academy presents advanced training programs to employees of the FBI and other federal, state, local, and international law enforcement agencies on an ongoing basis. These enable attendees to acquire new skills and enhance their knowledge and capabilities at all stages of their careers. Whether the Academy conducts technical training for FBI forensic scientists, counterterrorism programs for FBI special agents, tactical training for the Bureau's special response teams, or leadership courses for police commanders, the FBI Academy ensures that all training is up-to-date, based on solid research, and delivered by experts.

Several FBI Academy operational components combine expertise and other resources to design and deliver advanced training, such as the FBI National Academy, Field Police Training Unit, International Training Section, Investigative Training Unit, Law Enforcement Communication Unit, Leadership and Management Science Unit, Investigative Computer Training Unit, Forensic Science Research and Training Center, and the College of Analytical Studies, among others. Examples of advanced training programs for FBI special agents, support staff, and personnel from other agencies are discussed below.

Special Agent In-Service Training

FBI special agents can attend various advanced in-service training programs at the FBI Academy throughout their careers depending on the needs of individual agents, their responsibilities and special assignments, and the needs of the Bureau at any time. For example, many special agents attend in-service courses that focus on leadership, management, supervision, ethics, driving, information technology, and critical-incident stress. Agents also can attend the Academy's Law Enforcement Safety and Survival Course, as well as training that is concerned with counterterrorism, counterintelligence, cybercrime, national security investigations, financial crimes, hate crimes, bloodborne pathogens, recruiting and managing informants, the Foreign Intelligence Surveillance Act, and the USA PATRIOT Act. All special agents are required to complete at least 15 hours of in-service training annually.

Members of FBI special response teams attend much of their training at the FBI Academy. For example, special agents who serve on the FBI Hostage Rescue Team attend a four-month initial training program that consists of specialized tactical law enforcement instruction. This program and ongoing in-service training at the FBI

Academy focuses on hostage rescue fundamentals and planning, barricaded subject incidents, high-risk arrest and search operations, firearms, defensive tactics, rappelling, weapons of mass destruction, maritime operations, helicopter operations, mobile assaults, and cold-weather operations. Agents assigned to the Bureau's Crisis Negotiation Unit attend a two-week negotiation course and other programs at the FBI Academy. Special Weapons and Tactics team members attend training at the FBI Academy on high-risk arrest and search operations, drug raids, barricaded suspect incidents, sniper assaults, dignitary protection, intelligence gathering, operational planning, command and control operations, communications, threat assessment methods, strength and conditioning, legal issues, and other tactical matters.

Professional Support Staff In-Service Training

The FBI Academy is an important resource in the Bureau's ongoing effort to train its professional support staff at all levels in the latest technology, techniques, and initiatives, from entry-level administrative support staff to supervisors, managers, and executives. For example, FBI biologists attend courses at the Academy's Forensic Science Research and Training Center to learn and develop skills relating to scientific theories and principles, mitochondrial DNA analysis, serological techniques, biochemical analysis, evidence preservation, courtroom testimony, and other areas. FBI chemists are trained to identify various chemicals, poisons, controlled substances, explosives residues, paints, petroleum products, and many other substances. Initial training for FBI fingerprint examiners consists of a course at the Academy that focuses on examining and classifying fingerprints, fingerprint identification procedures, and FBI policies and procedures relating to fingerprint classification.

Training for the Bureau's information technology specialists is concerned with search and seizure of computers, data recovery, information linking, Internet investigations, computer security, data management, and other computer forensic techniques. FBI photographers attend courses that focus on crime-scene and arson photography, flash and infrared photography, photographic surveillance equipment, night-vision photography, camera systems, meters, lenses, filters, lighting techniques, photographic equipment maintenance, and other topics. Many other professional support personnel complete advanced training at the FBI Academy to keep up with changes in technology, procedures, laws, and other requirements. The Academy offers several leadership and management courses for FBI supervisors, managers, and executives.

Many of the advanced training programs completed by professional support personnel and employees of other law enforcement agencies worldwide are distance learning applications. These programs are produced by the FBI Training Network—a component of the Academy's Training Development Unit—which carries out broadcast and studio production operations from a television studio located in Hogan's Alley.

International Law Enforcement Training

The FBI Academy's International Training Section administers and coordinates all international mission-oriented training in support of the Bureau's international investigative responsibilities and other initiatives. The Academy has held many seminars attended by foreign law enforcement personnel relating to subjects such as counterterrorism, white-collar crime, drug enforcement, organized crime, internal affairs, ethics, police management, leadership, forensics, investigative techniques, interviewing, and the legal aspects of police work. Law enforcement officers, prosecutors, and judicial personnel from a wide range of countries in South

America, Asia, Europe, Africa, and other parts of the world have been trained at the Academy.

The Academy's involvement in international training encompasses activities such as conducting training needs assessments for foreign law enforcement agencies, presenting training programs in the U.S. and internationally to foreign law enforcement personnel, participating in the Mexican/American Law Enforcement Training initiative for police personnel working in the vicinity of the U.S.-Mexican border, participating in the Pacific Rim Training Initiative for officers serving with agencies in the Pacific region, and conducting the FBI National Academy program. The FBI also serves as the lead agency for coordinating activities at the ILEA in Hungary—a training center for police executives, prosecutors, judges, and criminal justice leaders from Eastern Europe, Russia, Ukraine, and the Baltic states—and also supports the ILEA in Thailand. The curricula of both ILEAs are based on the FBI National Academy model.

The FBI National Academy Program

The FBI National Academy—one of the Bureau's flagship training programs—provides leadership and management training for mid- and upper-level police commanders from around the world. The 10-week FBI National Academy program is offered on a quarterly basis and consists of intensive multidisciplinary training for which graduates can earn undergraduate and graduate credits from the University of Virginia. The National Academy program focuses on six academic disciplines, including leadership development, behavioral science, law, communication, health and fitness, and forensic science. Within these disciplines, attendees can take courses in white-collar crime, youth and gang crime, hate crimes, racial profiling, community policing, computer crime, communication skills, abnormal psychology, budgeting and finance, stress management, ethics, and other subjects. The program's instructors include permanent staff of the FBI Academy, personnel from various FBI field offices, and visiting scholars who are recognized experts in their fields. More than 30,000 law enforcement officers from the United States and more than 150 countries have graduated from the program since its inception in 1935. Each program is attended by about 250 students.

The DEA Training Academy

The DEA Training Academy is the centerpiece of the agency's comprehensive program for national and international drug law enforcement training. The DEA Academy provides technical and nontechnical training to all levels of DEA personnel and to other federal, state, local, and foreign law enforcement agencies. Training for DEA personnel includes entry-level courses for newly appointed special agents and certain support staff; specialized in-service courses for special agents and most other employees; executive development programs for DEA supervisors, managers, and executives; and ethics and integrity training for all levels of DEA personnel. The DEA Academy also conducts a wide range of training programs for state and local law enforcement officers, and presents training to foreign law enforcement personnel to assist in their drug law enforcement efforts.

Training Facilities

The DEA Training Academy is a 185,000-square-foot building that contains a 250-bed dormitory; classrooms; breakout training rooms; computer laboratories; practical training areas for instruction in fingerprinting, interviewing, and wiretap operations; office space for DEA training staff; health facility; cafeteria; banking facilities; laundry and dry cleaning facilities; warehouse; and gift shop. Training in firearms, defensive tactics, physical fitness, and defensive driving, as well as practical application exercises, are held at the Academy.

Basic Training Programs

The DEA Academy conducts basic training programs for special agents, diversion investigators, intelligence research specialists, and forensic chemists. These programs, which range from three to 16 weeks in duration, prepare newly hired personnel for their unique missions and specialized responsibilities.

DEA Basic Agent Training Program

To equip entry-level DEA Special Agents with the skills and abilities needed for the demands of worldwide drug law enforcement, newly appointed agents attend the 16-week DEA Basic Agent Training (BAT) program that introduces academic, tactical, practical, firearms, and legal instruction. This course covers all facets of drug law enforcement operations, from the perils of undercover work, through the intricacies of money laundering, to the legal requirements of virtually every aspect of DEA operations. Students must achieve an academic average of 80 percent on written examinations, qualify with firearms, demonstrate appropriate decision making and other competencies during tactical and other practical scenarios, and pass various physical task tests.

The program is organized such that classroom instruction provides a foundation for practical exercises. For example, after completing coursework in legal subjects and courtroom testimony, special agent recruits are cross-examined by defense attorneys during videotaped moot court exercises that simulate the stress associated with courtroom testimony and demonstrate the nature of court procedures.

Instruction in the BAT curriculum focuses on drug identification, drug smuggling, analytical investigations, law enforcement databases, clandestine laboratories, drug diversion, interviewing techniques, surveillance, undercover operations, wiretaps, money laundering, organized crime, raid planning and execution, defensive driving, vehicle stops, legal subjects, arrest techniques, evidence handling, photography, fingerprinting, courtroom testimony, crisis management, defensive tactics, physical fitness, ethics, and other subjects. BAT firearms training includes instruction in weapons safety, marksmanship, tactical shooting, and deadly-force decision making. Practical exercises—including scenarios that focus on surveillance, interviewing, search warrant operations, arrest situations, and other areas—measure trainees' judgment, knowledge of investigative and enforcement techniques, application of legal requirements, and leadership abilities.

Basic Diversion Investigator Training School

The DEA Basic Diversion Investigator (BDI) Training School is a 12-week program that provides an overview of drug diversion methods, the pharmaceutical and chemical industries, chemical control, and investigative techniques. This comprehensive course is presented through classroom lectures, case studies, and practical exercises. Examples of topics covered during the program include controlled substance laws and regulations, pharmaceutical drug scheduling and identification, drug manufacturing and distribution processes, pharmacy records auditing, drug diversion methods, security issues, case studies, interviewing and investigative techniques, courtroom procedures and testimony, clandestine laboratory operations, auditing techniques, report writing, and computer software tools. Approximately every two years thereafter, diversion investigators attend a one-week refresher course at the DEA Academy that covers legal updates, ethics and integrity, computer systems, and agency operational issues.

Basic Intelligence Research Specialist Training

The nine-week Basic Intelligence Research Specialist (BIRS) course emphasizes the development of analytical skills needed to participate in complex drug investigations, DEA programs, strategic planning, and national and international policy matters. This training program covers the mission and functions of the DEA, sources of information, legal aspects of intelligence, computer databases and software, information management, report writing, intelligence dissemination, and other aspects of drug trafficking and violent crime intelligence operations. Practical exercises in the BIRS program enable students to participate in various investigative processes, conduct analytical studies, and present their findings to DEA special agents, prosecutors, other law enforcement agencies, and policy makers.

Forensic Chemist Basic Training

Newly hired forensic chemists attend a three-week training program at the DEA Academy that is conducted in cooperation with the agency's Office of Forensic Sciences. This course provides an orientation to the functions of DEA laboratories and various laboratory technical procedures. The primary topics of instruction focus on laboratory operations, scientific instruments, evidence processing requirements, evidence sampling procedures, hazardous waste disposal, DEA-regulated drugs, the Controlled Substances Act, legal and administrative requirements, and pharmacology.

Advanced Training Programs

The DEA Academy's advanced training programs are specifically tailored to the needs of DEA personnel and the unique environments in which they carry out their responsibilities. Although these programs are carefully designed to address job-specific requirements that vary from one position to another, many DEA Academy courses are attended by DEA special agents and support staff alike, and also by personnel serving with state, local, and international law enforcement agencies.

Special Agent In-Service Training

The DEA Academy offers many professional development programs for special agents. For example, the one-week Advanced Agent Training School encompasses tactical training and classroom instruction concerning confidential sources, electronic surveillance, conspiracy, legal updates, functions of the DEA Special Operations Division, and other topics. The Academy's three-day Conspiracy and Complex Investigations School trains special agents and intelligence research specialists in strategies for developing complex conspiracy cases and presenting them to federal prosecutors. The three-day Confidential Source Management School—which is presented nationwide to DEA field divisions by the DEA Academy's Office of Training—addresses problems associated with confidential sources and issues relating to the recruitment and management of high-profile and high-risk informants. DEA Academy in-service training for special agents also focuses on subjects such as asset forfeiture, financial investigations, clandestine laboratory operations, firearms proficiency, tactical subjects, undercover operations, and legal updates.

Professional Support Staff In-Service Training

The nature of in-service courses for DEA professional support staff is diverse and constantly changing. Veteran intelligence research specialists can attend in-service training programs at the DEA Academy throughout their careers, such as the one-week Advanced Intelligence Training Program, the one-week Real-Time Analytical Intelligence Database course, the one-week Merlin File Management Training Program, and the one-week Strategic Intelligence Seminar. Diversion investigators attend the Academy's three-day Confidential Source Management School, a one-week asset forfeiture course, the one-week Diversion Chemical School, and other investigative training. DEA forensic chemists can attend courses and seminars sponsored by the Academy that focus on scientific techniques, instruments, problem-solving, computer software, and other forensics methods and issues. DEA supervisors attend the Academy's Group Supervisor Institute (GSI), which is a four-week leadership program, and the one-week Supervisor In-Service Program for first-line supervisors who have completed the GSI. Other advanced training for professional support staff focuses on computer skills, clandestine drug laboratories, digital evidence, legal updates, instructor development, and many other subjects.

State and Local Agency Training Programs

Training for state and local law enforcement agencies is one of the DEA's highest priorities. The Academy's Office of Training hosts or sponsors courses for police personnel at all levels. Police officers who are new to drug enforcement can attend the two-week Basic Narcotics School that focuses on the dynamics of drug investigations, clandestine laboratory investigations, cannabis eradication, drug trends, asset forfeiture, drug interdiction, and other subjects. Several courses are available for law enforcement supervisors and managers, such as the two-week Drug Unit Commanders Academy, which covers executive decision making, legal issues for managers, operational planning, tactical enforcement, confidential source management, and other topics; and the one-week Narcotics Commander Leadership Program, which teaches drug enforcement program leaders how to supervise, motivate, and evaluate narcotics officers and meet other drug program challenges.

International Training

The DEA Academy's International Training Section (ITS) conducts courses at the Academy and overseas to train foreign law enforcement officers in the latest and most effective drug enforcement strategies, and to increase cooperation and communication between foreign agencies and the DEA. These courses include the two-week Basic Drug Enforcement Seminar; the two-week Advanced Drug Enforcement Seminar; the three-week International Narcotics Enforcement Managers Seminar; and other specialized programs that are concerned with clandestine laboratory investigations, chemical diversion investigations, officer safety, airport interdiction operations, intelligence collection and analysis, asset forfeiture and money-laundering investigations, and forensic chemist training.

In cooperation with the State Department's ILEA in Hungary, Thailand, Botswana, and Costa Rica, ITS staff present instruction in subjects such as raid planning, counternarcotics strategies, tactical techniques, and supervision. The DEA Academy also operates a five-week Sensitive Investigative Unit Training Program to train foreign police agencies in drug enforcement operations. To facilitate the delivery of these courses, the Academy's international classroom has the capacity to simultaneously translate lectures into three different languages.

U.S. Postal Inspection Service Training Academy

U.S. Postal Inspection Service (USPIS) personnel are highly trained in an innovative atmosphere that targets multiple adult learning styles, extensive use of technology in the classroom, and a continuous thread of customer focus. The USPIS Career Development Division (CDD) conducts training for postal inspectors, postal police officers, and other USPIS employees.

Training Facilities

The national training academy for postal personnel is located at the William F. Bolger Training Center in Potomac, Maryland, an 83-acre campus situated 12 miles northwest of Washington, DC. This largely self-contained 525-bed complex is co-located with the Postal Service Leadership Center, and includes classrooms, practical scenario building, firearms facilities, fitness center, and dining facilities.

Basic Training Programs

The CDD conducts comprehensive entry-level basic training programs for USPIS postal inspectors and postal police officers at the Bolger Center. These residential programs are geared to the unique environments in which Postal Service law enforcement officers must carry out their duties.

Postal Inspector Basic Training Program

In 1997, the USPIS launched an innovative basic training program following the example of the Royal Canadian Mounted Police Training Academy. The new program mirrors USPIS field operations by assigning trainees to teams and minimizing lectures in favor of group problem-solving techniques and practical scenarios. The program employs multiple learning styles and extensive use of technology, with every team provided direct access to USPIS databases and the Internet in the classroom. Typical classroom sessions consist of teams engaged in brainstorming and various exercises in search of solutions to problems. Practical exercises are used extensively, including many nighttime operations. A continuous thread of customer focus is woven throughout the program, challenging students to view their efforts through the eyes of the community they serve.

Training modules in the program focus on subjects such as team building, problem solving, mail processing and delivery, case management, electronic surveillance, informants, undercover operations, controlled substances, interviewing and interrogation, statements and affidavits, report writing, financial investigations, accounting, search warrants, dynamic building entry, legal subjects, crime scene processing, evidence, photography, computer searches, crime lab operations, grand jury process, international security, risk assessment, defensive driving, felony vehicle stops, radio communication, firearms, defensive tactics, physical conditioning, first aid and CPR, and bloodborne pathogens.

Postal Police Officer Basic Training Program

The Postal Police Officer Basic Training Program is an intensive six-week course that includes instruction in patrol procedures, critical incident response, use of force, threat management, defensive tactics, officer safety and survival, firearms proficiency, communications, victim and witness interviewing techniques, criminal law, search and seizure, laws of arrest, report writing, bloodborne pathogens, CPR, and other topics. Similarly to the basic training program for postal inspectors, the Postal Police Officer Basic Training Program incorporates classroom instruction into carefully planned practical scenarios that emphasize problem-solving abilities, cognitive skills, and critical thinking.

Advanced Training Programs

CDD staff administer many specialized in-service programs for USPIS postal inspectors, postal police officers, technical surveillance specialists, investigative analysts, forensic document examiners, forfeiture specialists, and other USPIS personnel. Postal inspectors receive ongoing in-service training in subjects such as technical surveillance operations; threat management; mail processing and flow; information technology; asset forfeiture; hazardous materials; biohazard detection systems; legal updates; proficiency with handguns, shotguns, and submachine guns; and officer survival. Postal police officers are trained in legal subjects, defensive tactics, firearms, and many other subjects depending on their experience and responsibilities. Advanced training for USPIS supervisors and managers includes the Basic Law Enforcement Supervisory Training Program, Advanced Leadership Program, and other courses that focus on management skills, decision making, strategic planning, individual development, USPIS operations, and other topics. The USPIS International Affairs Group presents security and investigations training at the Bolger Center to foreign postal personnel, and also conducts safety and security reviews and law enforcement training for postal organizations internationally.

Specialized Training Facilities

Several federal law enforcement agencies offer special basic and advanced training programs not only for their staff, but also for personnel from other federal, state, local, and foreign law enforcement agencies. These agencies use their specialized expertise and resources to train law enforcement officers, technical and scientific personnel, prosecutors, compliance investigators, and other personnel in subjects such as arson investigation, ballistics, canine handling techniques, the investigation of hazardous waste dumping and other environmental crimes, and many other subjects. Three specialized federal training facilities—the National Firearms Examiner Academy, the Canine Enforcement Training Center, and the National Enforcement Training Institute—are profiled in the following sections.

National Firearms Examiner Academy, Bureau of Alcohol, Tobacco, Firearms and Explosives

The National Firearms Examiner Academy trains entry-level employees from the Bureau of Alcohol, Tobacco, Firearms and Explosives (ATF), and other federal, state, and local law enforcement agencies, in the fundamentals of firearm and toolmark examinations. The Academy, which is located within the ATF Forensic Science Laboratory in Ammendale, Maryland, conducts a firearm and toolmark examiner apprentice program that consists of four phases of instruction, including assignments prior to reporting to the Academy (phase 1); a 15-week session at the ATF Forensic Science Laboratory (phase 2); a four-month period in which students return to their duty stations and complete research projects and other tasks (phase 3); and a two-week follow-up school at the Academy that focuses on trial preparation and courtroom testimony (phase 4). The Academy also conducts several advanced courses—generally three days to two weeks in length—for experienced firearm and toolmark examiners, arson investigators, bomb technicians, and prosecutors.

Academy instruction covers subjects such as firearms identification, serial number restoration, black powder characteristics, firearms and ammunition characteristics and manufacturing, firearms test-firing, bullet examinations, shot patterns and distance determinations, toolmark identification and comparison, advanced fire cause and origin techniques, complex arson investigative techniques, explosives investigation techniques, post-blast investigative techniques, and courtroom testimony.

Canine Enforcement Training Center, U.S. Customs and Border Protection

Located on a 250-acre site in Front Royal, Virginia, the Canine Enforcement Training Center (CETC) is operated by U.S. Customs and Border Protection (CBP) to provide training for all CBP canine officer teams and to other federal, state, local, and foreign law enforcement agencies. CETC facilities include more than 100 kennel runs, a training building, a firearms range, vehicle training areas, training roads, classrooms, veterinary clinics, a laundry facility, a 150-car parking lot used for search techniques training, and a canine isolation and quarantine facility. CBP maintains two canine programs, including the Office of Field Operations program, which has more than 800 canine teams that are stationed mostly at airports, seaports, and land border crossings; and the Office of Border Patrol canine program, which has more than 450 canine teams that are responsible for all other areas.

CETC programs include a 13-week Basic Narcotic Detection Course; a 13-week Passenger Processing Course; a 13-week Technical Trainer Course for canine team supervisors; a 13-week Basic Currency Detection Course; and a three-day Administration and Technical Application Course for supervisory personnel. CBP canine teams also attend training at other facilities nationwide.

National Enforcement Training Institute, U.S. Environmental Protection Agency

Situated within the Environmental Protection Agency's (EPA's) Office of Enforcement and Compliance Assurance, the National Enforcement Training Institute (NETI) presents training programs for federal, state, local, and tribal lawyers, inspectors, civil and criminal investigators, regulatory personnel, and technical experts in various aspects of environmental law enforcement. NETI manages training sites in Washington, DC, and Lakewood, Colorado, and at the FLETC Glynco campus.

NETI courses and workshops focus on environmental crimes and investigations; legal subjects, interviewing and interrogation; evidence collection; forensics; criminal intelligence analysis; solid and hazardous waste sampling, identification, enforcement, and compliance; enforcement and compliance relating to the Clean Air Act, Clean Water Act, Endangered Species Act, National Environmental Policy Act, and National Historic Preservation Act; regulatory inspections; financial analysis; wetlands and flood plains; EPA Superfund enforcement; pesticide regulations; and other environmental issues.

INDEX

D

G

H

I

P–Q

W–Z